Bloom's Modern Critical Views

Bloom's Modern Critical Views

Alexander
  Solzhenitsyn
Sophocles
John Steinbeck
Tom Stoppard
Jonathan Swift
Amy Tan
Alfred, Lord Tennyson
Henry David Thoreau
J.R.R. Tolkien
Leo Tolstoy

Ivan Turgenev
Mark Twain
John Updike
Kurt Vonnegut
Derek Walcott
Alice Walker
Robert Penn Warren
Eudora Welty
Edith Wharton
Walt Whitman
Oscar Wilde

Tennessee Williams
Thomas Wolfe
Tom Wolfe
Virginia Woolf
William Wordsworth
Jay Wright
Richard Wright
William Butler Yeats
Emile Zola

Bloom's Modern Critical Views

WILLIAM SHAKESPEARE

Edited and with an introduction by
Harold Bloom
Sterling Professor of the Humanities
Yale University

CHELSEA HOUSE
PUBLISHERS
A Haights Cross Communications Company
Philadelphia

A Haights Cross Communications ⚏ Company

Printed and bound in the United States of America.
10 9 8 7 6 5 4 3 2 1

Library of Congress Cataloging-in-Publication Data

William Shakespeare / edited and with an introduction by Harold
Bloom.
    p. cm. — (Bloom's modern critical views)
Includes bibliographical references (p.) and index.
  ISBN 0-7910-7655-5 — ISBN 0-7910-7823-X (pbk.)
  1. Shakespeare, William, 1564-1616—Criticism and
interpretation. I. Bloom, Harold. II. Series.
  PR2976.W535 2003
  822.3'3—dc22

                                        2003020896

Chelsea House Publishers
1974 Sproul Road, Suite 400
Broomall, PA 19008-0914

http://www.chelseahouse.com

Contributing Editors: Brett Foster and Aaron Tillman

Cover designed by Terry Mallon

Cover: © Archivo/Iconografico, S.A./CORBIS

Layout by EJB Publishing Services

Contents

Editor's Note

This volume seeks to gather the best critical essays I could find (with the help of Brett Foster) that provide a sequence of commentaries on nearly all of Shakespeare's major plays. *Cymbeline* is a late exception (but then, much of it seems to me a Shakespearean self-parody) while the last play, "The Two Noble Kinsmen," was largely composed by John Fletcher, though the contributions by Shakespeare (Act I; Act III, scene i; Act V (excluding the second scene) are astonishing, and show what he might have done had he cared to continue.

My "Introduction: Foregrounding" revives the insight of the eighteenth century critic-administrator, Maurice Morgann, whose example teaches how Shakespeare wants us to infer the relationships between characters that existed before each play's opening. It indeed does matter how many children Lady Macbeth had in her first marriage.

The great Anglo-Irish short-story writer Frank O'Connor charts the emergence of Shakespeare's original genius from Marlowe's influence, with *The Merchant of Venice* as prime example.

The emergence of Richard Crookback is traced from *3 Henry VI* to *Richard III* by E. Pearlman, after which Erich Segal, novelist and play-doctor, gives a vivid account of the superb *The Comedy of Errors*.

I have included my own discussion of *The Taming of the Shrew* as a corrective to many current Feminist reading that regard Kate as Petruchio's victim, which is to neglect the superb Romantic comedy played out between them in one of Shakespeare's few happy marriages of equals.

A major Humanist scholar of European Renaissance literature, Thomas M. Greene, died recently, and I fear that something of great value, profound philology, ended with him. I represent him here with his superb essay upon *Love's Labour's Lost*, Shakespeare's gorgeous festival of language, in which the dramatist first discovered that his verbal resources were endless. Greene subtly demonstrates that the play turns upon variations in the use of the word "grace."

Greene is followed here by Harold C. Goddard's poignant interpretation of *Romeo and Juliet*, from his wise and humane book, *The Meaning of Shakespeare*, to which I am indebted throughout my own work.

Gilbert Keith Chesterton—poet, novelist, Catholic polemicist, wonderful critic of Chaucer, Dickens, and Browning—illuminates *A Midsummer Night's Dream* with his own deep love of the marvelous Bottom the Weaver.

One of my grand mentors, Northrop Frye, appears in this volume with his deft reading of *Richard II*, whom he sees as poised between history and imaginative vision.

Sir John Falstaff, Hamlet's only rival as the Shakespearean sublime, receives critical justice from the major Edwardian Shakespeare scholar A. C. Bradley, who memorably remarks that: "The bliss of freedom gained in humour is the essence of Falstaff," much the most magnificent comic creation in all of literature.

In a psychoanalytic essay, Joseph Westlund brilliantly remarks that: "In *The Merchant of Venice* trust comes a little too easily, and never to Shylock." I myself confess that I remain very uncomfortable in reading, teaching, or writing about what I am compelled to regard as being at once an extraordinary romantic comedy and an anti-Semitic work.

Barbara Everett, consistently one of the most distinguished of Shakespeareans, defends *Much Ado About Nothing* as the comedy of "two difficult lovers" falling in love with one another.

I turn back to the major English Romantic critic William Hazlitt's *Characters of Shakespeare's Plays* for his portraits of Henry V and Coriolanus. How do we like Henry V? Hazlitt asks, and charmingly replies: "We like him in the play. There he is a very amiable monster, a very splendid pageant." Of *Coriolanus* Hazlitt remarks that he dislikes the politics of the play but admires the poetry, and demonstrates his deep understanding of the protagonist's divided nature.

With authentic learning and skill, David Quint explains the intricate balance between history and poetry in *Henry V*, in which Shakespeare takes up a middle position between Humanist philosophy and Old Historicism (not the Foucault-and-soda-water sloganeering New Historicism).

Julius Caesar is read by Lawrence Danson in a mode parallel to Quint's: the tragedy of Brutus momentarily takes us into timelessness, but then we are cast back into history and its confusions.

One of my favorite younger scholar-critics of Shakespeare, James P. Bednarz learnedly relates *As You Like It* to "the Poet's War" fought between Shakespeare and his cohort of fellow-dramatists.

John Hollander, a central poet and distinguished Renaissance scholar-critic, demonstrates that *Twelfth Night* opposes itself to Ben Jonson's kind of comedy, though Hollander declines to argue that Malvolio is a satire upon Jonson, as I would.

A formidable authority upon Renaissance literary rhetoric, Richard A.

Lanham proposes an analysis of *Hamlet* that I find deeply congenial: "Human flesh is sullied with self-consciousness and with theatricality."

Patricia Parker organizes her formidable study of *All's Well That Ends Well* and *Troilus and Cressida* by centering upon Shakespearean metaphors of "increase," and with dialectical agility opens up fresh perspectives upon both these "problem plays."

In a sensitive account of *Measure for Measure*, Ronald R. Macdonald examines Shakespeare's final comedy and concludes it shows an ebbing faith in the comic genre.

Graham Bradshaw, one of the most original of Shakespearean critics, denies the scholarly myth of "double time" in *Othello*, and argues persuasively that the marriage between Othello and Desdemona is never consummated.

The important modern English critic, William Empson, defends *Macbeth* on many fronts, and preserves the integrity of Shakespeare's most ruthlessly economical drama.

Antony and Cleopatra frequently seems to set its poetry and its action into conflict, with each qualifying the other. Janet Adelman shows that we can believe neither the one nor the other when poetry and action diverge in the play.

Stephen Orgel, considering the poetics of *The Winter's Tale*, argues for deliberate opacity and even confusion as components in this drama. Whether Orgel proves his case may be disputable, but he opens the play to fecund further discussion.

Another of my favorites among contemporary Shakespearean critics, A. D. Nuttall, explores the double nature of *The Tempest*, at once skeptical and quasi-mystical, perhaps even Hermetic. Nuttall's grasp of the play is so beautifully firm that his emphasis upon its infinite suggestiveness is all the more convincing, and is an apt conclusion to the present volume.

HAROLD BLOOM

Introduction

FOREGROUNDING

I greet you at the beginning of a great career, which yet must have
had a long foreground somewhere, for such a start.
                                            —Emerson to Whitman, 1855

The "foreground" Emerson sees in Whitman's career is not, as he makes clear
by his strange and original use of the word, a background. That latter term has
been employed by literary historians during the twentieth century to mean a
context, whether of intellectual, social, or political history, within which works
of literature are framed. But Emerson means a temporal foreground of another
sort, a precursory field of poetic, not institutional, history; perhaps one might say
that its historiography is written in the poetry itself. *Foregrounding*, the verb,
means to make prominent, or draw attention to, particular features in a literary
work.

What is the long foreground of Sir John Falstaff, or of Prince Hamlet, or
of Edmund the Bastard? A formalist or textualist critic might say there is none,
because these are men made out of words. A contextualist or historicist critic
might say, There is background but no foreground. I have argued throughout
Shakespeare: The Invention of the Human that Shakespeare invents (or perfects,
Chaucer being there before him) a mode of representation that depends on his
foregrounding of his characters. Shakespeare calls upon the audience to surmise
just how Falstaff and Hamlet and Edmund got to be the way they are, by which
I mean: their gifts, their obsessions, their concerns. I am not going to ask what
made Falstaff so witty, Hamlet so skeptical, Edmund so icy. The mysteries or
enigmas of personality are a little to one side of Shakespearean foregrounding.

Shakespeare's literary art, the highest we ever will know, is as much an art

From *Shakespeare: The Invention of the Human.* © 1998 by Harold Bloom.

of omission as it is of surpassing richness. The plays are greatest where they are most elliptical. Othello loves Desdemona, yet seems not to desire her sexually, since evidently he has no knowledge of her palpable virginity and never makes love to her. What are Antony and Cleopatra like when they are alone together? Why are Macbeth and his fierce lady childless? What is it that so afflicts Prospero, and causes him to abandon his magical powers, and to say that in his recovered realm every third thought shall be of his grave? Why does no one behave other than zanily in *Twelfth Night*, or other than madly in *Measure for Measure*? Why must Shylock be compelled to accept Christian conversion, or Malvolio be so outrageously tormented? Foregrounding is necessary to answer these questions. I will begin with *Hamlet*, partly because I will argue that Shakespeare all but began with him, since there is no *Ur-Hamlet* by Thomas Kyd, and probably there was a *Hamlet* by Shakespeare as early as 1588. Another reason for starting with *Hamlet* is that the play, *contra* T. S. Eliot, indeed is Shakespeare's masterpiece, cognitively and aesthetically the farthest reach of his art.

In the final *Hamlet*, the prince we first encounter is a student home from Wittenberg, where his companions included Rosencrantz, Guildenstern, and Horatio. It is less than two months since the sudden death of his father, and only a month since his mother's marriage to his uncle, who has assumed the crown. Critics have been too ready to believe that Hamlet's melancholia results from these traumas, and from the Ghost's subsequent revelation that Claudius bears the mark of Cain. Yet the long foreground of Hamlet in Shakespeare's life and career, and of Hamlet in the play, suggests quite otherwise. This most extraordinary of all the Shakespearean characters (Falstaff, Iago, Lear, Cleopatra included) is, amidst much else, a despairing philosopher whose particular subject is the vexed relationship between purpose and memory. And his chosen mode for pursuing that relationship is the theater, of which he will display a professional's knowledge and an active playwright's strong opinions. His Wittenberg is pragmatically London, and his university must certainly be the London stage. We are allowed to see his art in action, and in the service of his philosophy, which transcends the skepticism of Montaigne and, by doing so, invents Western nihilism.

Hamlet's aptest disciple is Iago. As I have already noted, Harold Goddard, a now greatly neglected Shakespearean critic who possessed true insight, remarked that Hamlet was his own Falstaff. I would add that Hamlet also was his own Iago. A. C. Bradley suggested that Hamlet was the only Shakespearean character who could have written the play in which he appears. Again, I would add that Hamlet was capable of composing *Othello*, *Macbeth*, and *King Lear*. There is pragmatically something very close to a fusion of Hamlet and Shakespeare the tragedian, by which I do not mean that Hamlet was any more a representation of William Shakespeare than Ophelia was, or whom you will, but rather that Hamlet, in taking on Shakespeare's function as playwright-actor, assumes also the power of making Shakespeare his mouthpiece, his Player King who takes instruction. This is very different from Hamlet's serving as Shakespeare's mouthpiece. Rather, the creature usurps the creator, and Hamlet exploits Shakespeare's memory for purposes that belong more to the Prince of Denmark than to Shakespeare the man. Paradoxical as this must sound, Hamlet "lets be" Shakespeare's empirical self, while taking over the dramatist's ontological self. I do not think that this was Shakespeare's design, or his overt intention, but I suspect that Shakespeare, apprehending the process, let it be. Foregrounding Hamlet, as I will show, depends entirely on conclusions and inferences drawn only from the play itself; the life of the man Shakespeare gives us very few interpretative clues to help us apprehend Hamlet. But Hamlet, fully foregrounded, and Falstaff are clues to what, in a Shakespearean term, we could call the "selfsame" in Shakespeare. That sense of "selfsame" is most severely tested by the character of Hamlet, the most fluid and mobile of all representations ever.

Presumably, Shakespeare had read Montaigne in Florio's manuscript version. Nothing seems more Shakespearean than the great, culminating essay, "Of Experience," composed by Montaigne in 1588, when I suspect that Shakespeare was finishing his first Hamlet. Montaigne says that we are all wind, but the wind is wiser than we are, since it loves to make a noise and move about, and does not long for solidity and stability, qualities alien to it. As wise as the wind, Montaigne takes a positive view of our mobile selves, metamorphic yet surprisingly free. Montaigne, like Shakespeare's greatest characters, changes because he overhears what he himself has said. It is in reading his own text that Montaigne becomes Hamlet's precursor at representing reality in and by himself. He becomes also Nietzsche's forerunner, or perhaps melds with Hamlet as a composite precursor whose mark is always upon the aphorist of *Beyond Good and Evil* and *The Twilight of the Idols*. Montaigne's experiential man avoids Dionysiac transports, as well as the sickening descents from such ecstasies. Nietzsche unforgettably caught this aspect of Hamlet in his early *The Birth of Tragedy*, where Coleridge's view that Hamlet (like Coleridge) thinks too much is soundly repudiated in favor of the truth, which is that Hamlet thinks too well. I quote this again because of its perpetual insight:

> For the rapture of the Dionysian state with its annihilation of the ordinary bounds and limits of existence contains, while it lasts, a *lethargic* element in which all personal experiences of the past become immersed. This chasm of oblivion separates the worlds of everyday reality and of Dionysian reality. But as soon as this everyday reality re-enters consciousness, it is experienced as such, with nausea: an ascetic, will-negating mood is the fruit of these states.
>
> In this sense the Dionysian man resembles Hamlet: both have once looked truly into the essence of things, they have gained

knowledge, and nausea inhibits action; for their action could not change anything in the eternal nature of things; they feel it to be ridiculous or humiliating that they should be asked to set right a world that is out of joint. Knowledge kills action; action requires the veils of illusion: that is the doctrine of Hamlet, not that cheap wisdom of Jack the Dreamer who reflects too much and, as it were, from an excess of possibilities does not get around to action. Not reflection, no—true knowledge, an insight into the horrible truth, outweighs any motive for action, both in Hamlet and in the Dionysian man.

To see that for Hamlet knowledge kills action is to repeat the nihilist arguments that Hamlet composes for the Player King (quite possibly spoken by Shakespeare himself, upon stage at the Globe, doubling the role with the Ghost's). In his later *Twilight of the Idols*, Nietzsche returned to the Dionysiac Hamlet, though without mentioning him. Recalling the "O what a rogue and peasant slave am I!" soliloquy, where Hamlet denounces himself as one who "Must like a whore unpack my heart with words," Nietzsche arrives at a formulation that is the essence of Hamlet: "That for which we find words is something already dead in our hearts. There is always a kind of contempt in the act of speaking." With faith neither in language nor in himself, Hamlet nevertheless becomes a dramatist of the self who surpasses St. Augustine, Dante, and even Montaigne, for that is Shakespeare's greatest invention, the inner self that is not only ever-changing but also ever-augmenting.

J.H. Van den Berg, a Dutch psychiatrist from whom I've learned much, disputes Shakespeare's priority as the inventor of the human by assigning "the birth date of the inner self" to 1520, two generations before *Hamlet*. For Van den Berg, that undiscovered country was found by Martin Luther, in his discourse on "Christian Freedom," which distinguishes the "inner" man from the physical one. It is the inner man who has faith, and who needs only the Word of God. Yet that Word does not dwell within man, as it did for Meister Eckhart and Jakob Böhme, mystics extraordinary, and must come from above. Only the Ghost's word comes to Hamlet from above, and for Hamlet it both does and does not have authority. If you scorn to unpack your heart with words, then why have faith in the Ghosts act of speaking? The deadness in Hamlets heart long precedes the Ghost's advent, and the play will show us that it has been with Hamlet since early childhood. Foregrounding Hamlet is crucial (and anguishing), because it involves the prehistory of the first absolutely inner self, which belonged not to Martin Luther but to William Shakespeare. Shakespeare allowed something very close to a fusion between Hamlet and himself in the second quarter of the tragedy, which begins with the advent of the players in Act II, Scene ii, and continues through Hamlets antic glee when Claudius flees *The Mousetrap* in Act III, Scene iii.

We are overfamiliar with *Hamlet*, and we therefore neglect its wonderful outrageousness. The Prince of Denmark evidently is a frequent truant from Wittenberg and haunts the London playhouses; he is eager to hear all the latest gossip and fireworks of Shakespeare's theatrical world, and happily is brought up to date by the Player King. Clearly referring to Shakespeare and his company, Hamlet asks, "Do they hold the same estimation they did when I was in the city? Are they so followed?" and the Globe audience is free to roar when Rosencrantz answers, "No, indeed, are they not." The war of the theaters is discussed with great gusto in Elsinore, just down the street from the Globe. A greater outrageousness comes just a touch later when Hamlet becomes Shakespeare, admonishing the players to act what he has written. Not Claudius but the clown Will Kemp becomes the drama's true villain, and revenge tragedy becomes Shakespeare's revenge against poor players. Ophelia, in her lament for Hamlet, elegizes her lover as courtier, soldier, and scholar; as I have already mentioned, she might have added playwright, actor, and theater manager, as well as metaphysician, psychologist, and lay theologian. This most various of heroes (or hero-villains, as a few would hold) is more interested in the stage than all Shakespeare's other personages taken together. Playing a role is for Hamlet anything but a metaphor; it is hardly *second* nature, but indeed is Hamlet's original endowment. Fortinbras, crying out for military honors because Hamlet, had he ascended the throne, would have merited them, has gotten it all wrong. Had he lived, on or off a throne, Hamlet would have written *Hamlet*, and then gone on to *Othello*, *King Lear*, and *Macbeth*. Prospero, Shakespeare's redeemed Faustus, would have been Hamlet's final epiphany.

Shakespeare might have been everyone and no one, as Borges suggested, but from Act II, Scene ii, through Act III, Scene iii, Shakespeare can be distinguished from Hamlet only if you are resolved to keep the Prince and the actor-dramatist apart. Hamlet's relationship to Shakespeare precisely parallels the playwright's stance toward his own *Ur-Hamlet*; one can say that the Prince revises Shakespeare's career even as the poet revises the earlier protagonist into the Prince. It cannot be accidental that nowhere else in his work can we find Shakespeare risking so deliberate a conflation of life and art. The Sonnets dramatize their speaker's ejection, akin to the pathos of Falstaff's ruin, while no intrusion from the life of the theater is allowed in *Henry IV, Part Two*. It would make no sense to speak of "intrusions" in the "poem unlimited," *Hamlet*, where all is intrusion, and nothing is. The play as readily could have been expanded into a two-part work, because it could absorb even more of Shakespeare's professional concerns. When Hamlet admonishes and instructs the players, neither he nor the play is the least out of character: *The Mousetrap* is as natural to the world of *Hamlet* as is the crooked duel arranged by Claudius between Hamlet and Laertes.

But what does that tell us about Hamlet in his existence before the play begins? We cannot avoid the information that this was always a man of the theater, as much a critic as an observer, and very possibly more of an actual than a potential playwright himself. Foregrounding Hamlet will teach us his greatest paradox: that long before his father's murder and mother's seduction by Claudius, Hamlet was already a self-dramatizing genius of the theater, driven to it out of his contempt for the act of speaking what was already dead in his heart. The apocalyptic self-consciousness of this charismatic personality could have led to dangerous action, a murderousness prophetic of Macbeth's, had it not been for the outlet of this theatrical vocation. Hamlet is only secondarily a courtier, soldier, and scholar; primarily he is that anomaly (and knows it): a royal playwright, "The play's the thing" in every possible sense. Of all Shakespeare's works, this is the play of plays because it is the play of the play. No theory of the drama takes us further than the sequence from Act II, Scene ii, through Act III, Scene iii, if we realize that compared with it, everything that comes before and after in *Hamlet* is interruption. The mystery of Hamlet and the enigma of Shakespeare are centered here.

Backgrounding Shakespeare is a weariness, because it does nothing to explain Shakespeare's oceanic superiority to even the best of his contemporaries, Marlowe and Ben Jonson. Marlowe's Faustus is a cartoon; Shakespeare's Faustus is Prospero. Dr. Faustus in Marlowe acquires Mephistopheles, another cartoon, as familiar spirit. Ariel, Prospero's "sprite," though necessarily other than human, has a personality nearly as distinct as that of the great magus. What Shakespeare shared with his era can explain everything about Shakespeare, except what made him so different in degree from his fellows that at last it renders him different in kind. Foregrounding Shakespeare's characters begins by noting what Shakespeare himself implied about them; it cannot conclude by compiling what they imply about Shakespeare. We can make surmises, particularly in regard to Hamlet and Falstaff, who seem in many ways to live at the limits of Shakespeare's own consciousness. With just a handful of Shakespearean roles—Hamlet, Falstaff, Rosalind, Iago, Macbeth, Lear, Cleopatra—we sense infinite potential, and yet we cannot surpass Shakespeare's employment of them. With Lear—as to a lesser degree with Othello and Antony—we feel that Shakespeare allows us to know their limits as what Chesterton called "great spirits in chains." Perhaps the Falstaffian Chesterton thought of Hamlet as another such figure, since from a Catholic perspective Hamlet (and Prospero) are purgatorial souls at best. Dante foregrounds only Dante the Pilgrim; all others in him no longer can change, since those souls sustaining Purgatory only can be refined, not fundamentally altered. It is because of his art of foregrounding that Shakespeare's men and women are capable of surprising changes, even at the final moment, as Edmund changes at the close of King Lear. Unless you are adequately foregrounded, you can never quite overhear yourself.

Shakespeare is a great master of beginnings, but how far back does a Shakespearean play begin? Prospero foregrounds *The Tempest* in his early conversation with Miranda, but does the drama truly commence with his expulsion from Milan? Most would say it starts with the storm that rather oddly gives the play its title, a tempest that ends after the first scene. Since there is almost no plot—any summary is maddening—we are not surprised that scholars tell us there is no source for the plot. But the foreground begins with Shakespeare's subtle choice of a name for his protagonist, Prospero, which is the Italian translation of the Latin Faustus, "the favored one." Presumably Shakespeare, like Marlowe, knew that the name Faustus began as the cognomen that Simon Magus of Samaria took when he went to Rome, there to perish in an unlikely flying contest with St. Peter. *The Tempest*, most peculiarly, is Shakespeare's *Dr. Faustus*, all unlike Marlowe's last play. Think how distracting it would be had Shakespeare named his Mage Faustus, not Prospero. There is no devil in *The Tempest*, unless you argue with Prospero that poor Caliban is one, or at least a sea devil's child. The ultimate foregrounding of *The Tempest* is its magician's name, since its substitution for Faust means that Christianity is not directly relevant to the play. A distinction between "white" and "black" magic is not crucial; an art, Prospero's, is opposed to the sale and fall of a soul, Faustus's.

Hamlet, Prospero, Falstaff, Iago, Edmund: all have evolved through a foretime that itself is the implicit creation of Shakespeare's imaginings. While Hamlet and Prospero intimate dark sensibilities that preceded their catastrophes, Falstaff suggests an early turning to wit, even as Hamlet turned to theater and Prospero to hermetic magic. The despair of having thought too well too soon seems shared by Hamlet and by Prospero, while Falstaff, a professional soldier who long ago saw through chivalry and its glories, resolutely resolves to be merry, and will not despair. He dies of brokenheartedness, according to his fellow scamps, and so Hal's rejection does seem the Falstaffian equivalent of Hamlet's rejection of, and by, life itself.

It seems appropriate that I conclude this book with Falstaff and with Hamlet, as they are the fullest representations of human possibility in Shakespeare. Whether we are male or female, old or young, Falstaff and Hamlet speak most urgently for us and to us. Hamlet can be transcendent or ironic; in either mode his inventiveness is absolute. Falstaff, at his funniest or at his most reflective, retains a vitalism that renders him alive beyond belief. When we are wholly human, and know ourselves, we become most like either Hamlet or Falstaff.

FRANK O'CONNOR

Masterpieces

With *Romeo and Juliet*, *A Midsummer Night's Dream*, and *The Merchant of Venice* we reach the period of the great masterpieces.

Romeo is a betwixt-and-between play, of a rather curious kind, which at one extreme approximates less to the lyrical plays than to the earlier *Richard III* and at the other even surpasses the maturity of *The Merchant of Venice*. The reason may be that it was revised more than once. Of the textual disturbance in at least two scenes I am not competent to judge, but it is obvious that between the first and second quarto there was some rewriting; the marriage scene has been entirely rewritten, and the dying Mercutio (probably rightly) has been shorn of some of his bitter puns: I regret the loss of his proposed epitaph—

Tybalt came and broke the Prince's laws
And Mercutio was slain for the first and second cause.

But the real test for a literary man is the obviously archaic style of some scenes and the equally obvious mastery of others. Never did undergraduate so dreadfully display his ingenuity as Shakespeare does in the delighted dissection of lines like "Beautiful tyrant, fiend angelical"; "Come Montague for thou art early up to see thy son and heir now early down"; or the ghastly "This may flies do while I from this must fly." As in the Henry VI group we get the heaping up of useless words as in "Beguiled, divorced, wronged, spited, slain," and we seem

---

From *Shakespeare's Progress*. © 1960 by Frank O'Connor.

"to hear the lamentations of poor Anne" in the Nurse's "O woe, O woeful, woeful, woeful day," which rivals anything in the dramatic line of Bottom the weaver. On the other hand, there is the infallible sign of maturity we find in the love scenes; the length of the poetic phrase. In Mercutio's Queen Mab speech, using only his half voice, Shakespeare can produce marvels of delicacy and sweetness, but no momentary inspiration could account for the faultless phrasing of the full concert voice.

> O speak again, bright angel, for thou art
> As glorious to this night being o'er my head,
> As is a winged messenger of heaven
> Unto the white-upturned wondering eyes
> Of mortals that fall back to gaze on him
> When he bestrides the lazy puffing clouds
> And sails upon the bosom of the air.[1]

I think that here, as certainly in *The Merchant of Venice*, the main influence on his work is Marlowe's. One whole scene in *The Merchant of Venice* is cribbed directly from *Tamburlaine*. Marlowe's "The moon sleeps with Endymion every day," becomes Portia's "Peace ho! the moon sleeps with Endymion." He has rid himself entirely of his fondness for choplogic, and, tired of the tight, trim, niggling verse he had been writing, tries for great splashes of color. In the other two plays of the group the vivid, incantatory classicisms of Marlowe throw a smoky torchlight upon the scene.

> Did'st thou not lead him through the glimmering night
> From Perigenia whom he ravished,
> And make him with fair Aegles break his faith,
> With Ariadne and Antiopa?[2]

Or—from *The Merchant of Venice*—

> With no less presence but with much more love
> Than young Alcides when he did redeem
> The virgin tribute paid by howling Troy
> To the sea-monster.[3]

Or, once more, from the same play—

> In such a night
> Stood Dido with a willow in her hand
> Upon the wild sea-banks and waft her love
> To come again to Carthage.[4]

Like all actors, Shakespeare had an uncannily retentive ear which could not only recollect a cadence but embalm an error. In *Soliman and Perseda*, which he must have played in in his younger days, there is a line about "Juno's goodly swans"—a mistake, for the swans are Venus', not Juno's—but he saved them up for *As You Like It*: "Like Juno's swans still we went coupled and inseparable."[5] He must have been a born mimic; he loves to break up his speeches with parody, and has a kind of chameleon quality which makes him seize on any opportunity for a change of style. Those who believe his works were written for him by Marlowe, Greene, Peele, Kyd, and Chapman, have plenty of stylistic grounds, for just as in *A Midsummer Night's Dream* he can cheerfully plunge into a parody of a group of village mummers, he can adapt himself to almost any style. At the same time, being a man of original genius, he never stays adapted.

Even in *The Merchant of Venice* he does not stay adapted. In the second act there is a scene between two garrulous Venetian merchants, Salarino and Salanio. They describe the frenzy of Shylock after Jessica's elopement in a passage clearly modeled on Marlowe's *Jew of Malta*—"O girl! O gold! O beauty! O my bliss!"

My daughter, O my ducats, O my daughter!
Fled with a Christian, O my Christian ducats![6]

Then Salarino tells how on the previous day he had met a Frenchman

Who told me in the narrow seas that part
The French and English there miscarried
A vessel of our country richly fraught.

So far Marlowe's influence. But now we pass to the next scene but one, where again we meet the same two chatterboxes, but this time talking prose, and again we are informed that "Antonio hath a ship of rich lading wracked in the narrow seas; the Goodwins I think they call the place, a very dangerous flat and fatal, where the carcases of many a tall ship lie buried." Shylock appears and we get a characteristic Shakespearean scene of the period with its shattering repetitions—"a beggar that was used to come so smug on the mart—let him look to his bond! He was wont to call me usurer—let him look to his bond! He was wont to lend money for a Christian courtesy—let him look to his bond!" The chatterboxes go off, and to his fellow Jew, Tubal, Shylock bursts out in a terrific speech, and it is no longer a mere report of what has happened off stage, but the thing itself.

Why there, there, there, there, a diamond gone cost me two thousand ducats in Frankfort—the curse never fell on our nation till now; I never felt it till now—two thousand ducats in that and other precious, precious jewels: I would my daughter were dead at my foot and the jewels in her ear; would she were hearsed at my foot and the ducats in her coffin.[7]

Now, whether or not there was any interval between the writing of these two scenes, one does not have to be a literary critic to realize that they are the same scene, and that all Shakespeare has done is to take the hint contained in the Marlovian blank verse and expand it into the prose which by this time was becoming his favorite medium. They make an interesting contrast, for they show the direction in which he was moving. Though he might be lured into writing blank verse fantasy, his ultimate aim was a closer realism. He refused to stay adapted.

The part of Antonio is the last lingering echo of the Dark Lady episode. As Sir Edmund Chambers and others have pointed out, his melancholy is inexplicable unless we regard it as produced by Bassanio's forthcoming marriage. The melancholia broods over the play which has remarkably little cleverness. For the first and only time Shakespeare, in one dangerous line, says what Montaigne had already been saying in France—that tortured men will say anything. Was he thinking of Kyd, whose heartbroken preface to *Cornelia* he must have read?

But the most striking echo of the Dark Lady tangle escapes all the commentators. Bassanio has always been unpopular with them. He has no visible means of subsistence; he borrows money from Antonio, and his only notion of repairing his fortunes is by a wealthy marriage. What they have failed to note is that it is precisely his peculiar, half-loverlike relationship with Antonio which explains his fortune hunting. They see that Bassanio is a reflection of the young nobleman of the sonnets but they fail to see that this relationship of rank is also maintained in the play; and that an aristocrat in Bassanio's position could not have done otherwise than seek his fortune in marriage.

I think the distinction in rank has probably been somewhat obscured by rewriting. It is inevitably obscured for the modern reader and playgoer since he is entirely unaware of the light and shade represented for an Elizabethan by the changes rung on the formal second-person plural and the intimate second-person singular. As with ourselves and our use of Christian and surnames, the distinction was breaking down, but it never broke down to the point where a gardener called the lord of the manor by his first name or the mistress addressed the maid with the equivalent of "Miss Smith." Everyone in court must have known what Raleigh's fate was to be when Coke shouted, "I thou thee, thou traitor!" There are many episodes in Shakespeare where it is used with stunning effect, and whole scenes have lost their point by our modern inability to detect these changes of key. Half the fun of Malvolio's advances to Olivia is in the fact that he "thous" her; when Henry V dons Sir Thomas Erpingham's cloak to make his tour of the camp, his real disguise is not the cloak but the fact that even when "thoued" by Pistol he never forgets himself so far as to drop the formal "you"; when Falstaff accosts the young King on his procession through London his real offense is not that he claims intimacy with him but that he dares to "thou" him in public, which to any Elizabethan must have seemed like a capital offense. Here, I fancy, a foreigner could probably get more sense from Shakespeare than we can, for on the Continent this tradition is still very much alive.

There are two passages in *The Merchant of Venice* which reveal its significance. In the scene between Antonio and Bassanio the two friends use the formal "you" for the greater portion of the time. Then Bassanio mentions Portia, and it is as if a quiver of pain runs through Antonio. In his next speech he bursts out "Thou know'st that all my fortunes are at sea," and the whole scene becomes suffused with emotion. The second is the scene between Antonio and Shylock. Again Antonio uses the formal "you" until Shylock rates him for his anti-Semitism and Antonio snarls back "I am as like to call thee so again."

Anyone who reads the Belmont scenes with care will notice how Bassanio is addressed as "Your Honour," and though he "thous" Gratiano (a friend of Antonio's), is never, "thoued" by him.

> GRA.   My lord Bassanio and my gentle lady,
> I wish you all the joy that you can wish,
> For I am sure you can wish none from me:
> And when Your Honours mean to solemnize
> The bargain of your faith, I do beseech you
> Even at that time I may be married too.
> BASS.   With all my heart so thou can'st get a wife.
> GRA.   I thank your Lordship, you have got me one.
> My eyes, my Lord, can look as swift as yours.[8]

But Antonio is only one part of Shakespeare, the part that loved a lord. The other is Shylock. Shylock engaged the real contradiction in his nature, for he is the underdog out for revenge. Shakespeare takes great care to confine his aim to revenge. Though like Marlowe's Jew he is the villain of the play he is never allowed to say the sort of things Barabas says:

> As for myself, I walk abroad at night
> And kill sick people groaning under walls
> Sometimes I go about and poison wells.

Undoubtedly, Shakespeare has taken great pains to see that he never becomes a really unsympathetic character: in us, as in Shakespeare, there is an underdog who has felt "the insolence of office and the spurns that patient merit of the unworthy takes," and we know what it is to desire revenge, even to the extreme of murder. Heine tells the story of the English girl who sat near him during a performance, and who at the trial scene burst out with "O, the poor man is wronged!" That, of course, is the risk which Shakespeare ran Shylock, like

Falstaff after him, is the secondary character who steals the play, which tends to turn into the tragedy of the innocent Jew wrongfully deprived of his hard-earned pound of flesh; and it takes the whole subplot of the rings, the serenade, and the music to restore the key of comedy.

The greatness of this very great play is that it searches out the Shylock in each of us, and makes us bring in a verdict against judgment and conscience.

"The poor man is wronged."

NOTES

1. *R. and J.*, II. 2.
2. *M.N.D.*, I. 2.
3. *M. of V.*, III. 2.
4. *M. of V.*, V. 1.
5. *A.Y.L.*, I. 3.
6. *M. of V.*, II. 8.
7. *M. of V.*, III. 1.
8. *M. of V.*, III. 2.

E . PEARLMAN

The Invention of Richard of Gloucester *in* 3 Henry VI *and* Richard III

T he chronology of shakespeare's earliest plays is so uncertain that it is impossible to describe with any confidence the process by which the playwright learned to transmute the raw theatrical materials available to him in 1590 into the refined works he was able to produce less than a decade later. When Shakespeare first began to put to good use what he would modestly call his "rough, and all-vnable Pen," he had already absorbed a variety of deeply rooted theatrical genres. As a youth in Stratford, he had almost certainly heard companies of travelling professional actors perform the late moralities that were popular choices for the mayor's play. Shakespeare had also studied the works of Plautus and Seneca and, after his move to London, had paid careful attention to the liberating innovations of Kyd and Marlowe. In his first years as a playwright, Shakespeare discovered how to integrate a varied inheritance into a sophisticated drama that at its richest moments was simultaneously mimetic and symbolic.

Attempts to chart Shakespeare's progress as a dramatist often bog down in specialist bibliographical detail. It is good fortune that the circumstances out of which the astonishing Richard of Gloucester emerges are quite clear. Richard appears in two plays that antedate *Richard III*: he plays a brief part in *2 Henry VI* and one considerably more extensive in *3 Henry VI*, which was written and performed sometime before September 1592, when *Greene's Groatsworth of Wit* was entered in the Stationers' Register. (A sentence from the invective aimed by

From *Shakespeare Quarterly* 43, no. 4 (1992). © 1992 by the Folger Shakespeare Library.

Richard's father, the duke of York, at Margaret of Anjou—"Oh Tygres Heart, wrapt in a Womans Hide" [TLN 603; 1.4.137][1]—had been extracted by Robert Greene and transformed into an attack on Shakespeare himself.) The assumption that *3 Henry VI* must have preceded the composition of *Richard III* (usually dated about 1593 or 1594) has not been challenged.[2]

As he appears in *The Tragedy of Richard the Third*, Richard of Gloucester is the earliest of Shakespeare's inventions whose power and poetry continue to fascinate and amaze. When Shakespeare devised Richard, he created a character to whom no figure in the plays thought to precede this play—i.e., in the earlier history plays or *The Two Gentlemen of Verona* or *Errors* or *The Shrew* or *Titus Andronicus*—is even remotely comparable. The differentiation of Richard from the comparatively colorless orators and warriors who populate the *Henry VI* plays marks a turning point—perhaps *the* turning point—in Shakespeare's development into a dramatist of more than ordinary excellence.

When Shakespeare began to compose *3 Henry VI*, he may well have discovered that the Richard who had served adequately in a minor part in *2 Henry VI* was too flat and too unmarked for the more central role he would now enact. Over the course of the first two acts of *3 Henry VI*, Shakespeare appears to have conducted a series of experiments with the character. While Shakespeare does not seem to have been entirely satisfied with his first efforts, he did not bother to expunge the vestigial remnants of these trials from his manuscript. Not until the momentous scene in which Richard comments aside and then discourses at length on his brother Edward's lascivious wooing of the widow Lady Elizabeth Grey (3.2) does the ironic, leering, self-conscious, and devilish character with whom audiences have become familiar suddenly emerge. This reconceived Richard is amplified in the remainder of the play and was fully realized by the time Shakespeare sat down to compose the exceedingly accomplished opening soliloquy of *Richard III*.

Moreover, the transmutation of Richard seems to have taken place at a particularly heated psychological moment. The limbeck of emotion in which the new Richard was shaped was one of undisguised conflict between the siblings Edward and Richard and was especially charged by the furious sexual envy aimed by Richard at his callous older brother. Thus at the very same moment that Shakespeare invented the character of Richard, he also concentrated his imagination (possibly for the first time) on a closely linked pair of topics that reverberate in his writing *throughout* the next two decades. The first of these is, of course, the corrosive, insane jealousy that will dominate such characters as Othello, Posthumus, and Leontes; the second, and even more elemental, is the murderous competition between brothers, which will reappear in conflicts between Robert Falconbridge and his bastard brother Philip; between Oliver and Orlando; between Claudius and the elder Hamlet; between Edmund and Edgar; and between Prospero and Antonio. The evidence suggests that Shakespeare discovered his own genius while writing and revising a play that began as conventional chronicle history but that transmuted into a resonant study of jealousy and brotherhood.

In *2 Henry VI*, Richard is deformed, audacious, and bloodthirsty. The older Clifford (not an impartial witness, to be sure) accuses him of being a "heape of wrath, [a] foule indigested lumpe, / As crooked in thy manners, as thy shape" (TLN 3156–57; 5.1.157–58). Richard is a relentless warrior whose nature is epitomized in his striking aphorism "Priests pray for enemies, but Princes kill" (TLN 3294; 5.2.71). Shakespeare reintroduces his bold soldier in the first scene of *3 Henry VI*, where Richard, his older brother Edward, and a character named Montague[3] (historically a brother-in-law to the duke of York and therefore an uncle to the pair of brothers) vie for the duke's approval. Each produces his own trophy. First Edward, who proclaims that he has either slain or wounded the duke of Buckingham, presents a gory cloth or knife and says, "this is true (Father) behold his blood" (TLN 18; 1.1.13). Then Montague displays his bloody hands (or clothes) and boasts, "here's the Earle of Wiltshires blood" (TLN 19; l. 14). Finally, ferocious Richard trumps his brothers by bringing onstage not the blood but the stage-property head of the earl of Salisbury. Richard, pretending to address his defeated enemy ("Speake thou for me, and tell them what I did" [TLN 21; l. 16]), must then either throw the head to the ground or manipulate it as if it were a ventriloquist's dummy: "Thus do I hope to shake King *Henries* head" (TLN 25; l. 20). The primitive and bloodthirsty Richard who brings a decapitated head onstage to mock his enemy would be at home in a play like *Titus* or *Selimus* or *The Spanish Tragedy* but is as yet far wide of the devious, indirect, ambitious, and self-conscious figure he will soon become.

The character of Richard becomes more complex but also more confused in the second scene of the play, when he volunteers to advise his father York on a question of chivalry: namely, whether York must honor his oath to permit Henry VI to remain as king. Richard's argument is worthy of the closest attention:

> An Oath is of no moment, being not tooke
> Before a true and lawfull Magistrate,
> That hath authoritie ouer him that sweares.
> *Henry* had none, but did vsurpe the place.
> Then seeing 'twas he that made you to depose,
> Your Oath, my Lord, is vaine and friuolous.
> Therefore to Armes: and Father doe but thinke,
> How sweet a thing it is to weare a Crowne,
> Within whose Circuit is *Elizium*,
> And all that Poets faine of Blisse and Ioy.
> Why doe we linger thus? I cannot rest,

Vntill the White Rose that I weare, be dy'de
Euen in the luke-warme blood of *Henries* heart.
(TLN 335–47; 1.2.22–34)

This speech divides into three distinct sections, each of which is characterized by its own particular diction and tone. In the first six lines, Richard advances the argument that his father's oath is of no binding force. The colorless language of these lines does not distinguish Richard from hosts of other chronicle-play characters. It is marked by vagueness ("*Henry* had none"), awkwardly disposed verbs ("being not tooke"), and redundancies ("Then seeing 'twas he that made you to depose"). These lines reflect neither the simple brutality of Richard in his first appearance nor the complexity that he will ultimately acquire. His choplogic quibbling in fact recalls nothing so much as the performance of the young nobles in the Temple Garden scene of *1 Henry VI* in dispute about some "nice sharpe Quillets of the Law" (TLN 946; 2.4.17).

The second section (from the seventh through the tenth lines, i.e., from "Therefore ..." to "Blisse and Ioy") is logically distinct from the argument that precedes and follows it and is of an entirely more fanciful rhetorical sweep. Discarding lawyer-like argumentation, Richard now exhorts his father to greater ambition. For this Richard the throne is no longer merely a political target but has become a transcendent aim. Richard speaks these four declamatory lines as if he has been kidnapped and translated from *Tamburlaine*. He becomes a Marlovian overreacher-in-little who distinctly echoes the Scythian shepherd's famous sentences about the "sweet fruition of an earthly crown." At the same time, Richard puts forward an idea that is commonplace enough in the Marlowe universe but discordant and alien in the context of *3 Henry VI*—that the crown grants its wearer "all that Poets faine of Blisse and Ioy." That Richard can trundle forth so inauthentic a sentiment only demonstrates that the boundaries of his character are still quite porous. Shakespeare must have quickly recognized that there was little to be gained by replicating Tamburlainean aesthetics in his own play, and he managed to confine Richard's enthusiasm for royal bliss and poetry to this one derivative moment.

Having tried and thus far failed to propel the character of Richard in a new direction, Shakespeare then, in the final three lines, fell back upon the conception of Richard present in the shocking early moments of the play. The impatient and fierce Richard, eager to dye his white rose in "luke-warme blood," recalls the character who toyed with Somerset's decapitated head but is distinct from the legalistic Richard of the first part of this speech and from the celebrant of Elysium in its middle section. Richard's disjointed address makes an effective dramatic point, but its incorporation of three very different styles of speech reveals little of the character whom Richard would ultimately become.[4]

The portrayal of Richard in *3 Henry VI* remains fluid in 2.1, the scene in which he makes his next important appearance. The sequence of events in this crowded scene begins with Edward and Richard anxious to discover whether their father escaped the battlefield at St. Albans. While they wait, three suns miraculously appear in the heavens. A messenger then informs the brothers that their father—"the flowre of Europe, for his Cheualrie"—has been slain "after many scornes, many foule taunts" by "vn-relenting *Clifford*" and "ruthlesse" Queen Margaret (TLN 714–27; ll. 58–71). Soon after, the earl of Warwick confesses his culpability in the Yorkist disaster at St. Albans; a few moments later, he, Edward, and Richard determine to rally their friends and set out in haste for London. In all this business Richard is an active and voluble participant who continues to employ a variety of tongues. Especially troublesome and confusing is his piece of oratory while waiting for a messenger from St. Albans. To Edward's fraternal concern—"How fares my Brother? why is he so sad?"—Richard replies at length:

> I cannot ioy, vntill I be resolu'd
> Where our right valiant Father is become.
> I saw him in the Battaile range about,
> And watcht him how he singled *Clifford* forth.
> Me thought he bore him in the thickest troupe,
> As cloth a Lyon in a Heard of Neat,
> Or as a Beare encompass'd round with Dogges:
> Who hauing pincht a few, and made them cry,
> The rest stand all aloofe, and barke at him.
> So far'd our Father with his Enemies,
> So fled his Enemies my Warlike Father:
> Me thinkes 'tis prize enough to be his Sonne.
> See how the Morning opes her golden Gates,
> And takes her farwell of the glorious Sunne.
> How well resembles it the prime of Youth,
> Trimm'd like a Yonker, prauncing to his Loue?
> (TLN 660–76; ll. 8–24)

Richard decorates this leisurely statement with a variety of formal tropes. The comparison of York to a lion is commonplace, but the longer simile about the bear suggests that Shakespeare was aiming for classical, or Vergilian, grandeur. The pair of lines that climax the description of York's peril begins with a teeter-totter of antimetabole (father-enemies; enemies-father) and adds anaphora ("So far'd ... so fled ..."), alliteration, and a dollop of isocolon. Although the later Richard possesses formidable suasive powers, he never again resorts to rhetorical artifice of such formal pattern.

The most discordant element of this speech is its conclusion, where, in the final four lines ("See how the Morning opes her golden Gates ..."), Richard modulates to still another style of speech and calls attention to the miracle that

Edward makes explicit ("Dazle mine eyes, or doe I see three sunnes?" [TLN 677; l. 25]) and that is figured in the Q1 stage direction: "Three sunnes appeare in the aire" (sig. B³). The sonneteering expressions that come so inappropriately to Richard's lips—the "golden Gates" of morning, the archaizing verb "opes," the submerged reference to Phoebus, and above all the egregiously unricardian prancing "Yonker"—are unique to this moment.⁵

Throughout the remainder of the scene and up until the death of young Clifford, *3 Henry VI* itself veers in the direction of revenge tragedy, and Richard is consequently transformed into a revenger-hero very much in the manner of Hieronymo or Titus. In response to the report that his father has been killed, Richard commits himself to seek private justice. Once again his language alters to accommodate Shakespearean experimentation: "I cannot weepe: for all my bodies moysture / Scarse serues to quench my Furnace-burning hart" (TLN 735–36; ll. 79–80). He continues in this high-flying oratorical vein and brings his newest statement of self-definition to a stirring, if windy, conclusion: "Teares then for Babes; Blowes, and Reuenge for mee. / *Richard*, I beare thy name, Ile venge thy death, / Or dye renowned by attempting it" (TLN 742–44; ll. 86–88). Richard then urges Warwick to join with him to fight on Edward's behalf. He continues to play the part of the revenger who discards religion and public morality in order to seek private vengeance. "Shall we," he asks Warwick, employing genuinely animated language for the very first time,

> ... throw away our Coates of Steele,
> And wrap our bodies in blacke mourning Gownes,
> Numb'ring our Aue-Maries with our Beads?
> Or shall we on the Helmets of our Foes
> Tell our Deuotion with reuengefull Armes?
> (TLN 818–22; ll. 160–64)

Richard's incarnation as a revenger-hero has its finest moment when, in the midst of excursions, strokes, and blows on a battlefield near York, he informs Warwick, at this point still the leader of the Yorkist party, that the earl's brother has been killed by Clifford:

> Ah Warwicke, why hast thou withdrawn thy selfe?
> Thy Brothers blood the thirsty earth hath drunk,
> Broach'd with the Steely point of *Cliffords* Launce:
> And in the very pangs of death, he cryde,
> Like to a dismall Clangor heard from farre,
> Warwicke, reuenge; Brother, reuenge my death.
> (TLN 1074–79; 2.3.14–19)⁶

In this passage Richard speaks in the popular dramatic style of the early 1590s at its most overwrought—a language still far removed from the jaunty mockery that will eventually become his hallmark. When Richard exhorts Warwick to revenge, his speech is marred by too ample alliteration ("Brothers blood ... Broach'd"), by mandatory adjectives ("*thirsty* earth," "*Steely* point," "*dismall* Clangor"), by generalities when specificity is sorely needed ("heard *from farre*"), and by an overplus of gruesome detail. Elizabethan audiences would almost inevitably compare the words "Brother, reuenge" to similar expressions in *The Spanish Tragedy* and *Locrine* as well as to Thomas Lodge's famous ghost "which cried so miserally at the Theator, like an oisterwife, *Hamlet, reuenge*."[7] Shakespeare would one day parody this style of declamation by placing it in the mouths of Pistol and Bottom/Pyramus.

Richard the revenger makes a second notable appearance in *3 Henry VI*. Along with his brothers Edward and George and their ally Warwick, he attempts to poke fun at Clifford, pierced in the neck with an arrow, but is forestalled when it is discovered that his mortal enemy has breathed his last and that would-be mockery is directed at a corpse. At this point Richard delivers himself of the extraordinary sentiment that,

> If this right hand would buy two houres life,
> That I (in all despight) might rayle at him,
> This hand should chop it off: & with the issuing Blood
> Stifle the Villaine, whose vnstanched thirst
> Yorke, and yong Rutland could not satisfie.
> (TLN 1365–69; 2.6.80–84)

Richard's offer to mutilate his own body in order to triumph over his enemy is appropriate to the gorier moments in Senecan drama and finds Elizabethan parallels in Hieronymo's severed tongue and the barbarities visited upon Lavinia and Titus. It is pure rant, all strut and bellow. Perhaps Shakespeare resorted to such purple poesy in *3 Henry VI* in order to express the depth of Richard's commitment to honoring and revenging his father. It is tempting to try to salvage the lines by scrutinizing them for a telltale wink of irony, but in truth there is no hint either in word or deed that Richard has not unreservedly embraced the role of avenger of his father's death.

Shakespeare had now explored quite a variety of possible approaches to the character of Richard of Gloucester. He began with a figure who was little more than ugly and audacious and who spoke in the undifferentiated tones of chronicle history. He then borrowed in turn from Marlowe, from the epic, from Seneca, and from the revenge tradition. Throughout, Richard continued to be marked by an uncomplicated ferocity.

The innovative scene, 3.2, in which Richard achieves his new identity is comprised of two separate actions. In the first, Edward, soon to be proclaimed king, pays court to Lady Elizabeth Grey while his brothers George and Richard comment lubriciously aside. Edward is attractive to women and is portrayed as something of a philanderer. (Hall had given Shakespeare his cue by reporting that Edward "loued well both to loke and to fele fayre dammosels."[8]) Elizabeth approaches him with a suit to regain lands confiscated from her late husband. Edward indicates that he is prepared to return her property but only in trade for her virtue. Meanwhile Richard, looking on, indulges in a succession of lewd observations: "I see the Lady hath a thing to graunt" (TLN 1512; l. 12); "Fight closer, or good faith you'le catch a Blow" (TLN 1524; l. 23); "Hee plyes her hard, and much Raine weares the Marble" (TLN 1559–60; l. 50). But Elizabeth does not yield, and Edward, smitten, at last asks for her hand. Edward leaves the stage with peremptory instructions to his offended brothers: "Widow goe you along: Lords vse her honourable" (TLN 1645; l. 123). In the second part of the scene, Richard is left onstage to ruminate on his prospects.

In the course of the extraordinarily inventive seventy-one-line soliloquy that brings the scene to a close, old characteristics slough away, and a new Richard—theatrical, scheming, wicked, ironic—springs suddenly to life. At the beginning of the passage, Richard is angry but directionless. Alone onstage for the first time, he gives vent to unguarded passion.

> I, *Edward* will vse Women honourably:
> Would he were wasted, Marrow, Bones, and all,
> That from his Loynes no hopefull Branch may spring,
> To crosse me from the Golden time I looke for:
> And yet, betweene my Soules desire, and me,
> The lustfull *Edwards* Title buryed,
> Is *Clarence*, *Henry*, and his Sonne young *Edward*,
> And all the vnlook'd-for Issue of their Bodies,
> To take their Roomes, ere I can place my selfe:
> A cold premeditation for my purpose.
>   (TLN 1648–57; ll. 124–33)

His initial line about Edward's womanizing is no more than an extension of the emotion of his previous asides, while the unfigured colloquial outburst that follows ("Would he were wasted ...") expresses with genuine intensity an undiluted loathing and jealousy. By the time Richard brings the soliloquy to conclusion seventy lines later, his passion has transformed into self-control and his inchoate anger has been supplanted by a coherent and determined strategy. The Richard who emerges during the course of the soliloquy intends to employ his consummate skill at disguise and pretense (a skill that up to this moment has been neither described nor displayed) to overcome any obstacle that might stand between him and his ambitions. Richard enters the soliloquy frustrated and immobilized but exits smugly confident of his powers and contemptuous of his opponents. His concluding couplet—"Can I doe this, and cannot get a Crowne? / Tut, were it farther off, Ile plucke it downe" (TLN 1718–19; ll. 194–95)—epitomizes his new conviction that gaining the throne is mere child's play for the accomplished intriguer that he has suddenly become. During the course of this speech, the character of Richard of Gloucester undergoes a radical metamorphosis.

The structure of the soliloquy is unusual in that it twice raises and resolves the same question. Following the exordium quoted above, in which he expresses his hatred for his brother and his desire to supplant him as king, Richard describes the conflict between his present situation and the desired kingship in terms of an extended geographical simile.

> Why then I doe but dreame on Soueraigntie,
> Like one that stands vpon a Promontorie,
> And spyes a farre-off shore, where bee would tread,
> Wishing his foot were equall with his eye,
> And chides the Sea, that sunders him from thence,
> Saying hee'le lade it dry, to haue his way:
> So doe I wish the Crowne, being so farre off,
> And so I chide the meanes that keepes me from it,
> And so (I say) Ile cut the Causes off,
> Flattering me with impossibilities:
> My Eyes too quicke, my Heart o're weenes too much,
> Vnlesse my Hand and Strength could equall them.
>   (TLN 1658–69; ll. 134–45)

Richard compares his situation to someone who looks out across an immense body of water toward a distant shore, and he imagines that it would be as difficult to attain the crown as it would be to bail or drain this sea dry. Having created this modest allegorization of his psychic distress, he then, in lines 146–71 (TLN 1670–95), concedes that his ambition is intimately tied to his deformity: he seeks the crown because he is not a man to "be belou'd." But this revelation is immediately followed by a second dark conceit that in essence repeats the content of the first; this time, Richard describes his dilemma not in terms of a sea but in terms of a forest.

> And yet I know not how to get the Crowne,
> For many Liues stand betweene me and home:
> And I, like one lost in a Thornie Wood,
> That rents the Thornes, and is rent with the Thornes,
> Seeking a way, and straying from the way,
> Not knowing how to finde the open Ayre,
> But toyling desperately to finde it out,

Torment my'selfe, to catch the English Crowne:
And from that torment I will free my selfe,
Or hew my way out with a bloody Axe.
(TLN 1696–1705; ll. 172–81)

He then seems to discover that a way out of the wood is to "smile, and murther whiles I smile" (TLN 1706; l. 182)—and to his new-smiling villainy he rapidly adds a whole host of related accomplishments, all of which involve some degree of pretense.

The two sections ("Why then I doe but dreame ... equall them" and "And yet I know not how ... bloody Axe") are closely related. In each, Shakespeare translates internal psychological impediments into dreamlike figures of frustration and paralysis. The see-saw rhythms of Richard's miniature allegories (especially in lines 175–76 [TLN 1699–1700]) replicate the intrapsychic struggle between his overweening desire and the difficulties that impede him. The desperate torment that Richard repeatedly struggles to express is neither theatrical affectation nor dissimulation. On the contrary, the speech portrays a soul in such pain that there is no relief for Richard but to "hew [his] way out with a bloody Axe." When Shakespeare presents Richard's internal psychological conflicts in terms of a vast sea or thorny wood, he twice falls back on traditional allegorical techniques to approximate in language suitable for the stage a measure of intrapsychic struggle and conflict for which there was as yet no established dramatic or descriptive vocabulary.

If these two moderately allegorical psychological expressions—the far-off shore and the thorny wood—are thought of as the framing of a problem, then the passages that immediately follow may be regarded as resolutions of those problems. Each of these figurative descriptions of a troubled mind is followed by a sudden and imaginative leap forward in the portrayal of the emerging character. The first of these leaps takes place when Richard confronts his own deformity.

Well, say there is no Kingdome then for *Richard*:
What other Pleasure can the World affoord?
He make my Heauen in a Ladies Lappe,
And decke my Body in gay Ornaments,
And 'witch sweet Ladies with my Words and Lookes.
Oh miserable Thought! and more vnlikely,
Then to accomplish twentie Golden Crownes.
Why Loue forswore me in my Mothers Wombe:
And for I should not deale in her soft Lades,
Shee did corrupt frayle Nature with some Bribe,
To shrinke mine Arme vp like a wither'd Shrub,
To make an enuious Mountaine on my Back,
Where sits Deformitie to mocke my Body;

To shape my Legges of an vnequall size,
To disproportion me in euery part:
Like to a Chaos, or an vn-lick'd Beare-whelpe,
That carryes no impression like the Damme.
And am I then a man to be belou'd?
Oh monstrous fault, to harbour such a thought.
Then since this Earth affoords no Ioy to me,
But to command, to check, to o're-beare such,
As are of better Person then my selfe:
Ile make my Heauen, to dreame vpon the Crowne,
And whiles I liue, t'account this World but Hell,
Vntill my mis-shap'd Trunke, that beares this Head,
Be round impaled with a glorious Crowne.
                              (TLN 1670–95; ll. 146–71)

Richard's external shape has not changed in the slightest; he was a "Foule stygmaticke" in *2 Henry VI* (TLN 3215; 5.1.216), a "valiant Crook-back Prodigie" early in *3 Henry VI* (TLN 1538; 1.4.75). But until this moment his misshapen body has served only as the target of insult, and Richard's own attitude toward it has not been expressed in either language or action. Now, for the first time, Shakespeare links Richard's shape to his villainy. Responding directly to Edward's successful wooing of Elizabeth, Richard first admits that he is jealous of his brother and then confesses that the misfortunes of the womb have cut him off from normal relationships with women. He does not of course articulate his motivation in a modern psychological term such as compensation. Instead, he devises a conceit in which the abstractions Love and Nature contrive to visit him with Deformity. Richard's shrub of an arm and mountain back suddenly become not the insignia but the cause of his depravity. His misshapen body is no longer to be understood as a mere joke of nature but rather as the catalyst of his amoral ambition. Since he cannot be "a man to be belou'd," he will make his heaven not by lying in a lady's lap but by dreaming upon the crown. Richard's soliloquy departs from convention when it becomes a statement not only of self-description and intended malice but also of psychological causation. Self-portrayal becomes almost confessional, and motivation, which in the histories had almost invariably been of an external and public nature (most commonly dynastic loyalty), suddenly becomes internal and personal. The familiar starting point of *Richard III*—"I, that am not shap'd for sportiue trickes" (TLN 16; 1.1.14)—is the great discovery of this speech in the third act of *3 Henry VI*, and the shift from a descriptive to an etiological psychology is a momentous occasion in the invention of the new Richard.

Despite the stunning revelations of this first leap forward, Shakespeare immediately followed it with Richard's retreat into the frustration of the "Thornie Wood"—a step backward that prepares for yet another forward leap, an innovation in the portrayal of his character of equal or even greater power than the exploration of his deformity. At the very moment when Richard suddenly announces that "I can smile, and murther whiles I smile," Shakespeare brilliantly transfuses qualities identified with the quasi-supernatural Vice of the moralities into Richard's secular and up until this point entirely naturalistic character.[9]

> Why I can smile, and murther whiles I smile,
> And cry, Content, to that which grieues my Heart,
> And wet my Cheekes with artificiall Teares,
> And frame my Face to all occasions.
> Ile drowne more Saylers then the Mermaid shall,
> Ile slay more gazers then the Basiliske,
> Ile play the Orator as well as *Nestor*,
> Deceiue more slyly then *Vlisses* could,
> And like a *Synon*, take another Troy.
> I can adde Colours to the Camelion,
> Change shapes with *Proteus*, for aduantages,
> And set the murtherous *Macheuill* to Schoole.
>   (TLN 1706–17; ll. 182–93)

The Vice not only murders and smiles simultaneously; he regularly pretends to be exactly what he is not. Cloaked Collusion in Skelton's *Magnyfycence*, grandfather to a brood of Hickscorners, Newfangles, and Iniquities, brags that "I can dyssemble, I can bothe laughe and grone."[10] The assumption of an alternative identity is a perennial feature of the Vice—so Shift disguises himself as Knowledge, Hypocrisy claims to be Friendship, Revenge pretends to be Courage, and so on. A precedent for Richard's sudden transformation can be found in the characteristic ability of the Vice (Haphazard) in *Apius and Virginia* (a play that Shakespeare seems to have recalled here and elsewhere) to assimilate to himself a variety of figures.

> Yea but what am I, a Scholer, or a scholemaister,
>   or els some youth.
> A Lawier, a studient or els a countrie cloune
> A Brumman [i.e., broom-man], a Baskit maker, or a Baker of Pies,
> A flesh or a Fishmonger, or a sower of lies: ...
> A Caitife, a Cutthrote, a creper in corners,
> A herbraine, a hangman, or a grafter of horners:
> By the Gods, I know not how best to deuise,
> My name or my property, well to disguise....[11]

Haphazard's catalogue of lawyer, student, and clown is paralleled by Richard's integration of the qualities of Ulysses, Nestor, and Sinon. Once Shakespeare allowed Richard to absorb the characteristics of the Vice, he immediately transformed him from a confrontational warrior to a creature of indirection, irony, and dissembling. He also empowered Richard to claim free access to the highly developed linguistic vitality of the Vice—a great liberation for a character who until this point had failed to find a distinct or constant voice. And while the pre-Vice Richard did not bother to wet his cheeks with artificial tears—in fact, he confessed that he was incapable of expressing emotion—the later Richard would always be ready with whatever emotion would be convenient to display.

In the litany that begins "Ile drowne more Saylers then the Mermaid shall," Shakespeare ingeniously overlaid Haphazard's pattern of speech with a spacious classical reference. In addition he reached back to an earlier moment in the play to retrieve an aborted gesture toward Marlovian aspiration. Like Tamburlaine, Richard is in restless pursuit of "more": "*more* Saylers," "*more* gazers," "deceiue *more* slyly," "take *another* Troy," "*adde* Colours." Classical, morality, and Marlovian elements combine to produce a triumph of rhetorical power and momentum. But Shakespeare had still another surprise in store: with the mention of Machiavelli, he departed from the precedent he had so carefully established. Without warning or transition, Shakespeare abandoned his predictable list of mythological guises in order to incorporate a modern bogeyman. There is a world of difference between, on one hand, mermaids and basilisks and chameleons and, on the other, the fearsome contemporary political analyst Machiavelli (although it is also true that in popular imagination the traits of Machiavel and Vice—atheism, unholy glee, evil for evil's sake—tended to intersect and merge). Richard's climactic "And set the murtherous *Macheuill* to Schoole" anachronistically introduced the new political atheism into historical drama, making it clear that this play would not merely exploit the allegorical tradition but would also amplify and supplement its traditional abstractions with a modern horror. While the Vice may be semi-comic, the murderous "*Macheuill*," at least in this context, is deadly serious, and Richard intensifies the emotional power of his soliloquy when he boasts that in comparison to his own skill at intrigue and villainy, the infamous Machiavelli is but a schoolboy.[12] (Perhaps it is worth noting that, from this point on, Richard also seems to gain in sheer quickness of wit. This too sets him apart from members of the aristocracy in Shakespeare's early histories, who on the whole are marked more by blunt ferocity than by intelligence.)

The reduplicated pattern of Richard's soliloquy is now clear. Twice Shakespeare portrayed Richard's psychological paralysis in slightly allegorical passages and twice followed with passages that add significant new dimensions to the character. It was not until he supplemented the one idea—that Richard's deformity governs his jealousy, hatred, and ambition—with a second—that Richard incorporates the wicked dissimulation of the Vice—that Shakespeare completed his experimentation. For want of a better term, Shakespeare's first innovation may be called realistic or natural, while the second innovation may be called symbolic or supernatural. These two opposed yet complementary resolutions clearly indicate that the process of experimentation with the character was a restless and continuing effort. In fact, Shakespeare's great discovery in writing the soliloquy may be that a character can be deepened by providing independent but overlapping natural and supernatural explanations for his conduct. It is a triumph of dramaturgy and a minor miracle that in the course of the scene Richard becomes both *more* and *less* realistic.[13]

When Shakespeare later wrote *The Tragedy of Richard III*, he had already learned how to integrate the realistic and the symbolic. On the realistic level, throughout *Richard III* Richard's private history is a continuing concern, and the dynamics of his personal psychology and of his deeply riven family are not neglected but are set out in abundant detail. Richard is a creature of his deformity and jealousy, a character hated by his own mother and who hates all women in return. He is portrayed as having been a child whose birth was a "greeuous burthen" to his mother; who was "[t]etchy and wayward" in his infancy, "frightfull, desp'rate, wilde, and furious" as a schoolboy (TLN 2944–46; 4.4.168-70); and who arrived in the world (according to the outlandish canard repeated by Holinshed) "not vn-toothed." Following the precedent of the great soliloquy in *3 Henry VI*, Shakespeare supplemented so natural an account of Richard's malevolence with a second system of explanation. While *Richard III* is certainly a tragedy of unconscionable and distorted human ambition, it is also a play where the wounds of the murdered bleed again in the presence of the murderer, where the stumbling of a horse is a compelling omen, where dreams possess explanatory value, where ghosts return to influence and govern temporal events, and where prophecies are fulfilled not in vague and general outline but in specific detail. Richard is at once the ferociously envious and warped younger brother who compensates for lost love with ambition and villainy, and also an allegorized and devilish embodiment of evil. Natural and supernatural elements come into simultaneous play at the end of the story when Richard finds himself afflicted by burgeoning guilt. When the doomed king lies in uneasy sleep on Bosworth field and is haunted by the ghosts of those he has murdered, an audience that knows Richard is a there human mortal afflicted with naturally explicable remorse is also authorized to believe that supernatural beings have chosen a propitious moment to overthrow a satanic usurper. But at the moment of writing the hinge soliloquy in which Richard's character emerges, these innovations, though adumbrated, are still in Richard's future just as are, in Shakespeare's future, such characters as Iago and Edmund, in which similar configurations are exploited with even greater verve and power.

As a result of Richard's emergence as a challenger to King Edward, the thematic focus of the later scenes of *3 Henry VI* inevitably alters. While the first part of the play revolved around the competition for the throne between York and the earl of Warwick on the one hand and Henry and Margaret on the other, now the interplay between Edward, George, and Richard moves to centerstage. The cracking of the bond between son and father was once the primary theme: King Henry, when he adopted York as his successor, "vnnaturally" disinherited his son, Prince Edward (TLN 218; 1.1.199); furious Clifford murdered York's son Rutland ("thy Father slew my Father: therefore dye" [TLN 450–51; 1.3.46]); and Warwick boasted to the Lancastrians that "we are those which ... slew your Fathers" (TLN 103–4; 1.1.90–91). This reiterated pattern was generalized in the allegorical inset of the "*Sonne that hath kill'd his Father*" and the "*Father that hath kill'd his Sonne*" (TLN 1189–90; 2.5.55, 79)—an episode that is a triumph of abstraction and which brings the theme of fathers and sons to climax and conclusion. If the most coherent intellectual concern of the first part of the play was the conflict between the generations, that theme is now exhausted. After Richard's transitional soliloquy, the remainder of the play turns its attention to cooperation and division among the three brothers.

The always implicit rift between them widens when both Richard and George complain that Edward has neglected to provide them with heiress wives. Richard accuses Edward of attempting to "burie Brotherhood" (TLN 2081; 4.1.54). Echoing Richard's complaints, George angrily abandons his older brother: "Now Brother King farewell" (TLN 2151; l. 118). Warwick also defects, claiming that Edward has forgotten "how to vse your Brothers Brotherly" (TLN 2273; 4.3.38). The crucial political event of the second half of the play, although easy to overlook in so crowded a canvas, focuses directly on brotherhood. After Oxford, Montague, and Somerset rush to Coventry to join with Warwick in support of Henry and the Lancastrians, Warwick announces the arrival of George and his armies:

> And loe, where *George* of Clarence sweepes along,
> Of force enough to bid his Brother Battaile:
> With whom, in vpright zeale to right, preuailes
> More then the nature of a Brothers Loue.
> (TLN 2759–62; 5.1.76–79)

Shakespeare contrives the denouement so that Warwick's absolute conception of an "vpright zeale to right" is directly opposed to the natural instinct of brotherly love. If Clarence continues to support Warwick, the victory will go to the Lancastrian side; should he rejoin his brothers, the Yorkists will triumph. It is a moment of high drama in which all eyes are fixed on George, duke of Clarence. Shakespeare surprisingly allows the matter to be settled with a silent but florid gesture: Richard and George "whispers togither." Then, as Warwick looks on with misplaced confidence, George acts decisively. According to a Q1 stage direction that seems to reflect theatrical practice, "Clarence takes his red Rose out of his hat, and throwes it at *Warwike*" (sig. E2^r). Rejecting the Lancastrian side, he elects to support his brothers:

> ... Why, trowest thou, *Warwicke*,
> That *Clarence* is so harsh, so blunt vnnaturall,
> To bend the fatall Instruments of Warre
> Against his Brother, and his lawfull King....
> And so, prowd-hearted *Warwicke*, I defie thee,
> And to my Brother turne my blushing Cheekes.
>   (TLN 2768–71, 2781–82; ll. 88–91, 101–2)

Richard congratulates George for showing "Brother-like" loyalty (TLN 2788; l. 108). Brotherhood, the scene proclaims, is both natural and just. A Yorkist climax of a sort is enacted when "Lasciuious *Edward*," "periur'd *George*," and "mis-shapen *Dicke*" (TLN 3009–10; 5.5.34–35) each stab young Prince Edward, the son of Henry VI and Queen Margaret. Conjunct assassination represents the high watermark of union and mutuality among the three royal brothers.

Shakespeare supplements the attention he pays to the brothers York with a complementary depiction of fraternal relations on the Lancastrian side. He elects to depict at considerable length Warwick's reaction to the death of his brother Montague at the climactic battle of Barnet—a minor event that, except for its thematic relevance, might easily have been passed over in silence. Hall describes the incident very briefly: "Warwicke ... was in the middes of his enemies, striken doune and slain. The marques Montacute, thynkyng to succor his brother, whiche he sawe was in greate ieoperdy, and yet in hope to obtein the victory, was likewise otter throwen and slain."[14] Shakespeare expands this hint into a scene of remarkable fraternal tenderness. Fatally wounded, his "Glory smear'd in dust and blood" (TLN 2824; 5.2.23), the hitherto unsentimental Warwick calls out to his brother:

> ... Ah *Mountague*,
> If thou be there, sweet Brother, take my Hand,
> And with thy Lippes keepe in my Soule a while.
> Thou lou'st me not: for, Brother, if thou didst,
> Thy tears would wash this cold congealed blood,
> That glewes my Lippes, and will not let me speake.
>   (TLN 2835–40; 5.2.33–38)

Warwick's request that his "sweet Brother" unglue his bloody lips with tears is baroque emotionalism of a kind previously unknown in the play—and seems to have no other function than to reinforce the representation of fraternal loyalty which dominates these latter moments of the play.

It is in this context that Richard's return to the stage in the penultimate scene of *3 Henry VI* must be set. In the play's last significant action, Richard leaves behind his brothers and rushes alone to London to murder Henry VI, the king "fam'd for Mildnesse, Peace, and Prayer" (TLN 814; 2.1.156). It is after this desperate deed, in the soliloquy beginning "I that haue neyther pitty, loue, nor feare," that Richard speaks the most famous and the most rivetting lines in *3 Henry VI*. While the play as a whole has established the loyalty of brother to brother as its only credible value, Richard chillingly asserts:

> I haue no Brother, I am like no Brother:
> And this word [Loue] which Gray-beards call
> Diuine, Be resident in men like one another,
> And not in me: I am my selfe alone.
> (TLN 3156–59; 5.6.80–83)

The phrase "I haue no Brother, I am like no Brother" is powerfully resonant. Richard is, of course, blessed with brothers: not only Edward and George but also Edmund of Rutland, the "innocent Child" (TLN 408; 1.3.8) whose murder by Clifford is one of the drama's more odious atrocities. Richard's lines gain their power because in them he not only turns his face from his own natural brothers but from the ideal of brotherhood. His literal he reflects a deeper truth—and a truth from which both the murder of the duke of Clarence and the conscienceless villainy that marks Richard's subsequent career inevitably follow. Shakespeare laboriously constructs a pattern of fraternal loyalty that is then eloquently refuted by his fully metamorphosed villain.

Richard's nihilist aphorisms are so clearly designed to capitalize on the innovations of the great soliloquy and to repudiate the ideal of brotherhood that it may come as a surprise to recall that his famous lines appear in an alternative form in Q1. To Richard's sentences, Q1 prefixes one very interesting variant line:

> I had no father, I am like no father,
> I haue no brothers, *I* am like no brothers,
> And this word *Loue*, which graybeards tearme diuiue,
> Be resident in men like one another,
> And not in me, I am my selfe alone.
> (sigs. E6v–E7r)[15]

The F and Q1 versions differ crucially in emphasis. The presence of the line "I had no father" in Q1 unquestionably diffuses the intensity of Richard's summary statement. F, on the other hand, by concentrating entirely on the relation between the deformed younger brother and the first-born king in whom the privileges of primogeniture are augmented by happy successes with women, catches the psychological essence of the play's concluding moments. The economical F version establishes brotherhood as a metaphor for all human contact, while the version in Q1 is more dilute, less intense. When, as may be likely, Shakespeare returned to the Quarto passage to sacrifice "I had no father"—a credible if ultimately unprovable hypothesis—he made the last of the many courageous choices that were required to distill to its quintessence the fraternal theme of the play's latter half and to bring his emergent villain to full realization.

The antagonism between Richard and Edward (and George) seems to have fired Shakespeare's imagination. In finding this focus, Shakespeare tapped a well of Elizabethan resentment. Except for areas in Kent which still practiced gavelkind and for sections of the Celtic marches in which tanistry had persisted, England held strictly to primogeniture. The disenfranchisement of younger brothers, and even of the "younger sons to younger brothers" whom Falstaff dismisses so glibly, was a national grievance. The sentiment that animates Thomas Wilson's cry from the heart in *The State of England, 1600* must have been shared by many a member of Shakespeare's audience: younger brothers are only allowed "that which the cat left on the malt heap, perhaps some small annuity during his life, or what please our elder brother's worship to bestow upon us if we please him and my mistress his wife." But Wilson adds that such disadvantages may provoke ambition or revenge; a younger brother might take up either letters or arms as a profession, "whereby many times we become my master elder brother's masters, or at least their betters in honour and reputation...."[16] (Shakespeare himself was a first surviving child—three elder siblings had died before his birth—and nothing is known of the emotions he felt toward his younger brothers Edmund and Richard.)

None of Shakespeare's history plays stray very far from the subject of antagonism between brothers. Hal's rivalry with Hotspur would be understood as a conflict between surrogate brothers even if Henry Bolingbroke had not been so tactless as to wish that the Plantagenet and Percy sons had been exchanged in cradle-clothes. Prince Hal even has a surrogate brother in the person of Poins; Poins is an underfinanced "second brother" (*2 Henry IV*, 2.2.63), Hal an older brother alienated from his natural siblings. In *2 Henry IV*, Shakespeare dwells on the contrast between the playful Prince Hal and the sober-blooded and unscrupulous John of Lancaster. Moreover, the old king's deathbed fright is the prospect of war between his sons, and the new King Henry's first concern on succeeding to the crown is to allay such apprehensions:

> Brothers, you mix your sadness with some fear.
> This is the English, not the Turkish court;
> Not Amurath an Amurath succeeds,
> But Harry Harry....
>
> (5.2.46–49)

The worried younger brothers must be reassured that Hal does not plan a mass murder of the sort familiar from recent Ottoman history (well known to theatrical audiences from its lurid echoes in *Selimus* and *Soliman and Perseda*).

Of all the glosses on Richard's "I haue no Brother" in the history plays, the grandest appears when Henry V inspires his troops just before the battle of Agincourt. Henry exalts the fellowship of those who will fight on St. Crispin's day and on the subject of brotherhood adopts a position that is the polar opposite of Richard's.

> We few, we happy few, we band of brothers;
> For he to-day that sheds his blood with me
> Shall be my brother; be he ne'er so vile
> This day shall gentle his condition....
> *(Henry V,* 4.3.60–63)

While Richard sets himself apart even from his own brothers, King Harry proclaims a fraternity of shared pain. Harry's world is as inclusive as Richard's is exclusive, and his comprehensive vision of England is a generous alternative to the narrow and perverse individualism that makes Richard so dangerous a politician and so powerful a dramatic figure. The supersession of "I have no brother" by "we band of brothers" is a crucial marker in Shakespeare's long and epochal progress from a playwright whose initial and inherited subject was revenge to one who turned at last to reconciliation and forgiveness—to the realization that "the rarer action is / In virtue than in vengeance" (*The Tempest*, 5.1.27–28). The long journey could not begin until Shakespeare had contrived a villain who could dominate the stage with his demonism, psychological coherence, and brilliance of language.[17]

NOTES

1. Quotations of *2* and *3 Henry VI* are taken from *The First Folio of Shakespeare*, ed. Charlton Hinman (New York: W. W. Norton, 1968) and are cited by Hinman's through-line numbers and also by the lineation in A. S. Cairncross's Arden editions (London: Methuen, 1957 and 1964). Quotations of the quartos of *2* and *3 Henry VI* are from *Shakespeare's Plays in Quarto*, ed. Michael J. B. Allen and Kenneth Muir (Berkeley: Univ. of California Press, 1981) and are referenced by signature. Quotations from other plays of Shakespeare are drawn from the appropriate Arden editions.

2. The text of *3 Henry VI* presents a number of impediments to the study of Shakespeare's strategies of composition. Modern editors accept the authority of the Folio and incorporate occasional readings from the quarto (more precisely octavo, but generally recognized in the abbreviation Q1) edition of 1594, called

The true Tragedie of Richard Duke of Yorke. Q1 has been widely regarded as a "bad" or reported text since the complementary studies by Madeleine Doran (*Henry VI, Parts II and III: Their Relation to The Contention and the True Tragedy* [Iowa City: Univ. of Iowa Press, 1928]) and Peter Alexander (*Shakespeare's* Henry VI *and* Richard III [Cambridge: At the Univ. Press, 1929]). The editors of the new Oxford Shakespeare, who are not loath to challenge orthodoxies, agree that the report hypothesis "plausibly and economically accounts for the O [Q1] text, and ... [they] accept it with only slight qualification." Their qualification is that Q1 "reports an abridged and possibly otherwise revised version of the F text" (Stanley Wells and Gary Taylor, *William Shakespeare, A Textual Companion* [Oxford: Clarendon Press, 1987], p. 197). In taking this position, the Oxford editors follow Marco Mincoff ("*Henry VI Part III* and *The True Tragedy*," *English Studies*, 42 [1961], 273–88), who showed that some of Q1's "rather obvious corruptions seem to be due to interference with a written source rather than to memorial reconstruction" (p. 276). Mincoff argued that the differences in Q1 "seem on the whole to be the result of deliberate cutting rather than of the actors' forgetfulness" (p. 283). In a distinguished piece of detective work, Scott McMillin ("Casting for Pembroke's Men: The *Henry VI* Quartos and The *Taming of A Shrew*," *Shakespeare Quarterly*, 23 [1972], 141–59) also accepted the basic hypothesis of memorial reconstruction but with severe reservations. He pointed out that there were three major rearrangements of the order of events in Act 4 of Q1 which "appear to result from deliberate revisions" (p. 148); "Q seems to be not an accumulation of 'memorial' accidents but an accurate record of the history plays as they were performed by Pembroke's men" (p. 149). The discussion in the present essay will proceed as though Q1 represents a memorially reported version, reconstructed in part from written material and in part from the memory of a stage adaptation of Shakespeare's manuscript, but will not ignore the strong possibility, amounting almost to certainty, that Shakespeare continued to rethink and revise the play after the manuscript that ultimately became Q1 left his hands.

3. Montague as he appears in *3 Henry VI* is a puzzle. It seems clear that "Mountague" in F and "Marquis Montague" in Q1, who is treated as the brother [in-law] of York, was historically York's nephew by his marriage to Cecily Neville and therefore brother to the earl of Warwick. But Montague's line "And I vnto the Sea, from whence I came" (TLN 237; 1.1.216) and Margaret's inexplicable sentence "Sterne *Falconbridge* commands the Narrow Seas" (TLN 270; l. 246) strongly indicate that Shakespeare originally intended Montague's lines for a character who would be the York brother-in-law Falconbridge (whom Hall had confused with Falconbridge's bastard son of the same name and who was—also according to Hall—"Vice-admyrall of the sea, and had in charge so to kepe the passage betwene Douer and Caleys" [fol. 222r]; see A. S. Cairncross, "An 'Inconsistency' in '3 Henry VI'," *Modern Language Review*, 50 [1955], 492–94). As far as 1.1 is concerned, there is no reason why the change from a York brother-

in-law to a Warwick brother would matter at all. It may be that Shakespeare made the change when he decided to contrast the antagonism between the York brothers to the relation of loyalty between Warwick and his "brother" Montague.

4. At this early point in *3 Henry VI*, the character of the future Edward IV is no more developed than that of his brother Richard. Edward will shortly emerge as a willful and self-indulgent amorist, but in this scene he too speaks in terms that are clearly indebted to the example of Tamburlaine. On the question of York's oath, Edward is both aspiring and thoughtless: "But for a Kingdome any Oath may be broken: / I would breake a thousand Oathes, to reigne one yeere" (TLN 327–28; ll. 16–17). He becomes a far less hyperbolical speaker as the play proceeds.

5. Shakespeare found the omen of the three suns in Hall: "The duke of Yorke [i.e., Edward, successor to Richard, duke of York, and soon to be Edward IV] ... mett with his enemies in a faire playne, nere to Mortimers crosse, not farre from Herford east, on Candelmas day in the mornyng, at whiche time the sunne (as some write) appered to [him], like iii. sunnes, and sodainly ioined al together in one, and that vpon the sight therof, he toke suche courage, that he fiercely set on his enemies, & them shortly discomfited: for which cause, men imagined, that he gaue the sunne in his full brightnes for his cognisaunce or badge" (Edward Hall, *The Vnion of the Two Noble & Illvstrate Famelies of Lancastre and Yorke* [London: Richard Grafton, 1548], fols. 183v–84r). Shakespeare makes Richard (historically only eight years old at the time) a witness and analyst of the miracle. Richard sees the potential for an allegorical reading ("In this, the Heauen figures some euent" [TLN 684; 2.1.32]). Edward advances his own interpretation: "I thinke it cites vs (Brother) to the field, / That wee, the Sonnes of braue *Plantagenet*, / Each one alreadie blazing by our meedes, / Should notwithstanding ioyne our Lights together, / And ouer-shine the Earth, as this the World" (TLN 687–91; ll. 34–38). By allowing Richard to comment on the astronomical anomaly, Shakespeare develops the subject of cooperation and conflict between the "Sonnes of braue *Plantagenet*." If Shakespeare was attempting to arouse interest in fraternal relationships, as he certainly was at later points in the composition of the play, why, since he had already violated history by introducing Richard, did he not also include Richard's elder brother George of Clarence in the scene. Where was George? Why, that is, did Shakespeare note but fail to exploit the pregnant figure of the three suns/sons?

6. This particular passage is an instance in which evidence for revision is unassailable. Richard's speech survives in a variant but unquestionably authentic form in Q1, where the subject is not a Warwick brother but Warwick's father, old Salisbury (the brother—actually half-brother—in question in F would be [in Hall's phrase] "the bastard of Salisbury" [fol. 186r; see also Cairncross, *3 Henry VI*, pp. xxi–ii and 2.3.15n]). Q1 reads

Thy noble father in the thickest thronges
Cride still for *Warwike* his thrise valiant son,
Vntill with thousand swords he was beset,
And manie wounds made in his aged brest,
And as he tottering sate vpon his steede,
He waft his hand to me and aide aloud:
Richard, commend me to my valiant sonne,
And still he cride *Warwike* reuenge my death.
And with those words he tumbled off his horse,
And so the noble Salsbury gaue vp the ghost.

(sig. C[1]v)

Shakespeare seems to have revised *older* Q1 to *newer* F to shift the emphasis from a paternal to a fraternal theme. It should also be noted that Richard's style of speech in Q1 is less distinct than in F and the revenge theme comparatively muted.

7. *Wits Miserie and the Worlds Madness* (London: Adam Islip, 1596), p. 56.

8. fol. 195v. In reading in the chronicles about Edward, Shakespeare would have found Thomas More's description of Richard, taken from More's *History of King Richard Ill*. According to More, Richard was "close and secrete, a deepe dissimuler, lowlye of counteynaunce, arrogant of heart, outwardly coumpinable where he inwardely hated, not letting to kisse whome bee thoughte to kyll: dispitious and cruell, not for euill will alway, but ofter for ambicion, and either for the suretie or encrease of his estate. Frende and foo was muche what indifferent, where his aduauntage grew, he spared no mans deathe, whose life withstoode his purpose." Scene 2 of Act 3 also dearly reflects More's account of the events: "Whom, when the king beheld, & hard [Elizabeth Grey] speke, as she was both faire, of a good fauor, moderate of stature, wel made & very wise: he not only pitied her, but also waxed ennamored on her. And taking her afterward secretly aside, began to entre in talking more familiarly. Whose appetite when she perceiued, she verteousely denyed him. But that did she so wiseli, & with so good maner, & wordes so wel set, that she rather kindled his desire then quenched it. And fynally after many a meeting, much woing & many great promises, she wel espied the kinges affeccion toward her so greatly encresed, that she durst somewhat the more boldly say her minde, as to hym whose harte she perceiued more firmely set, then to fall of for a worde. And in conclusion she shewed him plaine, that as she wist herself to simple to be his wife, so thought she her self to good to be his concubine. The king much merueling of her constaunce, as he that had not ben wont els where to be so stiffely sayd naye, ... so muche estemed her contynence and chastitie, that he set her vertue in the stede of possession & riches. And thus taking counsaile of his desyre, determined in al possible hast to mary her" (both passages quoted here from *The Complete Works of St. Thomas More*, 15 vols., *Richard III*, Vol. 2, ed. Richard S. Sylvester

[New Haven and London: Yale Univ. Press, 1963–86], pp. 8 and 61). In More's version of the events, Richard and George do not eavesdrop, nor does Richard reflect on the conversation.

9. Richard's Vice inheritance is well established in criticism and is elucidated most fully in Bernard Spivack's *Shakespeare and the Allegory of Evil: The History of A Metaphor In Relation to His Major Villains* ([New York: Columbia Univ. Press, 1958] esp. pp. 386–407). Antony Hammond epitomizes Richard's indebtedness to the Vice tradition in his new Arden edition of *King Richard III* ([London: Methuen, 1981] pp. 99–102).

10. Noted by Wolfgang G. Müller, "The Villain as Rhetorician in Shakespeare's *Richard III*," *Anglia*, 102 (1984), 37–59, esp. pp. 47–48.

11. *Apius and Virginia, 1575*, ed. R. B. McKerrow (Oxford: Malone Society Reprints, 1911), ll. 210–19.

12. Q1 reads "And set the aspiring *Catalin* to schoole" (sig. C8"). This anomaly can be explained as the result either of memorial reconstruction or of revision. If the former, the classical tag may have replaced the mention of the "murtherous *Macheuill*" when the compiler of Q1 remembered the pre-1579 play of *Catiline's Conspiracies*, which the unconverted Stephen Gosson had written "too showe the rewarde of traytors" (*Schoole of Abuse* [London, 1579], p. 23). There may also have been a second play on the subject of Catiline by the Robert Wilson who was perhaps also an actor with the earl of Leicester's company (see *An Edition of Robert Wilson's* Three Ladies of London *and* Three Lords and Three Ladies of London, ed. H.S.D. Mithal [New York: Garland, 1988], p. lxvi). This section of Q1 is badly abbreviated. Richard's soliloquy is truncated to a mere twenty-eight lines and seems to present clear evidence of "badness." For example, Q1 inserts (after TLN 1651; 3.2.127) "For I am not yet lookt on in the world," a line that is triggered by the phrase "vnlook'd-for Issue" (TLN 1655; l. 131) but which just as clearly anticipates Richard's much later "For yet I am not look'd on in the world" (TLN 3193; 5.7.22). Moreover, in Q1, Richard regrets that Love has been able "To drie mine arme vp like a withered shrimpe" (sig. C8r) where F retains the less ridiculous "To shrinke mine Arme vp like a wither'd Shrub" (TLN 1680; l. 156). "Withered shrimpe" seems to be an actor's recollection that the Countess of Auvergne had once branded Talbot a "weake and writhled shrimpe" (*1 Henry VI*, TLN 859; 2.3.22). Both Talbot—"a Child, a silly Dwarfe"—and Richard were probably played by the same low-statured actor (Cairncross thinks *1 Henry VI* to be a play in the same Pembroke repertoire as the Q versions of *2* and *3 Henry VI* ["Pembroke's Men and Some Shakespearean Piracies," *SQ*, 11 (1960), 335–49]). The argument that a fragment of *1 Henry VI* found its way into "bad" Q1 will not be persuasive to those who hold that *1 Henry VI* postdates and is therefore what has lately come to be called a "prequel" of *3 Henry VI*—although it is not impossible that even if *1 Henry VI* was written after *3 Henry VI*, the *compilation* of Q1 might still come after performances of *1 Henry VI*.

On the other hand, although unlikely, it is not beyond possibility that "aspiring *Catalin*" was the original conception and "murtherous *Macheuill*" an inspired improvement. An intelligent assessment of the place of Machiavelli on the stage and in the English imagination is offered by Margaret Scott in "Machiavelli and the Machiavel," *Renaissance Drama*, n.s. 15 (1984), 147–74. Scott notes in passing that the "three parts of *Henry VI* ... reveal a world where all order is discounted, loyalty sacrificed to ambition, truth and trust set by, and the law of God and man displaced by force and fraud" (p. 171). Richard's invocation of Machiavelli would be, in this view, an inevitable outgrowth of implicit amorality.

13. It is tempting to hypothesize that the repetition in the structure of the soliloquy signals revision, and that, with the burst of imagination and inspiration in the passage beginning "And yet I know not how to get the Crowne," Shakespeare began again to come to terms with a recalcitrant problem. The passage in which Richard discusses his deformity seems to come to a full stop with "round impaled with a glorious Crowne"—a line that rings with finality. The ungainly repetition of "crowne" as the last word of two consecutive lines remains in the text as evidence of suture. (But counter-evidence is provided by the epistrophes at 1.1.13–14 and 114–15; 1.4.23–24; 2.1.4–5; and 5.6.13–14.)

14. fol. 218r.

15. It is difficult to dissent from Wells and Taylor et al.'s observation that "the sense of the [Q1] line is of sufficient complexity to make it an improbable memorial interpolation" (p. 205). Positing "eyeskip" on the part of the compositor, the Oxford editors print the line as genuine. But memorial interpolation is not the only possibility. Is it not more likely that in this instance Q1 preserves an earlier state of the speech which was not inadvertently omitted by the compositor but deliberately blotted by the author? At some point Shakespeare noticed that the line "I had no father" is inappropriate to Richard (who never wavers in his loyalty to his father) and only compromises both Richard's intensity and the thematic concerns of the last part of the play.

16. Quoted here from Joan Thirsk, "Younger Sons in the Seventeenth Century;" *History*, 54 (1969), 358–77, esp. p. 360. Younger sons are compared to bastards by Arthur Warren in *The Poore Mans passions. And Pouerties Patience* (London, 1605):

> Because we are not elder Brethren borne,
> Apparant Heyres to earthly Heritage,
> Hence hautie Worlds inheritors vs scorne,
> As not begot in lawfull Marriage,
> > The harme is ours, the iniury was theirs,
> > To take all, ere we borne were to be Heires.
>
> > > > (sig. C2v)

17. Most writers on *3 Henry VI* (a play that does not *enjoy* as rich a criticism as some) do not concern themselves with shifts in the portrayal of Richard. The tendency in the work of those few who take note has been to regard what is here understood as experimentation as the revelation of characteristics that were implicit but unstated. So E.M.W. Tillyard notes that when Richard overhears his brother wooing Elizabeth, the "ecstasy of jealousy thereby aroused ... both sharpens his malignity towards his brother and strengthens, in compensation for his own deficiencies in amorous scope, his already excessive ambitions" (*Shakespeare's History Plays* [London; Chatto and Windus, 1948], p. 195). The same assumption underlies a remark by M. M. Reese (*The Cease of Majesty: A Study of Shakespeare's History Plays* [London: Edward Arnold, 1961]) that until the soliloquy in 3.2., "the practised Machiavel has kept his ambitions hidden" (p. 204). Even stronger positions are taken by Bernard Spivack ("Richard has continuous existence through three plays.... The *character* of Richard remains consistent with itself from first to last" [*Shakespeare and the Allegory of Evil* (cited in n. 9, above), p. 388]) and Larry S. Champion ("[Richard's] characterization is firmly established [from his first appearance]" [*Perspective in Shakespeare's English Histories* (Athens: Univ. of Georgia Press, 1980)], p. 82). In contrast, Robert B. Pierce (*Shakespeare's History Plays: The Family and the State* [Columbus: Ohio State Univ. Press, 1971]) takes note of the change in Richard's character. Pierce adduces an oedipal explanation: Richard's personality can only emerge after the death of York; "when the strength of his nature is freed from its filial tie, the last remnant of an order into which he can fit, he inevitably becomes a destructive force" (p. 83). David L. Frey notes Richard's "metamorphosis" towards "an embodiment of the perfected Machiavel" (*The First Tetralogy: Shakespeare's Scrutiny of the Tudor Myth* [The Hague: Mouton, 1976], p. 42). Nearest to the position advocated in this essay is that of Kristian Smidt, who sees Richard as a "brave soldier and a man of honour" who develops into "a Machiavelli of the blackest Elizabethan dye." Smith notes that "a change of personality *seems* to occur after the arrival of Lady Grey and the beginning of Edward's impolitic infatuation" (*Unconformities in Shakespeare's History Plays* [Atlantic Highlands, NJ.: Humanities Press, 1982], pp. 33–34).

ERICH SEGAL

Shakespeare: Errors and Erōs

Even great poets begin by mimicking their masters. Yet already in his journeyman days, Shakespeare was incapable of merely aping his distinguished predecessors. For *The Comedy of Errors*, possibly his earliest play and certainly the shortest, is a great deal more than an adaptation of Plautus' *Brothers Menaechmus* (*Menaechmi*). Shakespeare's *vortere* represents a "departure as a dramatist [and] his borrowings from classical comedy show the direction in which his mind was moving."[1] Coleridge called the play the "only poetical farce in our language." Documentary evidence dates the play around 1594 (or even earlier), but its thematic richness has inspired Harold Bloom to argue—contrary to the majority of critics—that it "does not read or play like apprentice work."[2] Northrop Frye affirms that "here as in so many other places this early experimental comedy anticipates the techniques of the romances."[3] Shakespeare was a natural, and he infused his very first offering for the stage with a sophistication bordering on genius.

In the Plautine play, we recall, a young man leaves Syracuse to search the entire world—or at least *Graecia exotica*—for his long-lost twin, in whose memory he has been redubbed Menaechmus. He likens the task to finding "a needle—as they say—in a haystack."[4] (The original Latin, *in scirpo nodum quaeris*, translates literally as "you're looking for a knot in a bulrush.") At long last he reaches the town of Epidamnus, where he is mistaken for someone who bears both his name and his likeness (a rather obvious clue). After a series of comic

From *The Death of Comedy*. © 2001 by the President and Fellows of Harvard College.

episodes or errors, the fraternal mirror images are reunited and both sail for Syracuse—leaving the Epidamnian twin's wife behind.

But this was not enough for the young Shakespeare even in his maiden effort. He recast the material, not merely to conform to the Elizabethan convention of the triple plot, but to add a depth and dimension that greatly enhance the Latin original. For a start, he increased the number of players. To the Roman twins he adds a pair of identical servants, both named Dromio—an apt name for these *servi currentes* (Greek *drom-*, "to run")—who by incredible coincidence were born the same day as their masters. And whereas the Menaechmus boys' parents disappear after the prologue, Shakespeare has built a rich finale in which not only are both braces of brothers reunited, but the Antipholus twins' father and mother as well.

Yet these additions transcend the mere multiplication of *dramatis personae*. The piece is suffused with a Christian coloration which makes the theme one not merely of discovery but of redemption.[5] As we will see, the change of locale from the Plautine Epidamnus to Ephesus has a number of Christian implications. Nevertheless, Shakespeare retains the Plautine setting of "Epidamium" [*sic*] as a place in the twins' past. Thus the playwright both asserts his command of the ancient material, and underscores the important change of dramatic setting.

The overplot is somber. The music at the beginning of *Twelfth Night* may have a "dying fall," but *Errors* commences with a note more suited to tragedy than comedy: the threat of actual death. The elderly Egeon has been condemned because of the strife between the neighboring towns of Syracuse and Ephesus—the setting of the play: "If any Syracusian born / come to the bay of Ephesus he dies."[6] The exclusion of foreigners on pain of death is a motif familiar from Euripidean melodrama (*Iphigenia in Tauris*, for example). The only way Egeon can "redeem his life" is by paying one thousand marks; lacking the necessary ransom, the old man is resigned to his doom. This is the first of many instances in the play which mix religious and monetary imagery. For the currency of redemption—"marks"—finds a contrapuntal echo in two themes which pervade the play. First there is a running joke of the blows inflicted on the two slaves. More seriously, there is an ongoing allusion to the stigmata of Christ, with all its implications for the theme of resurrection.

In an expository dialogue with the Duke of Ephesus, Egeon recounts how many years ago his pregnant wife followed him to Epidamnus, where he was doing business. Not long thereafter she produced "two goodly sons," twins:

And which were strange, the one so like the other
As could not be distinguish'd but by name.[7]

By happy coincidence, on the same day another woman in the town, who was "exceeding poor," also gave birth to "twins both alike." Pitying her, Egeon purchased her newborn lads to be servants to his own identical neonates.

But on the voyage home all were caught in a storm and scattered from one another in the ensuing shipwreck—a motif whose comic significance we have already seen in Euripides. It represents the chaotic loss of identity and upheaval of natural order that is part of the *k?mos*. Shakespeare is certainly using the imagery consciously, as his carefully chosen words demonstrate:

> Our helpful ship was splitted in the midst;
> So that, in this unjust *divorce* of us,
> Fortune had left to both of us alike,
> What to delight in, what to sorrow for.[8]

As we will later learn, the mother with one son and his servant boy were picked up by one passing ship, while the father and the other two babes were rescued by a second vessel. By this time Egeon is in tears (thus the actor can give his voice a rest, and the audience a breather). Fascinated, the Duke bids him continue his sad tale: "For we may pity, though not pardon thee."[9]

Eighteen years later, the son who had survived with Egeon—renamed, as in the *Menaechmi*, in memory of his lost brother Antipholus—left Syracuse with his similarly renamed servant to search for their other halves. When after five years they did not return, Egeon set off in pursuit, now in search of four people. His quest has brought him to Ephesus where he has been arrested and condemned to death. Touched by this tale, the sympathetic Duke postpones the old man's execution until sunset, in the hope that he may somehow obtain the money he needs to save his life.

As they leave the stage, the traveling Antipholus II and his slave appear, concluding a business deal with Balthazar, a local merchant. By artful coincidence, the tradesman pays the visiting twin a thousand marks—precisely the sum of money needed for his father's salvation—which Antipholus II entrusts to Dromio II to take to their inn. The merchant warns the visitor of the harsh law that imperils the lad's countrymen—one of whom (he adds with parenthetical irony) is scheduled to be executed that very day for violating the law.

Left alone on stage, Antipholus II decides to take a walk in the city and "lose myself"[10] He explains his predicament to the audience:

> I to the world am like a drop of water
> That in the ocean seeks another drop,
> Who, falling there to find his fellow forth,
> (Unseen, inquisitive) confounds himself.[11]

The image of water drops seems to have been inspired by the exclamation of Messenio in the *Menaechmi* when he sees both twins together for the first time:

> Never have I seen two men more similar than you two

Water isn't more like water, milk's not more alike to milk
Than he to you and you to him.[12]

But whereas in Plautus this same speech comes toward the climax, Shakespeare
has introduced the theme at an early stage, and he carefully develops the imagery
throughout the play—harking back to the storm which divorced the Antipholus
family. Thus intertextual allusion once again demonstrates Shakespeare's self-
conscious awareness of the Latin play and the transformations he has wrought.
For Antipholus effectively betrays his awareness of Messenio's words toward his
own Latin incarnation, as though he himself had read Plautus.

Yet the contrast is intensified by the joy in Messenio's ejaculation versus the
more Terentian melancholy in Antipholus' speech:

So I, to find a mother and a brother,
In quest of them, unhappy, lose myself.[13]

Here we encounter another somber moment continuing the mood of the
opening scene, something that is quite anomalous for the beginning of a
rollicking farce. Why is Antipholus not happy? Plautus' twin has been searching
just as long and shows no such despondency. Even in this early play, we can see
Shakespeare's greater depth of character and seriousness as compared with
Plautus' Roman farce.

As Antipholus II strolls off stage, there follows the first of the many errors.
The local Dromio mistakes the traveling twin for his master, and urges him to
come home to dinner at his house, the Phoenix—an apt name in a play of rebirth.
Antipholus II of course has no idea what "his" servant is talking about and
demands, "as I am a Christian ... where is the thousand marks thou hadst of
me?"[14] The servant is confused. Dromio I only knows "his mistress's marks"
upon his shoulders:

The clock hath strucken twelve upon the bell;
My mistress made it one upon my cheek.[15]

The angry traveler immediately gives him some more marks for his face
and chases him off, confiding to the audience:

They say this town is full of cozenage
As nimble jugglers that deceive the eye,
Dark-working sorcerers that change the mind,
Soul-killing witches that deform the body,
Disguised cheaters, prating mountebanks,
And many such-like liberties of sin.[16]

This is perhaps Shakespeare's closest echo of Plautus. There, punning on "Epidamnus," Messenio warns his master of the usual perils of an urban red-light district: "no one leaves here un-epi-damaged."[17] By changing the dramatic setting from Epidamnus to Ephesus, Shakespeare has added not only the theme of transformation and deception, but also a Christian dimension, echoing St. Paul's description of Ephesus as a place where

> exorcists took upon them to call over them which had evil spirits ... Many of them also which used curious arts brought their books together, and burned them before all men.[18]

Shakespeare develops the theme of sorcery and witchcraft throughout the play. Moreover, his portrayal of the characters' perplexity goes far deeper than Plautus' silly dupes. For "damaged" is not "transformed," nor in any way psychotropic. As the play proceeds, Shakespeare will strengthen this Christian dimension, which reaches its fullest expression in the finale.

The second act begins with a scene that Plautus could never have written. Two freeborn young women are having an intimate conversation: Adriana, the wife of the local Antipholus, and her gracious sister Luciana (both of course paradoxically played by young boys). Adriana is complaining about her husband's infidelity. In Plautus the *fille de joie* is called Erotium, while the wife is left nameless. Shakespeare reverses this, giving the married woman "a local habitation and a name," leaving the courtesan merely as "wench."

It is clear where the playwright's interests lie. In a bygone age the local Antipholus might have invoked the Roman husband's privilege of extramarital promiscuity. But fidelity was a subject close to Shakespeare's heart. Though he himself was separated by distance from Anne Hathaway, he was nonetheless a fervent advocate of marriage and procreation. This theme is everywhere in his plays and in the sonnets:

> From fairest creatures we desire increase,
> That thereby beauty's rose might never die ...[19]

The two women present a contrast. Adriana, the bad-tempered wife, bitterly complains of her husband's indifference to her. Her unmarried sister reminds her that "a man is master of his liberty."[20] To this the wife retorts with a strikingly modern sentiment, "why should their liberty than ours be more?"[21] Luciana's subsequent discourse on her view of the proper role of a woman in a marriage contains St. Paul's advice ("Wives, submit your selves unto your husbands, as unto the Lord"),[22] paraphrased by Luciana in her remark, "Ere I learn love, I'll practice to obey."[23] She is clearly good wife material. But Adriana remains adamant. For this display of proto-feminism she has been called a shrew.

Yet hers is a voice of a genuine, plausible lament, and in a real sense these two women provide the emotional core of the play.

Dromio I comes in to report that "his master" is mad, since he kept asking him for a thousand marks. And when told that Adriana wanted him home for dinner, his outraged master had replied, "'I know,' quoth he, 'no house, no wife, no mistress.'" Thus, to the women's perception, Antipholus I has abrogated his marriage vows. Divorce looms.

After the slave is given more marks for his efforts, the scene concludes with Adriana's mournful plaint that her marriage is disintegrating. She pines away "and starves for a merry look":

> What ruins are in me that can be found
> By him not ruin'd? Then is he the ground
> Of my defeatures; My decayed fair
> A sunny look of his would soon repair.[24]

In a kind of reversal of the Petrarchan conceit that love bestows loveliness on the beloved, Beauty thinks that she has become the Beast as a result of her husband's neglect. Yet another scene concludes with a plangent note:

> Since that my beauty cannot please his eye,
> I'll weep what's left away, and weeping die.[25]

Adriana and Luciana soon confront Antipholus—the wrong one—who has been transformed into another person. They continually and unwittingly pun on the two connotations of "strangeness," the one in its modern meaning, the other in the sense of "foreign." It is as if Adriana subconsciously recognizes that he is an outlander:

> Ay, ay, Antipholus, look strange and frown ...
> How comes it now, my husband, O, how comes it,
> That thou art then estranged from thyself?—
> Thyself I call it, being strange to me,
> That undividable, incorporate,
> Am better than thy dear self's better part.[26]

Her remark that Antipholus' personality is somehow divided into good and bad is our first hint that in Shakespeare's mind, as in Plautus', the twins might be two parts of a schizophrenic whole. The local twin is terribly bourgeois, complacent, and oddly detached from his wife and family.

He is also unfaithful and in debt—which may be construed as feelings of guilt. As Ferenczi observed, "debt" and "guilt" are, in many languages, expressed by the same word. Indeed, "debt" is repeated most often in this of all the comedies, and three times in this scene alone—hammering home a cardinal element in the play, the sentence lying over old Egeon's head. For in Elizabethan times "debt" was pronounced the same as "death"—and in Egeon's case both meanings are clearly operative. We find a similar pun in *1 Henry 4*, where Prince Hal reminds Falstaff on Shrewsbury field:

> HAL: Why, thou owes't God a death.
> FALSTAFF: ... I would be loath to pay him before his day.[27]

The pedant Holofernes explains in *Love's Labour's Lost*:

> HOL.:   I abhor such fanatical phantasimes, such
>   insociable and point devise companions, such
>   rackers of orthography, as to speak "dout,"
>   fine, when he should say "doubt"; "det," when
>   he should pronounce "debt"—*d*, *e*, *b*, *t*, not *d*,
>   *e*, *t* ...[28]

By contrast, his alter ego the traveling Antipholus, innocent of the world despite his years of voyaging, arrives in Ephesus unattached and "unhappy, to lose myself." But is not his entire purpose to find his other self? This theme of alienation of the self is often associated with the word "strange," repeated in this context again and again. The passage quoted above develops a motif begun in Egeon's remark that even at birth the twins' complete similarity was "strange."[29] The traveling twin reports that he "is as strange unto your town as to your talk,"[30] while the merchant Balthasar finds it "strange" that the local Antipholus is being kept out of his own house.[31] When at the end the Duke confronts the various twins, he will remark "Why this is strange."[32] Likewise Egeon, staring at the "wrong" son, and pained that he does not recognize his own father, wonders: "Why look you so strange on me?"[33] In other words, each brother needs to unite with the other to restore chaos to order and become an entire person.

Despondent at her (putative) husband's strangeness, Adriana begs him not to break their marriage tie with "deep-divorcing vow." We recall the "unjust divorce" of the storm that separated the Antipholus brothers. She too invokes the simile of water drops, once again to suggest a single person with two personalities:

> For know, my love, as easy mayst thou fall
> A drop of water in the breaking gulf,
> And take unmingled thence that drop again
> Without addition or diminishing,
> As take from me thyself, and not me too.[34]

Shakespeare employs similar imagery to express the insolubility of love in other plays, as in the balcony scene of *Romeo and Juliet*, when the heroine says:

> My bounty is as boundless as the sea,
> My love as deep: the more I give to thee
> The more I have, for both are infinite.[35]

Taken aback, the traveling Antipholus protests that they could not possibly know each other because "In Ephesus I am but two hours old ..."[36] In other words, he has just been born again. Luciana, of course, does not understand, and reproves him for denying that he is married to her sister. She too employs the imagery of transformation: "Fie brother! How the world is *changed* with you!"[37]

Still protesting that he does not know these women, Antipholus reminds us of the archetypal association of comedy with dreams. False etymologies can sometimes be truer than real ones:[38]

> What, was I married to her in my *dream?*
> Or *sleep* I now, and think I hear all this?
> What error drives our eyes and ears amiss?[39]

The kinship between comedy and dream is never far from Shakespeare's mind, whether it be Sly's drunken hallucinations in the Induction to *The Taming of the Shrew*, or an episode as zany as "Bottom's Dream," a nocturnal fantasy on a midsummer's night. And of course Puck's epilogue:

> PUCK: If we shadows have offended,
>   Think but this and all is mended,
>   That you have but slumber'd here
>   While these visions did appear.[40]

Dreaming or not, the traveling Antipholus accepts "his wife's" invitation to dinner, and sets Dromio to keep any intruders out. (There will only be another Antipholus and another Dromio trying to disturb their own house.)

Yet it is more than the possibility of *kma* here. Before entering, Antipholus II expresses his stupefaction:

> Am I in earth, in heaven, or in hell?
> Sleeping or waking, mad or well advised?
> Known unto these, and to myself disguised![41]

Shakespeare here raises the notion of insanity for the first time, as Antipholus questions his own lucidity and identity. Can he really be true "to myself disguised"? In a play which presents the "other self," he imagines that new feelings of love have awakened a better identity within him. In fact, he has been "reborn" as a lover "two hours old." Sane or mad, he is bewitched into accepting the hospitality of these lovely women who profess to know him. He will certainly get a good meal—and who knows what else for dessert?

And here is another significant variation on the Plautine theme. In the Roman play, the visiting twin gets to enjoy a free dinner and free love from Erotium, his brother's *mistress*. There is a wholly different dimension to Shakespeare's version. For here the traveling brother receives an affectionate offer to wine and dine—and perhaps recline—with his brother's *wife*. In Plautus the twin's greatest risk would be being accused of robbery, while in the *Comedy of Errors* there is the hazard of incest with his brother's wife. According to scripture—*au pied de la lettre*—the act would be both a sin and a moral outrage.[42]

The errors compound. As Harry Levin observed, "there is an inherent lack of dignity—I am almost tempted to call it a loss of face—in being indistinguishable from, in always being mistaken for, someone else."[43] The visiting Dromio, left to guard the home gate, turns away the rightful owner and his slave, insisting "*my* name is Dromio." We need not wonder that Antipholus I does not notice the striking similarity between the two bondsmen. It requires of us what Coleridge would call a "willing suspension of disbelief ... which constitutes poetic faith." This causes his local twin to echo the lament of the slave Sosia in the *Amphitruo* when *he* is turned away from his own household by Mercury. After the god punches him into believing that he is *not* Sosia any more, the bondsman exclaims: "Where did I get lost? Where was I transformed? Where did I lose my self?"[44]

In Shakespeare the local servant complains to his newly discovered mirror image: "O villain, thou hast stol'n both my office and my name!"[45]—another echo of the *Amphitruo* where Sosia retreats in anguish from Mercury, exclaiming: "I've got to find myself another name."[46] It is only *now*, when locked out of his own house, that Antipholus thinks of his courtesan.

No sooner does the husband depart for his "licensed" adultery than Shakespeare presents his twin making amorous advances to, Luciana, his "wife's" sister. Luciana is shocked, but Antipholus II persists, twice referring to the "wonder" of her already knowing his name. He once again presents himself as a newborn baby: "Smother'd in errors, feeble, shallow, weak."[47] His astonishment re-emphasizes the theme of rebirth and metamorphosis through the power of love:

> Are you a god? Would you create me new?
> Transform me then, and to your power I'll yield.[48]

This anticipates Romeo's burst of affection when Juliet asks him "to doff thy name." He answers, "call me but love and I'll be new baptized."[49] In Shakespeare love is renewal, regeneration, and rebirth.

But in the *Comedy of Errors*, a quite similar expression of affection has the opposite effect on the affrighted Luciana. "Why call you *me* love?" she protests. The visiting twin insists, "It is thyself, mine own self's better part." Once again we have the intimation that the twin is but half of another person. But here it is more conventional-one thinks of the Latin proverb *amicus est alter ego*. In truth, this twin must find his own self's other part before gaining license to marry the woman with whom he has fallen in love at first sight. But in the meantime Luciana is horrified and runs off from the confused visitor.

Dromio too has an identity crisis as well as a possible metamorphosis. He rushes in and asks his master in a panic:

DROMIO:	Do you know me, sir? Am I Dromio? Am I your man? Am *I* myself?
ANTIPHOLUS:	Thou art Dromio, thou art my man, thou art thyself.
DROMIO:	I am an ass, I am a woman's man, and besides myself.[50]

In a parody of the main plot, the servant also experiences the transforming power of "love." He will prate on about being changed into various animals (ass, dog, and so on) as he suffers from the amorous advances of the kitchen wench, a "mad mountain of flesh" who has mistaken him for his twin brother, to whom she is married. In a vaudevillian turn, the slave likens various parts of her anatomy to different countries:

ANTIPHOLUS:	Where America, the Indies?
DROMIO:	O, sir, upon her nose, all o'er embellished with rubies, carbuncles, sapphires, declining their rich aspect to the hot breath of Spain ...
ANTIPHOLUS:	Where stood Belgia, The Netherlands?
DROMIO:	O, sir, I did not look so low ...[51]

He concludes: "I, amazed, ran from her as a witch."[52] His master concurs, and they plan to leave Ephesus immediately.

But before they can sail, Angelo the Goldsmith enters to give the visitor a chain commissioned by his indigenous brother. Antipholus II is confused—but naturally accepts the gift:

But this I think, there is no man so vain,
That would refuse so fair an offered chain.[53]

Five o'clock nears. In the end, the many gifts bestowed on the traveling twin must be paid for. And they will be—by the local twin, who, in a reversal of

Bentley's formulation of comedy, "is *denied* the outrage but pays the consequences." Thus the traveling twin could represent the libido, the local the superego. Antipholus of Ephesus, confused by Angelo's dunning him for the money he owes for the chain, denies that he has received it. But this is no time for levity. The Goldsmith needs to pay a merchant at five o'clock. The specific sum provides irony for the cleverer spectators, and serves to remind all others that this is the scheduled time of old Egeon's execution. As a debt collector arrests Antipholus for non-payment, he sends Dromio—the wrong one, of course—to run home and get bail money from his wife.

As these confusions come hard and fast, we have a scene between the two sisters. Luciana is troubled by the sudden change both in her "brother-in-law's" interior and his exterior. Adriana is more upset by her "husband's" attempted seduction of her sister. Neither can fathom what has happened, and the only charitable conclusion they can reach is that he is mad. Note the rhetorical emphasis on psychic symptoms made physical:

> He is deformed, crooked, old and sere,
> Ill face'd, worse bodied, shapeless everywhere;
> Vicious, ungentle, foolish, blunt, unkind,
> Stigmatical in making, worse in mind.[54]

To a play that emphasizes the similarity of exteriors (the Plautine model), Shakespeare has added the dimension of interior changes.

Meanwhile the traveling Dromio arrives to ask for bail money. Adriana is astonished that her husband is "in debt," but gives the gold to Dromio, who rushes off.

The following scene is an elaboration of a moment in the Plautine original, when Menaechmus of Sicily enters dazed and amazed by the fact that people recognize him in this strange city:

> What unworldly wonders have occurred today in wondrous ways:
> People claim I'm not the man I am and close their doors to me.
> Then this fellow said he was my slave and that I set him free!
> Then he says he'll go and bring a wallet full of money to me ...
> All this business seems to me like nothing other than a dream.[55]

Again we encounter the oneiric aspect of comedy. For, etymology aside, comedy is in a very real sense a wish-fulfillment. Just like his naive Plautine forebear, Antipholus II has not yet understood why everybody in Ephesus seems to recognize him:

> There's not a man I meet but doth salute me
> As if I were their well-acquainted friend;

And every one doth call me by my name:
Some tender money to me; some invite me ...
Sure, these are but imaginary wiles,
And Lapland sorcerers inhabit here.[56]

Once again Shakespeare has added the dimension of sorcery to the
Syracusan twin's hypnotic experience. But the local Antipholus is not having the
same good luck. For one man's pleasant dream is another man's nightmare.
When the (nameless) courtesan, who has provided entertainment, confronts the
local Antipholus for the chain he promised, as well as the ring he took at dinner,
the astounded twin denies having received either. The lady immediately
concludes, "Now out of doubt Antipholus is mad"[57]—a diagnosis she repeats
three times in eight lines. And in a comic reversal of the "other woman" who
normally keeps a low profile—if that is the word—she rushes off to tell his wife
he is "lunatic." It is clear to the audience which twin will *pay* for the swindle.

Adriana reappears with a psychiatric consultant-cum-conjurer, the
ridiculous Dr. Pinch. Much like the *medicus gloriosus* in Plautus' play, he
pronounces the patient insane ("both master and man is possessed")[58] and orders
his strong-armed helpers to grab hold of Antipholus and Dromio. His
prescription, that "they be bound and laid in some dark room,"[59] was a normal
therapy for insanity in Elizabethan times; Malvolio is subjected to the same
treatment in *Twelfth Night*. Here in the dark, one cannot help perceiving an
additional intra-uterine adumbration of the symbolic rebirth that is to come.
Now both father and son can only be redeemed by payment of a debt.

The final act takes place not in the familiar city street, but before a
Christian Priory (formerly the famous temple of Diana, one of the listed wonders
of the ancient world) in whose cloisters the visiting Antipholus and Dromio have
taken refuge to avoid the local brother's creditors. The lady Abbess is both a kind
of *dea ex machina* and an early marriage counselor. Adriana explains to her with
unconscious irony, "this week he hath been ... much different from the man he
was."[60] The holy woman immediately seeks to reconcile the estranged couple.
She begins by admonishing Adriana for her bad temper (taking Luciana's
position), and concluding that she was partially to blame for her husband's going
mad:

The consequence is, then, thy jealous fits
Hath scar'd thy husband from the use of wits.[61]

Moreover, although Adriana wants custody of her afflicted husband, the Mother
Superior insists upon keeping Antipholus under her supervision.

But Adriana takes her plea to a higher court. For at that moment the
merchant announces that "the dial points at five," and the noble Solinus himself
enters, leading Egeon to his imminent execution. Adriana appeals to him with a

cry—"Justice, most sacred Duke, against the Abbess!"—and begins to describe her husband's madness—just as he himself appears with a perfect antiphonal shout ("justice, most gracious Duke").

Both husband and wife put their case before the noble ruler, who then overrules the Roman double standard with Christian fidelity. Other voices are raised. The merchants, and even the courtesan, vent their ire. At this cacophony of indictments, the Duke exclaims:

> Why, what an intricate impeach is this!
> I think you all have drunk of Circe's Cup.[62]

Shakespeare yet again calls our attention to the witchcraft and transformations that permeate Ephesus. The comparison to the enchantress in the *Odyssey* is particularly apt. A pernicious *femme fatale*, Circe used her seductive appeal to bewitch men and turn them into pigs—itself a kind of metaphor for male sensuality. Nor is this the only reference in the play to Homer's "reunion poem." Like Odysseus, Antipholus has spent years wandering throughout farthest Greece. His love for Luciana is like the siren's song that distracts and lures him from his quest:

> ANTIPHOLUS: O, train me not, sweet mermaid, with thy note,
>   To drown me in thy [sister's] flood of tears.[63]

The twin's long travels have been a voyage of rebirth and discovery. Is this not the very theme of the *Odyssey*?

And yet, although comedy focuses on the swinish parts of man, this reductive view of the relationship between the sexes is about to be refuted with the purity of love displayed by the protagonist. Suddenly Egeon catches sight of a possible savior, and quickly questions the much-beleaguered local twin:

> EGEON: Is not your name, sir, called Antipholus?
>   And is not that your bondman, Dromio?[64]

Just as it seems that this gambit of identities can go no further, Shakespeare, by having Egeon appeal to the wrong set of twins, wrings one final twist from the conventional material. Neither his son, nor his son's slave, recognizes him. Egeon is staggered, but still persists:

> EGEON: O time's extremity,
>   Hast thou so crack'd and splitted my poor tongue
>   In seven short years, that here my only son
>   Knows not my feeble key of untun'd cares?[65]

To Plautus' simple reunion, Shakespeare has added a deft *non-cognitio* as the local Antipholus answers bluntly but truthfully, "I never saw you in my life till now." And when Egeon claims again to be Antipholus' father, the local twin protests—with a touch of sadness—"I never saw my father in my life."

And now tragedy looms. In a moment it will be too late to save Egeon's life. And so the playwright expediently sends the Abbess onstage, leading the Syracusan man and slave—who of course immediately recognize their father. At this climactic moment, Adriana's eyes widen as she exclaims, "I see two husbands, or my eyes deceive me."[66] And with equal astonishment, the Duke adds:

> One of these men is genius to the other;
> And so of these, which is the natural man
> And which the spirit? Who deciphers them?[67]

As the traveling twins affectionately embrace their elderly father, the Dromios introduce themselves. The family reunion is made astonishingly complete by the wholly unexpected cry of the Abbess, who suddenly realizes that she is Mrs. Deus Ex Machina: the doomed prisoner is none other than her long-lost husband. For his part, the wide-eyed old man exclaims, "If I dream not, thou art Emilia." And yet he is not dreaming: this is indeed his long-lost wife—back from the divorce of death. His son thinks it is a sleeping fantasy, and echoes his astonishment: "If this be not a dream I see and hear." We are continually brought back to the strong link between *kma* and comedy—if not etymologically, at least psychologically.

The Duke himself has a sudden *cognitio*—of the veracity of Egeon's plaint in the prologue. Not only two pairs of sons but a father and mother have unexpectedly reappeared from the depths of the ocean. The mysteries, mistakes, and merchandising of this mad day are straightened out—and, most important, the money that will redeem Egeon. Antipholus offers to ransom his father from death, but the Duke pardons the old man so his son can keep the money. It is an archetypal ending, a world of dreams and wish-fulfillment. All anger is dispelled, and love can triumph.

Best of all, the traveling twin can now marry Luciana. Unlike the identical heroes in the Plautine model, who return home to Syracuse insouciantly leaving the Epidamnian wife behind, Shakespeare celebrates the symbolic remarriage of all four couples in a mighty quadruple *gamos*. We can safely assume that the local Antipholus will never visit the courtesan again. And, thanks to the intercession of the Duke, Adriana will be a shrew no more. His twin will marry his beloved Luciana and remain deeply in love. Even Dromio and his frumpy kitchen wife are reunited. This is perhaps too much like a fairy tale. But Shakespeare believed in the sacrament of marriage in a way that transcends words.

The play ends on a very Christian note as the Abbess exclaims:

Thirty-three years have I but gone in travail [pains of childbirth]
Of you, my sons; and till this present hour
My heavy burdens ne'er delivered.[68]

It is a curious speech. We have already been told that the shipwreck
occurred *twenty-five* years ago when the twins were neonates. This is surely not,
as some pedestrian critics have argued, a mere *lapsus calami*: it is neither slip of pen
nor memory. In this play full of christological allusions, we immediately recognize
the age of Christ at the crucifixion—another direct reference to resurrection.[69] In
Frye's view, "the imagery of the final recognition scene suggests a passing through
death into a new world."[70] In other words, as Antipholus of Syracuse
demonstrates, you must lose yourself to find yourself. Everyone in the play has
experienced a rebirth, and the Mother Superior invites them to come to church
to celebrate "a gossips' feast"—a highly significant choice, for this was the
celebration of a newborn child's baptism. The bemused Duke puns, "with all my
heart I'll gossip at this feast." The local Dromio invites his brother to join "their
gossiping," and they joyfully leave the stage hand in hand.

Yet, strangely, the reunion of their masters is muted, to say the least.
Nowhere in the final scene does either of them exchange a single word of
affection or enthusiasm. Could this be a dramaturgical error?[71] After all, the
traveling twin earlier expressed his longing to meet his brother. Could it be that,
having lost himself, he will only find himself again when reunited with his other
self? The two can be viewed as two parts of a single whole—one married with
responsibilities, the other a carefree traveler.[72] They only share the same name
because of the loss which has now been recovered. Perhaps they need heavenly
benediction for the restoration of their wholeness, their humanity—and their
speech. Then at last the wandering twin will find himself.

This first comedy by Shakespeare set the tone for all those that followed.
For in one way or another, every one of them is about lost selves, absence,
recognition, and reunion—whether it be the parodic transformation of Bottom
into an Ass which mocks the lovers' imbroglios wrought by Puck, or time
recaptured in *The Winter's Tale* with the discovery of the lost Perdita and the
magical rebirth of her wronged mother, Hermione. Or Pericles reunited with his
wife Thiasa, long thought dead, now magically rescued from her watery tomb
and—like Emilia in *Errors*—serving as a nun at the temple of Diana in Ephesus.
Pericles, embracing his beloved wife, lovingly invites her, "come be buried / a
second time within these arms."[73] Ultimately, all these themes were refined into
the most delicate gold in *The Tempest*, with which Shakespeare ended his career.

NOTES

1. Leo Salingar, *Shakespeare and the Traditions of Comedy* (Cambridge, 1974),
p. 75.

2. Harold Bloom, *Shakespeare: The Invention of the Human* (London, 1999), p. 21; he continues: "[*Errors*] shows such skill, indeed mastery—in action, incipient character, and stagecraft—that it far outshines the three *Henry VI* plays and the rather lame *Two Gentlemen of Verona*." For the conventional evidence of the early dating, see, among others, R. A. Foakes's excellent Arden edition of *The Comedy of Errors* (Walton on Thames, 1962), p. xxiii. Kenneth Muir, *Shakespeare's Comic Sequence* (Liverpool, 1979), pp. 15–16, at first straddles the fence, saying: "The chronology of Shakespeare's early comedies is uncertain, but *The Comedy of Errors*, *The Two Gentlemen of Verona*, and *The Taming of the Shrew* (in whichever order) were the first three." He subsequently retreats to join the general consensus, conceding that "it seems probable, therefore, that the *Comedy of Errors* was the first to be written."

3. Northrop Frye, *A Natural Perspective: The Development of Shakespearean Comedy and Romance* (New York, 1965), p. 87.

4. Plautus *Menaechmi* 247.

5. The relevant New Testament passages are all printed in Appendix I of Foakes's edition.

6. *Comedy of Errors* 1.1.18–19.

7. Ibid., 1.1.51–52.

8. Ibid., 1.1.103–106.

9. Ibid., 1.1.97.

10. Ibid., 1.2.30.

11. Ibid., 1.2.35–38.

12. *Menaechmi* 1088–1090.

13. *Comedy of Errors* 1.2.39–40.

14. Ibid., 1.2.77–81.

15. Ibid., 1.2.45–46.

16. Ibid., 1.2.97–102.

17. *Menaechmi* 264, *nemo ferme huc sine damno devortitur.*

18. Acts 19.13–19.

19. Sonnet 1.1–2.

20. *Comedy of Errors* 2.1.7.

21. Ibid., 2.1.10.

22. Ibid., 2.1.18–24: "The beasts, the fishes, and the winged fouls / Are their males' subjects, and at their controls; / Man, more divine, the master of all these, / Lord of the wide world and wild wat'ry seas, / Indued with intellectual sense and souls, / Of more pre-eminence than fish and fowls, / Are masters to their females, and their lords ..."

23. Ibid., 2.1.29. Compare Ephesians 5.22.

24. *Comedy of Errors* 2.1.96–99.

25. Ibid., 2.1.114–115.

26. Ibid., 2.2.110; 119–123.

27. *1 Henry 4* 5.1.126.

28. *Love's Labour's Lost* 5.1.17–22.

29. *Comedy of Errors* 1.1.51.

30. Ibid., 2.2.149.

31. Ibid., 3.1.97.

32. Ibid., 5.1.281.

33. Ibid., 5.1.296. The adjective "strange" and its verb "estrange" occur frequently in Shakespeare's first play, reinforcing the sense of enchantment and magic that pervades his Ephesus. *Strange* swells to a veritable tidal wave in *The Tempest*, his final play, where it occurs no fewer than 21 times. He is not using it in the familiar modern sense, but rather to denote something that contains a certain magic and wonder—most famously expressed: "Full fathom five thy father lies / Of his bones are coral made; / Those are pearls that were his eyes: / Nothing of him that doth fade, / But doth suffer a sea-change / Into something *rich and strange.*" (*The Tempest* 1.2.399–404.)

34. Ibid., 2.2.125–129.

35. *Romeo and Juliet* 2.2.133–135.

36. *Comedy of Errors* 2.2.148.

37. Ibid., 2.2.152.

38. These false but apt etymologies include *lucus ex non lucendo* ("glade from shade") or asparagus from "sparrow grass."

39. *Comedy of Errors* 2.2.182–184.

40. *Midsummer Night's Dream* 5.1.423–426.

41. *Comedy of Errors* 2.2.212–214.

42. See Leviticus 18.16.

43. Harry Levin, *Refractions: Essays in Comparative Literature* (Oxford, 1966), p. 130.

44. *Amphitruo* 456.

45. *Comedy of Errors* 3.1.44.

46. *Amphitruo* 423, *aliud nomen quarendum est mihi*.

47. *Comedy of Errors* 3.2.35.

48. Ibid., 3.2.39–40.

49. *Romeo and Juliet* 2.2.50.

50. *Comedy of Errors* 3.2.72–77.

51. Ibid., 3.2.131–138.

52. Ibid., 3.2.143.

53. Ibid., 3.2.179–180.

54. Ibid., 4.2.19–22.

55. *Menaechmi* 1039–1043; 1047.

56. *Comedy of Errors* 4.3.1–4; 10–11.

57 Ibid., 4.3.78–90.

58. Ibid., 4.4.90.

59. Ibid., 4.4.92.

60. Ibid., 5.1.45–46.

61. Ibid., 5.1.85–86.

62. Ibid., 5.1.270–271.

63. Ibid., 3.2.45–46.

64. Ibid., 5.1.287–288.

65. Ibid., 5.1.307–310.

66. Ibid., 5.1.331.

67. Ibid., 5.1.332–334.

68. Ibid., 5.1.400–402.

69. Foakes, *Comedy*, p. 106, calls attention to the arithmetic but omits mention of christological evidence.

70. Frye, *Perspective*, p. 107.

71. Another more remote possibility is that, as in a production of *Comedy of Errors* in Stratford, Connecticut, in the early 1960s, both Antipholi were played by the same actor. This worked without masks. If the same tactic was adopted in Shakespeare's version, one of the twins would have been doubled in the finale by an extra who, though dressed the same, was unable to speak lines.

72. On the reunion of twins see Frye, *Perspective*, p. 78: "When they meet they are delivered, in comic fashion, from the fear of the loss of identity, the primitive horror of the Doppelganger which is an element in nearly all forms of insanity, something of which they feel as long as they are being mistaken for each other."

73. *Pericles* 5.3.43–44.

Romantic Comedy and Farce:
The Taming of the Shrew

The *Taming of the Shrew* begins with the very odd two scenes of the Induction, in which a noble practical joker gulls the drunken tinker, Christopher Sly, into the delusion that he is a great lord about to see a performance of Kate and Petruchio's drama. That makes their comedy, the rest of *The Taming of the Shrew*, a play-within-a-play, which does not seem at all appropriate to its representational effect upon an audience. Though skillfully written, the Induction would serve half a dozen other comedies by Shakespeare as well or as badly as it coheres with the *Shrew*. Critical ingenuity has proposed several schemes creating analogies between Christopher Sly and Petruchio, but I am one of the unpersuaded. And yet Shakespeare had some dramatic purpose in his Induction, even if we have not yet surmised it. Sly is not brought back at the conclusion of Shakespeare's *Shrew*, perhaps because his disenchantment necessarily would be cruel, and would disturb the mutual triumph of Kate and Petruchio, who rather clearly are going to be the happiest married couple in Shakespeare (short of the Macbeths, who end separately but each badly). Two points can be accepted as generally cogent about the Induction: it somewhat distances us from the performance of the *Shrew*, and it also hints that social dislocation is a form of madness. Sly, aspiring above his social station, becomes as insane as Malvolio in *Twelfth Night*.

Since Kate and Petruchio are social equals, their own dislocation may be their shared, quite violent forms of expression, which Petruchio "cures" in Kate

From *Shakespeare: The Invention of the Human.* © 1998 by Harold Bloom.

at the high cost of augmenting his own boisterousness to an extreme where it hardly can be distinguished from a paranoid mania. Who cures, and who is cured, remains a disturbing matter in this marriage, which doubtless will maintain itself against a cowed world by a common front of formidable pugnacity (much more cunning in Kate than in her roaring boy of a husband). We all know one or two marriages like theirs; we can admire what works, and we resolve also to keep away from a couple so closed in upon itself, so little concerned with others or with otherness.

It may be that Shakespeare, endlessly subtle, hints at an analogy between Christopher Sly and the happily married couple, each in a dream of its own from which we will not see Sly wake, and which Kate and Petruchio need never abandon. Their final shared reality is a kind of conspiracy against the rest of us: Petruchio gets to swagger, and Kate will rule him and the household, perpetually acting her role as the reformed shrew. Several feminist critics have asserted that Kate marries Petruchio against her will, which is simply untrue. Though you have to read carefully to see it, Petruchio is accurate when he insists that Kate fell in love with him at first sight. How could she not? Badgered into violence and vehemence by her dreadful father Baptista, who vastly prefers the authentic shrew, his insipid younger daughter Bianca, the high-spirited Kate desperately needs rescue. The swaggering Petruchio provokes a double reaction in her: outwardly furious, inwardly smitten. The perpetual popularity of the *Shrew* does not derive from male sadism in the audience but from the sexual excitation of women and men alike.

The *Shrew* is as much a romantic comedy as it is a farce. The mutual roughness of Kate and Petruchio makes a primal appeal, and yet the humor of their relationship is highly sophisticated. The amiable ruffian Petruchio is actually an ideal—that is to say an overdetermined—choice for Kate in her quest to free herself from a household situation far more maddening than Petruchio's antic zaniness. Roaring on the outside, Petruchio is something else within, as Kate gets to see, understand, and control, with his final approval. Their rhetorical war begins as mutual sexual provocation, which Petruchio replaces, after marriage, with his hyperbolical game of childish tantrums. It is surely worth remarking that Kate, whatever her initial sufferings as to food, costume, and so on, has only one true moment of agony, when Petruchio's deliberately tardy arrival for the wedding makes her fear she has been jilted:

> *Bap.*   Signor Lucentio, this is the 'pointed day
> That Katharine and Petruchio should be married,
> And yet we hear not of our son-in-law.
> What will be said? What mockery will it be
> To want the bridegroom when the priest attends
> To speak the ceremonial rites of marriage!
> What says Lucentio to this shame of ours?

Kath.	No shame but mine. I must forsooth be forc'd
	To give my hand, oppos'd against my heart,
	Unto a mad-brain rudesby, full of spleen,
	Who woo'd in haste and means to wed at leisure.
	I told you, I, he was a frantic fool,
	Hiding his bitter jests in blunt behaviour.
	And to be noted for a merry man
	He'll woo a thousand, 'point the day of marriage,
	Make feast, invite friends, and proclaim the banns,
	Yet never means to wed where he hath woo'd.
	Now must the world point at poor Katharine,
	And say 'Lo, there is mad Petruchio's wife,
	If it would please him come and marry her.'
Tra.	Patience, good Katharine, and Baptista too.
	Upon my life, Petruchio means but well,
	Whatever fortune stays him from his word.
	Though he be blunt, I know him passing wise;
	Though he be merry, yet withal he's honest.
Kath.	Would Katharine had never seen him though

Exit weeping [followed by Bianca and attendants].

[III.ii.1–26]

No one enjoys being jilted, but this is not the anxiety of an unwilling bride. Kate, authentically in love, nevertheless is unnerved by the madcap Petruchio, lest he turn out to be an obsessive practical joker, betrothed to half of Italy. When, after the ceremony, Petruchio refuses to allow his bride to attend her own wedding feast, he crushes what she calls her "spirit to resist" with a possessive diatribe firmly founded upon the doubtless highly patriarchal Tenth Commandment:

They shall go forward, Kate, at thy command.
Obey the bride, you that attend on her.
Go to the feast, revel and domineer,
Carouse full measure to her maidenhead,
Be mad and merry, or go hang yourselves.
But for my bonny Kate, she must with me.
Nay, look not big, nor stamp, nor stare, nor fret;
I will be master of what is mine own.
She is my goods, my chattels, she is my house,
My household stuff, my field, my barn,
My horse, my ox, my ass, my any thing,
And here she stands. Touch her whoever dare!
I'll bring mine action on the proudest he

That stops my way in Padua. Grumio,
Draw forth thy weapon, we are beset with thieves,
Rescue thy mistress if thou be a man.
Fear not, sweet wench, they shall not touch thee, Kate.
I'll buckler thee against a million.
            Exeunt PETRUCHIO, KATHARINA [and GRUMIO].
                                            [III.ii.220–37]

This histrionic departure, with Petruchio and Grumio brandishing drawn swords, is a symbolic carrying-off, and begins Petruchio's almost phantasmagoric "cure" of poor Kate, which will continue until at last she discovers how to tame the swaggerer:

Pet.   Come on, a God's name, once more toward our father's.
          Good Lord, how bright and goodly shines the moon!
Kath.   The moon? the sun! It is not moonlight now.
Pet.   I say it is the moon that shines so bright.
Kath.   I know it is the sun that shines so bright.
Pet.   Now by my mothers son, and that's myself,
          It shall be moon, or star, or what I list,
          Or e'er I journey to your father's house.—
          [*To Servants.*] Go on, and fetch our horses back again.—
          Evermore cross'd and cross'd; nothing but cross'd.
Hor.   Say as he says, or we shall never go.
Kath.   Forward, I pray, since we have come so far,
          And be it moon, or sun, or what you please.
          And if you please to call it a rush-candle,
          Henceforth I vow it shall be so for me.
Pet.   I say it is the moon.
Kath.   I know it is the moon.—
Pet.   Nay, then you lie. It is the blessed sun.
Kath.   Then, God be blest, it is the blessed sun.
          But sun it is not, when you say it is not,
          And the moon changes even as your mind.
          What you will have it nam'd, even that it is,
          And so it shall be so for Katharine.
                                            [IV.v.1–22]

From this moment on, Kate firmly rules while endlessly protesting her obedience to the delighted Petruchio, a marvelous Shakespearean reversal of Petruchio's earlier strategy of proclaiming Kate's mildness even as she raged on. There is no more charming a scene of married love in all Shakespeare than this little vignette on a street in Padua:

Kath.	Husband, let's follow, to see the end of this ado.
Pet.	First kiss me, Kate, and we will.
Kath.	What, in the midst of the street?
Pet.	What, art thou ashamed of me?
Kath.	No, sir, God forbid; but ashamed to kiss.
Pet.	Why, then, let's home again. Come, sirrah, let's away.
Kath.	Nay, I will give thee a kiss. Now pray thee, love, stay.
Pet.	Is not this well? Come, my sweet Kate.
	Better once than never, for never too late.

Exeunt.

[V.i.130–38]

One would have to be tone deaf (or ideologically crazed) not to hear in this a subtly exquisite music of marriage at its happiest. I myself always begin teaching the *Shrew* with this passage, because it is a powerful antidote to all received nonsense, old and new, concerning this play. (One recent edition of the play offers extracts from English Renaissance manuals on wife beating, from which one is edified to learn that, on the whole, such exercise was not recommended. Since Kate does hit Petruchio, and he does not retaliate—though he warns her not to repeat this exuberance—it is unclear to me why wife beating is invoked at all.) Even subtler is Kate's long and famous speech, her advice to women concerning their behavior toward their husbands, just before the play concludes. Again, one would have to be very literal-minded indeed not to hear the delicious irony that is Kate's undersong, centered on the great line "I am asham'd that women are so simple." It requires a very good actress to deliver this set piece properly, and a better director than we tend to have now, if the actress is to be given her full chance, for she is advising women how to rule absolutely, while feigning obedience:

Fie, fie! Unknit that threatening unkind brow,
And dart not scornful glances from those eyes,
To wound thy lord, thy king, thy governor.
It blots thy beauty as frosts do bite the meads,
Confounds thy fame as whirlwinds shake fair buds,
And in no sense is meet or amiable.
A woman mov'd is like a fountain troubled,
Muddy, ill-seeming, thick, bereft of beauty,
And while it is so, none so dry or thirsty
Will deign to sip or touch one drop of it.
Thy husband is thy lord, thy life, thy keeper,
Thy head, thy sovereign; one that cares for thee,
And for thy maintenance; commits his body
To painful labour both by sea and land,

To watch the night in storms, the day in cold,
Whilst thou liest warm at home, secure and safe;
And craves no other tribute at thy hands
But love, fair looks, and true obedience;
Too little payment for so great a debt.
Such duty as the subject owes the prince
Even such a woman oweth to her husband.
And when she is froward, peevish, sullen, sour,
And not obedient to his honest will,
What is she but a foul contending rebel,
And graceless traitor to her loving lord?
I am asham'd that women are so simple
To offer war where they should kneel for peace,
Or seek for rule, supremacy, and sway,
When they are bound to serve, love, and obey.
Why are our bodies soft, and weak, and smooth,
Unapt to toil and trouble in the world,
But that our soft conditions and our hearts
Should well agree with our external parts?
Come, come, you froward and unable worms,
My mind hath been as big as one of yours,
My heart as great, my reason haply more,
To bandy word for word and frown for frown.
But now I see our lances are but straws,
Our strength as weak, our weakness past compare,
That seeming to be most which we indeed least are.
Then vail your stomachs, for it is no boot,
And place your hands below your husband's foot.
In token of which duty, if he please,
My hand is ready, may it do him ease.

                                                    [V.ii.137–80]

    I have quoted this complete precisely because its redundancy and
hyperbolical submissiveness are critical to its nature as a secret language or code
now fully shared by Kate and Petruchio. "True obedience" here is considerably
less sincere than it purports to be, or even if sexual politics are to be invoked, it
is as immemorial as the Garden of Eden. "Strength" and "weakness" interchange
their meanings, as Kate teaches not ostensible subservience but the art of her
own will, a will considerably more refined than it was at the play's start. The
speech's meaning explodes into Petruchio's delighted (and overdetermined)
response:

Why, there's a wench! Come on, and kiss me, Kate.

If you want to hear this line as the culmination of a "problem play," then perhaps you yourself are the problem. Kate does not need to be schooled in "consciousness raising." Shakespeare, who clearly preferred his women characters to his men (always excepting Falstaff and Hamlet), enlarges the human, from the start, by subtly suggesting that women have the truer sense of reality.

THOMAS M. GREENE

Love's Labour's Lost:
The Grace of Society

The qualities of *Love's Labour's Lost* determine its limitations. The arabesques of wit, the elaborations of courtly artifice, the coolness of tone— these sources of its charm contribute to that brittleness and thinness and faded superficiality for which some critics of several generations have reproached it. For its admirers, a heavy stress upon these limitations is likely to appear irrelevant. But even admirers must acknowledge that, placed against its author's work, *Love's Labour's Lost* is distinguished by a certain slenderness of feeling, a delicate insubstantiality. It is most certainly not a trivial play, but its subtlety remains a little disembodied.

One source of that impression may be the play's lack, unique in Shakespeare, of any firm social underpinning. Not only is there missing any incarnation of responsible authority, any strong and wise center of political power, but there is equally missing any representative of a stable and dependable citizenry. There is nobody here who, however quirky or foolish or provincial, can be counted on, when he is multiplied enough times, to keep society functioning. Or if there is such a figure in the person of Constable Dull, we are struck with how very marginal a role his creator has permitted him. The patently comic figures—Armado, Holofernes, Costard, Nathaniel, Moth—are all too thin or specialized or socially peripheral to suggest any sort of living society. They may be contrasted with the mechanicals of *A Midsummer Night's Dream*, who, for all their splendid ineptness, do persuade us that a kind of Athenian proletariat exists. The earlier play may owe its peculiar airiness in part to a lack of that social solidity.

From *The Vulnerable Text: Essays on Renaissance Literature.* © 1986 by Columbia University.

Yet despite its lack of a ballasted society, the play is really about "society," in a slightly different sense of the word. Its true subject is caught in an offhand remark by one of its funny men: "Societie (saith the text) is the happiness of life" (IV.ii.177–78).[1] The play does not challenge Nathaniel's text, however insubstantial its dramatic sociology. It is much concerned with society, and the happiness of life in society. If it does not present a living society in action, it presents and comments on configurations of conduct which sustain living societies in and out of plays. It is concerned with styles, modes of language and gesture and action which befit, in varying degrees, the intercourse of civilized people. And being a comedy, it is concerned with the failures of inadequate styles, since this is the perennial source of elegant comedy from Homer to Proust. Only at the end, and much more surprisingly, does it turn out to reflect the failure of all style.

To distinguish most sensibly the play's hierarchy of moral styles, one may adopt the vantage point of the princess of France and her three attendant ladies. These four women, being women, cannot provide a strong political center, but they do constitute a certain spirited and witty center of social judgment. In their vivacious and spontaneous taste, limited in range and depth but not in accuracy, each is a poised, Meredithian arbitress of style. This power of discrimination is established by the first speech each lady makes onstage. In the cases of the three attendants, the speech consists in a sketch of the gentleman who is to become the given lady's suitor, and each speech, in its alert and finely qualified appreciation, does credit to the speaker as well as to its subject. Thus Maria:

> I know him Madame....
> A man of soveraigne parts he is esteem'd:
> Well fitted in Arts, glorious in Armes:
> Nothing becomes him ill that he would well.
> The onely soyle of his faire vertues glosse,
> If vertues glosse will staine with any soile,
> Is a sharp wit match'd with too blunt a Will:
> Whose edge hath power to cut whose will still wills,
> It should none spare that come within his power.
>
> (II.i.44, 48–55)

As regards the princess, it is her modesty, her impervious disregard of flattery, the sense of proportion regulating her pride of birth, which betoken most frequently her moral poise. The princess' first speech opens with a mild rebuke of the spongy Lord Boyet for his gratuitous compliments:

> Good L. *Boyet*, my beauty though but mean,
> Needs not the painted flourish of your praise: ...
> I am lesse proud to heare you tell my worth,

Then you much wiling to be counted wise,
In spending your wit in the praise of mine.

(II.i.16–17, 20–22)

She refuses coolly to be hoodwinked by the flattery her station conventionally attracts, with an acuteness which sets off the foolish egotism of the king. His first speech, the opening speech of the play, is full of tiresome talk of fame and honor, posturing predictions of immortality and glory. The princess' view of "glory" is plain enough after her quick disposal of Boyet, as it is in a later scene when she laughingly dismisses with a tip an unwitting blunder by the forester. Indeed she follows that incident with reflections which are painfully apposite to the king's foolish enterprise, even if they are ostensibly and deprecatingly directed at herself:

And out of question, so it is sometimes:
Glory growes guiltie of detested crimes,
When for Fames sake, for praise and outward part,
We bend to that, the working of the hart.

(IV.i.34–37)

This last phrase about bending to externals the working of the heart touches very nearly the heart of the play. For *Love's Labour's Lost* explores the relation of feeling and forms, feeling and the funny distortions of feeling which our social experience beguiles us to fashion. The four gentlemen, quite clearly, begin by denying the workings of their hearts and libidos for the outward part of fame, just as Armado squirms from his distressing passion for a girl who is outwardly—i.e., socially—his inferior. The distinction of the ladies is that their feelings and their style, their outward parts, are attuned; they know what they feel and they are in control of its expression. Although they are as quick to admire as the four gentlemen, they are slower to think they are falling in love. They are also, to their credit, far clearer about the physiological dimension of their in The freedom of their byplay about sex may have lost with time some of its comic sprightliness, but next to the dogged Petrarchan vaporizings of their suitors that freedom still emerges as the healthier and more refreshing mode of speech. The four ladies are, in the best sense, self-possessed, although the play does not try to pretend that the *scope* of their feelings or their experience is any wider than most girls'. An older person with no wider a scope would risk the hollowness of the ambiguous, slightly sterile Boyet. The ladies are so engaging because their spirited and untested freshness is tempered by instinctive good sense.

The roles of the gentlemen—Navarre and his three courtiers—are slightly more complicated. For they must justify to some degree the interest the ladies conceive in them. Longaville may not be quite the "man of sovereign parts" Maria says he is, but he must remain within hailing distance of that distinguished

man she thought she saw and liked. We must always be able to assume that the
gentlemen are salvageable as social animals and potential husbands, and need
only the kind of education provided by laughter and the penances to which, at
the close, they are assigned. But granting them a basic attractiveness, we have to
confess that they resemble a little—in their deplorable affectations, their
wayward rhetoric, their callow blindness to themselves—the caricatured figures
of the subplot. There is a difference of degree, not of kind, between the doggerel
of, say, Holofernes (IV.ii.66–76) and the mediocrity of Dumain's verses:

> A huge translation of hypocrisie,
> Vildly compiled, profound simplicitie
> (V.ii.55–56)

Like Holofernes, Armado, and Nathaniel, the gentlemen "have been at a great
feast of languages and stolen the scraps"; all steal indifferently from a common
alms-basket of words. They are failures as poseurs because their poses are never
original, and as Holofernes himself is able to recognize, "imitari is nothing." The
successive defeats of the gentlemen in their sets of wits with the ladies betray an
ineptitude of social intelligence and style.

Shakespeare will tolerate cheerfully enough the fashionable inanities of
sentimental rhetoric, but he sees the risk of mistaking rhetoric for real sentiment.
It is the risk which anguished Pirandello, but it works in this more comical world
to expose the gentlemen to their mistresses' ridicule. For the ladies, who are not
all wise, know enough to distinguish language in touch with feeling from the
language which does duty for feeling, or, more accurately, which papers over
adolescent confusions of feeling. The ladies' rhetoric, cooler, more bracing, more
alert than the lords', enlivened by the freedom of its casual license, finds a natural
recreation in a kind of amiable flyting, a "civil war of wits." The ladies vanquish
their suitors unfailingly in this civil badinage because they are, so to speak, in
practice. The suitors are not, having attempted to exclude from their still and
contemplative academy what they call "the world's debate." Or rather, they have
allowed the debate to impinge only at second hand, as a recreative fancy and
linguistic toy. They may hear, says the king, from Armado:

> In high-borne words the worth of many a Knight:
> From tawnie Spaine lost in the worlds debate.
> (I.i.184–85)

Perhaps it is their unwillingness to be so lost—save in fantasy, through the
mediation of high-colored language—which loses them the verbal battles under
the banner of Saint Cupid. The play will end with a calendary debate, reminding
us that nature itself, and the human lives it governs, are subject to the amoebean
conflicts of the seasons.

The war of wits is "civil" in more meanings than one, since the term *civility* gathers up all of the play's central values. The term as Elizabethans used it embraced all those configurations of political and social and moral conduct which can render society the happiness of life. The gentlemen, in their cocksure unworldliness, have only bungling conceptions of civility, and for all their fumbling efforts toward urbanity, their parochial manners unflaggingly show through. The ideal is defined partly by its breaches: the ascetic breach represented by the academy's austere statutes; or the inhuman breach of the decree which would deprive an interloping woman of her tongue: "a dangerous law against gentilitie" (I.i.139); or the inhospitable breach which denies the princess welcome to the court of Navarre; or the rhetorical breaches of the gentlemen's poetastical love complaints; or the fantastical breach of the Muscovite embassy:

> Their shallow showes, and Prologue vildely pen'd:
> And their rough carriage so ridiculous;
>
> (V.ii.342–43)

or the final blunder which asks the bereaved princess to listen still to her lover's suit. This variety of gaffes is filled out by the cruder affectations of the minor comic characters. Virtually all the men in the play violate, each in his peculiar way, the values of "civility," which meant at once civilization, social polish, government, courtesy, decorum, manners, and simple human kindness.

Of these various participant values, the play lays particular stress on the virtue of decorum, which becomes here a sense of the conduct appropriate to a given situation. Berowne's main charge against Navarre's academy appeals implicitly to that virtue:

> FERDINAND: *Berowne* is like an envious sneaping Frost,
> That bites the first borne infants of the Spring.
> BEROWNE: Wel, say I am, why should proud Summer boast,
> Before the Birds have any cause to sing?
> Why should I ioy in any abortive birth?
> At Christmas I no more desire a Rose,
> Then wish a Snow in Mayes new fangled showes:
> But like of each thing that in season growes.
> So you to studie now it is too late,
> That were to clymbe ore the house to unlocke the gate.
>
> (I.i.110–19)

Enterprise blossoms when, in Berowne's phrase, it is "fit in his place and time" (I.i.107); comedy wells up from the disjuncture of act and occasion. The lords' intuition of this great Renaissance virtue is blunted equally in their roles as students and as suitors, so that art especial irony tinges the king's summons to courtship:

> Away, away, no time shall be omitted,
> That will be time, and may by us be fitted.
>   (IV.iii.400–401)

That cry will receive an unwitting answer in Rosaline's fantasy:

> O that I knew he were but in by th'weeke,
> How I would make him fawne, and begge, and seeke,
> And wait the season, and observe the times.
>   (V.ii.65–67)

and finds another faint echo later in the princess' rejection of Navarre's last plea:

> KING: Now at the latest minute of the houre,
> Grant us your loves.
> QUEEN: A time me thinkes too short,
> To make a world-without-end bargaine in.
>   (V.ii.861–64)

This fault of abusing season and "time" is implicitly caught up in Berowne's incoherent apology for the misconduct of himself and his companions, whose errors he ruefully confesses to have sinned against decorum.

> Your beautie Ladies
> Hath much deformed us, fashioning our humors
> Even to the opposed end of our intents.
> And what in us hath seem'd ridiculous:
> As Love is full of unbefitting straines,
> All wanton as a childe, skipping and vaine ...
> Which partie-coated presence of loose love
> Put on by us, if in your heavenly eies,
> Have misbecom'd our oathes and gravities.
> Those heavenlie eies that looke into these faults,
> Suggested us to make. (V.ii.829–34, 839–43)

The key words are "deformed," "unbefitting," and "misbecom'd," suggesting offenses against that value of propriety which had not yet, in the sixteenth century, become the fossilized austerity we have learned to deplore.

The relationship of Berowne to the ideals of civility is rather more complex than his fellows', since he understands so much more than they without ever saving himself from their muddles. He has traits in common with Shaw's John Tanner: both are brilliant, ineffectual talkers who never quite learn how useless are even their best lines. Berowne for all his brilliance is easily put in his place by the securer wit of Rosaline. But despite his frustrations he remains the most original, interesting, and complicated character in the play. He is insincere from the outset; he knows of course that he will sign the articles of the academic oath, even as he calls attention to himself by pretending to refuse. He plays with life, and his life is a play within the play. It is the last word he speaks, in the famous regretful line that gives us—had we been so obtuse as to miss it—the key to his character: "That's too long for a play" (V.ii.955). Ironist, sophist, scoffer, he has one small, delusory faith: he believes in language, and it fails him. He is almost saved by his capacity to laugh at himself, but not quite; his worst muddle is his last, when he tries to chasten his rhetoric I before the fact of death, and cannot shake his inveterate cleverness:

> We to our selves prove false,
> By being once false, for ever to be true
> To those that make us both, faire Ladies you.
> (V.ii.845–47)

To themselves they do indeed prove false, and to the motto "Honest plain words, best pierce the ears of griefe" (V.ii.826).

Berowne's teasing dilettantism is not up to death—nor (more surprisingly?) is it up to sex. His sexuality, like his fellow suitors', is visual, not to say voyeuristic. Their obsession with the eye transcends the Petrarchan cliché; it betokens their callow and adolescent virginity. It is symptomatic that the most sleazy joke the gentlemen permit themselves has to do with looking;[2] when the ladies' talk is bawdy, they refer to the more relevant organs. Their ribaldry is the cleaner. None of these women would say of her lover what Berowne is so foolish to admit:

> O but her eye: by this light, but for her eye, I would not love her; yes, for her two eyes. (IV.iii.10–12)

And again later:

> From womens eyes this doctrine I derive.
> They sparcle still the right promethean fire,
> They are the Bookes, the Arts, the Achademes,
> That shew, containe, and nourish all the world.
> Else none at all in ought proves excellent.
> (IV.iii.369–73)

This fascination is echoed in the rhetoric of the other suitors, and enters the plot with the misleading exchange of favors:

> The ladies did change Favours; and then we
> Following the signes, woo'd but the signe of she.
>
>   (V.ii.521–22)

The sign of she! That is always the object of immature desire. To know and love the complex living creature takes more tune and a wiser heart.

The comedy of the gentlemen's sentimental inadequacies is reflected obliquely in the comedy of their inferiors. This reflection receives dramatic expression in Costard's mistaken interchange of Berowne's poem with Armado's letter. The confusion suggests a common element which we recognize as the vice of affectation, a vice which is only a few degrees more marked in the style of Armado and spills over into humor. One might almost say that we are invited to share Costard's error. But from another perspective the gentlemen as gallants emerge from the contrast with even less credit than the ostensible clowns. Costard at least represents the closest thing to good sense in the flights of folly of the opening scene; through his malapropising nonsense a few primitive truths are sounded which shatter all the foregoing silliness about asceticism:

> Now sir for the manner; It is the manner of a man to speake to a woman. (I.i.221–22)

> Such is the simplicitie of man to harken after the flesh. (I.i.229–30)

Armado of course is more closely parallel to the gentlemen because, unlike Costard, he fancies himself to be in love. Armado is the most suggestive of the comic figures and one of the richest of any in Shakespeare's early comedies, although his potentialities are not consistently developed. There is a resonance to his humor which is lacking, say, in the humor of his fellow pomposity, Holofernes. This is because Shakespeare invests Armado's grandiloquence with a touch of melancholy. We are allowed to catch a bat's squeak of pathos behind the tawny splendor, and a lonely desire for Jaquenetta behind the clumsy condescension to her. The pathos is really affecting when he must decline Costard's challenge and confess his shirtlessness, infamonized among potentates. Nothing so touching overshadows the presentation of the gentlemen. Armado's courtship is more desperate, more clouded, and more believable.

A conventional reading of the play places the main turning point at the end of the fourth act, with the fourfold exposure of the quondam academics and their abjuration of study in the name of Saint Cupid. But to read in this way is to be taken in by the gentlemen's own self-delusions. For their apparent conversion is at bottom a pseudo-conversion, the exchange of one pretentious fiction for

another, and we are meant to view ironically their naive release of enthusiasm, as
we view Caliban's "Freedom, high-day!" The Muscovite embassy represents the
culmination of the gentlemen's clumsy posing, their inept sophistication, and
their empty formalism. Never yet in the play have manner and mien been quite
so far from feeling, and we learn merely that courtship as performance can be just
as silly as the performance of monastic seclusion. The real turning point begins
with Berowne's second abjuration and its potentially deeper renunciation of
rhetorical affectation.

> Taffata phrases, silken tearmes precise,
> Three-pil'd Hyperboles, spruce affection;
> Figures pedanticall, these summer flies
> Have blowne me full of maggot ostentation.
> I do forsweare them. (V.ii.452–56)

Berowne underestimates the difficulty of the sacrifice, as Rosaline finds a way to
suggest, but we are allowed to hope that the seed of understanding has been
planted. Indeed the remaining action of this rich last scene—almost a one-act
play in itself—can be regarded as a progressive and painful exorcism of the
gentlemen's pretenses and pretensions. The first step involves a humiliating
sincerity.

> KING: Teach us sweete Madame, for our rude transgression, some
> faire excuse.
> QUEEN: The fairest is confession.
> Were you not heere but even now, disguis'd?
> KING: Madam, I was. (V.ii.478–82)

That step leads to the further humbling discovery of the exchanged favors and
mistaken identities, and that in turn to the puzzling but clearly important episode
of the Worthies' pageant.[3]

The intrusion of this interlude, so cruelly and even pathetically routed at
the climax of the action, has troubled more than one reader,[4] and indeed it is not
easily justified by our common standards of daily morality. Yet I think that
Shakespeare has given us a key to its interpretation, a key which no critic to my
knowledge has noticed. The essential point is the reluctance of the gentlemen to
watch the pageant, chastened as they already are at this point by their sense of
their own absurdity. Yet in fact they do watch. The exchange is notable that
immediately precedes this ambiguous entertainment:

> KING: *Berowne*, they will shame us: Let them not approach.
> BEROWNE: We are shame-proofe my Lord: and 'tis some policic,
> to have one shew worse then the Kings and his companie.

KING: I say they shall not come.
QUEEN: Nay my good Lord, let me ore-rule you now;
That sport best pleases, that does least know how.
Where Zeale strives to content, and the contents
Dies in the Zeale of that which it presents:
Their forme confounded, makes most forme in mirth,
When great things labouring perish in their birth.
BEROWNE: A right description of our sport my Lord.

(V.ii.567–79)

The clumsy pageant will imitate uncomfortably the fumbling Muscovite masquing. The analogy is painfully close, as both the king and Berowne are alert enough to perceive. The princess' wise insistence on the performance—"That sport best pleases, that does least know how"—creates a small moral dilemma for the lords which they come to resolve by mocking their own unwitting mockers. They recognize, not without a certain rueful courage, that the pageant represents a quintessential parody of their own offenses against propriety; so they choose to follow Boyet in turning upon that parody as though to exorcise their own folly. The telling line is Dumaine's:

Though my mockes come home by me, I will now be merrie.

(V.ii.704–5)

Unforgivable in itself, the routing of the pageant is dramatically right as ritual action, as a symbolic rejection of a mask beginning to be outworn. Indeed only the savage shame one feels toward an unworthy part of one's self could motivate the gentlemen's quite uncharacteristic cruelty.

Considered in this way, the ridicule of the pageant needs no palliation, and yet two palliative observations can be made. The first is that the ridicule is not heaped equally on all five performers. Moth as Hercules remains silent while presented by Holofernes-Maccabaeus and is allowed to leave the stage after the six-line presentation without any interruption. Costard is interrupted twice and corrected once at the outset, but is then heard out quietly, thanked by the princess, and complimented by Berowne. Nathaniel fares somewhat worse, but the most scathing ridicule is reserved for the two most outrageous (if charming) pomposities, Holofernes and Armado. This careful apportioning of embarrassment is not accidental, nor is the circumstance that the two most harried victims achieve individually their finest, and simplest, moments under fire. Holofernes' reproach is his last line and his one stroke of quiet dignity: "This is not generous, not gentle, not humble" (V.ii.696). Armado, the richer character, is vouchsafed by his creator a felicity close to eloquence:

The sweet War-man is dead and rotten,

Sweet chuckes, beat not the bones of the buried:
When he breathed he was a man (V.ii.731–33)

and by the end something like a transformation seems to be operating even upon his stiff and shallow playing-card magnificence. ("For mine owne part, I breath free breath: I have scene the day of wrong, through the little hole of discretion, and I will right my selfe like a soldier"—V.ii.795–97.) He too will serve a penance like his betters.[5] Thus the lash of comic criticism chastens with bitter success all the surquedry of this dramatic world. Thus all men are taught, with Nathaniel, not to o'erpart themselves.

The final and most telling chastisement appears with the entrance of Marcade, who brings the fact of death. Even a few minutes earlier, this fact would have shattered the play; now it can be borne. Heretofore death has been itself rhetorical, as in the very first lines:

Let *Fame*, that all hunt after in their lives,
Live registred upon our brazen Tombes,
And then grace us in the disgrace of death. (I.i.6–8)

Then an abstract unreality, death now is a particular event. No one of the characters has the emotional depth fully to command a rhetoric commensurate with the event, but in the speeches following Marcade's entry three degrees of rhetorical inadequacy can be distinguished. The princess falls short only in the reserve with which she receives her bereavement, a reserve which betrays no feeling and risks the appearance of coldness. Otherwise she is sensible, brief, even, briskly courteous, alert to the relative inconsequence of all the badinage that has preceded. In contrast, the poverty of the king's rhetoric is painfully manifest:

The extreme parts of time, extremelie formes
All causes to the purpose of his speed: (V.ii.813–14)

a rhetorical failure because it cannot conceal the underlying poverty of sympathy or even of decent respect. In essence, the king is making a request which is shockingly improper—that his courtship not be neglected because of her loss—and perhaps it is his consciousness of this indecorum that produces such monstrous linguistic convolutions and elicits her wryly polite answer: "I understand you not, my greefes are double" (V.ii.825). Berowne's essay at a valediction, as we have seen, opens with a gesture toward the proper simplicity but winds up with an equally inappropriate contortion. Berowne at least recognizes the rhetorical problem; the lesson of his failure seems to be that habits of feeling and language are not quickly overcome. Earlier he had confessed:

> beare with me, I am sicke.
> Ile leave it by degrees. (V.ii.464–65)

The degrees do indeed come slowly.

In the light of the lords' inadequacies before the fact of death, the penances set them by the ladies constitute a kind of final prodding toward maturation. Berowne's will test the relevance of his dilettantish jesting to human suffering[6] and thereby purge perhaps the frivolity of his ironies. In these closing moments of the last scene, one has the impression of the comedy turning back upon itself, withdrawing from those modes of speech and laughter which have in fact constituted its distinctiveness. Pater is surely right when he suggests that the play contains "a delicate raillery by Shakespeare himself at his own chosen manner"[7]—at least of the manner chosen for this work. The raillery has been there throughout, diffused and subtle, but now at the end it has become something more serious and has determined the conclusion. Could this final verdict have been introduced in the later version, "newly corrected and augmented," as the title page of the 1598 quarto informs us? The judgment on Berowne comes to seem like a judgment on the slenderness of a certain moral style that has been outgrown.

There could be no greater mistake than to conclude from this judgment that Shakespeare disliked rhetorics and forms, patterns of words and of experience. He was not, needless to say, in favor of the crude expression of raw passion. He knew that society, the happiness of life, depends on configurations and rituals. He represented the Muscovite masquing to be silly not because it was artificial but because, in his sense of the word, it was not artificial enough; it was "shallow" and "rough" and "vilely penned." This being so, one may ask whether Shakespeare did not provide within the play an instance of authentic artifice, and the answer is that he did provide it, in the form of the two concluding songs.

If we regard the presentation of these songs literally, as a part of the pageant they are designed to conclude, then their artistic finish is out of place. But if we regard them as rhetorical touchstones by which to estimate the foregoing funny abuses of language, they form an ideal ending. In their careful balance, elaborate refrain, and lyric poise, the songs are artificial in the good old sense, but in their freshness and freedom from stale tradition, they blithely escape the stilted modern sense. They violate the cliché preference of spring to winter and adumbrate a finer decorum; they "like of each thing that in season grows." They like of each thing, but not conventionally or sentimentally; the "unpleasing" word of the cuckoo sounds in the spring, while the wintry cry of the owl is "merry." Joseph Westlund points out suggestively that the more attractively "realistic" world of Hiems lies further from the effete world of the play itself, and closer to the experience the gentlemen must come to face.[8] The winter song achieves a mingling of the lyrical and the humbly truthful which none of the courtly poetasters in Navarre could manage.

"The Words of Mercurie, / Are harsh after the songs of Apollo" concludes
Armado (V.ii.1012–13). A recent editor paraphrases:

> i.e., let us end with the songs, because clever words of the god
> Mercury would come harshly after the songs of Apollo, the god of
> poetry.[9]

Such may well be Armado's meaning, but his words can bear an ulterior
construction. He might be taken to mean that the songs we have just heard, with
their bracing directness, are to the rest of the play and its pseudo-golden poetry
as Mercury is to Apollo. From the narrow world of neo-Petrarchan sentiment,
the experience of the songs may well seem "harsh," since they treat of cuckolds
and red noses and frozen milk. With that adjective in our ears, Armado ends the
comedy: "You that way; we this way" (V.ii.1014). Who is "you"? The actors on
the other side of the stage? Or we in the audience, who must leave the theater
and exchange one set of conventions and disguises for another, less tractable to
laughter?

Society may be, ideally, the happiness of life, but the end of the play has
not placed us in it. Perhaps Nathaniel's text is fallacious. But by one very faint,
almost surreptitious means, Shakespeare seems to me to remind us repeatedly of
the possible felicity into which society can flower. This means is the unusual
frequence and special prominence accorded the word "grace"—the word, we
remember, with which the opening sentence plays (quoted above). As the play
continues, the many extensions and intricate variations of "grace" in all its
meanings are explored with deliberate subtlety. In no other play by Shakespeare
is the address "Your Grace" to a sovereign so alive with suggestiveness. The
princess is represented explicitly and emphatically as endowed with "grace," from
the first mention of her:

> For well you know here comes in Embassie
> The *French* Kings daughter, with your selfe to speake:
> A Maide of grace and compleate maiestie
>
> (I.i.145–47)

and again at her first appearance, in Boyet's injunction:

> Be now as prodigall of all deare grace,
> As Nature was in making Graces deare,
> When she did starve the generall world beside,
> And prodigally gave them all to you. (II.i.12–15)

The princess' grace has something to do presumably with the comely carriage of
her physical bearing, but also with a certain courtesy and sweetness of manner

which transcend the body. As the multiple meanings of the word quietly exfoliated, educated Elizabethan playgoers may have remembered the quality of *grazia* in Castiglione's *Cortegiano*, that indefinable air which represents the courtier's supreme distinction, and which is repeatedly and emphatically opposed to affectation.[10] Such an echo could only heighten the ironies of the honorific "Your Grace" addressed to the king, and indeed on one occasion his fitness for it is indirectly questioned:

> Good heart, What grace hast thou thus to reprove
> These wormes for loving, that art most in love?
> (IV.iii.158–59)

The word in these contexts signifies a virtue a person can possess, but other contexts remind us that it is something that can be given to another. It is what lovers want, as Longaville's poem shows:

> Thy grace being gain'd, cures all disgrace in me
> (IV.iii.68)

and what the ladies determine to refuse:

> And not a man of them shall have the grace
> Despight of sute, to see a Ladies face. (V.ii.134–35)

> No, to the death we will not move a foot,
> Nor to their pen'd speech render we no grace.
> (V.ii.152–53)

Grace is what a wit desires from his audience, perhaps meretriciously:

> For he hath wit to make an ill shape good,
> And shape to win grace though she had no wit.
> (II.i.63–64)

> Why that's the way to choke a gibing spirit,
> Whose influence is begot of that loose grace,
> Which shallow laughing hearers give to fooles
> (V.ii.934–36)

but it is also the very ability to amuse:

> He is Wits Pedler, and retailes his Wares,
> At Wakes, and Wassels, Meetings, Markets, Faires.

And we that sell by grosse, the Lord doth know,
Have not the grace to grace it with such show.

> (V.ii.356–59)

These last passages suggest the paradoxical openness of this ability to perversion
or manipulation, and other usages imply the same double-edged danger:

Follie in Wisedome hatch'd:
Hath wisedoms warrant, and the helpe of Schoole,
And Wits own grace to grace a learned Foole? (V.ii.74–76)

But all these failures, real or potential, of the virtue never quite suppress the hope
which the word embodies: the hope for felicitous human conversation. And
although the hope is firmly rooted in the affairs of this world, at least one usage
holds the word open briefly to its theological sense:

For every man with his affects is borne,
Not by might mastred, but by speciall grace. (I.i.163–64)

That is Berowne on the resilience of human passion, to be echoed later by his flip
cynicism: "God give him grace to grone" (IV.iii.20). Is it fanciful to think that the
word is introduced deliberately, to enrich its resonance still further, in the
invitation of Holofernes to Nathaniel?

I do dine to day at the fathers of a certaine Pupill of mine, where it
(being repast) it shall please you to gratifie the table with a Grace, *I*
will ... undertake your *bien vonuto* ... I beseech your Societie.
     NATHANIEL: And thanke you to: for Societie (saith the text) is the
happinesse of life. (IV.ii.169–73, 175–78)

Here, just below the amusing surface, two or three meanings of the word seem
to coalesce.

The grace of entertainment, the grace of love, the grace of wit, the grace
of civility—*Love's Labour's Lost* is about the pursuit of all these fragile goals. Its
opening adumbrates the need of some ulterior, metaphysical principle to "grace
us in the disgrace of death," though the principle of fame proposed there is
quickly forgotten. The reader may ask what means the play holds out to us to
confront that disgrace, since in fact we are forced at the end to consider it, and
the disgrace also of "the speechless sick" and "the pained impotent." Perhaps the
upshot is a wry surrender and such a devaluation of grace as Kokeritz teaches us
to find in the irreverent play of *The Comedy of Errors* on the word's Elizabethan
homonym: "Marry, Sir, she's the kitchen-wench, and all grease."[11] But *Love's
Labour's Lost* is not, in the last analysis, devaluative, and in a sense its object is to

live with the best sort of grace—with enlightened intercourse between the sexes, with gaiety and true wit, with poise, taste, decorum, and charity. The ending does not discredit this object, even if it acknowledges the helplessness of wit before suffering, and even if it extends the realm of grace to unexpected social strata. For the play does not leave us with the princess; it leaves us with a pun on greasy Joan who keels the pot.

We can be grateful to the playwright for not attempting to put onstage the truly enlightened society. He leaves that achievement where it belongs, in the indefinite future, not altogether remote, but much too long for a play. In 1598 he was beginning to outgrow comedy as he knew it, and to question the truth of a comic resolution. Shortly he would reach his own Twelfth Night, an end to merriment. At the end of this comedy, we hardly know where we are, as Berowne goes off to the hospital and the king to a naked hermitage, and Armado to his plow, and the princess to her loss, all off to the world's debate, and we are left with our former mirth a little suspect, and are signaled to leave, almost enigmatically: "You that way; we this way."

NOTES

1. Quotations from *Love's Labour's Lost* are from the New Variorum Edition, H. H. Furness, ed. (Philadelphia: Lippincott, 1904).

2. BEROWNE: O if the streets were paved with thine eyes,

Her feet were much too dainty for such tread.
DUMAINE: O vile, then as she goes what upward lyes?
The street should see as she walk'd over head.

(IV.iii.295–98)

3. Still another step, just preceding and accompanying the pageant, is the reconciliation of Berowne to Boyet, upon whom Berowne has vented considerable irritation during this scene in two extended speeches (354–73, 513–34). The second speech (concluding bitterly, "You leere upon me, do you? There's an eie / Wounds like a Leaden sword") is met with a surprisingly soft reply:

BOYET: Full merrily hath this brave manage, this carreere bene run.
(V.ii.535–36)

That courtesy, a bit unexpectedly magnanimous and suggestive of a generosity beneath Boyet's mockery, elicits in turn Berowne's retirement from the quarrel:

Loe, he is tilting straight. Peace, I have don

(V.ii.537)

and anticipates the warmer rapprochement a few moments later:

Well said old mocker, I must needs be friends with thee.

(V.ii.609–10)

"Tilting straight" is generally taken to mean "tilting immediately"; it would make more sense if interpreted "in a straight-forward manner, without malice or irony." This interpretation would better fit Boyet's actual speech, and motivate better Berowne's retirement. In any case, the acceptance of Boyet, with his tougher and more "realistic" wit, by Berowne (and by extension his companions) is not without psychological and thematic importance.

4. To cite two critics:

"In contrast to that of the Princess, the behaviour of the men is incredibly unattractive, particularly that of Berowne. It is difficult to believe that this is the same man who spoke so eloquently a short time ago about the soft and sensible feelings of love, and promised Rosaline to mend his ways.... The laughter is unattractive, wild, and somehow discordant ... and it has little resemblance to the laughter we have heard in the play before this, delicate, sophisticated, sometimes hearty. But never really unkind" (Bobbyann Roesen, "*Love's Labour's Lost*," *Shakespeare Quarterly* [1953], 4:422–23).

"After this defeat, and especially after Berowne's self-criticism one might expect the men to begin acting with more discretion and self-consciousness; but any such expectation proves false, for in the pageant of the Nine Worthies, which breaks in on the men's defeat, their behavior attains to a new degree of crudity" (E. M. W. Tillyard, *Shakespeare's Early Comedies* [New York: Barnes and Noble, 1965], pp. 147–48).

5. "I am a Votarie, I have vow'd to *Iaquenetta* to holde the Plough for her sweet love three yeares" (V.ii.961–62).

6. Just as death has been an abstraction, so disease has heretofore served Berowne as a source of witty imagery:

Light Wenches may prove plagues to men forsworne.
                                                  (IV.iii.404)

Write *Lord have mercie on us*, on those three,
They are infected, in their hearts it lies:
They have the plague, and caught it of your eyes.
                                                  (V.ii.466–68)

7. Walter Pater, *Appreciations* (London: Macmillan, 1913), p. 166. Pater is speaking specifically hereof the style of Berowne; the larger context deals with the "foppery of delicate language" as it is toyed with throughout the play.

8. "All the wooers must learn to be patient, to wait out the full seasonal cycle which the songs represent.... The gaudy blossoms of Ver, the wonderful artifice of wit and wooing, are to be tried by the rigors of winter—of experience in the real world." Joseph Westlund, "Fancy and Achievement in *Love's Labour's Lost*," *Shakespeare Quarterly* (1967), 18:45.

9. The Signet edition of *Love's Labour's Lost*, John Arthos, ed. (New York and Toronto, 1965), p. 146.

10. "Sara adunque il nostro cortegiano stimato eccellente ed in ogni cosa averà grazia, massimamente nel parlare, se fuggirà l'affetazione." Baldassare Castiglione, *Il Cortegiano, con una scelta delle opere minori*, Bruno Maier, ed. (Turin: U.T.E.T., 1955), p. 129.

11. Helge Kokeritz, *Shakespeare's Pronunciation* (New Haven: Yale University Press, 1953), p. 110.

HAROLD C. GODDARD

The Meaning of Shakespeare:
Romeo and Juliet

I

One word has dominated the criticism of *Romeo and Juliet*: "star-cross'd."

From forth the fatal loins of these two foes,

says the Prologue-Chorus,

A pair of star-cross'd lovers take their life.

"Star-cross'd" backed by "fatal" has pretty much surrendered this drama to the astrologers. "In this play," says one such interpreter, "simply the Fates have taken this young pair and played a cruel game against them with loaded dice, unaided by any evil in men." That is merely an extreme expression of the widely held view that makes *Romeo and Juliet*, in contrast with all Shakespeare's later tragedies, a tragedy of accident rather than of character and on that account a less profound and less universal work. That this play betrays signs of immaturity and lacks some of the marks of mastery that are common to the other tragedies may readily be granted. But that its inferiority is due to the predominance of accident over character ought not to be conceded without convincing demonstration. The burden of proof is certainly on those who assert it, for nowhere else does

From *The Meaning of Shakespeare*. © 1951 by the University of Chicago.

Shakespeare show any tendency to believe in fate in this sense. The integrity of his mind makes it highly unlikely that in just one instance he would have let the plot of the story he was dramatizing warp his convictions about freedom.

The theme of *Romeo and Juliet* is love and violence and their interactions. In it these two mightiest of mighty opposites meet each other squarely—and one wins. And yet the other wins. This theme in itself makes *Romeo and Juliet* an astrological play in the sense that it is concerned throughout with Venus and Mars, with love and "war," and with little else. Nothing ever written perhaps presents more simply what results from the conjunction of these two "planets." But that does not make it a fatalistic drama. It all depends on what you mean by "stars." If by stars you mean the material heavenly bodies exercising from birth a predestined and inescapable occult influence on man, Romeo and Juliet were no more star-crossed than any lovers, even though their story was more unusual and dramatic. But if by stars you mean—as the deepest wisdom of the ages, ancient and modern, does—a psychological projection on the planets and constellations of the unconsciousness of man, which in turn is the accumulated experience of the race, then Romeo and Juliet and all the other characters of the play are star-crossed as every human being is who is passionately alive.

> In tragic life, God wot,
> No villain need be! Passions spin the plot,
> We are betrayed by what is false within.

The "villain" need not be a conspicuous incarnation of evil like Richard III or Iago; the "hero" himself may be the "villain" by being a conspicuous incarnation of weakness as was another Richard or a Troilus. Or the "villain" may consist in a certain chemical interplay of the passions of two or more characters. To seek a special "tragic flaw" in either Romeo or Juliet is foolish and futile. From pride down, we all have flaws enough to make; of every life and of life itself a perpetual and universal tragedy. Altering his source to make the point unmistakable, Shakespeare is at pains to show that, however much the feud between Capulets and Montagues had to do with it incidentally, the tragedy of this play flowed immediately from another cause entirely. But of that in its place. Enough now if we have raised a suspicion that the "star-crossed" of the Prologue should be taken in something other than a literal sense, or, better, attributed to the Chorus; not to the poet. The two are far from being the same.[1]

In retrospect, Shakespeare's plays, which in one sense culminate in *King Lear* and in another, in *The Tempest*, are seen to deal over and over with the same underlying subject that dominates the Greek drama: the relation of the generations. *Romeo and Juliet*, as the first play of its author in which this subject is central, assumes a profound seminal as well as intrinsic interest on that account. It points immediately in this respect to *Henry IV* and *Hamlet*, and ultimately to *King Lear* and *The Tempest*.

This theme of "the fathers" is merely another way of expressing the theme of "the stars." For the fathers are the stars and the stars are the fathers in the sense that the fathers stand for the accumulated experience of the past, for tradition, for authority and hence for the two most potent forces that mold and so impart "destiny" to the child's life. Those forces, of course, are heredity and training, which between them create that impalpable mental environment, inner and outer, that is even more potent than either of them alone. The hatred of the hostile houses in *Romeo and Juliet* is an inheritance that every member of these families is born into as truly as he is born with the name Capulet or Montague. Their younger generations have no more choice in the matter than they have choice of the language they will grow up to speak. They suck in the venom with their milk. "So is the will of a living daughter curbed by the will of a dead father," as Portia puts it in *The Merchant of Venice*. The daughter may be a son and the father may be living, but the principle is the same. Thus the fathers cast the horoscopes of the children in advance—and are in that sense their stars. If astrology is itself, as it is, a kind of primitive and unconscious psychology, then the identity of the stars and the fathers becomes even more pronounced.

Now there is just one agency powerful enough in youth to defy and cut across this domination of the generations, and that is love. Love is a "star" but in another and more celestial sense. Romeo, of the Montagues, after a sentimental and unrequited languishing after one Rosaline, falls in love at first sight with Juliet, of the Capulets, and instantly the instilled enmity of generations is dissipated like mist by morning sunshine, and the love that embraces Juliet embraces everything that Juliet touches or that touches her.

> My bounty is as boundless as the sea,
> My love as deep; the more I give to thee,
> The more I have, for both are infinite.

The words—music, imagery, and thought uniting to make them as wonderful as any ever uttered about love—are Juliet's, but Romeo's love is as deep—almost. It is love's merit, not his, that his enemies suddenly become glorified with the radiance of the medium through which he now sees everything. Hostility simply has nothing to breathe in such a transcendental atmosphere. It is through this effect of their love on both lovers, and the poetry in which they spontaneously embody it, that Shakespeare convinces us it is no mere infatuation, but love indeed in its divine sense. Passion it is, of course, but that contaminated term has in our day become helpless to express it. Purity would be the perfect word for it if the world had not forgotten that purity is simply Greek for fire.

II

Shakespeare sees to it that we shall not mistake this white flame of Romeo's love, or Juliet's, for anything lower by opposing to the lovers, two of the impurest characters he ever created, Mercutio and the Nurse. And yet, in spite of them, it has often been so mistaken. Mercutio and the Nurse are masterpieces of characterization so irresistible that many are tempted to let them arrogate to themselves as virtue what is really the creative merit of their maker. They are a highly vital pair, brimming with life and fire—but fire in a less heavenly sense than the one just mentioned. Juliet, at the most critical moment of her life, sums up the Nurse to all eternity in one word. When, in her darkest hour, this woman who has acted as mother to her from birth goes back on her completely, in a flash of revelation the girl sees what she is, and, reversing in one second the feeling of a lifetime, calls her a fiend ("most wicked fiend"). She could not have chosen a more accurate term, for the Nurse is playing at the moment precisely the part of the devil in a morality play. And Juliet's "ancient damnation" is an equally succinct description of her sin. What more ancient damnation is there than sensuality—and all the other sins it brings in its train? Those who dismiss the Nurse as just a coarse old woman whose loquacity makes us laugh fail hopelessly to plumb the depth of her depravity. It was the Nurse's desertion of her that drove Juliet to Friar Laurence and the desperate expedient of the sleeping potion. Her cowardice was a link in the chain that led to Juliet's death.

The Nurse has sometimes been compared with Falstaff—perhaps the poet's first comic character who clearly surpassed her. Any resemblance between them is superficial, for they are far apart as the poles. Falstaff was at home in low places but the sun of his imagination always accompanied him as a sort of disinfectant. The Nurse had no imagination in an proper sense. No sensualist—certainly no old sensualist—ever has. Falstaff loved Hal. What the Nurse's "love" for Juliet amounted to is revealed when she advises her to make the best of a bad situation and take Paris (bigamy and all). The man she formerly likened to a toad suddenly becomes superior to an eagle.

> Go, counsellor,

cries Juliet, repudiating her Satan without an instant's hesitation,

> Thou and my bosom henceforth shall be twain.

It is the rejection of the Nurse. But unlike Falstaff, when he is rejected, she carries not one spark of our sympathy or pity with her, and a pathetic account of her death, as of his, would be unthinkable. We scorn her utterly as Juliet does.

III

The contrast between Friar Laurence and the Nurse even the most casual reader or spectator could scarcely miss. The difference between the spiritual adviser of Romeo and the worldly confidant of Juliet speaks for itself. The resemblance of Mercutio to the Nurse is more easily overlooked, together with the analogy between the part he plays in Romeo's life and the part she plays in Juliet's. Yet it is scarcely too much to say that the entire play is built around that resemblance and that analogy.

The indications abound that Shakespeare created these two to go together. To begin with, they hate each other on instinct, as two rival talkers generally do, showing how akin they are under the skin. "A gentleman, nurse," says Romeo of Mercutio, "that loves to hear himself talk, and will speak more in a minute than he will stand to in a month." The cap which Romeo thus quite innocently hands the Nurse fits her so perfectly that she immediately puts it on in two speeches about Mercutio which are typical examples of *her* love of hearing herself talk and of saying things *she* is powerless to stand by:

> An a' speak any thing against me, I'll take him down, an 'a were lustier than he is, and twenty such jacks; and if I cannot, I'll find those that shall. Scurvy knave! I am none of his flirt-gills; I am none of his skains-mates. (*Turning to* PETER, *her man*) And thou must stand by too, and suffer every knave to use me at his pleasure! ... Now, afore God, I am so vexed, that every part about me quivers. Scurvy knave!

That last, and the tone of the whole, show that there was a genuinely vicious element in the Nurse under her superficial good nature, as there invariably is in an old sensualist; and I do not believe it is exceeding the warrant of the text to say that the rest of the speech in which she warns Romeo against gross behavior toward her young gentlewoman—quite in the manner of Polonius and Laertes warning Ophelia against Hamlet—proves that in her heart she would have been delighted to have him corrupt her provided she could have shared the secret and been the go-between. "A bawd, a bawd, a bawd!" is Mercutio's succinct description of her.

But, as usual, when a man curses someone else, he characterizes himself. In what sense Mercutio is a bawd appears only too soon. In the meantime what a pity it is that he is killed off so early in the action as to allow no full and final encounter between these two fountains of loquacity! "Nay, an there were two such, we should have none shortly." Mercutio himself says it in another connection, but it applies perfectly to this incomparable pair. Their roles are crowded with parallelisms even down to what seem like the most trivial details. "We'll to dinner thither," says Mercutio, for example, parting from Romeo in Act

II, scene 4. "Go, I'll to dinner," says the Nurse on leaving Juliet at the end of scene 5. A tiny touch. But they are just the two who would be certain never to miss a meal. In Shakespeare even such trifles have significance.

The fact is that Mercutio and the Nurse are simply youth and old age of the same type. He is aimed at the same goal she has nearly attained. He would have become the same sort of old man that she is old woman, just as she was undoubtedly the same sort of young girl that he is young man. They both think of nothing but sex—except when they are so busy eating or quarreling that they can think of nothing. (I haven't forgotten Queen Mab; I'll come to her presently.) Mercutio cannot so much as look at the clock without a bawdy thought. So permeated is his language with indecency that most of it passes unnoticed not only by the innocent reader but by all not schooled in Elizabethan smut. Even on our own unsqueamish stage an unabridged form of his role in its twentieth-century equivalent would not be tolerated. Why does Shakespeare place the extreme example of this man's soiled fantasies precisely before the balcony scene? Why but to stress the complete freedom from sensuality of Romeo's passion? Place Mercutio's dirtiest words, as Shakespeare does, right beside Romeo's apostrophe to his "bright angel" and all the rest of that scene where the lyricism of young love reaches one of its loftiest pinnacles in all poetry—and what remains to be said for Mercutio? Nothing—except that he is Mercutio. His youth, the hot weather, the southern temperament, the fashion among Italian gentlemen of the day, are unavailing pleas; not only Romeo, but, Benvolio, had those things to contend with also. And they escaped. Mercury is close to the sun. But it was the material sun, Sol, not the god, Helios, that Mercutio was close to. Beyond dispute, this man had vitality, wit, and personal magnetism. But personal magnetism combined with sexuality and pugnacity is one of the most dangerous mixtures that can exist. The unqualified laudation that Mercutio has frequently received, and the suggestion that Shakespeare had to kill him off lest he quite set the play's titular hero in the shade, are the best proof of the truth of that statement. Those who are themselves seduced by Mercutio are not likely to be good judges of him. It may be retorted that Mercutio is nearly always a success on the stage, while Romeo is likely to be insipid. The answer to that is that while Mercutios are relatively common, Romeos are excessively rare. If Romeo proves insipid, he has been wrongly cast or badly acted.

"But how about Queen Mab?" it will be asked. The famous description of her has been widely held to be quite out of character and has been so down as an outburst of poetry from the author put arbitrarily in Mercutio's mouth. But the judgment "out of character" should always be a last resort. Undoubtedly the lines, if properly his, do reveal an unsuspected side of Mercutio. The prankish delicacy of some of them stands out in pleasing contrast with his grosser aspects. The psychology of this is sound. The finer side of a sensualist is suppressed and is bound to come out, if at all, incidentally, in just such a digression as this seems to be. Shakespeare can be trusted not to leave such things out. Few passages in his plays, however, have been more praised for the wrong reasons. The account of Queen Mab is supposed to prove Mercutio's imagination: under his pugnacity there was a poet. It would be nearer the truth, I think, to guess that Shakespeare put it in as an example of what poetry is popularly held to be and is not. The lines on Queen Mab are indeed delightful. But imagination in any proper sense they are not. They are sheer fancy. Moreover, Mercutio's anatomy and philosophy of dreams prove that he knows nothing of their genuine import. He dubs them

> the children of an idle brain,
> Begot of nothing but vain fantasy.

Perhaps his are—the Queen Mab lines would seem to indicate as much. Romeo, on the other hand, holds that dreamers "dream things true," and gives a definition of them that for combined brevity and beauty would be hard to better. They are "love's shadows." And not only from what we can infer about his untold dream on this occasion, but from all the dreams and premonitions of both Romeo and Juliet throughout the play, they come from a fountain of wisdom somewhere beyond time. Primitives distinguish between "big" and "little" dreams. (Aeschylus makes the same distinction in *Prometheus Bound*.) Mercutio, with his aldermen and gnats and coach-makers and sweetmeats and parsons and drums and ambuscadoes, may tell us a little about the littlest of little dreams. He thinks that dreamers are still in their day world at night. Both Romeo and Juliet know that there are dreams that come from as far below the surface of that world as was that prophetic tomb at the bottom of which she saw him "as one dead" at their last parting. Finally, how characteristic of Mercutio that he should make Queen Mab a midwife and blemish his description of her by turning her into a "hag" whose function is to bring an end to maidenhood. Is this another link between Mercutio and the Nurse? Is Shakespeare here preparing the way for his intimation that she would be quite capable of assisting in Juliet's corruption? It might well be. When Shakespeare writes a speech that seems to be out of character, it generally, as in this case, deserves the closest scrutiny.

And there is another justification of the Queen Mab passage. Romeo and Juliet not only utter poetry; they are poetry. The loveliest comment on Juliet I ever heard expressed this to perfection. It was made by a girl only a little older than Juliet herself. When Friar Laurence recommends philosophy to Romeo as comfort in banishment, Romeo replies:

> Hang up philosophy!
> Unless philosophy can make a Juliet ...
> It helps not, it prevails not. Talk no more.

"Philosophy can't," the girl observed, "but poetry can—and it did!" Over against the poetry of Juliet, Shakespeare was bound, by the demands of contrast on which all art rests, to offer in the course of his play examples of poetry in various verbal, counterfeit, or adulterate estates.

> This precious book of love, this unbound lover,
> To beautify him, only lacks a cover.

That is Lady Capulet on the prospective bridegroom, Paris. It would have taken the play's booby prize for "poetry" if Capulet himself had not outdone it in his address to the weeping Juliet:

> How now! a conduit, girl? What, still in tears?
> Evermore showering? In one little body
> Thou counterfeit'st a bark, a sea, a wind;
> For still thy eyes, which I may call the sea,
> Do ebb and flow with tears; the bark thy body is,
> Sailing in this salt flood; the winds, thy sighs;
> Who, raging with thy tears, and they with them,
> Without a sudden calm, will overset
> Thy tempest-tossed body.

It is almost as if Shakespeare were saying in so many words: That is how poetry is not written. Yet, a little later, when the sight of his daughter, dead as all suppose, shakes even this egotist into a second of sincerity, he can say;

> Death lies on her like an untimely frost
> Upon the sweetest flower of all the field.

There is poetry, deep down, even in Capulet. But the instant passes and he is again talking about death as his son-in-law—and all the rest. The Nurse's vain repetitions in this scene are further proof that she is a heathen. Her O-lamentable-day's only stress the lack of one syllable of genuine grief or love such as Juliet's father shows. These examples all go to show what Shakespeare is up to in the Queen Mab speech. It shines; and even seems profound, beside the utterances of the Capulets and the Nurse. But it fades and grows superficial, beside Juliet's and Romeo's. It is one more shade of what passes for poetry but is not.

IV

The crisis of *Romeo and Juliet*, so far as Romeo is concerned, is the scene (just after the secret marriage of the two lovers) in which Mercutio and Tybalt are slain and Romeo banished. It is only two hundred lines long. Of these two hundred lines, some forty are introduction and sixty epilogue to the main action.

As for the other hundred that come between, it may be doubted whether Shakespeare to the end of his career ever wrote another hundred that surpassed them in the rapidity, inevitability, and psychologic truth of the succession of events that they comprise. There are few things in dramatic literature to match them. And yet I think they are generally misunderstood. The scene is usually taken as the extreme precipitation in the play of the Capulet–Montague feud; whereas Shakespeare goes out of his way to rove that at most the feud is merely the occasion of the quarrel. Its cause he places square in the temperament and character of Mercutio, and Mercutio, it is only too easy to forget, is neither a Capulet nor a Montague, but a kinsman of the Prince who rules Verona, and, as such, is under special obligation to preserve a neutral attitude between the two houses.

This will sound to some like mitigating the guilt of Tybalt. But Tybalt has enough to answer for without making him responsible for Mercutio's sins.

The nephew of Lady Capulet is as dour a son of pugnacity as Mercutio is a dashing one:

> What, drawn, and talk of peace! I hate the word,
> As I hate hell.

These words—almost the first he speaks in the play—give Tybalt's measure. "More than prince of cats," Mercutio calls him, which is elevated to "king of cats" in the scene in which he mounts the throne of violence. (It is a comment on the Nurse's insight into human nature that she speaks of this fashionable desperado as "O courteous Tybalt! honest gentleman!") Mercutio's contempt for Tybalt is increased by the latter's affectation of the latest form in fencing: "He fights as you sing prick-song, keeps time, distance, and proportion.... The pox of such antic, lisping, affecting fantasticoes; these new tuners of accents!" Yet but a moment later, in an exchange of quips with Romeo, we find Mercutio doing with his wit just what he has scorned Tybalt for doing with his sword. For all their differences, as far as fighting goes Mercutio and Tybalt are two of a kind and by the former's rule are predestined to extinction: "an there were two such, we should rule none shortly, for one would kill the other." When one kills the other, there is not one left, but none. That is the arithmetic of it. The encounter is not long postponed.

Tybalt is outraged when he discovers that a Montague has invaded the Capulet mansion on the occasion of the ball when Romeo first sees Juliet. But for his uncle he would assail the intruder on the spot:

> Patience perforce with wilful choler meeting
> Makes my flesh tremble[2] in their different greeting.
> I will withdraw; but this intrusion shall
> Now seeming sweet convert to bitter gall.

He is speaking of the clash between patience and provocation in himself, But he might be prophesying his meeting with Romeo. As the third ad opens, he is hunting his man.

Tybalt is not the only one who is seeking trouble. The first forty lines of the crisis scene are specifically devised to show that Mercutio was out to have a fight under any and all circumstances and at any price. As well, ask a small boy and a firecracker to keep apart as Mercutio and a quarrel. Sensuality and pugnacity are the poles of his nature. In the latter respect he is a sort of Mediterranean Hotspur, his frank southern animality taking the place of the idealistic "honour" of his northern counterpart. He is as fiery in a literal as Romeo is in a poetic sense.

The scene is a public place. Enter Mercutio and Benvolio. Benvolio knows his friend:

> I pray thee, good Mercutio, let's retire.
> The day is hot, the Capulets abroad,
> And, if we meet, we shall not 'scape a brawl,
> For now, these hot days, is the mad blood stirring.

Mercutio retorts with a description of the cool-tempered Benvolio that makes him out an inveterate hothead:

> Thou! why, thou wilt quarrel with a man that hath a hair more, or a hair less, in his beard, than thou hast. Thou wilt quarrel with a man for cracking nuts, having no other reason but because thou hast hazel eyes. What eye but such an eye would spy out such a quarrel? Thy head is as full of quarrels as an egg is full of meat, and yet thy head hath been beaten as addle as an egg for quarrelling. Thou hast quarrelled with a man for coughing in the street, because he hath wakened thy dog that hath lain asleep in the sun. Didst thou not fall out with a tailor for wearing his new doublet before Easter? with another for tying his new shoes with old riband?

This, the cautious and temperate Benvolio! As Mercutio knows, it is nothing of the sort. It is an ironic description of himself. It is he, not his friend, who will make a quarrel out of anything—out of nothing, rather, and give a local habitation and a name, as a poet does with the creatures of his imagination. Mercutio is pugnacity in its pure creative state. At the risk of the Prince's anger, he makes his friend Romeo's cause his own and roams the streets in the hope of encountering some Capulet with whom to pick a quarrel. The feud is only a pretext. If it hadn't been that, it would have been something else. The Chorus may talk about "stars," but in this case Mars does not revolve in the skies on the other side of the Earth from Venus, but resides on earth right under the jerkin of this particular impulsive youth, Mercutio. Or if this "fate" be a god rather than a planet, then Mercutio has opened his heart and his home to him with unrestrained hospitality. So Romeo, is indeed "star-cross'd" in having Mercutio for a friend.

Mercutio has no sooner finished his topsy-turvy portrait of Benvolio than Tybalt and his gang come in to reveal which of the two the description fits. Tybalt is searching for Romeo, to whom he has just sent a challenge, and recognizing Romeo's friends begs "a word with one of you." He wishes, presumably, to ask where Romeo is. But Mercutio, bent on provocation, retorts, "make it a word and a blow." Benvolio tries in vain to intervene. Just as things are getting critical, Romeo enters, and Tybalt turns from Mercutio to the man he is really seeking:

> Romeo, the love I bear thee can afford
> No better term than this,—thou art a villain.

Here is the most direct and galling of insults. Here are Mercutio, Benvolio, and the rest waiting to see how Romeo will take it. The temperature is blistering in all senses. And what does Romeo say?

> Tybalt, the reason that I have to love thee
> Doth much excuse the appertaining rage
> To such a greeting; villain am I none;
> Therefore farewell; I see thou know'st me not.

We who are in the secret know that "the reason" is Juliet and that his love for her is capable of wrapping all Capulets in its miraculous mantle, even "the king of cats."

But Tybalt is intent on a fight and will not be put off by kindness how-ever sincere or deep. "Boy," he comes back insolently,

>   this shall not excuse the injuries
> That thou hast done me; therefore turn and draw.

Romeo, however, is in the power of something that makes him impervious to insults:

> I do protest I never injur'd thee,
> But love thee better than thou canst devise
> Till thou shalt know the reason of my love;
> And so, good Capulet,—which name I tender
> As dearly as my own,—be satisfied.

The world has long since decided what to think of a man who lets himself be called a villain without retaliating. Romeo, to put it in one word, proves himself, according to the world's code, a mollycoddle. And indeed a mollycoddle might act exactly as Romeo appears to. But if Romeo is a mollycoddle, then Jesus was a fool to talk about loving one's enemies, for Romeo, if anyone ever did, is doing just that at this moment. And Juliet was demented to talk about love being boundless and infinite, for here Romeo is about to prove that faith precisely true. Those who think that Jesus, and Juliet, and Romeo were fools will have plenty of backing. The "fathers" will be on their side. They will have the authority of the ages and the crowd. Only a philosopher or two, a few lovers, saints, and poets will be against them. The others will echo the

> O calm, dishonourable, vile submission!

with which Mercutio draws his rapier and begins hurling insults at Tybalt that make Tybalt's own seem tame:

> MER.: Tybalt, you rat-catcher, will you walk?
> TYB.: What wouldst thou have with me?
> MER.: Good king of cats, nothing but one of your nine lives.

And Mercutio threatens to stick him before he can draw if he does not do so instantly. What can Tybalt do but draw? "I am for you," he cries, as he does so.

Such, however, is the power of Romeo's love that even now he attempts to prevent the duel:

> Gentle Mercutio, put thy rapier up.

But Mercutio pays no attention and the two go to it. If ever a quarrel scene defined the central offender and laid the responsibility at one man's door, this is the scene and Mercutio is the man. It takes two to make a quarrel. Romeo, the Montague, will not fight. Tybalt, the Capulet, cannot fight if Romeo will not. With Mercutio Tybalt has no quarrel. The poet takes pains to make that explicit in a startling way. "Peace be with you, sir," are the words Tybalt addresses to Mercutio when Romeo first enters. That from the man who once cried,

> peace! I hate the word,
> As I hate hell.

Now we see why Shakespeare had him say it. It was in preparation for this scene. Thus he lets one word exonerate Tybalt of the responsibility for what ensues between him and Mercutio.

And now, condensed into the fractional part of a second, comes the crisis in Romeo's life. Not later, when he decides to kill Tybalt, but now. Now is the moment when two totally different universes wait as it were on the turning of a hand. There is nothing of its kind to surpass it in all Shakespeare, not even in *Hamlet* or *King Lear*, not, one is tempted to think, in all the drama of the world. Here, if anywhere, Shakespeare shows that the fate we attribute to the stars lies in our own souls.

> Our remedies oft in ourselves do lie,
> Which we ascribe to heaven: the fated sky
> Gives us free scope.

Romeo had free scope. For, if we are free to choose between two compulsions, we are in so far free. Romeo was free to act under the compulsion of force or under the compulsion of love—under the compulsion of the stars, that is, in either of two opposite senses. Granted that the temptation to surrender to the former was at the moment immeasurably great, the power of the latter, if Juliet spoke true, was greater yet:

> My bounty is as boundless as the sea,
> My love as deep; the more I give to thee,
> The more I have, for both are *infinite*.

Everything that has just preceded shows that the real Romeo wanted to have utter faith in Juliet's faith. "Genius trusts its faintest intimation," says Emerson, "against the testimony of all history." But Romeo, whose intimations were not faint but strong, falls back on the testimony of all history that only force can overcome force. He descends from the level of love to the level of violence and attempts to part the fighters with his sword.

> Draw, Benvolio; beat down their weapons.
> Gentlemen, for shame, forbear this outrage!
> Tybalt, Mercutio, the prince expressly hath
> Forbidden bandying in Verona streets.
> Hold, Tybalt! good Mercutio!

Here, if anywhere, the distinction between drama and poetry becomes clear. Drama is a portrayal of human passions eventuating in acts. Poetry is a picture of life in its essence. On the level of drama, we are with Romeo absolutely. His purpose is noble, his act endearingly impulsive. We echo that purpose and identify ourselves with that act. In theater we do, I mean, and under the aspect of time. But how different under the aspect of eternity! There the scene is a symbolic picture of life itself, of faith surrendering to force, of love trying to gain its end by violence—only to discover, as it soon does, and as we do too, that what it has attained instead is death. A noble motive never yet saved a man from the consequences of an unwise act, and Romeo's own words to Mercutio as he draws his sword are an unconscious confession in advance of his mistake. Having put aside his faith in Juliet's faith, his appeal is in the name of law rather than of love: "The prince expressly hath forbidden." That, and his "good Mercutio," reveal a divided soul. And it is that divided soul, in a last instant of hesitation, that causes an awkward or uncoordinated motion as he interferes and gives the cowardly Tybalt his chance to make a deadly thrust at Mercutio under Romeo's arm. If Romeo had only let those two firebrands fight it out, both might have lost blood with a cooling effect on their heated tempers, or, if it had gone to a finish, both might have been killed, as they ultimately were anyway, or, more likely, Mercutio would have killed Tybalt. ("An there were two such, we should have none shortly, for one would kill the other.") In any of these events, the feud between the two houses would not have been involved. As it is, the moment of freedom passes, and the rest is fate.

The fallen Mercutio reveals his most appealing side in his good humor, at death. But why his reiterated "A plague o' both your houses"? He is one more character in Shakespeare who "doth protest too much." Four times he repeats it, or three and a half to be exact. How ironical of Mercutio to attribute his death to the Capulet–Montague feud, when the Capulet who killed him had plainly been reluctant to fight with him, and the chief Montague present had begged and begged him to desist. That "plague o' both your houses" is Mercutio's unwitting confession that his own intolerable pugnacity, not the feud at all, is responsible. And if that be true, how much that has been written about this tragedy must be retracted.

What follows puts a final confirmation on Romeo's error in trying to part the duelists by force. With Mercutio dead as a direct result of his interference, what can Romeo say? We heard him fall from love to an appeal to law and order while the fight was on. Now it is over, he descends even lower as he bemoans his, "reputation stain'd with Tybalt's slander." Reputation! Iago's word.

> O sweet Juliet,
> Thy beauty hath made me effeminate
> And in my temper soften'd valour's steel!

Were ever words more tragically inverted? That fire should soften metal must have seemed a miracle to the man who first witnessed it. How much greater the miracle whereby beauty melts violence into love! That is the miracle that was on the verge of occurring in *Romeo and Juliet*.

Instead, Benvolio enters to announce Mercutio's death. Whereat Romeo, throwing the responsibility of his own mistake on destiny, exclaims:

> This day's black fate on more days doth depend;
> This but begins the woe others must end.

Could words convey more clearly the fact that the crisis has passed? Freedom has had its instant. The consequences are now in control.

Tybalt re-enters. Does Romeo now remember that his love for Juliet makes every Capulet sacred? Does he recall his last words to her as he left the orchard at dawn?

> Sleep dwell upon thine eyes, peace in thy breast!
> Would I were sleep and peace, so sweet to rest!

Does he now use his sword merely to prevent bloodshed?

> Away to heaven, respective lenity,

he cries, implying without realizing it the infernal character of his decision,

> And fire-ey'd fury be my conduct now!

Fury! Shakespeare's invariable word for animal passion in man gone mad. And in that fury Romeo's willingness to forgive is devoured like a flower in a furnace:

> Now, Tybalt; take the villain back again
> That late thou gav'st me; for Mercutio's soul
> Is but a little way above our heads,
> Staying for thine to keep him company.
> Either thou, or I, or both, must go with him.

The spirit of Mercutio does indeed enter Romeo's body, and though it is Tybalt who is to go with the slain man literally, it is Romeo who goes with him in the sense that he accepts his code and obeys his ghost. Drawing his rapier, he sends Tybalt to instant death—to the immense gratification of practically everyone in the audience, so prone are we in the theater to surrender to the ancestral emotions. How many a mother, suspecting the evil influence of some companion on her small son, has put her arms about him in a desperate gesture of protection. Yet that same mother will attend a performance of *Romeo and Juliet*, and, seduced by the crowd, will applaud Romeo's capitulation to the spirit of Mercutio to the echo. So frail is the tenderness of the mothers in the face of the fathers.

In this respect the scene is like the court scene in *The Merchant of Venice* when we gloat over Shylock's discomfiture. Here, as there, not only our cooler judgment when we are alone but all the higher implications of the tragedy call for a reversal of our reaction when with the crowd. In this calmer retrospect, we perceive that between his hero's entrance and exit in this scene Shakespeare has given us three Romeos, or, if you will, one Romeo in three universes. First we see him possessed by love and a spirit of universal forgiveness. From this he falls, first to reason and an appeal to law, then to violence—but violence in a negative or "preventive" sense. Finally, following Mercutio's death, he passes under the control of passion and fury, abetted by "honour," and thence to vengeance and offensive violence. In astrological terms, he moves from Venus, through the Earth, to Mars. It is as if Dante's *Divine Comedy* were compressed into eighty lines and presented in reverse—Romeo in an inverted "pilgrimage" passing from Paradise, through Purgatory, to the Inferno.

This way of taking the scene acquits Romeo of doing "wrong," unless we may be said to do wrong whenever we fail to live up to our highest selves. Love is a realm beyond good and evil. Under the aspect of time, of common sense, possibly even of reason and morality, certainly of "honour," Romeo's conduct in the swift succession of events that ended in Tybalt's death was unexceptionable. What at else could he have done? But under the aspect of eternity, which is poetry's aspect, it was less than that. We cannot blame a man because he does not perform a miracle. But when he offers proof of his power and the very next moment has the opportunity to perform one, and does not, the failure is tragic. Such was the "failure" of Romeo. And he himself admits it in so many words. Death, like love, lifts us; for a moment above time. Just before he drinks the poison, catching sight of the body of Tybalt in the Capulet vault, Romeo cries, "Forgive my cousin." Why should he ask forgiveness for what he did in honor, if honor be the guide to what is right?

Romeo as an honorable man avenges his friend. But in proving himself a man in this sense, he proves himself less than the perfect lover. "Give all to love," says Emerson:

> Give all to love ...
> 'Tis a brave master;
> Let it have scope:
> Follow it utterly,
> Hope beyond hope ...
> Heartily know,
> When half-gods go,
> The gods arrive.

Juliet's love had bestowed on Romeo power to bring down a god, to pass even beyond the biblical seventy times seven to what Emily Brontë calls the "first of the seventy-first." But he did not. The play is usually explained as a tragedy of the excess of love. On the contrary it is the tragedy of a deficiency of it. Romeo did not "follow it utterly," did not give quite "all" to love.

V

Romeo's mental condition following the death of Tybalt is proof of the treason he has committed against his own soul. Up to this point in the scene, as we saw, Shakespeare has given us three Romeos. Now he gives us a fourth: the man rooted to the spot at the sight of what he has done. The citizens have heard the tumult and are coming. "Stand not amaz'd," cries Benvolio—and it is a case where one poet's words seem to have been written to illuminate another's. Wordsworth's lines are like a mental stage direction for the dazed Romeo:

> Action is transitory—a step, a blow,
> The motion of a muscle—this way or that—
> 'Tis done; and in the after-vacancy
> We wonder at ourselves like men betrayed:
> Suffering is permanent, obscure and dark,
> And has the nature of infinity.

"O! I am Fortune's fool," cries Romeo. "Love's not Time's fool," says Shakespeare, as if commenting on this very scene, in that confession of his own faith, the 116th sonnet:

> O, no! it is an ever-fixed mark,
> That looks on tempests and is never shaken;
> It is the star to every wandering bark,
> Whose worth's unknown, although his height be taken.

There is an astrology at the opposite pole from that of the Chorus to this play: Romeo's love looked on a tempest—and it was shaken. He apparently has just strength enough left to escape and seek refuge in Friar Laurence's cell, where, at the word of his banishment, we find him on the floor,

> Taking the measure of an unmade grave,

in a fit of that suicidal despair that so often treads on the heels of "fury." At is not remorse for having killed Tybalt that accounts for his condition, a nor even vexation with himself for having spoiled his own marriage, but same for having betrayed Juliet's faith in the boundlessness of love.

Meanwhile, at the scene of the duels, citizens have gathered, followed by the Prince with Capulets and Montagues. Lady Capulet, probably the weakest character in the play, is the first to demand more blood as a solution of the problem:

> Prince, as thou art true,
> For blood of ours, shed blood of Montague.

But the Prince asks first for a report of what happened.

> Benvolio, who began this bloody fray?

Benvolio mars what is otherwise a remarkably accurate account of the affair by failing utterly to mention Mercutio's part in instigating the first duel, placing the entire blame on Tybalt.

> He is a kinsman to the Montague,

cries Lady Capulet,

> Affection makes him false; he speaks not true.
> Some twenty of them fought in this black strife,
> And all those twenty could but kill one life.

Her sense of reality and character are on a level with her courage.

In Capulet's orchard, the Nurse brings to Juliet the rope ladder by which her husband is to reach her chamber—and with it the news of Tybalt's death and Romeo's banishment.

> O serpent heart, hid with a flowering face!
> Did ever dragon keep so fair a cave?

cries Juliet,

> O nature, what hadst thou to do in hell,
> When thou didst bower the spirit of a fiend
> In mortal paradise of such sweet flesh?

Even in the exaggeration of her anguish, Juliet diagnoses what has happened precisely as Shakespeare does: a fiend—the spirit of Mercutio—has taken possession of her lover-husband's body. Contrast her insight at such a moment with the Nurse's drivellings:

> There's no trust,
> No faith, no honesty in men; all perjur'd,
> All forsworn, all naught, all dissemblers.
> Ah, where's my man?

A fair sample of how well her inane generalizations survive the test of concrete need.

Back in Friar Laurence's cell, the stunned Romeo is like a drunken man vaguely coming to himself after a debauch. When he draws his sword to make away with himself, the Friar restrains him not by his hand,[3] as Romeo had once sought to restrain Mercutio at a similarly critical moment, but by the force of his words:

> Hold thy desperate hand!
> Art thou a man?

And he seeks to sting him back to manhood by comparing his tears to those of a woman and his fury to that of a beast.

> Thou hast amaz'd me ....
> Why rail'st thou on thy birth, the heaven, and earth?
> Since birth, and heaven, and earth, all three do meet
> In thee at once, which thou at once wouldst lose.

No nonsense about "star-cross'd lovers" for Friar Laurence. Shakespeare, like Dante before him and Milton after him, knew where the stars are new, knew that heaven and hell, and even earth, are located within the human soul. Romeo is the "skilless soldier" who sets afire the powder in his own flask.

VI

Juliet too in her despair can think of death. But with what relative calmness and in what a different key! The contrast between the two lovers at this stage is a measure of the respectively innocent and guilty states of their souls.

Their meeting at night is left to our imagination, but their parting at dawn is Shakespeare's imagination functioning at its highest lyrical intensity, with interwoven symbols of nightingale and lark, darkness and light, death and love. Then follow in swift succession the mother's announcement of her daughter's impending marriage with Paris, Juliet's ringing repudiation of the idea, the rejection of her, in order, by her father, her mother, and the Nurse—the first brutal, the second supine, the third Satanic. And then, with an instantaneousness that can only be called divine, Juliet's rejection of the Nurse. In a matter of seconds the child has become a woman. This is the second crisis of the drama, Juliet's, which, with Romeo's, gives the play its shape as certainly as its two foci determine the shape of an ellipse. If ever two crises were symmetrical, and opposite these are.

Romeo, in a public place, lured insensibly through the influence of

Mercutio to the use of force, falls, and as a direct result of his fall, kills Tybalt. Juliet, in her chamber, deserted by her father and mother and enticed to faithlessness by the Nurse, child as she is, never wavers for an instant, puts her tempter behind her, and consents as the price of her fidelity to be "buried" alive. Can anyone imagine that Shakespeare did not intend this contrast, did not build up his detailed parallelism between Mercutio and the Nurse to effect it? Romeo, as we said, does not give quite "all" for love. But Juliet does. She performs her miracle and receives supernatural strength as her reward. He fails to perform his and is afflicted with weakness. But eventually her spirit triumphs in him. Had it done so at first, the tragedy would have been averted. Here again the heroine transcends the hero. And yet Romeo had Friar Laurence as adviser while Juliet was brought up by the Nurse! The profounder the truth, the more quietly Shakespeare has a habit of uttering it. It is as if he were saying here that innocence comes from below the sources of pollution and can run the fountain clear.

To describe as "supernatural" the strength that enables Juliet "without fear or doubt" to undergo the ordeal of the sleeping potion and the burial vault does not seem excessive:

Give me, give me! O! tell me not of fear!

Long before—in the text, not in time—when she had wondered how Romeo had scaled the orchard wall below her balcony, he had said:

With love's light wings did I o'erperch these walls;
For stony limits cannot hold love out,
And what love can do that dares love attempt.

Juliet is now about to prove the truth of his words, in a sense Romeo never dreamed of, "in that dim monument where Tybalt lies." The hour comes, and after facing the terrors her imagination conjures up, Juliet goes through her "dismal scene" alone, is found "dead," and following a scene that anticipates but reverses Hamlet in that a wedding is turned into a funeral, is placed in the Capulet vault in accordance with Friar Laurence's desperate plan. But after force has had its instant way, fate in the guise of fear usually; has its protracted way, and to oppose it is like trying to stay an avalanche with your hand.

VII

The pestilence prevents the Friar's messenger from reaching Romeo. Instead, word is brought to him that Juliet is dead, and, armed with a drug of an apothecary who defies the law against selling poison, he ends his banishment to

Mantua and starts back to Verona to seek beside Juliet the eternal banishment of death. The fury with which he threatens his companion Balthasar, on dismissing him when they reach the churchyard, if he should return to pry, reveals Romeo's mood:

> By heaven, I will tear thee joint by joint
> And strew this hungry churchyard with thy limbs.
> The time and my intents are savage-wild,
> More fierce and more inexorable far
> Than empty tigers or the roaring sea.

And when he encounters and slays Paris, the contrast between his death and that of Mercutio, or even Tybalt, shows that we are dealing here not so much with the act of a free agent choosing his course in the present as with the now fatal consequences of an act in the past, of an agent then free but now no longer so. Paris is little more than the branch of a tree that Romeo pushes aside—and his death affects us almost as little. It is all like a dream, or madness. Finding the sleeping—as he supposes the dead—Juliet, Romeo pours out his soul in words which, though incomparable as poetry, err in placing on the innocent heavens the responsibility for his own venial but fatal choice:

> O, here
> Will I set up my everlasting rest,
> And shake the yoke of inauspicious stars
> From this world-wearied flesh.

And then, by one of those strokes that, it sometimes seems, only Shakespeare could achieve, the poet makes Romeo revert to and round out, in parting from Juliet forever, the same metaphor he had used when she first gazed down on him, from her balcony and he had tried to give expression to the scope and range of his love. How magically, placed side, by side, the two passages fit together, how tragically they sum up the story:

> I am no pilot; yet, went thou as far
> As that vast shore wash'd with the farthest sea,
> I would adventure for such merchandise.

> Come, bitter conduct, come, unsavoury guide!
> Thou desperate pilot, now at once run on
> The dashing rocks thy sea-sick weary bark!
> Here's to my love! (*Drinks.*) O true apothecary!
> Thy drugs are quick. Thus with a kiss I die. (*Dies.*)

Enter Friar Laurence—a moment too late. That fear is with him Shakespeare shows by another echo. "Wisely and slow; they stumble that run fast," the Friar had warned Romeo on dismissing him after his first confession of his love for Juliet, and now he says:

> How oft to-night
> Have my old feet stumbled at graves! ...
> ... Fear comes upon me.

He discovers the dead Romeo. Just then Juliet awakes. But at the same moment he hears a noise. The watch is coming! He cannot be found here.

> Come, go, good Juliet, I dare no longer stay,

and when she refuses to follow, he deserts her. With a glance into the empty cup in Romeo's hand and a kiss on the lips that she hopes keep poison for her own—anticipating touches at the deaths of both Hamlet and Cleopatra—she snatches Romeo's dagger and kills herself.

Why did Shakespeare, after building up so noble a character as Friar Laurence, permit him to abandon Juliet at so fatal a moment? Why add his name to the so different ones of Capulet, Lady Capulet, and the Nurse, no matter how much better the excuse for his desertion of her? For two reasons, I think: first, to show how far the infection of fear extends that Romeo's use of force had created. "Here is a friar, that trembles, sighs, and weeps," says the Third Watchman, and Laurence himself confesses, when he tells his story,

> But then a noise did scare me from the tomb.

And then, to show that Juliet, abandoned *even by religion*, must fall back for courage finally on love alone.

The pestilence plays a crucial part toward the end of the action. It is a symbol. Whatever literal epidemic there may have been in the region, it is plain that fear is the real pestilence that pervades the play. It is fear of the code of honor, not fate, that drives Romeo to seek vengeance on Tybalt. It is fear of the plague, not accident, that leads to the miscarriage of Friar Laurence's message to Romeo. It is fear of poverty, not the chance of his being at hand at the moment, that lets the apothecary sell the poison. It is fear of the part he is playing, not age, that makes Friar Laurence's old feet stumble and brings him to the tomb just a few seconds too late to prevent Romeo's death. It is fear of being found at such a spot at such a time, not coincidence, that lets him desert Juliet at last just when he does. Fear, fear, fear, fear, fear. Fear is the evil "star" that crosses the lovers. And fear resides not in the skies but in the human heart.

VIII

The tragedy ends in the reconciliation of the two houses, compensation, it is generally held, for the deaths of the two lovers. Doubtless the feud was not renewed in its former form. But much superfluous sentiment has been spent on this ending. Is it not folly to suppose that Capulet or Lady Capulet was spiritually transformed by Juliet's death? And as for Montague, the statue of her in pure gold that he promised to erect in Verona is proof in itself how incapable he was of understanding her spirit and how that spirit alone, and not monuments or gold, can bring an end to feuds. (Lady Montague, who died of a broken heart, was far and away the finest of the four parents.) Shakespeare's happy endings are, almost without exception, suspect. Or rather they are to be found, if at all, elsewhere than in the last scene and final speeches, and are "happy" in a quite untheatrical sense.

Cynics are fond of saying that if Romeo and Juliet had lived their love would not have "lasted." Of course it wouldn't—in the cynic's sense. You can no more ask such love to last than you can ask April to last, or an apple blossom. Yet April and apple blossoms do last and have results that bear no resemblance to what they come from—results such as apples and October—and so does such love. Romeo, in his last words, referred to the phenomenon known as "a lightning before death." Here is that lightning, and here, if it have one, is the happy ending of *Romeo and Juliet*:

> ROM: If I may trust the flattering truth of sleep,
>   My dreams presage some joyful news at hand.
>   My bosom's lord sits lightly in his throne,
>   And all this day an unaccustom'd spirit
>   Lifts me above the ground with cheerful thoughts.
>   I dreamt my lady came and found me dead—
>   Strange dream, that gives a dead man leave to think!—
>   And breath'd such life with kisses in my lips,
>   That I reviv'd and was an emperor.
>   Ah me! how sweet is love itself possess'd,
>   When but love's shadows are so rich in joy!

Enter Balthasar—with news of Juliet's death.

Dreams go by contraries, they say, and this seems to be an example. But is it?

NOTES

1. See the discussion of the Choruses of *Henry V* on this point.

2. *Nurse* (II, iv, 172): "Now, afore God, I am so vexed that every part about me quivers." Another revealing analogy.

3. The actor may easily make a mistake here and spoil Shakespeare's point.

G. K. CHESTERTON

A Midsummer Night's Dream

The greatest of Shakespeare's comedies is also, from a certain point of view, the greatest of his plays. No one would maintain that it occupied this position in the matter of psychological study, if by psychological study we mean the study of individual characters in a play: No one would maintain that Puck was a character in the sense that Falstaff is a character, or that the critic stood awed before the psychology of Peaseblossom. But there is a sense in which the play is perhaps a greater triumph of psychology than *Hamlet* itself. It may well be questioned whether in any other literary work in the world is so vividly rendered a social and spiritual atmosphere. There is an atmosphere in *Hamlet*, for instance, a somewhat murky and even melodramatic one, but it is subordinate to the great character, and morally inferior to him; the darkness is only a background for the isolated star of intellect. But *A Midsummer Night's Dream* is a psychological study, not of a solitary man, but of a spirit that unites mankind. The six men may sit talking in an inn; they may not know each other's names or see each other's faces before or after, but night or wine or great stories, or some rich and branching discussion may make them all at one, if not absolutely with each other, at least with that invisible seventh man who is the harmony of all of them. That seventh man is the hero of *A Midsummer Night's Dream*.

A study of the play from a literary or philosophical point of view must therefore be founded upon some serious realization of what this atmosphere is. In a lecture upon *As You Like It*, Mr. Bernard Shaw made a suggestion which is

From *Chesterton on Shakespeare*, ed. Dorothy E. Collins. © 1971 by Dorothy E. Collins.

an admirable example of his amazing ingenuity and of his one most interesting limitation. In maintaining that the light sentiment and optimism of the comedy were regarded by Shakespeare merely as the characteristics of a more or less cynical pot-boiler, he actually suggested that the title "As You Like It" was a taunting address to the public in disparagement of their taste and the dramatists's own work. If Mr. Bernard Shaw had conceived of Shakespeare as insisting that Ben Jonson should wear Jaeger underclothing or join the Blue Ribbon Army, or distribute little pamphlets for the non-payment of rates, he could scarcely have conceived anything more violently opposed to the whole spirit of Elizabethan comedy than the spiteful and priggish modernism of such a taunt. Shakespeare might make the fastidious and cultivated Hamlet, moving in his own melancholy and purely mental world, warn players against an overindulgence towards the rabble. But the very soul and meaning of the great comedies is that of an uproarious communion, between the public and the play, a communion so chaotic that whole scenes of silliness and violence lead us almost to think that some of the "rowdies" from the pit have climbed over the footlights. The title "As You Like It" is, of course, an expression of utter carelessness, but it is not the bitter carelessness which Mr. Bernard Shaw fantastically reads into it; it is the godlike and inexhaustible carelessness of a happy man. And the simple proof of this is that there are scores of these genially taunting titles scattered through the whole of Elizabethan comedy. Is "As You Like It" a title demanding a dark and ironic explanation in a school of comedy which called its plays, "What You Will", "A Mad World, My Masters", "If It Be Not Good, the Devil Is In It", "The Devil is an Ass", "An Humorous Day's Mirth", and "A Midsummer Night's Dream"? Every one of these titles is flung at the head of the public as a drunken lord might fling a purse at his footman. Would Mr. Shaw maintain that "If It Be Not Good, the Devil Is In It", was the opposite of "As You Like It", and was a solemn invocation of the supernatural powers to testify to the care and perfection of the literary workmanship? The one explanation is as Elizabethan as the other.

Now in the reason for this modern and pedantic error lies the whole secret and difficulty of such plays as *A Midsummer Night's Dream*. The sentiment of such a play, so far as it can be summed up at all, can be summed up in one sentence. It is the mysticism of happiness. That is to say, it is the conception that as man lives upon a borderland he may find himself in the spiritual or supernatural atmosphere, not only through being profoundly sad or meditative, but by being extravagantly happy. The soul might be rapt out of the body in an agony of sorrow, or a trance of ecstasy; but it might also be rapt out of the body in a paroxysm of laughter. Sorrow we know can go beyond itself; so, according to Shakespeare, can pleasure go beyond itself and become something dangerous and unknown. And the reason that the logical and destructive modern school, of which Mr. Bernard Shaw is an example, does not grasp this purely exuberant nature of the comedies is simply that their logical and destructive attitude have rendered impossible the very experience of this preternatural exuberance. We cannot realize *As You Like It* if we are always considering it as we understand it. We cannot have *A Midsummer Night's Dream* if our one object in life is to keep ourselves awake with the black coffee of criticism. The whole question which is balanced, and balanced nobly and fairly, in *A Midsummer Night's Dream*, is whether the life of waking, or the life of the vision, is the real life, the *sine quâ non* of man. But it is difficult to see what superiority for the purpose of judging is possessed by people whose pride it is not to live the life of vision at all. At least it is questionable whether the Elizabethan did not know more about both worlds than the modern intellectual; it is not altogether improbable that Shakespeare would not only have had a clearer vision of the fairies, but would have shot very much straighter at a deer and netted much more money for his performances than a member of the Stage Society.

In pure poetry and the intoxication of words, Shakespeare never rose higher than he rises in this play. But in spite of this fact the supreme literary merit of *A Midsummer Night's Dream* is a merit of design. The amazing symmetry, the amazing artistic and moral beauty of that design, can be stated very briefly. The story opens in the sane and common world with the pleasant seriousness of very young lovers and very young friends. Then, as the figures advance into the tangled wood of young troubles and stolen happiness, a change and bewilderment begins to fall on them. They lose their way and their wits for they are in the heart of fairyland. Their words, their hungers, their very figures grow more and more dim and fantastic, like dreams within dreams, in the supernatural mist of Puck. Then the dream-fumes begin to clear, and characters and spectators begin to awaken together to the noise of horns and dogs and the clean and bracing morning. Theseus, the incarnation of a happy and generous rationalism, expounds in hackneyed and superb lines the sane view of such psychic experiences, pointing out with a reverent and sympathetic scepticism that all these fairies and spells are themselves but the emanations, the unconscious masterpieces, of man himself. The whole company falls back into a splendid human laughter. There is a rush for banqueting and private theatricals, and over all these things ripples one of those frivolous and inspired conversations in which every good saying seems to die in giving birth to another. If ever the son of man in his wanderings was at home and drinking by the fireside, he is at home in the house of Theseus. All the dreams have been forgotten, as a melancholy dream remembered throughout the morning might be forgotten in the human certainty of any other triumphant evening party; and so the play seems naturally ended. It began on the earth and it ends on the earth. Thus to round off the whole midsummer night's dream in an eclipse of daylight is an effect of genius. But of this comedy, as I have said, the mark is that genius goes beyond itself; and one touch is added which makes the play colossal. Theseus and his train retire with a crashing finale, full of Humour and wisdom and things set right, and silence falls on the house. Then there comes a faint sound of little feet, and for a moment, as it were, the elves look into the house, asking which is the reality. "Suppose we are the realities and they the shadows." If that ending were acted properly any modern man would feel shaken to his marrow if he had to walk home from the theatre through a country lane.

It is a trite matter, of course, though in a general criticism a more or less indispensable one to comment upon another point of artistic perfection, the extraordinarily human and accurate manner in which the play catches the atmosphere of a dream. The chase and tangle and frustration of the incidents and personalities are well known to everyone who has dreamt of perpetually falling over precipices or perpetually missing trains. While following out clearly and legally the necessary narrative of the drama, the author contrives to include every one of the main peculiarities of the exasperating dream. Here is the pursuit of the man we cannot catch, the flight from the man we cannot see; here is the perpetual returning to the same place, here is the crazy alteration in the very objects of our desire, the substitution of one face for another face, the putting of the wrong souls in the wrong bodies, the fantastic disloyalties of the night, all this is as obvious as it is important. It is perhaps somewhat more worth remarking that there is about this confusion of comedy yet another essential characteristic of dreams. A dream can commonly be described as possessing an utter discordance of incident combined with a curious unity of mood; everything changes but the dreamer. It may begin with anything and end with anything, but if the dreamer is sad at the end he will be sad as if by prescience at the beginning; if he is cheerful at the beginning he will be cheerful if the stars fail. *A Midsummer Night's Dream* has in a most singular degree effected this difficult, this almost desperate subtlety. The events in the wandering wood are in themselves, and regarded as in broad daylight, not merely melancholy but bitterly cruel and ignominious. But yet by the spreading of an atmosphere as magic as the fog of Puck, Shakespeare contrives to make the whole matter mysteriously hilarious while it is palpably tragic, and mysteriously charitable, while it is in itself cynical. He contrives somehow to rob tragedy and treachery of their full sharpness, just as a toothache or a deadly danger from a tiger, or a precipice, is robbed of its sharpness in a pleasant dream. The creation of a brooding sentiment like this, a sentiment not merely independent of but actually opposed to the events, is a much greater triumph of art than the creation of the character of Othello.

It is difficult to approach critically so great a figure as that of Bottom the Weaver. He is greater and more mysterious than Hamlet, because the interest of such men as Bottom consists of a rich subconsciousness, and that of Hamlet in the comparatively superficial matter of a rich consciousness. And it is especially difficult in the present age which has become hag-ridden with the mere intellect. We are the victims of a curious confusion whereby being great is supposed to have something to do with being clever, as if there were the smallest reason to suppose that Achilles was clever, as if there were not on the contrary a great deal of internal evidence to indicate that he was next door to a fool. Greatness is a certain indescribable but perfectly familiar and palpable quality of size in the personality, of steadfastness, of strong flavour, of easy and natural self-expression. Such a man is as firm as a tree and as unique as a rhinoceros, and he might quite easily be as stupid as either of them. Fully as much as the great poet towers above the small poet the great fool towers above the small fool. We have all of us known rustics like Bottom the Weaver, men whose faces would be blank with idiocy if we tried for ten days to explain the meaning of the National Debt, but who are yet great men, akin to Sigurd and Hercules, heroes of the morning of the earth, because their words were their own words, their memories their own memories, and their vanity as large and simple as a great hill. We have all of us known friends in our own circle, men whom the intellectuals might justly describe as brainless, but whose presence in a room was like a fire roaring in the grate changing everything, lights and shadows and the air, whose entrances and exits were in some strange fashion events, whose point of view once expressed haunts and persuades the mind and almost intimidates it, whose manifest absurdity clings to the fancy like the beauty of first love, and whose follies are recounted like the legends of a paladin. These are great men, there are millions of them in the world, though very few perhaps in the House of Commons. It is not in the cold halls of cleverness where celebrities seem to be important that we should look for the great. An intellectual salon is merely a training-ground for one faculty, and is akin to a fencing class or a rifle corps. It is in our own homes and environments, from Croydon to St. John's Wood, in old nurses, and gentlemen with hobbies, and talkative spinsters and vast incomparable butlers, that we may feel the presence of that blood of the gods. And this creature so hard to describe, so easy to remember, the august and memorable fool, has never been so sumptuously painted as in the Bottom of *A Midsummer Night's Dream*.

Bottom has the supreme mark of this real greatness in that like the true saint or the true hero he only differs from humanity in being as it were more human than humanity. It is not true, as the idle materialists of today suggest, that compared to the majority of men the hero appears cold and dehumanized; it is the majority who appear cold and dehumanized in the presence of greatness. Bottom, like Don Quixote and Uncle Toby and Mr. Richard Swiveller and the rest of the Titans, has a huge and unfathomable weakness, his silliness is on a great scale, and when he blows his own trumpet it is like the trumpet of the Resurrection. The other rustics in the play accept his leadership not merely naturally but exuberantly; they have to the full that primary and savage unselfishness, that uproarious abnegation which makes simple men take pleasure in falling short of a hero, that unquestionable element of basic human nature which has never been expressed, outside this play, so perfectly as in the incomparable chapter at the beginning of *Evan Harrington* in which the praises of The Great Mel are sung with a lyric energy by the tradesmen whom he has cheated. Twopenny sceptics write of the egoism of primal human nature; it is reserved for great men like Shakespeare and Meredith to detect and make vivid this rude and subconscious unselfishness which is older than self. They alone with their insatiable tolerance can perceive all the spiritual devotion in the soul of a snob. And it is this natural play between the rich simplicity of Bottom and the simple simplicity of his comrades which constitutes the unapproachable excellence of the farcical scenes in this play. Bottom's sensibility to literature is perfectly fiery and genuine, a great deal more genuine than that of a great many cultivated critics of literature—"the raging rocks and shivering shocks shall break the locks of prison gates, and Phibbus' car shall shine from far, and make and mar the foolish fates", is exceedingly good poetical diction with a real throb and swell in it, and if it is slightly and almost imperceptibly deficient in the matter of sense, it is certainly every bit as sensible as a good many other rhetorical speeches in Shakespeare put into the mouths of kings and lovers and even the spirits of the dead. If Bottom liked cant for its own sake the fact only constitutes another point of sympathy between him and his literary creator. But the style of the thing, though deliberately bombastic and ludicrous, is quite literary, the alliteration falls like wave upon wave, and the whole verse, like a billow mounts higher and higher before it crashes. There is nothing mean about this folly; nor is there in the whole realm of literature a figure so free from vulgarity. The man vitally base and foolish sings "The Honeysuckle and the Bee"; he does not rant about "raging rocks" and "the car of Phibbus". Dickens, who more perhaps than any modern man had the mental hospitality and the thoughtless wisdom of Shakespeare, perceived and expressed admirably the same truth. He perceived, that is to say, that quite indefensible idiots have very often a real sense of, and enthusiasm for letters. Mr. Micawber loved eloquence and poetry with his whole immortal soul; words and visionary pictures kept him alive in the absence of food and money, as they might have kept a saint fasting in a desert. Dick Swiveller did not make his inimitable quotations from Moore and Byron merely as flippant digressions. He made them because he loved a great school of poetry. The sincere love of books has nothing to do with cleverness or stupidity any more than any other sincere love. It is a quality of character, a freshness, a power of pleasure, a power of faith. A silly person may delight in reading masterpieces just as a silly person may delight in picking flowers. A fool may be in love with a poet as he may be in love with a woman. And the triumph of Bottom is that he loves rhetoric and his own taste in the arts, and this is all that can be achieved by Theseus, or for the matter of that by Cosimo di Medici. It is worth remarking as an extremely fine touch in the picture of Bottom that his literary taste is almost everywhere concerned with sound rather than sense. He begins the rehearsal with a boisterous readiness, "Thisby, the flowers of odious savours sweete." "Odours, odours," says Quince, in remonstrance, and the word is accepted in accordance with the cold and heavy rules which require an element of meaning in a poetical passage. But "Thisby, the flowers of odious savours sweete", Bottom's version, is an immeasurably finer and more resonant line. The "i" which he inserts is an inspiration of metricism.

There is another aspect of this great play which ought to be kept familiarly in the mind. Extravagant as is the masquerade of the story, it is a very perfect aesthetic harmony down to such *coup-de-maître* as the name of Bottom, or the flower called Love-in-Idleness. In the whole matter it may be said that there is one accidental discord; that is in the name of Theseus, and the whole city of Athens in which the events take place. Shakespeare's description of Athens in *A Midsummer Night's Dream* is the best description of England that he or any one else ever wrote. Theseus is quite obviously only an English squire, fond of hunting, kindly to his tenants, hospitable with a certain flamboyant vanity. The mechanics are English mechanics, talking to each other with the queer formality of the poor. Above all, the fairies are English; to compare them with the beautiful patrician spirits of Irish legend, for instance, is suddenly to discover that we have, after all, a folklore and a mythology, or had it at least in Shakespeare's day. Robin Goodfellow, upsetting the old women's ale, or pulling the stool from under them, has nothing of the poignant Celtic beauty; his is the horseplay of the invisible world. Perhaps it is some debased inheritance of English life which makes American ghosts so fond of quite undignified practical jokes. But this union of mystery with farce is a note of the medieval English. The play is the last glimpse of Merrie England, that distant but shining and quite indubitable country. It would be difficult indeed to define wherein lay the peculiar truth of the phrase "merrie England", though some conception of it is quite necessary to the comprehension of *A Midsummer Night's Dream*. In some cases at least, it may be said to lie in this, that the English of the Middle Ages and the Renaissance, unlike the England of today, could conceive of the idea of a merry supernaturalism. Amid all the great work of Puritanism the damning indictment of it consists in one fact, that there was one only of the fables of Christendom that it retained and renewed, and that was the belief in witchcraft. It cast away the generous and wholesome superstition, it approved only of the morbid and the dangerous. In their treatment of the great national fairy-tale of good and evil, the Puritans killed St. George but carefully preserved the Dragon. And this seventeenth-century tradition of dealing with the psychic life still lies like a great shadow over England and America, so that if we glance at a novel about occultism we may be perfectly certain that it deals with sad or evil destiny. Whatever else we expect we certainly should never expect to find in it spirits such as those in *Aylwin* as inspirers of a tale of tomfoolery like the *Wrong Box* or *The Londoners*. That impossibility is the disappearance of "merrie England" and Robin Goodfellow. It was a land to us incredible, the land of a jolly occultism where the peasant cracked jokes with his patron saint, and only cursed the fairies good-humouredly, as he might curse a lazy servant. Shakespeare is English in everything, above all in his weaknesses. Just as London, one of the greatest cities in the world, shows more slums and hides more beauties than any other, so Shakespeare alone among the four giants of poetry is a careless writer, and lets us come upon his splendours by accident, as we come upon an old City church in the twist of a city street. He is English in nothing so much as in that noble cosmopolitan unconsciousness which makes him look eastward with the eyes of a child towards Athens or

Verona. He loved to talk of the glory of foreign lands, but he talked of them with the tongue and unquenchable spirit of England. It is too much the custom of a later patriotism to reverse this method and talk of England from morning till night, but to talk of her in a manner totally un-English. Casualness, incongruities, and a certain fine absence of mind are in the temper of England; the unconscious man with the ass's head is no bad type of the people. Materialistic philosophers and mechanical politicians have certainly succeeded in some cases in giving him a greater unity. The only question is, to which animal has he been thus successfully conformed?

NORTHROP FRYE

The Bolingbroke Plays
(Richard II, Henry IV)

I've mentioned the sequence of plays, four in all, that Shakespeare produced
early in his career, on the period of the War of the Roses between Lancaster and
York (so called because the emblem of Lancaster was a red rose and that of York
a white one). With *Richard II* we begin another sequence of four plays,
continuing through the two parts of *Henry IV* and ending with *Henry V*. The two
central characters of the whole sequence are Bolingbroke, later Henry IV, who
appears in the first three, and his son, later Henry V, who appears in the second,
third and fourth. Although there are ominous forebodings of later events in
Richard II, the audience would pick up the allusions, and we don't need to assume
that Shakespeare began *Richard II* with the ambition of producing another
"tetralogy" or group of four plays. The second part of *Henry IV* looks as though
it were written mainly to meet a demand for more Falstaff. Still, each play does
look back to its predecessors, so there is a unity to the sequence, whether planned
in advance or not. And, as the Epilogue to *Henry V* tells us, the story ends at the
point where the earlier sequence began.

I've provided a table of the intermarriages of English royalty between the
reigns of Edward III and Henry VII, the period that covers the eight history
plays. If you add Henry VIII, Henry VII's son, all the histories are covered that
Shakespeare wrote except *King John*. In order to show the important marriages,
I haven't always listed sons and daughters in order of age, from the left. We can
see that there were not many Romeo and Juliet situations: in the aristocracy at

From *Northrop Frye on Shakespeare*. © 1986 by Northrop Frye.

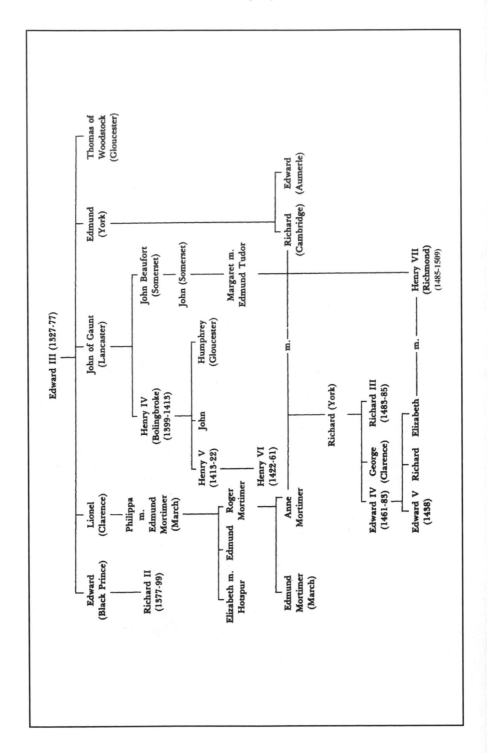

that time you simply married the man or woman who would do most for the fortunes of your family.

We start with Edward III's five sons. Shakespeare speaks of seven sons: the other two, both called William, died early on. Edward's eldest son and heir, Edward the "Black Prince," who would normally have succeeded his father, died the year before his father did, and the rules of succession brought his son, Richard, to the throne when he was still a boy. As some of his contemporaries remarked, "Woe to the land that's governed by a child!", and yet Richard lasted for twenty-two years, as long as Henry IV and Henry V together, Shakespeare's play covering only the last year or so of his reign.

The daughter of the second son, Lionel, married into the family of Mortimers; her daughter in turn married Hotspur of the Percy family. When Richard II's life ended in 1399, his heir, by the rules of succession, should have been the third Edmund Mortimer, Earl of March, who was also nominated, according to the conspirators in *Henry IV*, by Richard II as his successor. That was the issue that the revolt against Henry IV, which involved Hotspur so deeply, depended on. Bolingbroke was the son of John of Gaunt, Edward III's third son, and so not the next in line to the crown. However, he succeeded in establishing the Lancastrian house as the royal family, and was followed by his son and grandson. Apart from what the conspirators say, the fact that Bolingbroke seized the crown from Edmund as well as Richard is played down in this sequence, but there is a grimly eloquent speech from this Edmund, dying in prison, in *1 Henry VI* (although Shakespeare, if he wrote the scene, has confused him with someone else).

The Yorkist line came from the fourth son, Edmund, Duke of York, whose dramatic switch of loyalties from Richard to Bolingbroke, and the resulting conflict with his son Edward, called Aumerle, is the real narrative turning point of *Richard II*. The Yorkist line was not consolidated until the marriage of Aumerle's brother, Richard, to a descendant of Lionel produced Richard, Duke of York, who began the War of the Roses. The Yorkists got the upper hand in the war, and the Yorkist heir succeeded as Edward IV. Edward's two young sons, Edward (called Edward V because he had a theoretical reign of two months, although never crowned) and Richard, were supposed to have been murdered in the Tower by their wicked uncle, who became Richard III. Whether Richard III did this, or whether the story came from the Tudor propaganda machine, is still disputed: in any case Shakespeare bought it. Richard III, after a reign of about two years, was defeated and killed in battle by the Duke of Richmond, a descendant of John of Gaunt through a later wife. (She was not his wife when their son was born, and the line had to be legitimized by a special act of Richard II.) The Duke of Richmond then ascended the throne as Henry VII and founded what is called the House of Tudor, from the name of his father. Because of his descent from John of Gaunt, his victory technically restored the House of Lancaster, but one of the first things he did was to marry the Yorkist heiress

Elizabeth, and the marriage put a symbolic end to the war by uniting the red and white roses. References to this could easily be turned into a compliment to Queen Elizabeth's complexion: a sonnet by the poet Fulke Greville begins:

> Upon a throne I saw a virgin sit,
> The red and white rose quartered in her face.

The fifth son, Thomas of Woodstock, Duke of Gloucester, had been murdered just before the action of *Richard II* begins, and the duel that Bolingbroke and Mowbray are about to fight in the opening scene of the play results from Mowbray's being implicated in the murder. There was another well-known contemporary play on this subject, *Thomas of Woodstock* (anonymous). This play is probably a source for Shakespeare, as it seems to be earlier, although it loads the case against Richard more heavily than Shakespeare does. According to this play Woodstock lost his life because he was too persistent in giving Richard II advice, and Richard was as much involved with his death as Mowbray.

Shakespeare's play seems to have made a deep impression on his public, and there were six Quartos of it, five of them within his lifetime. The first three omitted the deposing scene at the end of Act IV; the fourth, the first one that had it, appeared five years after Queen Elizabeth's death. The cutting out of the deposing scene could have happened anyway, because of the official nervousness about showing or printing such things, but there is evidence that the play was revived during the conspiracy of Essex against Elizabeth, perhaps for the very purpose the censors worried about, that of accustoming the public to the thought of deposing a monarch. The queen herself made the connection, and is reported, to have said: "I am Richard II, know ye not that? This tragedy was played forty times in open streets and houses." We may perhaps take "forty" to be (literally) Elizabethan rhetoric for at least once," but even the commission of inquiry must have realized that there was no relation between the reckless and extravagant Richard and the cautious and stingy Elizabeth. It is perhaps a measure of her sense of insecurity, even at this period of her reign, that she thought there was.

As for Shakespeare's own dramatic vision, we have that curious garden scene (III.iv), for which scholars have never located a source, and which is two things that Shakespeare's writing practically never is, allegorical and sentimental. Considering the early date of the play (mid-1590s, probably), it is most unlikely that there was any contemporary allusion, but if the Essex group did revive the play for propaganda, this scene would have backfired on them, as it says that a capable ruler ought to cut ambitious nobles down to size before they get dangerous.

In *Richard II* Shakespeare had to make a marriage of convenience between the facts of medieval society, so far as they filtered down to him from his sources, and the Tudor mystique of royalty. That mystique regarded government by a central sovereign to be the form of government most in accord with both human nature and the will of God. It is true that no English sovereign except Henry VIII ever had the unlimited power that was very common on the Continent then and for many centuries thereafter. But still the reigning king or queen was the "Lord's anointed," his or her person was sacred, and rebellion against the sovereign was blasphemy and sacrilege as well as treason. The phrase "Lord's anointed" comes ultimately from the Bible. The Hebrew word Messiah, meaning "the anointed one," is applied in the Old Testament to a lawfully consecrated king, including even the rejected King Saul. The Greek equivalent of Messiah is Christ, and Jesus Christ was regarded as the king of the spiritual world, lawful kings in the physical world being his regents. If a lawful king happened to be a vicious tyrant, that was ultimately the fault of his subjects rather than of him, and they were being punished through him for their sins.

So when Richard II, during the abdication scene particularly, draws so many parallels between his trial and the trial of Christ, he is not comparing himself directly to Christ, but saying that the same situation, of the world rejecting the Lord's anointed, is being enacted once again. Of these echoes from the Passion in the Gospels, perhaps the most striking is that of Pilate's washing of his hands in a futile effort to make himself innocent of the death of Christ. Bolingbroke uses this image when he is making his first act as the next king, in ordering the execution of Bushy and Green; it is repeated in a contrasting context by Richard:

> Not all the water in the rough rude sea
> Can wash the balm off from an anointed king
>
> (III.ii. 54–55)

and explicitly linked with Pilate by Richard in the abdication scene. The closing lines of the play are spoken by Bolingbroke, and express his purpose of going on a crusade "To wash this blood off from my guilty hand."

One awkward question might be raised in connection with this doctrine of the sacredness of the royal person. Suppose you're second in line from the throne, and murder the one who's first in line, do you thereby acquire all the sanctity of the next Lord's anointed? Well, in some circumstances you do. Shakespeare's King John becomes king when his nephew, Prince Arthur, is really in line for the succession, and although the prince technically commits suicide by jumping out of a window, John is certainly not innocent of his murder. John thereby becomes by default the lawful king, and when he dies his son Prince Henry becomes his legitimate heir. The strongest man in the country at the time is Falconbridge, bastard son of Richard I, who would have been king if he were legitimate, and could probably seize power quite easily in any case. But he holds back in favour of Prince Henry, and the play comes to a resounding patriotic conclusion to the effect that nothing can happen "If England to itself do rest but true," which in the context means partly keeping the line of succession intact.

You may not find this particular issue personally very involving, but the general principle is that all ideologies sooner or later get to be circumvented by cynicism and defended by hysteria, and that principle will meet you everywhere you turn in a world driven crazy by ideologies, like ours.

A lawful king, as Shakespeare presents the situation, can be ruthless and unscrupulous and still remain a king, but if he's weak or incompetent he creates a power vacuum in society, because the order of nature and the will of God both demand a strong central ruler. So a terrible dilemma arises between a weak king de jure and a de facto power that's certain to grow up somewhere else. This is the central theme of *Richard II*. Richard was known to his contemporaries as "Richard the Redeless," i.e., a king who wouldn't take good advice, and Shakespeare shows him ignoring the advice of John of Gaunt and York. His twenty-year reign had a large backlog of mistakes and oppressions that Shakespeare doesn't need to exhibit in detail. In the scene where his uncle John of Gaunt is dying, John concentrates mainly on the worst of Richard's administrative sins: he has sold, for ready cash, the right of collecting taxes to individuals who are not restrained in their rapacity by the central authority. This forms part of what begins as a superbly patriotic speech: Shakespeare's reason for making the old ruffian John of Gaunt a wise and saintly prophet was doubtless that he was the ancestor of the House of Tudor. We also learn that Richard had a very undesirable lot of court favourites, spent far too much money on his own pleasures, and at the time of the play was involved in a war in Ireland that had brought his finances into a crisis. As we'll see later, getting into a foreign war is normally by far the best way of distracting a disaffected people, but Ireland roused no one's enthusiasm.

In the Middle Ages the effective power was held by the great baronial houses, which drew their income from their own land and tenants, many of them serfs; they could raise private armies, and in a crisis could barricade themselves into some very strong castles. In such a situation a medieval king had a theoretical supremacy, but not always an actual one, and, as his power base was often narrower than that of a landed noble, he was perpetually hard up for money. So if he were stuck with a sudden crisis, as Richard II is with the Irish war, he would often have to behave like a brigand in his own country and find pretexts for seizing and confiscating estates. What kind of law does a lawful king represent who resorts to illegal means of getting money? Or, who resorts to means that are technically legal, but violate a moral right?

Depends on what the moral right is. If it's abstract justice, protection of the poor, the representation of taxpayers in government, the right of the individual to a fair trial or the like, forget it. Shakespeare's *King John* never mentions Magna Carta, and *Richard II* never mentions the most important event of the reign, the Peasants' Revolt (twenty years earlier, but the social issues were still there). But if you take private property away from a noble house that's powerful enough to fight back, you're in deep trouble. The Duke of York tries to explain to Richard that his own position as king depends on hereditary succession, and that the same principle applies to a nobleman's right to inherit the property of his father. When Richard seizes John of Gaunt's property, he's doing something that will make every noble family in England say "Who next?" So John's son Henry Bolingbroke gets a good deal of support when he defies Richard's edict of banishment and returns to claim his own. We don't know much about what is going on in Bolingbroke's mind at any one time, and that's largely because he doesn't let himself become aware of the full implications of what he's doing. When he says at first that he merely wants his rights, it's possible that he means that. But this is the point at which Richard's spectacular incompetence as an administrator begins to operate. In the demoralized state of the nation a de facto power begins to gather around Bolingbroke, and he simply follows where it leads, neither a puppet of circumstances nor a deliberately unscrupulous usurper.

The rest of the play is the working out of this de jure and de facto dilemma. Some, like the Duke of York, come over to Henry's side and transfer the loyalty owed the Lord's anointed to him. So, when York's son Aumerle conspires in favour of Richard, York accuses his son of the same treason and sacrilege he'd previously accused Bolingbroke of before he changed sides. In the scene, where York insists on the king's prosecuting his son for treason and his duchess pleads for pardon, Bolingbroke is at his best, because he realizes the significance of what's happening. He's made the transition from being the de facto king to being the de jure king as well, and after that all he needs to do is get rid of Richard.

There are others, like the Bishop of Carlisle, who take the orthodox Tudor line, and denounce Bolingbroke for what he is doing to the Lord's anointed. As Shakespeare presents the issue, both sides are right. Henry becomes king, and makes a better king, as such things go, than Richard. When his nobles start quarrelling among themselves in a scene that reads almost like a reprise of his own challenge to Mowbray, he puts all the challenges "under gage," postpones all action, and squashes instantly what could become a dangerous brawl. But the way he came to the throne leaves a curse over the House of Lancaster that starts working out after Henry V's death twenty years or so later. Perhaps the only thing that would really resolve the situation is for Henry IV to go on the crusade he keeps talking about, because killing Moslems is so meritorious an act that it wipes out all previous sins, however grievous. John of Gaunt introduces the theme of crusade, as one of the things England was devoted to in its prime: he was doubtless thinking of the contrast between Richard and his namesake, Richard I, who spent so much of his ten-year reign fighting in the Third Crusade. But Henry's plans to go on a crusade are interrupted by revolts against him, and that again is inevitable: one revolt begets another. He carries on as best he can, and the comforting prophecy that he will die in Jerusalem turns out to apply to the name of a room in the palace of Westminster. It is a particularly savage irony, from Bolingbroke's point of view, that his enemy Mowbray, who, unlike him, was banished for life, should have died fighting in a crusade.

It should be clear by now that Shakespeare is not interested in what we would normally think of as history. What is really happening in history is extremely difficult to dramatize. Shakespeare is interested in chronicle, the personal actions and interactions of the people at the top of the social order. And the centre of his interest is in the kind of dramatic performance involved in being a leader in society, more particularly a king. All social relationships are in a sense theatrical ones: as soon as someone we know appears, we throw ourselves into the dramatic situation that our knowledge of him makes appropriate, and act it out accordingly. If we're alone, like Hamlet or like Richard in prison, we soliloquize; that is, we dramatize ourselves to ourselves. And what we all do, the prince makes history, or chronicle, by doing. In his vision of leadership, Shakespeare often comes curiously close to Machiavelli's *The Prince*. Curiously, because it is practically impossible that Shakespeare could have known Machiavelli's writings, and because Shakespeare's social vision is a deeply conservative one, whereas Machiavelli's was realistic enough to make the horrified idealists of his time give him a reputation in England and elsewhere as the voice of the devil himself. He comes in, for example, to emit cynical sentiments as the prologue speaker of Marlowe's *Jew of Malta*. But the theorist and the dramatist converge on two points: the dramatic nature of leadership and the fact that the qualities of the born leader are not moral qualities.

In ancient times stage actors usually wore masks, and the metaphor of the masked actor has given two words to the language. One is "hypocrite," which is Greek in origin and refers to the actor looking through the mask; the other is "person," which is Latin and refers to his speaking through it. Today we also use the word "persona" to mean the social aspect of an individual, the way he encounters other people. To some extent it's a misleading term, because it implies a real somebody underneath the masks, and, as the soliloquy reminds us, there's never anything under a persona except another persona. What there is is a consistency that limits the variety of social relations to a certain repertoire: that is, Hamlet always sounds like Hamlet, and Falstaff like Falstaff, whatever their roles at the moment. But for Shakespeare, as we'll see further later on, the question of identity is connected with social function and behaviour; in other words with the dramatic self, not with some hidden inner essence.

Well, "hypocrite" is a moral term and "person" is not: we accept that everyone has a personality, but it's supposed to be wrong for people to be hypocrites. Hypocrisy has been called the tribute that vice pays to virtue, but to know that you're saying one thing and thinking another requires a self-discipline that's practically a virtue in itself. Certainly it's often an essential virtue for a public figure. Situations change, and the good leader does what the new situation calls for, not what is consistent with what he did before. When Bolingbroke orders the execution of the king's favourites, one of his gravest charges against them is the way that they have separated the king from the queen, but an act or so later he himself is ordering a much more drastic separation of them. A successful leader doesn't get hung up on moral principles: the place for moral principles is in what we'd call now the PR job. The reputation of being virtuous or liberal or gracious is more important for the prince than the reality of these things, or rather, as in staging a play, the illusion is the reality.

Bolingbroke begins and ends the play, and the beginning and ending are in a most symmetrical relationship. At the beginning there is to be a public duel, or trial by battle, between Bolingbroke and Mowbray, over the murder of Thomas of Woodstock. Although Mowbray belongs to the house of Norfolk, not York, here is in embryo the theme of the eight historical plays: two noblemen quarrelling among themselves, with the king driven to stratagems to maintain his ascendancy. Perhaps a shrewder monarch would have left them to fight it out, on the ground that a duel to the death would get rid of at least one dangerous nobleman, but Richard stops the duel and banishes both, Mowbray for life, Bolingbroke for ten years, later reduced to six. The duellists talk so much that we suspect they're both lying, but it's Bolingbroke who drops the key image of civil war, Cain's murder of his brother Abel:

> That he did plot the Duke of Gloucester's death...
> Which blood, like sacrificing Abel's, cries
> Even from the tongueless caverns of the earth.
>
> (I.i. 100–105)

At the end of the play, no Bolingbroke, now Henry IV, hints that the death of the imprisoned Richard would be most convenient to him, and his follower Exton carries out the murder, and returns expecting a reward for faithful service. He forgot that leaders have to dissociate themselves immediately from such acts, whether they ordered them or not, and the play closes with Exton banished and Henry saying, "With Cain go wander thorough shades of night," echoing Mowbray's line about his banishment: "To dwell in solemn shades of endless night."

The play is thus enclosed by the image of the first human crime, Cain's murder of his brother, the archetype of all civil wars that follow. In the middle comes the scene of the queen and the gardener. The gardener is addressed as "old Adam's likeness," which, means that this is not a garden like Eden, where nothing was "unruly" and there were no weeds, but a garden made from the soil that Adam was forced to cultivate after his fall. Another phrase, of the queen's, "To make a second fall of cursed man," is repeated in a very curious context in *Henry V*. Every fall of every consecrated) ruler repeats the original fall of man. Since then, history has proceeded in a series of cycles: Shakespeare's audience was thoroughly familiar with the image he uses constantly in his plays, the wheel of fortune, and would see the entire action of this play, from the murder of Woodstock to the murder of Richard, as a single turn of that wheel. Richard's image for this is that of two buckets, one going up and the other down, "The emptier ever dancing in the air," a most sardonic comment on the sort of person who succeeds in the way that Bolingbroke has succeeded. One corollary from this conception of a wheel of fortune is that in history it is only the past that can be idealized or thought of as, heroic or peaceful. The *Henry VI* plays look back to the great and victorious Henry V; the play of *Henry V* looks back to the time of Richard as a time when there was no curse of usurpation on the royal house; and in this play we have John of Gaunt idealizing an earlier time, apparently the reign of Edward III, the reign that saw the Black Death and the beginning of the Hundred Years' War with France.

What keeps the wheel turning is the fact that people are conditioned to a certain reflex about it: whenever there's a change in personnel in the state, the assumption is normally that somehow or other an old age is going to be renewed. As the Duchess of York says to Aumerle after the king has pardoned him, "Come, my old son: I pray God make thee new." The joyful expectation on the part of the people that a new king will give a new life to the nation is put by York into its proper context:

> As in a theatre the eyes of men,
> After a well-graced actor leaves the stage,
> Are idly bent on him that enters next.   (V.ii. 23–25)

The illusion of movement in history corresponds to the processional aspect of a drama, the series of events that holds the interest. We have to listen on a deeper level, picking up such things as the Cain imagery, to realize that the beginning and the end are much the same point.

We feel this circularity of movement from the very beginning, the ordeal by battle that opens the play. Such ordeals, in medieval times, were surrounded by the most detailed ritual and punctilio. The combatants appeared before the king and formally stated their cases; the king would try to reconcile them; he would fail; he would then allow a trial by battle at a time and place duly stated. As the play goes on, the duel modulates to one between Bolingbroke and King Richard, but the same ritual formality continues, except that there is no longer any question of a fair fight. That is one reason why *Richard II* is written, contrary to Shakespeare's usual practice, entirely in verse: no contrasting force from outside the duelling ritual breaks in to interrupt the action.

Bolingbroke realizes that one of the qualities of the leader is inscrutability, giving the impression that there are great reserves of power of decision not being expressed. Of course many people look inscrutable who are merely stupid: Bolingbroke is not stupid, but he understands that the leaders who attract the greatest loyalty and confidence are those who can suggest in their manner that they have no need of it. Later, in *1 Henry IV*, Bolingbroke is telling his son Prince Hal that, in the dramatic show a leader puts on, the one essential is aloofness. He says that he appeared publicly very seldom, and always with calculation:

By being seldom seen, I could not stir
But like a comet I was wond'red at

(1 Henry IV, III.ii. 46–47)

and contrasts his own skilful performance with Prince Hal's wasting time with low company in Eastcheap, which he says is repeating the mistake of "the skipping king" Richard, who lost his crown mainly because he was seen too often and not with the right people. What Henry says may be true as a general political principle, though whether it was true of his own behaviour at the time or not is another question: certainly the communique from Richard's headquarters about Bolingbroke is very different from what Bolingbroke remembers of it:

Off goes his bonnet to an oyster-wench;
A brace of draymen bid God speed him well
And had the tribute of his supple knee

(Richard II, I.iv. 31–33)

One aspect of this question of leadership has been studied in a fine piece of scholarship, a book called *The King's Two Bodies,* by E.H. Kantorowicz. Oversimplifying a bit, the king's two bodies, as distinguished in medieval and Renaissance theory, are his individual body as a man and his symbolic aspect as the body of his nation in an individual form. To extend this in the direction of *Richard II*, if the individual man is A, and the symbol of the nation as a single body is B, then the real king is B, the consecrated and sacrosanct figure, the king de jure. But the stronger the king is as an individual, and the more de facto ability he has, the more nearly A will equal B, and the better off both the king and his society will be. In any case, whether A equals B or not, it is clear that A minus B equals nothing, and that equation is echoed in the words "all" and "nothing" that run through the abdication scene, and in fact are continuing as late as *King Lear*.

Richard has been brought up to believe in the sanctity of his office, and unfortunately that has not made him more responsible but less so. Hence he turns to magic and fantasy as soon as he is even momentarily frustrated. When he goes to see the dying John of Gaunt, thinking of how soon he can get his money, he soliloquizes:

Now put it, God, into the physician's mind
To help him to his grave immediately!   (I.iv. 59–60)

This is not the voice of a strong-willed and powerful king, but of a spoiled child, and those who talk in such accents can never get away with what they do for long. John of Gaunt tells him his flatterers have got inside his individual castle, and have cut him off from that identification with his society that every genuine king must have. Nobody could express the doctrine of the two bodies more clearly than John of Gaunt does:

A thousand flatterers sit within thy crown,
Whose compass is no bigger than thy head;
And yet, incaged in so small a verge,
The waste is no whit lesser than thy land.

(II.i. 100–103)

After his return from Ireland, Richard refuses for a time to believe that anything can affect an anointed king adversely. But after the roll call of disasters has been recited to him he suddenly reverses his perspective, fascinated by the paradox that an individual, as vulnerable and subject to accident as anyone else, could also be the body of his whole kingdom. In short, he turns introvert, and that is a dangerous thing for a ruler to be who expects to go on being a ruler.

It is obvious, long before his final murder, that Richard is no coward, but his growing introversion gives him some of the weaknesses that make other men cowards. One of them is an overreacting imagination that sketches the whole course of a future development before anyone else has had time to figure out the present one. Sometimes these flashes of the future are unconscious: at the beginning he tells Mowbray that he is not favouring Bolingbroke and would not "Were he my brother, nay, my kingdom's heir." That could pass as the straight thematic anticipation that we've met before in Shakespeare. So, more doubtfully, could his complaint about John of Gaunt's "frozen admonition":

chasing the royal blood
With fury from his native residence.   (II.i. 118–19)

But when disaster becomes objective he instantly begins to see himself as the central figure of a secular Passion. When Northumberland reports Bolingbroke's wish for Richard to come down and parley with him in the "base court" (the *basse cour* or lower courtyard of Flint Castle), the symbolism of the whole operation flashes at once through his mind:

Down, down I come, like glist'ring Phaeton ...
In the base court? Base court, where kings grow base ...
In the base court? Come down? Down, court! Down, king!

(III.iii. 178–82)

So active an imagination makes Richard a remarkable poet, but cripples him as a practical man, because his mental schedule is so different from those of people who advance one step at a time, like Bolingbroke. We are reminded here, as so often in Shakespeare, that successful action and successful timing are much the same thing. His being a day late in returning from Ireland has resulted in twelve thousand Welshmen, on a rumour that he was dead, deserting to Bolingbroke. Very little is said about fortune or fate or the stars here, because Richard has made so many mistakes in timing that something like this was bound to hit him sooner or later.

Eventually Richard comes to understand, if not consciously at first, that he is programming himself as a loser, and has thrown himself into the elegiac role of one who has lost his throne before he has actually lost it. This in its turn is a kind of self-indulgent retreat from the confronting situation: "that sweet way I was in to despair," as he calls it. In the abdication scene he makes what could look like a last throw of the dice:

> And if my word be sterling yet in England,
> Let it command a mirror hither straight
>
> (IV.i. 264–65)

It is Bolingbroke who gives the order to bring a looking glass: there is nothing sterling about Richard's word anymore. As far as history is concerned, Richard has had it: nothing remains but to find some device for murdering him. But as far as drama is concerned, Richard is and remains the unforgettable central figure, and Bolingbroke is a supporting actor. How does this come about? How does Richard manage to steal the show from Bolingbroke at the very moment when Bolingbroke is stealing his crown?

The reason goes back to the distinction we made earlier between the two forms of mask: the hypocrite and the person. We all have to be persons, and that involves our being hypocrites at times too: there's no way out of that. But Richard is surrounded with nobles solidly encased in hypocrisy of various kinds: many of them, as we'll discover more fully in the next play, are just gangsters glorified by titles and blank verse, and all of them, including Bolingbroke, are engaged in pretending that a bad king is being deposed for a good one. Some truth in it, of course; there's always a lot of truth in hypocrisy.

When Richard says he sees traitors before him, that is only what a loser would be expected to say. But when he goes on:

> Nay, if I turn mine eyes upon myself,
> I find myself a traitor with the rest.   (IV.i. 247–48)

he may sound as though he were saying what Northumberland is trying to bully him into saying, or signing: that he is justly deposed as a criminal. But in fact something else is happening: in that solid mass of rebels ritually carrying out a power takeover, Richard is emerging as a stark-naked personality, and the others can do nothing but stare at it.

There follows the inspired mirror scene, in which he dramatizes his phrase "turn mine eyes upon myself." He's still putting on an act, certainly; but it's a totally different act from what he was expected to put on. In one of his two aspects, the king is a human being: by forcing everyone to concentrate on him as a human being, while he stares in the mirror, a kind of royalty becomes visible from that humanity that Bolingbroke will never in this world find the secret of. We see a principle that we see later on in *King Lear*: that in some circumstances the real royalty is in the individual person, not in the symbolic one. Bolingbroke lives in a world of substance and shadow: power is substantial to him, and Richard with his mirror has retreated to a world of shadows. But a nagging doubt remains, of a kind related to the close of *A Midsummer Night's Dream*: which has the more effective power, the Duke of Athens or the king of shadows in the wood? In the context of a history the issue is clearer cut than in a fantastic comedy, of course, except for the audience's response. The audience takes Richard out of the theatre, and groups everyone else around him.

The contrast between what Bolingbroke has become and what Richard has been all along comes out in the two final episodes of the play. The first episode is the one we've glanced at already: Bolingbroke's pardoning of Aumerle, who conspired against him, in response to the impassioned pleas of the Duchess of York. In this episode there are two themes or verbal phrases to be noticed: the theme of the beggar and the king, and the theme of setting the word against the word. Bolingbroke is now king, and everyone else becomes in a sense a beggar: if a subject does anything that puts his life in danger, he must sue to the king for his life as a beggar would do. The "word" being discussed is the word of royal command, specifically the word "pardon." The Duke of York, as hot for prosecuting his son as ever, urges Bolingbroke to say pardon in French, where *pardonnez-moi* would have the general sense of "sorry, nothing doing." But Bolingbroke knows that he is now in a position where he is the source of the word of command, and must make all such words as unambiguous as possible, even when he does what he is soon to do to Exton.

This scene is immediately followed by Richard's great prison speech, which in many respects sums up the play, and repeats these two themes of the beggar and the king and of setting the word against the word. The prison is the final actualizing of the individual world dramatized by the mirror earlier, and Richard is fascinated by the number of personae he can invoke. His soul and brain become an Adam and an Eve, and they germinate between them a whole new world of thoughts. Some of the thoughts are ambitious, wanting only to get out; some are resigned (perhaps Boethius, writing *The Consolation of Philosophy* while awaiting execution in prison, is in the background here), but all of them are discontented. Not because of the prison: they'd be discontented anywhere. Here, setting "the word against the word" refers to the words of Scripture, the commands that come from the spiritual world and so often seem ambiguous; and the king and beggar are the same identity, different only in mask and context. He concludes:

> Nor I, nor any man that but man is,
> With nothing shall be pleased till be he eased
> With being nothing.   (V.v. 39–41)

Ever since the beginning of language, probably, "nothing" has meant two things: "not anything" and "something called nothing." Richard is saying here (not very grammatically) that every human being, including himself, is discontented, not pleased with anything, until he becomes that something we call nothing, i.e., in this context, dead. This double meaning becomes very central in *King Lear* later.

In *A Midsummer Night's Dream* the two worlds of the play, Theseus's court and Oberon's wood, represent two aspects of the mind, the conscious, rational, daylight aspect and the dreaming and fantasizing aspect. One dwells in a world of things and the other in a world of shadows; the shadow mind may live partly in the imaginary, in what is simply not there, but it may live partly also in the genuinely creative, bringing into existence a "transfigured" entity, to use Hippolyta's word, which is neither substantial nor shadowy, neither illusory nor real, but both at once. In *Romeo and Juliet* we got one tantalizing glimpse of this world in Mercutio's Queen Mab speech, but what we see of it mostly is the world created out of the love of the two young people, a world inevitably destroyed as the daylight world rolls over it, but possessing a reality that its destruction does not disprove.

Richard II is in a more complex social position, and has been caught in the paradox of the king, who, we remember, possesses both an individual and a sacramental body. The latter includes all the subjects in his kingdom; the former, only himself. In the prison, however, an entire world leaps into life within his own mind: the other world he was looking for in the mirror. He has as many thoughts as he has subjects, and, like his subjects, his thoughts are discontented, rebellious and conflicting. But the king's two bodies are also God's two realities, linked by the anointing of they king.

The imagery changes as music sounds in the background: Richard comments on the need for keeping time in music, and applies the word to his own life: "I wasted time, and time doth now waste me." From there two conceptions of time unfold: time as rhythm and proportion, the inner grace of life itself that we hear in music, and time as the mechanical progress of the clock, the time that Bolingbroke has kept so accurately until the clock brought him to power. Near the beginning of the play, John of Gaunt refuses to take active vengeance for Woodstock's death on the Lord's anointed. He leaves vengeance to heaven, which will release its vengeance "when they see the hours ripe on earth." The word "they" has no antecedent: John must mean something like "the gods," but the image of ripening, and of acting when the time is "ripe," brings in a third dimension of time, one that we don't see in this play, or perhaps fully anywhere else, although there are unconscious commitments to it like Edgar's "ripeness is all." There is a power in time, with its own rhythm and form: if we can't see it in action, perhaps it sees us, and touches the most sensitive people, such as Hamlet, with the feeling that it shapes our ends. If we did see it, perhaps the world of history would burst like an eggshell and a new kind of life would come forth.

A. C. BRADLEY

The Rejection of Falstaff[1]

Of the two persons principally concerned in the rejection of Falstaff, Henry, both as Prince and as King, has received, on the whole, full justice from readers and critics. Falstaff, on the other hand, has been in one respect the most unfortunate of Shakespeare's famous characters. All of them, in passing from the mind of their creator into other minds, suffer change; they tend to lose their harmony through the disproportionate attention bestowed on some one feature, or to lose their uniqueness by being conventionalised into types already familiar. But Falstaff was degraded by Shakespeare himself. The original character is to be found alive in the two parts of *Henry IV.*, dead in *Henry V.*, and nowhere else. But not very long after these plays were composed, Shakespeare wrote, and he afterwards revised, the very entertaining piece called *The Merry Wives of Windsor*. Perhaps his company wanted a new play on a sudden; or perhaps, as one would rather believe, the tradition may be true that Queen Elizabeth, delighted with the Falstaff scenes of *Henry IV.*, expressed a wish to see the hero of them again, and to see him in love. Now it was no more possible for Shakespeare to show his own Falstaff in love than to turn twice two into five. But he could write in haste— the tradition says, in a fortnight—a comedy or farce differing from all his other plays in this, that its scene is laid in English middle-class life, and that it is prosaic almost to the end. And among the characters he could introduce a disreputable fat old knight with attendants, and could call them Falstaff, Bardolph, Pistol, and Nym. And he could represent this knight assailing, for financial purposes, the

From *Oxford Lectures on Poetry*. © 1909 by Macmillan and Co.

virtue of two matrons, and in the event baffled, duped, treated like dirty linen, beaten, burnt, pricked, mocked, insulted, and, worst of all, repentant and didactic. It is horrible. It is almost enough to convince one that Shakespeare himself could sanction the parody of Ophelia in the *Two Noble Kinsmen*. But it no more touches the real Falstaff than Ophelia is degraded by that parody. To picture the real Falstaff befooled like the Falstaff of the *Merry Wives* is like imagining Iago the gull of Roderigo, or Becky Sharp the dupe of Amelia Osborne. Before he had been served the least of these tricks he would have had his brains taken out and buttered, and have given them to a dog for a New Year's gift. I quote the words of the impostor, for after all Shakespeare made him and gave to him a few sentences worthy of Falstaff himself. But they are only a few—one side of a sheet of notepaper would contain them. And yet critics have solemnly debated at what period in his life Sir John endured the gibes of Master Ford, and whether we should put this comedy between the two parts of *Henry IV.*, or between the second of them and *Henry V*. And the Falstaff of the general reader, it is to be feared, is an impossible conglomerate of two distinct characters, while the Falstaff of the mere playgoer is certainly much more like the impostor than the true man.

The separation of these two has long ago been effected by criticism, and is insisted on in almost all competent estimates of the character of Falstaff. I do not propose to attempt a full account either of this character or of that of Prince Henry, but shall connect the remarks I have to make on them with a question which does not appear to have been satisfactorily discussed—the question of the rejection of Falstaff by the Prince on his accession to the throne. What do we feel, and what are we meant to feel, as we witness this rejection? And what does our feeling imply as to the characters of Falstaff and the new King?

I.

Sir John, you remember, is in Gloucestershire, engaged in borrowing a thousand pounds from Justice Shallow; and here Pistol, riding helter-skelter from London, brings him the great news that the old King is as dead as nail in door, and that Harry the Fifth is the man. Sir John, in wild excitement, taking any man's horses, rushes to London; and he carries Shallow with him, for he longs to reward all his friends. We find him standing with his companions just outside Westminster Abbey, in the crowd that is waiting for the King to come out after his coronation. He himself is stained with travel, and has had no time to spend any of the thousand pounds in buying new liveries for his men. But what of that? This poor show only proves his earnestness of affection, his devotion, how he could not deliberate or remember or have patience to shift himself, but rode day and night, thought of nothing else but to see Henry, and put all affairs else in oblivion, as if there were nothing else to be done but to see him. And now he stands sweating with desire to see him, and repeating and repeating this one desire of his heart— 'to see him.' The moment comes. There is a shout within the Abbey like the roaring of the sea, and a clangour of trumpets, and the doors open and the procession streams out.

> FAL. God save thy grace, King Hal! my royal Hal!
> PIST. The heavens thee guard and keep, most royal imp of fame!
> FAL. God save thee, my sweet boy!
> KING. My Lord Chief justice, speak to that vain man.
> CH. JUST. Have you your wits? Know you what 'tis you speak?
> FAL. My King! my Jove! I speak to thee, my heart!
> KING. I know thee not, old man: fall to thy prayers;
> How ill white hairs become a fool and jester!
> I have long dream'd of such a kind of man,
> So surfeit-swell'd, so old and so profane;
> But being awaked I do despise my dream.
> Make less thy body hence, and more thy grace;
> Leave gormandizing; know the grave doth gape
> For thee thrice wider than for other men.
> Reply not to me with a fool-born jest
> Presume not that I am the thing I was;
> For God doth know, so shall the world perceive,
> That I have turn'd away my former self;
> So will I those that kept me company.
> When thou dost hear I am as I have been,
> Approach me, and thou shalt be as thou vast,
> The tutor and the feeder of my riots
> Till then, I banish thee, on pain of death,
> As I have done the rest of my misleaders,
> Not to come near our person by ten mile.
> For competence of life I will allow you,
> That lack of means enforce you not to evil:
> And, as we hear you do reform yourselves,
> We will, according to your strengths and qualities,
> Give you advancement. Be it your charge, my lord,
> To see perform'd the tenour of our word.
> Set on.

The procession passes out of sight, but Falstaff and his friends remain. He shows no resentment. He comforts himself, or tries to comfort himself—first, with the thought that he has Shallow's thousand pounds, and then, more seriously, I believe, with another thought. The King, he sees, must look thus to the world; but he will be sent for in private when night comes, and will yet make the fortunes of his friends. But even as he speaks, the Chief Justice, accompanied by Prince John, returns, and gives the order to his officers:

> Go, carry Sir John Falstaff to the Fleet;
> Take all his company along with him.

Falstaff breaks out, 'My lord, my lord,' but he is cut short and hurried away; and after a few words between the Prince and the Chief Justice the scene closes, and with it the drama.

What are our feelings during this scene? They will depend on our feelings about Falstaff. If we have not keenly enjoyed the Falstaff scenes of the two plays, if we regard Sir John chiefly as an old reprobate, not only a sensualist, a liar, and a coward, but a cruel and dangerous ruffian, I suppose we enjoy his discomfiture and consider that the King has behaved magnificently. But if we *have* keenly enjoyed the Falstaff scenes, if we have enjoyed them as Shakespeare surely meant them to be enjoyed, and if, accordingly, Falstaff is not to us solely or even chiefly a reprobate and ruffian, we feel, I think, during the King's speech, a good deal of pain and some resentment; and when, without any further offence on Sir John's part, the Chief Justice returns and sends him to prison, we stare in astonishment. These, I believe, are, in greater or less degree, the feelings of most of those who really enjoy the Falstaff scenes (as many readers do not). Nor are these feelings diminished when we remember the end of the whole story, as we find it in *Henry V.*, where we learn that Falstaff quickly died, and, according to the testimony of persons not very sentimental, died of a broken heart.[2] Suppose this merely to mean that he sank under the shame of his public disgrace, and it is pitiful enough: but the words of Mrs. Quickly, 'The king has killed his heart'; of Nym, 'The king hath run bad humours on the knight; that's the even of it'; of Pistol,

> Nym, thou hast spoke the right,
> His heart is fracted and corroborate,

assuredly point to something more than wounded pride; they point to wounded affection, and remind us of Falstaff's own answer to Prince Hal's question, 'Sirrah, do I owe you a thousand pound?' 'A thousand pound, Hal? a million: thy love is worth a million: thou owest me thy love.'

Now why did Shakespeare end his drama with a scene which, though undoubtedly striking, leaves an impression so unpleasant? I will venture to put aside without discussion the idea that he meant us throughout the two plays to regard Falstaff with disgust or indignation, so that we naturally feel nothing but pleasure at his fall; for this idea implies that kind of inability to understand Shakespeare with which it is idle to argue. And there is another and a much more ingenious suggestion which must equally be rejected as impossible. According to it, Falstaff, having listened to the King's speech, did not seriously hope to be sent for by him in private; he fully realised the situation at once, and was only making game of Shallow; and in his immediate turn upon Shallow when the King goes out, 'Master Shallow, I owe you a thousand pound,' we are meant to see his humorous superiority to any rebuff, so that we end the play with the delightful feeling that, while Henry has done the right thing, Falstaff, in his outward overthrow, has still proved himself inwardly invincible. This suggestion comes from a critic who understands Falstaff, and in the suggestion itself shows that he understands him.[3] But it provides no solution, because it wholly ignores, and could not account for, that which follows the short conversation with Shallow. Falstaff's dismissal to the Fleet, and his subsequent death, prove beyond doubt that his rejection was meant by Shakespeare to be taken as a catastrophe which not even his humour could enable him to surmount.

Moreover, these interpretations, even if otherwise admissible, would still leave our problem only partly solved. For what troubles us is not only the disappointment of Falstaff, it is the conduct of Henry. It was inevitable that on his accession he should separate himself from Sir John, and we wish nothing else. It is satisfactory that Sir John should have a competence, with the hope of promotion in the highly improbable case of his reforming himself. And if Henry could not trust himself within ten miles of so fascinating a companion, by all means let him be banished that distance: we do not complain. These, arrangements would not have prevented a satisfactory ending: the King could have communicated his decision, and Falstaff could have accepted it, in a private interview rich in humour and merely touched with pathos. But Shakespeare has so contrived matters that Henry could not send a private warning to Falstaff even if he wished to, and in their public meeting Falstaff is made to behave in so infatuated and outrageous a manner that great sternness on the King's part was unavoidable. And the curious thing is that Shakespeare did not stop here. If this had been all we should have felt pain for Falstaff, but not, perhaps, resentment against Henry. But two things we do resent. Why, when this painful incident seems to be over, should the Chief justice return and send Falstaff to prison? Can this possibly be meant for an act of private vengeance on the part of the Chief justice, unknown to the King? No; for in that case Shakespeare would have shown at once that the King disapproved and cancelled it. It must have been the King's own act. This is one thing we resent; the other is the King's sermon. He had a right to turn away his former self, and his old companions with it, but he had no right to talk all of a sudden like a clergyman; and surely it was both ungenerous and insincere to speak of them as his 'misleaders,' as though in the days of Eastcheap and Gadshill he had been a weak and silly lad. We have seen his former self, and we know that it was nothing of the kind. He had shown himself, for all his follies, a very strong and independent young man, deliberately amusing himself among men over whom he had just as much ascendency as he chose to exert. Nay, he amused himself not only among them, but at their expense. In his first soliloquy—and first soliloquies are usually significant—he declares that he associates with them in order that, when at some future time he shows his true character, he may be the more wondered at for his previous aberrations. You may think he deceives himself here; you may believe that he frequented Sir John's company out of delight in it and not merely with this cold-blooded design; but at any rate he *thought* the design was his one motive. And, that being so, two results follow. He ought in honour long ago to have given Sir John clearly to understand that they must say good-bye on the day of his accession. And, having neglected to do this, he ought not to have lectured him as his misleader. It was not only ungenerous, it was dishonest. It looks disagreeably like an attempt to buy the praise of the respectable at the cost of honour and truth. And it succeeded. Henry *always* succeeded.

You will see what I am suggesting, for the moment, as a solution of our problem. I am suggesting that our fault lies not in our resentment at Henry's conduct, but in our surprise at it; that if we had read his character truly in the light that Shakespeare gave us, we should have been prepared for a display both of hardness and of policy at this point in his career.And although this suggestion does not suffice to solve the problem before us, I am convinced that in itself it is true. Nor is it rendered at all improbable by the fact that Shakespeare has made Henry, on the whole, a fine and very attractive character, and that here he makes no one express any disapprobation of the treatment of Falstaff. For in similar cases Shakespeare is constantly misunderstood. His readers expect him to mark in some distinct way his approval or disapproval of that which he represents; and hence where *they* disapprove and *he* says nothing, they fancy that he does *not* disapprove, and they blame his indifference, like Dr. Johnson, or at the least are puzzled. But the truth is that he shows the fact and leaves the judgment to them. And again, when he makes us like a character we expect the character to have no faults that are not expressly pointed out, and when other faults appear we either ignore them or try to explain them away. This is one of our methods of conventionalising Shakespeare. We want the world's population to be neatly divided into sheep and goats, and we want an angel by us to say, 'Look, that is a goat and this is a sheep,' and we try to turn Shakespeare into this angel. His impartiality makes us uncomfortable: we cannot bear to see him, like the sun, lighting up everything and judging nothing. And this is perhaps especially the case in his historical plays, where we are always trying to turn him into a partisan. He shows us that Richard II. was unworthy to be king, and we at once conclude that he thought Bolingbroke's usurpation justified; whereas he shows merely, what under the conditions was bound to exist, an inextricable tangle of right and unright. Or, Bolingbroke being evidently wronged, we suppose Bolingbroke's statements to be true, and are quite surprised when, after attaining his end through them, he mentions casually on his death-bed that they were lies. Shakespeare makes us admire Hotspur heartily; and accordingly, when we see Hotspur discussing with others how large his particular slice of his mother-country is to be, we either fail to recognise the monstrosity of the proceeding, or, recognising it, we complain that Shakespeare is inconsistent. Prince John breaks a tottering rebellion by practising a detestable fraud on the rebels. We are against the rebels, and have heard high praise of Prince John, but we cannot help seeing that his fraud is detestable; so we say indignantly to Shakespeare, 'Why, you told us he was a sheep'; whereas, in fact, if we had used our eyes we should have known beforehand that he was the brave, determined, loyal, cold-blooded, pitiless, unscrupulous son of a usurper whose throne was in danger.

To come, then, to Henry. Both as prince and as king he is deservedly a favourite, and particularly so with English readers, being, as he is, perhaps the most distinctively English of all Shakespeare's men. In *Henry V.* he is treated as a national hero. In this play he has lost much of the wit which in him seems to have depended on contact with Falstaff, but he has also laid aside the most serious faults of his youth. He inspires in a high degree fear, enthusiasm, and affection; thanks to his beautiful modesty he has the charm which is lacking to another mighty warrior, Coriolanus; his youthful escapades have given him an understanding of simple folk, and sympathy with them; he is the author of the saying, 'There is some soul of goodness in things evil'; and he is much more obviously religious than most of Shakespeare's heroes. Having these and other fine qualities, and being without certain dangerous tendencies which mark the tragic heroes, he is, perhaps, the most *efficient* character drawn by Shakespeare, unless Ulysses, in *Troilus and Cressida*, is his equal. And so he has been described as Shakespeare's ideal man of action; nay, it has even been declared that here for once Shakespeare plainly disclosed his own ethical creed, and showed us his ideal, not simply of a man of action, but of a man.

But Henry is neither of these. The poet who drew Hamlet and Othello can never have thought that even the ideal man of action would lack that light upon the brow which at once transfigures them and marks their doom. It is as easy to believe that, because the lunatic, the lover, and the poet are not far apart, Shakespeare would have chosen never to have loved and sung. Even poor Timon, the most inefficient of the tragic heroes, has something in him that Henry never shows. Nor is it merely that his nature is limited: if we follow Shakespeare and look closely at Henry, we shall discover with the many fine traits a few less pleasing. *Henry IV.* describes him as the noble image of his own youth; and, for all his superiority to his father, he is still his father's son, the son of the man whom Hotspur called a 'vile politician.' Henry's religion, for example, is genuine, it is rooted in his modesty; but it is also superstitious—an attempt to buy off supernatural vengeance for Richard's blood; and it is also in part political, like his father's projected crusade. Just as he went to war chiefly because, as his father told him, it was the way to keep factious nobles quiet and unite the nation, so when he adjures the Archbishop to satisfy him as to his right to the French throne, he knows very well that the Archbishop wants the war, because it will defer and perhaps prevent what he considers the spoliation of the Church. This same strain of policy is what Shakespeare marks in the first soliloquy in *Henry IV.*, where the prince describes his riotous life as a mere scheme to win him glory later. It implies that readiness to use other people as means to his own ends which is a conspicuous feature in his father; and it reminds us of his father's plan of keeping himself out of the people's sight while Richard was making himself cheap by his incessant public appearances. And if I am not mistaken there is a further likeness. Henry is kindly and pleasant to every one as Prince, to every one deserving as King; and he is so not merely out of policy: but there is no sign in him of a strong affection for any one, such an affection as we recognise at a glance in Hamlet and Horatio, Brutus and Cassius, and many more. We do not find this in *Henry V.*, not even in the noble address to Lord Scroop, and in *Henry IV.* we find, I think, a liking for Falstaff and Poins, but no more: there is no more than a liking, for instance, in his soliloquy over the supposed corpse of his fat friend, and he never speaks of Falstaff to Poins with any affection. The truth is, that the members of the family of *Henry IV.* have love for one another, but they cannot spare love for any one outside their family, which stands firmly united, defending its royal position against attack and instinctively isolating itself from outside influence.

Thus I would suggest that Henry's conduct in his rejection of Falstaff is in perfect keeping with his character on its unpleasant side as well as on its finer; and that, so far as Henry is concerned, we ought not to feel surprise at it. And on this view we may even explain the strange incident of the Chief Justice being sent back to order Falstaff to prison (for there is no sign of any such uncertainty in the text as might suggest an interpolation by the players). Remembering his father's words about Henry, 'Being incensed, he's flint,' and remembering in *Henry V.* his ruthlessness about killing the prisoners when he is incensed, we may imagine that, after he had left Falstaff and was no longer influenced by the face of his old companion, he gave way to anger at the indecent familiarity which had provoked a compromising scene on the most ceremonial of occasions and in the presence alike of court and crowd, and that he sent the Chief Justice back to take vengeance. And this is consistent with the fact that in the next play we find Falstaff shortly afterwards not only freed from prison, but unmolested in his old haunt in Eastcheap, well within ten miles of Henry's person. His anger had soon passed, and he knew that the requisite effect had been produced both on Falstaff and on the world.

But all this, however true, will not solve our problem. It seems, on the contrary, to increase its difficulty. For the natural conclusion is that Shakespeare *intended* us to feel resentment against Henry. And yet that cannot be, for it implies that he meant the play to end disagreeably; and no one who understands Shakespeare at all will consider that supposition for a moment credible. No; he must have meant the play to end pleasantly, although he made Henry's action consistent. And hence it follows that he must have intended our sympathy with Falstaff to be so far weakened when the rejection-scene arrives that his discomfiture should be satisfactory to us; that we should enjoy this sudden reverse of enormous hopes (a thing always ludicrous if sympathy is absent); that we should approve the moral judgment that falls on him; and so should pass lightly over that disclosure of unpleasant traits in the King's character which

Shakespeare was too true an artist to suppress. Thus our pain and resentment, if we feel them, are wrong, in the sense that they do not answer to the dramatist's intention. But it does not follow that they are wrong in a further sense. They may be right, because the dramatist has missed what he aimed at. And this, though the dramatist was Shakespeare, is what I would suggest. In the Falstaff scenes he overshot his mark. He created so extraordinary a being, and fixed him so firmly on his intellectual throne, that when he sought to dethrone him he could not. The moment comes when we are to look, at Falstaff in a serious light, and the comic hero is to figure as a baffled schemer; but we cannot make the required change, either in our attitude or in our sympathies. We wish Henry a glorious reign and much joy of his crew of hypocritical politicians, lay and clerical; but our hearts go with Falstaff to the Fleet, or, if necessary, to Arthur's bosom or wheresomever he is.[4]

In the remainder of the lecture I will try to make this view clear. And to that end we must go back to the Falstaff of the body of the two plays, the immortal Falstaff, a character almost purely humorous, and therefore no subject for moral judgments, I can but draw an outline, and in describing one aspect of this character must be content to hold another in reserve.

2.

Up to a certain point Falstaff is ludicrous in the same way as many other figures, his distinction lying, so far, chiefly in the mere abundance of ludicrous traits. *Why* we should laugh at a man with a huge belly and corresponding appetites; at the inconveniences he suffers on a hot day, or in playing the footpad, or when he falls down and there are no levers at hand to lift him up again; at the incongruity of his unwieldy bulk and the nimbleness of his spirit, the infirmities of his age and his youthful lightness of heart; at the enormity of his lies and wiles, and the suddenness of their exposure and frustration; at the contrast between his reputation and his real character, seen most absurdly when, at the mere mention of his name, a redoubted rebel surrenders to him—*why*, I say, we should laugh at these and many such things, this is no place to inquire; but unquestionably we do. Here we have them poured out in endless profusion and with that air of careless ease which is so fascinating in Shakespeare; and with the enjoyment of them I believe many readers stop. But while they are quite essential to the character, there is in it much more. For these things by themselves do not explain why, beside laughing at Falstaff, we are made happy by him and laugh *with* him. He is not, like Parolles, a mere *object* of mirth.

The main reason why he makes us so happy and puts us so entirely at our ease is that he himself is happy and entirely at his ease. 'Happy' is too weak a word; he is in bliss, and we share his glory. Enjoyment—no fitful pleasure crossing a dull life, nor any vacant convulsive mirth—but a rich deep-toned chuckling enjoyment circulates continually through all his being. If you ask what he enjoys, no doubt the answer is, in the first place, eating and drinking, taking his ease at his inn, and the company of other merry souls. Compared with these things, what we count the graver interests of life are nothing to him. But then, while we are under his spell, it is impossible to consider these graver interests; gravity is to us, as to him, inferior to gravy; and what he does enjoy he enjoys with such a luscious and good-humoured zest that we sympathise and he makes us happy. And if any one objected, we should answer with Sir Toby Belch, 'Dost thou think, because thou art virtuous, there shall be no more cakes and ale?'

But this, again, is far from all. Falstaff's ease and enjoyment are not simply those of the happy man of appetite;[5] they are those of the humorist, and the humorist of genius. Instead of being comic to you and serious to himself, he is more ludicrous to himself than to you; and he makes himself out more ludicrous than he is, in order that he and others may laugh. Prince Hal never made such sport of Falstaff's person as he himself did. It is *he* who says that his skin hangs about him like an old lady's loose gown, and that he walks before his page like a sow that hath o'erwhelmed all her litter but one. And he jests at himself when he is alone just as much as when others are by. It is the same with his appetites. The direct enjoyment they bring him is scarcely so great as the enjoyment of laughing at this enjoyment; and for all his addiction to sack you never see him for an instant with a brain dulled by it, or a temper turned solemn, silly, quarrelsome, or pious. The virtue it instils into him, of filling his brain with nimble, fiery, and delectable shapes—this, and his humorous attitude towards it, free him, in a manner, from slavery to it; and it is this freedom, and no secret longing for better things (those who attribute such a longing to him are far astray), that makes his enjoyment contagious and prevents our sympathy with it from being disturbed.

The bliss of freedom gained in humour is the essence of Falstaff. His humour is not directed only or chiefly against obvious absurdities; he is the enemy of everything that would interfere with his ease, and therefore of anything serious, and especially of everything respectable and moral. For these things impose limits and obligations, and make us the subjects of old father antic the law, and the categorical imperative, and our station and its duties, and conscience, and reputation, and other people's opinions, and all sorts of nuisances. I say he is therefore their enemy; but I do him wrong; to say that he is their enemy implies that he regards them as serious and recognises their power, when in truth he refuses to recognise them at all. They are to him absurd; and to reduce a thing *ad absurdum* is to reduce it to nothing and to walk about free and rejoicing. This is what Falstaff does with all the would-be serious things of life, sometimes only by his words, sometimes by his actions too. He will make truth appear absurd by solemn statements, which he utters with perfect gravity and which he expects nobody to believe; and honour, by demonstrating that it cannot set a leg, and that neither the living nor the dead can possess it; and law, by evading all the attacks of its highest representative and almost forcing him to laugh at his own defeat; and patriotism, by filling his pockets with the bribes offered by competent soldiers who want to escape service, while he takes in their stead the halt and maimed and the gaol-birds; and duty, by showing how he labours in his vocation—of thieving; and courage, alike by mocking at his own capture of Colvile and gravely claiming to have killed Hotspur; and war, by offering the Prince his bottle of sack when he is asked for a sword; and religion, by amusing himself with remorse at odd times when he has nothing else to do; and the fear of death, by maintaining perfectly untouched, in the face of imminent peril and even while he *feels* the fear of death, the very same power of dissolving it in persiflage that he shows when he sits at ease in his inn. These are the wonderful achievements which he performs, not with the sourness of a cynic, but with the gaiety of a boy. And, therefore, we praise him, we laud him, for he offends none but the virtuous, and denies that life is real or life is earnest, and delivers us from the oppression of such nightmares, and lifts us into the atmosphere of perfect freedom.

No one in the play understands Falstaff fully, any more than Hamlet was understood by the persons round him. They are both men of genius. Mrs. Quickly and Bardolph are his slaves, but they know not why. 'Well, fare thee well,' says the hostess whom he has pillaged and forgiven; 'I have known thee these twenty-nine years, come peas-cod time, but an honester and truer-hearted man-well, fare thee well.' Poins and the Prince delight in him; they get him into corners for the pleasure of seeing him escape in ways they cannot imagine; but they often take him much too seriously. Poins, for instance, rarely sees, the Prince does not always see, and moralising critics never see, that when Falstaff speaks ill of a companion behind his back, or writes to the Prince that Poins spreads it abroad that the Prince is to marry his sister, he knows quite well that what he says will be repeated, or rather, perhaps, is absolutely indifferent whether it be repeated or not, being certain that it can only give him an opportunity for humour. It is the same with his lying, and almost the same with his cowardice, the two main vices laid to his charge even by sympathisers. Falstaff is neither a liar nor a coward in the usual sense, like the typical cowardly boaster of comedy. He tells his lies either for their own humour, or on purpose to get himself into a difficulty. He rarely expects to be believed, perhaps never. He abandons a statement or contradicts it the moment it is made. There is scarcely more intent in his lying than in the humorous exaggerations which he pours out in soliloquy just as much as when others are by. Poins and the Prince understand this in part. You see them waiting eagerly to convict him, not that they may really put him to shame, but in order to enjoy the greater lie that will swallow up the less. But their sense of humour lags behind his. Even the Prince seems to accept as half-serious that remorse of his which passes so suddenly into glee at the idea of taking a purse, and his request to his friend to bestride him if he should see him down in the battle. Bestride Falstaff! 'Hence! Wilt thou lift up Olympus?'

Again, the attack of the Prince and Poins on Falstaff and the other thieves on Gadshill is contrived, we know, with a view to the incomprehensible lies it will induce him to tell. But when, more than rising to the occasion, he turns two men in buckram into four, and then seven, and then nine, and then eleven, almost in a breath, I believe they partly misunderstand his intention, and too many of his critics misunderstand it altogether. Shakespeare was not writing a mere farce. It is preposterous to suppose that a man of Falstaff's intelligence would utter these gross, palpable, open lies with the serious intention to deceive, or forget that, if it was too dark for him to see his own hand, he could hardly see that the three misbegotten knaves were wearing Kendal green. No doubt, if he *had* been believed, he would have been hugely tickled at it, but he no more expected to be believed than when he claimed to have killed Hotspur. Yet he is supposed to be serious even then. Such interpretations would destroy the poet's whole conception; and of those who adopt them one might ask this out of some twenty similar questions:—When Falstaff, in the men in buckram scene, begins by calling twice at short intervals for sack, and then a little later calls for more and says, 'I am a rogue if I drunk to-day,' and the Prince answers, 'O villain, thy lips are scarce wiped since thou drunk'st last,' do they think that he was meant to deceive? And if not, why do they take it for granted that the others were? I suppose they consider that Falstaff was in earnest when, wanting to get twenty-two yards of satin on trust from Master Dombledon the silk-mercer, he offered Bardolph as security; or when he said to the Chief Justice about Mrs. Quickly, who accused him of breaking his promise to marry her, 'My lord, this is a poor mad soul, and she says up and down the town that her eldest son is like you'; or when he explained his enormous bulk by exclaiming, 'A plague of sighing and grief! It blows a man up like a bladder'; or when he accounted for his voice being cracked by declaring that he had 'lost it with singing of anthems'; or even when he sold his soul on Good-Friday to the devil for a cup of Madeira and a cold capon's leg. Falstaff's lies about Hotspur and the men in buckram do not essentially differ from these statements. There is nothing serious in any of them except the refusal to take anything seriously.

This is also the explanation of Falstaff's cowardice, a subject on which I should say nothing if Maurice Morgann's essay,[6] now more than a century old, were better known. That Falstaff sometimes behaves in what we should generally call a cowardly way is certain; but that does not show that he was a coward; and if the word means a person who feels painful fear in the presence of danger, and yields to that fear in spite of his better feelings and convictions, then assuredly Falstaff was no coward. The stock bully and boaster of comedy is one, but not Falstaff. It is perfectly clear in the first place that, though he had unfortunately a reputation for stabbing and caring not what mischief he did if his weapon were out, he had not a reputation for cowardice. Shallow remembered him five-and-fifty years ago breaking Scogan's head at the court-gate when he was a crack not thus high; and Shallow knew him later a good back-swordsman. Then we lose sight of him till about twenty years after, when his association with Bardolph began; and that that association implies that by the time he was thirty-five or forty he had sunk into the mode of life we witness in the plays. Yet, even as we see him there, he remains a person of consideration in the army. Twelve captains hurry about London searching for him. He is present at the Council of War in the King's tent at Shrewsbury, where the only other persons are the King, the two princes, a nobleman and Sir Walter Blunt. The messenger who brings the false report of the battle to Northumberland mentions, as one of the important incidents, the death of Sir John Falstaff. Colvile, expressly described as a famous rebel, surrenders to him as soon as he hears his name. And if his own wish that his name were not so terrible to the enemy, and his own boast of his European reputation, are not evidence of the first rank, they must not be entirely ignored in presence of these other facts. What do these facts mean? Does Shakespeare put them all in with no purpose at all, or in defiance of his own intentions? It is not credible.

And when, in the second place, we look at Falstaff's actions, what do we find? He boldly confronted Colvile, he was quite ready to fight with him, however pleased that Colvile, like a kind fellow, gave himself away. When he saw Henry and Hotspur fighting, Falstaff, instead of making off in a panic, stayed to take his chance if Hotspur should be the victor. He *led* his hundred and fifty ragamuffins where they were peppered, he did not *send* them. To draw upon Pistol and force him downstairs and wound him in the shoulder was no great feat, perhaps, but the stock coward would have shrunk from it. When the Sheriff came to the inn to arrest him for an offence whose penalty was death, Falstaff, who was hidden behind the arras, did not stand there quaking for fear, he immediately fell asleep and snored. When he stood in the battle reflecting on what would happen if the weight of his paunch should be increased by that of a bullet, he cannot have been in a tremor of craven fear. He *never* shows such fear; and surely the man who, in danger of his life, and with no one by to hear him, meditates thus: 'I like not such grinning honour as Sir Walter hath. Give me life: which if I can save, so; if not, honour comes unlooked-for, and there's an end,' is not what we commonly call a coward.

'Well,' it will be answered, 'but he ran away on Gadshill; and when Douglas attacked him he fell down and shammed dead.' Yes, I am thankful to say, he did. For of course he did not want to be dead. He wanted to live and be merry. And as he had reduced the idea of honour *ad absurdum*, had scarcely any self-respect, and only a respect for reputation as a means of life, naturally he avoided death when he could do so without a ruinous loss of reputation, and (observe) with the satisfaction of playing a colossal practical joke. For *that* after all was his first object. If his one thought had been to avoid death he would not have faced Douglas at all, but would have run away as fast as his legs could carry him; and unless Douglas had been one of those exceptional Scotchmen who have no sense of humour, he would never have thought of pursuing so ridiculous an object as Falstaff running. So that, as Mr. Swinburne remarks, Poins is right when he thus distinguishes Falstaff from his companions in robbery: 'For two of them, I know them to be as true-bred cowards as ever turned back; and for the third, if he fight longer than he sees reason, I'll forswear arms.' And the event justifies this distinction. For it is exactly thus that, according to the original stage-direction, Falstaff behaves when Henry and Poins attack him and the others. The rest run away at once; Falstaff, here as afterwards with Douglas, fights for a blow or two, but, finding himself deserted and outmatched, runs away also. Of course. He saw no reason to stay. *Any* man who had risen superior to all serious motives would have run away. But it does not follow that he would run from mere fear, or be, in the ordinary sense, a coward.[7]

3.

The main source, then, of our sympathetic delight in Falstaff is his humorous superiority to everything serious, and the freedom of soul enjoyed in it. But, of course, this is not the whole of his character. Shakespeare knew well enough that perfect freedom is not to be gained in this manner; we are ourselves aware of it even while we are sympathising with Falstaff; and as soon as we regard him seriously it becomes obvious. His freedom is limited in two main ways. For one thing he cannot rid himself entirely of respect for all that he professes to ridicule. He shows a certain pride in his rank: unlike the Prince, he is haughty to the drawers, who call him a proud Jack. He is not really quite indifferent to reputation. When the Chief Justice bids him pay his debt to Mrs. Quickly for his reputation's sake, I think he feels a twinge, though to be sure he proceeds to pay her by borrowing from her. He is also stung by any thoroughly serious imputation on his courage, and winces at the recollection of his running away on Gadshill; he knows that his behaviour there certainly looked cowardly, and perhaps he remembers that he would not have behaved so once. It is, further, very significant that, for all his dissolute talk, he has never yet allowed the Prince and Poins to *see* him as they saw him afterwards with Doll Tearsheet; not, of course, that he has any moral shame in the matter, but he knows that in such a situation he, in his old are, must appear contemptible—not a humorist but a mere object of mirth. And, finally, he has affection in him—affection, I think, for Poins and Bardolph, and certainly for the Prince; and that is a thing which he cannot jest out of existence. Hence, as the effect of his rejection shows, he is not really invulnerable. And then, in the second place, since he is in the flesh, his godlike freedom has consequences and conditions; consequences, for there is something painfully wrong with his great toe; conditions, for he cannot eat and drink for ever without money, and his purse suffers from consumption, a disease for which he can find no remedy.[8] As the Chief Justice tells him, his means are very slender and his waste great; and his answer, 'I would it were otherwise; I would my means were greater and my waist slenderer,' though worth much money, brings none in. And so he is driven to evil deeds; not only to cheating his tailor like a gentleman, but to fleecing Justice Shallow, and to highway robbery, and to cruel depredations on the poor woman whose affection he has secured. All this is perfectly consistent with the other side of his character, but by itself it makes an ugly picture.

Yes, it makes an ugly picture when you look at it seriously. But then, surely, so long as the, humorous atmosphere is preserved and the humorous attitude maintained, you do not look at it so. You no more regard Falstaff's misdeeds morally than you do the much more atrocious misdeeds of Punch or Reynard the Fox. You do not exactly ignore them, but you attend only to their comic aspect. This is the very spirit of comedy, and certainly of Shakespeare's comic world, which is one of make-believe, not merely as his tragic world is, but in a further sense—a world in which gross improbabilities are accepted with a smile, and many things are welcomed as merely laughable which, regarded gravely, would excite anger and disgust. The intervention of a serious spirit breaks up such a world, and would destroy our pleasure in Falstaff's company. Accordingly through the greater part of these dramas Shakespeare carefully confines this spirit to the scenes of war and policy, and dismisses it entirely in the humorous parts. Hence, if *Henry IV.* had been a comedy like *Twelfth Night*, I am sure that he would no more have ended it with the painful disgrace of Falstaff than he ended *Twelfth Night* by disgracing Sir Toby Belch.[9]

But *Henry IV.* was to be in the main a historical play, and its chief hero Prince Henry. In the course of it his greater and finer qualities were to be gradually revealed, and it was to end with beautiful scenes of reconciliation and affection between his father and him, and a final emergence of the wild Prince as a just, wise, stern, and glorious King. Hence, no doubt, it seemed to Shakespeare that Falstaff at last must be disgraced, and must therefore appear no longer as the invincible humorist, but as an object of ridicule and even of aversion. And probably also his poet's insight showed him that Henry, as he conceived him, would behave harshly to Falstaff in order to impress the world, especially when his mind had been wrought to a high pitch by the scene with his dying father and the impression of his own solemn consecration to great duties.

This conception was a natural and a fine one; and if the execution was not an entire success, it is yet full of interest. Shakespeare's purpose being to work a gradual change in our feelings towards Falstaff, and to tinge the humorous atmosphere more and more deeply with seriousness, we see him carrying out this purpose in the Second Part of *Henry IV.* Here he separates the Prince from Falstaff as much as he can, thus withdrawing him from Falstaff's influence, and weakening in our minds the connection between the two. In the First Part we constantly see them together; in the Second (it is a remarkable fact) only once before the rejection. Further, in the scenes where Henry appears apart from Falstaff, we watch him growing more and more grave, and awakening more and more poetic interest; while Falstaff, though his humour scarcely flags to the end, exhibits more and more of his seamy side. This is nowhere turned to the full light in Part I.; but in Part II. we see him as the heartless destroyer of Mrs. Quickly, as a ruffian seriously defying the Chief Justice because his position as an officer on service gives him power to do wrong, as the pike preparing to snap up the poor old dace Shallow, and (this is the one scene where Henry and he meet) as the worn-out lecher, not laughing at his servitude to the flesh but sunk in it. Finally, immediately before the rejection, the world where he is king is exposed in all its sordid criminality when we find Mrs. Quickly and Doll arrested for being concerned in the death of one man, if not more, beaten to death by their bullies; and the dangerousness of Falstaff is emphasised in his last words as he hurries from Shallow's house to London, words at first touched with humour but at bottom only too seriously meant: 'Let us take any man's horses; the laws of England are at my commandment. Happy are they which have been my friends, and woe unto my Lord Chief Justice.' His dismissal to the Fleet by the Chief Justice is the dramatic vengeance for that threat.

Yet all these excellent devices fail. They cause us momentary embarrassment at times when repellent traits in Falstaff's character are disclosed; but they fail to change our attitude of humour into one of seriousness, and our sympathy into repulsion. And they were bound to fail, because Shakespeare shrank from adding to them the one device which would have ensured success. If, as the Second Part of *Henry IV.* advanced, he had clouded over Falstaff's humour so heavily that the man of genius turned into the Falstaff of the *Merry Wives*, we should have witnessed his rejection without a pang. This Shakespeare was too much of an artist to do—though even in this way he did something—and without this device he could not succeed. As I said, in the creation of Falstaff he overreached himself. He was caught up on the wind of his own genius, and carried so far that he could not descend to earth at the selected spot. It is not a misfortune that happens to many authors, nor is it one we can regret, for it costs us but a trifling inconvenience in one scene, while we owe to it perhaps the greatest comic character in literature. For it is in this character, and not in the judgment he brings upon Falstaff's head, that Shakespeare asserts his supremacy. To show that Falstaff's freedom of soul was in part illusory, and that the realities of life refused to be conjured away by his humour—this was what we might expect from Shakespeare's unfailing sanity, but it was surely no achievement beyond the power of lesser men. The achievement was Falstaff himself, and the conception of that freedom of soul, a freedom illusory only in part, and attainable only by a mind which had received from Shakespeare's own the inexplicable touch of infinity which he bestowed on Hamlet and Macbeth and Cleopatra, but denied to Henry the Fifth.
1902.

Notes

1. In this lecture and the three that follow it I have mentioned the authors my obligations to whom I was conscious of in writing or have discovered since;

hut other debts must doubtless remain, which from forgetfulness I am unable to acknowledge.

2. See on this and other points Swinburne, *A Study of Shakespeare*, p. 106 ff.

3. Rötscher, *Shakespeare in seinen höchsten Charaktergebilden*, 1864.

4. That from the beginning Shakespeare intended Henry's accession to be Falstaff's catastrophe is clear from the fact that, when the two characters first appear, Falstaff is made to betray at once the hopes with which he looks forward to Henry's reign. See the First Part of *Henry IV.*, Act I., Scene ii.

5. Cf. Hazlitt, *Characters of Shakespear's Plays*.

6. See Note at end of lecture.

7. It is to he regretted, however, that in carrying his guts away so nimbly he 'roared for mercy'; for I fear we have no ground for rejecting Henry's statement to that effect, and I do not see my way to adopt the suggestion (I forget whose it is) that Falstaff spoke the truth when he swore that he knew Henry and Poins as well as he that made them.

8. Panurge too was 'naturally subject to a kind of disease which at that time they called lack of money'; it was a 'flux in his purse' (Rabelais, Book II., chapters xvi., xvii.).

9. I seem to remember that, according to Gervinus, Shakespeare did disgrace Sir Toby—by marrying him to Maria!.

NOTE

For the benefit of readers unacquainted with Morgann's Essay I reproduce here, with additions, some remarks omitted from the lecture for want of time. 'Maurice Morgann, Esq. the ingenious writer of this work, descended from an ancient and respectable family in Wales; he filled the office of under Secretary of State to the late Marquis of Lansdown, during his first administration; and was afterwards Secretary to the Embassy for ratifying the peace with America, in 1783. He died at his house in Knightsbridge, in the seventy-seventh year of his age, on the 28th March, 1802' (Preface to the edition of 1825). He was a remarkable and original man, who seems to have written a good deal, but, beyond this essay and some pamphlets on public affairs, all or nearly all anonymous, he published nothing, and at his death he left orders that all his papers should be destroyed. The *Essay on the Dramatic Character of Sir John Falstaff* was first published in 1777. It arose out of a conversation in which Morgann expressed his belief that Shakespeare never meant Falstaff for a coward. He was challenged to explain and support in print what was considered an extraordinary paradox, and his essay bears on its title-page the quotation, 'I am not John of Gaunt, your grandfather: but yet no coward, Hal'—one of Falstaff's few serious sentences. But Morgann did not confine himself to the question of

Falstaff's cowardice; he analysed the whole character, and incidentally touched
on many points in Shakespearean criticism. 'The reader,' he observes, 'will not
need to be told that this inquiry will resolve itself of course into a critique on the
genius, the arts, and the conduct, of Shakespeare: for what is Falstaff, what Lear,
what Hamlet, or Othello, but different modifications of Shakespeare's thought?
It is true that this inquiry is narrowed almost to a single point; but general
criticism is as uninstructive as it is easy: Shakespeare deserves to be considered in
detail; a task hitherto unattempted.'

The last words are significant. Morgann was conscious that he was striking
out a new line. The Eighteenth Century critics had done much for Shakespeare
in the way of scholarship; some of them had praised him well and blamed him
well; but they had done little to interpret the process of his imagination from
within. This was what Morgann attempted. His attitude towards Shakespeare is
that of Goethe, Coleridge, Lamb, Hazlitt. The dangers of his method might be
illustrated from the Essay, but in his hands it yielded most valuable results. And
though he did not attempt the eloquence of some of his successors, but wrote like
a cultivated ironical man of the world, he wrote delightfully; so that in all
respects his Essay, which has long been out of print, deserves to be republished
and better known. [It was republished in Mr. Nichol Smith's excellent *Eighteenth
Century Essays an Shakespeare*, 1903; and, in 1912, by itself, with an introduction
by W. A. Gill.]

Readers of Boswell (under the year 1783) will remember that Morgann,
who once met Johnson, favoured his biographer with two most characteristic
anecdotes. Boswell also records Johnson's judgment of Morgann's Essay, which,
says Mr. Swinburne, elicited from him 'as good a jest and as bad a criticism as
might have been expected.' Johnson, we are told, being asked his opinion of the
Essay, answered: 'Why, Sir, we shall have the man come forth again; and as he
has proved Falstaff to be no coward, he may prove Iago to be a very good
character.' The following passage from Morgann's *Essay* (p. 66 of the 1825
edition, p. 248 of Mr. Nichol Smith's book) gives, I presume, his opinion of
Johnson. Having referred to Warburton, he adds: 'Another has since undertaken
the custody of our author, whom he seems to consider as a sort of wild Proteus
or madman, and accordingly knocks him down with the butt-end of his critical
staff, as often as he exceeds that line of sober discretion, which this learned
Editor appears to have chalked out for him: yet is this Editor, notwithstanding,
"a man, take him for all in all," very highly respectable for his genius and his
learning.'

JOSEPH WESTLUND

The Merchant of Venice:
Merging with a Perfect World

The reparative effect of *The Merchant of Venice* is often diluted. Many viewers tend to "fuse" with its world, to merge with it so intensely that they cannot distinguish between what is in the play and what they wish, or fear, to find.[1] A. D. Moody chastises critics for romanticizing, for giving way to "a wish to find in the play an assurance that the world may be simple and good, in spite of its evidence to the contrary."[2] The impulse is especially noticeable among Christian interpreters: Portia becomes a figure of mercy or the new law, and the play takes on a strong religious tone.[3] Interpreters begin to ignore details such as the play's secular extravagance, bawdy jokes, and sexual romance. Psychoanalytic critics also idealize: they see Portia as benign and maternal, and view the drama as a contest "between a loving mother, Portia, and a castrating father, Shylock."[4] Such an interpretation ignores Portia's trickiness about the law and the rings; it also underestimates her ability to provoke the terrifying fantasy of a maternal figure who deceives, manipulates, and always wins.

Other critics go to the opposite extreme and "isolate" the play by degrading or limiting its effect. They keep the work at arm's length by concentrating on its unrealistic attitude toward trust and money, and its antisemitism; Shylock turns out to be something of a hero, and the Christians hypocrites. This impulse is the opposite extreme, a reaction against the impulse to fuse. Other festive comedies are less seductive, for they continually touch base with a realistic world. *As You Like It*, for example, reminds us that fantasies about

From *Shakespeare's Reparative Comedies: A Psychoanalytic View of the Middle Plays*. © 1984 by the University of Chicago.

ideal love and the golden world need to be brought down to earth. *The Merchant* can provoke extreme wariness. Moody sees the play as thoroughly amoral, although somehow instructively ironic: we see *through* the Christians' hypocrisy. Marilyn L. Williamson takes a detached look at the romantic heroine, and finds that in the ring plot she "exercises a last petty tyranny on her open, unsuspecting bridegroom," and contrives a situation in which she will have to reveal her central role in saving Antonio.[5] Vera M. Jiji seeks to present an unidealized account of Portia, but instead degrades her by dwelling on the bad side, by finding her acerbic, mocking, tormenting, and even "the agent of death—her weapon, the genital trap."[6] We are far from Holland's comfortable sense of the play working "with the feeling of trust a child needs to have toward his mother" (p. 330).

As Norman Rabkin demonstrates, intelligent critics offer "interpretations opposed so diametrically that they seem to have been provoked by different plays."[7] Unlike Rabkin, I think that *The Merchant* triggers peculiarly unsettling emotions. In the process, crucial aspects drop out of sight; for instance, critics wary of the play's idealism forget that Shylock attempts murder, Portia is largely benign, and the romantic and Christian values which infuse the play are not all touched with irony. Wheeler remarks that "psychologically, *Merchant* is inhabited by helpless, dependent children, whose fates turn on the contest" between Portia and Shylock (p. 172). This is true, and since we identify with the characters, in varying degrees, the play must negotiate with our unconscious fear and rage at finding ourselves in such a spot. Here is one reason for the extreme responses to *The Merchant*. Most critics seem to deal with this fear by finding either Portia *or* Shylock estimable, or by damning both of them; however, I think that they both stand for something which we value.

Many think Portia stands for trust; they often refer to Erik Erikson's idea of "basic trust," but not to his qualification of this term. Trust is not an achievement, but the principal one of two potentials: "a person devoid of the capacity to mistrust would be as unable to live as one without trust."[8] The play strongly conveys both potentials. Mistrust can be a positive attitude; it is, for instance, a useful way to assert autonomy, as in Portia's complaints about the lottery and her behavior in the trial. On the other hand, mistrust can be negative and lead to isolation such as Shylock's. Since the play can encourage too much trust, to the point where viewers fuse or isolate, Shylock must be convincingly drawn to serve as a counterweight.

Because of his arresting nature, we are faced with two compelling characters; what they represent becomes polar. An unsettling situation readily develops: characters seem split into all good or all bad. Critics debate, however, about who is which; this probably indicates that we are meant to be ambivalent about Portia and Shylock—as, say, we are about the Duke in *Measure for Measure*. If we could feel of two minds about Shylock, the play would seem realistic, rather than a possibly frightening fantasy: we could respect his mistrust as an outsider in a hostile world, and yet perceive its self-destructive nature. If we could feel ambivalent about him, the comedy would prove less disturbing. This would also be the case if we were able to admire Portia for her deep trust *and* for her wariness. However, such even-tempered responses are rare, as critics bear witness. Shakespeare's characterization is more complex than in the earlier comedies, more ambitiously detailed, yet the mixture of traits fails to coalesce. This distorts the reparative effect. The central characters rarely temper basic trust with mistrust, or convince us that their actions are believable. Since the characters are either not very consistent (the gentiles) or seem fragmented (Shylock in his isolation and rage) it is difficult to identify with them, to use them as models. The fantasies awakened by *The Merchant* can be potent, and viewers seem distressed to find none of the characters able to contain and transcend them.

II

Before going into this further, let us look at the first scene of the play, for here Shakespeare sets up contrasting attitudes in an analogous attempt to offer alternatives and to temper extremes. Antonio has no fear of losing his ships—just as he later has no qualms about losing a second loan to Bassanio, or signing Shylock's bond, or dying at Shylock's hands. Such wondrous poise can encourage us to follow suit, as can the whole play. Yet we know better, so it would help if we sensed that the play, and significant characters, were not so out-of-touch with the danger—or "so very very far above money."[9] Salerio and Solanio protest they would worry had they so many ships at sea:

> should I go to church
> And see the holy edifice of stone
> And not bethink me straight of dangerous rocks,
> Which touching but my gentle vessel's side
> Would scatter all her spices on the stream,
> Enrobe the roaring waters with my silks,
> And in a word, but even now worth this,
> And now worth nothing?
>
> (1.1.29–36)

Antonio replies to this poignant expression of loss not in a grandly venturesome but in a carefully down-to-earth manner:

> Believe me no, I thank my fortune for it—
> My ventures are not in one bottom trusted,
> Nor to one place; nor is my whole estate
> Upon the fortune of this present year:

Therefore my merchandise makes me not sad.
                                        (1.1.41–45)

He sounds curiously prudent here, given his behavior during most of the play. His doggedly measured terms and their repeated negatives make him for a moment akin to Shylock (although the latter thinks him mad to take so many chances with crazed vessels). The scene gives a sense of possibilities other than the gentiles' extravagant trust. Salerio's account of the ship being engulfed conveys the danger of merchant enterprise. On a deeper level, it suggests that venturing in the larger sense is a going out of self which can result in being engulfed, lost, and destroyed: "but even now worth this, / And now worth nothing." Antonio's first appearance begins the play's series of contradictory impressions. He begins by being aloof, and ends the scene by being on intimate terms with Bassanio, almost to the point of fusing (or losing) himself with his friend. At the outset he denies being melancholy because of love, yet by the scene's end we know his melancholy stems from the departure of his good friend. He begins by being prudent (1.1.41–45); he ends by contradicting what he claimed earlier: now "all my fortunes are at sea, / Neither have I money, nor commodity / To raise a present sum" (1.1.177–79).

Such details do not constitute a character about whom we can feel "ambivalent," for they hardly seem aspects of one psyche. Instead, the opposed aspects are simply contradictory. This also happens later when Antonio treats Shylock at first in a civil manner, then grows haughty and outraged: "The devil can cite Scripture for his purpose,— / An evil soul producing holy witness / Is like a villain" (1.3.93–95). Antonio sounds self-righteously vigorous, whereas during the trial he sounds pathologically passive: "I am a tainted wether of the flock, / Meetest for death" (4.1.114–15). He seems not so much a well-rounded character as one com-posed of minor contradictions which give us a sense of his being imperfect, hard to understand completely, and thus vaguely realistic. He shows that he knows about evil, tries to prevent the consequences of Shylock's usury, and yet trusts that things will work out. This can quiet some of our fears about being caught up in a fictional world which denies the validity of mistrust. Still, Antonio signs the bond. And Bassanio uses the money to woo Portia. Most of the characters pay no attention to danger and live in a never-never land.

III

Portia bears the burden of making us feel that reality has not been totally ignored, and that trust is not a dangerous fantasy. Unusually powerful for a heroine in a festive comedy, she runs the risk of being felt too much in charge. At first she has too little power, for she must rely on the lottery, and this momentarily troubles her. But during the trial she has too much control as both lawyer and judge; also, she would not need to assert herself so much if she were actually as trusting as the play would have us believe. She becomes progressively more assertive and prudent as the potential for danger increases.

As we look at her behavior during the play, we find a curious situation: her trusting and mistrusting attitudes remain contradictory rather than cohere into some comprehensible unity. We logically assume that an important character in Shakespeare is most likely a unified one, but this may not be the case with Portia (or Antonio). William Empson argues that at times, for instance in the song sung while Bassanio chooses a casket, "We are concerned ... with a sort of dramatic ambiguity of judgment which does not consider the character so much as the audience."[10] Still, as we experience a play we probably expect a character's actions and words to become more than a bundle of facts and traits. With Portia and Antonio, though, the viewer has to create the unity, to labor in a vain attempt to conceive of the character as *being* ambivalent. Since Portia seems not to integrate her feelings—unlike, say Beatrice or Rosalind—critics find it almost impossible to do so. Moody, for example, notes that she is "a warmly and resourcefully human person" (p. 37), but he continually finds her deeply suspect- and, perhaps as a result, makes her a larger and more disturbing figure than warranted. Shakespeare has introduced canny mistrust into a highly romanticized heroine, a fairy-tale princess.

Portia chafes at the potential risk when she discusses the lottery. Unlike Antonio, who blithely signs Shylock's bond, and Bassanio, who lets him do so and proceeds to hazard for her, she momentarily finds taking a chance irritating and irrational: "I may neither choose who I would, nor refuse who I dislike, so is the will of a living daughter curb'd by the will of a dead father" (1.2.22–25). Nerissa easily—too easily—persuades her that the right man will reveal himself by his choice, for it will indicate his attitude toward her and toward life: he will have to be willing to give and hazard all, to venture out of himself to love her. Still, when Bassanio appears and she falls in love, Portia tries to postpone the test, fearing that he might lose. For a moment we find someone in the play realistic about taking chances. Later, this fear grows pronounced: we can wonder if she cheats by giving him a hint in the song sung "the whilst Bassanio comments on the caskets to himself " (3.2.63). Whether the song is a clue or not remains contested by critics (Arden edition, p. 80). And rightly so, for we are not supposed to be sure, but to wonder if her mistrust has overwhelmed her. Here is a conflict such as we ourselves might feel. We know that Bassanio probably needs no clue, but Portia does not. He hazards all the time: taking another loan, he draws an analogy to shooting a second arrow to find the first; he seems perfectly at home in the Venetian world of venturers. She says that she will not cheat, but the song's rhymes on "lead" could serve as a clue. It would be very odd, though, if she cheated, for she seems loyal to her father's will. Perhaps Shakespeare directs the clue to the audience: we are allowed to wonder if it is Portia's trick, but never to be sure.

The practical and mercantile terms which the lovers use during their love scene also help to bring it down-to-earth. Bassanio says "I come by note to give, and to receive" (as if a bill or note of dues prompted him), and he doubts "whether what I see be true, / Until confirm'd, sign'd, ratified by you" (3.2.140,147–48). She says: "Myself, and what is mine, to you and yours / Is now converted" (3.2.166–67). All ventures out of the self, especially in love, are ones which can entail a fear of fusion—which is why people often either avoid them, or recoil once they make them. The mercantile and legal terms help to make the lovers' venture less threatening: such terms indicate that some control is available, as it more often is in daily business and legal relationships than in highly romantic situations.[11]

IV

In the minor love plot involving Jessica and Lorenzo we find lovers who are pitted against a more formidable obstacle than the lottery set up by Portia's father (a test we know must be benign). Latent anxieties about love emerge more openly here. Unlike Portia, Jessica must throw off parental restraint, for she knows Shylock would prevent her marriage. Nor does Jessica bravely, foolishly, leave herself open to adversity. She firmly takes matters into her own hands, disobeys her father, and steals money from him. We are in the world of conventional comedy, which is unusual for Shakespeare: a miserly father would prevent the marriage of true lovers. To judge from critical commentary, Shakespeare may have avoided such situations because the consequences can be disruptive.[12] Viewers are disturbed in unexpected ways. For instance, the psychoanalyst Theodore Reik identifies himself so completely with Shylock that he sees himself, and his own daughter and her suitor locked in a painful relationship which he finds in the play itself (by projection, I think).[13] We can to some extent sympathize with a badly deceived father. However, that Shylock should wish Jessica dead and the ducats in her coffin should keep us at a distance from such grotesque love. Many people try to sympathize with Shylock by wishing away his clear lack of affection. Spedding, for example, would like to excise Jessica's theft so that "the secret that [Shylock] really cared more for the ducats than the daughter would not be forced upon the knowledge of his admirers, who regard paternal tenderness as one of his most conspicuous virtues" (Variorum edition, p. 99). Critics seem to deny the guilt which Shylock can stir up in us—in that we identify with his destructive response to being deprived. Others seem to deny the guilt which Jessica can stir up—in that we identify with her rebellion against her father. The scene often leaves a bad taste, or gets explained in evasive ways.

That Jessica steals money is a strongly potent issue (one Reik took very much to heart). Why she does so is not clear, especially in a world where Antonio and Portia dispense money so lavishly. The play instills a deeper sense of mistrust hy using such details: Jessica cannot be sure of how to get along once she elopes. In addition, her theft makes us suspicious about her: can a daughter who steals from her father be good? It seems not, for she squanders the money—and her mother Leah's ring. Shylock's sense of loss grows credible and our sympathy turns to him, and away from the otherwise ideal young lovers. At the very moment she goes off to gild herself with more of Shylock's ducats, Lorenzo idealizes her (without meaning to be ironic): "wise, fair, and true, / Shall she be placed in my constant soul" (2.6.56–57). Alexander Leggatt notes that "metaphorically, Jessica is taking love from her father and transferring it to her husband; but the throwing of the casket and the extra detail of her disappearing to get more ducats put the focus on the literal wealth she is stealing."[14] Jessica is possessive and mistrustful like her father. This love plot is more realistic, less idealized; we begin for the first time to find the conflict about trust out in the open. This minor love plot can have unexpected effects: viewers are unsettled by the theft, by Shylock's destructive anger, and, ultimately, by the reverberations we may feel when faced with an outraged parent and an abusive child.

V

Greed and possessiveness taint Jessica and Lorenzo, but form Shylock's center of being. He can easily dominate the play and overwhelm us with his sense of mistrust. Viewers have seen Shylock in strikingly different ways; it is impossible to know the original intention or best reading. He was played by comedians very early in the eighteenth century (although Rowe was sure that he was "design'd Tragically by the Author"); by the middle of the century more serious actors played the role. In 1814 he was given a "terrible energy" in Kean's innovative interpretation, one which led Hazlitt to find Shylock "honest in his vices; [the Christians] are hypocrites in their virtues." (As early as 1796 the idea was recorded that he is not wholly malignant.) Sir Henry Irving, who in 1879 produced an immensely successful *Merchant*, pronounced Shylock "a bloody-minded monster,—but you mustn't play him so, if you wish to succeed; you must get some sympathy with him" (for this summary, see the Arden edition, pp. xxxiii–xxxv). Irving's view seems closest to what the text suggests (although he made much of Shylock as a member of a despised race).

We can make Shylock's contradictory aspects cohere more readily than we can Portia's. Perhaps we more easily comprehend evil characters who display a few sympathetic traits than we do good characters with bad ones (as in the case of Isabella). And yet, Shylock's sympathetic traits are difficult to find. He has no obvious virtues. His love for Jessica is possessive and selfish. He even seems to have little of the pride often ascribed to him; for instance, he readily backs down once defeated by the law, and then leaves without even complaining about being misled. (If he did so, of course, the play might grind to a halt.) Monstrous, and at times comically so, he holds values not entirely bad: they are ours, in part, and this contributes to our sense of his dignity. Harold C. Goddard acutely suggests that the Christians "project on him what they have dismissed from their own consciousness as too disturbing."[15] Rather than attribute this to projection by the characters, who seem too thinly drawn for such activity, I think that *viewers* project on Shylock what they have dismissed from their own consciousness as too disturbing. Then he can be damned for their feelings. Viewers can also project good traits (prudence, dignity, honesty) onto Shylock, and value them.[16]

Ever alert to risks, Shylock tries to anticipate and prevent bad consequences. When he goes out he locks up his daughter. He gladly rids himself of a servant who allegedly eats too much. When Shylock sees a chance to get rid of Antonio, his competitor (as he sees it), he tries to catch him with his merry jest. In court Shylock relentlessly insists upon his "rights," and when they vanish he tries to get his money back. Even his sense of religion has a self-sufficient and narrowly prudent quality: he takes no chances on mercy (although a good Jew should), for he thinks that he can justify himself. These traits, odd though it seems, are basically congenial to a part of many of us; we, too, profoundly hope that to "fast bind" is to "fast find." His profession is unsavory to us—and was even more so to Shakespeare's audience—but has its own inner logic: he minimizes risks as, say, a banker, or insurance agent, or doctor should. We sympathize with his loss of his daughter (who really seems dead to him), and of his ducats, because we grieve for our own losses. In seeking to ward off adversity, he isolates himself so thoroughly that it can be terrible to see—especially if the viewer sometimes errs in this direction.

The play gives a hearing to Shylock's feelings, but since its predominant attitude encourages trust, and since we need the capacity for both trust and mistrust, the reparative strategy is to try to manage our identification. Some ways of distancing Shylock from viewers have vanished, or so we like to think: especially the assumption that Jews are exotic, alien, subhuman creatures. We may not understand the moral outrage against usurers in the way Shakespeare's audience did, but we still know the evil of usurious rates and the lender's cold malice—"I will feed fat." That Shylock is a comic miser, too, and a ridiculously inept and callous father, continue to keep us at a distance. We prefer to imagine that Shylock is not our sort.

Nonetheless, many try to excuse Shylock. Perhaps it is simply because he is Jewish: gentiles feel guilt, and Jews outraged sympathy. Or perhaps he points out the hypocrisy and complacency of the predominant group in his society, and that cannot be all bad. On the deepest level, however, I suspect that Shylock's wish to control his world overstimulates our identification with him. To some degree we must feel as he does: the world is full of dangerous possibilities. He adduces many reasons why Antonio is not "sufficient" as a potential debtor:

> ventures he hath squand'red abroad,—but ships are but boards, sailors but men, there be land-rats, and water-rats, water-thieves, and

land-thieves, (I mean pirates), and then there is the peril of waters,
winds, and rocks.

(1.3.19–23)

Unlike Salerio and Solanio, who also foresee trouble, Shylock concentrates
upon the probable failings of people (sailors are but men), or a paranoid view of
them (as water-thieves and land-thieves). Even the land-rats and water-rats
worry him. Then he briefly mentions what *no one* can control: "waters, winds,
and rocks." Only the latter inanimate forces beyond man's control capture the
imagination of the trusting Salerio and Solanio in their lyrical account of
shipwreck.

Shylock does not even take much of a chance in loaning money to Antonio
(he thinks), for he wins either way if Antonio cannot discharge the debt. The loss
of money would be well worth it: "I will have the heart of him if he forfeit, for
were he out of Venice I can make what merchandise I will"—that is, drive
usurious bargains (3.1.116–18). If Antonio can pay, then Shylock merely loses his
chance. Everything is legal, he thinks, and thus he should be safe.

VI

Shylock's attempt to control the outcome of events reaches its high point during
the trial. Now we find the two principal characters both exercising control: the
issue becomes central, yet critics rarely agree about the resolution. Some praise
the trial as an allegory of "Justice and Mercy, of the Old Law and the New"
(Coghill, p. 21). But Shylock cannot represent justice or the old law, for he is a
comic, murderous figure; nor can we feel comfortable that Portia's theatrical
interpretation is allegorically related to the workings of mercy or the new law.
Other critics find her conduct reprehensible: she sings "the praises of mercy
when she is about to insist that the Jew shall have the full rigours of justice
according to the strict letter of the law."[17]

The trial has a number of theatrical surprises. Just before it, Shylock seems
certain to win, for "the duke cannot deny the course of law." Antonio begins to
behave oddly, and becomes baroquely coercive: "pray God Bassanio come / To
see me pay his debt, and then I care not" (3.3.35–36). This remark anticipates the
gentiles' covertly manipulative approach during the trial. Shylock, on the other
hand, is perfectly open about his need to control, and grandiosely omnipotent:
"What judgment shall I dread doing no wrong?" Antonio's inability to do
anything makes him degrade himself.

> I am a tainted wether of the flock,
> Meetest for death,—the weakest kind of fruit
> Drops earliest to the ground, and so let me;
> You cannot better be employ'd Bassanio,

Than to live still and write mine epitaph.

$$(4.1.114–18)$$

Antonio's impotence sounds pathological, and makes us eager for someone who can take charge. Shylock's omnipotence also disturbs us: he fuses with the law—"I crave the law" (4.1.202).

When Portia enters we are ready to put up with a great deal in order to repair the damage which is being done. She talks about mercy, and although we know that Shylock will render none, it helps to have the issue of control deflected from human affairs to a higher level: mercy drops from heaven and is beyond our control, for it is "an attribute to God himself" (4.1.191). The religious frame of reference helps to make her discovery of a way out seem providential—even though we may upon reflection find her tactics distressing. Before setting to work she acknowledges human fallibility, something which we can forget because of Shylock's omnipotence and his seemingly airtight case:

> in the course of justice, none of us
> Should see salvation: we do pray for mercy,
> And that same prayer, doth teach us all to render
> The deeds of mercy.

$$(4.1.195–98)$$

Soon we see how she might catch Shylock, for he questions the need for a surgeon to staunch the blood: "Is it so nominated in the bond?" His reliance on the bond as a magical entity—it has all the answers—may suggest the solution to Portia, who replies, "It is not so express'd, but what of that?" Before she exerts the control we have been waiting for, Antonio has a final disconcerting speech, one which makes his impotence almost as odious as Shylock's grandiosity:

> Give me your hand Bassanio, fare you well,
> Grieve not that I am fall'n to this for you:
> . . . .
> Repent but you that you shall lose your friend
> And he repents not that he pays your debt.

$$(4.1.261–62, 274–75)$$

Some of this is noble sentiment—"bid her [Portia] be judge / Whether Bassanio had not once a love" (4.1.272–73); but most of it is passive-aggressive. He puts the blame on Bassanio, not himself. "grieve not that I am fall'n to this for you." If Antonio really wants to assuage his friend's guilt, he should not at the same time say that it is his fault. Again, we are tempted to find an inner logic to Antonio's remarks, but if we do he turns out to be far too troubling for his role—and for the approbation of his community. I think that Shakespeare has a limited goal in mind, but the effect can be unsettling. Antonio's loss of self-esteem is supposed to make us long even more for someone who will resolve this painful situation. Characters now seem so helpless before Shylock that we are ready to accept almost anything. Even Bassanio and Gratiano make oddly unreal statements: they would be willing to sacrifice themselves, or their wives. Portia and Nerissa greet this with wry disbelief, which confirms that at last such high-minded sentimentalizing must be set aside.

Portia's intervention—"Tarry a little, there is something else"—strikes just the right note: calm, controlled, reasonable. She works out her bold deed in legalistic terms. Some critics think the outcome demonstrates that "the vicious circle of the bond's law can be transformed into the ring of love ... through a literal and unreserved submission to the bond as absolutely binding."[18] This seems too extreme, and makes it difficult to see how an ordinary, sensible person would react to the scene if under pressure to feel this. Portia says that the law is absolutely binding; but she interprets it in a way which many find suspiciously creative; lawyers find it downright illegal (Arden edition, p. li). Her emphasis on legal points and quibbles, along with her delay in discovering them, discourages fusion with an idealized law. The Venetians discover that they can trust the law because it anticipates danger, hedges itself about with mistrust, and leaves itself open to the interpretation along lines which it helps to delimit. In a word, the law is not, as it seems to Shylock, a magically perfect entity. For instance, the law apparently discriminates against an alien who seeks to take the life of any citizen (whether it protects an alien against a citizen we do not know, for we need not know here). The trust which the trial scene encourages in a viewer is not merely in the law, or in Portia, or in society—but in all of them working together under providence. Insofar as the power is spread out, the play helps to establish a clear relation to reality—with the law's quibbles, the judge's rather arbitrary interpretation, and the prevalence of common sense in deciding matters of life and death. To the degree that the trial keeps us *away from* fantasy, it works well.

Unfortunately, some of this "reality" can be interpreted differently. On a conscious level, Portia is tricky and the law readily manipulated to serve powerful members of society. On an unconscious level, one that is influenced by the apparent tricks and manipulation, fantasy destroys the reparative sense that life can be trusted to be benevolent and supportive. Portia seems a powerful, arbitrary, deceptive female who endangers Antonio, briefly, and then Shylock. Society appears hypocritical and prejudiced against anyone different from the norm. Life can seem out to get us. Viewers who strongly respond to the details of plot and characterization along these lines—many critics do in various degrees—will find that the reparative effect of *The Merchant* has derailed. Since such viewers are already prone to be mistrustful, the fact that Shylock voices such feelings, and then is punished, will add to their discomfort. Perhaps such derailment occurs more often now than when the play was first presented—because, say, we now suspect the *status quo* more readily, or are more sensitive to persecution of Jews, or simply think too much about what is, first of all, a theatrical experience in which a man's life is saved. Or, Shakespeare may not yet be fully in control of what he writes.

VII

The remainder of *The Merchant* at last begins to confront the need for prudence. The deep mistrust which Shylock raises begins to subside when he leaves the stage; but it lingers on, as it must. At this point mistrust becomes respectable, not an easily repudiated trait tied to Shylock. So far, reservations about giving and hazarding have surfaced only fitfully. For the first time, the lovers seriously entertain the need to be possessive. The ladies stress the outward signs of love, the rings, just as Portia and others stressed the exact proscriptions of the bond and lottery. As I noted in discussing the odd responses of Bassanio and Gratiano during the trial, the husbands' characteristic generosity appears for the first time excessive—ridiculous even for a romantic and theatrical moment. When Bassanio says that to save Antonio he would give my "life itself, my wife, and all the world" (4.1.280); Portia wryly dashes cold water on the notion: "Your wife would give you little thanks for that." To Gratiano's similar gesture, Nerissa trenchantly remarks "'Tis well you offer it behind her back, / The wish would make else an unquiet house."

When Portia has defeated Shylock, Bassanio gratefully presses her (that is, Balthazar) to "take some remembrance of us as a tribute, / Not as a fee." She asks for his ring, with the result that for the first time in the entire play the unbelievably generous Venetians find themselves in a dilemma: "Good sir, this ring was given me by my wife, / And when she put it on, she made me vow / That I should neither sell, nor give, nor lose it" (4.1.437–39). The wedding ring stands for fidelity and chastity, and serves, in effect, as a contractual bond; it cannot be given away as ships and money can. Unlike other ventures—going out of oneself to be loving, friendly, and altruistic—giving up the rings entails more than the possibility of losing oneself. Someone in addition to the venturer has a stake in the risk. Thus the need for prudence here is clearer and not contaminated with selfishness; here to give and hazard would be to betray the trust placed in one by another person. In the back of our minds we may remember Jessica's willful, distressing act of giving away Leah's ring. Our unease at Bassanio risking Antonio's life by accepting and spending the money may lurk about. If we think Bassanio sufficiently developed as a character who could feel guilt, we might see his gift of the ring as an attempt to repair the almost fatal damage to Antonio. Still, Bassanio has no right to give the ring no matter how good the cause. We find a real conflict here. It differs from the previous stylized conflict between attitudes identified with different figures: now conflict is *within* individuals.

In the last act, Jessica and Lorenzo (who are far from being ideal) talk about famous lovers (all ill-fated), and heavenly music (which they cannot hear).

Portia and Nerissa talk about light, music, and song (all perceived in relative terms). Bassanio and Gratiano enter and are closely questioned about their fidelity (which they cannot prove, having given away the rings). The play separates ideal from actual with a clarity unknown before. The wives mock their husbands and threaten to be as liberal with their own bodies as the men were with the wedding rings. Now mistrust has explicitly religious overtones: although God must be trusted absolutely, the rings remind the husband and wife that they must be careful and possessive in marriage. Mistrust becomes a virtue, not a passing fear such as Portia's about the lottery or the potential subversion of the state—as it would be if acted upon by the friends of Antonio with regard to observing the bond. Portia tells Bassanio that it was his "own honour to contain the ring" (5.1.201). The playful squabbling can be reparative for viewers in that the wives' retentiveness is legitimate, as is the husbands' demand that their wives not play around with other men. Shylock's mistrust—"fast bind, fast find"—now emerges as the counterpart of trust. The poesy on Gratiano's ring, "love me, and leave me not," is a version of Shylock's motto. Without a bit of mistrust, of fear that the partner may be too liberal, the trusting relationship would have little chance to survive the potential unkindness of real circumstances.

More than elsewhere Portia now behaves like the controlling characters of the other comedies; her power is limited, which was not true during the trial. She and Nerissa "manage," rather than manipulate. Like the Duke in *Measure for Measure*, the ladies offer an occasion for characters to rise to the task of controlling themselves and assisting in the creation of a happy outcome. This, I think, can be reassuring to an audience. Bassanio and Gratiano always knew that they should not give away the rings, and are ready to agree with their wives. In contrast, Shylock could not be brought to be merciful. The husbands and wives can face mistrust because it has been safely contained by the situation. Bassanio and Gratiano, and Antonio as well, find that they were too generous; but since Portia and Nerissa themselves received the rings, there are no serious consequences such as those which face Antonio about the bond. Since the husbands are ready to match their inner sense of what they ought to do with what their wives insist upon, they can take the trick in good humor and without fear of being manipulated. The need for prudence arises within the context of an underlying trust in one another. The ring episode creates a situation similar to the one in *Much Ado* where Beatrice and Benedick find themselves tricked into admitting what they already know to be true.

In *The Merchant of Venice* trust comes a little too easily, and never to Shylock: the play's numerous qualifications prove too slight to quiet possible objections to such an expansive view. In *Much Ado about Nothing*, probably the next comedy Shakespeare wrote, we find nearly the opposite pattern: instead of moving from trust to some reservations about it, *Much Ado* begins with such strong reservations that the possibility only gradually, fitfully, emerges. It is located almost exclusively in Beatrice and Benedick rather than in an entire society. The note of constriction on which *The Merchant* ends, and which assists in making the play's world somewhat more like our own, becomes the predominant tone in the next comedy.[19]

NOTES

1. This process can be normal or pathological. Although the terms are briefly explained in my text, I will for convenience relate them to one another here. *Fusion* is losing oneself, and one's limitations and imperfections, through merging with something omnipotent and perfect—say, God, or art, or the ideal mother. We seek to merge with what we *idealize* as a source of excellence in which we can partake, and which reflects our own perfection. Ultimately; if carried far enough, this is a regression to an infant's narcissistic bliss, a state free from the frustration and impotence which limit us in the real world. However, we cannot tolerate coming close to complete fusion, for we would lose our identity by merging in such a union. The prototype of fusion is our relation to mother before we separate and become individuals (on this see my reference to Margaret S. Mahler in chap. 1, n. 16). To approach such fusion with people is terrifying: it causes a sharp reaction toward an opposite state of *isolation* from others—and concurrently, the *degradation* of them and of what they could offer. The shift is between two poles (and I simplify here): the one, fusion, idealization, and trust; the other, isolation, degradation, and mistrust.

I concentrate upon the shift between these poles—and the play's effect in reducing such fluctuation—in my chapters on the three earlier plays. *The Merchant* encourages fusion; *Much Ado* (except for Beatrice and Benedick) encourages isolation; and *As You Like It* seems the first of these comedies to convey a serene sense of autonomy. Richard Y. Wheeler nicely summarizes the psychological process which I concentrate upon in these chapters: "The longing for merger threatens to destroy precariously achieved autonomy; the longing for complete autonomy threatens to isolate the self from its base of trust in actual and internalized relations to others"; *Shakespeare's Development*, 206.

2. A.D. Moody, *Shakespeare: The Merchant of Venice* (Woodbury, N.Y.: Barron's Educational Series, 1964), 15. This is an excellent, if too antiromantic, reading.

3. See, for example: Barbara K. Lewalski, "Biblical Allusion and Allegory in *The Merchant of Venice*," *SQ* 13 (1962): 327–43; Nevil Coghill, "The Basis of Shakespearean Comedy," *Essays and Studies 3* (1950): 1–28; and René E. Fortin, Launcelot and the Uses of Allegory in *The Merchant of Venice*," *SEL* 14 (1974): 259–70. John S. Coolidge in "Law and Love in *The Merchant of Venice*," *SQ* 27 (1976): 243, argues that "the play is in fact a kind of hermeneutic drama, reflecting the contest between Christian and Jew for the possession of Hebrew scriptures."

4. Norman Holland, *Psychoanalysis and Shakespeare* (1964; reprint New York: Farrar, Straus & Giroux, 1976), 236. Wheeler argues that "the triumph over Shylock protects *Merchant* from the threat of the vengeful, possessive father," and with this play masculine values based on competition and conquest (such as found in Shakespeare's histories) disappear from the festive comedies. In these plays he sees, "more than the release of sexual desire ... a rhythm of frustration and fulfillment grounded in trust, focused specifically through the presence of a trust-worthy woman" (*Shakespeare's Development*, 175).

5. Marilyn L. Williamson, "The Ring Episode in *The Merchant of Venice*," *South Atlantic Quarterly* 71 (1972): 591.

6. Vera M. Jiji, "Portia Revisited: The Influence of Unconscious Factors Upon Theme and Characterization in *The Merchant of Venice*," *Literature and Psychology* 26 (1976): 11. Jiji wisely observes that the need "to keep Portia divine, or to delight in her surrender to Bassanio, may betray some distortion of their [romanticizing critics'] vision of women rather than an understanding of Shakespeare's" (p. 6).

7. Norman Rabkin, *Shakespeare and the Problem of Meaning* (Chicago: University of Chicago Press, 1981), 5.

8. Erikson, *Identity, Youth, and Crisis*, 325, n. 8. He specifically addresses what he sees as a common misunderstanding of his idea about basic trust.

9. C.L. Barber, *Shakespeare's Festive Comedy* (Princeton: Princeton University Press, 1959), 190.

10. William Empson, *Seven Types of Ambiguity* (1930; reprint London: Chatto and Windus, 1947), 43.

11. The love scene can be read differently, and in a way which gives Portia's character greater coherence. The intensity of her speech when she gives Bassanio everything may indicate why she takes such delight in controlling him by means of the ring plot:

> But now I was the lord
> Of this fair mansion, master of my servants,
> Queen o'er myself: and even now, but now,
> This house, these servants. and this same myself
> Are yours,—my lord's!—I give them with this ring.

(3.2.167–71)

She tries to get back the control which of necessity she gave up in marrying, and this can be disturbing to us. (The insight is Janet Adelman's and not published.)

12. On this see Rabkin, *Problem of Meaning*, 17–19; the Arden edition, xlv; and Leonard Tennenhouse, "The Counterfeit Order of *The Merchant of Venice*," in *Representing Shakespeare*, 58. Jessica's betrayal, Tennenhouse argues, "is presented in such a way as to *deny* that it is in fact a betrayal, an illusion that those who are disturbed by Jessica's behavior find reassuring to accept. And yet the

justifications that Shakespeare has built into this plot seem to reflect a real ambivalence on his part." Also see my chap. 2, n. 19.

13. Theodore Reik, "Jessica, My child," in *The Secret Self* (New York: Farrar, Straus & Giroux, 1952): reprinted in *The Design Within: Psychoanalytic Approaches to Shakespeare*, ed. M.D. Faber (New York: Science House, 1970). 441–62.

14. Alexander Leggatt, *Shakespeare's Comedy of Love* (London: Methuen, 1974), 125.

15. Harold C. Goddard, *The Meaning of Shakespeare* (Chicago: University of Chicago Press, 1951), 85. Moody quotes this (*Shakespeare*, 32); he remarks that "in condemning Shylock they [the Christians] are condemning their own sins" of worldliness and inhuman behavior.

16. On "projective identification" see Melanie Klein, "Notes on Some Schizoid Mechanisms" (1946), and "On Identification" (1955), in *Envy and Gratitude and Other Works, 1946–1963*, ed. R.E. Money-Kyrle (London: Hogarth Press, 1975). Also see Segal, *Introduction to the Work of Melanie Klein*, 126. Projective identification is "the result of the projection of parts of the self into an object. It may result in the object being perceived as having acquired the characteristics of the projected part of the self but it can also result in the self becoming identified with the object of its projection." This basic, complex process seems to account for viewers unconsciously seeing themselves as Shylock—and then reacting with unconscious and extreme scorn, or admiration.

17. John Palmer, *Comic Characters of Shakespeare* (1946; reprint London: Macmillan, 1961), 87. Palmer and Coghill ("The Basis of Shakespearean Comedy"), are cited in the concise summary in the Arden edition, l–lii.

18. Sigurd Burckhardt, *Shakespearean Meanings* (Princeton: Princeton University Press, 1968), 210.

19. Tennenhouse ("The Counterfeit Order of *The Merchant of Venice*," 63), and many others feel this note of constriction in Antonio being left without a mate at the end; nothing has changed for him except that he is restored to his riches by Portia's mysterious message. If we take his isolation during the trial seriously, and relate it to his melancholy at the beginning and his being without a wife at the end, we may be troubled for him. However, at the end of *Much Ado* Benedick tells Don Pedro: "thou art sad; get thee a wife, get thee a wife"; at the end of *As You Like It* the converted Duke and Jaques are to be left in Arden; and Malvolio leaves in fury at the end of *Twelfth Night*. All are solitary, outside the community, and not married. Perhaps this is a gesture to indicate that the demands of reality have not been completely overlooked.

BARBARA EVERETT

Much Ado About Nothing:
the unsociable comedy

Social workers sometimes speak of people 'falling through the net'. That's what it can seem that *Much Ado About Nothing* has done, critically speaking. Audiences and readers rarely like it quite as much as the two comedies by Shakespeare which follow it, *As You Like It* and *Twelfth Night*: they feel that by comparison it lacks some sort of magic. Professional critics can take this vague disappointment much further, almost echoing the nineteenth-century charge that the heroine Beatrice is an 'odious woman'. In case it appears that we have changed all that, it may be worth mentioning that what is probably still the only full-length handbook on the play describes Beatrice (at least in her earlier unreformed phase) as 'self-centred', 'the embodiment of pride', a person who '*cannot love*', 'a crippled personality, the very antithesis of the outgoing, self-giving character [Shakespeare] values most highly'. Nor is this study by J. R. Mulryne exceptional. A leading paperback edition cites it approvingly and itself describes both Benedick and Beatrice as 'posing', 'showing themselves off as a preparation for mating'; and it regrets that this pair of lovers fails to 'arouse in an audience the warmth of feeling' evoked by a Portia or a Rosalind. The writer of this Introduction, R.A. Foakes, can only conclude that 'The contrast between [Claudio and Hero] and Beatrice and Benedick was surely designed in part to expose the limitations of both couples.'

'This lookes not like a nuptiall', Benedick murmurs helpfully as the catastrophic Wedding Scene of *Much Ado* gets under way: and the reader of the

From *English Comedy*, ed. Michael Cordner, Peter Holland, and John Kerrigan. © 1994 by Cambridge University Press.

play's criticism can often feel the same. Particularly given that we are considering a love-comedy by Shakespeare, the remarks I have quoted all seem to me to be startling judgements. For opinions to differ so much can provoke useful thought. Perhaps Shakespeare's mature comedies, once recommended literary fodder for school-children on the grounds of their charming pure-minded simplicity, are—whatever their other characteristics—not so simple after all. When Shakespeare first staged *Much Ado*, fairly certainly in 1598 or '99, he was coming to the end of a decade of extraordinary achievement and invention. The first Tragedies, the earlier Histories and Comedies lay behind him, *The Merchant of Venice* immediately preceded *Much Ado*, and Shakespeare had probably written most of both parts of *Henry IV*. The dramatist of *The Merchant of Venice* and *Henry IV* was in no way unsophisticated or unambitious. If he gave the three comedies we now choose to call 'mature' his most throwaway titles, they aren't throwaway plays. Possessed as they are of a profound sense and vitality which suggest the popular audience they were written for, their lightness nonetheless recalls that 'negligent grace' (*sprezzatura*) which the aristocratic culture of the Renaissance aspired to. The very unpretension of *Much Ado About Nothing*, its affectionate straightforward transparency have been invented to deal with human experience dense enough and real enough to produce notably different reactions from given human beings.

These comedies have become so familiar that it can be hard to think of them freshly. I want therefore to begin by approaching *Much Ado* from a slightly unexpected angle—because sometimes, when we are surprised, we see things more clearly. I'm going to start by thinking about one of the comedy's textual cruces, involving a few words spoken by Leonato in the first scene of Act 5. An interestingly shaped play, whose structural rhythm the dramatist was to use again in *Othello* (a fact which alone may say something about the work's seriousness), *Much Ado* has its main plot's climax, which turns out to be a pseudo- or anti-climax, in Act 4: in the big, bustling, peopled and very social Wedding Scene, which sees the gentle Hero, unjustly shamed by the machinations of the villains, publicly humiliated and jilted by her courtly fiance Claudio—though the fidelity to her of her witty though here grieving cousin, Beatrice, brings to Beatrice's side her own lover, the humorous Benedick.

In marked contrast, Act 5 opens with a quiet scene between two suddenly aged men, Hero's father Leonato and his brother Antonio. Critics have often thought it the most feeling moment in a drama they otherwise find cool. Leonato rebuffs his brother's philosophical comfort; he will be stoical, Leonato says bitterly, only if so advised by one who has suffered precisely as, and as much as, himself:

> If such a one will smile and stroke his beard ...
> Patch griefe with proverbs, make misfortune drunke
> With candle-wasters: bring him yet to me,
> And I of him will gather patience.

I have edited this, cutting out a line which both the early texts, the 1600 Quarto and the 1623 Folio, are agreed on, but which the great late-Victorian New Variorum edition fills two and a half of its large minutely printed pages of Notes discussing: and which all modern editors emend, in various slightly unconvincing ways. In the authentic texts, Leonato says that his despised comforter would be one to

> stroke his beard,
> And sorrow, wagge, crie hem, when he should grone,
> Patch griefe with proverbs

—and so on.

I want to talk for a few moments about what I think Leonato really said (which is not quite what modern editors make him say). It's necessary to add that, as the New Variorum records in its textual apparatus, fortunately or unfortunately an excellent American scholar named Grant White printed in his edition of 1854 the emendation I'm going to propose: but, since he dropped the emendation in his second edition, and didn't explain or gloss it in the first place, the field remains reasonably clear. He thought, and I too had thought independently, that Leonato describes his would-be comforter angrily as 'sorrow's wagge'—'And, sorrow's wagge, crie hem, when he should prone': a compositorial mistake very easy to account for; for, in the old Secretary hand which Shakespeare had learned to write in, the terminal letter 's' to a word was written as a kind of scrawled loop very like a topped comma. Let the comma lose its top because of a shortage of ink and the text reads just as in the Quarto and Folio.

It's an interesting fact that the editor of the New Variorum, the scholar Furness, urges us to find these early texts 'irredeemably corrupt'—not even to try, that is, to emend their version of the line. And he does so because the line shocks him as it stands. No editor, however authoritative (he says) 'can ever persuade me that Shakespeare put such words, at this passionate moment, into Leonato's mouth. There is a smack of comicality about "wag" which is ineffaceable.'

There is indeed. But perhaps Shakespeare put it there. The seriousness, even the genius of *Much Ado* may be to bring in precisely that 'smack of comicality' where we least expect it—just as its dramatist invents peculiarly English constables for his Sicilian play, to stumble fat-headedly into arresting the villains and bringing about the play's happy ending. A 'wag' is a word and a social phenomenon that is nearly obsolete now, though I can remember my own mother using it drily, with something of Furness's rebuke. A wag is or was a person who habitually, even desperately, tries to be funny. But in Shakespeare's time the word hadn't progressed to this degraded condition—it had not, so to speak, grown up: it remained the 'little tine boy' of Feste's song. For the most

familiar colloquial usage of 'wag' in the poet's own day was in the tender phrase,
'Mother's wag'. The word denoted a mischievous small prankster, amusingly
naughty as little boys often are. Only a few years before *Much Ado*, Greene in his
Menaphon has, 'Mothers wagge, prettie boy'—and Falstaff calls Hal his 'sweet
Wagge' in Part I of *Henry IV*.

Leonato says that the father who, having lost a child, could still find or
accept words of comfort would be 'Sorrow's wagge': he means the man would be
himself a child, immature. And the phrase has an element of oxymoron that
defines his shock and outrage. Like Furness after him, this decently conventional,
hierarchical, even conservative old man thinks that certain conjunctions of what
they would have called the grave and the gay, of grief and humour, are
'irredeemably corrupt'.

Before we agree with them both, we ought perhaps to pause and ask
whether Shakespeare has not shaped this encounter of the two old men so as to
prevent us doing just that. The 'passionate moment' which the Victorian editor
points to is surely something odder than passionate—and is odd in a way that is
relevant. For (and this is my chief topic here) *Much Ado About Nothing*'s real
achievement may be to make us think very hard indeed about this quality of the
'passionate' in human beings.

In this scene, Leonato and Antonio wear something that is easy to call, at
sight, the dignity of the bereaved; and they wear it consciously. But this is odd
because, though Hero may be disgraced, she is certainly not dead. And both
Leonato and Antonio know it. Moreover, we in the audience know that even
Hero's disgrace is rapidly melting into air: for the grieving scene is linked to the
Church Scene by, and is immediately preceded by, the comic bridge-scene in
which the ludicrous constables—the more senior proclaiming, with something of
Leonato's own self-important fury, that he 'hath had losses'—have apprehended
the villains and are at this moment hotfoot bringing a full disclosure to Leonato.

Later in this Fifth Act, Don Pedro and Claudio will make solemn
acknowledgement at the quasi-tomb of Hero. This action has its own meaning—
the moment's music allows the gesture a dimension of the symbolic: the scene
mutedly articulates some sadness which all grown-up 'understanders' of this
highly civilised, social comedy know to be intrinsic to most passion seeking social
embodiment. In the very preceding scene, 5.2, Benedick has lightly told Beatrice
that she doesn't live in 'the time of good neighbours', if it ever existed; that 'if a
man doe not erect in this age his owne tombe ere he dies, hee shall live no longer
in monuments, then the Bels ring, & the Widdow weepes'—i.e., not long. But
symbols are one thing, and facts another, even in our greatest poetic dramatist.
Hero still isn't dead. And the fact that she isn't, and that we know that she isn't,
and that her family, too, know that she isn't, turns this grieving ceremony at the
tomb into something like the masked dances which characterise this
sophisticated comedy: an art, a game, a pretence—a deception exonerated by
having been proposed in good faith and by a man, so to speak, of the cloth.

Much Ado's tomb-trick may in short be considered as not unlike those bed-tricks in the two later, much darker comedies, *Measure for Measure* and *All's Well That Ends Well*. Greater, much more intense, these two plays tell us far more about Shakespeare's interest in the tragi-comic—though neither they, nor any other play written by him is truly identifiable with the genre as the Continental aristocracy of the period knew it. But *Much Ado* shares one striking characteristic with them. It has the tragi-comic concern with love in society, a society for which some version of the political, the power-issue, is serious: a world which defers to Courtship and to social hierarchy. From this point of view, the tomb-trick is like the bed-tricks in working as a special kind of 'good deceit' or virtuous untruth, a device of worldly accommodation in a light but moral art. The clever courtiers, with Don Pedro at their head, have descended on Leonato's provincial family, and have done these simpler if still socially aspiring people some harm. Now the tables are pleasingly turned, the foolers are fooled, and Leonato and Antonio regain something of their lost honour merely by the silent superiority of knowing what they know.

But if this is conceded, something else must follow. The tomb-trick is peculiarly like those forms of wise comfort (and the word comfort actually means 'self-strengthening') angrily rejected in the grieving scene by the passionate Leonato. The music of the tomb-scene, shortly after, though saying nothing true, can still both calm and resolve. It thus performs the act at first denied by Leonato in the scene I started from: it can, like the wag's wisdom, 'Charme ache with ayre, and agony with words'. While the old man scorns sorrow's wags, something wise in the play embraces them.

I have used the word 'embrace' here deliberately—and not only because it is a love-comedy we are concerned with. For Elizabethans, the chief image of Love itself was as a 'wag': as the Puck-like armed baby, Cupid—naughtily dangerous, even disturbing to the coolly rationalistic eye of the Renaissance, yet in these comedies also the medium of great good. Puck himself is, after all, in the service of Oberon the King. Yet Puck moves in the night, 'Following darkenesse like a dreame', and the wood where the lovers wander is a distressing and frightening place. These complexities make Shakespeare's Love, and love's Happiness, a pair of twins, springing from the circumstances of sorrow: sorrow's wags.

I am hoping to suggest that in this casual phrase, a local crux in the text of a light comedy, we have some suggestion of the kind of rich complexity, of fruitful half-paradox, which gives *Much Ado* the vitality and depth by which it now survives. The comedy's Italian director, Franco Zeffirelli, once referred to it as a 'very dull play'. And *Much Ado* is indeed simple if we compare it, for instance, to its predecessor *The Merchant of Venice*. But that play's fascinating intellectual battles, its energy of contrasts embodied in Portia and Shylock, the marketplace and Belmont, leave behind at the end a disquieting dissatisfaction, a sense of something unjust or unresolved. This is a subject I shall return to. For the moment I want only to suggest that *Much Ado* may have chosen to be a 'very dull play', to be simple to the eye.

But its simplicity is a solidity. Shakespeare uses the novelle sources from which he has taken his main plot to generate a special, almost novelistic sense of the real, of a world where people live together to a degree that is socially and psychologically convincing, and new in the poet's work. And this realistic, even novelistic comedy deepens itself by containing, indeed we may say, with Leonato in mind, by *embracing* contradictions everywhere beneath its smooth and civil surface. If there is, to Leonato's mind, a troubling indecorum, an unconventionality in the juxtapositions, momentarily glimpsed by him, of sorrow with joy and of play with love, then it has to be said that such vital oppositions pervade the play, and are its life. Let me touch on one famous passage. At one point Don Pedro finds himself proposing marriage to Beatrice. He does not love her, nor she him. He has been led into it by his belief in the kindness of his own impeccable manners: a self-defeating trap from which he is released by Beatrice, who of course has led him into it in the first place, with the neat licentious speed of some brilliant Court Fool. Panting slightly, the courtly Don Pedro tells Beatrice that she was 'born in a merry howre'. She wins again, both wittily and touchingly: 'No sure my Lord, my Mother cried, but then there was a starve daunst, and under that was I borne.' This nicely hints at some of the reasons why this (to my mind) superb heroine has been and can still be disliked by a whole host of male scholars, both past and present. She is Shakespeare's true heroine, woman as 'wag', the sharp and comical child of sorrow.

Beatrice does something far more waggish than merely walking along a razor's edge of good behaviour with a visiting grandee. Indecorum is embodied in the fact that she and her story, which a formal criticism calls 'the sub-plot', take over the play, edging aside the main-plot story of Claudio and Hero. It's well known that Charles I wrote against the title of his text of the play 'Benedik and Betrice', and the sympathy of most succeeding readers has agreed with him. But the high originality of this comic structure can leave editors behind. Much in accord with the New Penguin Introduction which I quoted earlier, the New Arden confronts as the chief critical problem the question, 'What can or should be done to balance the play?' and proposes as answer: 'Hero and Claudio can gain in prominence; Benedick and Beatrice can be less salient.' But perhaps the comedy has its own balance, which can only be impaired by these adjustments: and this balance has to do with the delicate poise of energies suggested by the phrase, 'sorrow's wag'. I have lingered over this conceit because of all it can suggest about the essential principles involved in a Shakespearean comedy: principles necessitating both light and dark, both seriousness and laughter.

It can be a struggle to explain why these romantic comedies carry the value that they do—why, seeming to be 'About Nothing' (as their ironic or nonchalant titles suggest) they nonetheless evoke from those who truly like them, words like 'true' or 'brilliant' or 'profound'. The 'Nothing' of the *Much Ado* title is now, of course, somewhat undercut by our understanding that Elizabethans could pronounce 'Nothing' as 'Noting'. The plot of the comedy certainly turns on what this pun implies: note-taking, spying, eavesdropping. No other play in Shakespeare introduces so much eavesdropping—each new turn of the action depends on it. The confusions of Don Pedro's wooing of Hero for his protégé Claudio, the machinations by which his bastard brother Don John deceives Claudio into believing Hero unchaste, the trick by which Beatrice and Benedick are persuaded that each loves the other, the discovery of the villains by the comic constables—all these are effected by the incessant system of eavesdropping. Yet underneath the noting there is nothing. The play's first act is filled by a flurry of redoubled misunderstanding which scholars often assume to be textual confusion or revision. This seems to me a mistake. The dramatist plainly wanted his comedy to be this way: he wanted the world he had invented to be swept through by these currents of pointless energetic bewilderment. Later, after all, he almost unwinds the villainy of the main plot before our eyes, by having the pretend-Hero address her villainous lover as 'Claudio', a naming which would have left the heroine all but guiltless. Shakespeare's change of all his sources in this main plot is important here: what they presented as evidence, he converts to mere inference. An editor once complained that the omission of the 'Window Scene' does an injustice to Claudio. Perhaps; but it was meant to. And this stress in Shakespeare's play on the insecurities of mere social inference even touches the other lovers. In the last scene, the obdurately individual Beatrice and Benedick show signs of being as near as makes no matter to a readiness to back out of each other's arms: loving each other 'no more then reason', 'in friendly recompence', taking each other 'for pittie', yielding 'upon great perswasion'.

Much Ado About Nothing reminds us, both as title and play, that, though life is indeed serious, most human beings pass much of their time in little things, unseriousness; that the ordinary, social fabric of life can be very thin, made up of trivia, and we can often feel a kind of real nothingness underneath ('hee shall live no longer in monuments, then the Bels ring, & the Window weepes... an hower in clamour and a quarter in rhewme'). Benedick's light definition of human void is a striking one, peculiarly apt in the theatrical world which has produced it, where revels are always 'now ... ended'. He evokes it in a context congenital to Shakespearean comedy, that of the presence or absence of real human feeling: love in a world which is defined as recognisably *not* 'the time of good neighbours', and in which the sound of the bells is short, of weeping even shorter.

Shakespeare's comedies are a 'Nothing' concerned with serious things: and these serious things are the principles of true human feeling, in a world in which a wise man knows that so much is nothing. To be at ease in such reflections demands at once ironic detachment and feeling participation. Consonantly, if we are trying to describe the power, the real survival-value of even the poet's earliest comedies, it has to do with his ability to bring laughter together with tenderness.

We think of Launce and his dog in *The Two Gentlemen of Verona*; of the tough slapstick of *The Taming of the Shrew*, resolving into Katherine's sober devotion; or the weeping of the angrily jealous Adriana in the brilliant fast farce of *The Comedy of Errors*. The coolest and most intellectual of aristocratic revues, *Love's Labour's Lost* ends with a father dead and Berowne sent, in the name of love, to 'move wilde laughter in the throate of death'; and it includes the memory of a girl, Katherine's sister, who died of love: 'He made her melancholy, sad, and heavy, and so she died: had she beene Light like you, of such a merrie nimble stirring spirit, she might a bin a Grandam ere she died.' Titania, similarly, in *A Midsummer Night's Dream*, tells of her loyalty to the friend who died in childbirth, like so many Elizabethan women:

> she being mortall, of that boy did die,
> And for her sake I doe reare up her boy,
> And for her sake I will not part with him.

I quoted Beatrice's 'No sure my Lord, my Mother cried.' Immediately after, with Beatrice sent out of the room, Leonato tells that, by Hero's report, Beatrice has 'often dreamt of unhappinesse, and wakt her selfe with laughing'. Something very similar might be said of Shakespeare's comedies in themselves: their character from the beginning has to do with finding a way of being 'sorrow's wag'. His art recognises the interdependence of the dark and the light in life, especially at those points of love and friendship where feeling is most acute, and often most complex. The mature comedies seek to perfect a style or condition in which happiness exists not just despite unhappiness but through it, because of it, yet charitably and sympathetically, like Patience smiling at grief. There must in the end be the co-existence, the smiling and the grief. In *The Merchant of Venice*, for all its brilliance, there is no final co-existence: something has been sacrificed to the desired achievement of extreme contrarieties, of the play of light and dark. As the sociable Bassanio has to use the lonely loving Antonio, so in the end the golden Portia must destroy the embittered, dark-housed Shylock, the greatest personage in the comedies.

It's in the art of co-existence that *Much Ado*'s supremacy lies: this, the first of Shakespeare's mature comedies in which very different human beings believably live together. Its 'dullness' (to quote Zeffirelli) is only the prosaic quality of the novel as against the poem. Yet this temperate, equable and witty world Shakespeare has created has surprising resonances, depths and possibilities. If prose is the comedy's dominant medium, the work's very coherence and inventiveness is a poetic achievement of a high kind.

That creativity is first manifested by Shakespeare's making of 'Messina'. That the dramatist calls his play's setting Messina, and makes his elderly Leonato, father to Hero and uncle to Beatrice, Governor of it, does not have to be taken too seriously—seriously in the sense of literally. 'Messina' is any romantic place lived in by rich and relatively important people. But, off the literal level, 'Messina' has extraordinary self-consistency and convincingness. The fantasy-place also functions as the grounding of the real; and, immediately below the surface, things hold together. I will give one small example from the first lines of the play: it says something about the way the poet's imagination has worked on his fantasy-place, and may even give some hint as to why Shakespeare chose this Sicilian port as his locality. *Much Ado* begins with the descent of grand visitors, heralded by formal letter and Gentleman-Messenger, on the excited and grateful Leonato: the visitors being the well-born and triumphant young warriors, Don Pedro and friends. The stage 'Messina' is thus flooded by a desired and aspired-to standard of Court behaviour, one evidenced in the battle just won (the chief occupation of a Court culture was warfare); and also in the good manners everywhere, the formal wit, the letters, the vivid sense of worldly hierarchies.

But directly this Court standard is initiated, we feel its ambiguity. Don Pedro brings with him the brother he has just defeated, the villainous Don, John. The opening words of the drama speak of the distinguished visitor by his Spanish title-he is *'Don Peter of Arragon'*; and his brother Don John's title can hardly fail to remind an Elizabethan audience of that Don John of Austria who was similarly a Spaniard, a natural son of Philip II. Oddly enough, it was at the port of Messina that the fleets gathered before the great battle of Lepanto, where 'Don John of Austria' rode 'to the wars'. Catholic Spain was at Lepanto the defender of what Renaissance Christians held to be true civilisation against the barbarian hordes of the East. But she was also the lasting, unchanging threat to English supremacy at sea—and she represented a Church thought by many of Protestant Elizabeth's subjects to be wickedly authoritarian: a double face, as the play's courtliness will shift between light and dark.

For, though Leonato welcomes Don Pedro's visit as a high honour, Don Pedro brings with him the bastard brother, Don John, the at least nominal source of all the play's troubles, his dark, surly, lonely ill-nature an interesting shadow to Don Pedro's all-too-glittering sociality. And young Claudio, Don Pedro's friend, is as amiably disagreeable as he is conventional. It is entirely unsurprising that he should later indicate his interest in Hero by making certain that she is her father's heir; that his deception by the villains should be as rapid as his consequent repentance; and that the girl he readily accepts at Leonato's hand as second bride should be 'Another Hero'. In the triviality of their love is the necessary stability of their society.

The story of his two independent individualists, Beatrice and Benedick, Shakespeare seems to have invented for himself. But the main Hero-and-Claudio plot of his play he took from the great stock of international Renaissance romance. These facts are perhaps suggestive: they may tell us something about the kind of world Shakespeare saw himself creating in this comedy of 'Much Ado'. 'Messina' is a figure for the most courtly, most worldly aspirations of ordinary people. The society of 'Messina' is governed by decorum, convention and fashion. Its only alternative, bred within itself, is the hostile isolationist Don John, the lawless brother who has determined 'not to sing in my cage'. Everyone else does sing in the cage—the cage being Leonato's great house with its arbour—full of secrets for a garden, a world of spiky high-level chatter where formal compliments intertwine with informal insults. It's not surprising that the comic policemen get the impression that the villains are led by one Deformed, a man of some fashion. Even Shakespeare himself sings in his cage: amusedly inventing at one point the babble of *Vogue* magazine, telling us that Hero's wedding-dress will be worth ten of the Dutchesse of Millaine's 'cloth a gold and cuts, and lac'd with silver, set with pearles, downe sleeves, side sleeves, and skirts, round underborn with a blewish tinsel'.

'Messina' is tinsel itself, and yet very real. It can't be satirised or politicised out of existence, nor even assumed to be a mere preserve of the rich. The constables who enter the play in its third act to resolve the problems of their nominal superiors are just as much given to chat and argument as anyone else in Messina, and as interested too in social status. They are rustic, obdurately English instead of Sicilian, and often very funny ('We will rather sleepe than talke, wee know what belongs to a Watch'—'Nothing' operates here, too). 'Messina' represents a mundane if aspiring social reality which we recognise at sight: that social world which is, as Wordsworth remarked, the 'world / Of all of us', and in it, we 'find our happiness, or not at all'. When Benedick resolves to marry, he remarks briskly that 'the world must be peopled', and we all (of course) laugh. Yet he is serious too; and this is what *Much Ado* portrays in 'Messina'—the world of people that 'must be peopled'.

This wonderfully real and recognisable world Shakespeare brings alive in the very style and structure of his comedy. 'Messina' talks a fine and formal, conversational yet mannered prose, which in the genuinely intelligent becomes admirably flexible. Only those who are unusually deeply moved (Beatrice in love, Hero's family in and after the Church Scene) speak in verse, and that not often. The play is a very Elizabethan work, yet it sometimes sounds to the ear almost like Restoration Comedy, at moments even like Wilde. Its structure has the same tacit expressiveness. The action falls naturally into Messina's large crowded scenes of social encounter—the opening arrival of the soldiers, the evening dance in mask, the church wedding, the final celebration. It is because of these thronged and bustling scenes that the moment when Benedick and Beatrice speak their love to each other, left alone on the stage after the interrupted marriage, has such startling effect.

Despite the eventfulness of what we call the main plot, nothing really happens to the more social characters of the play, who are precisely defined as people to whom nothing can happen (hence, 'Another Hero'). Late in the play, after Hero has been cruelly rejected on her wedding-day and is believed to be dead by all but her family and friends, there is a decidedly subtle and embarrassing encounter between the young men, as Don Pedro and Claudio think to take up again their old verbal teasing of Benedick, and can't realise by how much he has now outgrown it. This unawareness is the continuity of the social, the process by which it survives: 'Messina' lives in a perpetual present, where salvation depends on the power to forget. It has all been, after all, 'Much Ado About Nothing'. And yet there is of course an exception to this. Beatrice and Benedick do change. And the index of this change, their falling in love, is the great subject of the comedy.

Beatrice and Benedick are most certainly inhabitants of Messina. Hero's cousin and Claudio's friend, they belong in their world, possessed by a social realism summed up in Beatrice's 'I can see a Church by daylight.' Moreover, there is a real sense in which we are glad to see the cousins and friends join hands again at the end of the play, with a sensible patient warmth foreshadowing that romantic yet worldly wisdom which keeps the families joined, if at some distance, at the end of *Pride and Prejudice*.

Yet Beatrice and Benedick do still change. Modern Shakespeareans who work assiduously to banish this change, to work the hero and heroine back into those borders of the action from which they come, seem to me to be in serious error, and to be breaking the back of a work of art. *Much Ado*'s very originality of action and structure, that power of mind which animates Shakespeare's lightest comedies, here depends on the growing importance of two people who, though their intelligence gives them authority from the beginning, are socially on the margins of the action, subordinate in interest to the possibly younger Hero and Claudio. But, where the trick played on Claudio by Don John destroys his shallow love for Hero, Don Pedro's fooling only releases real depths of feeling in Beatrice and Benedick, the two unsociable individuals who think themselves determined to resist the enforcements of matrimony.

There has been in much recent criticism a comparable resistance to the originality of *Much Ado* itself, one evidenced by the repeated insistence that Beatrice and Benedick do not change and fall in love in the course of the play: they are (the argument goes) in love when it begins. Again, I have to say that I find this near-universal assumption entirely mistaken. Despite all the sophisticated techniques of the modern psychological novel, the analysis of actual human feeling often lags far behind Shakespeare still. Beatrice and Benedick begin their play attracted to each other, but not in love. Both are children of 'Messina'; both play its games; both belong to a social world for which such attraction is an ordinary datum of experience. 'Messina' assumes that men and women are always after each other and always betraying each other: 'Men were deceivers ever'; and Benedick joins in with Leonato's social by-play of distrusting his own child's legitimacy.

But both from the first see beyond, and through, the merely social, as Benedick really prefers 'my simple true judgement' to what he is 'professed' or supposed to think. This soldierly preference for sincerity suggests that he might similarly like to be truly in love with Beatrice. But he isn't. When he finally does fall, he is honest enough—in a fashion both comic and heroic—to tell her how 'strange' he finds it to feel so much. Earlier, though, what has angered Beatrice is this sense of a mere conditionality in Benedick, which might never have become fact. With an allusive dimension of past and future which distinguishes the two senior lovers from the rest of timeless Messina, Beatrice has two curious references to time past which have puzzled critics. She tells of the moment when Benedick 'challenged Cupid at the Flight', and was in turn challenged by Leonato's fool. This narrative anecdote works, I believe, as a conceit of analysis, a definition for a pre-psychological age: she is saying that Benedick may think his resistance to love so clever and aristocratic, but really it is just stupid. This is Beatrice the 'odious woman', descended from Katherine the Shrew; but Shakespeare has deepened the moment and justified the rudeness. With a touch of Lear's Fool in her, Beatrice is the true human heart, struggling against the mere manners of Messina.

And this becomes plainer in her Second-Act answer to Don Pedro, who tells her she has 'lost the heart of Signior *Benedicke*':

> Indeed my Lord, hee lent it me a while, and I gave him use for it, a
> double heart for a single one, marry once before he wonne it of mee,
> with false dice, therefore your Grace may well say I have lost it.

This is less private history than a fine open act of analysis. Beatrice describes what the courtly Don Pedro, without knowing it, means by 'heart': a world of mere lending and borrowing, a scene of mere winning and losing. The dice are false. Charmingly, wittily and sometimes politely, Beatrice is looking for something else again. Her brisk, tough and cool character belongs—and this is Shakespeare's profound insight, in the most psychologically interesting romantic comedy he has yet written—to one of the most romantic and idealistic of human beings. But she isn't intending to discuss her heart in Messina, a world which is, in her own words, 'civill as an Orange, and something of a jealous complexion'.

With these views, Beatrice may well, as she knows herself, 'sit in a corner and cry, heigh ho for a husband'. And Benedick is as true an individual as herself. Despite the friendly effervescence of his successful social being, there is another Benedick who is most himself when he 'sits in a corner'. In a curious small scene (2.3) he complains of the change in Claudio: and his soliloquy is prefaced, in a way that editions don't explain, by his sending of his boy to fetch the book 'in my chamber window' for him to read 'in the orchard'. The vividness of this is on a par with the thorough realism elsewhere in *Much Ado*: and it throws up a sudden image of the solitude of the real Benedick, whom we see when no one else is there. The book in the hand is for Elizabethans a symbol of the solitary.

In short, here are two people who could easily have remained divided from each other, in a state of irritated or quietly melancholy resentment at themselves and at life. This Elizabethan comedy brings alive what we may think of as a datum of peculiarly modern experience, the randomness, the accidentality of existence: the fact that many things in the life of feeling remain 'a perpetual possibility / Only in a world of speculation'. Attraction starts up socially but there need be no happy endings; there is only 'Much Ado About Nothing', a waste of wishes and desires.

The two difficult lovers owe much to the courtiers for bringing them together, a debt which justifies the forgivingness of the last scene. Yet neither Beatrice nor Benedick is precisely dependent on the tricks of a trivial milieu for their feeling. Orthodox Elizabethans believed that God indeed made 'Much' out of 'Nothing', the Creation out of Void. The change of these two intelligent and principled lovers asks to be comparably explained. They come together over the quasi-dead body of Hero, at the end of the Church Scene. They are, that is to say, drawn together by their shared sympathy for the wronged girl. It is this tertium quid outside themselves that permits Benedick to say at last, 'I do love nothing in the world so well as you, is not that strange?' and Beatrice to answer, 'As strange as the thing I know not, it were as possible for me to say, I loved nothing so well as you.'

I am hoping to suggest that there is a paradox here not far from the oddity of 'sorrow's wag'. The moment is so romantic because not romantic—or not so in the Messina sense; it is the true romanticism of the real. Benedick is at heart a kind man, which to Elizabethans meant 'kinned', 'brotherly'. He is deeply grateful to Beatrice, and besides can't bear to watch her crying. All this, on top of her usual attraction for him. She responds in precisely the same way, not merely changing the subject when she says firmly: 'I am sorry for my cousin.' It's as if she were drawing up the rule-book for the rest of their lives. Both Beatrice and Benedick are individuals who have feared love because it means so much to them; when they do lose their heart, as here, it won't be a 'double' one, in the sense of *dishonest*. What brings them together at last is neither trick nor fluke, but the conjunction of shared principle—a principle which depends on their independence, even their loneliness as human beings. As a result, their professions of love are deep with risk and danger, which is why their bond is involved with a girl in some sense dead, and why Beatrice must ask Benedick to 'Kill *Claudio*'. He doesn't, and it's as well that he doesn't obey the whim of a wildly angry woman. But he's ready to. There is therefore a kind of death in their love, for both of them. 'Sitting in the corner' is the posture of a prizefighter or duellist; when the two advance to the centre, someone may lose, and something must die. There is a delightful, comic, humorous charm and truth in the fact that, as soon as the trick is afoot and love declared, both start to feel terrible: Benedick gets toothache and Beatrice a fearful cold. Many critics assume a pretence on their part, but I think not.

When Shakespeare borrowed his immensely widely disseminated main-plot story from many sources, he did something strange to it. He used a legend that turned on strong evidence of infidelity, and he took the evidence away. There is no 'Window-Scene' in our comedy. The poet has thereby transformed a tale of jealousy into something much nearer to a definition of love, which asks the question: 'How in the world do we ever *know*?' The answer of *Much Ado* is: 'By whatever we take to be the dead body of Hero'—a character whose very name is suggestive. Leaving aside the Leander-loss, we may say that in *Much Ado About Nothing* one kind of hero and heroine is replaced by another. Comparably, one kind of social, winning-and-losing false-dicing love finds itself quietly upstaged by something quite different: a feeling intensely romantic, because involving real individuals, yet grounding itself on something as sober, or we could even say 'dull', as an extreme and responsible human kindness. And the true lovers are kind, to each other and others, because they are aware that life necessitates it even from the romantic. They are both, that is to say, sorrow's wags.

Beatrice and Benedick, 'sitting in the corner' of life, each resent marriage because they are helplessly individual beings. But their very independence and individuality, their corner-view, gives them what no one else in the comedy really has—truth of feeling. Their thinking and feeling for themselves has as its high-water-mark that famous moment, already quoted, at which Beatrice, always quick off the mark, thinks almost too much for herself. As she weeps angrily in the church after Hero's rejection, Benedick makes his vital move—he lets Don Pedro's party leave without him, and stays to comfort Beatrice, asking gently if he can help her. Yes, she says, he can; he can kill Claudio. The play is a comedy precisely because Benedick, always the sounder in sizing up the mark he is being asked to get off, doesn't have to kill Claudio; and we can hardly regret the fact that 'Messina' survives. Here is a co-existence we can like as well as finding likely. But we can't regret either the two individuals who are, as Benedick says, 'Too wise to wooe peaceablie'. The comedy needs their wisdom, just as it needs the constables' folly. Intensely romantic, therefore, as well as consistently funny, *Much Ado* is serious in its concerns while always wearing the air of being entertainingly 'About Nothing'.

WILLIAM HAZLITT

Shakespeare's Characters:
Henry V and Coriolanus

HENRY V

Henry V is a very favourite monarch with the English nation, and he appears to have been also a favourite with Shakespeare, who labours hard to apologize for the actions of the king, by showing us the character of the man, as 'the kind of good fellows'. He scarcely deserves this honour. He was fond of war and low company:—we know little else of him. He was careless, dissolute, and ambitious—idle, or doing mischief. In private, he seemed to have no idea of the common decencies of life, which he subjected to a kind of regal license; in public affairs, he seemed to have no idea of any rule of right or wrong, but brute force, glossed over with a little religious hypocrisy and archiepiscopal advice. His principles did not change with his situation and professions. His adventure on Gadshill was a prelude to the affair of Agincourt, only a bloodless one; Falstaff was a puny prompter of violence and outrage, compared with the pious and politic Archbishop of Canterbury, who gave the king *carte blanche*, in a genealogical tree of his family, to rob and murder in circles of latitude and longitude abroad—to save the possessions of the Church at home. This appears in the speeches in Shakespeare, where the linden motives that actuate princes and their advisers in war and policy are better laid open than in speeches from the throne or woolsack. Henry, because he did not know how to govern his own kingdom, determined to make war upon his neighbours. Because his own title to the crown was doubtful, he laid claim to that of France. Because he did not know

From *Characters of Shakespeare's Plays*. © 1916 by Oxford University Press.

how to exercise the enormous power, which had just dropped into his hands, to any one good purpose, he immediately undertook (a cheap and obvious resource of sovereignty) to do all the mischief he could. Even if absolute monarchs had the wit to find out objects of laudable ambition, they could only 'plume up their wills' in adhering to the more sacred formula of the royal prerogative, 'the right divine of kings to govern wrong,' because will is only then triumphant when it is opposed to the will of others, because the pride of power is only then shown, not when it consults the rights and interests of others, but when it insults and tramples on all justice and all humanity. Henry declares his resolution 'when France is his, to bend it to his awe, or break it all to pieces'—a resolution worthy of a conqueror, to destroy all that he cannot enslave; and what adds to the joke, he lays all the blame of the consequences of his ambition on those who will not submit tamely to his tyranny. Such is the history of kingly power, from the beginning to the end of the world—with this difference, that the object of war formerly, when the people adhered to their allegiance, was to depose kings; the object latterly, since the people swerved from their allegiance, has been to restore kings, and to make common cause against mankind. The object of our late invasion and conquest of France was to restore the legitimate monarch, the descendant of Hugh Capet, to the throne: Henry V in his time made war on and deposed the descendant of this very Hugh Capet, on the plea that he was a usurper and illegitimate. What would the great modern catspaw of legitimacy and restorer of divine right have said to the claim of Henry and the title of the descendants of Hugh Capet? Henry V, it is true, was a hero, a king of England, and the conqueror of the king of France. Yet we feel little love or admiration for him. He was a hero, that is, he was ready to sacrifice his own life for the pleasure of destroying thousands of other lives: he was a king of England, but not a constitutional one, and we only like kings according to the law; lastly, he was a conqueror of the French king, and for this we dislike him less than if he had conquered the French people. How then do we like him? We like him in the play. There he is a very amiable monster, a very splendid pageant. As we like to gaze at a panther or a young lion in their cages in the Tower, and catch a pleasing horror from their glistening eyes, their velvet paws, and dreadless roar, so we take a very romantic, heroic, patriotic, and poetical delight in the boasts and feats of our younger Harry, as they appear on the stage and are confined to lines of ten syllables; where no blood follows the stroke that wounds our ears, where no harvest bends beneath horses' hoofs, no city flames, no little child is butchered, no dead men's bodies are found-piled on heaps and festering the next morning-in the orchestra!

So much for the politics of this play; now for the poetry. Perhaps one of the most striking images in all Shakespeare is that given of war in the first lines of the Prologue.

O for a muse of fire, that would ascend
The brightest heaven of invention,

A kingdom for a stage, princes to act,
And monarchs to behold the swelling scene!
Then should the warlike Harry, like himself,
Assume the port of Mars, and *at his heels*
Leash'd in like hounds, should famine, sword, and fire
Crouch for employment.

Rubens, if he had painted it, would not have improved upon this simile.

The conversation between the Archbishop of Canterbury and the Bishop of Ely relating to the sudden change in the manners of Henry V is among the well-known *Beauties* of Shakespeare. It is indeed admirable both for strength and grace. It has sometimes occurred to us that Shakespeare, in describing 'the reformation' of the Prince, might have had an eye to himself—

Which is a wonder how his grace should glean it,
Since his addiction was to courses vain,
His companies unletter'd, rude and shallow,
His hours fill'd up with riots, banquets, sports;
And never noted in him any study,
Any retirement, any sequestration
From open haunts and popularity.
  Ely. The strawberry grows underneath the nettle,
And wholesome berries thrive and ripen best
Neighbour'd by fruit of baser quality
And so the prince obscur'd his contemplation
Under the veil of wildness, which no doubt
Grew like the summer-grass, fastest by night,
Unseen, yet crescive in his faculty.

This at least is as probable an account of the progress of the poet's mind as we have met with in any of the Essays on the Learning of Shakespeare.

Nothing can be better managed than the caution which the king gives the meddling Archbishop, not to advise him rashly to engage in the war with France, his scrupulous dread of the consequences of that advice, and his eager desire to hear and follow it.

And God forbid, my dear and faithful lord,
That you should fashion, wrest, or bow your reading,
Or nicely charge your understanding soul
With opening titles miscreate, whose right
Suits not in native colours with the truth.
For God doth know how many now in health
Shall drop their blood, in approbation

Of what your reverence shall incite us to.
Therefore take heed how you impawn your person,
How you awake our sleeping sword of war;
We charge you in the name of God, take heed.
For never two such kingdoms did contend
Without much fall of blood, whose guiltless drops
Are every one a woe, a sore complaint
'Gainst him, whose wrong gives edge unto the swords
That make such waste in brief mortality.
Under this conjuration, speak, my lord;
For we will hear, note, and believe in heart,
That what you speak, is in your conscience wash'd,
As pure as sin with baptism.

Another characteristic instance of the blindness of human nature to everything but its own interests is the complaint made by the king of 'the ill neighbourhood' of the Scot in attacking England when she was attacking France.

For once the eagle England being in prey,
To her unguarded nest the weazel Scot
'Comes sneaking, and so sucks her princely eggs.

It is worth observing that in all these plays, which give an admirable picture of the spirit of the *good old times*, the moral inference does not at all depend upon the nature of the actions, but on the dignity or meanness of the persons committing them. 'The eagle England' has a right 'to be in prey', but 'the weazel Scot' has none 'to come sneaking to her nest', which she has left to pounce upon others. Might was right, without equivocation or disguise, in that heroic and chivalrous age. The substitution of right for might, even in theory, is among the refinements and abuses of modern philosophy.

A more beautiful rhetorical delineation of the effects of subordination in a commonwealth can hardly be conceived than the following:

For government, though high and low and lower,
Put into parts, doth keep in one consent,
Congruing in a full and natural close,
Like music.
            —Therefore heaven doth divide
The state of man in divers functions,
Setting endeavour in continual motion;
To which is fixed, as an aim or butt,
Obedience: for so work the honey bees;
Creatures that by a rule in nature, teach

The art of order to a peopled kingdom.
They have a king, and officers of sorts
Where some, like magistrates, correct at home;
Others, like merchants, venture trade abroad;
Others, like soldiers, armed in their stings,
Make boot upon the summer's velvet buds
Which pillage they with merry march bring home
To the tent-royal of their emperor;
Who, busied in his majesty, surveys
The singing mason building roofs of gold;
The civil citizens kneading up the honey;
The poor mechanic porters crowding in
Their heavy burthens at his narrow gate;
The sad-eyed justice, with his surly hum,
Delivering o'er to executors pale
The lazy yawning drone. I this infer,—
That many things, having full reference
To one consent, may work contrariously
As many arrows, loosed several ways,—
Fly to one mark;
As many several ways meet in one town;
As many fresh streams meet in one salt sea;
As many lines close in the dial's centre;
So may a thousand actions, once a-foot,
End in one purpose, and be all well borne
Without defeat.

Henry V is but one of Shakespeare's second-rate plays. Yet by quoting passages, like this, from his second-rate plays alone, we might make a volume 'rich with his praise,'

As is the oozy bottom of the sea
With sunken wrack and sumless treasuries.

Of this sort are the king's remonstrance to Scroop, Grey, and Cambridge, on the detection of their treason, his address to the soldiers at the siege of Harfleur, and the still finer one before the battle of Agincourt, the description of the night before the battle, and the reflections on ceremony put into the mouth of the king.

O hard condition; twin-born with greatness,
Subjected to the breath of every fool,
Whose sense no more can feel but his own wringing!

What infinite heart's ease must kings neglect,
That private men enjoy? and what have kings,
That privates have not too, save ceremony?
Save general ceremony?
And what art thou, thou idol ceremony?
What kind of god art thou, that suffer'st more
Of mortal griefs, than do thy worshippers?
What are thy rents? what are thy comings-in?
O ceremony, show me but thy worth!
What is thy soul, O adoration?
Art thou aught else but place, degree, and form,
Creating awe and fear in other men?
Wherein thou art less happy, being feared,
Than they in fearing.
What drink'st thou oft, instead of homage sweet,
But poison'd flattery? O, be sick, great greatness,
And bid thy ceremony give thee cure!
Think'st thou, the fiery fever will go out
With titles blown from adulation?
Will it give place to flexure and low bending?
Can'st thou, when thou command'st the beggar's knee,
Command the health of it? No, thou proud dream,
That play'st so subtly with a king's repose,
I am a king, that find thee: and I know,
'Tis not the balm, the sceptre, and the ball,
The sword, the mace, the crown imperial,
The enter-tissu'd robe of gold and pearl,
The farsed title running 'fore the king,
The throne he sits on, nor the tide of pomp
That beats upon the high shore of this world,
No, not all these, thrice-gorgeous ceremony,
Not all these, laid in bed majestical,
Can sleep so soundly as the wretched slave;
Who, with a body fill'd, and vacant mind,
Gets him to rest, cramm'd with distressful bread,
Never sees horrid night, the child of hell:
But, like a lacquey, from the rise to set,
Sweats in the eye of Phoebus, and all night
Sleeps in Elysium; next day, after dawn,
Doth rise, and help Hyperion to his horse;
And follows so the ever-running year
With profitable labour, to his grave
And, but for ceremony, such a wretch,

Winding up days with toil, and nights with sleep,
Has the forehand and vantage of a king.
The slave, a member of the country's peace,
Enjoys it; but in gross brain little wots,
What watch the king keeps to maintain the peace,
Whose hours the peasant best advantages.

Most of these passages are well known: there is. one, which we do not remember to have seen noticed, and yet it is no whit inferior to the rest in heroic beauty. It is the account of the deaths of York and Suffolk.

> *Exeter.* The duke of York commends him to your majesty.
> *K. Henry.* Lives he, good uncle? thrice within this hour,
> I saw him down; thrice up again, and fighting;
> From helmet to the spur all blood he was.
> *Exeter.* In which array (brave soldier) doth he lie,
> Larding the plain: and by his bloody side
> (Yoke-fellow to his honour-owing wounds)
> The noble earl of Suffolk also lies.
> Suffolk first died: and York, all haggled o'er,
> Comes to him, where in gore he lay insteep'd,
> And takes him by the beard; kisses the gashes,
> That bloodily did yawn upon his face;
> And cries aloud—*Tarry, dear cousin Suffolk!*
> *My soul shall thine keep company to heaven:*
> *Tarry, sweet soul, for mine, then fly a-breast;*
> *As, in this glorious and well foughten field,*
> *We kept together in our chivalry!*
> Upon these words I came, and cheer'd him up:
> He smil'd me in the face, raught me his hand,
> And, with a feeble gripe, says—*Dear my lord,*
> *Commend my service to my sovereign.*
> So did he turn, and over Suffolk's neck
> He threw his wounded arm, and kiss'd his lips;
> And so, espous'd to death, with blood he seal'd
> A testament of noble-ending love.

But we must have done with splendid quotations. The behaviour of the king, in the difficult and doubtful circumstances in which he is placed, is as patient and modest as it is spirited and lofty in his prosperous fortune. The character of the French nobles is also very admirably depicted; and the Dauphin's praise of his horse shows the vanity of that class of persons in a very striking point of view. Shakespeare always accompanies a foolish prince with a satirical courtier, as we see in this instance. The comic parts of *Henry V* are very inferior to those of *Henry IV*. Falstaff is dead, and without him, Pistol, Nym, and Bardolph are satellites without a sun. Fluellen the Welshman is the most entertaining character in the piece. He is good-natured, brave, choleric, and pedantic. His parallel between Alexander and Harry of Monmouth, and his desire to have 'some disputations' with Captain Macmorris on the discipline of the Roman wars, in the heat of the battle, are never to be forgotten. His treatment of Pistol is as good as Pistol's treatment of his French prisoner. There are two other remarkable prose passages in this play: the conversation of Henry in disguise with the three sentinels on the duties of a soldier, and his courtship of Katherine in broken French. We like them both exceedingly, though the first savours perhaps too much of the king, and the last too little of the lover.

CORIOLANUS

Shakespeare has in this play shown himself well versed in history and state affairs. *Coriolanus* is a store-house of political commonplaces. Any one who studies it may save himself the trouble of reading Burke's *Reflections*, or Paine's *Rights of Man*, or the Debates in both Houses of Parliament since the French Revolution or our own. The arguments for and against aristocracy or democracy, on the privileges of the few and the claims of the many, on liberty and slavery, power and the abuse of it, peace and war, are here very ably handled, with the spirit of a poet and the acuteness of a philosopher. Shakespeare himself seems to have had a leaning to the arbitrary side of the question, perhaps from some feeling of contempt for his own origin; and to have spared no occasion of baiting the rabble. What he says of them is very true: what he says of their betters is also very true, though he dwells less upon it.—The cause of the people is indeed but little calculated as a subject for poetry: it admits of rhetoric, which goes into argument and explanation; put it presents no immediate or distinct images to the mind, 'no jutting frieze, buttress, or coigne of vantage' for poetry 'to make its pendant bed and procreant cradle in'. The language of poetry naturally falls in with the language or power. The imagination is an exaggerating and exclusive faculty: it takes from one thing to add to another: it accumulates circumstances together to give the greatest possible effect to a favourite object. The understanding is a dividing and measuring faculty: it judges of things, not according to their immediate impression on the mind, but according to their relations to one another. The one is a monopolizing faculty, which seeks the greatest quantity of present excitement by inequality and disproportion; the other is a distributive faculty, which seeks the greatest quantity of ultimate good, by justice and proportion. The one is an aristocratical, the other a republican faculty. The principle of poetry is a very anti-levelling principle. It aims at effect, it exists by contrast. It admits of no medium. It is everything by excess. It rises above the ordinary standard of sufferings and crimes. It presents a dazzling appearance. It shows its head turretted, crowned, and crested. Its front is gilt and blood-stained. Before it 'it carries noise, and behind it tears'. It has its altars and its victims, sacrifices, human sacrifices. Kings, priests, nobles, are its train-bearers, tyrants and slaves its executioners. 'Carnage is its daughter.' Poetry is right-royal. It puts the individual for the species, the one above the infinite many, might before right. A lion hunting a flock of sheep or a herd of wild asses is a more poetical object than they; and we even take part with the lordly beast, because our vanity or some other feeling makes us disposed to place ourselves in the situation of the strongest party. So we feel some concern for the poor citizens of Rome when they meet together to compare their wants and grievances, till Coriolanus comes in and with blows and big words drives this set of 'poor rats', this rascal scum, to their homes and beggary before him. There is nothing heroical in a multitude of miserable rogues not wishing to be starved, or complaining that they are like to be so: but when a single man comes forward to brave their cries and to make them submit to the last indignities, from mere pride and self-will, our admiration of his prowess is immediately converted into contempt for their pusillanimity. The insolence of power is stronger than the plea of necessity. The tame submission to usurped authority or even the natural resistance to it has nothing to excite or flatter the imagination: it is that assumption of a right to insult or oppress others that carries an imposing air of superiority with it We had rather be the oppressor than the oppressed. The love of power in ourselves and the admiration of it in others are both natural to man: the one makes him a tyrant, the other a slave. Wrong dressed out in pride, pomp, and circumstance has more Attraction than abstract right.—Coriolanus complains of the fickleness of the people: yet the instant he cannot gratify his pride and obstinacy at their expense, he turns his arms against his country. If his country was not worth defending, why did he build his pride on its defence? He is a conqueror and a hero; he conquers other countries, and makes this a plea for enslaving his own; and when he is prevented from doing so, he leagues with its enemies to destroy his country. He rates the people 'as if he were a God to punish, and not a man of their infirmity'. He scoffs at one of their tribunes for maintaining their rights and franchises: 'Mark you his absolute *shall?*' not marking his own absolute will to take everything from them, his impatience of the slightest opposition to his own pretensions being in proportion to their arrogance and absurdity. If the great and powerful had the beneficence and wisdom of Gods, then all this would have been well: if with a greater knowledge of what is good for the people, they had as great a care for their interest as they have themselves, if they were seated above the world, sympathizing with the welfare, but not feeling the passions of men, receiving neither good nor hurt from them, but bestowing their benefits as free gifts on them, they might then rule over them like another Providence. But this is not the case. Coriolanus is unwilling that the senate should show their 'cares' for the people, lest their 'cares' should be construed into 'fears', to the subversion of all due authority; and he is no sooner disappointed in his schemes to deprive the people not only of the cares of the state, but of all power to redress themselves, than Volumnia is made madly to exclaim

> Now the red pestilence strike all trades in Rome,
> And occupations perish.

This is but natural: it is but natural for a mother to have more regard for her son than for a whole city; but then the city should be left to take some care of itself. The care of the state cannot, we here see, be safely entrusted to maternal affection, or to the domestic charities of high life. The great have private feelings of their own, to which the interests of humanity and justice must curtsy. Their interests are so far from being the same as those of the community, that they are in direct and necessary opposition to them; their power is at the expense of our weakness; their riches of our poverty; their pride of our degradation; their splendour of our wretchedness; their tyranny of *our* servitude. If they had the superior knowledge ascribed to them (which they have not) it would only render them so much more formidable; and from Gods would convert them into Devils. The whole dramatic moral of *Coriolanus* is that those who have little shall have less, and that those who have much shall take all that others have left. The people are poor; therefore they ought to be starved. They are slaves; therefore they ought to be beaten. They work hard; therefore they ought to be treated like beasts of burden. They are ignorant; therefore they ought not to be allowed to feel that they want food, or clothing, or rest, that they are enslaved, oppressed, and miserable. This is the logic of the imagination and the passions; which seek to aggrandize what excites admiration and to heap contempt on misery, to raise power into tyranny, and to make tyranny absolute; to thrust down that which is low still lower, and to make wretches desperate: to exalt magistrates into kings, kings into gods; to degrade subjects to the rank of slaves, and slaves to the condition of brutes. The history of mankind is a romance, a mask, a tragedy, constructed upon the principles of *poetical justice*; it is a noble or royal hunt, in which what is sport to the few is death to the many, and in which the spectators halloo and encourage the strong to set upon the weak, and cry havoc in the chase, though they do not share in the spoil. We may depend upon it that what men delight to read in books, they will put in practice in reality.

One of the most natural traits in this play is the difference of the interest taken in the success of Coriolanus by his wife and mother. The one is only anxious for his honour; the other is fearful for his life.

> *Volumnia.* Methinks I hither hear your husband's drum:
> I see him pluck Aufidius down by th' hair
> Methinks I see him stamp thus—and call thus—
> Come on, ye cowards; ye were got in fear

Though you were born in Rome; his bloody brow
With his mail'd hand then wiping, forth he goes
Like to a harvest man, that's tasked to mow
Or all, or lose his hire.
    Virgilia. His bloody brow! Oh Jupiter, no blood.
    Volumnia. Away, you fool; it more becomes a man
Than gilt his trophy. The breast of Hecuba,
When she did suckle Hector, looked not lovelier
Than Hector's forehead, when it spit forth blood
At Grecian swords contending.

When she hears the trumpets that proclaim her son's return, she says in the true spirit of a Roman matron:

These are the ushers of Martius: before him
He carries noise, and behind him he leaves tears.
Death, that dark spirit, in's nervy arm doth lie,
Which being advanced, declines, and then men die.

Coriolanus himself is a complete character: his love of reputation, his contempt of popular opinion, his pride and modesty, are consequences of each other. His pride consists in the inflexible sternness of his will: his love of glory is a determined desire to bear down all opposition and to extort the admiration both of friends and foes. His contempt for popular favour, his unwillingness to hear his own praises, spring from the same source. He cannot contradict the praises that are bestowed upon him; therefore he is impatient at hearing them. He would enforce the good opinion of others by his actions, but does not want their acknowledgements in words.

Pray now, no more: my mother,
Who has a charter to extol her blood,
When she does praise me, grieves me.

His magnanimity is of the same kind. He admires in an enemy that courage which he honours in himself: he places himself on the hearth of Aufidius with the same confidence that he would have met him in the field, and feels that by putting himself in his power, he takes from him all temptation for using it against him.

In the title-page of *Coriolanus* it is said at the bottom of the Dramatis Personae, 'The whole history exactly followed, and many of the principal speeches copied from the life of Coriolanus in Plutarch.' It will be interesting to our readers to see how far this is the case. Two of the principal scenes, those between Coriolanus and Aufidius and between Coriolanus and his mother, are thus given in Sir Thomas North's translation of Plutarch, dedicated to Queen Elizabeth, 1579. The first is as follows:

It was even twilight when he entered the city of Antim, and many people met him in the streets, but no man knew him. So he went directly to Tullus Aufidius' house, and when he came thither, he got him up straight to the chimney-hearth, and sat him down, and spake not a word to any man, his face all muffled over. They of the house spying him, wondered what he should be, and yet they durst not bid him rise. For ill-favouredly muffled and disguised as he was, yet there appeared a certain majesty in his countenance and in his silence: whereupon they went to Tullus, who was at supper, to tell him of the strange disguising of this man. Tullus rose presently from the board, and coming towards him, asked him what he was, and wherefore he came. Then Martius unmuffled himself, and after he had paused awhile, making no answer, he said unto himself, If thou knowest me not yet, Tullus, and seeing me, dost not perhaps believe me to be the man I am indeed, I must of necessity discover myself to be that I am. 'I am Caius Martius, who hath done to thyself particularly, and to all the Volsces generally, great hurt and mischief, which I cannot deny for my surname of Coriolanus that I bear. For I never had other benefit nor recompence of the true and painful service I have done, and the extreme dangers I have been in, but this only surname: a good memory and witness of the malice and displeasure thou shouldest bear me. Indeed the name only remaineth with me; for the rest, the envy and cruelty of the people of Rome have taken from me, by the sufferance of the dastardly nobility and magistrates, who have forsaken me, and let me be banished by the people. This extremity hath now driven me to come as a poor suitor, to take thy chimney-hearth, not of any hope I have to save my life thereby. For if I had feared death, I would not have come hither to put myself in hazard: but pricked forward with desire to be revenged of them that thus have banished me, which now I do begin, in putting my person into the hands of their enemies. Wherefore if thou hast any heart to be wrecked of the injuries thy enemies have done thee, speed thee now, and let my misery serve thy turn, and so use it as my service may be a benefit to the Volsces: promising thee, that I will fight with better good will for all you, than I did when I was against you, knowing that they fight more valiantly who know the force of the enemy, than such as have never proved it. And if it be so that thou dare not, and that thou art weary to prove fortune any more, then am I also weary to live any longer. And it were no wisdom in thee to save the life of him who hath been heretofore thy mortal enemy, and whose service now can nothing help, nor pleasure thee.' Tullus hearing what he said, was a marvellous glad man, and taking him by the hand, he said unto him 'Stand up, O Martius, and be of good cheer, for in proffering thyself unto us, thou doest us great honour and by this means thou mayest hope also of greater things at all the Volsces' hands.' So he feasted him for that time, and entertained him in the honourablest manner he could, talking with him of no other matter at that present: but within few days after, they fell to consultation together in what sort they should begin their wars.

The meeting between Coriolanus and his mother is also nearly the same as in the play.

Now was Martius set then in the chair of state, with all the honours of a general, and when he had spied the women coming afar off, he marvelled what the matter meant: but afterwards knowing his wife which came foremost, he determined at the first to persist in his obstinate and inflexible rancour. But overcome in the end with natural affection, and being altogether altered to see them, his heart would not serve him to tarry their coming to his chair, but coming down in haste, he went to meet them, and first he kissed his mother, and embraced her a pretty while, then his wife and little children. And nature so wrought with him, that the tears fell from his eyes, and he could not keep himself from making much of them, but yielded to the affection of his blood, as if he had been violently carried with the fury of a most swift-running stream. After he had thus lovingly received them, and perceiving that his mother Volumnia would begin to speak to him, he called the chiefest of the council of the Volsces to hear what she would say. Then she spake in this sort 'If we held our peace, my son, and determined not to speak, the state of our poor bodies, and present sight of our raiment, would easily betray to thee what life we have led at home, since thy exile and abode abroad; but think now with thyself, how much more unfortunate than all the women living, we are come hither, considering that the sight which should be most pleasant to all others to behold, spiteful fortune had made most fearful to us: making myself to see my son, and my daughter here her husband, besieging the walls of his native country: so as that which is the only comfort to all others in their adversity and misery, to pray unto the Gods, and to call to them for aid, is the only thing which plungeth us into most deep perplexity. For we cannot, alas, together pray, both for victory to our country, and for safety of thy life also: but a world of grievous curses, yea more than any mortal enemy can heap upon us, are forcibly wrapped up in our prayers. For the bitter sop of most hard choice is offered thy wife and children, to forgo one of the two: either to lose the person of thyself, or the nurse of their native country. For myself, my son, I am determined not to tarry till fortune in my lifetime do make an end of this war. For if I cannot persuade the rather to do good unto both parties, than to overthrow and destroy the one, preferring love and nature before the malice and preferring of wars, thou shalt see, my son, and trust unto it, thou shalt no sooner march forward to assault thy country, but thy foot shall tread upon thy mother's womb, that brought thee first into this world. And I may not defer to see the day, either that my son be led prisoner in triumph by his natural countrymen, or that he himself do triumph of them, and of his natural country. For if it were so, that my request tended to save the country, in destroying the Volsces, I must confess, thou wouldest hardly and doubtfully resolve on that. For as to destroy thy natural country, it is altogether unmeet and unlawful, so were it not just and less honourable to betray those that put their trust in thee. But my only demand consisteth, to make a gaol delivery of all evils, which delivereth equal benefit and safety, both to the one and the other, but most honourable for the Volsces. For it shall appear, that having victory in their hands, they have of special favour-granted us singular graces, peace and amity, albeit themselves have no less part of both than we. Of which good, if so it came to pass, thyself is the only author, and so halt thou the only honour. But if it fail, and fall out contrary, thyself alone deservedly shalt carry the shameful reproach and burthen of either party. So, though the end of war be uncertain, yet this notwithstanding is most certain, that if it be thy chance to conquer, this benefit shalt thou reap of thy goodly conquest, to be chronicled the plague and destroyer of thy country. And if fortune overthrow thee, then the world will say, that through desire to revenge thy private injuries, thou hast for ever undone thy good friends, who did most lovingly and courteously receive thee.' Martius gave good ear unto his mother's words, without interrupting her speech at all, and after she had said what she would, he held his peace a pretty while, and answered not a word. Hereupon she began again to speak unto him, and said 'My son, why dost thou not answer me? Dost thou think it good altogether to give place unto thy choler and desire of revenge, and thinkest thou it not honesty for thee to grant thy mother's request in so weighty a cause? Dost thou take it honourable for a nobleman, to remember the wrongs and injuries done him, and dost not in like case think it an honest nobleman's part to be thankful for the goodness that parents do show to their children, acknowledging the duty and reverence they ought to bear unto them? No man living is more bound to show himself thankful in all parts and respects than thyself; who so universally showiest all ingratitude. Moreover, my son, thou hast sorely taken of thy country, exacting grievous payments upon them, in revenge of the injuries offered thee; besides, thou hast not hitherto showed thy poor mother any courtesy. And therefore it is not only honest, but due unto me, that without compulsion I should obtain my so just and reasonable request of thee. But since by reason I cannot persuade thee to it, to what purpose do I defer my last hope?' And with these words herself, his wife and children, fell down upon their knees before him: Martius seeing that, could refrain no longer, but went straight and lifted her up, crying out, 'Oh mother, what have you done to me?' And holding her hard by the right hand, 'Oh mother,' said he, 'you have won a happy victory for your country, but mortal and unhappy for your son: for I see myself vanquished by you alone.' These words being spoken openly, he spake a little apart with his mother and wife, and then let them return again to Rome, for so they did request him; and so remaining in the camp that night, the next morning he dislodged, and marched homeward unto the Volsces' country again.

Shakespeare has, in giving a dramatic form to this passage, adhered very closely and properly to the text. He did not think it necessary to improve upon the truth of nature. Several of the scenes in *Julius Caesar*, particularly Portia's appeal to the confidence of her husband by showing him the wound she had given herself, and the appearance of the ghost of Caesar to Brutus, are, in like manner, taken from the history.

DAVID QUINT

"Alexander the Pig": Shakespeare on History and Poetry

In one satirical scene of *Henry V*, Shakespeare criticizes a tradition of humanist ideas about the writing and reading of history. He specifically questions the assumption that the past possesses an inherently normative authority for the present, that the function of history is to produce exemplary models for human behavior. At the same time, he challenges the claim of the historian to provide a fully objective account of past events, uncolored by his own present circumstances and self-interest. The play thus denies to itself either of two canonical readings of the historical text: it presents itself neither as a collection of improving moral and political exemplars, nor as a true and impartial narration of historical fact.

Shakespeare's play thus finds a middle ground in the quarrel between humanism and historicism, a quarrel which was initiated in the self-reflections of Renaissance humanism and which has received its most distinguished modern contribution in the thought of Hans-Georg Gadamer. What Gadamer terms the "effective-historical consciousness" (*wirkungsgeschichtliches Bewusstsein*) is constituted not only by an historicism that understands the temporal distance separating present from past, but also by a recognition that both past and present belong to the same continuum of historical tradition. This recognition, by which the present observer grasps the historical limitations—what Gadamer sees as a constantly shifting "horizon"—that contain and condition his own understanding, provides a common ground between present and past and is the

From *Boundary* 2, no. 10 (1982). © 1982 by Duke University Press.

basis for a dialogue between the two that is Gadamer's modified version of the hermeneutic circle. The undisguised ulterior motive of Gadamer's philosophical project is a saving of the past and its "classic" tradition: these remain an inexhaustible source of self-understanding for the present interpreter, even after a historicist critique has deprived them of any normative exemplarity. For Gadamer, this critique is a *fait accompli* of nineteenth-century intellectual history, and his own latter-day humanism is a reaction against an historicism which aims to acquire an objective, scientific mastery over the past; this mastery would isolate the past from the subjective experience of the present interpreter and rule out any exchange between them.[1] The quarrel between humanism and historicism thus operates between, at one pole, the present's uncritical acceptance of the authority of the past, and, at the other, an equally uncritical investment of the present with authority over the past. These two positions also define the historical progress of the quarrel which arose when Renaissance humanists began to recognize the anachronism inherent in their attempts to imitate and relive the classical past and which has reopened to counter the triumph of historicism and of a modernism that announces its own definitive break with past tradition.

Shakespeare's criticism of historiography belongs to this quarrel's early stages. For most Renaissance humanists, the past retained the status of a classic; history was to be read as an exemplary text, a series of models held up for imitation. But the humanist cultural program was subject to self-criticism, produced by a nascent historicism that at once challenged the authority of the past and initiated a dialogue with it.[2] The reflections of *Henry V* upon its own presentation of history allude to and grow out of this humanist self-criticism. The play, moreover, suggests how the rhetorical self-consciousness peculiar to the literary text could provide a model for a historical consciousness that succeeds in placing itself at a critical distance from the past. Whereas both ancient and humanist thought had defined the proper writing and reading of history in opposition to poetry—the latter conceived as an inauthentic rhetoric of persuasion—Shakespeare insistently points to the poetic components of his history-play and implies that such rhetorical structures inevitably shape the historical understanding. This literary mediation which reveals its own workings effectively separates the present from the past which it represents, and contributes to a sense of the past's otherness. At the same time the transformation of history into a non-authoritative literary discourse allows the present interpreter to form a subjective critical response to the past rather than to find himself mastered by the force of historical example. In Shakespeare's poetic treatment, history ceases to be the didactic instrument of classical humanism and becomes instead an occasion for historicist self-reflection.

*   *   *

The co-captains of the all-British Isles team which King Henry fields at Agincourt include the Welshman Fluellen, the Scot Jamy, the Irishman MacMorris, and the Englishman Gower. This collection of nationalities underscores the patriotic theme of *Henry V*, and provides intermittent comic relief from the battle carnage in the form of ethnic humor. One of the play's running jokes is Fluellen's inability to pronounce the letter B. The joke, it turns out, is to be taken seriously.

In Act IV, scene 7, Fluellen and Gower express their somewhat mistaken appreciation of Henry's gallantry. At the end of the preceding scene, the King has ordered all the French prisoners killed, thereby operating "expressly against the law of arms." Henry's action comes not, as his two captains believe, in reprisal for the massacre of the English boys and baggage carriers, but rather as a tactical ploy in the face of a new French offensive.[3] The pedant-soldier Fluellen tries to discover a resemblance between Henry and the outstanding military commander of antiquity.

> *Flu.* Ay, he was porn at Monmouth, Captain Gower. What call you the town's name where Alexander the Pig was porn?
> *Gow.* Alexander the Great.
> *Flu.* Why, I pray you, is not pig great? the pig, or the great, or the mighty, or the huge, or the magnanimous, are all one reckonings, save the phrase is a little variations.
> *Gow.* I think Alexander the Great was born in Macedon: his father was called Philip of Macedon, as I take it.
> *Flu.* I think it is in Macedon where Alexander is porn. I tell you, captain, if you look in the maps of the 'orld, I warrant you sail find, in the comparisons between Macedon and Monmouth, that the situations, look you, is both alike. There is a river in Macedon, and there is also moreover a river in Monmouth: it is called Wye at Monmouth; but it is out of my prains what is the name of the other river; but 'tis all one, 'tis alike as my fingers is to my fingers, and there is salmons in both. If you mark Alexander's life well, Harry of Monmouth's life is come after it indifferent well; for there is figures in all things. Alexander, God knows, and you know, in his rages, and his furies, and his wraths, and his cholers, and his moods, and his displeasures, and his indignations, and also being a little intoxicates in his prains, did, in his ales and his angers, look you, kill his best friend, Cleitus.
> *Gow.* Our king is not like him in that; he never killed any of his friends.
> *Flu.* It is not well done, mark you now, to take the tales out of my mouth, ere it is made and finished. I speak but in the figures and comparisons of it: as Alexander killed his friend Cleitus, being in his

ales and his cups, so also Harry Monmouth, being in his right wits
and his good judgments, turned away the fat knight with the great-
belly doublet: he was full of jests, and gipes, and knaveries, and
mocks; I have forgot his name.
        Gow. Sir John Falstaff.[4]   (IV, vii, 12–53)

Whatever Henry might make of Fluellen's comparison, he is in no position to
complain, having himself invoked the example of Alexander to exhort his
troops once more into the breach at Harfleur (III, i, 19). The allusion to
Alexander's murder of Cleitus focuses attention upon the character who is
never onstage: despite Gower's disclaimer and Fluellen's eventual twisting of
his "figure" to transform Alexander into Henry's opposite, their exchange may
second the opinion of the Hostess that the King has killed Falstaff's heart (II,
I, 91) or, as Nym puts it, "The King hath run bad humors on the knight ..." (I,
iii, 124). Alive or dead, Falstaff haunts the play from the wings. Shakespeare
intensifies rather than alleviates the feelings of uneasiness about Henry's
character aroused by the rejection of the fat old knight at the end of *Henry IV,
Part 2.*

        The story of Alexander the Great and Cleitus was familiar to Renaissance
schoolboys in the Latin *History of Alexander* of Quintus Curtius, a work translated
into English by J. Brend in 1553.[5] In Curtius' dramatic account of the incident,
Alexander, swelled with wine and pride in his conquests, belittles the
achievements of his father, Philip of Macedon. Irritated by the boastfulness of the
younger generation at the expense of the Macedonian veterans, Cleitus, one of
Philip's officers, counters with a verse of Euripides to the effect that kings steal
away the glory won by the blood of others. He further mocks Alexander's
pretensions to be the son not of Philip, but of Jupiter Ammon. Enraged, the
young king seizes a spear and runs his trusted lieutenant through. But Alexander
is immediately filled with remorse, remembering that the same Cleitus had once
saved his life.

        This classical instance of unbridled violence, loaded with parricidal
overtones, corresponds to Nym's earlier assessment of the Henry who rejects the
false father, Falstaff. Nym asserts:

        The king is a good king: but it must be as it may; he passes some
        humors, and careers.   (II, i, 128–129)

But Fluellen is quick to explain that Henry is precisely not a violently
"humorous" or capricious ruler: he is the sober king who banishes drunken vice
from his court. In fact, Gower and Fluellen have reversed themselves. They
began by praising Henry for being anything but cool-headed—for slitting the
throats of the French prisoners out of revenge. The audience, however, knows
that Henry actually acted from policy, the "good judgments" which the two

captains attribute to the banishment of Falstaff. Yet, at the end of the captain's colloquy, Henry himself appears, fresh from the heat of battle.

> I was not angry since I came to France
> Until this instant.   (IV, vii, 57–58)

The king now seems to be out for blood, and he repeats his order to kill the prisoners. The Shakespearean complexity not only makes a puzzle out of Henry's motivation but also suggests the confusion of values in the minds of the captains who attempt to judge him. The question may be posed, however, whether it makes any difference to the slaughtered prisoners or to the dead Falstaff whether Henry acts out of anger or wise restraint. Fluellen insists that Henry is a second Alexander. But Alexander, after all, was a pig.

1. Excursus: Alexander, History, and Poetry

Fluellen's classical exemplum refers the play's ambivalence towards Henry to a Renaissance debate over Alexander's moral character, a debate whose larger subject was the didactic usefulness of reading history. This debate was formulated in the humanist manuals on education written during the first four decades of the sixteenth century, and its terms had become commonplaces by the century's end. Humanist educators regarded Alexander's career as proof of the effectiveness of their pedagogical theories, which stressed the practical application of classroom learning to politics and the business of living. Alexander had been instructed by Aristotle, the greatest philosopher-teacher of his age, and the result was the conquest of the world and countless deeds of prowess and virtue. Beginning in the Italian *quattrocento*, anecdotes about Aristotle and Alexander crop up with regularity in humanist educational treatises, demonstrating the link between the liberal arts and political achievement. The damaging incident of Cleitus remained to be explained, but here the humanists turned to the testimony of Quintillian. Before employing Aristotle, Philip had placed Alexander under the tutelage of one Leonidas, a man of unspecified bad habits which were transmitted to the young prince. The effects of a vice inculcated in childhood surfaced many years later in the drunken banquet and murder of Cleitus. The negative example of Leonidas, an unaccountable human error in the formation of the future hero, only confirmed the humanist belief in the power of education, and underscored the need for parental vigilance in the choice of a proper teacher.[6]

Alexander's curriculum under Aristotle resembled the one which the humanists proposed for their own pupils: he read the classics. The young prince's primary texts were the Homeric poems. Sir Thomas Elyot, in *The Book Named the Governor* (1531), uses the example of Alexander to demonstrate Homer's utility in the classroom.

For in his books he contained and most perfectly expressed, not only the documents martial and discipline of arms, but also incomparable wisdom, and instructions for political governance of people, with the worthy commendation and laud of noble princes; wherewith the readers shall be so all inflamed that they most fervently shall desire and covet, by the imitation of their virtues, to acquire semblable glory. For the which occasion, Aristotle, most sharp-witted and excellent learned philosopher, as soon as he had received Alexander from King Philip his father, he before any other thing taught him the most noble works of Homer; wherein Alexander found such sweetness and fruit that ever after he had Homer not only with him in all his journeys but also laid him under his pillow when he went to rest, and often times would purposely wake some hours of the night to take as it were his pastime with that most noble poet.[7]

Homer's main lessons are political and military, the appropriate fare for the future magistrates and civil servants, towards whom, as his title suggests, Elyot directed his educational program. Elyot describes the imitation of literary models which lies at the core of nearly all humanist pedagogical method. The student is inspired to copy the example of the great men he encounters in his reading. Alexander particularly venerated Achilles, from whom he claimed descent.[8]

This same method of study, with its emphasis on imitation, could be applied to historical writing. Elyot again has recourse to a classical precedent, Scipio Africanus, who was said to have learned the rules of good government and soldiership from Xenophon's didactic history of Cyrus. Similarly, Alexander's own life and deeds became a textbook for the Renaissance schoolboy. Included on Elyot's recommended reading list is

Quintus Curtius, who writeth the life of King Alexander elegantly and sweetly. In whom may be found the figure of an excellent prince, as he that incomparably excelled all other kings and emperors in wisdom, hardiness, strength, policy, agility, valiant courage, nobility, liberality, and courtesy, wherein he was a spectacle or mark for all princes to look on. Contrariwise when he was once vanquished with volupty and pride his tyranny and beastly cruelty abhorreth all readers. (*BNG*, 37)

The misgivings about Alexander's later career, which includes the murder of Cleitus, are presented almost as a parenthetical afterthought. The Macedonian conqueror remains for Elyot a "spectacle," a mirror for magistrates-in-training in which all human virtues are reflected. Twenty-two separate appeals to Alexander's example are scattered through the pages of *The Governor*. Alexander enjoys a similar prominence in the *De l'Institution du Prince* (1540) of the French humanist Guillaume Budé, a work that is largely a collection of moralizing biographical anecdotes about the great men of antiquity. To judge from the space and number of anecdotes devoted to him, Alexander ranks second only to Pompey in Budé's estimation.[9]

For his pedagogical purpose, Elyot recognizes little distinction between poetic fiction and historical fact. Both poetry and history are repositories of the edifying classical exemplum held up for modern imitation. Their twin status in the humanist literary education is suggested in a passage where Elyot announces a recent addition to the humanist curriculum.

> It would not be forgotten that the little book of the most excellent doctor Erasmus Roteradamus (which he wrote to Charles, now being Emperor and then Prince of Castile), which book is entitled *The Institution of a Christian Prince*, would be as familiar alway with gentleman at all times and in every age as was Homer with the great King Alexander, or Xenophon with Scipio.... (*BNG*, 40)

While Alexander carried Homer with him throughout his campaigns, Scipio "was never seen without his book of Xenophon" (*BNG*, 37). If the notable results of these intensive reading courses were any indication—and there is little to choose between Alexander and Scipio in a contest of ancient virtues—the poet and the historian seemed to be equally effective counsellors and teachers to the schoolboy-leader.

Erasmus' *Institutio Principis Christiani* was published in 1516. Elyot's enthusiastic recommendation is somewhat peculiar, since the Erasmian treatise constitutes a radical revision of those pedagogical premises which the continental Renaissance inherited from Italian humanism, premises which still inform the thought of the *Governor*.[10] Erasmus' new outlook can be detected from the very beginning of the *Institutio*, in his dedicatory epistle to Charles which contains an extended comparison of the future emperor to his ancient counterpart, Alexander.

> But as much as you surpass Alexander in good fortune, mighty prince Charles, so much do we hope you will surpass him in wisdom. For he had gained a mighty empire, albeit one not destined to endure, solely through bloodshed. You have been born to a splendid kingdom and are destined to a still greater one. As Alexander had to toil to carry out his invasions, so will you have to labor to yield, rather than to gain, part of your power. You owe it to the powers of heaven that you came into a kingdom unstained with blood, bought through no evil connection. It will be the lot of your wisdom to keep it bloodless and peaceful.[11]

The sentiment that Charles may surpass the achievements of Alexander goes beyond the usual flattery to princes that precedes most Renaissance books. Erasmus intends to found the ethical basis of humanist education in religion, a plan which does not so much alter the basic method of imitation as the subject matter to be imitated. The Christian king described in the title of his treatise and outlined in its pages is a pacifist in principle who has no use for the ancient military heroes. His proper model, as for all Christians, is the example of Christ in the gospels.

> Now what could be more senseless than for a man who has received the sacraments of the Christian church to set up as an example for himself Alexander, Julius Caesar, or Xerxes, for even the pagan writers would have attacked their lives if any of them had had a little sounder judgment? (*ECP*, 203)

This opinion is echoed by Rabelais in the person of old King Grandgousier in the *Gargantua*.

> Le temps nest plus d'ainsi conquester les royaulmes avecques dommaige de son prochain frere christian. Ceste imitation des anciens Hercules, Alexandres, Hannibalz, Scipions, Cesars, et aultres telz, est contraire a la profession de l'Evangile....[12]

Reading and emulating the classics may indeed produce a negative effect, feeding the dreams of military glory which Rabelais satirizes in Picrochole, whom his counsellors promise to make "le plus heureux, le plus chevalureux prince qui oncques feut depuis la mort de Alexandre Macedon" (*G*, chap. 31, 193). In his *De Causis Corruptarum Artium* (1531), the Spanish Erasmian Juan Luis Vives sees a direct literary link in the murderous chain of historical events.

> The name of Achilles incited Alexander, Alexander Caesar, Caesar many others; Caesar killed in his various battles 192,000 men, not counting the civil wars.[13]

For Vives, each despot imitates and tries to outdo the predecessor about whom he reads. This kind of classical education leads to more and more bloodshed. Among his other efforts to emulate Achilles, Alexander ordered the heels of his valiant captive Betis to be pierced, and then dragged him behind his chariot as Homer's hero had treated the body of Hector. Montaigne gives prominence to this story by recounting it in the first of his *Essais*.[14]

Vives couples Achilles and Alexander as negative models, assuming that both poetry and history are read in order to be imitated. The failure of the humanist literary education to define different reader's responses to fiction and non-fiction will create the dilemma of Don Quixote who imitates the outlandish heroes of chivalry *as if* they were historical figures. The possibility of such a confusion of poetry and history may account for the mistrust of imaginative literature which occasionally surfaces in humanist thought. In the *De Corruptio*, Vives inveighs precisely against the "Spanish Amadis and Florisand, Lancelot and the French round table, and the Italian Roland," quixotic books of pure fable which corrupt their readers "not otherwise than those of delicate stomach, who are the most indulged, and who are sustained by sugary and honeyed condiments, spitting out any solid food."[15] Vives disjoins the traditional Lucretian metaphor of the sugar-coated pill, the combination of the *dulce*, the pleasurable, and the *utile*, the useful, the metaphor which Tasso would use to justify his inclusion of Roland-like chivalric fictions into his historical epic of the First Crusade.[16] Vives insists upon the necessity of keeping history and poetry apart. When historians mix lies with facts, they are following the example of poets who,

> because they strove after only the pleasure of their hearers and, as it were, the tickling of their ears, only pursued those things which give pleasure; and because occasionally they did not trust to succeed with the real truth of things, they both mixed false things with true ones, and distorted that same truth in the direction where they thought it would have more grace and admiration: they abused to that end figures of speech, metaphors, allegories, ambiguities, analogies between things and between names.[17]

Vives' remarks occur in the context of a discussion of historiography. In spite of his rejection of history as a subject for imitation, he rehearses a series of classical criticisms that formed the standard humanist rules for good history-writing. These almost all derive from the treatise, *How to Write History*, by the second century A.D. Greek satirist, Lucian of Samosata. Translated into Latin by Pirckheimer in 1515, the work was the most influential and widely read ancient theoretical discussion of history in the Renaissance.[18] Lucian succinctly spells out the problem of the pleasurable and the useful.

> Now some think they can make a satisfactory distinction in history between what gives pleasure and what is useful, and for this reason work eulogy into it as giving pleasure and enjoyment to its readers; but do you see how far they are from the truth? In the first place, the distinction they draw is false: history has one task and one end—what is useful—and that comes from truth alone.[19]

Lucian decries the practice among his contemporary historians to eulogize the often less-than-great men whose deeds they record. Their methods include formal panegyric and the inclusion of mythological episodes: "But if history introduces flattery of that sort, what else does it become but a sort of prose poetry ...?" (*HWH*, 13). Vives similarly accuses certain Greek historians of performing the Lucianic rhetorical trick of turning a gnat into an Indian elephant by so extolling a mediocre man that "if you consider with what praise they adorn him, you would expect to be reading about someone more outstanding than Alexander, Caesar, or Pompey."[20] Vives further notes the patriotic biases of contemporary historians who expand upon the glories and conceal the faults of their particular nations: "The fools do not realize that this is not writing history, but taking up the cause of that nation, which is the way of an advocate, not of a historian."[21]

Despite his insistence upon the separation of history and poetry, Lucian does not deny a kind of artistry to historical style. He describes the task of the historian

> to give a fine arrangement to events and illuminate them as vividly as possible. And when a man who has heard him thinks thereafter that he is actually seeing what is being described and then praises him— then it is that the work of our Phidias of history is perfect and has received its proper praise.[22]

The aim of writing history is to make the truth appear true. Lucian compares the ideal history to the lifelike sculpture of Phidias. The historian's craft produces a heightened verisimilitude which causes the reader to forget the literary medium of the text. The ability to make the narrated events seem to take place before the reader's eyes is the source of the power of the historical text—a power which may be abused. Guillaume Budé echoes Lucian's precepts with a warning.

> Car la nature de l'Histoire nest aultre chose, que suiure la pure verité des faicts, & les reciter de telle sorte, qu'il semble qu'ilz se facent plus tost lors qu'on les list, que qu'ilz soient escripts. Aultrement, si on n'observoit la verite: l'Histoire se deueroit nommer une honteuse fable, & non pas estre honorée d'un si honneste tiltre, que lon doibt tenir aussy certain, que la certitude propre. (*DIP*, 115)

Truth is absolutely essential to a history whose style aims to persuade the reader of the factuality of the deeds it depicts. Lucian dwells upon the need for impartiality and independence, enjoining the prospective historian to tell the truth no matter whom it pleases or displeases. He cites specific examples.

> He must not be concerned that Philip has had his eye put out by Aster of Amphipolis, the archer at Olynthus—he must show him exactly as he was. Nor must he mind if Alexander is going to be angry

when he gives a clear account of the cruel murder of Cleitus at the banquet. (*HWH*, 53)

The murder of Cleitus, the bloody stain upon Alexander's glorious career, is a classical test case for objectivity in historical writing.[23]

But it is precisely the historian's refusal to prettify his subject matter with a flattery which Lucian equates with poetry[24] that makes history unacceptable for the humanist schools of Erasmus and Vives. The dilemma in which their advocacy of historical impartiality placed the humanist teachers who sought to instruct through literary models could be viewed in terms of a contradictory understanding of the relationship of history to poetry: history was to be *read* in the same way as poetry but *written* in opposition to poetic norms. Sir Philip Sidney seizes upon this contradiction in his *Apology for Poetry* (1595) in order to demonstrate the didactic superiority of poetry to history. Sidney follows a long line of sixteenth-century Italian critics who rediscovered in Aristotle's *Poetics* the dictum that poetry is more philosophical than history because the poet deals with universals while the historian is confined to particular events: poetry shows man as he should be, not as he too often is.[25] This critical tradition asserted that Xenophon's idealized portrait of Cyrus in the *Cyropaedia* is not—as Elyot had maintained—history at all, but a kind of poetry.[26] But this poetic heightening of the pages of history, according to Sidney, redeems history for the classroom.

> But if the question be for your own use and learning, whether it be better to have it set down as it should be or as it was, then certainly is more doctrinable the feigned Cyrus in Xenophon than the true Cyrus in Justin, and the feigned Aeneas in Virgil than the right Aeneas in Dares Phrygius.[27]

Sidney defends the poetic supplements to history which Vives, following Lucian, had condemned. Rather than keeping poetry and history apart, Sidney claims that poetic embellishment will produce a more "doctrinable" textbook out of history. By contrast, the historian who must stick to the facts can only present an ambivalent portrait of human behavior.

> ... the historian, bound to tell things as things were, cannot be liberal (without he will be poetical) of a perfect pattern, but as in Alexander or Scipio himself, show doings, some to be liked, some to be misliked. And then how will you discern what to follow but by your own discretion, which you had without reading Quintus Curtius? (*APP*, 32–33)

Sidney adapts his Aristotelian defense of poetry to the pedagogical concerns shared by the humanist educators, and his argument exploits the division in their thought which followed the Erasmian rejection of secular history from the moral curriculum. As the example of Alexander attests, history mixes depictions of virtue and vice and provides no absolute model for the student to follow. The absolute model that the Erasmians found in the imitation of Christ Sidney posits in the "perfect pattern" of the poetic hero.[28]

2. SHAKESPEARE, THE POET-HISTORIAN

Fluellen would obviously prefer a perfect Henry to the ambiguous Alexander.[29] The Welshman "poetizes" history, displaying all the vices which Lucianic advocates of impartial, factual historiography most deplore: he abuses analogy, he devotes himself to panegyric, he is guided by nationalistic prejudice, he inflates his king into another Alexander. But this same rhetoric betrays him. Adducing the salmons and rivers of Monmouth and Macedon, Fluellen's argument for the similarity of Henry and Alexander is preposterously weak, but Henry does indeed begin to look like Alexander precisely at the moment when Fluellen reverses himself and protests their dissimilarity. Fluellen can neither persuade the audience that Henry resembles Alexander *in bono* nor that Henry does *not* resemble Alexander *in malo*, the murderer of Cleitus. The result is not a poetically embellished portrait of the perfect prince, but rather the complicated, morally indeterminate Henry of Shakespeare's play. By satirizing Fluellen's inept use of the encomiastic style, the play portrays a poetic temptation to the historian to which it apparently knows better than to succumb. Furthermore, at the moment when Henry has committed his one unmitigatedly blameworthy deed—the killing of the French prisoners—the play refers to Alexander's murder of Cleitus, the retelling of which, according to Lucian, exemplified the need for objective history. Showing Henry's action as it was, rather than joining Fluellen and Gower in trying to find justification and praise for it, the play seems to come down squarely on the side of the historian against the poet.

Fluellen is neither the play's worst nor most ludicrous offender in the practice of panegyric flattery. That distinction must belong to the French Dauphin who writes sonnets on the glories of his horse (III, vii). Renaissance readers knew that the ancients had set for themselves the rhetorical exercise of composing eulogies in praise of trivial subjects—salt, gnats, and the like—and Erasmus' revival of the custom produced one of the comic masterpieces of their age. The Dauphin, however, seems to be quite literal about his horse.[30]

> it is a
> theme as fluent as the sea; turn the sands into elo-
> quent tongues, and my horse is argument for them
> all.   (III, vii, 34–37)

The inexhaustible subject requires a comparable eloquence and the Dauphin's equine encomium seems to call for a comic version of the rhetorical *copia* which Erasmus and his fellow humanist educators sought to inculcate in their pupils.[31] The ideal orator should not only have something to say on an infinite number of subjects, but be able to speak on any one subject in an infinite number of ways. The eulogizing Fluellen seems to have a special predilection for this rhetorical method ("his rages, and his furies, and his wraths, and his cholers, and his moods, and his displeasures, and his indignations ..." "jests, and gipes, and knaveries, and mocks ..."). He appeals to *copia* to defend his substitution of "Alexander the Pig" for "Alexander the Great."

> Why, I pray you, is not pig great? the pig, or the great, or the mighty, or the huge, or the magnanimous, are all one reckonings, save the phrase is a little variations.

By "little" variation, "great" becomes "big," which becomes "pig." Here, too, Fluellen's language comically backfires, and his attempt to improve his subject with rhetorical elegance merely introduces ambiguity, not only about Alexander and Henry, but about all the other great, mighty, huge and magnanimous.

The joke, however, works two ways. The bungling Fluellen satirizes the poetizers of history, but Fluellen is himself a poetic character with no historical existence outside the fiction of the play. His difficulty with the letter B is a poetic choice—the more so since Fluellen pronounces his B's correctly on occasion (between, but, being). There is a providence in the slip of the tongue, the providence of the playwright who here asserts his control over the script. When Fluellen Welshes "big" into "pig," the play sends up his version of history only to fall back upon its own: where the minimal phonemic difference between two labial consonants attests to the inability of "historical meaning" to be independent of the language through which it is transmitted. No less than the playwright, the writer of history has the last word because he uses words—which are not interchangeable parts of an ornamental whole, "all one reckonings," as the copious rhetorician Fluellen appears to think, but which rather fragment the empirical historical event into a series of discrete descriptive possibilities from which the historian chooses his authorized version.

The disclosure of an authorial presence violates one of the stylistic canons of Renaissance historiography. The verisimilar style defined by Lucian, which aims to make the reader an eyewitness to the historical event, suppresses the literary mediation of the historian to the point where his own narrative voice virtually disappears. Sir Thomas North's translation (1579) of Jacques Amyot's preface to his French translation of Plutarch's *Lives* (1559) commends this "lively" style for allowing the reader a full if vicarious identification with its historical subject matter.

> as in the very reading of them we see our minds to be so touched by
> them, not as though the things were already done and past, but as
> though they were even then presently in doing, and we find ourselves
> carried away with gladness and grief through fear or hope, well near
> as though we were then at the doing of them....[32]

There is an implicit link between the verisimilitude which almost makes the
reader a participant in the event itself, and the truth and objectivity of the
historian; for Budé, the style does not merely reflect but also enjoins the writer's
impartiality. By pointing through Fluellen to its own playwright-historian and
breaching the verisimilar style, Shakespeare's play criticizes such stylistic
assumptions. This criticism reverses the relationship of style and content,
suggesting that the historian's verisimilitude *creates the appearance* of his
impartiality, thereby reducing historical objectivity to a trick of style, a rhetorical
trope. Whereas the clumsy rhetorician Fluellen lets his biases show and cannot
convince the audience of a word he says, the considerably adroit Shakespeare
may be more persuasive. The audience may accept the play's truthlike version of
history as historical truth unless the playwright steps forward to call his
representation into question.

Instead, Shakespeare sends the magniloquent Chorus of *Henry V* onstage.
Appearing before each act and as an epilogue, the Chorus ostensibly seeks to
create or enhance the verisimilitude of the performance. The spectator is asked
to suspend disbelief and supplement the stage business with his imagination. But
the Chorus simultaneously criticizes the play's lack of verisimilitude—otherwise
his own function would be superfluous. He laments the inadequacy of theatrical
representation for the great subject at hand.

> But pardon, gentles all,
> The flat unraised spirits that hath dar'd
> On this unworthy scaffold to bring forth
> So great an object: can this cockpit hold
> The vasty fields of France? or may we cram
> Within this wooden O the very casques
> That did affright the air at Agincourt?
>
> (Prologue, 8–14)

> There is the playhouse now, there must you sit;
> And thence to France shall we convey you safe
> And bring you back, charming the narrow seas
> To give you gentle pass; for, if we may,
> We'll not offend one stomach with our play.
>
> (II, Pro., 36–40)

And so our scene must to the battle fly;
Where, O for pity! we shall much disgrace
With four or five most vile and ragged foils,
Right ill-dispos'd in brawl ridiculous,
The name of Agincourt. Yet sit and see;
Minding true thing by what their mock'ries be.

(IV, Pro., 48–53)

The theatrical illusion which the Chorus seems to promote with one hand—the illusion of verisimilitude which might lead the spectator to take the actions of the play for the "true things" of history—he apologetically dispels with the other, showing those actions up as "mock'ries." The Chorus exposes the actors, scene changes, and stage properties for what they are as well as for what they represent. The imperfect verisimilitude he describes preserves rather than reduces the distance between the audience and the play, a distance spelled out in spatial terms by the conceit of the playhouse as a ferryboat crossing and recrossing the Channel to follow the action on its stage.

Shakespeare frequently finds devices to distance the spectator from the stage action of his plays. In the discourse of *Henry V*, the willed aesthetic distance—maintained both inside the action by Fluellen's unintentionally comic history-within-a-history and outside the action by the speeches of the Chorus—corresponds to a recognition of *historical distance*. Dramatizing rather than concealing the hybrid nature of his play which is both history and poetry, Shakespeare points to the literary mediation separating the audience from the historical event. The play's focus upon the literary act which re-creates the event both denies to history-writing its aura of unmediated and empirical truth and suggests that the truth about the event may be ultimately irrecoverable across the gap of time. This skepticism is underscored thematically by the play's confusing, contradictory portrait of Henry. If even the eyewitnesses Gower and Fluellen cannot discern the motivation of their king, who is now one thing, now another, how can the historian-poet who was not present at Agincourt?[33]

No less than the indecision about Henry which deprives the play of a clear-cut model prince, the perception of historical distance inhibits imitation, the stock didactic response to history advocated in humanist educational theory. Imitation would collapse the distance between the reader-playgoer and the historical event. So would the historical analogy: if, as Fluellen claims, "there is figures in all things," the identity found between events blurs their historical specificity. The anachronism of imitation and analogy finds literary expression in the verisimilar style, and it is thus not surprising to find the same humanists who recommend the imitation of historical models also upholding an historical style which creates the illusion of simultaneity between the act of reading and the events which that style narrates. The preservation of distance in Shakespeare's play allows a critical response to the historical event which perceives its otherness from the experience of the present interpreter. The recognition of the difference between past and present pulls apart historical analogies and questions the validity of finding norms for human behavior in the actions of the past.[34] The distanced interpreter of *Henry V* must judge its action for himself, and the play demands from him an act of self-reflection just as it reflects upon its own act of writing and interpreting history.

It may seem paradoxical that Shakespeare should demonstrate an historicist understanding of the past by turning it into a poetic text. But it is possible that Renaissance thought could more easily recognize the historical otherness of texts than of events. The humanist revolution in historical thought originated in the discipline of philology which developed critical principles for the reading of texts.[35] This reading, to be sure, was put in the service of a rhetorical program and applied to practical affairs. But the twin aims of humanism, supposed to be complementary, proved contradictory. By placing the text in a given historical context, philology calls into question its applicability to the present rhetorical moment. This is essentially the same contradiction explored in Shakespeare's play, which replaces the historical event with a literary text of which the event is only one of several constituent parts that philology can break down and analyze. Such analysis discovers that historical meaning does not consist in a series of prescriptive models which the past may hand down and impose upon a passive present age, but is rather the product of an active process of interpretation by which the present may also define itself in relationship to the past. A critical understanding of the past may thus have first emerged through the recognition of the historical text as text. This critical understanding, with its unsettling effects upon a humanism which rests upon tradition and imitation, lies at the basis of Shakespeare's historical enterprise.

NOTES

An earlier version of this paper was presented as a public lecture at Bowdoin College. I should like to thank Bowdoin and the members of the Stahl Lecture Committee for their generous hospitality.

1. Gadamer, *Truth and Method* (1960; English trans., New York, 1975), pp. 153–341. For a discussion of the classical exemplum, see pp. 253-258.

2. For a discussion of the critical understanding of the past which could be attained by a humanism that was informed by a new perception of historical distance, see Thomas M. Greene, "Petrarch and the Humanist Hermeneutic," in *Italian Literature: Roots and Branches*, ed. Giose Rimanelli and Kenneth Jon Atchity (New Haven, 1976), pp. 201–04.

3. Shakespeare's source is the following passage in Holinshed's *Chronicles*: "But when the outcry of the lackeys and boys, which ran away for fear of the

Frenchmen thus spoiling the camp, came to the King's ears, he (doubting lest his enemies should gather together again and begin a new field, and mistrusting further that the prisoners would be an aid to his enemies or the very enemies to their takers if they were suffered to live), contrary to his accustomed gentleness, commanded by sound of trumpet that every man (upon pain of death) should incontinently slay his prisoner. When this dolorous decree and pitiful proclamation was pronounced, pity it was to see how some Frenchmen were suddenly sticked with daggers, some were brained with poleaxes, some slain with mauls, others had their throats cut and some their bellies paunched, so that in effect, having respect to the great number, few prisoners were saved." *Shakespeare's Holinshed*, ed. Richard Hosley (New York, 1968), p. 133.

4. All citations of *King Henry V* are taken from the Arden edition, ed. J. H. Walter (London, 1954). There is a discussion of Fluellen's comparison of Henry to Alexander in Ronald S. Berman, "Shakespeare's Alexander: Henry V," *College English* 22 (1961–62), 532–39. Berman confines his discussion to the portrait of Alexander in Plutarch's *Lives*, which I do not believe is Shakespeare's primary source in this scene. For perceptive remarks on the scene and on Fluellen's role in the play, see Gordon Ross Smith, "Shakespeare's *Henry V*: Another Part of the Critical Forest," *Journal of the History of Ideas* 37 (1976), 3–26, pp. 22–24.

5. Quintus Curtius, *History of Alexander the Great of Macedon*, VIII, i, 22–ii, 12.

6. "Nescio, qui error Leonide locum fecit," writes Aeneas Sylvius in the *De Liberorum Educatione*, trans. Brother Joel Stanislaus Nelson, The Catholic University of America Studies in Medieval and Renaissance Latin Language and Literature, Vol. XII (Washington, 1940), p. 98. The Quintillian passage, *Institutio Oratoria* I, i, 9, is also cited by Erasmus in the *Declamatio de Pueris Statim ac Liberaliter Instituendis*, ed. and trans. Jean-Claude Margolin (Geneva, 1966), p. 418. With the episode of Cleitus clearly in mind, Sir Thomas Elyot, in *The Book Named the Governor* (ed. S. E. Lehmberg [London and New York, 1962], pp. 19–20 [hereafter cited as *BNG*]), speculates on the nature of Leonidas' vice: "some suppose it to be fury and hastiness, other superfluous drinking of wine." For an especially notable discussion of Aristotle as the teacher of Alexander, see Castiglione's *Il Libro del Cortegiano* 4, 47.

7. Elyot, p. 30. For a discussion of the educational thought of *The Governor*, see Fritz Caspari, *Humanism and the Social Order in Tudor England* (1954; rpt. New York, 1968), pp. 160–78.

8. Quintus Curtius, VIII, iv, 26. Arrian, *History of Alexander*, I, xii, 1; VIII, xiv, 4. Plutarch, *Life of Alexander*, XV, 4–5.

9. Budé, *De l'Institution du Prince* (1547; facsimile rpt. Farnborough, 1966), pp. 105–108 (hereafter cited as *DIP*).

10. The Italian humanists were not, however, unaware of the ethical problems contained in the imitation of historical models, problems which the

Erasmians would emphasize. See Felix Gilbert, *Machiavelli and Guicciardini* (Princeton, 1965), pp. 216–18.

11. Erasmus, *The Education of a Christian Prince*, trans. Lester K. Born (1936; rpt. New York, 1968), pp. 134–35 (hereafter cited as *ECP*). For humanist attitudes towards war and military conquest, see Robert P. Adams, *The Better Part of Valor: More, Erasmus, Colet and Vives on Humanism, War, and Peace* (Seattle, 1962).

12. *Gargantua*, ed. Ruth Calder and M. A. Screech (Geneva and Paris, 1970), Chapter 44, p. 258 (hereafter cited as *G*).

13. "Achillis nomen Alexandrum accendit; Alexander Caesarem; Caesar permultos: occidit Caesar variis praeliis C, XCII M. hominum, sine bellis civilibus." Vives, *Opera Omnia* (1745; facsimile rpt. London, 1964), Vol. 6, p. 105.

14. Montaigne, *Essais*, ed. Pierre Villey (Paris, 1965), pp. 9–10. The episode of Betis is recounted in Quintus Curtius, IV, vi, 29. The figure of Alexander, the great man who behaves with inhumanity towards his fellow men, frames the *Essais* as a whole. His example is invoked at the end of the first essay of the collection and also reappears in the closing paragraphs of Montaigne's concluding essay, "De L'Experience" (3, 13).

15. "... non aliter quam delicata quidam stomachi et quibus plurimum est indultum, saccareis modo et melleis quibusdam condituris sustentantur, cibum omnem solidum respuentes." Vives, *Opera Omnia*, 6, p. 109.

16. Lucretius, *De Rerum Natura* I, 936–49. Tasso, *Gerusalemme Liberata* 1, 3, 5-8.

17. "... qui quod solam captarent audientium voluptatem, et aurium quandam titillationem, ea sola consectati sunt, quae delectarent; quod quum efficere se interdum germana rerum veritate non considerent, et veris miscuerunt falsa, et ipsa eadem vera alio detorserunt, ubi plus putarent habitura vel gratiae vel admirationis: abusi sunt ad eam rem loquendi figuris, metaphoris, allegoriis, amphibologiis, similitudinibus rerum, aut nominum ..." Vives, *Opera Omnia*, 6, p. 102.

18. For the canonical status of *How to Write History* in later Renaissance historical thought, see Giorgio Spini, "I Trattatisti dell'Arte Storica nella Controriforma Italiana" in *Contributi alla Storia del Concilio di Trento e della Controriforma*, ed. Luigi Russo (Florence, 1948), 109–36, pp. 112–13. Lucian's treatise is discussed as a model for Robortello and the target of Patrizi in Girolamo Cotroneo, *I Trattatisti dell' "Ars Historia"* (Naples, 1971), pp. 164–67, 209–12. Pirckheimer's translation was included by Johann Wolfius in his collection of eighteen essays on the art of history, the *Artis Historiae Penus* (1579). This collection is discussed by Beatrice Reynolds, "Shifting Currents in Historical Criticism" in *Renaissance Essays*, ed. Kristeller and Weiner (New York and Evanston, 1968), 115–36.

19. I am quoting from the English translation of *How to Write History* in Vol. 6 of the Loeb Classical Library edition of *Lucian*, trans. K. Kilburn (London and Cambridge, Mass., 1959), p. 15 (hereafter cited as *HWH*).

20. "si cogites quibus eum ornent laudibus, aliquem te lecturum speres Alexandro, aut Caesare, aut Pompejo praestantiorem." Vives, *Opera Omnia*, 6, p. 106. The image of a gnat or fly turned into an elephant is found in the last sentence of Lucian's mock encomium to *The Fly*, and is included in Erasmus' *Adagia* I, 9, 69.

21. "stulti non intelligunt hoc non esse historiam scribere, sed causam illius gentis agere, quod patroni est, non historici." Vives, *Opera Omnia*, VI, pp. 107–108.

22. *How to Write History*, p. 65. Lucian's formulation runs counter to Cicero's opinion, often invoked in the Renaissance, which classifies history as a branch of epideictic rhetoric. See the *Orator*, Chapters 11 and 20.

23. This passage is repeated in the *De Scribenda Historiae* (Antwerp, 1569) of Giovanni Antonio Viperano, who speaks thus of the impartial historian: "qui nec metuat quemquam, nec ab ullo quicquam speret, vel si Alexander sicut in Clytum acerbus existat . . ." (p. 65). Viperano's treatise has been reprinted by Eckhard Kessler, *Theoretiker Humanistischer Geschichtsschreibung* (Munich, 1971).

24. Erasmus' Folly similarly identifies the lyres of Orpheus and Amphion with flattery in *The Praise of Folly*. Erasmus, *Ausgewählte Schriften* (Darmstadt, 1975), Vol. II, 56. The Lucianic equation of poetry and flattery is taken to its farthest logical extension in the episode of the moon in Canto 35 of the *Orlando Furioso*.

25. *Poetics*, 9. For the adaptation of Aristotle's vindication of poetry over history in Italian critical thought, see Baxter Hathaway, *The Age of Criticism* (Ithaca, 1962), pp. 129–43.

26. For the re-evaluation of the *Cyropaedia*, see Hathaway, pp. 146 ff.

27. Sidney, *An Apology for Poetry*, ed. Forrest G. Robinson (Indianapolis and New York, 1970), pp. 31–34 (hereafter cited as *APP*).

28. Erasmus, *The Education of a Christian Prince*, p. 162, also suggests the construction of a "perfect pattern" for the student's emulation. "Let the teacher paint a sort of celestial creature, more like to a divine being than a mortal: complete in all the virtues; born for the common good; yes, sent by the God above to help the affairs of mortals by looking out and caring for everyone and everything...." The language suggests that the teacher's fiction inevitably turns into the perfect model, Christ.

29. Some critics of the play have also wished to see Henry as a model hero. J. H. Walter, in his introduction to the Arden edition, pp. xi–xlii, sees Henry as the Renaissance's "ideal king." "The modern was naturally compared with the ancient, Henry with Alexander. Calvary apart there could be no greater praise"

(p. xxiii). For a balanced view of Henry's progress from Prince to King, which measures the human cost of his political mastery, see Alvin B. Kernan, "The Henriad: Shakespeare's Major History Plays" in Kernan, ed., *Modern Shakespearean Criticism* (New York, 1970), pp. 245–75.

30. The encomium of the perfect horse is, in fact, a well-developed literary genre by the time of its comic appropriation in Luigi Pulci's *Morgante* (1483). See Paolo Orvieto, *Pulci Medievale* (Rome, 1978), pp. 86–105.

31. For *copia*, see R. R. Bolgar, *The Classical Heritage and Its Beneficiaries* (1954; rpt. New York, 1964), pp. 271–75. Erasmus' treatise, *De Copia*, is translated and annotated by Betty I. Knott in Volume 24 of the *Collected Works of Erasmus* (Toronto, Buffalo and London, 1978), pp. 279–659.

32. *Plutarch's Lives Englished by Sir Thomas North*, ed. W. H. D. Rouse (London, 1898), Vol. 1, p. 19.

33. Francesco Patrizi had undertaken a skeptical attack upon the knowability of historical truth in the *Della historia dieci dialoghi* (1560). Patrizi's treatise is reprinted in Kessler, *op. cit.* His arguments are outlined by Julian H. Franklin in *Jean Bodin and the Sixteenth-Century Revolution in Methodology of Law and History* (New York and London, 1963), pp. 96–101.

34. This shift in Renaissance attitudes towards the utility of history is mirrored in Guicciardini's quarrel with Machiavelli. See Gilbert, pp. 271–301. See also Myron P. Gilmore, "The Renaissance Conception of the Lessons of History" in *Facets of the Renaissance*, ed. William H. Werkmeister (New York, 1963). G.W. Pigman III explores "the confrontation of a nascent historicist view of the past with the traditional humanistic belief in the utility of history" in "Imitation and the Renaissance sense of the past: the reception of Erasmus' *Ciceronianus*," *The Journal of Medieval and Renaissance Studies* 9 (1979), 155–77. There is a fine discussion of the effects of a new historical consciousness upon the idea of a normative tradition in Lawrence Manley, *Convention: 1500–1750* (Cambridge, Mass., and London, 1980), pp. 203–26.

35. For Renaissance historicism and philology, see Donald R. Kelley, *Foundations of Modern Historical Scholarship* (New York and London, 1970).

LAWRENCE DANSON

Julius Caesar

In the previous chapter I suggested that the answer to the problems Hamlet confronts is *Hamlet* itself: the perfected form of the play successfully subsumes, and in that sense solves, the various linguistic crises within it. Now having with one hand put forward this purely formal, esthetic answer, I want with the other hand to begin, tentatively, to withdraw it. I would like, that is, to have the position reached in the discussion of *Hamlet* to be maintained provisionally as a possibility: it has, I believe, its portion of truth, but it is no shame to confess that, as with most things Shakespearean, it must share its truth with other, competing truths. The limited nature of this particular truth is indicated by my own characterization of it as formal and esthetic; for the question which immediately occurs is whether any such "truth" (the only standard for which remains that offered by Keats's Grecian Urn) can be wholly satisfying.

In regard to theories of tragedy, Murray Krieger asks "whether we have not been beguiled by aesthetic satisfactions and whether the utterly stripped tragic vision may not after all be, less illusory than the fullness which shines through tragedy."[1] He suggests, that is, that tragedy's "calm of mind, all passion spent" is the result of a formal resolution which may be at odds with the play's "stripped" thematic content. Similarly, Clifford Leech remarks that "the control of art need suggest nothing more than that man has a certain faculty for ordering his experience: it does not transform the nature of that experience, and it does not necessarily suggest that either he or a creator can control the totality of

From *Tragic Alphabet: Shakespeare's Drama of Language*. © 1974 by Yale University.

experience."[2] Now I am not convinced that the stripping of an artist's vision is a worthwhile pursuit, nor do I underestimate the importance of our ability to order even parts of our experience; still, the objections which have been leveled against a formalist approach to tragedy are powerful and cannot be dismissed.

In the next chapter, on *Troilus and Cressida*, I intend to give these objections their due: in that play, I will argue, Shakespeare himself is most fully skeptical about the possibility of substituting the control of art for the chaos of experience. But even with *Hamlet* I must acknowledge the presence of this alternative. Conceived in formal terms, the ending of *Hamlet* ought, indeed, to leave us satisfied, filled with the sense that, yes, we have come through—that, yes, the world is once again in joint. Yet even as the trumpets sound and Hamlet is borne like a soldier to the stage, certain doubts may refuse to be stilled. How appropriate, really, is this military fanfare for the Hamlet we have known? Can the brash Fortinbras ever be expected to understand the story which the scholarly Horatio is bid to tell? Though our passion is spent in the tragic close, is there not also the hint of mere waste? Fortinbras, we may even suspect, is more appropriately the heir to Claudius's limitations than to Hamlet's brilliance. At the same instant that Shakespeare affirms the order which his play has brought out of chaos, he subtly mocks the pretension of that affirmation.

In *Julius Caesar*, to which we now turn, a similar doubleness emerges. But the critic, who is fated to the discursive mode, cannot speak (Weird Sister-like) simultaneously of two opposite truths. I have chosen, therefore, to follow out the basic pattern we have seen in *Hamlet*. I will speak as if a formal, esthetic solution were indeed possible for the various linguistic problems we discover, and locate that solution in the fullness of the tragic form. At the end of the discussion, before proceeding to *Troilus and Cressida*, I will recur to the other possibility, Shakespeare's recognition of the insufficiency of the formal solution. In *Troilus and Cressida* that latter recognition is primary in Shakespeare's treatment of his material; in *Hamlet* and *Julius Caesar* it remains a muted, troubling doubt.

In *Julius Caesar* we find, more starkly and simply than in *Hamlet*, those problems of communication and expression, those confusions linguistic and ritualistic, which mark the world of the tragedies. The play opens with the sort of apparently expository scene in which Shakespeare actually gives us the major action of the play in miniature. Flavius and Marullus, the tribunes, can barely understand the punning language of the commoners; had they the wit, they might exclaim with Hamlet, "Equivocation will undo us." It is ostensibly broad daylight in Rome, but the situation is dreamlike; for although the language which the two classes speak is phonetically identical, it is, semantically, two separate languages. The cobbler's language, though it sounds like the tribunes', is (to the tribunes) a sort of inexplicable dumb show.

And as with words, so with gestures; the certainties of ceremonial order are as lacking in Rome, as are the certainties of the verbal language. The commoners present an anomaly to the tribunes simply by walking "Upon a labouring day without the sign / Of [their] profession." To the commoners it is a "holiday," to the tribunes (although in fact it is the Feast of Lupercal), a "labouring day." The commoners have planned an observance of Caesar's triumph—itself, to the tribunes, no triumph but rather a perversion of Roman order—but the tribunes send the "idle creatures" off to perform a quite different ceremony:

> Go, go, good countrymen, and for this fault
> Assemble all the poor men of our sort;
> Draw them to Tiber banks, and weep your tears
> Into the channel, till the lowest stream
> Do kiss the most exalted shores of all.
>
> [I.i.57]

Thus, in a Rome where each man's language is foreign to the next, ritual gestures are converted into their opposites; confusion in the state's symbolic system makes every action perilously ambiguous. The tribunes, having turned the commoners' planned ritual into its opposite, go off bravely to make their own gesture, to "Disrobe the images" of Caesar; but shortly we learn that they have actually been made to play parts in a bloodier ritual (one which, as we shall see, becomes increasingly common in the play). And when, in a later scene, we find Brutus deciding upon his proper gesture, the confusions of this first scene should recur to us.[3]

The second scene again opens with mention of specifically ritual observance, as Caesar bids Calphurnia stand in Antony's way to receive the touch which will "Shake off [her] sterile curse" (I.ii.9). Perhaps Shakespeare intends to satirize Caesar's superstitiousness; at least we can say that Calphurnia's sterility and the fructifying touch introduce the question, what sort of ritual can assure (political) succession in Rome? Directly, the Soothsayer steps forth, warning Caesar, "Beware the ides of March." But this communication is not understood: "He is a dreamer; Let us leave him. Pass" (I.ii.24).

What follows, when Caesar and his train have passed off the stage leaving Brutus and Cassius behind, is an enactment—virtually an iconic presentation—of the linguistic problem. More clearly even than the first scene, this scene gives us the picture of Rome as a place where words and rituals have dangerously lost their conventional meanings. As Cassius begins to feel out Brutus about the conspiracy—telling him of Rome's danger and wishes, of Caesar's pitiful mortality, of Brutus's republican heritage—their conversation is punctuated by shouts from offstage, shouts at whose meaning they can only guess. (The situation brings to mind the one in *Hamlet* when the men on the battlements question each other about the strange new customs in Denmark.)

Casca, an eyewitness to the ritual in the marketplace, finally arrives to be their interpreter; but even he has understood imperfectly. Caesar (he says) has been offered the crown, but

> I can as well be hang'd as tell the manner of it: it was mere foolery; I
> did not mark it. I saw Mark Antony offer him a crown—yet 'twas not
> a crown neither, 'twas one of these coronets....   [I.ii.234]

Caesar refused the crown, but Casca suspects "he would fain have had it." "The
rabblement hooted," and Caesar "swooned and fell down at" the stench. As for
the rest, Cicero spoke, but again the language problem intervened: "He spoke
Greek." There is other news: "Marullus and Flavius, for pulling scarfs off
Caesar's images, are put to silence." And, "There was more foolery yet, if I could
remember it" (I.ii.286).

The dramatic point of it all lies not so much in the conflict between
republican and monarchical principles, as in the sheer confusion of the reported
and overheard scene. It is all hooting and clapping and uttering of bad breath,
swooning, foaming at the mouth, and speaking Greek. Casca's cynical tone is well
suited to the occasion, for the farcical charade of the crown-ritual, with Caesar's
refusal and Antony's urging, is itself a cynical manipulation. The crowd clapped
and hissed "as they use to do the players in the theatre" (I.ii.260)—and rightly so.

These two opening scenes give us the world in which Brutus is to
undertake his great gesture. When we next see Brutus, his decision is made: "It
must be by his death" (II.i.10). Behind Brutus's decision is that linguistic and
ceremonial confusion which is comic in the case of the commoners and sinister
in the case of Caesar's crown-ritual. The innovations in Rome's ceremonial order
give evidence to Brutus for the necessity of his gesture. But those same
innovations, attesting to a failure in Rome's basic linguistic situation, also make
it most probable that his gesture will fail. Brutus is not unlike Hamlet: he is a
man called upon to make an expressive gesture in a world where the
commensurate values necessary to expression are lacking. The killing of Caesar,
despite the honorable intentions that are within Brutus and passing show, will
thus be only one more ambiguous, misunderstood action in a world where no
action can have an assured value. Brutus's grand expression might as well be
Greek in this Roman world.

Brutus's position is not unlike Hamlet's, but he does not see what Hamlet
sees. Indeed, he does not even see as much as his fellow conspirators do. To
Cassius, the dreadful and unnatural storm over Rome reflects "the work we have
in hand" (I.iii.129); to the thoughtful Cassius, the confusion in the heavens is an
aspect of the confusion in Rome. But Brutus is, typically, unmoved by the storm,
and calmly makes use of its strange light to view the situation: "The exhalations,
whizzing in the air, / Give so much light that I may read by them" (II.i.44). And
what he reads by this deceptive light is as ambiguous as the shouts of the crowd
at the crown-ritual: the paper bears temptations slipped into his study by the
conspirators, words that mislead and may betray. On the basis of this mysterious
communication, revealed by a taper's dim light and the unnatural "exhalations"
above, Brutus determines to "speak and strike." Every sign is misinterpreted by

Brutus; and the world that seems to him to make a clear demand for words and gestures is in fact a world where words are equivocal and where gestures quickly wither into their opposites.

The situation, as I have so far described it, forces upon us the question critics of the play have most frequently debated: who is the play's hero? A simple enough question, it would seem: the title tells us that this is *The Tragedy of Julius Caesar*. But that answer only serves to show the actual complexity of the question, for if Caesar (who is, after all, dead by the middle of the play) is to this play what, say, Hamlet is to his, then *Julius Caesar* is, structurally at least, a most peculiar tragedy. The question of the hero—and a glance at the critical literature shows that the position is indeed questionable—bears upon fundamental matters of meaning and structure.[4]

Now it is a curious fact about Shakespeare's plays (and, to an extent, about all drama) that the questions the critics ask have a way of duplicating the questions the characters ask, as though the playwright had done his best to make all criticism redundant. As if the play were not enough, nor the characters sufficient unto their conflicts, the critical audience continues to fight the same fights and ask the same questions the characters in the play do. Of *Julius Caesar*, as I have said, the question we most often ask concerns the play's hero: Caesar or Brutus? I have not bothered to tally the choices; for our purposes it is more interesting to notice the mode of critical procedure and the way in which it tends to imitate the actions of the characters in the play. Both critics and characters tend to choose sides in their respective conflicts on the bases of political prejudice and evaluations of moral rectitude. Since the moral and political issues in *Julius Caesar* are themselves eternally moot, it is not surprising that the critical debate continues unresolved.

About Caesar, for instance: if we try to make our determination of herohood on the basis of Caesar's moral stature, we are doing precisely what the characters do; and we find, I think, that he becomes for us what he is for Shakespeare's Romans, less a man than the object of men's speculations. Caesar is the Colossus whose legs we may peep about but whom we can never know; characters and audience alike peep assiduously, each giving us a partial view which simply will not accord with any other. Within the play, Caesar is virtually constituted of the guesses made about him: Casca's rude mockery, Cassius's sneers, Brutus's composite portrait of the present Caesar (against whom he knows no wrong) and the dangerous serpent of the future, Antony's passionate defense, the mob's fickle love and hate: these are the guesses, and contradictory as they are, they give us the Caesar of the play—and of the play's critics.

Of Caesar's, or for that matter of Brutus's, moral status we can have little more certain knowledge than the characters themselves have. What we are in a privileged position to know is the *structure* of the play: the characters' prison, the play's encompassing form, is our revelation. What I propose to do, therefore, is to look at the implicit answer Brutus gives (through his actions) to the question, who is the play's tragic hero?, and compare that answer to the answer revealed by the play's unfolding structure.

Everything Brutus does (until the collapse of the conspiracy) is calculated to justify the title of the play, to make it indeed *The Tragedy of Julius Caesar*. As we watch Brutus directing the conspiracy, we watch a man plotting a typical Shakespearean tragedy; and it is crucial to the success of his plot that Caesar indeed be its hero-victim. The assassination, as Brutus conceives it, must have all the solemnity and finality of a tragic play. The wonder of the spectacle must, as in tragedy, join the audience (both within and without the play) into a community of assent to the deed. For his part, Brutus is content with a necessary secondary role, the mere agent of the hero's downfall—a kind of Laertes, or a more virtuous Aufidius to Caesar's Coriolanus.

But of course Brutus's plot (in both senses of the word) is a failure. The withholding of assent by the audience (again, both within and without the play) proves his failure more conclusively than do moral or political considerations. Brutus misunderstands the language of Rome; he misinterprets all the signs both cosmic and earthly; and the furthest reach of his failure is his failure to grasp, until the very end, the destined shape of his play. Brutus's plot is a failure, but by attending to the direction he tries to give it we can find, ironically, a clear anatomy of the typical tragic action.

Brutus makes his decision and in Act II, scene i he meets with the conspirators. Decius puts the question, "Shall no man else be touch'd but only Caesar?" Cassius, whose concerns are wholly practical, urges Antony's death. But Brutus demurs: the assassination as he conceives it has a symbolic dimension as important as its practical dimension; and although Brutus is not able to keep the two clearly separated (he opposes Antony's death partly out of concern for the deed's appearance "to the common eyes") he is clear about the need for a single sacrificial victim. His emphasis on sacrifice indicates the ritual shape Brutus hopes to give the assassination:

> Let's be sacrificers, but not butchers, Caius.
> We all stand up against the spirit of Caesar,
> And in the spirit of men there is no blood.
> O that we then could come by Caesar's spirit,
> And not dismember Caesar! But, alas,
> Caesar must bleed for it! And, gentle friends,
> Let's kill him boldly, but not wrathfully;
> Let's carve him as a dish fit for the gods,
> Not hew him as a carcass fit for hounds....
> We shall be call'd purgers, but not murderers.
>   [II.i.166, 180]

The "sacrifice" must not be confused with murder, with mere butchery. The name of the deed becomes all important, indicating the distance between a gratuitous, essentially meaningless gesture, and a sanctioned, efficacious, unambiguous ritual.

But Brutus's speech, with a fine irony, betrays his own fatal confusion. "In the spirit of men there is no blood," but in this spirit—this symbol, this embodiment of Caesarism—there is, "alas," as much blood as Lady Macbeth will find in Duncan. Whatever we may feel about Brutus's political intentions, we must acknowledge a failure which has, it seems to me, as much to do with logic and language as with politics: Brutus is simply unclear about the difference between symbols and men. And his confusion, which leads to the semantic confusion between "murder" and "sacrifice," and between meaningless gestures and sanctioned ritual, is the central case of something we see at every social level in Rome. The assassination Brutus plans as a means of purging Rome dwindles to just more of the old ambiguous words and empty gestures. The assassination loses its intended meaning as surely as the commoners' celebration did in scene i.

The assassination is surrounded by Brutus with all the rhetoric and actions of a sacrificial rite. It becomes ritually and literally a bloodbath, as Brutus bids,

> Stoop, Romans, stoop,
> And let us bathe our hands in Caesar's blood
> Up to the elbows, and besmear our swords.
> [III.i.106]

Even the disastrous decision to allow Antony to address the mob arises from Brutus's concern that "Caesar shall / Have all true rites and lawful ceremonies" (III.i.241). In Brutus's plot, where Caesar is the hero-victim whose death brings tragedy's "calm of mind, all passion spent," no one, not even Antony, should be left out of the ceremonious finale. With the conspirators' ritualized bloodbath, indeed, the implied metaphor of the assassination-as-drama becomes explicit—if also horribly ironic:

> *Cas.*   Stoop then, and wash. How many ages hence
> Shall this our lofty scene be acted over
> In states unborn and accents yet unknown!
> *Bru.*   How many times shall Caesar bleed in sport....
> [III.i.112]

Trapped in their bloody pageant, these histrionic conspirators cannot see what, in the terms they themselves suggest, is the most important point of all: this lofty scene occurs, not at the end, but in the middle of a tragic play.

Brutus's plot is not Shakespeare's; and immediately after the conspirators have acted out what should be the denouement of their tragic play, the actual shape of the play (the one they cannot see as such) begins to make itself clear.

Antony, pointedly recalling Brutus's distinction between "sacrificers" and "butchers," says to the slaughtered symbol of tyranny, "O, pardon me, thou bleeding piece of earth, / That I am meek and gentle with these butchers!" (III.i.255), and announces the further course of the action:

> And Caesar's spirit, ranging for revenge,
> With Ate by his side come hot from hell,
> Shall in these confines with a monarch's voice
> Cry 'Havoc!' and let slip the dogs of war,
> That this foul deed shall smell above the earth
> With carrion men, groaning for burial.
>
> [III.i.271]

Brutus's revolutionary gesture, which was intended to bring to birth a stabler order, has been (in an esthetic as well as a political sense) premature. His ritual has failed, and now, as Caesar's spirit ranges for revenge (for there is blood in the spirits of men), it still remains for the proper ritual to be found. Now Brutus will at last assume his proper role: Brutus must be our tragic hero.

Of course he does his best to deny that role. His stoicism—the coolness, for instance, with which he dismisses Caesar's ghost: "Why, I will see thee at Philippi, then" (IV.iii.284)—is hardly what we expect of the grandly suffering tragic hero. Still, it is to Brutus that we owe one of the finest descriptions of the peculiar moment in time occupied by a Shakespearean tragedy:

> Since Cassius first did whet me against Caesar,
> I have not slept.
> Between the acting of a dreadful thing
> And the first motion, all the interim is
> Like a phantasma or a hideous dream.
> The Genius and the mortal instruments
> Are then in council; and the state of man,
> Like to a little kingdom, suffers then
> The nature of an insurrection.
>
> [II.i.61]

The moment is suspended, irresolute, but charged with the energy to complete itself. The separation of "acting" from "first motion," of "Genius" from "mortal instruments," is an intolerable state—the measure of it is the insomnia—which demands resolution. In *Macbeth* we will see this moment protracted and anatomized; it is the tragic moment, and Brutus, for all his Roman calm, must pass through it to its necessary completion.

The acting of the "dreadful thing"—or, rather, what Brutus thinks is the dreadful thing, Caesar's death—does not bring the promised end; that is made immediately clear. Antony's funeral oration shows that Brutus's grand gesture has changed little. Antony easily converts Brutus's sacrifice into murder. In Rome (as in Elsinore) men's actions merely "seem," and Antony can shift the intended meaning of Brutus's action as easily as the tribunes had changed the intended meaning of the commoner's actions in Act I, scene i. Antony can use virtually the same words as the conspirators—he can still call Brutus an "honourable man" and Caesar "ambitious"—and yet make condemnation of approval and approval of condemnation. Even after the revolutionary moment of Caesar's death, this Rome is all of a piece: a volatile mob, empty ceremonies, and a language as problematic as the reality it describes.

Even names are problematic here. It was with names that Cassius first went to work on Brutus:

> 'Brutus' and 'Caesar'. What should be in that 'Caesar'?
> Why should that name be sounded more than yours?
> Write them together: yours is as fair a name.
> Sound them: it doth become the mouth as well.
> Weigh them: it is as heavy. Conjure with 'em:
> 'Brutus' will start a spirit as soon as 'Caesar'.
>
> [I.ii.142]

Cassius's contemptuous nominalism reminds one of Edmund in *King Lear*, who also thinks that one name—that of "bastard," for instance—is as good as any other. Names, to Cassius and Edmund, are conventional signs having reference to no absolute value, and they may be manipulated at will.

In his funeral oration, Antony also plays freely with names; and with the repetition of those two names "Brutus" and "Caesar" he does indeed conjure a spirit. It is the spirit of riot, of random violence, and its first victim (with a grotesque appropriateness) is a poet and a name:

> 3 *Pleb.* Your name sir, truly.
> *Cin.* Truly, my name is Cinna.
> 1 *Pleb.* Tear him to pieces; he's a conspirator!
> *Cin.* I am Cinna the poet, I am Cinna the poet.
> 4 *Pleb.* Tear him for his bad verses, tear him for his bad verses!
> *Cin.* I am not Cinna the conspirator.
> 4 *Pleb.* It is no matter, his name's Cinna; pluck but his name out of his heart, and turn him going.
> 3 *Pleb.* Tear him, tear him!
>
> [III.iii.26]

"Pluck but his name out of his heart, and turn him going": it is like Brutus's impossible, "And in the spirit of men there is no blood." Again, it is the confusion between symbol and reality, between the abstract name and the blood-filled man who bears it. Poets, whose genius it is to mediate symbol and reality and to find the appropriate name to match all things, generally have rough going in *Julius Caesar*. Brutus the liberator shows how he has insensibly aged into a figure indistinguishable from the tyrant when he dismisses. a peace-making poet with a curt, "What should the wars do with these jigging fools?" (IV.iii.135). And Caesar, too, had rebuffed a poetical soothsayer.

The gratuitous murder of Cinna the poet reflects ironically upon the murder of Caesar. The poet's rending at the hands of the mob is unreasonable, based solely on a confusion of identities (of names, words), and while it bears some resemblance to the sacrifice of a scapegoat figure, it is really no sacrifice at all but unsanctioned murder. Caesar's death, similarly, was undertaken as a sacrificial gesture, but quickly became identified with plain butchery. In the mirror of the Cinna episode the assassination is seen as only one case in a series of perverted rituals—a series that runs with increasing frequency now, until the proper victim and the proper form are at last found.

Immediately following the murder of Cinna we see the new triumvirate pricking the names of its victims. The death of Caesar has released the motive force behind the tragedy, and that force runs unchecked now until the final sacrifice at Philippi. From the very first scene of the play we have witnessed ritual gestures that wither into meaninglessness; with the conspiracy and Caesar's death, we become aware of sacrifice as the particular ritual toward which the world of the play is struggling: the series of mistaken rituals becomes a series of mistaken sacrifices, culminating at Philippi.[5]

The wrong sacrifice, the wrong victim: the play offers an astonishing gallery of them. It has been noticed that all of the major characters implicate themselves in this central action:

> each character in the political quartet in turn makes a similar kind of theatrical gesture implying the sacrifice of his own life: to top his refusal of the crown, Caesar offers the Roman mob his throat to cut; Brutus shows the same people that he has a dagger ready for himself, in case Rome should need his death; with half-hidden irony, Antony begs his death of the conspirators; and in the quarrel scene, Cassius gives his "naked breast" for Brutus to strike.[6]

The idea of sacrifice is imagistically linked to the idea of hunters and the hunted. Caesar, says Antony, lies "like a deer strucken by many princes" (Ill.i.210). The ruthless Octavius feels, improbably enough, that he is "at the stake, / And bay'd about with many enemies" (IV.i.48). But it was the conspirators themselves who first suggested the analogy between sacrifice and hunting: their blood-bathing ceremony suggests (as Antony makes explicit) the actions of a hunter with his first kill. And finally, appropriately, the sacrifice-hunting imagery fastens on Brutus: "Our enemies have beat us to the pit" (V.v.23).

From a slightly different perspective, the final scenes at Philippi might be a comedy of errors. Military bungles and mistaken identities follow quickly on each other's heels; the number of suicides, especially, seems excessive. Of the suicide of Titinius, a relatively minor character, Granville-Barker asks, "why, with two suicides to provide for, Shakespeare burdened himself with this third?"[7] The answer to his question, and the explanation for the apparent excesses generally, must be found, I believe, in the context of false sacrifice throughout the play. Caesar's death was one such false sacrifice; Cinna the poet's a horrible mistake; the political murders by the triumvirate continued the chain; and now Cassius sacrifices himself on the basis of a mistake, while Titinius follows out of loyalty to the dead Cassius. Brutus embarked on the conspiracy because he misinterpreted the confused signs in, and above, Rome; the intended meaning of his own gesture was in turn subverted by Antony and the mob. And now Cassius has misinterpreted the signs: friendly troops are mistaken for hostile, their shouts of joy are not understood; thus "Caesar, thou art reveng'd," as Cassius dies, in error, "Even with the sword that kill'd thee" (V.iii.45). And, because Cassius has "misconstrued every thing" (as Titinius puts it [V.iii.84]), Titinius now dies, bidding, "Brutus, come apace."

Titinius places a garland on the dead Cassius before he dies himself; and Brutus, entering when both are dead, pronounces a solemn epitaph:

> Are yet two Romans living such as these?
> The last of all the Romans, fare thee well!
> It is impossible that ever Rome
> Should breed thy fellow. Friends, I owe moe tears
> To this dead man than you shall see me pay.
> I shall find time, Cassius, I shall find time.
>
> [V.iii.98]

The words and the actions form an appropriate tragic device of wonder—but this is no more the end than it was when Brutus spoke an epitaph for Caesar. The death of Cassius is still not the proper sacrifice, and the play has still to reach its culminating ritual.

At Philippi, Brutus at last accepts his role. Against the wishes of Cassius, Brutus insists upon meeting the enemy even before (as the enemy puts it), "we do demand of them." The ghost of Caesar has appeared and Brutus has accepted its portent: "I know my hour is come" (V.v.20). Most significant in Brutus's final speeches is their tone of acceptance:

> Countrymen,
> My heart doth joy that yet in all my life
> I found no man but he was true to me.
> I shall have glory by this losing day,

More than Octavius and Mark Antony
By this vile conquest shall attain unto.
So fare you well at once; for Brutus' tongue
Hath almost ended his life's history.
Night hangs upon mine eyes; my bones would rest,
That have but labour'd to attain this hour.

                                                    [V.v.33]

The expressed idea of the glorious defeat is an authentic sign of Shakespearean tragedy: in a later play, Cleopatra will address similar lines to the wretchedly victorious Octavius. Brutus recognizes here the necessary end of "his life's history": all, from the very start, has tended to this gesture. In it we may find, as in Hamlet's death, "the vision of life in its entirety, the sense of fulfillment that lifts [the hero] above his defeat."[8] Brutus's death is the action which resolves the phantasmal "interim" and ends the "insurrection" in "the state of man."

And this gesture receives, as the assassination of Caesar did not, the requisite assent. Brutus "hath honour by his death," says Strato; and Lucilius, "So Brutus should be found." The opposing parties join together now in Octavius's service, and it is Antony himself who can pronounce the epitaph, "This was the noblest Roman of them all." His words and the gestures are universally accepted.

But what of Rome and its future? I said at the outset of this chapter that the esthetic satisfaction of the perfected tragic form is a "truth" to be accepted only provisionally—and it is the close involvement of Julius Caesar with widely known historical facts which forces upon us the recognition of that truth's limitations. Indeed, the play contains hints—the bloody, divisive course of the triumvirate has been made plain, for instance—which, even without prior historical knowledge, might make us temper our optimism over the play's conclusion. With Brutus's death the play has revealed its tragic entelechy; the destined shape has been found, and the discovery brings its esthetic satisfactions. That the price of our pleasure is the hero's death is not (as in *King Lear* it will so terribly be) a source of discomfort. But what we cannot dismiss is our knowledge that every end is also a beginning. History will have its way; "fate" will defeat men's "wills"; and the "glory" of this "losing day" will tarnish and become, in the movement of time, as ambiguous as the glorious loss on the ides of March.

Thus we must entertain two apparently opposite points of view. With Brutus's sacrificial gesture the ritual has been found which can satisfy the dramatic expectations created by the play. The final words are spoken, the language is understood; and thus the play has given us what Robert Frost demanded of all poetry, "a momentary stay against confusion." But if we stress in Frost's definition his modifying word *momentary*, we find ourselves cast back upon history; and once out of the timeless world of the play, "confusion" predominates. Shakespeare, I believe, recognized this. In *Hamlet* we saw some aspects of his meditation on the problem of time. In *Troilus and Cressida* we will see more, and see in particular some ramifications of that problem for the nature of his art.

NOTES

1. *The Tragic Vision* (New York, 1960), p. 21.

2. *Shakespeare's Tragedies and Other Studies in Seventeenth Century Drama* (London, 1950), p. 8.

3. Cf. the discussion of this scene, and of "mock-ceremony" generally in the play, in Brents Stirling, *Unity in Shakespearean Tragedy* (New York, 1956).

4. Herewith a brief sampler of alternatives. John Dover Wilson, in his New Cambridge edition of the play (Cambridge, 1949) finds that "the play's theme is the single one, Liberty *versus* Tyranny." Since Dover Wilson believes that "Caesarism is a secular threat to the human spirit," it obviously follows that Brutus is our hero (pp. xxi–xxii). But the editor of the Arden *Julius Caesar*, T. S. Dorsch (London, 19555), while admitting that "Caesar has some weaknesses," thinks that the assassination is an "almost incredible piece of criminal folly," for (he asks confidently), "Can it be doubted that Shakespeare wishes us to admire his Caesar?" (pp. xxxviii–xxxix). Another approach is tried by R. A. Foakes: "The three main characters are all noble and yet weak; none has the stature of hero or villain" ("An Approach to *Julius Caesar*," *Shakespeare Quarterly* 5 [Summer 1954]: 270). And, for the sake of symmetry, a final example: "There are ... two tragic heroes in *Julius Caesar*, Brutus and Caesar, although one is more fully treated than the other" (Irving Ribner, *Patterns in Shakespearian Tragedy* [London, 1960], p. 56).

5. John Holloway does not discuss *Julius Caesar* in his *The Story of the Night* (Lincoln, Neb., 1961), but his description of the sacrificial pattern of Shakespearean tragedy is pertinent. That pattern "has as its centre a very distinctive role pursued by the protagonist over the whole course of the play: a role which takes him from being the cynosure of his society to being estranged from it, and takes him, through a process of increasing alienation, to a point at which what happens to him suggests the expulsion of a scapegoat, or the sacrifice of a victim, or something of both" (p. 135). The audience can see that this pattern (which Brutus tries to impose on *his* "Tragedy of Julius Caesar") more aptly describes Brutus's career than Caesar's.

6. Adrien Bonjour, *The Structure of "Julius Caesar"* (Liverpool, 1958), p. 30, n. 33.

7. *Prefaces to Shakespeare* (Princeton, N.J., 1947), 2: 401.

8. Langer, *Feeling and Form* (New York, 1953), p. 356.

JAMES P. BEDNARZ

As You Like It *and the Containment*
of Comical Satire

*'I do now remember a saying, 'The fool doth think he is wise, but the wise
man knows himself to be a fool.'"*

As You Like It

T he anonymous author of *2 Return from Parnassus* implies that Shakespeare
purged Jonson in reaction to *Poetaster*, and the preponderance of evidence
corroborates the theory that he did so in *Troilus and Cressida*, a play that
assimilated and negated the poetics of comical satire. Support for this view is
found not only in *Troilus and Cressida* but also in the metatheatrical commentaries
of *As You Like It* and *Twelfth Night* that precede it. In these three comedies written
between 1600 and 1601, Shakespeare responded with increasing forcefulness to
Every Man Out, *Cynthia's Revels*, and *Poetaster*. The first pairing of dramaturgical
statement and response, *Every Man Out* and *As You Like It*, premiered at the
newly opened Globe theater during its first year of operation. During this crucial
first year at the Globe, the Chamberlain's Men appealed to their audience's
heterogeneous tastes by offering them Jonson's comical satire, invented to
abolish festive comedy, and Shakespeare's festive comedy, designed to deflate
comical satire. Rather than simply defending Shakespeare's popular genre against
Jonson's elitist critique, they sponsored alternative versions of comedy. The
result was a dynamic repertoire that balanced Shakespeare's proven form against
Jonson's provocative experiment. With *Every Man Out* the company met the
growing demand for satire (whetted by the success of *Every Man In*) with a sequel

From *Shakespeare and the Poets' War*. © 2001 by Columbia University Press.

that intensified Jonson's new emphasis on invective. Then, with *As You Like It*, the company's "ordinary poet" defended his embattled genre in a play whose title advertised its continuity with his prior successful comedies at the Theater and Curtain.[1] While Aristophanic Jonson advocated revolutionary standards of art, reason, and satire, Plautine Shakespeare tested them against the opposing standards of nature, instinct, and imagination.

Every Man Out would not have been performed without Shakespeare's consent. As both a sharer in the company and its principal poet, he would have been among those charged with selecting its repertoire. He allowed or even encouraged the players to stage Jonson's comedy because he found it intellectually challenging, even though its principles repudiated his own. He would have understood that he was—in Jonson's schema—closer to Antonio Balladino than to Asper. But the fact that he did not serve as one of the play's principal comedians, as he had in *Every Man In*, symbolizes his alienation from its argument. His absence from the cast of *Every Man Out*, combined with evidence that he appeared in *As You Like It*, shows a pattern of oppositional self-definition through which he first explored the terms of the playwrights' growing estrangement.

That the Chamberlain's Men produced both the neoclassically inspired *Every Man Out* and the popular *As You Like It* is symptomatic of the company's historical position. The opening of the Globe in 1599 marks a midpoint in the troupe's evolution from its organization in 1594 to control of both the Globe and Blackfriars theaters in 1608. At this time Jonson began to aim his work at the "gentlemen," while Shakespeare split his attention between the general audience Jonson dismissed and the elite segment he courted. The Chamberlain's Men didn't have to choose between *As You Like It* and *Every Man Out*. Both were deployed as part of a strategy to consolidate the company's hold on a heterogeneous audience while seeking new ways to increase its attraction for that audience's most sophisticated and profitable members. Jonson's challenge was unmistakable: in *Every Man Out* he posited—for the first time—a distinction between his own self-conscious artistry and Shakespeare's instinctive artlessness. Asper informs the Globe's audience that *Every Man Out* is such an objectively good drama that "if we fail, / We must impute it to this only chance, / '*Art* hath an enemy call'd *Ignorance*'" ("After the Second Sounding," lines 217–19). Marston succinctly defined Jonson's credo as: "Art above Nature, Judgement above Art."[2]

In *As You Like It* Shakespeare answered Jonson's objections to festive comedy in two interconnected ways. First, he tested the standards of "art" and "judgment" against the imperatives of "nature" and "folly" in a metatheatrical subplot involving Jaques (the satirist), Touchstone (the fool), and William (the clown). Through this new topical material he personalized the superiority of festive comedy over comical satire. His purge of Jonson as Ajax in the subplot of *Troilus and Cressida* recapitulates the literary joke he first made in bestowing the name "Jaques"—which in Elizabethan pronunciation is a homonym for "Ajax"—on the melancholy satirist who rejects festive solutions. In his response to *Every Man Out*, Shakespeare began "to run in that vile line" from Jaques of *As You Like It* to Ajax of *Troilus and Cressida*.

Second, Shakespeare used the pastoral element of festive comedy, with its bias toward nature, to counter Jonson's conception of art. By writing a festive comedy that included the "cross-wooing" and "clown" Jonson had censured and a plot based on Thomas Lodge's recent novella, Shakespeare acknowledged affiliations that would have struck Jonson as artless. Since *Much Ado About Nothing* had been urban, Shakespeare's return to pastoral seems strategic. He chose a genre, as Frank Kermode and Edward Tayler have indicated, that was constructed on the all-embracing categories of nature and art.[3] These dialectically opposed yet mutually dependent divisions of experience would become in future criticism synonymous with "Shakespeare" and "Jonson." Yet *As You Like It* is complex; though it seems to justify a natural teleology, it also suggests the inextricable entanglement of nature and art in Rosalind's counterfeit courtship and her concluding masque of Hymen. Shakespeare's drama is remarkable for its tendency to challenge its own premises: the play's benign naturalism mocks its own grinning. Orlando saved Oliver's life because he was motivated by "kindness, nobler ever than revenge, / And nature, stronger than his just occasion" (4.3.128–29). But by being "natural" in *As You Like It* one becomes a "fool": "Nature's natural, the cutter off of nature's wit" (1.2.49–50). The "natural philosopher" Corin strikes a perfect balance when he explains that "he that hath learn'd no wit by nature, nor art, may complain of good breeding, or comes of a very dull kindred" (3.2.29–31). Wit springs from either art or nature, so the witless can cite the absence of either as the cause of their deficiency. Yet one of the most striking paradoxes of *As You Like It* is that the most seemingly natural literary kind is also the most artificial.

Shakespeare discovered in pastoral's dialectic the terms for defusing comical satire, as he countered Jonson's heuristic program with a skeptical humanism underwritten by Socratic ignorance and Erasmian folly. Here Jonson's mockery of the "ridiculous" surrenders to the irony of the "ludicrous," as Asper's assertion of unequivocal truth gives way to Touchstone's determination that "the truest poetry is the most feigning" (3.3.19-20).[4]

I

Shakespeare's main source for *As You Like It* was Thomas Lodge's popular novella *Rosalind: Euphues' Golden Legacy* (1590).[5] And even when we take into consideration Shakespeare's proclivity for finding instead of inventing plots, his comedy is unique in its fidelity to this single antecedent. *As You Like It* follows Rosalind so closely that their main plots can be conflated into a single narrative.[6] Onto this stock, however, Shakespeare grafts three new characters—Jaques,

Touchstone, and William—designed to offer a metatheatrical commentary on the issues Jonson had raised.

Ever since Campbell popularized the theory that Jaques "serves as an amusing representative of the English satirists" and their "doctrines," critics have agreed that Shakespeare intended the character to reflect the rise of satire at the end of the 1590s.[7] We first hear of Jaques when Duke Senior's retainers recall his railing, as "most invectively he pierceth through / The body of the country, city, court" (2.1.58–59). Shakespeare created him, Peter Phialas stresses, "not only to introduce into the scheme of the play allusions to the less attractive features of human life but also to satirize a particular type as well as the general attitude of the new satiric school at the turn of the century."[8] David Bevington suggests that he represents Shakespeare's assimilation of contemporary influences and that his "satirical voice in the forest of Arden offers a valuable if limited contribution" to the play's "many-sided view of humanity."[9] His speech on the seven ages of man is one of the play's most memorable passages, and Shakespeare would increasingly give credence to this perspective as he moved from *As You Like It* through *Twelfth Night* to *Troilus and Cressida*. Yet here he exhibits his strongest resistance to its allure as Jaques, "the agent and the object" of satire, reduces its motivating spirit to an arbitrary and extreme humour.[10]

"My often rumination," Jaques explains, "wraps me in a most humorous sadness" (4.18–20). His satire is a symptom of melancholy, not a cure. "Monsieur Melancholy" is a satirist like Asper and a humourist like Macilente, who can only "rail against ... the world, and all our misery" (3.2.278–79). When Duke Senior states, "I love to cope him in these sullen fits, / For then he's full of matter" (2.1.67–68), he puns on the source of Jaques' "matter" of invention: the diseased bodily fluids that produce satire. Jaques' melancholy reveals a partial truth about experience, but in *As You Like It* joy is privileged over grief. "I had rather have a fool to make me merry," Rosalind explains, "than experience to make me sad" (4.1.27–29). *Every Man Out* isolates the satirist from the humourist, while *As You Like It* negates this distinction.

Thus, while "few critics accept that Jaques himself represents Jonson," writes Russ McDonald, "his satiric credo may fairly be called Jonsonian." In particular, he notes, Jaques' colloquy on satire with Duke Senior in 2.7 "is Jonsonian in spirit and diction," although "complicated by dramatic circumstances."[11] It is here that the satirist allegorizes his name when he asks the Duke for authority to *purge* his sick auditors:

> give me leave
> To speak my mind, and I will through and through
> Cleanse the foul body of th'infected world,
> If they will patiently receive my medicine.
>
> (2.7.58–61)

Jaques' phrasing evokes the purge metaphor of comical satire in a passage that reveals the source of his name, which we should not be misled into pronouncing with a French accent. Anglicized in the early modern period, the name was regularly punned with the word "jakes," which in the first quarto of *King Lear* (1608) is spelled "iaques" (sig. Eɪᵛ; 2.2.67). This pronunciation is the basis for Harington's anecdote in *The Metamorphosis of Ajax* about a flustered lady-in-waiting who introduces one Mr. Jaques Wingfield as "*M. Privy Wingfield.*"[12] That is why Touchstone slyly refers to him as "Master What-ye-call't" (3.3.73). The satirist who vows to "Cleanse the foul body of th'infected world"—to purge it through satire—is the conduit and receptacle of filth. As Helen Gardner observes, he is "discredited before he opens his mouth by the unpleasantness of his name."[13] According to Renaissance medical theory, melancholy caused constipation, making Jaques a "jakes." When in *Every Man In* Stephano, who feigns a fashionable melancholy, is offered the use of Matheo's study, he responds: "I thank you sir, ... have you a close stool there?" (3.1.87–88). Since "Jaques" and "Ajax" are homonyms; Shakespeare uses *the same pun* to score the same topical point—"running in that vile line" from Jaques in *As You Like It* to Ajax in *Troilus and Cressida*—in parodies that bracket his involvement in the Poets' War.

In *As You Like It* Duke Senior rejects the would-be purger because he lacks moral authority and only contributes to the current malaise. And when Jaques presses his case—"What, for a counter, would I do but good?"—the duke responds that he would only further sicken society by committing "Most mischevious foul sin, in chiding sin":

> For thou thyself hast been a libertine,
> As sensual as the brutish sting itself,
> And all th' embossed sores, and headed evils,
> That thou with license of free foot hast caught,
> Wouldst thou disgorge into the general world.
> (2.7.64–69)

Jaques' corrective satire is diseased vomit; he can only verbally disgorge the "embossed sores, and headed evils" he has acquired through sexual license. Such criticism at the Globe can only infect "the general world." "I will chide no breather in the world but myself," Orlando informs him, "against whom I know most faults" (3.2.280–81). But instead of directly addressing the Duke's charge, Jaques defends satire as an impersonal indictment of vice. When he attacks the citizen's wife or poor gallant for vanity, he objects, his critique is general and hence legitimate:

> Why, who cries out on pride
> That can therein tax any private party?

Doth it not flow as hugely as the sea,
Till that the weary very means do ebb?
What woman in the city do I name,
When that I say the city-woman bears
The cost of princes on unworthy shoulders?
Who can come in and say that I mean her,
When such a one as she, such is her neighbor?
Or what is he of basest function,
That says his bravery is not on my cost,
Thinking that I mean him, but therein suits
His folly to the mettle of my speech?
There then! how then? what then? Let me see wherein
My tongue hath wrong'd him; if it do him right,
Then he hath wrong'd himself. If he be free,
Why then my taxing like a wild goose flies,
Unclaim'd of any man.

(2.7.70–87)

This condemnation of fashion mongers—middle-class women and lower-class men who dress above their station—would likely have reminded listeners of Fallace, the spendthrift merchant's wife, and her lover Fastidious Brisk, the bankrupt but ostentatiously dressed pseudocourtier in *Every Man Out*. Cordatus had similarly claimed that Jonson's characters did not represent his contemporaries:

For that were to affirm, that a man, writing of NERO, should mean all Emperors: or speaking of MACHIAVEL, comprehend all Statesmen; or in our SORDIDO, all Farmers; and so of the rest; than which, nothing can be utter'd more malicious, or absurd. Indeed, there are ... narrow-ey'd decipherers ... that will extort strange ... meanings out of any subject, be it never so conspicuous and innocently deliver'd. But to such (where ere they sit conceal'd) let them know, the author defies them, and their writing-tables....

(2.6.166–75)

To name one is not to attack all. But elsewhere Jonson concedes that he does at times obliquely refer to living individuals in some of his characters. He acknowledges having "tax'd" some of the players in Poetaster, a drama he admitted to having written "on" Marston. In defending *Volpone* he would boast that his personation was almost too subtle to be detected: "Where have I been particular? where personal? except to a mimic, cheat, bawd, or buffoon, creatures (for their insolencies) worthy to be tax'd? Yet, to which of these so pointingly, as he might ... have ... dissembled his disease?" (5:18).

"Possibly enough Jonson may be glanced at," Herford and Simpson concur, since Jaques' "vindication of satire" is "substantially Jonson's."[14] But the question of whether Jonson was the model for Jaques hardly does justice to the sophisticated manner in which Shakespeare implies that this is the case while deploying the character in a symbolic narrative. "That Jonson, and Jonson only, is 'translated' in the person of Jaques is, I think, beyond doubt," writes Arthur Gray. Although "Shakespeare's criticism of Jonson is general," he continues, his "identity is proclaimed in the date of *As You Like It*, in personal incidents, in character, in dramatic motive."[15] But though Jaques' language of purgation and denial of personal reference are Jonsonian, both are also mainstays of the new satiric movement. While Marston builds personal details into his Jonson caricature, Shakespeare's subtler innuendo verges on being "Unclaim'd of any man." Jaques represents an attitude shared by a new generation of writers, including Donne, Guilpin, Rankins, Weever, Hall, Harington, Jonson, and Marston. Those who saw themselves in its mirror deserved to be so viewed. Still, in the Elizabethan commercial theater this kind of satirist appears only in *Every Man Out* and *Histriomastix* before stepping forward in *As You Like It*.[16]

II

Though he invokes Jonsonian satire, however, Jaques is part of a dramatic fiction more symbolic than mimetic. A third of his lines praise the clown Touchstone, an estimation Jonson would have detested. None of the modern commentators who identify Jaques' attitude with Jonson's account for the fact that when he lauds Touchstone's wit and asks to serve as the duke's retainer in motley—his "only suit"—his reverence is counter-referential, an ironic inversion of a Jonsonian paradigm. In *Ben Jonson's Parodic Strategy*, Robert Watson observes that his characters often serve as literary markers—"strategic reductions" of his rivals' work—that encode literary theory in a "hierarchy of texts." "Jonson's comedies," he writes, "are acts of theatrical imperialism" in "a proud campaign for sovereignty in drama" through which he transforms his competitors into "self-dramatizing characters" acting out "unhealthy literary forms."[17] *As You Like It* turns this strategy against Jonson.

Shakespeare insists that the fool not only subsumes the satirist but is superior to him, insofar as he admits that folly rather than wisdom is the universal condition of human experience. Touchstone, like Rosalind, exemplifies C. L. Barber's notion of "a mocking reveller," a character who yields to festivity by accepting the natural as irrational.[18] At the turn of the seventeenth century a renewed interest in the fool led to such plays as George Chapman's *All Fools* and a flurry of publications, such as *Fool upon Fool* (1600), Pasquil's *Foolscap* (1600), and *The Hospital of Incurable Fools* (1600). By adapting an Erasmian defense with roots in Socratic ignorance and Christian folly, Shakespeare aligns himself with the most skeptical manifestation of Renaissance humanism to bolster his case against Jonson. In contrast to Jonson's attempt to distinguish the judicious from the humoured, Shakespeare emphasizes their common fallibility. Whereas Jonson's satirist makes absolute moral judgments and resists desire, Shakespeare's fool derides a natural condition he embraces.

Once the Poets' War had become more aggressive in its second phase, Shakespeare imagined this same subordination of critic to fool with greater vehemence in the punitive fantasy of *Twelfth Night*. Jaques' respect for Touchstone's wit and Malvolio's disdain for Feste's folly are variations on a single theme. The only difference is that *Twelfth Night* shows greater irritation in reiterating the same hierarchy, as the critic resists identifying with the fool until he is forced to acknowledge their resemblance.

Touchstone embodies festive comedy in all its contradictions. Robert Armin, the actor for whom the role was created, wrote a book, *Fool upon Fool*, that distinguished between "natural" and "artificial" varieties, between idiots who stumbled on wit and professional jesters. In practice, however, they were often difficult to differentiate, as in the case of Touchstone, who is both "the cutter off of Nature's wit" (1.2.49–50) and a "deep contemplative" (2.7.31). It is necessary, then, not to draw too firm a line between clown and fool—rustic buffoon and court jester—since Shakespeare blurs this distinction. "Touchstone" is generically labeled "Clown" in the First Folio's speech-prefixes, while in the dialogue he is also called a "motley" or "clownish fool." Like Lear's fool, he never has a name: he only takes on the *alias* "Touchstone" when entering the forest of Arden. If the clown is associated with nature and the fool with art, Touchstone fuses both. The scope of his satire, moreover, is remarkably comprehensive; if he criticizes the tenets of comical satire, exposing the flaws of art, he ridicules festive comedy as well, even as he submits to its imperatives.

Jaques' long endorsement of Touchstone and his recognition of the satiric potential of clowning (2.7.12–34) constitute Shakespeare's first explicit praise of folly. Earlier clowns, beginning with the Dromios of *The Comedy of Errors*, show wit on occasion, but none exhibits his talents as ostentatiously as Touchstone and none receives such glowing reviews within the play. "The wise man's folly," Jaques explains, "is anatomized / Even by the squand'ring glances of the fool" (2.7.56–57). "He uses his folly like a stalking horse," Duke Senior agrees, behind which he "shoots his wit" (5.4.106–7). And when Celia threatens to have him "whipt for taxation" for mocking her father, the usurping Duke Frederick, Touchstone's retort summarizes his special status: "The more pity that fools may not speak wisely what wise men do foolishly" (1.2.86–87).

In Renaissance neoclassicism from Sidney through Jonson, the clown is a vilified personification of commercial theater. Tallying the "gross absurdities" of popular dramatists in the *Apology*, Sidney had famously complained that "mongrel tragi-comedies" had begun "mingling kings and clowns not because the matter so carrieth it, but thrust in clowns by head and shoulders, to play a part in majestical matters, with neither decency nor discretion."[19] Jonson went so far as to urge the character's elimination from his native genre, which he achieved in his last two comical satires. In *Every Man Out*, however, he only debased the clown's function and diminished his wit. After Musco (later called Brainworm) of *Every Man In*, Jonson's last sympathetic Plautine clown, the fools of *Every Man Out*, such as Carlo Buffone and Sogliardo, became one-dimensional humourists.[20]

Jonson personalizes his argument through analogy by comparing Shakespeare to the social-climbing country clown Sogliardo, whom he describes as "*An essential Clown ... so enamour'd of the name of a Gentleman, that he will have it, though he buys it*" (characters, lines 78–80). Returning from the Heralds, he brags, "I can write myself a gentleman now; here's my patent, it cost me thirty pounds" (3.4.52–53). Sogliardo is not a caricature of Shakespeare, but when Puntarvolo suggests that the "word" of his new coat of arms should be "*Not without mustard*" (3.4.86), parodying Shakespeare's "*Non sanz droict*," the hit is palpable. Indeed, this quip might have sparked Touchstone's jest about the knight who did not lie when he swore that "the pancakes" were "good" and "the mustard was naught," although the pancakes were bad and the mustard good, because he swore "*by his honor*," and "if you swear by that that is not, you are not forsworn" (1.2.63–77). Shakespeare's joke about honor and mustard turns Jonson's critique on its head and mocks the social pretension Shakespeare had been accused of exhibiting.

Having acquired a coat of arms in 1596 in his father's name, with a motto probably of his own devising, Shakespeare could call himself a "gentleman." But in 1599, the issue of his gentility had become potentially embarrassing when he attempted to upgrade his shield by placing the Arden pattern of his mother's more prestigious side of the family on its sinister side and moving the Shakespeare crest to its dexter half. Jonson could have known of these affairs at the College of Arms through his friendship with William Camden, the Clarenceux King-of-Arms, who assisted Sir William Dethick, Garter King-of-Arms, in drawing up the grant for the impalement, which was not issued. The problem was that the heralds found it difficult to know from which branch of this ancient family the Ardens of Wilmcote had descended and had used the pattern of the Ardens of Park Hall before scratching it out and adding that of the Ardens of Cheshire. In 1602, the original bid for gentrification by "Shakespeare the Player" was included in the charges Ralph Brooke, the York Herald, planned to bring against Camden and Dethick for certifying "mean" persons.[21] Sogliardo's suggested coat of arms differs from Shakespeare's, being organized around "A swine without a head, without brain, wit, any thing indeed, ramping to gentility" (3.4.64–66). But it is hard to miss Jonson's imputation that Shakespeare was clownish in his bid to purchase honor.[22]

Shakespeare answered Jonson's attack on clowning by identifying poetry with Ovidian desire instead of Horatian reason. "I am here with thee and thy goats," Touchstone tells the shepherdess Audrey, "as the most capricious [variable and goatlike] poet, honest Ovid, was among the Goths [pronounced 'goats'].'' Ovid, whose seducer's manual *The Art of Love* and alleged affair with Augustus's granddaughter were thought to have caused his exile to bleak and barbaric Tomis, embodied a defiance of humanist ideals.[23] And when Audrey asks if "poetry" is "a true thing," Touchstone replies:

> No, truly; for the truest poetry is the most feigning, and lovers are given to poetry; and what they swear in poetry may be said as lovers they do feign.
>
> (3.3.19–22)

To counter Plato's accusation in the *Republic* that poets are liars, a charge repeated in Stephen Gosson's *School of Abuse*, Sidney had described poetry as an art in which "feigning may be tuned to the highest key of passion" to move its audience to virtuous action. Indeed, the "feigning" of "notable images," he argued, was a "right describing note to know a poet by."[24] Touchstone agrees that for poets fiction is as good as fact, but he reverses Sidney's polemic by insisting that poets "feign" or "pretend" because they "fain" or "desire" and are willing to lie to achieve their amorous ends. Sidney had begun *Astrophil and Stella* with the line, "Loving in truth and fain in verse my love to show," and Touchstone recovers this sense of the word to reject the didactic aims of English neoclassicism. Poetry, then, to reverse Sidney's critical dictum, was the expression not of "erected wit" but of "infected will."

Rather than being the play's spokesman, however, Touchstone's ironic voice is destabilized by Shakespeare, and his affair with Audrey is as far from the festive norm epitomized by Orlando and Rosalind as Silvius's Petrarchan love for Phebe. He enters the forest without enthusiasm: "Ay, now am I in Arden, the more fool I" (2.4.16), and, lacking commitment, he serves as a parody of desire on its lowest level. He wants Sir Oliver Martext to wed him to Audrey, he tells Jaques, so that "not being well married, it will be a good excuse for me hereafter to leave my wife" (3.3.92–94). As an unreliable spokesman, he incorporates in his folly a debased naturalism that balances Silvius's bloodless devotion. Between the extremes of Silvius and Touchstone, Rosalind balances attachment and detachment, synthesizing their polarity.

Shakespeare's conception of his ironic fool as a response to Jonson's self-righteous satirist was stimulated by Robert Armin's replacement of William Kemp in the Chamberlain's Men in 1600. In *2 Return from Parnassus*, when Kemp laughs with Burbage about how Shakespeare has purged Jonson, he shares in his revenge as an actor and a clown. But though Kemp still served as the personification of all that Jonson detested, by the time this scene was written he had already left the company. A court deposition by John Heminges and Henry Condell in 1619 states that although Kemp had been among the original members of the Chamberlain's Men who held a moiety of the Globe's lease, he had surrendered his share "about the time of the building of the said Playhouse ... or shortly after." The Globe's construction began after the company signed a contract with the builder Peter Street on 26 February 1599. By 16 May, it had, as Park Honan notes, at least "a partial existence," and by September, Thomas Platter ventured "over the water" to see *Julius Caesar*.[25] Bernard Beckerman has suggested that "before the stage of the Globe was painted and the spectators admitted," Kemp "severed his connection with the Lord Chamberlain's Men."[26] But it is possible that he stayed on until the beginning of the following year. His only allusion to this event appears in his dedication to *Nine Days' Wonder*, which describes his dance marathon from London to Norwich, between 11 February and 11 March 1600, as a consequence of his departure from the Globe: "Some swear ... I have trod a good way to win the world: others that guess righter, affirm, I have without good help danced my self out of the world."[27] "It was odd," notes Gerald Bentley, "for an actor as famous as Kempe to leave the leading company of the time."[28] It seems likely that Kemp either experienced friction with the other members of the company or was drawn to other opportunities, such as being a solo performer, or both.[29]

Kemp was notorious for his jigs and stage antics and his success as a comic numbskull in the roles of Bottom and Dogberry. Shakespeare, however, included no important clowns in either *Henry V* or *Julius Caesar*, both written in 1599. And he even shares a measure of Jonson's anxiety when he has Hamlet urge the traveling actors to "let those that play your clowns speak no more than is set down for them," since unscripted improvisation prompts "barren spectators" to laugh when "some necessary question of the play" should be considered. It has long been suspected that Kemp is here being reprimanded for a proclivity to that "villainous" disruption that "shows a most pitiful ambition in the fool that uses it" (3.2.38–45). Although it is difficult to pinpoint when Armin replaced him, through the recent examination of the problem by Evelyn Joseph Mattern it seems likely that Armin premiered as Touchstone early in 1600.[30]

This would account for the lavish praise and topicality that Shakespeare writes into the role. As Leslie Hotson first noticed, the clown's alias, "Touchstone," alludes to two of Armin's professional affiliations. A touchstone was used by goldsmiths to test the quality of metals rubbed against it, and he had served his apprenticeship in the Goldsmiths' Company (the heraldic crest of which shows a "woman clothed, holding in one hand a touchstone"). He might even have later returned to the trade or at least enjoyed the guild's privileges.[31] But the pseudonym Touchstone evoked his comic persona as well, since Armin had probably already created for himself the role of the clown Tutch in *The Two Maids of More-Clacke*. Playing on his name, Tutch confesses his double nature as truth teller and liar: "now am I tried on my own touch, / I am true metal one way, but counterfeit another." Thus, with a single stroke, Shakespeare not only named Touchstone in homage to Armin but sanctioned his status as the character who, despite his flaws, cleverly assessed the value of others.[32] The Chamberlain's Men was a repertory company, and Shakespeare shaped his plays to his fellows' skills. A versatile performer, Armin reprised Kemp's russet roles, including the broad humor of Dogberry, while fleshing out the new motley jesters Shakespeare created for him. The new poet-player was able to master Shakespeare's comic patter with a fluency that John Davies of Hereford attributed to his ability to "*wisely play the fool.*"[33] Through him, Shakespeare explored a range of new possibilities—especially his mastery of mock academic discourse—in a collaboration that climaxed in *King Lear*. In 1600, then, Armin was a new actor who could make explicit the philosophical acceptance of folly upon which festive comedy was based.

III

Shakespeare is, for the most part, what George Steiner calls an "altruistic" dramatist who submerges his voice in that of his characters, gaining immortality at the price of anonymity. Yet an amusing exception occurs in *As You Like It* when, in the last of his three topical overlays, Shakespeare represents himself as a Jonsonian caricature to seal his acceptance of the wisdom of folly. The main purpose of this short episode is to admit his own folly—that is, his own wisdom— by subjecting himself to Touchstone's censure. In the first scene of the fifth act, without the slightest forewarning, a country clown named William emerges from the forest of Arden, briefly converses with Audrey and Touchstone, and is flouted off the stage. It is likely that William, who shares both the author's first name and his birthplace, was an assay in the personally allusive style of the Poets' War, enabled by the pastoral convention of self-reference.

From the classical period to the Renaissance, pastoral poets regularly included themselves among their shepherds, from Virgil's Tityrus through Sannazaro's Ergasto, Sidney's Philisides, and Spenser's Colin Clout. The standard technique of self-portraiture in the Renaissance was to follow Sannazaro's example in *Arcadia* by depicting oneself as a mournful lover, often the victim of cross-wooing. Indeed, the attraction of pastoral self-reference was so strong that even Anthony Munday became "shepherd Tonie" in *England's Helicon* (1600). What is more, the great English examples—Philisides in the *Arcadia* and Colin Clout in *The Shepherd's Calendar* and Book Six of *The Fairy Queen*—involved cameo appearances hidden in tangled plots. These characters were planted in self-reflexive episodes for readers in the know who were meant to be surprised by the sudden emergence of truth in feigning. Having satirized a proto-Jonsonian satirist in "Jaques," Shakespeare felt obligated to generate laughter at his own expense, and he did so by re-creating himself as "William."[34] There is, furthermore, circumstantial evidence that Shakespeare acted this role alongside Armin during the play's initial run in order to implicate himself in the inescapable folly that determines the plot *of As You Like It* and the shape of human experience.

Enter William

TOUCHSTONE   It is meat and drink to me to see a clown. By my troth, we that have good wits have much to answer for; we shall be flouting; we cannot hold.

WILLIAM   Good ev'n, Audrey.

AUDREY   God ye good ev'n, William.

WILLIAM   And good ev'n to you, Sir.

TOUCHSTONE   Good ev'n, gentle friend. Cover thy head, cover thy head; nay, prithee be cover'd. How old are you, friend?

WILLIAM   Five and twenty, sir.

TOUCHSTONE   A ripe age. Is thy name William?

WILLIAM   William, Sir.

TOUCHSTONE   A fair name. Wast born i' the forest here?

WILLIAM   Ay, Sir, I thank God.

TOUCHSTONE   "Thank God"—a good answer. Art rich?

WILLIAM   Faith Sir, so, so.

TOUCHSTONE   "So, so" is good, very good, very excellent good; and yet it is not, it is but so, so. Art thou wise?

WILLIAM   Ay, Sir, I have a pretty wit.

TOUCHSTONE   Why, thou say'st well. I do now remember a saying, "The fool doth think he is wise, but the wise man knows himself to be a fool." The heathen philosopher, when he had a desire to eat a grape, would open his lips when he put it into his mouth, meaning thereby that grapes were made to eat and lips to open. You do love this maid?

WILLIAM   I do, Sir.

TOUCHSTONE   Give me your hand. Art thou learned?

WILLIAM   No, Sir.

TOUCHSTONE   Then learn this of me: to have is to have. For it is a figure in rhetoric that drink, being pour'd out of a cup into a glass, by filling the one doth empty the other. For all your writers do consent that *ipse* is he: now, you are not *ipse*, for I am he.

WILLIAM   Which he, Sir?

TOUCHSTONE   He, sir, that must marry this woman. Therefore, you clown, abandon—which is in the vulgar leave—the society—which in the boorish is company—of this female—which in

> the common is woman; which together is,
> abandon the society of this female, or clown,
> thou perishest; or to thy better understanding,
> diest; or (to wit) I kill thee, make thee away,
> translate thy life into death, thy liberty into
> bondage. I will deal in poison with thee, or in
> bastinado, or in steel; I will bandy with thee in
> faction; I will o'errun thee with policy; I will kill
> thee a hundred and fifty ways: therefore
> tremble and depart.

AUDREY   Do, good William.

WILLIAM   God rest you merry, sir. Exit.

                                                (5.1.10–59)

This one-sided *moromachia* between the learned fool and the country clown—between art and nature—becomes wittier when it is read in terms of an original performance that capitalized on Armin and Shakespeare's presence on-stage as theatrical celebrities. The caricature that Shakespeare draws of himself entering the forest of his fiction constitutes a comic etiology through which the established London poet recounts his provincial background and identifies himself as a dim-witted country bumpkin—like Jonson's Sogliardo—baffled by the mock "wisdom" of a learned fool. Shakespeare completed his play when he was thirty-five; William, who is twenty-five, functions as a retrospective glance at his rural past that distanced him from his current married status and London residence. Spenser, at twenty-five, had presented himself in *The Shepherd's Calendar* as Colin Clout, a "shepherd's boy"; Shakespeare, ten years older, casts himself as a baffled but good-natured "youth" of the forest.

The Touchstone–Audrey–William triangle has roots not only in *The Shepherd's Calendar* (1579) but also in Book Six of *The Fairy Queen* (1596), which suggested the narrative outline for Touchstone's adventure in Arden. Shakespeare comically reconfigures Sir Calidore's pastoral interlude in Book Six in Touchstone's violation of the knight's exemplary performance. Spenser's Sir Calidore, the knight of Courtesy, voluntarily becomes a shepherd and praises country life to old Meliboe (6.9.19), after having fallen in love with Pastorella, a shepherdess later discovered to be an aristocratic foundling. In courting her, Calidore is contrasted with the clownish Coridon, a country rival to whom he is always considerate, even while proving his own natural superiority, especially his courage. Furthermore, in the same episode, in a surprising moment of self-reference, Calidore inadvertently disrupts Colin Clout's vision of the Graces and causes the poet's beloved (who appears at its center) to vanish. Distraught by her disappearance and deprived of his harmonic rapture, Spenser's hapless persona smashes his bagpipe and moans (6.10.18). Shakespeare's rewriting of Spenser's pastoral episode on the lowest mimetic level is one of the play's better literary jokes. Touchstone, in place of Calidore, exchanges court life for a bucolic existence, but he does so only reluctantly and details his ambivalent feelings about it to old Corin, whom he ridicules for lacking courtly manners and pandering, to the rams of his flock. Once in the country, he romances an ignorant shepherdess, Audrey (without royal connections), and menaces her ex-beau, his rustic competitor, William, whom he threatens to murder. Instead of accidentally upsetting the author's persona—as Calidore had done to Colin Clout—Touchstone deliberately abuses William, whom he viciously replaces in Audrey's favor. Using the pastoral convention of self-reference, Spenser and Shakespeare thus make brief appearances near the ends of their works, in scenes specifically created to show them being deprived of the pastoral happiness their fictions celebrate. Unlike Spenser, however, Shakespeare fashioned this episode of dramatic self-effacement to demonstrate the Socratic paradox that the admission of ignorance is the securest form of knowledge. And it is through this encounter that the "gentle" poet's "pretty wit" upsets "learned" distinctions in the Ur-text of all defenses of Shakespeare's natural genius. When, at the end of the seventeenth century, John Ward wrote in his diary that "Mr. Shakespeare was a natural wit, without any art at all," he unknowingly repeated a version of the poet's self-created myth, stripped of its *sprezzatura*.[35]

In the dialogue between Touchstone and Audrey that precedes William's entry, the court clown confronts her with the suspicion that "there is a youth ... in the forest lays claim to you." "Ay, I know who 'tis," Audrey responds, while insisting that "he hath no interest in me in the world" (5.1.6–9). Since, William Jones points out, the Globe was sometimes called "the world" (by Kemp, among others) Audrey is ironically made, on a metatheatrical level, to deny that Shakespeare had any proprietary interest in a character in a play he had written for a playhouse he partially owned.[36]

The joke that the tongue-tied country clown William represented Shakespeare as Shakespeare represented *him* is developed through the sequence of questions Touchstone asks. These not only reveal the youth's name and birthplace but also describe him as having "a pretty wit," although he is not "learned." The self-portrait that emerges fleshes out Jonson's critique but reverses its implications. At the play's opening, Celia identifies "Nature" as the source of "wit" (1.2.45), and it is in this sense—as inspiration—that Shakespeare employs it. During the Renaissance, "wit" acquired a double meaning. In Old English, the word originally referred to "the power of thinking and reasoning," but during the sixteenth century it came to mean "the ability to speak facetiously." This second meaning distinguishes Shakespeare's artful self-portrait, which exhibits what Fuller later calls "the quickness of his Wit." What "William" lacked was William's specialty, as the play's first audience was coaxed to look through the character to the poet-player who impersonated him. The punning begins when Armin/Touchstone, hearing his rival call himself William, concurs that it is a "fair" name, meaning both "attractive" and "appropriate."

William, after all, plays "William playing 'William.'" Touchstone's otherwise bland response would have been amusing only if the audience recognized that the name of the nonce character he addressed was that of the actor playing "a poet playing a clown." What is most daring about this self-representation is that it breaks the Renaissance taboo requiring pastoral pseudonyms. Here Shakespeare returns to the norm of Old Comedy, which specifically named its targets. And just as Socrates in a famous anecdote about Aristophanes' *Clouds* acknowledged his resemblance to the distorted comic mask of the actor who parodied him, Shakespeare admitted his nearness to the doltish clown he played.

In *Shakespeare's Clown: Actor and Text in the Elizabethan Playhouse*, David Wiles detects the personal dimensions of this exchange but explains it with only partial success. He correctly assumes that the audience was "encouraged to decipher the name 'Touchstone' as an alias for the real clown, Robert Armin," but misidentifies his straight man as Kemp. "The other clown's name— 'William'—is repeated three times," he notes, "so that the audience will not miss the contrast between the departing company clown, William Kemp, and the new fool/clown," as the "traditional simple-minded rustic" was "symbolically dismissed from the new Globe stage."[37] But it is improbable that Kemp would have allowed himself to be humiliated in this manner, especially since he had already been replaced by Armin. Wiles misses an important clue: Armin's question "Wast born i' the forest here?" would have prompted a laugh only if Shakespeare replied, "Ay, Sir, I thank God." Still, anyone who was alert enough to have expected William Kemp to appear would have been doubly amused to find another William in his place. If Phyllis Rackin is right, William of *As You Like It* is but one of a series of instances in which "Shakespeare associates a character who shares his own name with inarticulate, humble life obliterated by the elite textualized world of his betters."[38]

Arden is a theatrical construct populated by pastoral types. "For the learned and literary," Helen Gardner writes, "this is one of Shakespeare's most allusive plays."[39] That Arden is posited as a natural world that dramatizes its artificiality is apparent when the shepherdess Phebe displays her knowledge of current poetry and literary biography in a couplet that eulogizes Christopher Marlowe by naming him after his famous lyric, "The Passionate Shepherd," and quoting a line (I.176) from *Hero and Leander* (1598):

> Dead shepherd, now I find thy saw of might,
> "Who ever lov'd that lov'd not at first sight?"
> (3.5.81–82)

This concise pastoral elegy is yet another example of the play's compendium of generic motifs; Arden becomes a forest of the literary imagination even as it takes on a more familiar geographical contour. "Ardennes" is a fictional forest lifted from Lodge's *Rosalind*, which was based on the actual territory, located in present-day France, Belgium, and Luxembourg. But when re-creating it as the "Arden" of *As You Like It*, Shakespeare gave it a native English inflection, suggested by the rustic greetings "Good even, Audrey," and "God ye good even, William." This layer of referentiality superimposed over Lodge's exotic setting the Forest of Arden in Warwickshire, which surrounded the town of Stratford where he was born. "To William Shakespeare this was native ground," writes Stuart Daley, who explains how a London audience would have responded to the mention of its name:

> To many Elizabethans ... the Forest of Arden ... was anything but a *terra incognita* in a remote corner of the Kingdom. A dominant geographical feature of the central Midlands since the Middle Ages, by the sixteenth century the Forest or Woodland of Arden had become a famous and storied region covering over two hundred square miles in the heart of England.[40]

Shakespeare, who shares Kemp's first name, seems to have revived his part as the country clown in mock deference to Armin. But he also appears to have created the role of William of Arden—reflecting the maternal lineage he had hoped to add to his coat of arms—in answer to Jonson's charge that his artlessness had caused him to lapse into absurdity in his comedies of cross-wooing. This self-caricature is the only instance during the Poets' War in which Shakespeare is impersonated, and its deftness probably discouraged further *ad hominem* criticism.

The probability that Shakespeare played William when *As You Like It* premiered is strengthened by a late oral tradition indicating that he acted the part of old Adam, Orlando's servant. In the middle of the eighteenth century, William Oldys noted that "one of Shakespeare's younger brothers," who had been "a spectator of him as an actor in some of his plays," had identified him as wearing "a long beard" and seeming "so weak ... that he was ... carried ... to a table, at which he was feasted." The story is too late to have come from Shakespeare's brother, and when Edward Capell repeated it, he attributed it instead to a relative and explained why he found it credible:

> A traditional story was current some years ago about Stratford—that a very old man of that place,—of weak intellects, but yet related to Shakespeare,—being ask'd by some of his neighbors, what he remembered about him; answer'd—that he saw him once brought on the stage upon another man's back; which answer was apply'd by the hearers, to his having seen him perform in this scene the part of Adam: That he should have done so, is made not unlikely by another constant tradition,—that he was no extraordinary actor, and therefore took no parts upon him but such as this.[41]

If we accept the plausibility of Shakespeare's having acted the role of old Adam, it is likely that once Orlando had "set down" his "venerable burthen" (2.7.167–68) and Adam vanished at the end of the scene, the actor who played him could also double as young William. "For the professional players," Gerald Bentley explains, "doubling" was "a normal feature of casting."[42] Like Armin, who, due to his skill as a singer, must have doubled as Amiens, Shakespeare probably played both Adam and William. By taking on these roles in 1600 he would have informed the play's original meaning with a unique metatheatricality: a middle-aged man of thirty-five would have personified an entire cycle of life in the three (if not seven) ages of man. And since he probably knew, as Camden notes in *Remains* (1605), that "Adam" in Hebrew meant "man," he would have fused in the same performance generic and specific versions of his identity.[43]

Touchstone's triumph over William in the fifth act is achieved through belligerent pseudophilosophical rhetoric aimed at Arden's natural man. The comic manipulation of academic jargon—a prime feature of Renaissance wit in the style of Erasmus and Rabelais—was one of Armin's specialties. Here its pseudoauthentication is backed by the threat of violence. Touchstone begins by citing "the heathen philosopher," perhaps Aristotle, who maintains that a thing is defined by its use. Hence, he implies, deploying a pastoral metaphor, Audrey is a grape ripe for eating. Arden presents a banquet for the omnivorous Touchstone, who feeds on William as well: it is, he admits, "meat and drink to me to see a clown." But how does he prove that he is "the man" to replace William? Mastery of rhetoric—the art of persuasion based on classical models—includes an understanding of the laws of identity, possession, and cause and effect. Since pouring water from a cup into a glass empties the former into the latter, rhetoric determines that only one rival can win. Which "he"? In Latin, *ipse* means "he himself," and Touchstone usurps the word's privileged cultural authority to insist on his superior status. But the phrase "*ipse*, he" had a specific literary connotation that Touchstone evokes to clinch his case: in Lyly's *Euphues* it denotes the successful suitor Curio, who causes Lucilla to reject the work's titular hero.[44] Jonson, who would later comment on Shakespeare's "small Latin and less Greek," quotes Cicero in Latin to justify comical satire. "Learned" Touchstone uses this same tactic to claim Audrey before translating his threat into "the boorish" to beat William. Learning for Touchstone is a weapon to bully a bumpkin; all he offers to support his assumption of privilege is the tautology "to have is to have." Unfortunately for William (the empty cup), the opposite is also true. And at this point the one-sided war between sly and dry clowns comes to a halt as William, encouraged by Audrey to leave, hospitably bids Touchstone farewell, exhibiting what Jonson would later call Shakespeare's "open and free nature."

As You Like It, Chambers writes, "does for the Elizabethan drama what the long string of pastoral poets, Spenser and Sidney, Lodge and Greene.... and the rest, had already done." And when "it goes beyond *Rosalind*," Edwin Greenlaw adds, it does so "in conformity to the typical pastoral plot lines of Sidney and Spenser."[45] The William episode combines two prominent love triangles in Renaissance pastoral, the self-reflexive episode and a kind of pastourelle, in which an amorous courtier seduces a country girl away from an ignorant country bumpkin. At first glance, the William–Audrey–Touchstone love triangle seems merely to repeat the Costard–Jaquenetta–Armado cross-wooing in *Love's Labor's Lost*. *As You Like It*, however, invests this mock triumph of art over nature with self-reflexive irony. Those familiar with the formula for self-representation in Renaissance pastoral had to have been surprised at Shakespeare's radical subversion of its typical expression. In the most famous use of a pastoral persona in the English Renaissance, Spenser had originally represented himself in *The Shepherd's Calendar* as the victimized Colin Clout, who loved Rosalind until his rival Menalcus "by treachery" destroyed her "faultless faith" and "the truest shepherd's heart made bleed" ("June," lines 43–48; 102–11).[46] Less original authors, faced with Shakespeare's choices, might have written themselves into the mournful Silvius yearning for Phebe or the melancholy Jaques abandoning love. But here, in a wholly parodic register, we find a nasty scene of infidelity centering on Audrey (not Rosalind), whose name suggests her worthlessness since "in the sixteenth century, the word tawdry was coined from Audrey, a name favored by the poorer classes, to suggest any cheap or garish goods."[47]

In representing himself in this manner, moreover, Shakespeare aligned himself with the native medieval tradition of poetic self-effacement. Two hundred years earlier, William Langland in *Piers Plowman* had ironically depicted himself as "Long Will," a man too weak and tall for field labor.[48] And Chaucer had poked fun at himself in *The Canterbury Tales* as a fat "elvyssh" loner whose "drasty rymyng is nat worth a toord!"[49] Both Chaucer and Shakespeare contrive to have their personae ostracized by other characters. Among a company of raconteurs, Geoffrey is censured for his artless tale of Sir Thopas, and in a play that unites four couples (a record number for festive comedy), "William's unharvested ripeness represents an opportunity not taken, and he is banished from the possibility of love."[50]

Part of the joke of Touchstone's abuse of William is the way in which he leads him through the first stages of a mock marriage ceremony—"You do love this maid?" "I do, sir." "Give me your hand"—only to dash his hopes. As the odd man out in his own work, like Bottom in *A Midsummer Night's Dream*, Shakespeare excludes himself (as Jaques does) from the scene of social bonding that gives closure to festive comedy. The title of Shakespeare's play—*As You Like It*—admits its commitment to its audience as the arbiter of theatrical value. Bequeathed to Shakespeare as the paradoxical mark of a superior poet, Chaucer's legacy is the definitive example of an author willing to depend on his audience's favor to redress his self-imputed weakness. Shakespeare repeats that paradigm, consolidating it not only with pastoral self-reference but also with the semi-autobiographical narrative he had previously devised to represent his amorous betrayal.

Although the *Sonnets* would not be published until 1609, by the time *As You Like It* was staged Shakespeare had already represented himself in them as a frustrated lover caught in a triangle involving a dark lady and a young man. In *Palladis Tamia* (1598), Francis Meres shows familiarity with Shakespeare's drama as well as "his sugared Sonnets among his private friends," which were then circulating in manuscript.[51] In 1599 two of these sonnets—"When my love swears that she is made of truth" and "Two loves I have of comfort and despair" (138 and 144)—were anthologized at the opening of *The Passionate Pilgrim*, a collection wrongfully attributed by William Jaggard wholly to "W. Shakespeare." What readers discovered in the two poems was a brief version of the *Sonnets*: a love triangle that moved from mutual self-deception to betrayal. Evidence that this erotic tale had originated several years earlier—around the time that *Venus and Adonis* (1593) and *The Rape of Lucrece* (1594) were dedicated to Henry Wriothesley, earl of Southampton—is found in a cryptic text entitled *Willobie His Avisa* (1594). What makes Henry Willobie's work so intriguing is that it contains an early biographical myth about Shakespeare—"W.S."—written by a contemporary who had read some sonnets. Willobie seeks to recruit Shakespeare's persona to strengthen the praise he offers his own idealized mistress, "Avisa" or "A." He consequently uses Shakespeare's triangle as the basis for his own fantasia. H.W. tells W.S., who "not long before had tried the courtesy of the like passion," that he loves A., and W.S., knowing better, encourages him to pursue her as a kind of theatrical audition:

> because he would see whether another could play his part better than himself, and in viewing a far off the course of his loving Comedy, he determined to see whether it would sort to a happier end for this new actor than it did for the old player. But at length this Comedy was like to have grown to a Tragedy, by the weak and feeble estate that H. W. was brought unto ... till Time and Necessity ... brought him a plaster.... In all which discourse is lively represented the unruly rage of unbridled fancy ... which Will, set loose from Reason, can devise....[52]

Shakespeare's initials reveal his identity, which is hinted at again in the play on his nickname in Willobie's allusion to the "sundry changes of affections" that "Will, set loose from Reason, can devise." In the *Sonnets*, the poet had similarly used his name to signify desire, telling his mistress, "Whoever hath her wish, thou hast thy Will" (135). H.W. are the initials of Henry Wriothesley, a likely candidate for the young man of the *Sonnets*. Willobie, who probably knew the poet, fuses allusions to Shakespeare's theatrical career with details of his sonnet persona. Shakespeare refers to himself as an actor in the public theater (sonnets 110 and 111) and as older than his male friend (sonnet 73). In *Willobie*, W.S. uses H.W. to see if "another could play his part better than ... the old player."

Willobie's W.S., however, like Shakespeare, is a dramatist as well as an actor, who encourages H.W. to pursue A. until the "loving Comedy" he scripted "was like to have grown a Tragedy."[53]

In the 1590s, through a process of biographical mythmaking, the poet had become Shakespeare in love, identified with Ovid as well as Plautus. For Meres, "the sweet witty soul of Ovid" lived in the "mellifluous and honey-tongued *Shakespeare*" of *Venus and Adonis*, *The Rape of Lucrece*, and the *Sonnets*.[54] By the turn of the century, the foppish Gullio of *1 The Return from Parnassus* mixes paraphrases of lines from *Romeo and Juliet* (2.4.39–43) and *Venus and Adonis* (1–2; 5–6), then sighs, "O sweet Mr. Shakespeare, I'll have his picture in my study at the court." In Gullio's religion of love, Shakespeare's portrait is a devotional relic. "Let this duncified world esteem of Spenser and Chaucer," he rhapsodizes, "I'll worship sweet Mr. Shakespeare, and to honour him will lay his Venus and Adonis under my pillow," imitating Alexander the Great, who "slept with Homer under his bed's head." In the play's sequel, even Judicio admits that Shakespeare's "sweeter verse" contains "heart-robbing lines."[55]

In the *Sonnets* and *As You Like It*, Shakespeare's personae—"Will" and "William"—are betrayed and displaced. But in the tales that start to be told about him at this time, he is both the transgressor and the victor. In his *Diary* on 13 March 1602, John Manningham records a dirty joke about Shakespeare that imagines him in a fabliau as a deceptive seducer who outwits the charismatic Burbage:

> Upon a time when Burbage played Richard III there was a citizen grew so far in liking with him, that before she went from the play she appointed him to come that night unto her by the name of Richard III. Shakespeare overhearing their conclusion went before, was entertained, and at his game ere Burbage came. Then message being brought that Richard III was at the door, Shakespeare caused return to be made that William the Conqueror was before Richard III.

Manningham's variation on the bed-trick concludes with a note that explains its jest: "Shakespeare's name William."[56] This tale reflects the stereotype of actors as unscrupulous libertines, but it also makes Shakespeare win for a change—through the exercise of wit. William the Conqueror would succeed as well in rumor dating from the late seventeenth century about the poet's affair with Mrs. Davenant, yet another of the triangulated stories about Shakespeare, the maker of such fictions.

IV

At its most general level, the debate between Jonson and Shakespeare in *Every Man Out* and *As You Like It* centers on the philosophical distinction between art and nature. Since Shakespeare chose pastoral for his response, one would expect him to summon an ideal Arcadian nature to contest Jonson's reformative art. From this standpoint, the play becomes, in Rosalie Colie's words, "a celebration, in varying degrees of devotion, of what is 'natural' and sustaining in human life and human environment."[57] *Every Man Out* begins in the country and ends at court; *As You Like It* reverses that movement. Here nature is "More free from peril than the envious court" (2.1.4), and Rosalind and Celia follow Duke Senior "To liberty, and not to banishment" (1.3.138). A sense of natural teleology is inscribed in the play's comic formula. Its progression from unnatural conflicts to a natural community wrought by love—for all except William and Jaques—recapitulates the movement from conflict through release to reconciliation that C. L. Barber described as the underlying structure of "Shakespeare's festive comedy."

In the main plot, flight to the green world of Arden is an escape from a society controlled by "unnatural" siblings (4.3.124). In symmetrical acts of transgression, Duke Frederick, a younger brother, deposes his older brother Duke Senior, while Oliver, an older brother, plans his younger brother Orlando's murder. Both acts are reversed when Duke Frederick senses his connection with the divine and Oliver acknowledges his bond to nature. Having met an "old religious man" in the forest, "After some question with him," Frederick is "converted / Both from his enterprise and from the world" (5.4.161–62). Rescued from death by his mistreated brother, Oliver too is instantly changed when he recognizes his capacity for love. "'Twas I; but 'tis not I," he informs Rosalind. "I do not shame / To tell you what I was, since my conversion / So sweetly tastes, being the thing I am" (4.3.135–37). In each case a self-alienating complex of narcissism, anger, and envy is voluntarily abandoned as the generators of public and private dissension submit freely to the moral norm of Shakespearean comedy. Both *Every Man Out* and *As You Like It* are cathartic fictions of moral transformation. The conversions of Oliver and Duke Frederick, like those of their analogues in *Every Man Out*, argue for the possibility of social renewal. But despite this similarity, it would be difficult to find two comedies in the English Renaissance that rest on such contradictory premises. In *Every Man Out*, catharsis culminates in a necessary alienation from society. In *As You Like It*, the main characters surrender to others and learn to live according to nature, whose aim is to make odds even.

Still, in a characteristically dialectical maneuver, Shakespeare acknowledges that nature is neither rational nor wholly benign. Part of the difficulty of understanding *As You Like It* is that the play systematically undermines the normative standard it advocates. Just as Touchstone balances the virtues and vices of pastoral in his clever parody of the *beatus ille* tradition (3.2.13–22), *As You Like It* espouses the benefits of living according to nature even as it suggests both the difficulty of knowing exactly what that would mean and the danger such a life would involve.

The presence of the virgin queen at the conclusion of *Every Man Out* sanctions Jonson's art by establishing a parallel between the sovereign and the poet, both of whom restrain desire through judgment. The epiphany that concludes *As You Like It* validates the play's natural teleology by evoking the concept of a supernatural art coincident with nature. "I have, since I was three year old," Rosalind reveals, "convers'd with a magician, most profound in his art" (5.2.59–61). Shakespeare links the natural to the artistic and the artistic to the marvelous. "I bar confusion," announces the god Hymen, whom Rosalind's art has secured to officiate over the play's masquelike ending; "'Tis I must make conclusion / Of these most strange events" (5.4.125–27). No precedent for this scene can be found in *Rosalind*, and Shakespeare uses it to sanctify experience through mythology, which binds together the natural, the human, and the divine as coordinated elements in a single all-inclusive order. Affirming a poetics of correspondence, Hymen imparts a divine sanction to natural events: "Then is there mirth in heaven, / When earthly things made even / Atone together" (5.4.108–10).

Yet Shakespeare does not assert desire to be either rational or amenable to reason. "Love," explains Rosalind, "is merely a madness, and I tell you, deserves as well a dark house and a whip as madmen do; and the reason why they are not so punish'd and curd is, that the lunacy is so ordinary that the whippers are in love too" (3.2.400–4). "We that are true lovers," Touchstone admits, "run into strange capers; but as all is mortal in nature, so is all nature in love mortal in folly," to which Rosalind replies, "Thou speak'st wiser than thou art ware of" (2.4.54–57). Furthermore, Jonson's plan to purge desire is implicitly mocked by Rosalind, disguised as Ganymede, who tells Orlando that she can cure him through the "physic" of "counsel," if he is prepared to be driven "from his mad humor of love, to his living humor of madness" (3.2.418–19). But Orlando curtly rejects this offer: "I would not be curd" (3.2.425). From the perspective of festive comedy, acceding to this madness is the closest we can come to wisdom. It is necessary to submit to a mysterious power beyond rational comprehension, symbolized by Hymen's epiphany. *Every Man Out* upholds the moral power of an art that Shakespeare supposedly lacked, while *As You Like It* meditates on the primal opposition between the intellectual categories of nature and art that Jonson's comical satire presupposes. The play is an encomium to nature that questions its own entanglement in the artistic and the artificial. The bathetic figure of William—the prototype of Shakespeare in love—epitomizes this dialectical engagement.

V

The myth of an artful Jonson and a natural Shakespeare that evolved over the ensuing four centuries into the controlling paradigm for understanding their relationship began as a collaborative effort at self-definition. Indeed, the playwrights confronted each other over the theory of comedy in two coordinated periods during which they explored their differences through the dialectic of nature and art. These periods of symbiotic self-reference commemorate the beginning and end of their interconnected lives as poets in the public theater. Their first exchange took place during the Poets' War. Their second began a decade later, near the end of Shakespeare's career, when in *The Winter's Tale* (1610) and *The Tempest* (1611) he nostalgically returned to pastoral comedy and was criticized again by Jonson in the new address "To the Reader," added to the first quarto of *The Alchemist* (1612); the Induction to *Bartholomew Fair* (1614); and the new Prologue (composed between 1612 and 1616) for the First Folio's revised *Every Man In*. In this case, however, Shakespeare seems to have deliberately provoked Jonson, as E.A.J. Honigmann and Harry Levin have argued, by using his final comedies in an elegiac manner to insist on the writers' difference as comedians. In these late plays we find a continuation of the debate begun a decade earlier. Levin notes that the "conjunction of Jonson and Shakespeare was never closer ... than in the successive seasons of 1610 and 1611, when His Majesty's Servants introduced *The Alchemist* and *The Tempest* respectively." It was this proximity, he concludes, that prompted Shakespeare to use his comedy to comment on Jonson's, giving him a final "opportunity to reflect and reply, as he is said to have done in the so-called War of the Theaters."[58]

The myth that arose from their argument consequently made Shakespeare nature's paragon. By 1615, Francis Beaumont, in a jocular epistle to his friend Jonson, vows to write in a style that will let "slip (If I had any in me) scholarship, and from all Learning keep these lines as clear / as Shakespeare's best are." Preachers will henceforth cite this poet, he contends, as an example of just "how far sometimes a mortal man may go / by the dim light of Nature."[59] Beaumont's Shakespeare is Jonson's artless but witty opposite who prospers by his natural faculties. This is the Shakespeare whose flashes of genius were offset by ridiculous errors (such as a Bohemia that lies by the sea). This is the Shakespeare Dryden would prefer to Jonson, despite or even because of his imputed flaws. "Those who accuse him to have wanted learning," Dryden says, "give him the greater commendation. He was naturally learned; he needed not the spectacles of books to read nature. He looked inwards and found her there."[60]

One of the most vehement defenses of Shakespeare by a contemporary is Leonard Digges's opening elegy in John Benson's collection of Shakespeare's *Poems* (1640), in which he rejects Jonson's scholarship and plagiarism in favor of the untutored genius, "born not made," whose plays are "Art without Art unparalleled as yet."[61] The embodiment of an extreme Renaissance romanticism, Digges's Shakespeare never imitates, since to do so would be a sign of weakness. His poems are not burdened, as Jonson's are, with Greek and Latin phrases translated "Plagiary-like" (line 15) into leaden English. In his study of Digges's tribute to Shakespeare, John Freehafer cogently notes how the poem "joins forcefully in the continuing argument over the relative places of Nature and Art in the production of great poetry—an argument in which Shakespeare and Jonson came to be ... the paradigms of the opposing principles, so that the success or failure of one of these men could be virtually equated with the success or failure of a whole philosophy of artistic creation." But Freehafer mistakenly assumes that only "men like Digges and Jonson were prepared to quarrel" over literary theory, while "Shakespeare himself seemingly was not."[62] Despite the efforts that have been made to contextualize Shakespeare's plays, contemporary criticism is still dominated by the belief that he was above the fray, that he did not respond to Jonson's censure, preferring to leave controversy to others. Shakespeare, however, was an active participant in shaping his own myth, and in *As You Like It* the quick master of dialectic first confounded the categories that Jonson used to describe him.

   Among those who viewed *As You Like It* at the Globe, none made better use of its metatheatrical critique of Jonson than Marston, who reprised the play's combination of pastoral comedy and antisatirical satire in *Jack Drum's Entertainment* to create his first malicious treatment of the humour poet. How Marston used what he had learned from Shakespeare to amplify his attack on Jonson is the focus of the next chapter.

NOTES

1. For their relative dating, see the Chronological Appendix.

2. *Ben Jonson: The Critical Heritage, 1599–1798*, ed. D. H. Craig (London: Routledge, 1990), 92.

3. See Edward W. Tayler's *Nature and Art in Renaissance Literature* (New York: Columbia University Press, 1964) and Frank Kermode's introductions to *English Pastoral Poetry: From the Beginnings to Marvell* (New York: Norton & Co., 1972) and *The Tempest* (London: Methuen, 1954). More recently, Derek Attridize explores the problems involved in this dialectic in "Puttenham's Perplexity: Nature, Art, and the Supplement in Renaissance Poetic Theory," *Literary Theory/Renaissance Texts*, eds. Patricia Parker and David Quint (Baltimore: Johns Hopkins University Press, 1986), 257–79.

4. Harry Levin, *Playboys and Killjoys: An Essay on the Theory and Practice of Comedy* (New York: Oxford University Press, 1982), 12, contrasts these terms.

5. From its initial publication in 1590 to 1642, *Rosalind* went through a remarkable ten editions.

6. Consider how closely Shakespeare follows Lodge. Both *Rosalind* and *As You Like It* have double plots: the first involves a usurper, Torismond (Shakespeare's Duke Frederick), who sends the rightful king, Gerismond (Duke Senior), into exile in the forest of Ardennes (Arden); the second concerns the conflict between two brothers, the unnaturally cruel Saladyne (Oliver) and his

innocent younger sibling Rosader (Orlando), whom he deprives of his inheritance. The plots are brought together when Rosalind, the daughter of the exiled ruler, and her friend Alinda (Celia), daughter of the usurper, watch Rosader (Orlando) win a match with a professional wrestler during which Rosalind also "falls" for him. Following his victory, threatened by his older brother, he escapes into the forest with Adam, a faithful old servant. Nevertheless, the lovers' reunion is assured when Torismond (Duke Frederick) forces Rosalind to leave court and his own daughter Alinda (Celia) willingly accompanies her into the same forest in search of her exiled father. To disguise their identities, the latter then adopts the name Aliena and the former, to shield them from assault, cross-dresses, calling herself Ganymede.

When they enter the forest, Aliena and Ganymede encounter an aged shepherd, Corydon (Corin), and his friend, the young Montanus (Silvius), who is in love with a disdainful mistress, Phebe. The women purchase the farm on which the old shepherd works and, by the end of the play, Rosalind discovers love, as does Alinda (Celia); unites the pastoral Petrarchan lovers; and presents herself to her father. The integration of the two main plots continues when the disguised Rosalind again meets Rosader (Orlando), who has fallen in love with her and hangs poems in her honor on the surrounding trees. Taken in by her disguise, he agrees to practice courting Ganymede as a surrogate Rosalind and she uses this opportunity to question and criticize love. The first movement toward closure occurs when Saladyne (Oliver), who seeks his brother in Ardennes (Arden), is reconciled with him, becomes morally transformed, and is engaged to Aliena. Ganymede, who has become the love object of Phebe, then promises to satisfy all the discontented lovers at her next appearance. Returning dressed in female attire, she joins the beguiled Phebe to Montanus (Silvius) and satisfies her own lover. The marriage of the two brothers is then coordinated with the political restoration of her father Gerismond (Duke Senior).

7. Oscar James Campbell, "Jaques," *The Huntington Library Bulletin* 8 (1935): 94.

8. Peter G. Phialas, *Shakespeare's Romantic Comedies: The Development of Their Form and Meaning* (Chapel Hill: University of North Carolina Press, 1966), 232.

9. David Bevington, "Shakespeare vs Jonson on Satire," *Shakespeare 1971, Proceedings of the World Shakespeare Congress*, eds. Clifford Leech and J.M.R. Margeson (Toronto: University of Toronto Press, 1972), 121.

10. Campbell, "Jaques," 91.

11. Russ McDonald, *Shakespeare & Jonson/Jonson & Shakespeare* (Lincoln: University of Nebraska Press, 1988), 8, 78.

12. Sir John Harington's *A New Discourse of a Stale Subject, called The Metamorphosis of Ajax*, ed. Elizabeth Story Donno (New York: Columbia University Press, 1962), 82. Donno notes on the same page that the first name of

this same person, sometimes called James Wingfield, is also recorded in official documents of the period as "Jaques" or "Jakes."

13. Helen Gardner, "*As You Like It*," in *More Talking of Shakespeare*, ed. John Garrett (London: Longmans, 1959), 31.

14. Quoted from *Ben Jonson*, eds. C. H. Herford and Percy Simpson, 11 vols. (Oxford: Clarendon, 1925–1952), I:28*n*.

15. Arthur Gray, *How Shakespeare 'Purged' Jonson: A Problem Solved* (Cambridge: W. Heffer & Sons, 1928), 20. Gray assumes that *As You Like It* contains Shakespeare's purge of Jonson mentioned in *2 Return from Parnassus*, even though it was said to have been administered the following year, after *Poetaster*.

16. Campbell, "Jaques," 101, stresses the character's connection to Jonson but blunders in arguing that Feliche, the satirist of *Antonio and Mellida*, Marston's second play, also serves as a precedent for Jaques, through whom "Shakespeare deprecates the savage manner of Marston and Jonson." But Shakespeare could only have had *Every Man Out* in mind, since *Antonio and Mellida* followed *As You Like It*. Marston's Rossaline, who makes witty sexual innuendos in that play, is an imitation of Shakespeare's character. See the Chronological Appendix (number 3).

17. Robert N. Watson, *Ben Jonson's Parodic Strategy: Literary Imperialism in the Comedies* (Cambridge: Harvard University Press, 1987), 1–2. See also Terrance Dunford, "Consumption of the World: Reading, Eating, and Imitation in *Every Man Out of His Humour*," *English Literary Renaissance* 2 (1984): 131–47.

18. C.L. Barber, *Shakespeare's Festive Comedy: A Study of Dramatic Form and its Relation to Social Custom* (Princeton: Princeton University Press, 1959), 223–39.

19. Sir Philip Sidney, *An Apology for Poetry*, ed. Forrest G. Robinson (Indianapolis: Bobbs-Merrill, 1970), 77. In *The Pilgrimage to Parnassus* (1598/99), Dromio enters, drawing "*a clown in with a rope*," and explains that "clowns have been thrust into plays by head and shoulders, ever since Kemp could make a scurvy face" (lines 665–67), in *The Three Parnassus Plays, 1598–1601*, ed. J. B. Leishman (London: Ivor Nicholson & Watson, 1949).

20. For background on Charles Chester, the model for Carlo Buffone, see Charles Nicholl, *A Cup of News: The Life of Thomas Nashe* (London: Routledge and Kegan Paul, 1984), 103–6.

21. See S. Schoenbaum, *William Shakespeare: A Documentary Life* (New York: Oxford University Press, 1975), 166–73. Jonson dedicated the folio version of *Every Man In* to his former tutor and friend in 1616.

22. What might have been equally galling was that Sogliardo is a rich country clown whose brother Sordido, like several of Shakespeare's Stratford neighbors, illegally kept corn off the market during a time of famine. For this they were cited in a Privy Council letter of 22 August 1597 as being "more like to wolves

or cormorants than to natural men." Quoted by E. K. Chambers, *William Shakespeare: A Study of Facts and Problems*, 2 vols. (Oxford: Clarendon, 1930), 2:100. Park Honan, *Shakespeare: A Life* (Oxford: Oxford University Press, 1998), 240–42, mentions the "Note of Corn and Malt," drawn up by Adrian Quiney on 4 February 1598, which lists Shakespeare's household as possessing considerable holdings (eighty bushels) during this period of continuing shortages and social unrest at Stratford.

23. Jonson would render his own account of Ovid's exile in *Poetaster*, when he shifted the terms of his opposition to Shakespeare from a Greek to a Roman context, as he moved from an Aristophanic to an Horatian perspective.

24. Sidney, *An Apology for Poetry*, 33, 21.

25. For the actors' testimony, see the suit of "John Witter v. John Heminges and Henry Condell" in Charles William Wallace, "Shakespeare and His London Associates," *University of Nebraska Studies* 10 (1910): 54. Honan, *Shakespeare: A Life*, 268, cites a reference to the Globe's construction in the inquisition into the assets of Sir Thomas Brend, on whose land the theater was erected. Platter's diary is quoted from S. Schoenbaum, *William Shakespeare: A Compact Documentary Life* (New York: Oxford University Press, 1980), 209.

26. Bernard Beckerman, *Shakespeare at the Globe* (New York: Columbia University Press, 1962), x.

27. William Kemp, *Nine Days' Wonder (1600)*, ed. G. B. Harrison (London: John Lane, The Bodley Head, 1923), 3.

28. Gerald Eades Bentley, *The Profession of Player in Shakespeare's Time* (Princeton: Princeton University Press, 1984), 43.

29. Kemp's emancipation left him free for further travel. To the ballad-mongers who composed rhymes of his exploits he boasts that "I William Kemp," who had almost been "rent in sunder with your unreasonable rhymes, am shortly God willing to set forward as merrily as I may" (*Nine Days' Wonder* 29). David Wiles, *Shakespeare's Clown: Actor and Text in the Elizabethan Playhouse* (Cambridge: Cambridge University Press, 1987), 36–39, speculates about Kemp's trips to Italy and Germany, before returning to England to join Worcester's Men.

30. See the Chronological Appendix (number 3 in *Shakespeare & The Poets' War*).

31. Armin's association with the goldsmiths' guild and their emblem in his role as Touchstone is pointed out by Hotson in *Shakespeare's Motley* (London: Rupert Hart-Davis, 1952), 115. Jane Belfield, "Robert Armin, 'Citizen and Goldsmith of London,'" *Notes and Queries* 27 (1980): 158–59, indicates that Armin was an apprentice to the goldsmith John Louyson in 1581. He belatedly became free of the company in January 1604 and on 15 July 1608 took James Jones as an apprentice.

Most scholars who have considered the question agree that the parts of Touchstone and Feste were written with Armin in mind. Discussions of his career, aside from Hotson's sometimes misleading *Shakespeare's Motley*, include: T. W. Baldwin, "Shakespeare's Jester," *Modern Language Notes* 39 (1927): 447–55; Austin K. Gray, "Robert Armine, the Foole," *PMLA* 42, (1927): 673–85; and Charles Felver, "Robert Armin, Shakespeare's Fool: A Biographical Essay," *Research Studies 5, Kent University Bulletin* 49 (1961).

A general appraisal of the fool's social function is found in: Barbara Swain, *Fools and Folly During the Middle Ages and the Renaissance* (New York: Columbia University Press, 1932); Enid Welsford, *The Fool: His Social and Literary History* (London: Faber and Faber, 1935); Robert Goldsmith, *Wise Fools in Shakespeare* (East Lansing: Michigan State University Press, 1955); Walter Kaiser, *Praisers of Folly: Erasmus, Rabelais, Shakespeare* (Cambridge: Harvard University Press, 1963); and William Willeford, *The Fool and His Scepter: A Study in Clowns and Jesters and Their Audience* (Evanston: Northwestern University Press, 1969).

32. *The Collected Works of Robert Armin*, ed. J. P. Feather, 2 vols. (New York: Johnson Reprint Company, 1972), 2:sigs. D^{r-v}. Charles Felver, "Robert Armin: Shakespeare's Source for Touchstone," *Shakespeare Quarterly* 7 (1956): 135–37, corrects Hotson's assumption that Armin referred to himself as "Tutch" to imitate Shakespeare's character.

33. John Davies, line 30 of "*To honest-gamesome* Robin Armin" in *The Scourge of Folly* (London: 1611?), 229.

34. The only viable treatment of this autobiographical reference is by William M. Jones in "William Shakespeare as William in *As You Like It*," *Shakespeare Quarterly* 2 (1960): 228–31. Jones stresses the detachable quality of the episode and conjectures that "the boy from Stratford" had "been in London long enough to joke about his own clownish origins" (229). He also believes that Shakespeare designed the role for himself and uses it to satirize "the pedantic learning that Jonson sometime boasted" (231).

35. John Ward is quoted from S. Schoenbaum, *Shakespeare's Lives* (Oxford: Clarendon, 1970), 297.

36. Jones, "William Shakespeare as William," 231.

37. Wiles, *Shakespeare's Clown*, 146.

38. Phyllis Rackin, *Stages of History: Shakespeare's English Chronicles* (Ithaca: Cornell University Press, 1990), 244. Another good example is the schoolboy William Page in *The Merry Wives of Windsor* (4.1), who struggles through a lesson in Latin grammar.

39. Gardner, "*As You Like It*," 17.

40. Stuart Daley, "Where Are the Woods in *As You Like It?*" *Shakespeare Quarterly* 34 (1983): 175. See also Mark Eccles, "The Shakespeares and the

Ardens," in *Shakespeare in Warwickshire* (Madison: University of Wisconsin Press, 1961), 3–23.

41. Both quotations are from Schoenbaum, *William Shakespeare: A Documentary Life*, 149. Unfortunately, all that the old narrator's selective memory could recall of this performance was seeing another old man.

42. Bentley, *The Profession of Player in Shakespeare's Time*, 228.

43. William Camden, *Remains of a Greater Work* (London, 1605), 40: "Man, earthly, or red."

44. T. W. Baldwin, *William Shakespeare's Small Latine and Lesse Greeke*, 2 vols. (Urbana: University of Illinois Press, 1944), I:116–20, grounds Touchstone's learned fooling in the rhetorical strategies of Aristotle, Cicero, and Quintilian. Agnes Latham notes the reference to Lyly's *Euphues* (5.1.43–44) in her edition of *As You Like It* (London: Methuen, 1975).

45. E. K. Chambers, *Shakespeare: A Survey* (New York: Hill and Wang, 1958), 158, and Edwin Greenlaw, "Shakespeare's Pastorals," *Studies in Philology* 13 (1916): 131. Publication of pastoral literature first written in the 1580s and 1590s prolonged its influence. The period's finest collection of pastoral verse, *England's Helicon*, was printed in 1600, the same year *As You Like It* premiered. Two years earlier a translation of Montemayor's *Diana* (the original of which inspired Sidney) and Marlowe's *Hero and Leander* (both alluded to by Shakespeare) were issued.

46. Quoted from *Spenser's Poetical Works*, eds. J. C. Smith and E. De Selincourt (Oxford: Clarendon, 1970).

47. Murray Levith, *What's in Shakespeare's Names* (Hamden, Conn.: Archon, 1978), 89, and S. A. Tannenbaum, "The Names in *As You Like It*," *The Shakespeare Association Bulletin* 15 (1940): 255–56.

48. *The Vision of William Concerning Piers the Plowman*, ed. Walter W. Skeat, 2 vols. (1886; reprint, Oxford: Oxford University Press, 1969), 1: B, Passus XV, 148, and C, Passus VI, 22–25.

49. *The Canterbury Tales* (Fragment VII, lines 703 and 930) in *The Works of Geoffrey Chaucer*, ed. F. N. Robinson (Boston: Houghton Mifflin, 1957).

50. Donn Ervin Taylor, "'Try in Time in Despite of a Fall': Time and Occasion in *As You Like It*," *Texas Studies in Literature and Language* 24 (1982): 129.

51. Francis Meres, *Palladis Tamia, Wit's Treasury, Being the Second Part of Wit's Commonwealth* (London, 1598), 281–82.

52. Henry Willobie, *Willobie His Avisa*, ed. G. B. Harrison (New York: Barnes and Noble, 1966), 115–17.

53. Ibid., 121. Shakespeare is cited as the author of *The Rape of Lucrece* in the opening poem (19). Park Honan, *Shakespeare: A Life*, 359, notes that Willobie's elder brother "married Eleanor Bampfield, whose sister in the same month

married Thomas Russell," the overseer of Shakespeare's will. He also mentions "a semi-erotic" verse by H.M. of the Middle Temple ("The Strange Fortune of Alerane, or My Lady's Toy") that pairs references to *Willobie His Avisa* and *The Rape of Lucrece*.

54. Meres, *Palladis Tamia*, 281.

55. Anonymous, *The Return from Parnassus*, lines 1032–1033, 1200–1203, and *2 Return from Parnassus*, line 302, in *The Three Parnassus Plays (1598-1601)*, ed. J. B. Leishman (London: Ivor Nicholson & Watson, 1949).

56. *The Diary of John Manningham of the Middle Temple 1662–1663*, ed. Robert Parker Sorlien (Hanover, N.H.: The University Press of New England, 1976), 75.

57. Rosalie L. Colie, *Shakespeare's Living Art* (Princeton: Princeton University Press, 1974), 284.

58. See E. A. J. Honigmann, *Shakespeare's Impact on His Contemporaries* (Totowa, N.J.: Barnes and Noble, 1982), 109–20, and Harry Levin, "Two Magian Comedies: *The Tempest* and *The Alchemist*," in *Shakespeare and the Revolution of the Times* (New York: Oxford University Press, 1976), 2, 19, 231. An example of this later engagement occurs, as Honigmann points out, when Polixenes describes "streak'd gillyvors" as being created through grafting, "an art which ... shares with great creating Nature," and in doing so proves that "art itself is Nature" (4.4.82–97). Annoyed by this witty suggestion that art and nature are indistinguishable, Jonson regrets in "To the Reader" of *The Alchemist* that he ever used these terms to clarify his difference from Shakespeare:

But how out of purpose, and place, do I name Art? when the Professors are grown so obstinate contemners of it, and presumers on their own Naturals, as they are deriders of all diligence that way, and, by simple mocking at the terms, when they understand not the things, think to get off wittily with their Ignorance. Nay, they are esteem'd the more learned, and sufficient for this, by the Many, through their excellent vice of judgment. (5:291)

The plural screens a singular indictment. Shakespeare was a "professor" (or practitioner) of "Art" who preferred his copious imagination. Jonson rebukes him for overestimating his wit, depending on his "natural" ability (his instinct or folly), and even gaining a reputation for being "learned" in his "Ignorance" for subverting the distinction between art and nature. Thomas Cartelli further explores Jonson's reaction to Shakespeare's late pastoral comedy in "*Bartholomew Fair* as Urban Arcadia: Jonson Responds to Shakespeare," *Renaissance Drama* 14 (1983): 151–72.

59. Quoted from Chambers, *William Shakespeare: A Study of Facts and Problems*, 2:224.

60. *An Essay of Dramatic Poesy* in *The Works of John Dryden*, ed. Keith Walker (Oxford: Oxford University Press, 1987), 110.

61. "Upon Master William Shakespeare, the Deceased Author and His Poems," in *Poems Written by William Shakespeare, Gentleman* (London, 1640), lines 1 and 10.

62. John Freehafer, "Leonard Digges, Ben Jonson, and the Beginning of Shakespeare Idolatry," *Shakespeare Quarterly* 21 (1970): 75.

JOHN HOLLANDER

Twelfth Night
and the Morality of Indulgence

To say that a play is "moral" would seem to imply that it represents an action which concretizes certain ethical elements of human experience, without actually moralizing at any point, and without having any of the characters in it state univocally a dogma, precept, or value that would coincide completely with the play's own moral intention. It was just this univocal didacticism, however, which characterized what was becoming in 1600 a prevailing comic tradition. The moral intent of the Jonsonian "comedy of humours" was direct and didactic; its purpose was to show

> the times deformitie
> Anatomiz'd in euery nerue and sinnew
> With constant courage, and contempt of feare.[1]

For moral purposes, a humour is an identifying emblem of a man's moral nature, graven ineradicably onto his physiological one. In the world of a play, a humour could be caricatured to such a degree that it would practically predestine a character's behavior. It was made to

> ... so possesse a man, that it doth draw
> All his affects, his spirits and his powers,
> In their confluctions, all to runne one way,
> This may be truly said to be a Humour.

From *The Sewanee Review* 68, no. 2 (Spring 1959). © 1959 by John Hollander.

The emblematic character of the humour, and the necessity for its use, were affirmed even more directly by Sidney, whose dramatic theory Jonson seems to have greatly admired:

> Now, as in Geometry the oblique must bee knowne as wel as the right, and in Arithmeticke the odde as well as the euen, so in the actions of our life who seeth not the filthiness of euil wanteth a great foile to perceiue the beauty of vertue. This doth the Comedy handle so in our priuate and domestical matters, as with hearing it we get as it were an experience, what is to be looked for of a nigardly *Demea*, of a crafty *Dauus*, of a flattering *Gnato*, of a vaine glorious *Thraso*, and not onely to know what effects are to be expected, but to know who be such, by the signifying badge giuen them by the Comedian.

Now *Every Man In His Humour* was first acted in 1598, and it is known that Shakespeare appeared in it. He seems in *Twelfth Night* (for which I accept the traditional date of 1600–1601) to have attempted to write a kind of moral comedy diametrically opposed to that of Jonson, in which "the times deformitie" was not to be "anatomiz'd," but represented in the core of an action. For a static and deterministic Humour, Shakespeare substituted a kinetic, governing Appetite in the action, rather than in the bowels, of his major characters. In his plot and language, he insists continually on the fact and importance of the substitution. Characters in a comedy of humours tend to become caricatures, and caricatures tend to become beasts, inhuman personifications of moral distortions that are identified with physiological ones. I believe that it was Shakespeare's intention in *Twelfth Night* to obviate the necessity of this dehumanization by substituting what one might call a moral process for a moral system. While it is true that the play contains quite a bit of interesting discussion of humours as such, and that there is some correspondence between appetites and humours, it is equally true that the only person in the play who believes in the validity of humourous classifications, who, indeed, lives by them, is himself a moral invalid. I will have more to say about this later. At this point I merely wish to suggest that the primary effective difference between Shakespeare's and Jonson's techniques in making moral comedy is the difference between what is merely a display of anatomy, and a dramatization of a metaphor, the difference between a Pageant and an Action.

II

The Action of *Twelfth Night* is indeed that of a Revels, a suspension of mundane affairs during a brief epoch in a temporary world of indulgence, a land full of food, drink, love, play, disguise and music. But parties end, and the reveller eventually becomes satiated and drops heavily into his worldly self again. The fact that plays were categorized as "revells" for institutional purposes may have appealed to Shakespeare; he seems at any rate to have analyzed the dramatic and moral nature of feasting, and to have made it the subject of his play. His analysis is schematized in Orsino's opening speech.

The essential action of a revels is: To so surfeit the Appetite upon excess that it "may sicken and so die". It is the Appetite, not the whole Self, however, which is surfeited: the Self will emerge at the conclusion of the action from where it has been hidden. The movement of the play is toward this emergence of humanity from behind a mask of comic type.

Act I, Scene 1, is very important as a statement of the nature of this movement. Orsino's opening line contains the play's three dominant images:

> If music be the food of love, play on.
> Give me excess of it, that, surfeiting,
> The appetite may sicken, and so die. (I. i. 1–3)

Love, eating, and music are the components of the revelry, then. And in order that there be no mistake about the meaning of the action, we get a miniature rehearsal of it following immediately:

> That strain again! It had a dying fall.
> Oh, it came o'er my ear like the sweet sound
> That breathes upon a bank of violets
> Stealing and giving odor! Enough, no more.
> 'Tis not so sweet now as it was before.
> O spirit of love, how quick and fresh art thou!
> That, notwithstanding thy capacity
> Receiveth as the sea, naught enters there,
> Of what validity and pitch soe'er,
> But falls into abatement and low price,
> Even in a minute! So full of shapes is fancy
> That it alone is high fantastical. (I. i. 4–15)

A bit of surfeiting is actually accomplished here; what we are getting is a proem to the whole play, and a brief treatment of love as an appetite. The substance of a feast will always fall into "abatement and low price" at the conclusion of the feasting, for no appetite remains to demand it. We also think of Viola in connection with the "violets / Stealing and giving odor," for her actual position as go-between-turned-lover is one of both inadvertent thief and giver. The Duke's rhetoric is all-embracing, however, and he immediately comments significantly upon his own condition.

> Oh, when mine eyes did see Olivia first,
> Methought she purged the air of pestilence!
> That instant was I turned into a hart,
> And my desires, like fell and cruel hounds,
> E'er since pursue me. (I. i. 19–23)

Like Actaeon, he is the hunter hunted; the active desirer pursued by his own desires. As embodying this overpowering appetite for romantic love, he serves as a host of the revels.[2]

The other host is Olivia, the subject of his desire. We see almost at once that her self-indulgence is almost too big to be encompassed by Orsino's. Valentine, reporting on the failure of his mission, describes her state as follows:

> So please my lord, I might not be admitted,
> But from her handmaid do return this answer:
> The element itself, till seven years' heat,
> Shall not behold her face at ample view;
> But, like a cloistress, she will veiled walk
> And water once a day her chamber round
> With eye-offending brine—all this to season
> A brother's dead love, which she would keep fresh
> And lasting in her sad remembrance. (I. i. 24–32)

"To season a brother's dead love": she is gorging herself on this fragrant herb, and though she has denied herself the world, she is no true anchorite, but, despite herself, a private glutton. The Duke looks forward to the end of her feast of grief,

> ... when liver, brain, and heart,
> These sovereign thrones, are all supplied, and filled
> Her sweet perfections with one self king! (I. i. 37–39)

The trinitarian overtone is no blasphemy, but a statement of the play's teleology. When everyone is supplied with "one self king", the action will have been completed.

The first three scenes of the play stand together as a general prologue, in which the major characters are introduced and their active natures noted. Viola is juxtaposed to Olivia here; she is not one to drown her own life in a travesty of mourning. It is true that she is tempted to "serve that lady" (as indeed she does, in a different way). But her end in so doing would be the whole play's action in microcosm; the immersion in committed self-indulgence would result in the revelation of her self

And might not be delivered to the world
Till I had made mine own occasion mellow,
What my estate is. (I. ii. 42–44)

She will serve the Duke instead, and use her persuasive talents to accomplish the ends to which his own self-celebrating rhetoric can provide no access. "I can sing," she says, "and speak to him in many sorts of music." Her sense of his character has been verified; the Captain tells her that his name is as his nature. And "what is his name?" she asks. "Orsino," answers the Captain. Orsino—the bear, the ravenous and clumsy devourer. Her own name suggests active, affective music; and the mention of Arion, the Orpheus-like enchanter of waves and dolphins with his music, points up the connotation. Orsino's "music," on the other hand, is a static well of emotion in which he allows his own rhetoric to submerge; Viola's is more essentially instrumental, effective, and convincing.[3]

The third scene of Act I completes the prologue by further equating the moral and the physiological. Here we first encounter the world of what Malvolio calls "Sir Toby and the lighter people" (it is indeed true that there is none of Malvolio's element of "earth" in them). The continued joking about *dryness* that pervades the wit here in Olivia's house, both above and below stairs, is introduced here, in contrast to Olivia's floods of welling and self-indulgent tears. The idea behind the joking in this and the following scenes is that drinking and merriment will moisten and fulfill a dry nature. As Feste says later on, "Give the dry fool drink, then the fool is not dry." Toby's sanguine temperament and Aguecheek's somewhat phlegmatic one are here unveiled. They are never identified as such, however; and none of the wit that is turned on the associations of "humours," "elements" and "waters," though it runs throughout the play, ever refers to a motivating order in the universe, except insofar as Malvolio believes in it.

What is most important is that neither Feste, the feaster embodying not the spirit but the action of revelry, nor Malvolio, the ill-wisher (and the *bad appetite* as well), his polar opposite, appears in these introductory scenes. It is only upstairs in Olivia's house (I, v) that the action as such commences. The revels opens with Feste's exchange with Maria in which she attempts three times to insist on innocent interpretations of "well-hanged" and "points." But Feste is resolute in his ribaldry. Thus Olivia, momentarily voicing Malvolio's invariable position, calls Feste a "dry fool," and "dishonest"; Malvolio himself refers to him as a "barren rascal." From here on in it will be Feste who dances attendance on the revelry, singing, matching wit with Viola, and being paid by almost everyone for his presence. To a certain degree he remains outside the action, not participating in it because he represents its very nature; occasionally serving as a comic angel or messenger, he is nevertheless unmotivated by any appetite, and is never sated of his fooling. His insights into the action are continuous, and his every remark is telling. "*Cucullus non facit monachum.* That's as much as to say I wear not motley in my brain."[4] Indeed, he does not, but more important is the fact that his robe and beard are not to make him a *real* priest later on. And neither he as Sir Thopas, nor Olivia as a "cloistress," nor Malvolio in his black suit of travestied virtue, nor the transvestite Viola is what he appears to be. No one will be revealed in his true dress until he has doffed his mask of feasting. And although neither Feste nor Malvolio will change in this respect, it is for completely opposite reasons that they will not do so.

Every character in the play, however, is granted some degree of insight into the nature of the others. It is almost as if everyone were masked with the black side of his vizard turned inwards; he sees more clearly past the *persona* of another than he can past his own. Valentine, for the Duke, comments on Olivia, as we have seen before. Even Malvolio is granted such an insight. Olivia asks him "What manner of man" Caesario is; unwittingly, his carping, over self-conscious and intellectualized answer cuts straight to the heart of Viola's disguise: "Not yet old enough for a man, nor young enough for a boy, as a squash is before 'tis a peascod, or a codling when 'tis almost an apple. 'Tis with him in standing water, between boy and man. He is very well–favored and he speaks very shrewishly. One would think his mother's milk were scarce out of him." (1. v. 165-171)

The puns on "cod" and "codling" insist on being heard here, and as with the inadvertently delivered obscenity about Olivia's "great P's" and their source in the letter scene, Malvolio does not know what he is saying. The point is that Malvolio asserts, for an audience that knows the real facts, that Viola can scarcely be a male creature.

A more significant case of this hide-and-seek is Olivia's retort to Malvolio in the same scene: "O you are sick of self-love, Malvolio, and taste with a distempered appetite"; it provides the key to his physiological-moral nature. "Sick of self-love" means "sick with a moral infection called self-love," but it can also mean "already surfeited, or fed up with your own ego as an object of appetite." Malvolio's "distempered appetite" results from the fact that he alone is not possessed of a craving directed outward, towards some object on which it can surfeit and die; he alone cannot morally benefit from a period of self-indulgence. Actually this distemper manifests itself in terms of transitory desires on his part for status and for virtue, but these desires consume him in their fruitlessness; he is aware of the nature of neither of them. This is a brilliant analysis of the character of a melancholic, and Shakespeare's association of the melancholy, puritanic and status-seeking characters in Malvolio throws considerable light on all of them. The moral nature of the plot of *Twelfth Night* can be easily approached through the character of Malvolio, and this, I think, is what Lamb and his followers missed completely in their egalitarian sympathy for his being no "more than steward." For Malvolio's attachment to self-advancement is not being either aristocratically ridiculed or praised as an example of righteous bourgeois opposition to medieval hierarchies. In the context of the play's moral physiology, his disease is shown forth as a case of indigestion due to his self-love, the result of a perverted, rather than an excessive appetite.[5] In the world of feasting, the values of the commercial society outside the walls of the party go topsy-turvy: Feste is given money for making verbal fools of the donors thereof; everyone's desire is fulfilled in an unexpected way; and revellers are shown to rise through realms of unreality, disguise and luxurious self-deception. We are seduced, by the revelling, away from seeing the malice in the plot to undo Malvolio. But whatever malice there is remains peculiarly just. It is only Malvolio who bears any ill-will, and only he upon whom ill-will can appear to be directed. He makes for himself a hell of the worldly heaven of festivity, and when Toby and Maria put him into darkness, into a counterfeit-hell, they are merely representing in play a condition that he has already achieved.

The plot against Malvolio, then, is no more than an attempt to let him surfeit on himself, to present him with those self-centered, "time-pleasing" objects upon which his appetite is fixed. In essence, he is led to a feast in which his own vision of himself is spread before him, and commanded to eat it. The puritan concern with witchcraft and the satanic, and its associations of them with madness are carried to a logical extreme; and once Malvolio has been permitted to indulge in his self-interest by means of the letter episode, he is only treated as he would himself treat anyone whom he believed to be mad. His puritanism is mocked by allusions to his praying made by Toby and Maria; a priest (and a false, dissembling one at that, the answer to a puritan's prayer) is sent to him; and the implications of the darkness are eventually fulfilled as his prison becomes his hell.

It is interesting to notice how carefully Shakespeare analyzed another characteristic of the melancholic in his treatment of Malvolio. L. C. Knights has suggested[6] that the vogue of melancholy at the turn of the 17th century was occasioned to some degree by the actual presence in England of a large number of "*intellectuels en chômage*" (in Denis de Rougement's words), unemployed, university-trained men whose humanistic education had not fitted them for any suitable role in society. Malvolio is no patent and transparent university intellectual (like Holofernes, for example). He contrives, however, to over-rationalize his point (where the Duke will over-sentimentalize it) on almost every occasion. Even his first introduction of Viola, as has been seen before, is archly over-reasoned. His venture into exegesis of a text is almost telling.

It is not merely self-interest, I think, that colors the scrutiny of Maria's letter. His reading is indeed a close one: he observes that, after the first snatch of doggerel, "The numbers altered." But Malvolio is incapable of playing the party-game and guessing the riddle. Of "M, O, A, I doth sway my life," he can only say "And yet, to crush this a little it would bow to me, for every one of these letters are in my name." He even avoids the reading that should, by all rights, appeal to him: Leslie Hotson has suggested that "M, O, A, I" probably stands for *Mare*, *Orbis*, *Aer* and *Ignis*, the four elements to which Malvolio so often refers. Malvolio himself fails as a critic, following a "cold scent" that, as Fabian indicates, is "as rank as a fox" for him in that it tantalizes his ambition.

But he continues to aspire to scholarship. In order to "let his tongue tang with arguments of state, he intends to "read politic authors". His intrusion on the scene of Toby's and Andrew's merry-making involves a most significant remark: "Is there no respect of persons, time or place in you?", he asks. In other words, "Do you not observe even the dramatic unities in your revelling? Can you not apply even the values that govern things as frivolous as plays to your lives?" Coming from Malvolio, the ethical theorist, the remark feels very different from the remark made to Sir Toby by Maria, the practical moralist: "Aye, but you must confine yourself within the modest levels of order." Maria, presiding over the festivities, would keep things from getting out of hand. It is not only the spirit in which Malvolio's comment is uttered that accounts for this difference, however. I think that one of the implications is quite clearly the fact that Jonson's ordered, would-be-classic, but static and didactic comedy would disapprove of *Twelfth Night* as a moral play, and mistake its intention for a purely frivolous one.

The prank played on Malvolio is not merely an "interwoven" second story, but a fully-developed double-plot. Like the Belmont episodes in *The Merchant of Venice*, it is a condensed representation of the action of the entire play. In *Twelfth Night*, however, it operates in reverse, to show the other side of the coin, as it were. For Malvolio there can be no fulfillment in "one self king". His story effectively and ironically underlines the progress toward this fulfillment in everybody else, and helps to delineate the limitations of the moral domain of the whole play. In contrast to Feste, who appears in the action at times as an abstracted spirit of revelry, Malvolio is a model of the sinner.

The whole play abounds in such contrasts and parallels of character, and the players form and regroup continually with respect to these, much in the manner of changing of figurations in a suite of *branles*. Viola herself indulges in the festivities in a most delicate and (literally) charming way. She is almost too good a musician, too effective an Orpheus: "Heaven forbid my outside have not charmed her," she complains after her first encounter with Olivia. But as soon as she realizes that she is part of the game, she commits herself to it with redoubled force. If her "outside" is directed towards Olivia, her real identity and her own will are concentrated even more strongly on Orsino. In the most ironic of the love-scenes, she all but supplants Olivia in the Duke's affections. Orsino, glutting himself on his own version of romantic love, allows himself to make the most extravagant and self-deceptive statements about it:

> Come hither, boy. If ever thou shalt love,
> In the sweet pangs of it remember me;
> For such as I am all true lovers are,
> Unstaid and skittish in all motions else
> Save in the constant image of the creature
> That is beloved. (II. iv. 15–20)

This skittishness, beneath the mask of the ravenous and constant bear, is obvious to Feste, at least: "Now, the melancholy god protect thee, and the tailor make thy doublet of changeable taffeta, for thy mind is a very opal. I would have men of such constancy put to sea, that their business might be everything and their intent everywhere; for that's it that always makes a good voyage of nothing." (II. iv. 75–80)

Orsino also gives us a curious version of the physiology of the passions on which the plot is based; it is only relatively accurate, of course, for he will be the last of the revellers to feel stuffed, to push away from him his heaping dish.

> There is no woman's sides
> Can bide the beating of so strong a passion
> As love doth give my heart, no woman's heart
> So big to hold so much. They lack retention.
> Alas, their love may be called appetite—
> No motion of the liver, but the palate—
> They suffer surfeit, cloyment and revolt.
> But mine is all as hungry as the sea
> And can digest as much. (II. iv. 96–104)

Viola has been giving him her "inside" throughout the scene, and were he not still ravenous for Olivia's love he could see her for what she is: a woman with a constancy in love (for himself and her brother) that he can only imagine himself to possess. She is indeed an Allegory of Patience on some baroque tomb at this point. She is ironically distinguished from Olivia in that her "smiling at grief" is a disguising "outside" for her real sorrow, whereas Olivia's is a real self-indulgent pleasure taken at a grief outworn. It is as if Olivia had misread Scripture and taken the letter of "Blessed are they that mourn" for the spirit of it. Her grief is purely ceremonial.

The "lighter people," too, are engaged in carrying out the action in their own way, and they have more business in the play than merely to make a gull of Malvolio. Toby's huge stomach for food and drink parallels the Duke's ravenous capacity for sentiment. The drinking scene is in one sense the heart of the play. It starts out by declaring itself in no uncertain terms. "Does not our life consist of the four elements?" catechizes Sir Toby. "Faith, so they say," replies Andrew, "but I think it rather consists of eating and drinking." No one but Feste, perhaps, really knows the extent to which this is true, for Andrew is actually saying "We are not merely comic types, mind you, being manipulated by a dramatist of the humours. The essence of our lives lies in a movement from hunger to satiety that we share with all of nature."

When Toby and Andrew cry out for a love song, Feste obliges them, not with the raucous and bawdy thing that one would expect, but instead, with a direct appeal to their actual hostess, Olivia. This is all the more remarkable in that it is made on behalf of everyone in the play. "O Mistress Mine" undercuts the Duke's overwhelming but ineffectual mouthings, Viola's effective but necessarily misdirected charming, and, of course, Aguecheek's absolute incompetence as a suitor. The argument is couched in purely naturalistic terms: "This feast will have to end, and so will all of our lives. You are not getting younger ('sweet and twenty' is the contemporaneous equivalent of 'sweet and thirty,' at least). Give up this inconstant roaming; your little game had better end in your marriage, anyway." The true love "That can sing both high and low" is Viola-Sebastian, the master-mistress of Orsino's and Olivia's passion. (Sebastian has just been introduced in the previous scene, and there are overtones here of his being invoked as Olivia's husband). Sebastian has, aside from a certain decorative but benign courtly manner, no real identity apart from Viola. He is the fulfillment of her longing (for she has thought him dead) and the transformation into reality of the part she is playing in the *ludus amoris*. The prognostication is borne out by Sebastian's own remark: "You are betrothed both to a man and maid." He is himself characterized by an elegance hardly virile; and, finally, we must keep in mind the fact that Viola was played by a boy actor to begin with, and that Shakespeare's audience seemed to be always ready for an intricate irony of this kind.

But if Viola and Sebastian are really the same, "One face, one voice, one habit, and two persons, A natural perspective that is and is not," there is an interesting parallel between Viola and Aguecheek as well. Both are suitors for Olivia's hand: Andrew, ineffectively, for himself; Viola for Orsino, and (effectively) for Sebastian. Their confrontation in the arranged duel is all the more ironic in that Andrew is an effective pawn in Toby's game (Toby is swindling him), whereas Viola is an ineffective one in the Duke's (she is swindling him of Olivia's love).

Feste's other songs differ radically from "O Mistress Mine." He sings for the Duke a kind of languorous ayre, similar to so many that one finds in the songbooks.[7] It is aimed at Orsino in the very extravagance of its complaint. It is his own song, really, if we imagine him suddenly dying of love, being just as ceremoniously elaborate in his funeral instructions as he has been in his suit of Olivia. And Feste's bit of handy-dandy to Malvolio in his prison is a rough-and-tumble sort of thing, intended to suggest in its measures a scrap from a Morality, plainly invoking Malvolio in darkness as a devil in hell. Feste shows himself throughout the play to be a master of every convention of fooling.

If Feste's purpose is to serve as a symbol of the revels, however, he must also take a clear and necessary part in the all-important conclusion. *Twelfth Night* itself, the feast of the Epiphany, celebrates the discovery of the "True King" in the manger by the Wise Men. "Those wits," says Feste in Act I, Scene 5 "that think they have thee [wit] do very oft prove fools, and I that am sure I lack thee may pass for a wise man." And so it is that under his influence the true Caesario, the "one self king," is revealed.[8] The whole of Act V might be taken, in connection with "the plot" in a trivial sense, to be the other *epiphany*, the perception that follows the *anagnorisis* or discovery of classic dramaturgy. But we have been dealing with the Action of *Twelfth Night* as representing the killing off of excessive appetite through indulgence of it, leading to the rebirth of the unencumbered self. The long final scene, then, serves to show forth the Caesario-King, and to unmask, discover and reveal the fulfilled selves in the major characters.

The appearance of the priest (a real one, this time) serves more than the simple purpose of proving the existence of a marriage between Olivia and "Caesario." It is a simple but firm intrusion into the world of the play of a way of life that has remained outside of it so far. The straightforward solemnity of the priest's rhetoric is also something new; suggestions of its undivided purpose have appeared before only in Antonio's speeches. The priest declares that Olivia and her husband have been properly married

> And all the ceremony of this compact
> Sealed in my function, by my testimony.
> Since when, my watch hath told me, toward my grave
> I have travelled but two hours. (V. i. 163–166)

It is possible that the original performances had actually taken about two hours to reach this point. At any rate, the sombre acknowledgment of the passage of time in a real world is there. Antonio has prepared the way earlier in the scene; his straightforward confusion is that of the unwitting intruder in a masquerade who has been accused of mistaking the identities of two of the masquers.

That the surfeiting has gradually begun to occur, however, has become evident earlier. In the prison scene, Sir Toby has already begun to tire: "I would we were well rid of this knavery." He gives as his excuse for this the fact that he is already in enough trouble with Olivia, but such as this has not deterred him in the past. And, in the last scene, very drunk as he must be, he replies to Orsino's inquiry as to his condition that he hates the surgeon, "a drunken rogue." Self knowledge has touched Sir Toby. He could not have said this earlier.

As the scene plays itself out, Malvolio alone is left unaccounted for. There is no accounting for him here, though; he remains a bad taste in the mouth. "Alas poor fool," says Olivia, "How have they baffled thee!" And thus, in Feste's words, "the whirligig of time brings in his revenges." Malvolio has become the fool, the "barren rascal." He leaves in a frenzy, to "be revenged," he shouts, "on the whole pack of you." He departs from the world of this play to resume a role in another, perhaps. His reincarnation might be as Middleton's De Flores, rather than even Jaques. His business has never been with the feasting to begin with, and now that it is over, and the revellers normalized, he is revealed as the true madman. He is "The Madly-Used Malvolio" to the additional degree that his own uses have been madness.

For Orsino and Viola the end has also arrived. She will be "Orsino's mistress and his fancy's queen." He has been surfeited of his misdirected voracity; the rich golden shaft, in his own words, "hath killed the flock of all affections else" that live in him. "Liver, brain and heart" are indeed all supplied; for both Olivia and himself, there has been fulfillment in "one self king." And, lest there be no mistake, each is to be married to a Caesario or king. Again, "Liver, brain and heart" seems to encompass everybody: Toby and Maria are married, Aguecheek chastened, etc.

At the end of the scene, all exit. Only Feste, the pure fact of feasting, remains. His final song is a summation of the play in many ways at once. Its formal structure seems to be a kind of quick rehearsal of the Ages of Man. In youth, "A foolish thing was but a toy": the fool's bauble, emblematic of both his *membrum virile* and his trickery, is a trivial fancy. But in "man's estate," the bauble represents a threat of knavery and thievery to respectable society, who shuts its owner out of doors. The "swaggering" and incessant drunkenness of the following strophes bring Man into prime and dotage, respectively. Lechery, trickery, dissembling and drunkenness, inevitable and desperate in mundane existence, however, are just those activities which, mingled together in a world of feasting, serve to purge Man of the desire for them. The wind and the rain accompany him throughout his life, keeping him indoors with "dreams and imaginations" as a boy, pounding and drenching him unmercifully, when he is locked out of doors, remaining eternal and inevitable throughout his pride in desiring to perpetuate himself. The wind and the rain are the most desperate of elements, that pound the walls and batter the roof of the warm house that shuts them out, while, inside it, the revels are in progress. Only after the party is ended can Man face them without desperation.

It is the metaphor of the rain that lasts longest, though, and it recapitulates the images of water, elements and humours that have pervaded the entire play. Feste himself, who tires of nothing, addresses Viola: "Who you are and what you would are out of my welkin—I might say 'element' but the word is over-worn." He adroitly comments on Malvolio's line "Go to; I am not of your element" by substituting a Saxon word for a Latin one. The additional association of the four elements with the humours cannot be overlooked. It is only Malvolio, of course, who uses the word "humour" with any seriousness: "And then to have the humour of State," he muses, as he imagines himself "Count Malvolio." Humours are also waters, however. And waters, or fluids of all kinds, are continually being forced on our attention. Wine, tears, sea-water, even urine, are in evidence from the first scene on, and they are always being metaphorically identified with one another. They are all fluids, bathing the world of the play in possibilities for change as the humours do the body. Feste's answer to Maria in the prison scene has puzzled many editors; if we realize, however, that Feste is probably hysterically laughing at what he has just been up to, "Nay, I'm for all waters" may have the additional meaning that he is on the verge of losing control of himself.

He is "for all waters" primarily in that he represents the fluidity of revelling celebration. And finally, when all is done, "The rain it raineth every day," and Feste reverts to gnomic utterance in a full and final seriousness. Water is rain that falls to us from Heaven. The world goes on. Our revels now are ended, but the actors solidify into humanity, in this case. "But that's all one, our play is done / And we'll strive to please you every day."

<h1 style="text-align:center">III</h1>

In this interpretation of *Twelfth Night*, I have in no sense meant to infer that Malvolio is to be identified as Ben Jonson, or that the play functioned in any systematic way in the war of the theatres. There are, of course, a number of propitious coincidences: Marston's *What You Will*, coming some six or seven years after *Twelfth Night*, devotes much effort to lampooning Jonson. What could have been meant by the title, however, as well as Shakespeare's real intention in his subtitle, remains obscure. Perhaps they both remain as the first part of some forgotten proverb to the effect that what you will (want) may come to you in an unexpected form. Perhaps they are both merely throwaway comments to the effect that the play is really "whatyoumaycallit". (It has been frequently suggested that it is a translation of Rabelais' "*Fay ce que vouldras*.") Then there is the dig, in *Every Man Out of His Humour*, at a comedy with a romantic (Italianate) plot more than vaguely resembling that of *Twelfth Night*. *Every Man Out* has been dated in 1599, but the idea that Shakespeare may have chosen just such a "romantic" story with which to oppose Jonson's comic theories is not inconceivable.

My point, however, is that *Twelfth Night* is opposed by its very nature to the kind of comedy that Jonson was not only writing, but advocating at the time; that it is a moral comedy, representing human experience in terms of a fully dramatized metaphor rather than a static emblematic correspondence; and, finally, that it operates to refute the moral validity of comedy of humours in its insistence on the active metaphor of surfeiting the appetite, upon which the whole plot is constructed. It is only romantic in that it shares, with *As You Like It* (and with *Love's Labour's Lost*, too, for that matter) a hint of the world of transformation of the last plays. Its moral vision is as intense as that of the problem comedies.

<h2 style="text-align:center">NOTES</h2>

1. Ben Jonson, *Every Man Out of His Humour* (1599), Induction, ll. 120–122.

2. See the extremely provocative commentary on the Duke's opening lines in Kenneth Burke, *The Philosophy of Literary Form* (Baton Rouge, 1941), pp. 344–349.

3. See my own "Musica Mundana and Twelfth Night" in *Sound and Poetry*, ed. Northrop Frye (New York, 1957), pp. 55–82, for an extended treatment of the use of "speculative" and "practical" music in the play.

4. Cf. *Measure for Measure*, V, i, 263, where Lucio refers in the identical words to the Duke disguised as Friar Lodowick.

5. And Leslie Hotson has pointed out that his yellow stockings, as he later appears in them, are the true color of the Narcissus, as well as of the craven. See *The First Night of Twelfth Night* (London, 7954), p. 98f.

6. *Drama and Society in the Age of Jonson* (Manchester, 1936), pp. 315–332.

7. The Rev. E. H. Fellowes, in *English Madrigal Verse* (Oxford, 1929), lists four different ayres with the conventional opening phrase, "Come away."

8. For my interpretation of the last act I am indebted to Professor Roy W. Battenhouse's suggestions.

RICHARD A. LANHAM

Superposed Plays:
Hamlet

Shakespeare uses a variation on the sonnets strategy in *Hamlet*. He writes two plays in one. Laertes plays the revenge tragedy hero straight. He does, true enough, veer toward self-parody, as when he complains that crying for Ophelia has interfered with his rants: "I have a speech o' fire, that fain would blaze / But that this folly drowns it" (4.7.189–90).[1] But he knows his generic duty and does it. No sooner has his "good old man" (Polonius's role in the straight, "serious" play) been polished off than he comes screaming with a rabble army. He delivers predictably and suitably stupid lines like "O thou vile king, / Give me my father" (4.5.115–16). And the Queen can scarcely manage a "Calmly, good Laertes" before he begins again: "That drop of blood that's calm proclaims me bastard, / Cries cuckold to my father, brands the harlot / Even here between the chaste unsmirched brows / Of my true mother" (4.5.117–20). And just before the King begins to calm him, to the villainous contentation of both: "How came he dead? I'll not be juggled with. / To hell allegiance, vows to the blackest devil, / Conscience and grace to the profoundest pit!" (4.5.130–32). He plays a straight, hard-charging revenge-hero.

Against him, Ophelia reenacts a delightfully tear-jerking madwoman stage prop. The King mouths kingly platitudes well enough ("There's such divinity doth hedge a king ..." [4.5.123]), comes up with a suitably stagey, two-phase fail-safe plot, and urges the hero on ("Revenge should have no bounds"). And the whole comes suitably laced with moralizing guff. So the King plays a Polonius-

From *The Motives of Eloquence: Literary Rhetoric in the Renaissance*. © 1976 by Yale University.

of-the-leading-questions: "Laertes, was your father dear to you?" Laertes, with unusual common sense, returns, "Why ask you this?" And then the King is off for a dozen Polonian lines on love's alteration by time: "Not that I think you did not love your father, / But that I know love is begun by time ..." 4.7.109–10). Only then can he get back to, as he phrases it, "the quick o' th' ulcer." And the Queen plays out a careful scene on the brookside where Ophelia drowned. And wrestling in Ophelia's grave, Hamlet, annoyed at being upstaged by Laertes, protests, "I'll rant as well as thou." And, as superb finale, Laertes, at the fencing match, stands there prating about honor with the poisoned rapier in his hand. The poisoner-poisoned motif releases the Christian forgiveness that forgives us, too, for enjoying all that blood. *Hamlet* offers, then, a story frankly calculated to make the audience as well as the compositor run out of exclamation points.

Hamlet obligingly confesses himself Laertes' foil. "In mine ignorance / Your skill shall, like a star i'th'darkest night, / Stick fiery off indeed" (5.2.244–46). It is the other way about, of course. Laertes foils for Hamlet. Shakespeare is up to his old chiasmatic business, writing a play about the kind of play he is writing. The main play overlaps as well as glossing the play criticized—again, a strategy of superposition. Polonius plays a muddling old proverb-monger, and a connoisseur of language, in the Hamlet play, as well as good old man in the Laertes play. Ophelia, though sentimental from the start, is both more naive and more duplicitous in the Hamlet play; and so with the King and Queen, too, both are more complex figures. Shakespeare endeavors especially to wire the two plots in parallel: two avenging sons and two dead fathers; brother's murder and "this brother's wager"; both Hamlet and Laertes in love with Ophelia; both dishonest before the duel (Hamlet pretending more madness than he displays when he kills Polonius), and so on.

Now there is no doubt about how to read the Laertes play: straight revenge tragedy, to be taken—as I've tried to imply in my summary—without solemnity. We are to enjoy the rants as rants. When we get tears instead of a rant, as with the Laertes instance cited earlier, an apology for our disappointment does not come amiss. We are not to be caught up in Laertes' vigorous feeling any more than in Ophelia's bawdy punning. We savor it. We don't believe the fake King when he maunders on about Divine Right, the divinity that doth hedge a king. We don't "believe" anybody. It is not that kind of play. For explanation, neither the ketchup nor the verbal violence need go further than enjoyment. The more outrageous the stage effects, the more ghastly the brutality, the more grotesque the physical mutilation, the better such a play becomes. Shakespeare had done this kind of thing already and knew what he was about. Such a vehicle packed them in. Just so, when part-sales were falling, would Dickens kill a baby.

The real doubt comes when we ask, "What poetic do we bring to the Hamlet play?" As several of its students have pointed out, it is a wordy play. Eloquence haunts it. Horatio starts the wordiness by supplying a footnote from ancient Rome in the first scene, by improving the occasion with informative reflection. Everybody laughs at Polonius for his moralizing glosses but Hamlet is just as bad. Worse. Gertrude asks him, in the second scene, why he grieves to excess and he gives us a disquisition on seeming and reality in grief. The King follows with his bravura piece on grief. Everybody moralizes the pageant. The Hamlet play abounds with triggers for straight revenge-tragedy response. The whole "mystery" of Hamlet's hesitant revenge boils down to wondering why he doesn't go ahead and play his traditional part, complete with the elegant rants we know he can deliver.

The rhetorical attitude is triggered not only by obvious stylistic excess, as we have seen, or by *de trop* moralizing, but by talking about language, by surface reference to surface. This surface reference occurs at every level of the Hamlet play in *Hamlet*, as well as, of course, throughout the Laertes play. Polonius plays a main part here. His tedious prolixity ensures that we notice everyone else's tedious prolixity. And his relish of language, his speech for its own sake, makes us suspect the same appetite in others and in ourselves. The Queen's rejoinder to the marvelous "brevity is the soul of wit" speech in 2.2 could be addressed to almost anybody in the play, including the gravedigger: "More matter, with less art."

Everyone is manipulating everyone else with speechifying and then admitting he has done so. Every grand rhetorical occasion seems no sooner blown than blasted. Polonius offers the famous Gielgud encore about being true to oneself and then sends off Reynaldo to spy and tell fetching lies. The King plays king to angry Laertes then confesses to Gertrude that he has been doing just this. Ophelia is staked out to play innocent maiden so Hamlet can be drawn out and observed. *Hic et ubique.* Is she a stage contrivance or a character? What kind of audience are we to be? Everyone is an actor, Hamlet and his madness most of all. The play is full of minor invitations to attend the surface, the theme of speaking. Even the ghost has to remind himself to be brief—before continuing for thirty-odd lines (1.5). Theatrical gestures are not simply used all the time but described, as in Hamlet's inky cloak and windy suspiration for grief, or the costuming and gesture of the distracted lover, as the innocent Ophelia describes Hamlet's visit:

> My lord, as I was sewing in my closet,
> Lord Hamlet, with his doublet all unbraced,
> No hat upon his head, his stockings fouled,
> Ungartered, and down-gyved to his ankle,
> Pale as his shirt, his knees knocking each other,
> And with a look so piteous in purport
> As if he had been loosed out of hell
> To speak of horrors—he comes before me.
>
> . . . .
> He took me by the wrist and held me hard.

Then goes he to the length of all his arm,
And with his other hand thus o'er his brow
He falls to such perusal of my face
As 'a would draw it. Long stayed he so.
At last, a little shaking of mine arm
And thrice his head thus waving up and down,
He raised a sigh so piteous and profound
As it did seem to shatter all his bulk
And end his being. That done, he lets me go,
And with his head over his shoulder turned
He seemed to find his way without his eyes,
For out o'doors he went without their helps
And to the last bended their light on me.

[2.1.77–84, 87–100]

This might have come from an actor's manual. Do we take it as such, respond as professional actors?

The Hamlet play turns in on itself most obviously when the players visit. Dramatic self-consciousness retrogresses a step further as the tragedians of the city talk about themselves doing what they are just now doing in a play depicting them doing just what.... The debate is about rightful succession, of course, like both the Laertes and the Hamlet plays. "What, are they children? Who maintains 'em? How are they escorted? Will they pursue the quality no longer than they can sing? Will they not say afterwards, if they should grow themselves to common players (as it is most like, if their means are no better), their writers do them wrong to make them exclaim against their own succession?" (2.2.338–44). Who are the children in the "real" plays? Hamlet had invoked a typical cast a few lines earlier (314 ff.) such as *Hamlet* itself uses and stressed that "he that plays the king shall be welcome." Hamlet will use the play, that is, *as a weapon*, the propaganda side of rhetorical poetic, to complement the Polonius-pleasure side. But before that, there is a rehearsal, for effect, to see whether the players are good enough to play the play within the play. Here, even more clearly than in the Laertes play, we confront the connoisseur's attitude toward language. Polonius supplies a chorus that for once fits: "Fore God, my lord, well spoken, with good accent and good discretion" (2.2.454–55). This to Hamlet, a good actor, as Polonius was in his youth. They proceed in this vein, nibbling the words; "That's good. 'Mobled queen' is good."

The main question pressing is not, How does the feedback work? What relation is there, for example, between rugged Pyrrhus and Hamlet, or Laertes? Or what relation with the King, who also topples a kingdom? And why is Hamlet so keen to reach Hecuba? The main question is, How does all this connoisseurship affect the "serious" part of *Hamlet*? *Hamlet* is one of the great tragedies. It has generated more comment than any other written document in

English literature, one would guess, reverent, serious comment on it as a serious play. Yet finally can we take *any* of its rhetoric seriously? If so, how much and when? The play is full of the usual release mechanisms for the rhetorical poetic. And, at the end, the Laertes play is there as stylistic control, to mock us if we have made the naive response. But what is the sophisticated response?

Hamlet focuses the issue, and the play, the plays, when he finally gets to Hecuba. He who has been so eager for a passionate speech is yet surprised when it comes and when it seizes the player:

> O, what a rogue and peasant slave am I!
> Is it not monstrous that this player here,
> But in a fiction, in a dream of passion,
> Could force his soul so to his own conceit
> That from her working all his visage wanned,
> Tears in his eyes, distraction in his aspect,
> A broken voice, and his whole function suiting
> With forms to his conceit? And all for nothing,
> For Hecuba!
> What's Hecuba to him, or he to Hecuba,
> That he should weep for her? What would he do
> Had he the motive and the cue for passion
> That I have?
>
> > [2.2.534–46]

Hamlet makes the point that dances before us in every scene. Dramatic, rhetorical motive is stronger than "real," serious motive. Situation prompts feeling in this play, rather than the other way round. Feelings are not real until played. Drama, ceremony, is always needed to authenticate experience. On the battlements Hamlet with ghostly reinforcement—makes his friends not simply swear but make a big scene of it. Laertes keeps asking for *more ceremonies* for Ophelia's burial and is upset by his father's hugger mugger interment. Hamlet plays and then breaks off ("Something too much of this") a stoic friendship scene with Horatio in 3.2. The stronger, the more genuine the feeling, the greater the need to display it.

The answer, then, to "What would he do ...?" is, presumably, "Kill the King!"? Not at all. "He would drown the stage with tears I And cleave the general ear with horrid speech" (2.2.546–47). He would rant even better. And this Hamlet him-self, by way of illustration, goes on to do:

> Yet I,
> A dull and muddy-mettled rascal, peak
> Like John-a-dreams, unpregnant of my cause,
> And can say nothing. No, not for a king,

Upon whose property and most dear life
A damned defeat was made. Am I a coward?
Who calls me villain? breaks my pate across?
Plucks off my beard and blows it in my face?
Tweaks me by the nose? gives me the lie i'th'throat
As deep as to the lungs? Who does me this?
Ha, 'swounds, I should take it, for it cannot be
But I am pigeon-livered and lack gall
To make oppression bitter, or ere this
I should ha' fatted all the region kites
With this slave's offal. Bloody, bawdy villain!
Remorseless, treacherous, lecherous, kindless villain!
O, vengeance!

[2.2.551–67]

Hamlet is here having a fine time dining off his own fury, relishing his sublime passion. He gets a bit confused, to be sure: saying nothing is not his problem. If somebody did call him villain or pluck his beard it would be better, for his grievance would then find some dramatic equivalent, would become real enough to act upon. But he enjoys himself thoroughly. He also sees himself clearly, or at least clearly enough to voice our opinion of his behavior: "Why, what an ass am I! This is most brave, / That I, the son of a dear father murdered, / Prompted to my revenge by heaven and hell, / Must like a whore unpack my heart with words" (2.2.568–71).

Hamlet is one of the most appealing characters the mind of man has ever created but he really is a bit of an ass, and not only here but all through the play. He remains incorrigibly dramatic. Do we like him because he speaks to our love of dramatic imposture? Because his solution, once he has seen his own posturing as such, is not immediate action but more playing? "I'll have these players / Play something like the murder of my father / Before mine uncle" (2.2.580–82). Playing is where we will find reality, find the truth. The play works, of course, tells Hamlet again what he already knows, has had a spirit come specially from purgatory to tell him. But that is not the point. Or rather, that is the point insofar as this is a serious play. The rhetorical purpose is to sustain reality until yet another dramatic contrivance—ship, grave scene, duel—can sustain it yet further.

We saw in the sonnets how a passage can invoke opaque attitudes by logical incongruity. Something of the sort happens in the scene after this speech, the "To be or not to be" centerpiece. Plays flourish within plays here, too, of course. The King and Polonius dangle Ophelia as bait and watch. Hamlet sees this. He may even be, as W. A. Bebbington suggested,[2] reading the "To be or not to be" speech from a book, using it, literally, as a stage prop to bemuse the spyers-on, convince them of his now-become-suicidal madness. No one in his right mind will fault the poetry. But it is irrelevant to anything that precedes. It fools Ophelia—no difficult matter—but it should not fool us. The question is whether Hamlet will act directly or through drama? Not at all. Instead, is he going to end it in the river? I put it thus familiarly to penetrate the serious numinosity surrounding this passage. Hamlet anatomizes grievance for all time. But does *he* suffer these grievances? He has a complaint indeed against the King and one against Ophelia. Why not do something about them instead of meditating on suicide? If the book is a stage prop, or the speech a trap for the hidden listeners, of course, the question of relevancy doesn't arise. The speech works beautifully. But we do not usually consider it a rhetorical trick. It is the most serious speech in the canon. But is it? It tells us nothing about Hamlet except what we already know—he is a good actor. Its relevance, in fact, may lurk just here. The real question by this point in the play is exactly this one: is Hamlet or not? Or does he just act? What kind of self does he possess?

The whole play, we know, seeks authenticity, reality behind the arras, things as they are. Hamlet, we are to assume, embodies the only true self, the central self amidst a cast of wicked phonies. The play, seen this way, provided a natural delight for both the Victorians and the existentialists; their sentimentalism about the central self ran the same way. Yet the question really is whether Hamlet is *to be*, to act rather than reenact. Much has been written on the Melancholy-Man-in-the-Renaissance and how his problems apply to Hamlet. Much more has been written on Hamlet's paralysis. Yet, how irrelevant all this commentary is to the real problem, not *what* Hamlet's motive is but *what kind of* motive. Why can't he act? Angels and ministers of grace, he does nothing else. Polonius, Rosencrantz and Guildenstern, Laertes, Claudius, all go to it. But Hamlet never breaks through to "reality." His motives and his behavior remain dramatic from first to last. So, in spite of all those bodies at the end, commentators wonder if *Hamlet* amounts to a tragedy and, if so, what kind. Hamlet lacks the serious, central self tragedy requires. We are compelled to stand back, hold off our identification, and hence to locate the play within rhetorical coordinates, a tragicomedy about the two kinds of self and the two kinds of motive.

We see this theme in that Q_2 scene (4.4) where Fortinbras and his army parade, with seeming irrelevance—at least to many directors, who cut it—across the stage. They parade so that Hamlet can reflect upon them. The theme is motive. The scene begins as a straightforward lesson in the vanity of human wishes. They go, the Captain tells Hamlet, "to gain a little patch of ground / That hath in it no profit but the name" (4.4.18–19). Hamlet seems to get the point, "the question of this straw," the absurd artificiality of human motive, and especially of aristocratic war, war for pleasure, for the pure glory of it. But then out jumps another non sequitur soliloquy:

How all occasions do inform against me
And spur my dull revenge! What is a man,

> If his chief good and market of his time
> Be but to sleep and feed? A beast, no more.
> Sure he that made us with such large discourse,
> Looking before and after, gave us not
> That capability and godlike reason
> To fust in us unused. Now, whether it be
> Bestial oblivion, or some craven scruple
> Of thinking too precisely on th' event—
> A thought which, quartered, hath but one part wisdom
> And ever three parts coward—I do not know
> Why yet I live to say, "This thing's to do,"
> Sith I have cause, and will, and strength, and means
> To do't.
>
> [4.4.32–46]

What has reason to do with revenge? His question—why, with all his compelling reasons, doesn't he go on—is again well taken. Shakespeare has carefully given him the realest reasons a revenge hero ever had—father murdered, mother whored, kingdom usurped, his innocent maiden corrupted in her imagination. The answer to Hamlet's question marches about on the stage before him. As usual, he does not fully understand the problem. It is the Player King's tears all over again. Fortinbras's motivation is sublimely artificial, entirely dramatic. Honor. It has no profit in it but the name. Hamlet cannot act because he cannot find a way to dramatize his revenge. Chances he has, but, as when he surprises Claudius praying, they are not dramatic. Claudius is alone. To fall upon him and kill him would not be revenge, as he says, not because Claudius will die shriven but because he will not see it coming, because nobody is watching.

So, when Hamlet continues his soliloquy, he draws a moral precisely opposite to the expected one. Again, logical discontinuity triggers stylistic attitude:

> Examples gross as earth exhort me.
> Witness this army of such mass and charge,
> Led by a delicate and tender prince,
> Whose spirit, with divine ambition puffed,
> Makes mouths at the invisible event,
> Exposing what is mortal and unsure
> To all that fortune, death, and danger dare,
> Even for an eggshell. Rightly to be great
> Is not to stir without great argument,
> But greatly to find quarrel in a straw
> When honor's at the stake. How stand I then,
> That have a father killed, a mother stained,

Excitements of my reason and my blood,
And let all sleep, while to my shame I see
The imminent death of twenty thousand men
That for a fantasy and trick of fame
Go to their graves like beds, fight for a plot
Whereon the numbers cannot try the cause,
Which is not tomb enough and continent
To hide the slain? O, from this time forth,
My thoughts be bloody, or be nothing worth!

[4.4.46–66]

He sees but does not see. In some way, Fortinbras represents where he wants to go, what he wants to be, how he wants to behave. But he doesn't see how, nor altogether do we. If ever an allegorical puppet was dragged across a stage it is Fortinbras. Yet he haunts the play. His divine ambition begins the action of the play; he gets that offstage introduction Shakespeare is so fond of; he marches to Norway to make a point about motive; and he marches back at the end, inherits Denmark. Yet he stays cardboard. It is not real motive he represents but martial honor much rather.

Shakespeare sought to give *Hamlet* a pronounced military coloration from first to last. The play begins on guard; the ghost wears armor; Denmark is a most warlike state. Military honor is the accepted motive in a Denmark Fortinbras rightly inherits. Honor will cure what is rotten in Denmark, restore its proper values. Hamlet cannot set the times right because he cannot find in martial honor a full and sufficient motive for human life. Hamlet, says Fortinbras, would have done well had he been king, but we may be permitted to doubt it. He thinks too much. Yet honor and the soldier's life provide the model motive for *Hamlet*. All his working life, Shakespeare was fascinated and perplexed by how deeply the military motive satisfied man. It constituted a sublime secular commitment which, like the religious commitment, gave all away to get all back. Hamlet's self-consciousness keeps him from it, yes, but even more his search for real purpose. Chivalric war—all war, perhaps—is manufactured purpose. Hamlet can talk about clutching it to his bosom but he cannot do it, for there is nothing *inevitable* about it.

Military honor is finally a role, much like Laertes' role as revenge hero. Both roles are satisfying, both integrate and direct the personality. But once you realize that you are playing the role for just these reasons, using it as a self-serving device, its attraction fades. As its inevitability diminishes, so does its reality. War and revenge both prove finally so rewarding because they provide, by all the killing, the irrefutable reality needed to bolster the role, restore its inevitability. Thus Shakespeare chose them, a revenge plot superposed on a Fortinbras—honor plot, for his play about motive. They provided a model for the kind of motive men find most satisfying; they combine maximum dramatic satisfaction with the irrefutable reality only bloody death can supply. In the Elizabethan absurdity as in our own, men kill others and themselves because that is the only real thing left to do. It is a rare paradox and Shakespeare builds his play upon it.

But even death is not dependable. We can learn to make sport of it, enjoy it. So the gravedigger puns on his craft. So, too, I suppose, Fortinbras laconically remarks at the end of the play: "Such a sight as this / Becomes the field, but here shows much amiss." Death's reality can vanish too. All our purposes end up, like the skull Hamlet meditates on, a stage prop. It is not accidental that the language which closes the play is theatrical. Hamlet even in death does not escape the dramatic self. When the bodies are "high on a stage ... placed to the view" Horatio will "speak to th' yet unknowing world," will authenticate the proceeding with a rhetorical occasion. Hamlet's body, Fortinbras commands, is to be borne "like a soldier to the stage, / For he was likely, had he been put on, I To have proved most royal."

Nor is it accidental that Hamlet kills Polonius. The act is his real attempt at revenge, Polonius his real enemy. Polonius embodies the dramatic self-consciousness which stands between Hamlet and the roles—Avenger and King—he was born to play. But Polonius pervades the whole of Hamlet's world and lurks within Hamlet himself. Only death can free Hamlet. Perhaps this is why he faces it with nonchalance. Much has been said about Hamlet's stoicism, but how unstoical the play really is! Honest feeling demands a dramatic equivalent to make it real just as artifice does. Stoicism demands a preexistent reality, a central self beyond drama, which the play denies. Stoicism is death and indeed, in *Hamlet*, the second follows hard upon the avowal of the first. We have no choice but to play.

And so Hamlet chooses his foil and plays. I have been arguing that the play invokes rhetorical coordinates as well as serious ones. It makes sense, if this is so, that it should end with a sublime game and the triumph of chance. Hamlet never solves his problem, nor does chance solve it for him, nor does the play solve it for us. No satisfactory model for motive, no movement from game to sublime, is suggested. Hamlet can finally kill the King because the King thoughtfully supplies a dramatic occasion appropriate to the deed. And Hamlet can kill Laertes because dramatic motive has destroyed naive purpose. And vice versa. But Hamlet cannot get rid of his dramatic self, his dramatic motives. The duel allegorizes the quarrel between kinds of motive which the play has just dramatized. And the duel, like the play, is a zero-sum game. Interest for both sides adds up to zero. The play leaves us, finally, where it leaves Hamlet. We have savored the violence and the gorgeous poetry and been made aware that we do. We have been made to reflect on play as well as purpose. We have not been shown how to move from one to the other. Nor that it *cannot* be done. We are left, like those in the play, dependent on death and chance to show us how to put our two motives, our two selves, together.

Shakespeare as a mature playwright is not supposed to be an opaque stylist. The great unity of his mature tragedies is a style we look through, not at. The gamesman with words fades out with the nondramatic poems and early infatuations like *Love's Labor's Lost*. *Hamlet* shows, by itself, how wrong this view of Shakespeare's development is. The play depends upon an alternation of opaque and transparent styles for its meaning. The alternation almost is the meaning. *Hamlet* is a play about motive, about style, and thus perhaps, of the mature plays, an exception? I don't think so. Where Shakespeare is most sublime he is also most rhetorical and both poetics are likely to be present in force. To illustrate such a thesis would constitute an agreeable task. The lines it would follow are clear enough. They would yield explanation of the double plot more basic than the comic/serious one. They would render the comic/tragic division altogether less important than it now seems.

In play after play the same stylistic strategy illustrates the same juxtaposition of motive, of play and purpose. Richard cannot learn the difference. Hal must. Lear can play the king but he has never *been* a king. *Antony and Cleopatra* juxtaposes not only public and private life but two poetics and two selves. The double plot becomes, over and over, a serious plot-poetic and a play plot-poetic. The fatal innocence of Shakespeare's characters turns out, over and over, to be innocence about the real nature of their motivation. All through the *Henriad* political rhetoric must be *seen* as rhetoric. Egypt is meant to be *seen* as more wordy and more metaphorical than Rome. *Romeo and Juliet* depends on our seeing the Petrarchan rhetoric as such, else we will mistake the kind of play it is, a play where death authenticates game. Lear on the heath, that centerpiece of Shakespearean sublimity, alters his outlines considerably within rhetorical coordinates. Shakespearean tragedy may come to seem, as in *Hamlet*, a juxtaposition of the two motives with a hole in the middle, with no way to connect them. The comedies collapse them. And the problem plays and romances try to make a path between the two, see them in dynamic interchange. The two things that obsessed Shakespeare were style and motive, and his career can be charted coherently from beginning to end in terms of their interrelation. In this he typifies the stylistic strategy of the Renaissance as a whole. The real question of motive lay beyond good and evil. It was the principal task of the self-conscious rhetorical style to point this moral. Human flesh is sullied with self-consciousness, with theatricality, and these will be the ground for whatever authentic morality any of us can muster.

NOTES

1. Ed. Willard Farnham.
2. "Soliloquy?," *Times Literary Supplement*, 20 March 1969, p. 289.

PATRICIA PARKER

Dilation and Inflation: Shakespearean Increase
in All's Well That Ends Well,
Troilus and Cressida

> a more spacious ceremony .... a more dilated farewell.
> *All's Well That Ends Well*

From as early as the first of Shakespeare's sonnets, a signally important motif in the Shakespeare canon as a whole is the figure of *increase*. In the sonnets themselves, the so-called procreation sequence that begins "From fairest creatures we desire increase" (1) depends on a mixture of economic and sexual terms—*increase, spend, dear, usury, use,* and the double-meaning *husbandry*, linked both to the "tillage" of an "unear'd womb" (3) and to the economic management of an equally double-meaning "house" (13). An older language of agricultural and sexual "abundance," "substance" (1, 37), and "breed" (12) is joined there by a bourgeois language of a different kind of "copy," "penury," inflation, and "store" (84).[1] And the language of increase—both in the sexual and generative sense of increase and multiply and in the sense of the *copia* of words as another form of wealth or store—continues in the canon in multiple forms, not just in the mode of celebration, fertility, or abundance but in the more problematic mode of *King Lear*, with its darker vision of negative increase (the "nothing" that comes of "nothing"), or the "rank" increase of *Hamlet*, product of a poisoned union that turns the copious *ubertas* of abundance into a tuberous proliferation of "words, words, words."

What I propose, then, to do in this chapter is to suggest first the ways in which increase (in both the economic and the generative sense of increase and multiply) becomes the nodal preoccupation of Shakespeare's problematic

From *Shakespeare from the Margins: Language, Culture, Context.* © 1996 by the University of Chicago.

comedy, *All's Well That Ends Well*, and then to go on, beyond the boundaries of this play, to consider the problem of inflation in several of its senses in the late sixteenth and early seventeenth centuries, before returning to the Shakespearean network of dilation and increase, briefly in *Hamlet* and then, more extensively, in *Troilus and Cressida*.

I will begin once again from what seems a simply marginal or inconsequential passage. In Act II of *All's Well That Ends Well*, Parolles (the Shakespearean character whose name means "words") advises Bertram to employ more words in his "adieu" to the lords of the French court by taking what he calls a "more dilated farewell":

> Use a more spacious ceremony to the noble lords; you have restrain'd yourself within the list of too cold an adieu. Be more expressive to them, for they wear themselves in the cap of the time....
> After them, and take *a more dilated farewell*. (II.i.50–57)

Parolles, who is studying to be the "perfect courtier" (I.i.203), here instructs Bertram—described as an immature or "unseason'd courtier" (I.i.67)—in the verbal fashions of the court. But the terms he suggests, of recourse to a more "spacious ceremony" and "more dilated farewell," also appear again, in different form, in the later scene where Parolles himself is "granted space" (IV.i.88) after he has almost lost his life for want of "language" (IV.i.70).

Parolles's counsel to Bertram to "take a more dilated farewell" sounds in a play that is literally filled with farewells—from Bertram's initial departure for Paris and his subsequent stealing away to Florence to Helena's departure on her pilgrimage and the final return of characters to Rossillion—but also with iterations of *farewell* in its double sense of an ending or separation and a wish for the way to come. The play inherits these repeated displacements from its narrative source, Boccaccio's story of Giletta of Narbona in *Decameron* 3. 9, summarized in William Painter's *Palace of Pleasure*:

> Giletta a Phisition's doughter of Narbon, healed the French King of a Fistula, for reward whereof she demaunded Beltramo Counte of Rossiglione to husband. The Counte being maried against his will, for despite fled to Florence, and loved another. Giletta, his wife, by pollicie founde meanes to lye with her husbande, in place of his lover, and was begotten with childe of two sonnes: which knowen to her husband, he received her againe, and afterwards he lived in great honour and felicitie.[2]

With name changes to Helena and Bertram, a streamlining of the bed trick to a single night and pregnancy, the feigned death of the wife, and a much less "felicitous" atmosphere at its end, this narrative is essentially the plot Shakespeare follows in *All's Well*. To it, however (notoriously, in the view of many critics), the play adds not only the figure of Parolles but a great deal whose interconnection still remains largely uninterpreted: including the scenes of wordplay between Bertram's mother the countess, the counselor Lafew, and Lavatch the clown; its repeated evocations of the specter of incest; and its variations on the multiple senses of increase. What I want to suggest, then, in what follows—under the rubric of dilation or increase—are precisely the unnoticed interstitial or marginal links be-tween the various characters, scenes, and "businesses" added by Shakespeare to his much more "straightforward" source.[3]

Increase in the sense of "increase and multiply" is, of course, the command delivered to Adam and Eve at the beginning of Genesis, the command that makes possible the extension of time and history as well as the multiplication of life that ensues. It is also the command repeatedly evoked in texts contemporary with *All's Well* that treat of the loss of virginity required in order to amplify, extend, or dilate the branches of a family tree, an act of increase that depends on the dilation or opening of something constricted or closed.[4] All of the traditional arguments against virginity oppose its premature end or "fine" to the extension, and generational reprieve from death, made possible through such an opening to increase, from the discourse of Genius in the *Roman de la Rose* to the texts that echo it.[5] This generative form of opening, in the arguments marshaled traditionally against virginity, depends on inducing something closed to open and dilate (a tradition we will also explore in the final chapter). The *increase* of such sexual opening had its hermeneutic and verbal counterparts, in the understanding of interpretation, for example, as opening up to increase a closed, hermetic, or forbidding text ("dilating or enlarging a matter by interpretation," as one text puts it),[6] and the dilation of discourse whose parodic double was empty inflation or mere words. Increase and multiply, in both the sexually generative and this hermeneutic sense, is the subject of the chapter of Augustine's *Confessions* that links the command in Genesis to the interpreter's opening of a scriptural text, a link also forged in the early modern tradition of verbal *copia* as an amplification of speech that proceeds by increasing a smaller, more restricted, stock of words.[7] What I want to suggest in focusing on dilation in both its sexual and its other contemporary senses in *All's Well* is that this linking of verbal, hermeneutic, and generative or generational under the heading of increase also provides a way into the subtle interconnections between this play's otherwise apparently unconnected scenes, an important interstitial context for its buried linkages.

Whether or not it is the play corresponding to Francis Meres's mysterious reference to a *Love's Labors Wonne*, *All's Well That Ends Well* is Shakespeare's most conspicuously teleological title, suggestive of the comic plot of fulfillment achieved after a long period of trial. Yet the Shakespearean play whose title appears to emphasize final closure, end, or fine is not only notoriously ambiguous in its own dramatic close but filled with more pressing, and more immediate, senses of premature ending or closing off.[8] By contrast, both in the scene in which Parolles counsels Bertram to "take a more dilated farewell" ("Use a more spacious ceremony") and in the scene in Act IV where this same Parolles is threatened with immediate death for want of "language" before he is "granted space" (IV.iii.96), the extension of discourse, as of life, is linked with the creation of an intervening space. Such an association is not restricted to scenes actually involving Parolles, or "words": it also extends to the play's repeated enactment of something constricted or closed that needs to be "granted space," or opened up.

Like several other plays of Shakespeare, *All's Well* begins with a heavy sense of conclusion or end—not, here, as in *The Comedy of Errors*, with a literal doom or sentence of death, but with a different kind of sentence, one whose constrictions need to be countered in order for the play itself to be granted space. In particular, it opens with the need to increase the space between birth and death, son and husband, in the despairing lines uttered by the countess at the moment of her son's farewell. The play's own first sentence—the countess's "in delivering my son from me, I bury a second husband"—summons a sense of delivery as birth that is immediately short-circuited by its heavier sense of burial, or death. Birth and death are here too close. The constricted interval between them involves the opposite of a more spacious interim or "dilated farewell," just as the potentially incestuous conflation of the space between husband and son as "second husband" produces an incestuous sense of generational constriction.

Ironically, however, it is the farewell the countess fears will be a second death—Bertram's departure for the French court—that Lafew goes on to present as a different kind of second, in a play that is to be filled with seconds and surrogates. Lafew's response—"You shall find of the King a husband, madam; you, sir, a father" (6–7)—deflects the potentially incestuous conflation of husband and son in the countess's opening line by displacement onto a substitute or surrogate father. It also converts a gloom-filled sentence, or apparent end, into a starting point and Bertram's farewell (with its introduction of geographical space or distance) into a form of "delivery." As in *The Comedy of Errors*, whose opening contains a play on opening, *All's Well* depends at its beginning on the opening up of space within something more constricted—both the threatening nearness or proximity of incest and the sense of stillbirth that would, to paraphrase Bertram's later line, otherwise cause the play itself to "end" ere it "begin" (II.v.27).

I start with the oppressive sense of ending at the beginning of *All's Well* not simply to introduce the importance in this play of spacing out and opening up but also to address one of its chief interpretive cruxes—the question of why this opening scene should also include its puzzling exchange between Parolles and Helena on the subject of increase. At the beginning of this exchange, Helena is immersed in her own despairing meditation on ending ("I am undone, there is no living, none, / If Bertram be away," I.i.84–85). And it is in the midst of this new despairing assumption of conclusion—after the marking of the deaths of fathers (Helena's as well as Bertram's) and allusion to the mortal malady of the king—that the play first introduces Parolles, the character whose name means not just one but many words (V.ii.36–40), along with his counsel of increase and multiply.

Parolles enters the scene as Helena herself is lamenting the departure of Bertram, the same departure the countess had mourned as a form of burial or death; and the sparring between them—an exemplary instance of what Stephen Greenblatt has called Shakespeare's warming verbal "friction"—is on the subject of virginity as another kind of death ("virginity murthers itself," I.i.139).[9] The punning that ensues on pregnancy as the "blowing up" of virgins and on tumescence and detumescence as "blow-[ing] up" and then "blowing ... down" a man (119-24) quickly leads to the extended exchange on the subject of increase:

> PAROLLES: ... Loss of virginity is rational increase, and there was
>   never virgin got till virginity was first lost.... Virginity, by being
>   once lost, may be ten times found; by being ever kept, it is ever
>   lost. 'Tis too cold a companion; away with't! ... 'tis against the
>   rule of nature.... Keep it not, you cannot choose but lose by't.
>   Out with't! Within tone year it will make itself two, which is a
>   goodly increase, and the principal itself not much the worse.
>   (I.1.127–49)

The imagery of the entire passage links generational and monetary increase, increase of the principal through interest and propagation as a form of increase and multiply, the two forms of wealth linked in the period as ways to "encrease" a "stock."[10] The fact that it is the notoriously inflated (or "blown up") Parolles who enters the play as the champion of increase forges, however, a further linking with verbal increase; and the entrance of the figure whose name means "words" accompanies the opening up of the play itself to a more dilated farewell. As if to call attention to the link, the scene's description of virginity as "too cold a companion" or as an "old courtier" who "wears her cap out of fashion" and knows not how to suit either "fashion" or "time" (I.i.156–57) verbally anticipates the later scene of Parolles's "more dilated farewell," with its contrasting of those who "wear themselves in the cap of the time" to "too cold an adieu" (II.i.49–56).[11]

All's Well That Ends Well begins, then, with an oppressive sense of death and with a "farewell" that appears at first to the countess and to Helena as the equivalent of a death, an ending beyond which there is "no living, none." But in the case of Helena, who will be the prime genetrix of the plot to come, the exchange with a character called "words" on the subject of increase seems to open up this initial oppressive sense of end in a way not unlike the opening up of the surrogate death or "fine" of virginity. Parolles—figure in the play of an increase or dilation that is finally *only* inflated or blown up—enters the play just as Helena, focused on death, is in another sense "meditating on virginity." And by the end of this sparring with the character called "Parolles," Helena has passed from despair to a more active sense that "Our remedies oft in ourselves do lie," from passivity before unalterable necessity ("now he's gone, and my idolatrous fancy / Must sanctify his relics") to the generation of a plot, her plan to travel to Paris to offer a cure to the king and win Bertram as a result:

> Who ever strove
> To show her merit, that did miss her love?
> The King's disease—my project may deceive me,
> But my intents are fix'd, and will not leave me.
>
> (I.i.226–29)

The intervening space introduced by Bertram's farewell becomes, then, after the exchange with Parolles on increase, the generative space of Helena's project, both in the sense of a plot with an end in view and in the sense of something projected toward the future rather than focused on the past. Opening up a space within constriction, achieving a reprieve in the face of an oppressive sense of end or fine, is what enables the play called *All's Well That Ends Well* itself to open to increase. The exchange with Parolles provides both for the play and for Helena, its prime mover, the parole his name suggests,[12] both the word she takes up in a scene where she has the final word and the reprieve from ending her project proceeds to provide. The verbal sparring of this opening scene, then, establishes an association between Parolles, or words, and the dilation that is simultaneously the generational, monetary, and verbal fulfillment of the command to increase and multiply.

This early exchange between Parolles and Helena on the subject of increase proleptically anticipates Helena's own eventual pregnancy after she has found a way to "blow up" her virginity according to her own designs and present Bertram with evidence of that increase. But the importance of increase in all of its senses—and hence the importance of this puzzling early exchange—is also underlined in a succession of scenes apparently so minor that they have remained strikingly underinterpreted in criticism of *All's Well*, though they provide some of the best examples of the importance in Shakespeare of the apparently marginal. The link between verbal and generational increase established in the early sparring between Parolles and Helena is reaffirmed almost immediately within Act I itself—when the steward's wordy, or Parolles-like, preamble (iii.3–7) serves as a form of stalling for time, filling up the space before the countess notices the presence of the clown Lavatch, who has come to express his own desire to increase and multiply ("I think I shall never have the blessing of God till I have issue a' my body," I.iii.24–25>).[13] The link between words and bearing, or generational increase—along with the disparagement of merely empty or inflated words—has already been established just before this scene, in the king's praise of Bertram's father as one whose "plausive words" were "scatter'd not in ears, but grafted ... To grow there and to bear" (I.ii.53–55). And the image is explicitly recalled in the clown's "He that ears my land spares my team" (I.iii.44) as a comic argument for cuckoldry as an increase of husbandry.

Increase also pervades the multiple allusions through the play to alchemy as a means of renewing or extending life, as the "multiplying medicine" (V.iii.102) associated with the command in Genesis to increase and multiply.[14] But the sense of increase as opening up a space within something constricted even more strikingly suggests links between the first act's insistence on increase and its equally insistent emphasis on incest, an emphasis found nowhere in the play's narrative source. We have already noted the way in which the countess's opening line ("In delivering my son from me I bury a second husband") not only collapses the space between birth and death, but also incestuously conflates husband and son.[15] But the threat of incest only hinted at in this opening sentence is directly foregrounded in the scene within Act I in which Helena strenuously objects to calling Bertram's mother her mother:

COUNTESS: You know, Helen,
    I am a mother to you.
HELENA: Mine honorable mistress.
COUNTESS: Nay, a mother,
    Why not a mother? When I said "a mother,"
    Methought you saw a serpent. What's in "mother"
    That you start at it? I say I am your mother,
    And put you in the catalogue of those
    That were enwombed mine....

    . . . .
    ... does it curd thy blood

    . . . .
    To say I am thy mother? What's the matter,

    . . . .
    —Why, that you are my daughter?
HELENA: That I am not.
COUNTESS: I say I am your mother.
HELENA: Pardon, madam;
    The Count Rossillion cannot be my brother:
    I am from humble, he from honored name;
    No note upon my parents, his all noble.
    My master, my dear lord he is, and I
    His servant live, and will his vassal die.

He must not be my brother.

COUNTESS: Nor I your mother?

HELENA: You are my mother, madam; would you were—
    So that my lord your son were not my brother—
    Indeed my mother! Or were you both our mothers,
    I care no more for than I do for heaven,
    So I were not his sister. Can't no other,
    But, I your daughter, he must be my brother?

COUNTESS: Yes, Helen, you might be my daughter-in-law.

(I.iii.138–67)

In relation to the series of chess moves Helena must make if she is to be "mated" as she desires (I.i.91),[16] becoming the "daughter" of the countess would resolve one of the obstacles she faces—the hierarchical or class distance from Bertram as one too far above her (I.i.82–92). But it would do so only by creating another obstacle, the dangerous proximity of consanguinity. Helena therefore invokes here the distance in social position she had earlier bemoaned ("The Count Rossillion cannot be my brother. / I am from humble, he from honored name"). "Daughter"—the term that in early modern usage could name both daughter by marriage and daughter by birth—is displaced or spaced into its more distant correlative ("you might be my daughter-in-law"), exogamous extension rather than endogamous collapse. The separation of ambiguously paired identities, originally contained within a "double-meaning" (IV.iii.99) name, comes in this scene as the answer to one of the play's first riddles, in ways that remind us how close the links are between incest, with its conflation of familial identities, and the kind of riddling whose solution depends on such spacing or separating out.[17] The sense of incest as involving something too near-and the need to create a space between relations that threaten to come too close—is underscored verbally just before this exchange by the steward's otherwise gratuitous "I was very late more *near* her than I think she wish'd me" (I.iii.106–7).

    The whole extended space of *All's Well That Ends Well*—whose plot proceeds through a series of displacements or farewells—is required to provide the corresponding answer to this early scene of incest and its riddling, just as later in Pericles a series of geographical displacements and a relentlessly narrative *espacement* intervene to separate out an opening incest's riddling conflation of generations and identities. The plot of *All's Well* from this point forward involves a series of displacements as well as a putting off of conclusions that are premature or threaten to be too near. The heavy sense of ending with which the play begins and the exchange between Parolles and Helena on the death wish of virginity have their counterpart first in the literal death wish of the ailing king, in a scene (II.i) in which the word *farewell* is sounded throughout. The king's gesture of parting from the young French lords on their way to war in Italy is joined by his sense of his own end as unalterably at hand ("FIRST LORD: 'Tis our hope, sir, /

After well-ent'red soldiers, to return / And find your Grace in health. / KING: No, no, it cannot be," II.i.5–8). And it is, again, in this scene—as the king temporarily retires to another part of the stage—that Parolles appears, uttering here the counsel to "take a more *dilated* farewell" (II.i.57).

Parolles's urging of this "more spacious ceremony" is inserted, in fact, between two iterations of the king's sense of the imminence and inevitability of his end, the second of which is explicitly a form of death wish:

> LAFEW: But, my good lord, 'tis thus: will you be curd
>   Of your infirmity?
> KING: No.
> LAFEW: O, will you eat
>   No grapes, my royal fox?
>
>   (II.i.68–70)

It is at this point—in the same scene as Parolles's "more spacious ceremony" and "more dilated farewell"—that Helena arrives as the "Doctor She" (II.i.79) provided with an enabling "physic." Once again, the exchange between Helena and the king has to do with the granting of a space (II.i.159). The king's conviction that he is "one near death" (131) is countered by Helena's reminders that

>   great floods have flown
> From simple sources; and great seas have dried
> When miracles have by the great'st been denied.
> Oft expectation fails, and most oft there
> Where most it promises; and oft it hits
> Where hope is coldest, and despair most [fits].
>
>   (II.i.139–44)

The king's fixation on ending is countered not only by the hope offered through Helena's physic but through this series of images recalling the miracles, and "parole," of Exodus—water from rock and the drying of the Red Sea—at precisely those points where what had at first seemed an imminent end opens into a space of reprieve. "Coldest" here, it needs to be observed, gathers echoes both from the symbolic death of "cold" virginity in the early exchange on increase and from the "cold" of Parolles's counteradvice to take "a more dilated farewell" ("you have restrain'd yourself within the list of *too cold* an adieu").[18]

The king's exchange with Helena, though it leads first to his refusal of what he terms a "senseless help" (124) for a "past-cure malady" ("fare thee well, kind maid, / Thy pains not us'd must by thyself be paid," 145–46), results finally in the granting to Helena of the requested "space" (159) in which to try her cure, and the king's readiness to be her "resolv'd patient" (204) in all the multiple senses of that phrase. In the fertility imagery appropriate for a king whose ailment, a fistula or "pipe," also suggests a kind of impotence,[19] Helena herself becomes a form of "physic." The scene of Exodus's imagery of water from rock or barren ground is filled, as has often been remarked, with innuendoes of sexual rejuvenation that begin with Lafew's comparing himself to "Cressid's uncle" (97) as he leaves the two alone together ("I have seen a medicine / That's able to breathe life into a stone, / Quicken a rock ... powerful to araise King Pippen, nay, / To give great Charlemain a pen in's hand / And write to her a love-line," II.i.72–78). The king's becoming "Lustick" or "lusty" (II.iii.41) as a result of the cure of this Doctor She is hence related to a specifically sexual increase through the familiar associations of this phallic pen, long linked with fulfillment of the command to increase and multiply. By contrast, the fistula, not just "water-pipe" (Latin, *fistula*) but a "running" sore, provides a parody of this fertility, of flowing liquid from a stone. As a choice for the opposite of genuine fertility it also forges a link with the inflated pseudoincrease or parody fertility of Parolles, or "words," since the association between a fistula or running sore and an unstoppable loquacity was proverbial ("Loquacity," as one contemporary text puts it, is "the Fistula of the minde").[20]

The king's "lustique" cure also, however, both procures a reprieve for him and performs, once again, a transition for Helena from the threat of death ("If I break time, or flinch in property / Of what I spoke, unpitied let me die," II.i.187–88) to the possibility of increase, expressed through the images of genealogical branches and of grafting in lines that eschew the right to have her "low and humble name to propagate / With any branch or image" as lofty as the king's (II.i.197–98). The familiar image of generational increase through the branches of a family tree, invoked in Helena's disclaimer as she chooses Bertram instead, will by the end of the play, as at the end of *Cymbeline*, be linked as well with the ramifications or branches of a dilated discourse. But even here the king's progression from the death wish of his anticipated end parallels the reprieve and regeneration of Helena after the exchange with Parolles on the subject of increase. The involvement of Parolles, or "words," in both scenes—first as the proponent of increase and multiply as opposed to the death wish of virginity and then as the counselor of a "more spacious ceremony" and "more dilated farewell" in the scene of the king's valedictory—suggests that he is paired not only with Helena but, more generally, with a form of increase that puts off immediate ends, and specifically with one that depends on paroles.

The play whose title foregrounds closure appears, then, from its very beginning to gain its own life or increase—as well as the achievement within it of the project of a Doctor She—from the opening up of space and the putting off of ends, as well as from the tension between mere verbal dilation as empty or blown up and a dilation that would finally be more fruitful, including the dilation of a play whose length is underscored by the epilogue's reference to the audience's patience as well. The subtle juxtaposition with Helena at both points in its early acts establishes a link between the two—Helena's argument to the king recalling Parolles's argument against the death wish of virginity—and hence begins to suggest a relationship of counterfeit or parodic imitation between the kind of wordy inflation he represents and the increase represented by her, a difference underlined by Helena's "I am not an imposture" (II.i.155) in the same scene in which Parolles asks to be remembered ("Say to him I live") to one "Captain *Spurio*" (II.i.43), whose name literally means "counterfeit."[21] To see Shakespeare's insertion into his source of the figure of Parolles—often regarded as a supernumerary irrelevance—as related instead to all the multiple senses of increase is not only to suggest a link as well as an opposition between this "manifold linguist" and the figure of Helena who directs its plot but the subtle links between the many scenes within the play often similarly treated as marginal or supernumerary.

As if, for example, to emphasize the dramatic connection between the extension of life and the extending of words, as between the play's various forms of putting off, the entrance of Helena through which the king is offered a respite from death (II.i.93) is preceded by lines that give to his counselor Lafew (whose name might promise a contrasting "in few") a verbosity associated elsewhere with Parolles ("Thus he his special nothing ever prologues," II.i.92). Most striking, however, in this regard is the fact that the offstage interval in which the king's death is postponed through Helena's physic is filled by an extraordinary scene of wordplay on the theme of putting off (yet another Shakespearean addition to the source), a scene whose verbal sparring involves the intersection of natural and other forms of increase. (It begins, for example, with a double-meaning reference to the clown's "breeding," II.ii.1-2). That such a pyrotechnical verbal exchange on putting off should come immediately after the counsel of Parolles to take a dilated farewell as well as after the king's agreement to the "space" that puts off his death makes it yet another of this play's apparently marginal but strategically suggestive scenes. In the series of parallels through which the clown parodically iterates the larger plot, Lavatch declares that his "business is but to the court" (II.ii.4) in lines that directly echo Parolles's studying to be the "perfect courtier" in the scene just before ("I am so full of businesses, I cannot answer thee acutely. I will return perfect courtier," I.i.206–7). And putting off in the exchange that follows in this scene ranges through various meanings from "selling" to "palming off on some one" to taking off one's cap before it settles into an extended parody of the very forms of putting off that Parolles in his counseling of a more dilated farewell had instructed the "unseason'd courtier" Bertram to learn—the technique of extending or amplifying through the courtier's apparently endless supply of words.[22]

As the wordplay of this scene proceeds, putting off is also linked with the clown's description of "an answer [that] will serve all men," a description to which the countess responds first, "that's a bountiful answer that fits all questions," and then, "it must be an answer of most monstrous size that must fit all demands." The answer that will fit all demands becomes, as the scene proceeds, the clown's stalling "O Lord, sir" which puts off or evades through a copious supply of intervening words, the empty "nothings" associated with Parolles elsewhere in the play ("CLOWN: Ask me if I am a courtier...? / COUNTESS: I pray you, sir, are you a courtier? / CLOWN: O Lord, Sir! There's a simple putting off," II.ii.36–41). Putting off is here a form of filling up both space and time, postponing a more direct answer to a question through a Parolles-like ability to extend through words. But what is signal in this scene is the fact that it not only calls attention to the idea—and multiple forms—of putting off but also reminds us that putting off cannot last forever, as the clown himself discovers as the scene approaches its own conclusion:

> CLOWN: I ne'er had worse luck in my life in my "O Lord, Sir!"
>   I see things may serve long, but not serve ever.
> COUNTESS: I play the noble huswife with the time,
>   To entertain it so merrily with a fool.
> CLOWN: O Lord, sir!—Why, there't serves well again.
> COUNTESS: An end, sir; To your business: give Helen this,
>   And urge her to a present answer back.
>
>   (57–64)

"Things may serve long, but not serve ever" provides a motto that might be applied to all this play's forms of putting off, from the physic that, even in the hands of Gerard de Narbon, can extend life but not ultimately put off death (I.i.28–29),[23] to the wordy "nothing" (II.iv.2–26) Parolles whose "spurious" counterfeiting will be ultimately exposed. Both "An end, sir," and the countess's call for a "present answer" remind us of ends that, though deferred, do finally come, even to a play whose own extension and increase depends on putting off.

The sheer multiplicity of changes on the theme of putting off in this scene of wordplay between the countess and the clown, however, also forges links with the different forms of putting off that follow Act II—an act that at first looks as if it might provide a more immediate folktale ending in the conclusion of the project through which Helena wins a husband by curing the king. For this same clown, in yet another parody of the larger plot, announces in his next exchange with the countess his intention to put off his intended wife ("I have no mind to Isbel since I was at court," III.ii.12), just after Bertram has evaded the wife who chooses him rather than the other way around. The entire comic scene on the forms of putting off (II.ii) is linked by unmistakable verbal echo to the kind of putting off that thus generates the plot a second time, when Helena is wedded to, but not bedded by, a now again departing Bertram. This time the putting off is not verbal but erotic. But this delay of consummation is announced once again through Parolles, or words, sent to deliver another farewell:

Madam, my lord will go away to-night,
A very serious business calls on him.
The great prerogative and rite of love,
Which, as your due, time claims, he does acknowledge,
But *puts it off* to a compell'd restraint;
Whose want, and whose delay, is strew'd with sweets,
Which they distill now in the curbed time,
To make the coming hour o'erflow with joy,
And pleasure drown the brim.

(II.iv.39–47)

Bertram's earlier farewell, his departure for Paris, had introduced the distance that led first to Helena's despairing sense of an end ("there is no living, none") and then to her first more active project, the curing of the king and fulfillment of the play's first comic plot. This, his second displacement, now for Italy, creates a space of putting off that reaches its end only after she relies not on her father's medicine but on her own devices.

Once again, the displacement introduced by Bertram's new farewell creates what the king had earlier called a "coming space" (II.iii.181), which here becomes the space before consummation that Helena, like Desdemona, experiences as a "heavy interim" (*O*, I.iii.258). It is in this new period of put-off ends that attention is repeatedly called to Bertram's being under the influence of Parolles, as if the play were aligning verbal and erotic putting off in its larger plot as it does more microscopically in its interweaving of asides referring both to the putting off of Helena and to the lengthy travelers' tales associated with Parolles's bombast (II.v.15–31). Verbal echoes link Bertram with a Parolles-like inflation as the "Proud, scornful boy" rebuked by the king for disparaging Helena's humble social origins ("Where great additions *swell's*, and virtue none, / It is a dropsied honor," II.iii.127–28). The "answer" Bertram offers to the king's command to "Speak" is a speech of wordy nothings that in retrospect appear to have been, no less than the clown's "O Lord, sir," a form of putting off (II.iii.167–73). And while Lafew's repeated references to the spurious or counterfeit dilation of travelers' tales (II.iii.202, II.v.28–31) have Parolles as their clearly intended referent, his "A good traveller is something at the latter end of a dinner, but one that lies three thirds and uses a known truth to pass a thousand nothings with, should be once heard and thrice beaten" (II.v.28–31) applies just as appropriately to Bertram, who is about to practice such a deception on Helena and on Diana, this second plot's now second (as well as substitute) virgin.

Bertram intends his departure from France to be another definitive and unalterable end ("tonight, / When I should take possession of the bride, / *End* ere I do begin," II.v.25–27). It is therefore at this point that he delivers both the letter to the countess announcing "I have wedded her, not bedded her, and sworn to make the 'not' eternal" (III.ii.21–22) and the second letter, whose curt farewell or intended last word is punningly termed a "dreadful sentence," simultaneously a final statement and a doom ("When thou canst get the ring upon my finger, which never shall come off, and show me a child begotten of thy body that I am father to, then call me husband; but in such a 'then' I write a 'never,'" III.ii.57–60). This deferral of consummation by Bertram's farewell creates yet another intervening space—now described as a "breadth" or "long distance" (III.ii.24)—which Helena first, passively and Griselda-like, calls a time of waiting upon her husband's will (II.iv.54), as if Bertram were a stand-in for another Lord, as in the familiar allegorization of the Griselda story. But it also becomes the space of a different and specifically female "plot" (III.vii.44), a project that opens up this "dreadful sentence" by converting it from a final word into a form of riddling question, turning Bertram's "not" (III.ii.22) into a knot to be hermeneutically untied and his apparently definitive "never" into the temporal trajectory of a demand to be answered or fulfilled. Helena calls it her "passport" (III.ii.56), in the sense of something that licenses her to wander from her home; and her displacement takes the form of a pilgrimage, traditionally the sign both of displacement and of an exodus that distances or separates.[24]

This second departure and second project bring together with extraordinarily concentrated internal echoes the play's several overlapping forms of increase as well as a dilation and delay simultaneously erotic and verbal. The space of Helena's plot becomes the space of a doubled deferral of consummation or erotic holding off. One of these is presented in its most conventional form as the virginity of a figure named Dian, a name also added by Shakespeare to the play's narrative source and explicitly identified with the "titled goddess" (IV.ii.2) of virginity. The other, more problematically, converts the delaying of consummation from a female to a male introduction of space or distance, and the withholding object of desire from a woman to the "Peevish, proud, idle" (I.i.144) boy whose conditions Helena finally fulfills.[25] In the first, Bertram's rhetorical appeals to Diana to "Stand no more off" (IV.ii.34) directly echo Parolles's arguments against virginity in the early exchange with Helena on the subject of increase ("you are cold and stern, / And now you should be as your mother was / When your sweet self was got," IV.ii.8–10). And Bertram's wooing of a Dian invokes the traditional misogynist lexicon of female "angling" or delay presented in its commercial form as what Parolles had called a "vendible commodity" (I.i.153–55). In the second, the fact that the actively questing Helena must now "blow up" a man—or, in the language of the exchange with Parolles in Act I, inspire the tumescence necessary to increase—introduces one of this problem comedy's most problematic elements, the tonal problems of such a reversal of the orthodox pattern of wooing, the sexual pursuit of a reluctant male by an active and finally successful woman.

The early exchange between Parolles and Helena (I.i) on the subject of virginity had already presented it as a commodity that "the longer kept" is "the less worth" ("Off with't while 'tis vendible," I.i.154–55). But the economics of putting off—of gauging how long to put off the sale in order to increase but not to jeopardize the price—is also the burden of Parolles's counsel to Diana on how to handle men like Bertram whose interest is only in "scoring," a word also linked to accounting or tallying ("When he swears oaths, bid him drop gold, and take it; / After he scores, he never pays the score. / Half won is match well made; match, and well make it; / He ne'er pays after-debts, take it before," IV.iii.223–26).[26] This is the conventional misogynist topos—of feminine delay as a way of raising "rate" or price—that Bertram rehearses as an aggressive defense when he is confronted by this "Dian" in Act V:

> She knew her distance, and did angle for me,
> Madding my eagerness with her restraint,
> As all impediments in fancy's course
> Are motives of more fancy, and in fine,
> Her inf'nite cunning, with her modern grace,
> Subdu'd me to her rate.
>
>   (V.iii.212–17)

The conventional delay of a "Dian" of virginity (whose "infinite cunning" achieves a desired fine or end by putting off another one) and Bertram's putting off of consummation with Helena, his "compell'd" wife (IV.ii.15), become, then, the motive forms of putting off that generate the play's second, and more extended, plot, as well as the different plotting of a Doctor She. This explicit evocation of the tradition of erotic delay and its link with artfully inflated rate or increase is, like the early exchange between Helena and Parolles, yet another Shakespearean addition, not to be found in the play's narrative source. Like the comic wordplay on the forms of putting off in the scene between the clown and countess in Act II, it suggests that what Shakespeare added to the narrative from Boccaccio, apart from Parolles, the "manifold linguist," is an emphasis on increase itself, in all the different forms it takes in *All's Well*.

As if to continue the complex exchange between Helena's plot of increase and the form of increase or putting off represented by Parolles, or words, the scenes in Act IV that effect the "blowing up" of her own virginity in the bed trick are presented in direct parallel with the scenes in which the ambushed Parolles, the play's figure for the inflation of mere words, is correspondingly deflated or blown down. Act IV, for example, begins with the plot to expose Parolles as an inflated "bubble" or "wordy nothing" (III.vi.5) when he hopes to counterfeit the recovery of his "drum" by simply filling the time for long enough (IV.i.24–25). It then proceeds to interleave these scenes with those of Helena's delivery to "fill the time" (III.vii.33) in the parallel counterfeiting of the bed trick. In the scene at the French court in Act II, Parolles's counsel to Bertram to "use a more spacious ceremony" and "take a more dilated farewell" (II.i.49–56) associated him explicitly with the amplification of discourse as well as with the prolonging of a farewell; and throughout the play, the figure of Parolles combines the courtier's verbal amplitude with the stage character of the blown-up or inflated braggart.

The scene of the ambush in Act IV—and its deflation of Parolles, the play's "manifold linguist" (IV.iii.236)—depends once again on a foregrounding of language, or "paroles." The "choughs' language: gabble enough and good enough" (IV.i.19–20) that the ambushers conspire to speak is parodically both empty sound or nonsensical "nothings" and the prattle of the "chough" or chatterer Parolles shares with Osric in *Hamlet* and other Shakespearean send-ups of the loquacious "new man."[27] when Parolles is ambushed by men who pretend not to understand his "tongue," not only does a lack or want of language entail the threat of immediate death for the figure named "words" (IV.i.70, "I shall lose my life for want of language"); but after his plea for an extension of life ("O, let me live, / And all the secrets of our camp I'll show," IV.i.83–84), he too is "granted space" (IV.i.88) for long enough to expose himself as the "counterfeit module" (IV.iii.99) or wordy nothing he is. His discourse becomes a parody of the "confession" (IV.iii.113) such a delaying of a doom is traditionally provided for, an elaborate "running" stream (or fistula) of words in which he spills the "secrets" of others as the "answers" to the "demands" of his ambushers' "inter'gatories" (IV.iii.183).

This interspersing of the scenes of the "plot" to deflate the swelling of Parolles with Helena's fulfillment of the conditions of Bertram's letter by being blown up in a different sense brings to a climax the link and contest between Helena and Parolles that began with the early sparring on increase. The space granted to Parolles as a reprieve or putting off of death (IV.i.iii) is provided in scenes that also coincide with Diana's imposing of erotic delay and Bertram's "Stand no more off" (IV.ii.34). On the same night as Parolles, pretending to be something he is not, exposes himself to a deflating recognition scene, and has all his "knots" untied except on his "scarf" (IV.iii.323–24), Helena, avoiding recognition by pretending to be someone she is not, effects her own plot by "filling the time" (III.vii.33–44) in the bed of a virginal "Dian" for long enough to convert Bertram's eternal "not" into a marriage knot and become pregnant with the demanded issue. The inflated Parolles is "crush'd with a plot" and finally "undone" (IV.iii.312–13), though as long as the play continues, he continues to live as "simply the thing" he is (IV.iii.333). On the same night, Helena accomplishes the sexual "doing" that effects her plot and the blowing up that is to serve as a sign of her increase. If one of the major preoccupations of *All's Well* is the relation between words and deeds, Parolles, or empty words, is deflated on the same night as the bodily increase of Helena provides her with a sign of marriage in deed as well as word.

We have already noted the long-standing link between natural and hermeneutic increase, between the opening up of virginity and the opening of a closed or forbidding text. Bertram considers the forbidding text or "dreadful sentence" (III.ii.61) he sends to Helena to be a final word, just as he hopes his "scoring"—the consummation of his quest to conquer a virginal "Dian"—will be the "end" of the "business" (IV.iii.96), as opposed to the blowing up of pregnancy or pursuit that from the perspective of a man like Bertram is simply another kind of female plot, a way of converting what should be an end or fine into a beginning. It is in this doubled space of deferred consummation—Bertram's putting off of Helena and Diana's putting off of him—that Helena, however, effects the plot that finally converts Bertram's closed sentence from a final word into the pretext for her *own* version of increase and multiply, both generational *and* interpretive. She becomes in the process both a lower-caste woman opening an aristocratic family up to exogamous increase and a successful hermeneut, opening the closed or virgin text of a recalcitrant Bertram to more fertile meaning. In the terms of the early exchange between Parolles and Helena, Helena's fulfillment of the conditions of Bertram's "dreadful sentence" involves her opening up of its closure to increase, just as the bed trick that accomplishes this project involves the blowing up of virginity in a sense very different from Bertram's reckoning.

Helena's increase, then, takes a hermeneutic as well as a bodily or generational form. On the same night as Parolles, or "words," is granted space to expose himself as a "counterfeit module," Bertram's forbidding text is opened to a fulfillment that simultaneously fulfills and alters it. The space that includes both kinds of extension is the interval of "patience" (epil. 5) that is the elapsed time of the play itself, by the end of which Helena, as Doctor She, has opened a closed or concluding "sentence," won Bertram a second time (V.iii.308), which the space of delay has served to render different from the first, and finally supplied in her own dilated body the expanded and bountiful "answer"[28] that fits all of this play's several riddles or questions, including the riddling of a "Dian" in its final scene:

> He knows himself my bed he hath defil'd,
> And at that time he got his wife with child.
> Dead though she be, she feels her young one kick.
> So there's my riddle: one that's dead is quick—
> And now behold the meaning.
>   [*Helena enters*]
>
>   (V.iii.300–304)

Helena's increase—both hermeneutic and generational—renders the play, however, a problematic one in part because it involves a reversal of gender as well as a more threatening version of increase and multiply. In Diana's final riddling, Helena herself is the multiple answer, in a play literally filled with such riddling questions or demands. The intervening space of language between question and answer is linked in this play with the space of delay between courtship and consummation in the very scene where Parolles advises Bertram to take a more dilated farewell. The king here addresses the young French lords about to set off for war in Italy, in lines whose phallic "questant" and feminine "demand" are echoed in the questions and answers of the wordplay that follows in the scene between countess and clown on the theme of putting off:

> see that you come
> Not to woo honor, but to wed it, when
> The bravest questant shrinks....
>
> . . . .
>
> Those girls of Italy, take heed of them.
> They say our French lack language to deny
> If they demand.
>
> (II.i.14–21)

Language here is cast as something that puts off demands or questions, or something interposed between a demand and its corresponding answer. The "lack" of language that here implies more immediate consummation or ending is echoed within the play both in the clown's comic variations on the forms of putting off and in the ambush scene, where a lack or "want of language" entails, for Parolles, the threat of immediate death before he gives way to his interrogators' demands (IV.iii). But apart from its evocation of war's homoerotic context, the phallic sense of "questant" and the reference to the "girls of Italy" gives to these lines the unsettling suggestion of a questing that reverses the orthodox gender positions. Diana, indeed, becomes this girl of Italy, as the demand for the ring (III.vii.22) and the phrasing of Bertram's first lying account of her suggests in Act V in saying that he had no answer for her amorous demand (V.iii.98). She is also the demander of riddles, in the series of paradoxes that baffle the court and endanger her case until she produces Helena back from supposed death as their manifold answer.

In the curiously phallic language of the king's address to his men—with its undertone of the sexual sense of answer and its evocation, once again, of tumescence and detumescence ("when / The bravest questant *shrinks*")—the sense of gender reversal before these aggressive girls of Italy and their possibly unsatisfiable demands gives to the passage a sense of "de-manned" as well as "demand." If "Not to woo honour, but to wed it" recalls the aggressive male context of Theseus's "I wood thee with my sword" in *A Midsummer Night's Dream*, both the shrinking here and the reference to a female demand suggests something more troubling for the orthodox or conventional. Phyllis Gorfain has described the way in which *All's Well*, in snaking women the demanders of riddles as well as the stage managers of the plot (in Helena's case making demand even of a king), reverses the normative power structures both of society and of riddling. And it is this reversal—of women as demanders and hence, in a patriarchal culture, de-manners—that provides us with much of the problem of this problem play.[29]

The tonal uneasiness resulting from this reversal is part of what Susan Snyder ascribes to the play's conversion of Helen of Troy—the quintessentially passive object of desire—into the Helen or Helena who is here the active pursuer of a man. In this context, Helena's "passport" associates her not only with a license to wander but with the assumed licentiousness of the wandering woman who follows a man.[30] Within the play, explicit discomfort with a woman's demanding (or commanding) a man sounds not only through Bertram's evident misogyny and surly resistance but through the scenes with the clown Lavatch, whose exclamation—"That man should be at woman's command, and yet no hurt done!" (I.iii.92–93)—evokes the more orthodox Pauline strictures on the proper order of female and male. The servant Lavatch, commanded by the countess, his gender subordinate but social superior, is the source both of the play's one explicit reference to Helen of Troy and of the misogynist moral that there is only "One good woman in ten" (I.iii.82). It may be—as with the presentation of Helena as a "most weak / And debile minister" (II.iii.33–34) yet one who demands—that the unease with female ordering in this play makes it, along with *A Midsummer Night's Dream* and *Troilus and Cressida*, an indirect glance at that Elizabeth who (both in her virginity and in her stage-managing of male subordinates) frequently invited such resentment and such aggressive double entendre.[31] The sexual double meanings of Lavatch's claim to "understand" his mistress the countess "most fruitfully" (II.ii.69–70), from one who "stands under" her as her servant or social inferior, release the salacious (and ambivalent) senses of *serve* used several times within this play, including the Petrarchan language that, as Diana points out, is part of the rhetoric of men who "serve" in love until they achieve the consummation through which women "serve" them, and hence the actual power relations beneath the Petrarchan niceties (IV.ii.17–18).[32]

It is within this context that we may turn, finally, to the threat of increase in the bed trick itself. Helen becomes, through its substitution, not the imposed and rejected wife but the sought-for Dian of male imagining, the object whose virginity attracts all the Petrarchan epithets attached to it in the exchange with Parolles in Act I.[33] The scene in which the trick is conceived by its female coconspirators goes out of its way to stress that the substitution is a "lawful" one:

> HELENA: You see it lawful then. It is no more
> But that your daughter, ere she seems as won,
> Desires this ring; appoints him an encounter;
> In fine, delivers me to fill the time,
> Herself most chastely absent.
>
> (III.vii.30–34)

HELENA: Why then to-night
  Let us assay our plot, which if it speed,
  Is wicked meaning in a lawful deed,
  And lawful meaning in a lawful act.

                                          (III.vii.43–46)

The bed trick presented as lawful, however, depends, like the counterfeiting of Parolles, upon duplicity, not just in the mundane sense of fooling Bertram (who appears not to notice any difference in the dark) but in the literal sense of manipulating the relationship between one and two. The riddle presented by Diana in the final scene ("He knows himself my bed he hath defiled") depends literally upon such duplicity, on one figure's being displaced or separated out into two. It plays on the Helena who, in the bed of Diana, simultaneously is and becomes "no longer Dian" in two riddling senses, no longer virginal (or "Dian") and not the Dian Bertram intends, in lines where Helena's responding "When I was like this maid" (V.iii.309) means similarly "when I counterfeited her likeness" and "when I was a 'maid,' like her."

Helena's devising of the bed trick has opened her critically to the charge of "strumpet," notwithstanding all the protestations of a "lawful meaning in a lawful act." If, in fulfillment of the early exchange with Parolles, the originally virginal Helen, now "no longer Dian," provides an answer to Bertram's dooming "sentence" by opening her body—and closed virginity—to increase, this same opening and active pursuit leaves her, in a patriarchal setting (as it does Desdemona), open to questioning. In the exchange of wordplay on "bountiful" answers and answers of "most monstrous size" in the scene between the clown and the countess in Act II, a "bountiful" answer is described as "like a barber's chair that fits all buttocks" (II.ii.17). But these lines also link it to the proverbial slang for whore, as when Stephen Gosson refers to Venus as "a notorious strumpet ... that made her self as common as a Barbars chayre."[34] The answer of "most monstrous size" that can fit all questions (or the "barber's chair that fits all buttocks") is like the "common place" of the Dark Lady Sonnets, open to all men.[35] In lying with Bertram, Helena, like her, also lies.

There is another sense, however, in which the bed trick involves duplicity as well as an unexpected form of increase. In a play that goes out of its way to stress surrogates or seconds as well as second times, Helen herself is double rather than single. This splitting of Helen is underlined by its contrast to the first words spoken about her, by the countess, in the play: "where an unclean mind carries virtuous qualities, there commendations go with pity: they are virtues and traitors too. In her they are the better for their *simpleness*" (I.1.41–44). The female figure whose medicine already associates her with "simples" and a "simple touch" (II.i.75) is associated here with a simpleness routinely glossed in its sense as singleness, as something without mixture or addition.[36] "Simple" is the term repeatedly attached to Helena in the play's early scenes ("I am a simple maid, and therein wealthiest / That I protest I simply am a maid," II.iii.66–67). But even in the "simple touch" (II.i.75) of her link with simples or medicinal herbs in the curing of the king, this simple maid is ambiguously double—a virgin, or maid, who risks the "Tax of impudence / A strumpet's boldness" (II.i.170–71) by the "demands" she makes (II.i.86, 191), in a curing scene filled with sexual innuendo and double entendre. Her patron is a Dian she wishes could be "both herself and Love" (I.iii.213), in a line that already names the tension in the play between the "titled goddess" of virginity and the "strumpet" Venus, a split between virgin and whore linked to the polarizations of masculine fantasy in this play.[37]

This splitting—or doubleness—comes with the substitution of the name Helen for the source's Giletta, and that name's explicit linking with Helen of Troy (I.iii.70–71). In the version of Stesichorus well known and frequently exploited in early modern texts,[38] the wanton Trojan Helen was a surrogate or spurious substitute for the true and chaste one, whose chastity was by contrast preserved by being removed from the scene of strumpetry, herself (to borrow a phrase from the bed trick) "most chastely absent." (The reference to the lover who "sees Helen's beauty in a brow of Egypt"—the single allusion in *A Midsummer Night's Dream* to the Helen of Troy with whom Shakespeare's only other Helena shares her name—suggests just such a glancing at the Stesichorus legend, where Egypt is the place of the chastely distanced double or look-alike.) Stesichorus's version, in other words, already splits a single female figure into chaste and whore: a figure called Helen remains chaste or Dian because of the female surrogate who takes her place, just as in *All's Well*, Dian is kept apart and virginal in a bed trick in which a figure named Helen now takes her place.

Such splitting or doubling—as well as the substituting of a surrogate—also enables the riddling distinctions of the bed trick that both link and separate Diana from the Helen who is "no longer Dian" in *All's Well*. Whereas before, each figure had threatened to embody the opposite of the associations of her name—Helena the married wife left still virginal by her husband's rejection, Diana the virgin associated with the goddess of virginity but inviting Bertram to her bed—Helena in the bed trick substitutes for Diana in a way that involves duplicity and doubling but paradoxically preserves the chastity of both. Helena is both the "other" woman and herself, in an echo of the clown's paradoxical changes on the benefits of being seconded in husbandry.

The Helena of *All's Well* is disturbing to more "simple" or singular conceptions because she embodies the fear that women are always double or duplicitous. When this Shakespearean Helen goes to "Paris" to seek her own ends, Lafew calls her "Cressida," linking her even further with the Troy legends of duplicitous women. Diana is not just duplicitous but triplicate: "Diana" and "Fontybell" appear as names for her in the text, but so, mysteriously, does "Violenta."[39] The bed trick—a scandal to Victorian audiences and part of what in the play, according to Dover Wilson, sets "our" teeth on edge, in the exclusive male "our" of such earlier criticism—embodies the anxiety that it is never possible to go to bed with only one woman, that the woman in question is always split. Approach a Dian, the ultimate male conquest, and you get, instead, a Helen, the infamous strumpet or, what is worse, female sexuality with its own different and more active agenda.

For Bertram, the bed trick plotted by women acting not as rivals but as coconspirators makes his night of consummation—to him apparently a simple end—into what we might call a nightmare of increase. One woman, the desired one, turns out to be duplicitous, or two. It is not just that consummating his desire may be anything but an end to the business—for a man who seems very much not to want to "blow up" virgins in Parolles's sense of the "rational increase" of pregnancy—but that what he had projected as both a conquest and a telos turns out to be anything but simple. They palter with him in a double sense: the object of consummation is "no longer Dian" in a sense very different from what he had planned, and the wife he thought he had abandoned is the sought-after virgin he deflowers. If his intended scoring, to use Parolles's term, carries the meaning of an accounting, the number he tallies is increased in a way beyond his simpler reckoning.

The play that places so much stress on end or fine is finally, at its own end, still open to increase. The king's "Let us from point to point this story know" is a version of the invitation to further dilation of all the branches of a story that in so many Shakespearean endings forecasts a continuation beyond a more limited dramatic close. And his famous "All yet *seems* well, and *if* it end so meet, / The bitter past, more welcome is the sweet" (V.iii.333–34) opens up closure itself to contingency, to an increase that may not be amenable to closural forms. Not only is there an offstage extension promised after its end—a narrative that in the source is told, instead, *before* Giletta is accepted by her husband—but Helena is still only pregnant at the end, unlike Giletta, who has already produced the demanded issue in the form of twin sons.[40] We are not surprised that a play that has placed such stock on deferral should continue to do so in its own final lines, shifting the relative certainties of its source to a projection that keeps these ends still at a distance. But the play entitled *All's Well That Ends Well* ends with an epilogue that also stresses its dependence on audience approval ("It is ended, *if* you will approve it") in a way that begs the question of whether a plot that so clearly reverses the orthodox roles of gender and class can so simply be approved. The teleological title summons assumptions of the conventional comic end (already altered, however, in Shakespeare as early as *Love's Labor's Lost*). But *All's Well That Ends Well* continues to be a "problem" comedy, despite attempts to dispel that designation for it.

There is another way, for example, that the problem of gender in particular is related to the plotting here of increase and multiply. The interpretive activity seen as inducing an opening in an otherwise closed text is, as we have seen, an activity that is itself already explicitly gendered, linked to the opening of a closed female figure to increase. In the masculinist logic of Parolles's variations on the blowing up of virgins, Helena is cast as the closed or narrow "o" (to use Helkiah Crooke's term) to be dilated. But as the active Venus whose virginal Adonis is reluctantly won, as the figure who in the bed trick herself accomplishes (in all senses) a blowing up, and as the hermeneut who induces an opening in Bertram's closed "sentence" that opens *it* to increase, Helena not only upsets the orthodox positions of class and gender but occupies too many positions at once. The structures of comedy that are summoned in Act V to provide closure for a scene that refuses, whatever the title, to be satisfyingly closed are those wed to the orthodoxies these more conventional roles provide. But the fact that in this story of increase Helena has to play, in a more desperate sense than Bottom, all the roles at once leaves unresolved, and perhaps unresolvable, its relation to the more traditional distribution of gendered parts.

The spurned lower-caste girl wins a husband of her choice, and the family incorporates a household servant whose folktale fulfillment of impossible tasks finally pays the price of entrance. But it is still only a constrained class and gender victory; and she remains his "servant" (I.iii.159) in at least one of the play's multiple senses of that term. If "women are words, men deeds"—an ubiquitous early modern proverb still echoed on the Great Seal of the State of Maryland— and Parolles is effeminated through his association with words, Helena is dramatically not only the acknowledged accomplisher of deeds but a figure who has to shrink back into the more passive female role in time for a conventional comic close.

If the bed trick is the ultimate sign of her active achievement, it is also (doubly) the place where she takes the place of the passive object of desire, becoming the traditional vessel of bearing in a tradition where the pregnant female body was the seal and sign of that passivity.[41] Bertram's family expands just enough to take in its "foreign seeds," and Helena's increase is accepted as Bertram's issue rather than the spurious one it might have been. But Helena's dilation, like that of the pregnant votaress of *A Midsummer Night's Dream*, is still uneasily conscripted to a patriarchal familial structure, albeit a more enfeebled one. What the female characters of this play manage to effect is, by contrast to the male bonding of Parolles and Bertram, consistently impressive. But the project—in the form, perhaps, still of a sentence to be fulfilled—is uneasily in this play still the project of an order within whose constrictions there may be only a severely limited space to plot.

Spacing, delivery, and distancing of the kind we have here traced links *All's Well*, like *Pericles* or in different ways *The Winter's Tale*, to genealogical as well as familial imperatives of displacement and differentiation, the distancing of son from mother, for example, that psychoanalytic readings of this play have traced. Its transformation of incestuous or endogamous nearness into exogamous increase also, however, takes this sense of spacing into the dynastic and political.

The plot is the story, finally, not just of the interposing of a distance that avoids the danger of potential incest but also of the opening of an older aristocratic family to a hierarchically exogamous increase, an opening and incorporation that links it with the famous images of grafting from *The Winter's Tale* ("we marry / A gentler scion to the wildest stock, / And make conceive a bark of baser kind / By bud of nobler race," IV.iv.92–95). Despite his best efforts to prevent it, Bertram's noble family expands just enough to graft onto itself a slip of baser stock, an image used several times in this play for the "breeding" that enables such increase (in, for example, the countess's "'Tis often seen / Adoption strives with nature, and choice breeds / A native slip to us from foreign seeds," I.iii.144–46), a breeding that runs counter to breeding in the aristocratic sense of pedigree.

We have already alluded to the sense of the spurious or counterfeit introduced into this play by its reference to "Captain Spurio," in the scene whose inclusion of Parolles's "more spacious ceremony" and "more dilated farewell" links the spacious with the spurious, and hence with the inflation associated with the dilation of this "counterfeit module." This apparently gratuitous introduction of the spurious, however, is even more telling for this play, including the proliferation within it of counterfeits or surrogates and its evocation of hybridization as a form of increase. Here too, Parolles and Helena are linked. *Spurio* in the period meant not just counterfeit or spurious but also "one base borne" (as well as "a whores sonne," or bastard), a definition that would fit the spurious offspring that might have been born of Bertram's lying adulterously with Diana (if this "Dian," instead of Helena, had been impregnated in that bed). *Spuriare* is also linked with the sense of adulteration already associated with adultery, with a hybridization or mixing that links *bastard* with *base*, and the spurious more generally with the contamination of the adulterated and illegitimate.[42] This is the reason, as Michael Neill has recently demonstrated, that Spurio in *The Revenger's Tragedy* proclaims, "Adultery is my nature" (I.ii.177), in a play that links his bastardy with the adulterate, the hybrid, and the counterfeit.[43] Bastardy as a form of illegitimacy is combined with the metaphorics of grafting (or hybrid mixing) different kinds of stocks in the lines already quoted from *The Winter's Tale* ("do not call them bastards," IV.iv.99); and the sense of the pollution of a stock by the adulteration of adultery is also conveyed by the "bastard graff" of Shakespeare's *Lucrece* ("This bastard graff shall never come to growth. / He shall not boast who did thy stock pollute," ll. 1062–63). It is this combination of the senses of the counterfeit, the spurious, the adulterated, and the illegitimate that the Spurio linked with Parolles introduces into *All's Well*, in the scene in which a lower-class Helena comes to perform the deed that will graft her onto Bertram's aristocratic stock (if not, higher up, the king's).

Spurious in the sense of illegitimate would, then, name the bastard offspring of the formerly "Dian" if the bed trick in *All's Well* had in fact been an act of adultery. Adulteration in this more restricted sense is prevented, the play's riddling lines suggest, by the substitution of a lawful wife (the "no longer Dian" already grafted onto Bertram's aristocratic family by a marriage in word that she confirms by this evidence of marriage in deed). But, in another way, the hybridization that grafts this lower-caste or baser slip (though lawful wife) onto Bertram's noble stock involves adulteration in the other contemporary sense of baser mixture—contributing, perhaps, to the uneasy sense of adultery that still surrounds her accomplishment of this otherwise lawful deed. (She is named, we might recall, not after Diana but after the famously adulterous Helen.) In a play that calls repeated attention to the simultaneous gender and class reversal involved in Helena's accomplishment of both of her impossible tasks, the sense of contamination that attaches to the Helen who is no longer virginal or Dian in a sexual sense is joined by this sense of adulteration at the level of class as well as of gender, the hybrid grafting of baser slip onto nobler stock that evokes even as it eschews the contamination of bastardy. What, then, Janet Adelman (approaching the bed trick from the perspective of the psychoanalytic, in a play that evokes both incest and Bertram's attempts to escape a bride associated with his mother) rightly points to here as the sense of pollution attaching to sexual contact with women has also its crucial class correlative, the contamination or adulteration involved (from the perspective of Bertram the aristocrat as well as husband) in a baser mixture.[44]

In this sense as well, the figure of Parolles shadows that of Helena, the character with whom his first exchange in the play is on the subject of increase. Commentators have linked Parolles not just with the empty inflation of words but with the hybridization associated with other Shakespearean figures of the proliferating new man—Osric in *Hamlet*, Oswald in *Lear*, or the social-climbing upstarts of the early histories, associated with the new regime of words rather than the older warrior aristocracy of deeds. (Parolles for all his martial rhetoric is a "counterfeit module" here as well, his boasted exploits finally just a punningly empty "drum".) Richard Halpern, in his comments on the counterfeit as well as hybrid nature of this new man as "a class and sexual hybrid," a "mixture of masculine and feminine, common and gentlemanly," relates this pervasive Elizabethan and Jacobean figure to the "inflation of honors" chronicled by Lawrence Stone and the proliferation of simulacra that accompanied the spiraling monetary inflation of the period. For Halpern, "Oswald, the phony courtier, represents the outermost curve of this inflationary spiral, leading to complete dilution and debasement of aristocratic status."[45] The grafting of such newer types onto the older stock and traditions of an aristocratic England produced hybridization as well as inflation. And the contradiction precipitated in early modern England was between this new inflation and older conservative and aristocratic values based on land that could be both abundant in itself and yield a metaphorics of abundance (like the servant Lavatch's praise of the father of Bertram, avatar of the nobility of this older aristocracy, as a "Copie" to these younger times). The older agricultural language of increase—including Lavatch's

summoning of this language in his own desire to "increase and multiply" (I.iii)—
coexists in this problem comedy with the newer lexicon of increase linked with
money or capital, a different kind of stock associated with usury as the breeding
of "barren metal" rather than breeding in either the aristocratic or the
agricultural sense. *Copia* itself, in the sense of abundance or fertility, also had its
double in the simulacra-like copies represented by inflated or counterfeit new
men.

     The inflation of values and prices was part of the crisis of inflation in all of
its senses, including the inflation of honors described by historians of the period.
The corresponding debasement of the coinage, though countered by the
Elizabethan recoinage in an attempt to bring down soaring prices, was a
continuing preoccupation of the second half of the sixteenth century. Inflation
itself was linked with the counterfeited, empty, or spurious through royal abuses
of coining that had led in the middle of the century to a general economic crisis
in England.[46] Contemporary texts such as John Ponet's *A Shorte Treatise of
Politicke Power* (1556) assigned to the crown in particular the responsibility for a
debased currency and inflated prices, complaining of "evil governors and rulers
... that contrary to all laws ... counterfeit the coin that is ordained to run between
man and man, turning the substance from gold to copper, from silver to worse
than pewter, and advancing and diminishing the price at their pleasure." The
rampant inflation of prices was linked with the crisis of an aristocracy whose own
economic insufficiency was reflected in the troubles of the Crown, part of the
larger crisis of a period of "proliferating Oswalds" and "bankrupt Lears."[47] And
it contributed to the larger historical phenomenon of grafting and hybridization
through which this older aristocracy, tied to land and to older kinds of increase,
had increasingly to supplement its deficiency through the newer forms of
monetary increase, with all the stooping to the base (and base means) this
involved. The new monetary idiom was grafted even onto older forms of charity,
in the hope, for example, of figures such as William Perkins "for the principall
with the increase at the yeares end." Thomas Wilson (in his *Discourse upon Usury*,
1572) expressed the "perplexing absence of solidity" that he and others associated
with the barren "breeding" of usury and the attendant loss of "manliness"—a set
of associations that resonate beside the figure of Parolles, the effeminated new
man, who counsels such forms of breeding in the exchange with Helena that
leads to her conceiving of a project or scheme. *Increase* participated in both
lexicons, of fruitful bodily (and generational) "increase and multiply" linked with
an older kind of breeding, and the "rational increase" of Parolles's new language
of interest, principal, and stock. Helena, after her exchange with Parolles in Act
I on the subject of increase in all of these senses, conceives of the project that is
ultimately fulfilled by the "bountiful answer" of her dilated or pregnant body; but
those linked with interest and monetary increase were also (pejoratively) called
"projectors," projecting into the future an increase to come.[48]

     All's Well That Ends Well, then, combines the older language of abundance or "increase and multiply" with the different kinds of increase that inform its apparently marginal or inconsequential scenes, including the monetary as well as verbal increase associated with Parolles, its wordy "new man." The play thus links economic and linguistic, in ways endemic in a culture where a word like *utterance* could refer to both words and wares.[49] And its foregrounding of the relation between dilation and inflation juxtaposes the dilation that is a generative opening (accomplished by the sexual opening of a virgin and by Helena's practical as well as hermeneutic opening of Bertram's "knot") with the dilation (or "spacious ceremony") associated ambivalently with the inflated speech of its spurious or "counterfeit module."

Shakespeare himself, however, was also part of the phenomenon of the new man bred by the inflation of honors that historians of the period have variously described—both a counterfeit gentleman and associated with "parolles." Figures such as Francis Bacon and contemporary anti-Ciceronians could decry the spurious dilation of the verbally inflated, "superfluity of talking" or "swelling of style," advising (as Thomas Sprat would, in the later manifesto of the Royal Society in favor of a more "masculine" plain style) a return to "the primitive purity and shortness, when men deliver'd so many things almost in an equal number of words."[50] But Shakespeare the playwright (like Jonson, who was more disingenuous in this regard) could not eschew altogether the increase associated with verbal dilation in particular. He himself was accused of producing plays that depended on this kind of spurious increase, Parolles—like wordiness or inflated speech—in attacks that also included class imputations of the base, the product of the inflation of honors associated with the social-climbing new man. Robert Greene's famous attack in *A Groatsworth of Wit* (1592) described the "upstart Crow" who "supposes he is as well able to *bombast out a blanke verse* as the best of you," a reminder of the links between *bombast* and the inferior social status of this player, or "rude groom." Puttenham in his treatment of "Bomphiologia, or Pompous Speech" condemns the use of "bombasted wordes, as seeme altogether farted full of winde," and associates it not only with an inflation that is "too high and loftie for the matter" but with the base orders of "popular rhymers." It has long been thought as well that the popular "Shake-scene" attacked by Greene was the same one that Nashe had attacked three years earlier as one of the "idiot art-masters" of the players "that intrude themselves ... as the alchemists of eloquence, who (mounted on the stage of arrogance) think to out brave better pens with the swelling bombast of bragging blank verse."[51]

Shakespeare's plays, however, also frequently call attention to as well as exploit their own dependence on verbal inflation, bombast, or stuffing for their dilation or increase. Puttenham's "farted" recalls the play on forcing, farting, or stuffing that is an implicit part of the copious Shakespearean combination of different materials or stuffs as early as *The Comedy of Errors*, as well as explicitly in *Henry V* ("we'll digest the abuse of distance, *force* a play"). The humanist

Lipsius (a model for Jonson) could write, "As those who are thin in body, fill themselves out in clothes, so those who are deficient in talent or knowledge, spread themselves out in words," while Roger Ascham, in *The Schoolmaster* (1570), could treat of the verbal "fullness" that must be chastened by the gravity of "age" and "weightier affairs" as well as of the need to purge of its "grossness" a style that is "overfat and fleshy."[52] But the plays of Shakespeare point repeatedly to their dependence on such dilation and its inflated simulacrum or double—not just in the comedies (including *The Comedy of Errors*'s "dilate at full") or the verbal inflations of Falstaff ("sweet creature of bumbast," *1H4*, II.iv.326) but also in the "bombast circumstance" ("Horribly *stuff'd* with epithites of war," I.i.13–14) of *Othello*, a tragedy filled with speeches and scenes (including Othello's "dilated" traveler's tale) excoriated as mere wordy filler by Rymer and other neoclassicizing critics.

    Othello, and in different ways *Hamlet*, suggest that the end of tragedy is related to the violent cessation of an increase associated both with female sexuality and with words. In this sense, as we have seen, the variations on *increase* in *All's Well That Ends Well*, whose own teleological title highlights end or "fine," suggest the dependence of the play itself on the figure of Parolles, or "words," even as he also represents a satiric addition of the effeminated new man to the plot's more straightforward source. In light of the tension between dilation and inflation contemporary with this comedy, however, such apparently metadramatic commentary, far from being restricted to intrinsic or formal properties, becomes part of its emplotment of different—and conflicting—forms of increase. In this respect, *All's Well* stages problems it shares with at least two of its near-contemporaries: *Hamlet*, which comments on its own diseased increase, as well as highlighting the proliferation of counterfeits; and *Troilus and Cressida*, a play preoccupied with the inflation of values, bodies, and words, as well as with the hybrid or spurious.[53]

Descriptions of verbal dilation in the period routinely pair it with its spurious tumid, swelling, and diseased simulacrum, in the opposition of *uber* and *tuber* that Terence Cave has remarked.[54] Tumid or inflated words are repeatedly linked in contemporary descriptions with the generally "puffed up," "swelling," or "blown up," in ways that recall the combination of inflated puffery and verbosity in Parolles.[55] Barret's *Alvearie*, under "to swell," gives "to be puffed up with pride or anger" (*tumeo*), a "swelling or puffing up" (*tumidus, turgidus, inflatus*), and "a mushroom: also a swelling," the counterpart of *tuber*, diseased or cancerous growth. The words *tumidus* and *inflatus* were routinely used in early modern writing for the bombastic or pretentious. With this inflation came the sense of an unhealthy bodily swelling, associated with the dropsical and with tumorous growths, along with the problem of distinguishing a healthy dilation or plumpness from the hydroptic swelling that was its spurious simulacrum or counterfeiting double.[56]

All's Well That Ends Well explicitly evokes these connections in the lines that link Bertram (in his association with Parolles) with the puffing up of pride ("Where great additions *swell's* and virtue none, / it is a dropsied honor," II.iii.127–28). *All's Well* is also centrally involved with the fistula of the king linked (as a running sore) with loquacity as the "fistula of the minde." A fistula (or "fester") was a morbid, pipelike ulcer, linked with an increase and multiplication both diseased and out of controls.[57] In the passage from *The Schoolmaster* already cited, Ascham goes on in ways that may remind us of the preoccupation in *All's Well* with illness and with physicians, including this royal fistula, the curative physic of Gerard de Narbon, and the ministrations of Helena as the Doctor She who cures the king's ailment and may (though less surely) finally cure the "dropsied" pride of Bertram himself. The disease of "overmuch fullness" or superfluity of words, according to Ascham and others, also stands in need of a cure, since "men's bodies be not more full of ill humors than commonly men's minds (if they be young, lusty, proud, like and love themselves well, as most men do) be full of fancies, opinions, errors and faults, not only in inward invention but also in all their utterance, either by pen or talk."[58] And the imagery of disease that in this sense associates the verbal with the bodily, a fistula, ulcer, or running sore with the parody-dilation of excessive wordiness, is an imagery that not only juxtaposes bodily dilation with verbal inflation in *All's Well* but links inflation, tumidity, and increase, in different ways, in *Hamlet* and *Troilus and Cressida*.

If, in *All's Well That Ends Well*, the command in Genesis to increase and multiply—combined with newer kinds of increase—informs Helena's early exchange with Parolles and the play's continuing association of verbal and generational, the evocation of increase and multiply in *Hamlet* yields a diseased increase, one also involving both generation and words, a tuberous or "unweeded garden / That grows to seed" (I.ii.135–36). Dilation as delay in *Hamlet* is associated with the empty proliferation of "words, words, words" (II.ii.192), the ineffectual wordiness of the "drab (II.ii.586) that attaches imputations of effeminacy to the prince who delays or puts off end or fine. Words themselves are coupled in this play with a sense of pestilent breeding, in Claudius's fear that Laertes "wants not buzzers to infect his ear / With pestilent speeches of his father's death" (IV.v.90–91) or in the concern about what "ill-breeding minds" (IV.v.7–15) will conjecture from Ophelia's mad speech.[59] A proliferating and diseased increase is linked with the poison poured into the ear of Old Hamlet ("a most instant tetter bark'd about, / Most lazar-like, with vile and loathsome crust," I.v.71–72)—a spreading poison that infects both the king's body and the body politic—as with the words by which the "ear" of Denmark is "rankly" abused (I.v.36–38). The sense of increase in *Hamlet* as diseased as well as out of control is heightened by the "plurisy" that gathers (spuriously from *pluris* or *plus*) the meaning of superfluity or excess ("goodness, growing to a plurisy, / Dies in his own too much," IV.vii.117–18). And it is linked in these same lines to "abatements and delays" (IV.vii.117–20), as well as the sense elsewhere in the play of adulteration or mixture, the poisonous "mixture rank" of the *Mousetrap* scene (III.ii.257) and the "baser matter" associated with Hamlet's adulterous mother (I.v.102–5).[60]

Hamlet explicitly reverses the Genesis command of "increase and multiply" in a speech whose contrasting counsel of virginity suggests that the Genesis Eden is itself a rank and unweeded garden: "Get thee to a nunn'ry, why wouldst thou be a breeder of sinners?" (III.i.120ff.). His "we will have no moe marriage" (147) involves a retreat not only from increase or breeding but from the adulteration associated with the frailty and sexual appetite of woman ("As if increase of appetite had grown / By what it fed on.... Frailty, thy name is woman!" I.ii.144–46). As an attempt to forestall increase, Hamlet's countermanding of Genesis and its "increase and multiply" counterfeits that apocalyptic end or "fine" where there is neither marrying nor giving in marriage (Gal. 3), an end to breeding as well as to the generations generated by the command in Genesis. What mimics or counterfeits apocalypse here, however, is a premature end or fine linked to a poisoning of the source of increase, the adulterous and incestuous union that may make Hamlet himself a spurious or illegitimate counterfeit, a bastard contaminated with "baser matter."[61] *Dilation* in its sense of amplification as well as delay becomes in this play a multiplication of occasions and images for the postponement or putting off of end or "fine," including the interim of life itself between the Eden of Genesis and Apocalypse. But incest, once again, as at the beginning of *All's Well*, collapses or conflates, bringing beginning and end too near (or "kin"); and the problem of what happens in *Hamlet* (for all of its dilation or delay) becomes in part a question of whether its apparent extension is finally anything but an interim foreclosed from the beginning, a tropical trap in which the poisoned union of its end is already contained within the poisoned union of its beginning.

Hamlet is filled with a sense of the spurious or counterfeit, as with a proliferation of seconds that includes the "second husband" of Gertrude who may have "seconded" Old Hamlet in husbandry. It also suggests the sense of bodily swelling linked with verbal inflation and tumidity in *All's Well* and other contemporary descriptions, in ways that recall the loquacity of Parolles (in the garrulity of Polonius, the wordiness of the effeminate courtier Osric, or the verbal dilations and delays of Hamlet himself). The dilation of discourse or words is introduced into the play by Claudius, the "bloat king" of Hamlet's later description (III.iv.182), through the "dilated articles" of his commission to Old Norway in Act I (I.ii.38).[62] This is the sense of verbal dilation repeated in Claudius's commission to the king of England in Act V ("an exact command, / *Larded* with many several sorts of reasons," V.ii.19–20) and parodied by Hamlet in the self-conscious amplifications (V.ii.39–43) of the counterfeit or spurious substitute that sends Rosencrantz and Guildenstern to their deaths. Claudius's dilated articles are part, then, of the amplified or "larded" style of this "bloat" king. In the commission to Norway near the beginning of the play, they bring an apparently successful end to the "business" (II.ii.85). But they also stand as a forecast of a dilation or amplification that elsewhere in this play does not bring about a satisfying end or "fine."

Both the linking of dilation with inflation in *All's Well* and the combination of the "bloat," enlarded, or dilated in *Hamlet* with the imagery of a diseased increase bring us, finally, to *Troilus and Cressida*, the play with which *All's Well* shares its suspect Helen. Dilation is, once again, explicitly introduced into this play, in the description of the "spacious and dilated parts" of Ajax (II.iii.250), part of Ulysses' own rhetorically swollen address to the figure who is to serve as a simulacrum or surrogate for Achilles. But the sense of "dilated parts" in this dramatic simulacrum of epic also includes the inflated, swollen, or tumid bodies that are its counterfeit or spurious doubles both of more fruitful dilation and of the grand epic style. The classic description of this grand style—also known as the *gravis* (both serious and weighty)—was for early modern readers the one provided in the *Rhetorica ad Herennium*, a text known to have been used by Shakespeare. Received with the authority of Cicero, this influential text outlined not just the elevated or grand suited to elevated subjects (including the magnanimity as well as gravity of epic), but also its tumid, swollen, or inflated double: "bordering on the Grand style ... there is a style to be avoided.... the Swollen (*sufflata*, "blown up").... For just as a swelling (*tumor*) often resembles a healthy condition of the body, so ... turgid and inflated language (*turget et inflata*) often seems majestic.... Most of those who fall into this type ... are misled by the appearance of grandeur and cannot perceive the tumidity."[63]
This particular association of bodily swelling or inflation with a tumid, inflated, or swelling style runs through the entire rhetorical tradition inherited by early modern England, a tradition in which body and style were already inseparably connected. The *Ad Herennium*'s description of the counterfeiting of the truly grand by the merely inflated or blown up—a description whose *sufflata* ("blown up") recalls the language linked with Parolles in *All's Well*—was repeated again and again in contemporary commentary. Vives writes that though "the inflated and tumid style gives the appearance not only of complete health but of a fortunate and strong constitution," inside it is "corrupt." In England, Richard Sherry described this simulacrum of the elevated or "great" as the spuribus counterfeit that merely "*seemeth* a grave oracion" because it "*swelleth* and is *puffed up*." The "high and lofty" become the merely "tumid" inflation of "petty and inferior things" is described in the passage from Jonson's *Discoveries* that treats of the "fleshy style" whose "circuit of words" (or "bombast circumstance") grows "fat and corpulent."[64] And the counterfeit greatness of the merely inflated or puffed up is described by Puttenham in a passage that might well be put beside the spurious epic "greatness" of *Troilus and Cressida*:

the high stile is disgraced and made foolish and ridiculous by all
wodes affected, counterfeit, and puffed up, as it were a windball
carrying more countenance then matter, and can not be better
resembled then to these midsommer pageants in London, where to
make the people wonder are set forth great and uglie Gyants
marching as if they were alive, and armed at all points, but within
they are stuffed full of browne paper and tow, which the shrewd
boyes underpeering, do guilefully discover and turne to a great
derision.[65]

The simulacrum, then, of the magnified, high, or grand style is the merely tumid
or inflated, the bombastic or swelling mimickry of genuine epic *gravitas*.[66] This
inflated or corpulent double was also linked with the unmanly or effeminate, in
a tradition stemming (among other sources) from Quintilian's description of the
tempering of *copia* necessary to preserve manliness from becoming "dissolute"
(*iucunda non dissoluta, grandia non tumida*).

Timothy Bright's *Characterie* (1588) gives "Greate" (or to make great) as a
synonym for dilate.[67] But Ulysses' description of Ajax's "spacious and dilated
parts" in *Troilus and Cressida* occurs in the context (to borrow again from *Hamlet*)
of a "bloat" or inflated greatness that mimics greatness, as well as the swelling or
inflation of bodies and pride. Like *All's Well*, Shakespeare's *Troilus* links the
spacious with the spurious, dilation with the inflation that is its merely blown up
look-alike; and it does so in a context of adultery and adulteration, or hybrid
mixture. The amplified, magnified, or great in this spurious simulacrum of
Homeric epic is presented again and again as the merely inflated or "blown
up"—not just in the bloated epic *materia* of the war described by Thersites as
nothing but "a whore and a cuckold" (II.iii.72–73), product of the adultery of
another "Helen," but also in the tumid inflations of the play's own interminable
verbosity, what Troilus (like Hamlet) calls "words, words, mere words"
(V.iii.107). Words, in this inflated economy, consume deeds, as its amplified
speeches and debates replace action on the battlefield.[68] Agamemnon's response
to Aeneas's inflated rhetoric—"The men of Troy / Are ceremonious courtiers"
(I.iii.234)—links such verbal dilation with the "more spacious ceremony" of the
would-be courtier Parolles of *All's Well*. And the verbosity or verbal inflation of
the play is paralleled by the "dilated parts" of its own bloated bodies or corpulent
parodies of epic greatness, the tumid embodiment of the pride of the "princes
orgillous" (prol. 2), linked with the inflation both of value and of rhetoric.

Among these "princes orgillous," the "large" (I.iii.162) and "broad"
(I.iii.190) Achilles—the "great and complete man" (III.iii.181) of Ulysses'
description, evocative of the tradition of epic magnanimity—is elsewhere simply
that "great bulk" (IV.iv.128) that Hector is to recognize by his "large and portly
size" (IV.v.162).[69] As the "proud lord / That bastes his arrogance with his own
seam" or grease (II.iii.184–85), Achilles is the figure the Greeks hesitate to

entreat because it would "enlard his fat-already pride" (II.iii.195), a description that comes just before the praise of his surrogate Ajax's "spacious and dilated parts" (250). "Enlarding" here is once again a term that participates in both the bodily and the rhetorical—the engrossing of the body and the interlarding that, like bombast or verbal stuffing, was a notorious means of dilating or swelling a discourse.[70] In ways that recall both the "rank" increase of *Hamlet* and the link in *All's Well* between Helena's fruitfully dilated body and Parolles as the merely inflated or blown up, Achilles' "puff'd" (IV.v.9) or "blown up" pride is described in terms that suggest both a grotesque pregnancy and a rank breeding or increase:

> the seeded pride
> That hath to this maturity blown up
> In rank Achilles must or now be cropp'd,
> Or shedding, breed a nursery of like evil,
> To overbulk us all.
>
> (I.iii.316–20).

The same scene that ends by describing Achilles as a corpulent "hulk" or "bulk" too heavy to be easily transported ("let Achilles sleep: / Light boats sail swift, though greater hulks [F, greater bulks] draw deep," II.iii.265–66), also argues that his "price" is inflated ("Go tell him this, and add, / That if he overhold his price so much, / We'll none of him; but let him, like an engine / Not portable, lie under this report," 132–35), in lines whose "overhold" is used in the sense of "overestimate." Achilles is linked explicitly with the inflation of discourse, with the "Achillean argument" (an argument without end)[71] evoked in Ulysses' enigmatic lines on the "matter" that Ajax will find in him (II.i.9), and with the "swol'n" discourse of Ulysses' description of his equally swollen pride:

> Things small as nothing, for request's sake only,
> He makes important. Possess'd he is with *greatness,*
> And speaks not to himself but with a *pride*
> That quarrels at self-breath. Imagin'd worth
> Holds in his blood such *swoll'n and hot discourse.*
>
> (II.iii.169–73)

Pride, like emulation, the play makes clear, is itself a form of inflation in the sense of the overheld or overesteemed, in ways that couple it with the question of value or price the play elsewhere endlessly debates.[72] The inflated pride of Achilles or of his surrogate Ajax, with his "spacious and dilated parts," is finally no different from the pride that includes all of the "princes orgillous" and the inflation that blows up the bloated matter of the war. The "bond of air" that characterizes Nestor's inflated eloquence in the Greek council scene (I.iii.66) is linked by image to Achilles' pride and "airy fame" (144). The danger of "enlarding" Achilles' own "fat-already pride" is repeated with reference to Menelaus in Thersites' "to what form but that he is, should wit *larded* with malice and malice *forced* with wit turn him to?" (V.i.56–58).[73] The "forcing" or "farting" linked with enlarding, fattening, and bombast or stuffing in Puttenham's description of "bombasted wordes ... farted full of winde" becomes part of the plan to "force" (or stuff) the pride of Ajax as Achilles' surrogate, beginning with Ulysses' inflated praise of his "spacious and dilated parts." And the play itself is bloated, forced/farted, or stuffed, beginning from the language of digestion that sounds in its "Prologue arm'd" for epic "argument," treating of what "may be *digested* in a play" (prol. 29), in a metaphorics of cramming or forcing that links its counterfeiting of epic magnitude with the figure of "forcing," farting, or stuffing in *Henry V*, where the apparent greatness of its matter is forced or stuffed into the "O" of the stage ("Linger your patience on; and we'll *digest* / Th'abuse of distance; *force* a play").[74]

The merely tumid, counterfeit, or spurious associated with the "spacious and dilated" parts of Ajax and with Achilles' bulk also affects this play's other representations of epic *gravitas* or greatness, including that of Priam, patriarch of Troy.[75] Troilus's "Weigh you the worth and honor of a king / So great as our dread father's in a scale / Of common ounces?" (II.ii.26–28) speaks even as it eschews a language that transforms a putatively inestimable aristocratic greatness into the weighing of a commodity whose value depends, in more bourgeois fashion, literally on its weight. His

> Will you with *compters* sum
> The past-proportion of his infinite,
> And buckle in a *waist most fathomless*
> With spans and inches so diminutive...?"
>
> (II.ii.28–31)

puns on aristocratic "waste" even as it makes use of the bourgeois language of counting and accounting.[76] Aeneas advises Achilles (of the celebrated greatness of Hector) to "weigh him well" (IV.v.81), but when Achilles finally does weigh his epic rival, it is in the burgher-butcher mode of "quoting ... joint by joint" (IV.v.233). Aristocratic and epic greatness in this play (in an era that produced the formulation "merchant prince" for a hybrid figure like Thomas Gresham) is repeatedly adulterated or mixed with the baser language of bourgeois measurement. Troilus's rhetorical question on summing and "compters" or counting is joined by the language elsewhere of a "substance" whose "grossness" is "summed up" by "little characters" (I.iii.324–25)—lines whose "substance" is simultaneously matter, wealth or riches, and contents or purport—and by the simultaneously commercial and textual figure of indexes in which,

(although small pricks
To their subsequent volumes) there is seen
The baby figure of the giant mass
Of things to come at large.

(I.iii.343–46)

The inflation or bloating that affects both bodies and words in *Troilus* also affects its presentation of its epic theme, matter, or argument, repeatedly said to represent an overheld or inflated value. Inflation of price is already reflected in this play—in ways that recall Parolles's or Bertram's misogynist calculus of a woman as a "vendible commodity" whose delay or holding off raises her rate—in the position of Cressida within this male economy.[77] In the debate in the Trojan council in Act II, Helen, the other woman of the play and the double-meaning argument of the war itself, is linked with the images elsewhere of both inflated value and "spacious and dilated parts." As the "prize" that is "inestimable" (II.ii.88), the "theme of honour and renown" that is "A spur to valiant and magnanimous deeds" (II.ii.199–200), this Helen is described by Paris as a figure whom the "world's large spaces cannot parallel" (II.ii.162). As the "contaminated carrion *weight*" (IV.i.72) of a more negative description, however, she is linked with the play's spurious simulacra of epic *gravitas*, the merely gravid or heavy. Paris's comparison, with its "magnanimous" and "large," is followed by Hector's figure of heaviness ("thus to persist / In doing wrong extenuates not wrong, / But makes it much more heavy," II.ii.186–88), an imagery repeated when Diomedes, asked by Paris "Who, in your thoughts, deserves fair Helen best, / Myself, or Menelaus?" (IV.i.54–55), answers that both are "heavier for a whore" (67). The lines here suggest a diseased or contaminated breeding rather than a fruitful or legitimate increase ("You like a lecher out of whorish loins / Are pleas'd to breed out your inheritors," 64–65), a figure, once again, of diseased *grossness* rather than a productive *grossesse*. The contamination of adultery associated with this Helen stands, we might recall, as the parallel in the drama of secular history to the Fall associated with the fault of Eve, that figure of female frailty that informs *Hamlet*'s imagery of diseased increase.[78]

The sense that the Helen of *Troilus and Cressida*—namesake of the pregnant or fruitfully dilated Helen of *All's Well*—is simply a gross, overestimated, or inflated commodity (in a play that links her prizing, at the level of the personal or erotic, with the political wooing of Achilles) is suggested by the juxtaposition of Hector's speech on her "value" as too "dear" (II.ii.20–23) with the scene of Thersites' description of Ajax's inflated price as the surrogate object of the Greeks' wooing or "suit" ("I will buy nine sparrows for a penny, and his *pia mater* is not worth the ninth part of a sparrow," II.i.70–72). The deflationary rhetoric of Troilus's initial refusal to fight for the thin argument represented by so "starv'd a subject" (I.i.92–93)—lines that exploit, once again, the sense of bodily corpulence as the inflation or blowing up of insignificants into a simulacrum of greatness—is joined by Thersites' deflating reminder that the vaunted heroic matter of Troy is simply the inflated value of a "placket" (II.iii.20).[79] The inflationary parallel between Achilles (or Ajax) and Helen extends here, as in his later "All the argument is a whore and a cuckold" (II.iii.72–73), to the play's presentation of its Homeric matter as the bloated or blown up, its epic *materia* reduced to the bodily "matter" (II.i.9) of the merely swelling and diseased, issuing from a diseased or "botchy core" (II.i.6).[80]

Inflation, then, in its multiple senses—of body, of discourse, of price, and of the space before end or fine—pervades the whole of *Troilus and Cressida*, and not just in the explicit summoning of dilation in Ulysses' praise of Ajax's "spacious and dilated parts." If in *All's Well That Ends Well*, the inflation of Parolles, or words, is contrasted with the pregnancy of Helena as evidence of an effective deed and promise of a final issue, the imagery of pregnancy in *Troilus* becomes a merely tumid and spurious counterfeit that fails to yield either issue or end. *Troilus* is filled with such figures of pregnancy. Ulysses' "I have a young conception in my brain, / Be you my time to bring it to some shape" (I.iii.312–13) prefaces the references to the "seeded pride" that in "rank Achilles" threatens to "breed a nursery of ... evil / To overbulk us all" (316–20). Cressida refers to pregnancy as "swelling" in an early exchange with the wordy Pandarus that recalls Parolles's exchange with Helena on the blowing up of virgins ("If I cannot ward what I would not have hit, I can watch you for telling how I took the blow—unless it swell past hiding, and then it's past watching," I.ii.267–70). But, like an endless or "Achillean" argument, the play itself-for all of its repeated images of teleology or ending, including the long-awaited telos of the war presented in the traditional images of a delayed Apocalypse—has notoriously no real end or "fine."[81] The association of Nestor's age with Time itself (IV.v.201–3) is accompanied by a reminder of the protracted or seemingly endless extension of a war that Time will only "one day" end ("The end crowns all, / And that old common arbitrator, Time, / Will one day end it," IV.v.224–26). But references to such a crowning end or fine produce not an "all's well that ends well"—or even that play's tentative sense of ending—but rather a protracted dilation that is finally only a bloated middle, whose stopping brings with it no sense of culmination or fruition. The play's various simulated pregnancies yield no issue, not even the projected end or object of the conception that began with Ulysses' praise of Ajax's "spacious and dilated parts." Like the gross simulacrum of pregnancy suggested in the description of Achilles' "seeded pride," the only increase that issues from this inflation is "rank" or diseased. Lacking any satisfactory end or "fine," the play itself is all distended middle, figuring the grotesque possibility of a bloated simulacrum of pregnancy, or blowing up, presided over by the syphilitic figure of Pandarus, the very emblem of the space *between*.[82]

The play that begins, then, with reference to delaying—in the "tarrying" of wheat (I.i.15–26) known as its "dilation" and the erotic dilation or delay that puts off the conventional end of comedy—is finally all tumid or inflated middle, for all of its apocalyptic (or politically strategic) projections of an end or "fine." Its figures of that tumid or inflated middle include not only the diseased body of Pandarus, the prototypical go-between, but also the hybridity or betweenness of Ajax himself, the "blended knight, half Troyan and half Greek" (IV.v.86) whose "spacious and dilated parts" are thus themselves a hybrid or mongrel product of that mixture, and the hybrid or bastard Thersites. Described in Chapman's Homer as having "in his *ranke* minde *coppy* [i.e., *copia*] ... of unregarded wordes"[83] and functioning in this play as a more scurrilous counterpart to the wordy Parolles, Thersites combines the senses of the hybrid, of illegitimacy, and of counterfeiting introduced into *All's Well* by its marginal "Spurio," writ large in this self-consciously spurious, counterfeit, and hybrid play. "Bastard begot, bastard instructed, bastard in mind, bastard in valor, in every thing illegitimate" (V.vii.16–18). Thersites figures not only its wordiness but its notoriously hybrid status—as the play that virtually embodies the suspect intermingling or cross-breeding condemned by Sir Philip Sidney as "mongrel tragicomedy," a bastardizing of the older hierarchies of degree in its own mingling of kings and clowns, including Ajax's mistaking of the clownish Thersites for Agamemnon (III.iii.261–62). Shakespeare's *Troilus* is the "hybrid prodigy" (as Swinburne dubbed it) that subverts both distinctions of class and the pedigree of genre by its own adulterate or hybrid nature: variously a "history," a "commedy," and (in F) *The Tragedie of Troilus and Cressida*, grafting spurious or bastard kinds onto the aristocratic stock of Homeric epic, sullying the purity of generic breeding even as it contaminates the professed singleness of "truth's simplicity" (III.ii.169) by an adulteration associated (as in *All's Well*) with the duplicity of women.[84]

Troilus and Cressida presents, then, a world of inflation in every sense—of words, of emulation or honors (the contemporary form of inflation evoked in Ulysses' speech on degree), of value or price, and of a "matter" that is part of "truth tired with iteration," a well-worn and perhaps finally bankrupt epic tradition.[85] Its "Mistress Thersites" (II.i.36)—together with its pervasive figures of effeminacy—calls attention not just to courtiers as men of words, associated with the effeminacy of Parolles and the wordy new man, but also institutions like the Inns of Court linked with the need to cure language of its excesses, whether or not there is anything to their association with an intended performance of this play.[86] Shakespeare's *Troilus* is a play that lends itself to topical analysis, not just in relation to a War of the Theaters in which bombast figured so prominently, but also in its protracted and unheroic War of Troy, which may have been inspired by the seemingly interminable and anything but heroic contemporary campaign in Ireland.[87] Like both *All's Well That Ends Well* and *Hamlet*, plays that share its figures of inflation and increase, *Troilus* suggests not just the inflationary social and economic milieu or the inflation of honors (and hysteria of imitation and emulation) contemporary with it but also the legacy of the last years of Elizabeth, including the tensions between an increasingly ineffectual erotic politics still wielded by this queen and the courtly male (homosocial and homoerotic) cult that was its rival.[88] The technique of erotic dilation or holding off—the staple of romantic comedy here linked more cynically to the raising of rate or price—was inextricably associated with the policy of Elizabeth, for whom it was a form of manipulation and control even as its description as a feminine device was itself an index of contemporary misogyny. Elizabeth's own tensely complex relationship with her male courtiers and her increasingly decaying body (and virginity) may indeed inform the differently inflected voices of misogyny, as well as the imagery of disease, in all three of the plays we have considered in this chapter. Such topical applications—like the Inns of Court in the case of *Troilus*— are tantalizing even as they are also, finally, only speculative. But whatever the links between these plays and the specific historical events and personages of the complex and difficult times from which they issued, each of them raises, in a different way, questions about the relation between dilation or increase and inflation or tumidity, about the hybrid or adulterate, and about the relationship to all of these of the "parolles" that inform the plays themselves.

NOTES

1. See Thomas M. Greene, "Pitiful Thrivers: Failed Husbandry in the Sonnets," in *Shakespeare and the Question of Theory*, ed. Patricia Parker and Geoffrey Hartman (New York: Methuen, 1985), 230–44. Some of the material in this chapter appeared in an earlier version in "*All's Well That Ends Well*: Increase and Multiply," in David Quint et al., eds., *Creative Imitation: New Essays on Renaissance Literature in Honor of Thomas M. Greene* (Binghamton, New York: Medieval and Renaissance Texts and Studies, vol. 95, 1992), 355–390.

2.. William Painter, *The Palace of Pleasure*, 1575 ed., novel 38, in Geoffrey Bullough, *Narrative and Dramatic Sources of Shakespeare* (New York: Columbia University Press, 1957), vol. 2.

3. See G. K. Hunter, ed., *All's Well That Ends Well* (London: Methuen, 1959), xxix. The original Cambridge editors, in numbering it among Shakespeare's "worst" plays, commend Boccaccio's more "simple" narrative line and praise Painter's as "straighter and more dignified than the plot of *All's Well*, straighter, because it keeps to its theme, without pushing in the business of Parolles, Lafeu, and the clowning of the Clown; more dignified in that it conducts Helena ... to her determined purpose, yet consistently with the behaviour of a great lady." Their complaints against Shakespeare's less dignified Helena echo Victorian horror at a plot that stresses a woman's active (and explicitly sexual) pursuit of a man rather than her role as passive object or long-suffering wife. The New Cambridge edition, ed. Russell Fraser (Cambridge: Cambridge University Press, 1985), provides a useful historical survey of views of the play. See also David McCandless, "Helena's Bed-trick: Gender and

Performance in *All's Well That Ends Well*," *Shakespeare Quarterly* 45 (Winter 1994): 449–468.

4. For the use of "dilation" for the sexual opening of a woman see, for example, *The Works of Aristotle, the Famous Philosopher* (rpt. New York: Arno Press, 1974), 10, 81; with the citations in chap. 7. For the importance of the biblical "increase and multiply" in early modern discussions of propagation, see Thomas Laqueur's *Making Sex* (Cambridge, Mass.: Harvard University Press, 1990).

5. See, for example, Francis Marker's praise, in *The Booke of Honour* (1625), of "those who have dilated and made excellent their bloods, by the great happiness of their fortunate issues" (II.ii.47) and Herbert of Cherbury's "Ode upon a Question Mov'd" ("So when one wing can make no way / Two joyned can themselves dilate, / So can two persons propagate, / When singly either would decay").

6. See the definition of paradiastole in John Smith, *Mysterie of Rhetorique Unveil'd* (London, 1657), a later text that sums up a long tradition; and John Chamberlin, *Increase and Multiply* (Chapel Hill: University of North Carolina Press, 1976) on the *ars praedicandi* tradition of the preacher-hermeneut's "opening" a brief or difficult text of Scripture.

7. I first explored these traditions in relation to *All's Well* in "Dilation and Delay: Renaissance Matrices," *Poetics Today* 5 (1984): 519–29.

8. On endings and intermediate endings in this play, see, among other treatments, Ian Donaldson, "*All's Well That Ends Well*: Shakespeare's Play of Endings," *Essays in Criticism* 27 (1977): 34ff.; Gerard J. Gross, "The Conclusion to *All's Well That Ends Well*," *Studies in English Literature, 1500 1900*, 23 (1983): 257–76; Thomas Cartelli, "Shakespeare's 'Rough Magic': Ending as Artifice in *All's Well That Ends Well*," *Centennial Review* 27 (1983), 117–34. For a different reading of second times and second chances, see David M. Bergeron, "The Structure of Healing in *All's Well That Ends Well*," *South Atlantic Bulletin* 37 (November 1972): 25–34.

9. I am alluding here to Stephen Greenblatt's notion of the warming of verbal friction, in his "Fiction and Friction," in *Shakespearean Negotiations* (Berkeley and Los Angeles: University of California Press, 1988).

10. On usury and increase, see Marc Shell's reading of *The Merchant of Venice* in *Money, Language, and Thought* (Berkeley and Los Angeles: University of California Press, 1982). Thomas Wilson's *A Discourse upon Usury* (London, 1572) gives as its definition of usury (fol. 85): "As for example, I doe lende to receive more then I layde out ... and my chiefe purpose in laying out my moneye is, by my principal to encrease my stocke, and hope by my lending, to receive an overplus." Wilson's text strongly opposes usury, contrasting the "plenty" of merchants with the true plenty of what it calls "spiritual usury."

11. Hunter (13n), suggests that Helena here, like Desdemona in *Othello* II.i (a scene that Rymer famously complained of as mere wordy filler), is simply filling the time in this exchange with Parolles.

12. In *"All's Well That Ends Well* and Shakespeare's Helens: Text and Subtext, Subject and object," *English Literary Renaissance* 18 (1988): 66–67, Susan Snyder reads this exchange as one of the points in the play where Helen shifts from passive to active. *Parole* in the sense of being "on parole" comes ultimately from "parole of honour" (*parole d'honneur*), whose first English usage is recorded in the *OED* as 1616. Another entry, for 1658, records this borrowing from the French as a "new" usage in English; but it is impossible to have a sense from the *OED* of familiarity with this meaning in the early 1600s, when the play is now dated. John Minsheu, *Ductor in Linguas or a Guide into the Tongues* (London, 1617) gives the French "parole" as "used ... for a plee in Court" and cites as well its sense of "a lease by word of mouth."

13. Hunter, ed., *All's Well*, 21, comments that "the steward's preamble is very wordy and it is possible to believe that he is playing for time till the Countess notices the clown's presence."

14. See, for example, II.iv.35–37, V.iii.102.

15. In this respect, the creation of a space within incestuous conflation in *All's Well* anticipates *Pericles*, where the original incestuous pairing of father and daughter is spaced out through the incremental repetitions of a plot that finally displaces these relations into father, mother, daughter, and son-in-law. See also *The Winter's Tale*, where Mamillius, the son who is a copy or exact likeness of his father, dies and is in a sense replaced by Florizel, a son-in-law. The spacing described by Peter Brooks, in *Reading for the Plot* (Oxford: Clarendon Press, 1984), is thus anticipated by these Shakespearean workings out of the threat of incest through narrative extension. *All's Well* contains a father described as a "copy" for his son, as well as featuring a sense of potentially incestuous proximity between Bertram and the mother Shakespeare adds to the play's source.

16. Helena, the "hind that would be mated by the lion" (I.i.91), is also called "queen" (106).

17. On incest and riddling, see Phyllis Gorfain, "Riddles and Reconciliation: Formal Unity in *All's Well That Ends Well*," *Journal of the Folklore Institute* 13 (1976): 263–81.

18. *Cold* is one of several linking words in this play. It is also used for Diana's virginity ("I spoke with her but once / And found her wondrous cold," III.vi.112–13; and again "you are cold and stern, / And now you should be as your mother was / When your sweet self was got," IV.ii.8–10). Just before the exchange with Parolles on increase, Helena has recourse to this image in lines that ambiguously prefer this "notorious liar" to "virtue's steely bones," which look "bleak i' th'cold wind," with the comment that "full oft we see / Cold wisdom waiting on superfluous folly" (I.i.103–5).

19. See *The Workes of that famous Chirurgion Ambrose Parey*, trans. Thomas Johnson (London, 1634), bk. 13, chap. 21: "It tooke its denomination from the similitude of a reeden [Fistula] that is, a pipe, like whose hollownes it is"; it sometimes "drops with continuall moisture"; some have "run for many yeares" (484); bk. 13, chap. 22: it can "penetrate even to the bowells, which come into the parts orespread with large vessells or Nerves which, happen to effeminate and tender persons" (485). The meditation on endings in *All's Well* involves, as in *Love's Labor's Lost* and other plays, a linking with bodily ends. See also Frank Whigham, "Reading Social Conflict in the Alimentary Tract: More on the Body in Renaissance Drama," *ELH* 55 (1988): 333–50; and chap. 2, above.

20. Thomas Blount, *The Academie of Eloquence* (London, 1654), 76: "Loquacity is the Fistula of the minde, ever running, and almost incurable. A talkative fellow is the unbrac't drum, which beats a wise man out of his wits." Both images apply to Parolles, the unstoppable flowing "tongue" or "manifold linguist" who is called "Tom Drum" in V.iii.321. See also the *OED* citation of Bulwer, *Chiron* (1644), 5: "The mouth is but a running sore and hollow fistula of the minde."

21. According to Florio's *A Worlde of Wordes* (London, 1598), "spuriare" means "to adulterate, to sophisticate, to counterfeit." See the discussion below.

22. "[H]e that cannot make a leg, put off's cap, kiss his hand, and say nothing, has neither leg, hands, lip, nor cap; and indeed such a fellow, to say precisely, were not for the court" (II.ii.9–13).

23. At the point where the king is cured, the name of Paracelsus is mentioned, perhaps not just because he was a rival of the Galen with whom he is explicitly paired but because he was author of a treatise (*De Vita Longa*) on extending life, and of treatises on alchemy as a miraculous form of multiplying. His real name was Theophrastus *Bombastus* von Hohenheim.

24. Contemporary definitions of *passport* include John Barret's *An Alvearie or Quadruple Dictionary* (London: H. Denhamus, 1580) ("safe conduct to passe") and Minsheu's *Ductor in Linguas*: "Passeport, is compounded of two French words (Passer, i. transire, & port, i. portus). It signifieth with us a Licence made by any that hath authoritie, for the safe passage of any man from one place to another."

25. See Carol Thomas Neely, *Broken Nuptials in Shakespeare's Plays* (New Haven: Yale University Press, 1985), 70.

26. Barret's *Alvearie or Quadruple Dictionary* gives for *score* a "tallie of wood, whereon a number of things delivered, is marked." The Latin equivalent he cites is *tessera*.

27. On wordiness as a feature of the sixteenth-century movement away from an older military society to a society of humanists and courtiers (the new men featured in Shakespeare from as early as the Suffolk/Talbot contrast in the early histories), see Joan Kelly's now classic essay "Did Women Have a Renaissance?"

in *Women, History, and Theory* (Chicago: University of Chicago Press, 1984), 44ff.

28. An answer in early modern English also implies something that accords or agrees with the original question. See Barret's *Alvearie* ("to Answere: to accorde and agree wyth some thing: to be like, or to resemble"); and Joel Altman, *The Tudor Play of Mind* (Berkeley and Los Angeles: University of California Press, 1978), 391: "The aim of the play is discovering the most comprehensive truth, not proving the validity of one side or the other. This is why the 'answer' usually embraces both." See also William G. Crane, *Wit and Rhetoric in the Renaissance* (New York: Columbia University Press, 1937), 90, 102. In her chapter on *All's Well* in *Broken Nuptials*, Neely notes (88) that Helena's pregnancy actually alters the letter of the "sentence" of Bertram's demand. See also Gorfain, "Riddles and Reconciliation," 267.

29. For an excellent summary of the "problem play" or "problem comedy" designation, see Neely, *Broken Nuptials*, 58–62. For women as demanders of riddles in this play, see Gorfain, "Riddles and Reconciliation," 40, 45.

30. On Helen of Troy, see Snyder, *"All's Well."* In "Naming Names in *All's Well That Ends Well*," *Shakespeare Quarterly* 43, no. 3 (1992): 265–79, Susan Snyder also observes that Helena as the name in *All's Well* is an arbitrary (if familiar) editorial choice, since Helen (the name she is frequently called) could be used instead in speech prefixes and stage directions. See also Random Cloud (Randall McLeod), "'The Very Names of the Persons': Editing and the Invention of Dramatick Character," *Staging the Renaissance*, ed. David Scott Kastan and Peter Stallybrass (New York: Routledge, 1991), 88–96. The aggressive female wooer is already a tonally ambivalent Ovidian motif, epitomized by the sexually aggressive Salmacis incorporated into the Venus of Shakespeare's *Venus and Adonis*, where the conventional gender roles of pursuer and pursued (subject and object) are similarly reversed. On the aggressive female wooer generally, see William Keach, *Elizabethan Erotic Narratives* (New Brunswick, N.J.: Rutgers University Press, 1977), 19; on Salmacis, see Leonard Barkan, *The Gods Made Flesh* (New Haven: Yale University Press, 1986), 57–58. Randle Cotgrave's definition in *A Dictionarie of the French and English Tongues* (London, 1611) forges a link between *passport* as a licence for travel and a "light" woman: *"Elle a son passe-port.* She hath somewhat about her that makes her way wheresoever she goes; (Said of a light, and wandering housewife)."

31. On Elizabeth and *A Midsummer Night's Dream*, see Louis A. Montrose, "'Shaping Fantasies': Figurations of Gender and Power in Elizabethan Culture," *Representations* 2 (1983): 61–94. See also Eric Mallin's "Emulous Factions and the Collapse of Chivalry: *Troilus and Cressida*," *Representations* 29 (1990): 145–79.

32. On this Petrarchan dynamic, see Nancy Vickers's "Diana Described: Scattered Woman and Scattered Rhyme," *Critical Inquiry* 8 (1981): 265–79. In the Petrarchan dialectic of "service" and mastery, the "Dian" who stands as the object of praise is also the virgin to be mastered; and the language of idealized

service dissimulates its own will to control. On the "Petrarchan" politics of the Elizabethan Age, see Stephen Greenblatt, *Renaissance Self-Fashioning* (Chicago: University of Chicago Press, 1980), 165ff.; and Montrose's application of Vickers's model to *A Midsummer Night's Dream* in "Shaping Fantasies."

33. The Folio text for this scene may not, in this respect, need editorial amendment when it places a colon after "Not my virginity yet" and then proceeds to list the Petrarchan commonplaces associated with it. In the Oxford single volume Shakespeare, Gary Taylor adds a reference to the court. See Snyder, *"All's Well,"* 68.

34. See Stephen Gosson, *An Apologie of the Schoole of Abuse* (1579), printed with *The Schoole of Abuse* (1597), (London, 1868), 66, and its description of Venus as "a notorious strumpet ... that made her self as common as a Barbars chayre." This semantic complex in *All's Well* is shared by *Othello*'s crossing of "barbarian" with the "maid of Barbary" / the strumpet of the Moor. *Barbiera* was slang for "whore." See Frankie Rubinstein's *A Dictionary of Shakespeare's Sexual Puns and Their Significance* (London: Macmillan, 1984), 21 and xii; and Ben Jonson's *Alchemist* and *Epicoene*, especially Morose's "That cursed barber! I have married his cittern that is common to all men." "Barbar" and "barber's chair" might equally be read in a homoerotic context in the period.

35. We need also to note here the relation between the semantic complexes of dilation and increase in *All's Well* and the Shakespearean uses—here and in other plays—of the sexual double entendres of "stretching." *All's Well* makes repeated use of the figure of stretching—both in its description of the skill of the physician Gerard de Narbon, which "had it stretched so far, would have made nature immortal" (I.i.19–20) and in the king's reference to the "gift" that "doth stretch itself as 'tis received" (II.i.4). But the latter image—stretching in order to receive—appears elsewhere in Shakespeare in an explicitly sexual sense, for the opening up or stretching of female sexuality to "fit" whatever it receives:—in the image of the chevril glove ("Here's a wit of cheverel, that stretches from an inch narrow to an ell broad!—I stretch it out for that word 'broad'") in *Romeo and Juliet* (II.iv.83–85) and in the old lady's reference, in *Henry VIII*, to the ambivalent "capacity" of Ann Bullen ("The capacity / Of your soft cheveril conscience would receive, / If you might please to stretch it," II.iii.31–33). The image of the chevril glove is linked to female wantonness in the scene in *Twelfth Night* where Feste invokes it in lines that refer to making his sister "wanton." But it is also explicitly summoned for Diana's duplicitous "angling," in the final scene of *All's Well* when, in her riddling double entendres, she begins to look perilously close to the prostitute or "common customer" (V.iii.276) Bertram seeks to portray her as ("This woman's *an easy glove*, my lord, she goes off and on at pleasure," V.iii.277–78). The link between dilation or stretching as sexual opening—in the case of virginity, a painful stretching—and other kinds of "service" is suggested as well in the double entendres of Philostrate's description

of the mechanicals' play as "nothing, nothing in the world; / Unless you can find sport in their intents, / Extremely stretch'd, and conn'd with cruel pain, / To do you service" in *A Midsummer Night's Dream* (V.i.78–81), where though the surface meaning of "extremely stretch'd" is something like "strained to the uttermost" (Riverside), there is also a sense of the sexualized language of class difference as the metaphor of sexual service extending to all servants. See chapter 4 and Rubinstein's *Dictionary*, under "con," "stretch," "nothing." (This context—along with *Romeo and Juliet* and other plays—also reminds us of the homo- as well as heterosexual application of this sexual imagery of stretching.) The painful opening/dilating/stretching of a virgin is described in Helkiah Crooke's *A Description of the Body of Man* (London, 1615): "when the yarde entreth into the necke of the wombe, then the fleshy membranes ... are torn even to their rootes, and the Caruncles are so fretted and streatched, that a man would beleeve they were never ioyned" (236): it is rare, he comments (236), that "the Membranes are *dilated* with little or no paine.... For all virgins although they be never so mellow, yet have their first coition painfull." See also chap. 7. The fact that the "answer" that must be "of most monstrous size" could refer to male tumescence as easily as to female (for example) "stretching" might lead us into the exploration in Shakespeare of what Derrida calls "double invagination," where the dilation or opening of a woman (for example), as a figure for the dilation of discourse, is joined by the tradition of narrative prologance (see Mercutio's double entendres on cutting his "tale short" in *Romeo and Juliet*).

36. See the gloss to *All's Well*, I.i.30–34, in the New Cambridge edition, 42. On the "simple" in *The Merry Wives of Windsor*, see chap. 4.

37. See, among others, Neely, *Broken Nuptials*, 73, 85–86. Neely also points out Helena's links with the harlot/saint Mary Magdalene, through Maudlin (a vernacular form of Magdalene, as well as a noun meaning "a penitent"), the name of the wife Bertram pledges to marry when Helena is assumed dead: "Mary Magdalene's traditional roles as reformed harlot and weeping penitent figure forth Bertram's own penitence and reform; they coincide with those of the promiscuous Diana and the saintly Helena that Bertram images and foreshadow the surprises still to come in the play" (85). Neely (80) sees this transformation of Helena, the rejected wife, into the desired "Dian" as part of Bertram's separation of himself, in the play's second part, from the authority of his mother and the surrogate-paternal authority of the king. This sense of the need to gain distance or "space" is foregrounded both in the threat of incest added to the source and in the dominance of the older generation in the plot. For psychoanalytic readings of both, see Richard Wheeler, *Shakespeare's Development and the Problem Comedies* (Berkeley and Los Angeles: University of California Press, 1981), chap. 2; Janet Adelman, "Bed Tricks: On Marriage as the End of Comedy in *All's Well That Ends Well* and *Measure for Measure*," in *Shakespeare's Personality*, ed. Norman N. Holland et al. (Berkeley and Los Angeles: University of California Press, 1989), 151–74, and chapter 4 of her *Suffocating Mothers* (New

York: Routledge, 1992); and Ruth Nevo, "Motive and Meaning in *All's Well That Ends Well*," in *"Fanned and Winnowed Opinions": Shakespearean Essays Presented to Harold Jenkins*, ed. John W. Mahon and Thomas A. Pendleton (London: Methuen, 1987), 26–51.

38. See, for example, Spenser's evocation of Stesichorus's version in the splitting, for example, of true and false Florimel, discussed by Nohrnberg in *The Analogy of "The Faerie Queene,"* 115. Nohrnberg notes Stesichorus's story of the two Helens in Plato's versions in the *Phaedrus* and the *Republic*. See also Euripides' *Helen*.

39. See "Shakespeare's *All's Well That Ends Well*, lines 2017–2018," in *Explicator* 41 (fall 1982): 6–9, whose reading, however, differs sharply from my own.

40. See Gross, "Conclusion," 262; and on the play's problematic ending, James Calderwood, "Styles of Knowing in *All's Well That Ends Well*," *Modern Language Notes* 25 (1964): 292–94; Gross, 257–76; Neely, *Broken Nuptials*, 87–92; Gorfain, "Riddles and Reconciliation," 264, 271ff., 275–76; and Anne Barton's Riverside introduction.

41. Part of the complexity of the bed trick is that it is also a sign of Bertram's inability to escape Helena's power even here. See Adelman, *Suffocating Mothers*, chap. 4.

42. See Florio, *Queen Anna's World of Words*, where *spurio* is translated as "a bastard, a baseborne" as well as "adulterate or counterfeit."

43. See Michael Neill, "'In Everything Illegitimate': Imagining the Bastard in Renaissance Drama," *The Yearbook of English Studies*, 23 (1993), 270–92, esp. 277–79, who notes that Latin *adulter* acquired the meaning not just of an adultery (or the bastard offspring of adultery) but also (generally in the form *adulter solidorum*), "a counterfeiter or adulterator of coin," while *adultero* likewise acquired the sense of "to falsify, adulterate, or counterfeit." See also the discussion of adultery and adulteration in chapters 4 and 5. The link between bastard and base appears, for example, in the "Why bastard? Wherefore base?" of Edmund in *King Lear*. See Neill, 271.

44. See Adelman's reading of the bed trick in *Suffocating Mothers*, chap. 4. Peter Erickson also raises the question of class in the play (along with parallels between Helena and Shakespeare) in his *Rewriting Shakespeare, Rewriting Ourselves* (Berkeley and Los Angeles: University of California Press, 1991), 70–73. See also the epilogue of *All's Well*, whose "The king's a beggar" (epil. 1) points as well to the crossing of class boundaries within the Shakespearean theater, by its player-kings. For a critique of modes of psychoanalytic explanation that exclude the social or political, see Kenneth Burke's observation that "psychoanalysis too often conceals ... the nature of exclusive social relations behind inclusive (i.e., universal) terms for sexual relations," in *A Rhetoric of Motives* (1950; rpt. Berkeley and Los Angeles: University of California Press,

1969), 279–80; Lisa Lowe, "'Say I Play the Man I Am': Gender and Politics in *Coriolanus,*" *Kenyon Review* 8 (fall 1986), esp. 89; and Frank Whigham, "Incest and Ideology," *PMLA* 100 (1985): 167–86, whose discussion of incest, exogamy, and class contamination is highly suggestive for *All's Well*. On the conflict between social/economic endogamy (e.g., marriages within aristocratic groupings) and cross-class mixing in the period, see also, among others, Lawrence Stone, *The Family, Sex, and Marriage in England, 1500–1800* (London: Weidenfeld, 1977), 60–61. For critiques of Stone, see Keith Thomas's review in *Times Literary Supplement,* 21 October 1977; and Christopher Hill, "Sex, Marriage, and the Family in England," *Economic History Review* 31 (1978): 450–63.

45. See Halpern, *The Poetics of Primitive Accumulation: English Renaissance Culture and the Genealogy of Capital* (Ithaca, N.Y.: Cornell University Press, 1991), 244 and 257; Douglas Bruster's *Drama and the Market in the Age of Shakespeare* (Cambridge: Cambridge University Press, 1992); and Lars Engle, *Shakespearean Pragmatism* (Chicago: University of Chicago Press, 1993), both generally and in relation to *Troilus and Cressida*. On the "inflation of honors," see, among others, Lawrence Stone, *The Crisis of the Aristocracy, 1558–1641,* abridged edition (New York: Oxford University Press, 1967), 65–128. *Inflation* in the monetary sense was, according to the *OED,* not yet in use in the period; but the sense of the dilation or inflating both of social status and of self-importance was. The *OED* cites Richard Taverner's 1539 translation of Erasmus's *Adages,* warning that "we dylate not our selves beyond our condition and state." Halpern remarks (*245*) that while "the proliferation of hybrids corroded the boundaries of the aristocratic signifier, the multiplying effects of simulacra 'inflated' it and debased its value."

46. See Salter, *Sir Thomas Gresham* (London: L. Parsons, 1925), 143, 156; and Whitney R. D. Jones, *The Tudor Commonwealth, 1529–1559* (London: Athlone Press, 1970), 733-34. Stone, *Crisis of the Aristocracy* (139), argues that between 1559 and 1602 prices rose 79 percent.

47. See John Ponet, *A Shorte Treatise of Politicke Power* (1556), sigs. Fii–Fiii, cited by Jones in *Tudor Commonwealth,* 140; and Halpern, *Poetics of Primitive Accumulation,* 258. The debasement of English currency was halted, but only for a time, by royal proclamation in 1560. On inflation as well as the general economic crises of early modern England, see Joan Thirsk, *Economic Policy and Projects: The Development of a Consumer Society in Early Modern England* (Oxford: Clarendon Press, 1978); and Bernard Supple, *Commercial Crisis and Change in England 1600–1642* (Cambridge: Cambridge University Press, 1959). See also Wayne A. Rebhorn, "The Crisis of the Aristocracy in *Julius Caesar,*" *Renaissance Quarterly* 43 (1990): 75–111, and Barry Taylor, *Vagrant Writing: Social and Semiotic Disorders in the English Renaissance* (London: Harvester Wheatsheaf, 1991), chap. 2.

48. See Jean-Christophe Agnew, *Worlds Apart: The Market and the Theater in*

Anglo-American Thought, 1550–1750 (Cambridge: Cambridge University Press, 1986), esp. 69 and 71. On "dry exchange," see Raymond de Roover, "What Is Dry Exchange? A Contribution to the Study of English Mercantilism," *Journal of Political Economy* 52 (1994): 250–66. Shakespearean play elsewhere on *engrossing* may also be relevant in relation to this play. Helena's fruitful dilation or generational increase is figured by her pregnant body, image of a fruitful *grossesse*; the merely gross or engrossed in the bodily sense is, by contrast, a frequent Shakespearean image of a merely swollen tumidity. See the discussion of *Troilus and Cressida* below. Engrossing in the commercial or property sense involved the activity of "engrossers" who "sought to 'corner' supplies in a commodity in order to raise its price" (Agnew, 214 n. 44), a "cornering" that may bring to mind the Shakespearean imagery of angling or cornering that appears in Bertram's charge against Diana in *All's Well* (see the first postscript to chap. 5, above). To engross in early modern English carried both this sense and the sense (from French *engrosser*) of "to make big, thick, or gross." It also meant "to write in large letters; chiefly ... to write in a peculiar character appropriate to legal documents" and by extension "to arrange." See the *OED*, *engross*, which cites, for the meaning of monopolize or "buy up the whole stock, or as much as possible" for the sake of raising the price, Florio's "*Monopolo*, an engrossement of any merchandise into one mans handes." Shakespeare exploits this sense in *1 Henry IV* ("Percy is but my factor ... / To engross up glorious deeds on my behalf," III.ii.147–48); and various forms of "engross" and "engrossment" appear in *2 Henry IV* ("this bitter taste yields his engrossments," IV.v.78–79), in *Merry Wives* ("I have ... engross'd opportunities to meet her," II.ii.194–96), in *Antony and Cleopatra* ("Your mariners are muleters, reapers, people / Ingross'd by swift impress," III.vii.35–36); and in *All's Well* ("If thou engrossest all the griefs are thine, / Thou robb'st me of a moi'ty," III.ii.65–66). The Shakespeare canon also exploits the sense of "to render gross, dense, or bulky" (from French *engrosser*), or "to make (the body) gross or fat" as well. See *Richard III*, II.vii.76.

49. See *OED*, "utterance," with Agnew, *Worlds Apart*, 62 and 221 n. 14; and Raymond Southall on the mouth as a mint of words in *Literature and the Rise of Capitalism* (London: Laurence and Wishart, 1973). Shakespeare exploits the linking of verbal and monetary in *Two Gentlemen of Verona* ("open your purse, that the money and the matter may be both at once deliver'd," I.i.129–30). See also chapter 7 on the ambiguity of "purse" elsewhere in Shakespeare.

50. The passage from Sprat is quoted in *Classical Rhetoric for the Modern Student*, 2d ed. (New York: Oxford University Press, 1971), 616. On the anti-Ciceronian movement and articulation of desire for a more "masculine" style, see my *Literary Fat Ladies* (New York: Methuen, 1987), chap. 2. On Shakespeare in relation to the inflation of honors, see William Harrison, "A Description of England," in *Holinshed's Chronicles of England, Scotland, and Ireland* ..., 6 vols. (London, 1807–8), 1:273, and the discussion in chapter 1, above.

51. For the above, see Robert Greene, *A Groatsworth of Wit*, ed. G. B. Harrison, 45; the Arden edition of *I Henry IV*, 74; and on Greene's attack Alfred Harbage, *Shakespeare and the Rival Traditions* (New York: Macmillan, 1952), 94; George Puttenham, *The Arte of English Poesie* (1906; rpt. Kent, Ohio: Kent State University Press, 1970), book III ("Of Ornament"). Nashe's preface to Greene's *Menaphon* (London, 1589) speaks of players as "taffata fools tricked up with our feathers," while in *Never Too Late* (1590) Greene makes Cicero say to Roscius, "Why art thou proud with Aesop's crow being pranked with the glory of other feathers." Marston famously, in *Histriomastix or The Player Whipt* (London, 1599–1600), part of the War of the Theaters that was preoccupied with such class distinctions, has his Chrisogonus (a poet and scholar unappreciated by the players) rail against the "ballad-monger" who, appealing to the "common sort," "all applauded and puff't up with pride, / Swell(s) in concept and load(s) the stage with stuff." See Harbage, *Shakespeare and Rival Traditions*, 102–3. Francis Beaumont's verse epistle to Jonson laments the use of "fustian Metaphors to stuff the brain." See *The Works of Francis Beaumont and John Fletcher*, ed. Arnold Glover and A. M. Waller (Cambridge: Cambridge English Classics, 1905–12), 10:71, 199; and E. A. J. Honigmann, "Shakespeare's 'Bombast'," in *Shakespeare's Styles: Essays in Honour of Kenneth Muir*, ed. Philip Edwards et al. (Cambridge: Cambridge University Press), esp. 153–54, which cites *Ben Jonson*, ed. D. H. Herford, Percy Simpson, and Evelyn Simpson, 11 vols. (Oxford: Clarendon Press, 1925–52), 8:587, and Dryden's later observation that "in reading some bombast speeches of *Macbeth*, which are not to be understood [Jonson] used to say that it was horror; and I am much afraid that this is so." In the induction to Jonson's *Cynthia's Revels* (1601), one of the actors expresses the wish that "your Poets would leave to bee promoters of other mens jests, and to way-lay all the stale apothegmes, or olde bookes, they can heare of ... to *farce* their Scenes withall." See Russ McDonald, *Shakespeare and Jonson, Jonson and Shakespeare* (Lincoln: University of Nebraska Press, 1988), and Harbage, *Shakespeare and Rival Traditions*, 109ff., which notes (115) that part of Jonson's polemic is against the popular theater and Shakespeare in particular.

52. See Justus Lipsius, *Institutio Epistolica*, vii, 9–10, in the edition appended to *Justi Lipsi Epistolarum Selectarum*; with Wesley Trimpi, *Ben Jonson's Poems* (Stanford, Calif.: Stanford University Press, 1962); and Roger Ascham, *The Schoolmaster* (1570), ed. Lawrence V. Ryan (Ithaca, N.Y.: Cornell University Press, 1967), 109.

53. The likeliest dating of these three plays puts *All's Well* last (1602–3), after *Hamlet* (1600–1601) and *Troilus and Cressida* (1601–2), but several critics believe *All's Well* to have been begun as early as 1594–95. In this chapter, reference to "recalls" of *All's Well* have to do with the order in which the plays are discussed here, rather than any argument related to their chronology.

54. See Terence Cave, *The Cornucopian* Text (Oxford: Clarendon Press, 1979).

55. See, among other examples, John Hoskins's *Directions for Speech and Style*, ed. Hoyt H. Hudson (Princeton: Princeton University Press, 1935), 24.

56. See, for example, Carol Clark, *The Web of Metaphor* (Lexington, Ky.: French Forum Publishers, 1978), 50: "Among Latin writers on style, the words *tumidus* and *inflatus* were in regular use in literary contexts, with a meaning more or less equivalent to our *pretentious, bombastic....* Allied to this usage was a recurring metaphor comparing bombast in writing to the unhealthy swelling of dropsical bodies.... Longinus, in his treatise *On the Sublime*, remarks that 'Tumours are bad things, whether in books or bodies, those empty inflations, void of sincerity.... For as they say, there's nought so dry as dropsy.'" Clark remarks of this passage: "The difficulty, of course, is to distinguish this hydroptic swelling from the actual plumpness of health."

57. The *OED* cites "*Fistula* ... the fester is a postume that rootyth wythin" (from 1398), a text from 1581 that treats of "the fretting Fistula within the bowels of the Christian commonwealth," and another (from 1622) that speaks of "an heart diseased with that grievous fistula of hypocrisie." It also draws the link with its synonym, *fester*. For its connection with a diseased and uncontrolled increase, see, for example, *An Account of the Causes of Some Particular Rebellious Distempers* (London, 1547): "where one Fistula is occasion'd by any other means, ten proceeds from that." See also David Hoeniger, "The She-Doctor and the Miraculous Cure of the King's Fistula in *All's Well That Ends Well*," in his *Medicine and Shakespeare in the English Renaissance* (Newark: University of Delaware Press, 1992), 287–306; and Ann Lecercle, "Anatomy of a Fistula, Anomaly of a Drama," in *All's Well That Ends Well: Nouvelles perspectives critiques*, ed. Jean Fuzier and Francois Laroque (Montpellier: Publications de l'Université de Paul Valéry, 1985), 105–24. I am grateful for this last reference to Frank Whigham. It would be fascinating to trace the links between this Shakespearean "fistula" (the Latin term for "pipe" used for the spouting of Pyramus's blood in the source-story for the artisans' play in *A Midsummer Night's Dream*), Lavinia's bleeding body likened in *Titus Andronicus* to "a conduit with three issuing spouts" (II.iv.30), and the "statue spouting blood in many pipes" in *Julius Caesar* (II.ii.85). Both the conduit of Lavinia and these pipes from *Julius Caesar* are linked to a feminizing incontinence in Gail Kern Paster's *The Body Embarrassed: Drama and the Disciplines of Shame in Early Modern England* (Ithaca, N.Y.: Cornell University Press, 1993). See her chapter "Blood as Trope of Gender in *Julius Caesar*," which also cites the "bubbling fountain" (*Titus Andronicus*, II.iv.23) associated with "lost virginity."

58. Ascham, *The Schoolmaster*, 112–13.

59. Calderwood, "Styles of Knowing," 92, notes that even words like *nunnery* breed in this play and, on 93, that the traditional flowers of rhetoric—source of the tradition of *copia* as a fruitful increase—here become an unweeded garden. This is the image already used in the rhetorical tradition of an inflated or overblown use of words. See, for example, Quintilian II.xviii, sec. 2.

60. On "plurisy," see the Arden editor's note on its mistaken derivation from Latin *plus, pluris*. On "mixture rank" and its echoes of the implication of Gertrude in Hamlet's "thy commandement all alone shall live / Within the book and volume of my brain, / *Unmix'd* with *baser matter*. Yes, by heaven! / O most *pernicious woman!*" (I.v.102–5), see Adelman, *Suffocating Mothers*, chap. 2, and the discussion of the parthenogenic copying of father in son in chapter 5, above. On ears and the poison spreading over the king's "smooth body," see Ann Thompson and John O. Thompson, *Shakespeare: Meaning and Metaphor* (Iowa City: University of Iowa Press, 1987), 102–3 and 107.

61. Both Michael Neill and Ruth Nevo make the important point that the doubts surrounding Gertrude's sexuality also raise the possibility of Hamlet's own illegitimacy. Neill argues that this also imports the network of the spurious or the counterfeit (as well as "bastardy") into this play. See Neill, "In Everything Illegitimate," 271–72, which cites Nevo's paper "Mousetrap and Rat Man: An Uncanny Resemblance," delivered at the Shakespeare Congress in Tokyo in 1991. On incest in the period, see Marc Shell, *The End of Kinship* (Stanford, Calif.: Stanford University Press, 1988) and Bruce Thomas Boehrer, *Monarchy and Incest in Renaissance England* (Philadelphia: University of Pennsylvania Press, 1992).

62. On the textual variants "dilated" and "delated," see the discussion in chapter 7.

63. Cited from the Loeb translation of the *Ad Herennium*, trans. Harry Caplan (Cambridge, Mass.: Harvard University Press, 1954), IV.viii.11–12 and IV.x.15. On Shakespeare's familiarity with this text, see T. W. Baldwin, *William Shakspere's Small Latine and Lesse Greeke*, 2 vols. (Urbana: University of Illinois Press, 1944), 2:133. See also Debora K. Shugar, *Sacred Rhetoric: The Christian Grand Style in the English Renaissance* (Princeton: Princeton University Press, 1988).

64. See Jonson, *Discoveries*, in *Ben Jonson*, 8:626. The Vives passage, above, is cited in Trimpi, *Ben Jonson's Poems*, 101. See also Trimpi's exposition of the three styles (plain style, middle style, and grand style) (6) and on the swollen style (265); Morris Croll, "Attic Prose," in *Style, Rhetoric, and Rhythm: Essays by Morris Croll*, ed. Max Patrick et al. (Princeton: Princeton University Press, 1969); Richard Sherry, *A Treatise of Schemes & Tropes* (London, 1550), 6; Hoskins, *Directions*, 24, treating of "superfluity of words." Hoskins gives an example he describes as "too swelling."

65. Puttenham, *Arte of English Poesie*, 165.

66. See Trimpi, *Ben Jonson's Poems*; with Norhnberg *Analogy*, 49–50, on the high epic style of "magnifying" that lies behind the magnifying of Spenser's Arthur, and its tumid counterpart in Orgoglio. This tumid double was routinely used to ridicule spurious epic pretensions—as when Jonson himself, in "The Famous Voyage" (*Ben Jonson*, 8:84), ridicules bombastic epic "stuffings."

67. Timothy Bright's *Characterie: An Arte of Shorte, Swifte, and secrete writing by Character* (London, 1588), gives "Great" as a synonym for *dilate* in its "Table of English Words."

68. See the discussion of this play's preoccupation with words rather than action in Kenneth Palmer, ed. *Troilus and Cressida* (London: Methuen, 1982), 40. In appendix 2 (309), Palmer notes that *Troilus* "contains some of Shakespeare's most accomplished oratory, two full-dress debates, discussions of topics (as in Hector's arguments) that would directly interest a lawyer, and much that is potentially ironic." It has been conjectured by John Bayley (*Uses of Division: Unity and Disharmony in Literature* [London: Chatto and Windus, 1976]), among others, that this may be because of an Inns of Court audience, but as Palmer's appendix points out, this remains only speculation. Palmer also suggests (7ff.) that some passages peculiar to the Folio text may represent cuts from the Quarto because it was thought too wordy or inept. The play is, certainly, preoccupied with wordiness. Pandarus calls attention to the wordiness of Troilus and Cressida even in the scene of the anticipated consummation or sexual "deed." Helen says in response to Pandarus's own wordiness, "Dear lord, you are full of fair words" (III.i.47), while Cressida remarks of one of Pandarus's tediously inflated anecdotes that it was "a great while going by" (I.ii.168). Ulysses' speech on degree is termed "a tale of length" (I.iii.136), thus calling explicit attention to its own protracted dilation as oratory. Agamemnon's contrasting of Thersites' railing with Ulysses' eloquence is itself delivered in a convoluted and wordy speech.

69. Lee Patterson has suggested to me that the play exploits the medieval tradition of Achilles' corpulence, associated with his indolence and withdrawal from active participation in the war. The Arden editor glosses "broad Achilles" as follows: "Probably alluding to Achilles' size, although editors have suggested 'puffed up.'" On the description of greatness or magnanimity in Aristotle's *Nicomachean Ethics* (a text famously, and anachronistically, echoed in *Troilus*), see appendix 3 of the Arden edition, esp. 314–16.

70. See the reference as well to Falstaff ("sweet creature of bumbast") as the "hill of flesh" (*1H4*, II.iv.243) who "lards the lean earth as he walks along" (II.ii.109). On "interlard," see *OED*, citing Foxe's *Actes and monuments* (1563–87): "To interlard a tale of untruth, with some parcell of truth nowe and then among." See also Thomas Newton's *Seneca His Tenne Tragedies* (1581; Bloomington, Indiana, 1968), 4–5: "And whereas it is by some squeymish Areopagites surmyzed, that the readinge of these Tragedies, being enterlarded with many Phrases and sentences ... cannot be digested without great dauger [sic] of infection ..."

71. "ULYSSES: No: you see, he is his argument, that has his argument, Achilles." The Arden note here observes (174): "Ulysses says, in effect 'Observe that Achilles, having stolen Thersites, is now Ajax' theme, and Ajax has thereby

acquired matter for everlasting dispute' [ie. an Achillean = endless argument]."
Zachery Grey, *Critical, Historical and Explanatory Notes on Shakespeare*, (London,
1754), 2:240, first called attention to the definition of an "Achillean argument"
in Erasmus's *Adagio* (chil. 1, cent. 7, prov. 41): "Denique rationem aut
argumentum *Achilleum* vocant, quod sit insuperabile & insolubile."

72. The set of linkages between overvaluation, inflation, corpulency, and
pride exploited in this play is one that persists at least as late as Richard
Flecknoe's *Fifty Five Enigmatical Characters, all Very Exactly Drawn to the Life*
(London, 1665), on the character of "a huge overvaluer of himself" (24), which
begins: "He affects a certain Corpulency in al his Actions, makes them rather
appear inflate and swoln than great and solide."

73. I prefer the Arden editor's adoption of the Folio's "forced" here rather
than the "fac'd" that the Riverside editor adopts from the Quarto text. See also
David Bevington, ed., *The Complete Works of Shakespeare*, 3d ed. (Glenview, Ill.:
Scott, Foresman, 1980), 536, which adopts "forced," glossing it as "stuffed." This
is another instance where particular networks of wordplay may be importantly
related to choices between variant texts.

74. The Arden *Henry V* gloss here is "'digest' = 'set in order our changes of
place.' ... There is a possible quibble on the normal meaning of 'digest.'" The
Arden editor there gives "compel" for "force," but Dover Wilson reads "force"
here as "farce," that is, cram or stuff, and adds "a culinary word, following close
upon digest." The Riverside gives "'force' = 'stuff' (with incidents)." Arden
editor Palmer insists that the "digested" of its prologue is "*Not* part of the food
imagery of the play." But the prologue to Troilus is clearly punning on both
meanings of *digested*, as rhetorically "arranged, disposed, distributed" and as
digested in the alimentary sense. This would be appropriate to the play's echoes
of epic precursors, since digestion was one of the most common of early modern
humanist figures for the process of literary imitation and incorporation.
Shakespeare also plays on both kinds of digestion in *The Merchant of Venice* ("JES.:
Nay, let me praise you while I have a stomach. / LOR.: No, pray thee, let it serve
for table-talk; / Then howsome'er thou speak'st, 'mong other things / I shall
digest it," III.v.7–90). *Troilus* itself several times evokes digestion in its alimentary
sense (II.ii.6, II.iii.41 and 111). Ulysses also refers to "fusty stuff" in his
description of the theatrics of Achilles and Patroclus. The Arden gloss on "fusty"
resists Deighton's suggestion of "fustian" as well as "mouldy," but once again the
phrase manages to participate in both registers, the inflated or bombastically
verbal and the alimentary, as does digestion used both for Thersites ("my
digestion," II.iii.41) and in its discursive sense of arrangement or disposition in
the prologue to the play.

75. Ajax may be a figure for Ben Jonson. For this tradition, see, among
others, McDonald, *Shakespeare and Jonson*.

76. For other Shakespearean uses of this more bourgeois language of

counting and accounting, in contexts that transform (or adulterate) an older more heroic or aristocratic context, see chapter 5; the discussion of Troilus by Bruster in *Drama and the Market*; and Engle's *Shakespearean Pragmatism*.

77. For dilation as delay in this erotic sense in this period, see Parker, *Literary Fat Ladies*, chap. 1. In relation to Cressida's capitulation in *Troilus and Cressida*, see René Girard, "The Politics of Desire in *Troilus and Cressida*," in Parker and Hartman, *Question of Theory*, 188ff., and his *A Theater of Envy: William Shakespeare* (New York: Oxford University Press, 1991), chaps. 14–18; Adelman, *Suffocating Mothers*, 46–51; Engle, *Shakespearean Pragmatism*, 153; and Linda Chames, *Notorious Identity: Materializing the Subject in Shakespeare* (Cambridge, Mass.: Harvard University Press, 1993), 94. Mallin, "Emulous Factions" (e.g., 145–46, 152, 155, and 157) analyses this motif in Troilus in relation to Elizabeth's policy of erotic manipulation and delay.

78. See the discussion of the links between women and *translation* in chapter 5.

79. The Arden gloss on "starv'd" here gives "trivial, lacking matter," while the Riverside gives "thin, empty (of sustenance)." Both, however, are conveyed, once again, by an imagery that links the bodily with the discursive. For contemporary debates concerning the Trojan War, see Marion Trousdale, *Shakespeare and the Rhetoricians* (Chapel Hill: University of North Carolina Press, 1982), 4ff., which (in the context of a discussion of *copia*) quotes Rainold's "Could wise men, and the most famous nobles of Grece: So occupie their heddes, and in the same, both to hasarde their lives for a beautifull strumpet or harlot" (fol. 26) and "It semeth a matter of folie, that so many people, so mightie nacions should bee bewitched, to raise so mightie a armie, hassardying their lives, leavying their countrie, their wives, their children, for one woman" (fol. 25v).

80. *Greatness* is deflated elsewhere in Shakespeare by being reduced to its merely bodily sense of size. See, for example, the lines on "Pompey the Great" in *Love's Labor's Lost*.

81. On this play's lack of clear end or telos, see, among others, Jonathan Dollimore, *Radical Tragedy: Religion, Ideology, and Power in the Drama of Shakespeare and His Contemporaries* (Chicago: University of Chicago Press, 1984), 43–44; Richard D. Fly, "'Suited in Like Conditions as Our Argument': Imitative Form in Shakespeare's *Troilus and Cressida*," *Studies in English Literature, 1500–1900* 15 (1975): 273–92, esp. 291; and Chames's chapter on the play in *Notorious Identity*.

82. On the status of the final lines spoken by Pandarus, see, for example, the introduction to the Arden edition.

83. The New Variorum (50) notes that Thersites is described as "full of words" in Chapman's translation of the *Iliad* ("full of words many and disorderly"), a translation based on the Latin verse translation in Spondanus (*Homeri quae extant omnia* [Basle, 1582], 33): "Thersites adhuc solus immoderate

verbosus crocitabat," a line Chapman translates as "Thersites sole except, a man of tongue, whose ravenlike voice, a tuneles iarring kept, Who in his *ranke* minde *coppy* had of unregarded *wordes*" (1598 ed., sig. EIV). Thersites' "coppy" or *copia* of words described as overblown or "rank" also calls to mind the term used for the "seeded pride" of Achilles. The Arden editor of *Troilus*, 35, notes that Thersites also appeared in a sixteenth-century interlude as a boastful coward. Thersites is famously garrulous: see, for example, the reference to him in Apthonius, *Progymnasmata* (Oxford, 1555), 117.

84. See here and above Neill's discussion in "In Everything Illegitimate" of Thersites in relation to the "spurious" generally in Troilus, esp. 289–90; and Adelman, *Suffocating Mothers*, 41ff., on the imagery of mixture in the play and its rhetoric of male simplicity and female duplicity; with the discussion of *Troilus and Cressida* in chapter 5, above. For Swinburne's description of "this hybrid ... prodigy," see A. C. Swinburne, *A Study of Shakespeare* (1880), in *Troilus and Cressida: A Casebook*, ed. Priscilla Martin (London: Macmillan, 1976), 55. For Sidney's strictures against "mongrel tragicomedy" and "mingling kings and clowns," see Sir Philip Sidney, "An Apology for Poetry," in *English Critical Essays (Sixteenth, Seventeenth, and Eighteenth Centuries)*, ed. Edmund D. Jones (London: Oxford University Press, 1947), 46.

85. On this play's underscoring that it treats a well-worn theme, see Elizabeth Freund, "'Ariachne's Broken Woof': The Rhetoric of Citation in *Troilus and Cressida*," in Parker and Hartman, *Question of Theory*, 19–36.

86. On the theory that this play was written for performance at one of the Inns of Court (first propounded by Peter Alexander in 1928–29), see the Arden *Troilus and Cressida*, appendix 2, 307–10. On the relation between the Inns of Court and movements to reform language in the period, see, among others, Trimpi, *Ben Jonson's Poems*.

87. See, among others, Mallin, "Emulous Factions," esp. 169.

88. See the readings of *All's Well* and *Hamlet* in Erickson, *Rewriting Shakespeare, Rewriting Ourselves*; and Mallin's analysis of Achilles in particular in relation to Essex in "Emulous Factions." On *Hamlet* in relation to the late years of Elizabeth's reign, see Annabel Patterson, *Shakespeare and the Popular Voice* (Oxford: Basil Blackwell, 1989), esp. 13–31 and 93–119; Tennenhouse, *Power on Display*, 85; Robert Weimann, "Mimesis in *Hamlet*," in Parker and Hartman, *Question of Theory*, 275–91; and Steven Mullaney, "Mourning and Misogyny: Hamlet, The Revenger's Tragedy, and the Final Progress of Elizabeth I, 1600–1607," *Shakespeare Quarterly* 45 (1994): 139–62, esp. 139–40, which discusses these years in relation to misogyny in particular.

RONALD R. MACDONALD

Measure for Measure:
The Flesh Made Word

It is generally conceded that *Measure for Measure* is Shakespeare's last comedy, properly speaking, though no one perhaps would care to argue that he never wrote a funny line after 1604, the date usually assigned to this very dark, if not the very darkest, of all his comedies. If Shakespeare abandoned comedy six or seven years before the end of his theatrical career, he never abandoned the comic at all, and *The Tempest* contains passages of inspired fooling as hilarious as anything the earlier plays have to offer. But if *The Tempest* can be said to be, at least in part, a very funny play, that does not make it a comedy, no more than the universally recognized somberness of *Measure for Measure* makes it a tragedy. The earlier play undoubtedly adheres to the familiar formulas of dramatic comedy, however grudgingly it may seem to do so.

Perhaps Shakespeare abandoned comedy simply because he thought he had exhausted its potential as far as his particular talent was concerned. It is a restrictive genre, after all, binding the author to certain well-established protocols, and, as Northrop Frye remarks, it "has been remarkably tenacious of its structural principles and character types." Frye goes on to remind us of G. B. Shaw's only half-joking remark that "a comic artist could get a reputation for daring originality by stealing his method from Molière and his characters from Dickens: if we were to read Menander and Aristophanes for Molière and Dickens the statement would be hardly less true, at least as a general principle."[1] It is possible to speculate on the basis of *Measure for Measure* that Shakespeare was

From *Studies in English Literature 1500–1900* 30 (1990). © 1990 by William Marsh Rice University.

simply becoming impatient with comedy. Of the three projected marriages that mark its conclusion two amount to judicial sentences for the male characters, a point Lucio drives home by protesting, "Marrying a punk, my lord, is pressing to death, whipping, and hanging" (V.i.522–23), while the third is so unexpected that the Duke's proposal apparently strikes the heroine dumb. Certainly no one, not even those who find no problems with this problem play, would fault the finale of *Measure for Measure* on grounds of excessive festivity.

Indeed, if we assume what seems to be the case, that romantic comedy is in some sense always about the arousal, shaping, and subsequent containing of the sexual passions by including them within the social institution of marriage, then *Measure for Measure* begins to look like a signal failure, an extension of comic form beyond an arena where it can produce plausible resolution.[2] Part of the problem, as has been often noted (recently with a distinct psychoanalytic twist), is that the play seems to offer no hope of mediating between pure and unbridled lust on the one hand and an absolute and equally uncompromising abstinence on the other.[3] The play makes it difficult to imagine what the earlier comedies apparently take for granted, that a man and a woman in a relationship of physical intimacy may and should have feelings of what we would now call "affection" for one another, feelings that prompt an attitude of mutual cherishing rather than the kind of crude gratification-on-the-run that seems to shadow sexual encounter in the play. Indeed, the word "affection" in itself raises the problem, for though it could mean in Shakespeare's English (and had meant as far back as the Middle English of Wyclif and Chaucer) very much what it means to us, it is regularly used in *Measure for Measure* in the now obsolete sense of "unbridled lust," as in Angelo's "by the affection that now guides me most" (II.iv.168). Every time the word appears in this sense we are reminded that the world of the play provides no real occasion for its gentler alternative.

There can be little wonder, then, that *Measure for Measure* has come to be classed as a "dark comedy" or "problem play," and surely one of the most important ways in which the sense of the problematic has changed since F.S. Boas introduced the latter term in 1898 is to be found in a shift of focus from the thematic to the generic.[4] If criticism is no longer quite so preoccupied with the way *Measure for Measure* addresses the difficulties of governing, for instance, difficulties that are of undoubted pragmatic relevance to the political tangles of our own world, it remains fascinated by, if always somewhat unsure about, certain formal and psychological matters, the peculiar tensions, for instance, generated by a play that looks like a comedy and yet feels at every step far more like a tragedy. As Northrop Frye has elsewhere put the matter, "The 'problem' comedies anticipate the romances more clearly than Shakespeare's other earlier comedies, and *Measure for Measure*, in particular, anticipates them in the way that it contains, instead of simply avoiding, a tragic action."[5] Frye's distinction is undoubtedly important, for the mere containment or forestalling of a tragic movement is a very long way from the imposition of a thoroughgoing comic vision with its promise of a harmony that will remain stable beyond the boundaries of the action in which it has been achieved. A tragedy contained suggests a tragedy kept for the moment at bay, no more. It is the strength or weakness of *Measure for Measure* (depending on point of view) to leave us pondering deeply whatever reservations we may harbor about the "happily ever after" formula—reservations that the romantic comedies encourage us to put aside.

I

No one can doubt that a staple of comic writing since the inception of the genre has been the reversal of intention or purpose by powers which elude the control of the individual. The hilarity in the fifth act of *A Midsummer Night's Dream*, for instance, is in great measure owing to the fact that all the artisans' attempts to secure solemn dignity for their play have the happy result of producing quite the opposite. But the very possibility of tragedy veering around into comedy in this manner suggests the reverse effect: comedy can just as well veer into tragedy, and if arriving at just the thing you have strenuously tried to avoid is indubitably funny in the case of the artisans' tragedy-as-comedy in *A Midsummer Night's Dream*, it is as well to remember that encountering a fate you thought you were fleeing is a central element of tragic stories from Sophocles' *Oedipus the King* to Chaucer's *The Pardoner's Tale* and onward through premodern and modern novels such as Hardy's *The Mayor of Casterbridge* and O'Hara's *Appointment in Samarra*. Whether we find such reversals terrifying or merely funny seems to depend on how and to what degree their consequences are contained. A bungled stage play, particularly when it is embedded in a larger one that has all the marks of technical mastery, is scarcely threatening. But a man who flees what he takes to be his native city precisely to avoid the fate of murdering his father and marrying his mother, only to end up carrying out both unspeakable acts anyway, must make us wonder to what extent any of us is in control of his life and destiny. In the fate of Oedipus the voice of the Other in the form of the Delphic Oracle has the final word.[6]

Perceptions from within *Measure for Measure* of the way purposes reverse themselves prove to be pervasively of a tragic order. "Merely, thou art death's fool," the disguised Duke tells the condemned Claudio, "For him thou labor'st by thy flight to shun, / And yet run'st toward him still" (III.i.11–13). Claudio himself has earlier confessed to a sense of inevitable reversal, of desires reverting to their opposites, in a speech which, even by the standards of *Measure for Measure*, is remarkable for its pessimism:

> As surfeit is the father of much fast,
> So every scope by the immoderate use
> Turns to restraint. Our natures do pursue,

Like rats that ravin down their proper bane,
A thirsty evil, and when we drink we die.
(I.ii.126–30)

And in both *All's Well That Ends Well* and *Measure for Measure* the device of the
bed trick has the oedipal effect of throwing the central male character into the
embrace of the very woman he has spent all his energies trying to avoid.

The hero's unwitting return to the one embrace he has shunned before all
others suggests a disturbing analogy to the Duke's observation about the
inevitably thwarted attempt to avoid death: the men of Shakespeare's final
comedies do tend to see women as an overmastering threat to their identities,
and the sexual disgust widely recognized in these plays may have its source in a
characteristically male fear of being subsumed in the feminine, along with a
related fear of procreation, shared in some degree by both sexes, a fear, in effect,
of creating the generation that will replace the current one.[7] As Lavatch in *All's
Well* remarks in a mock rueful way of Bertram's flight from his marriage with
Helena, "The danger is in standing to't; that's the loss of men, though it be the
getting of children" (III.ii.41–42).

The clown's remark with its bawdy punning suggests the antagonism
between generations in particularly clear form. The getting of children is, simply,
the loss of men; men create further life only at the expense of their own. In the
late comedies the perennial Elizabethan pun on the verb "to die" in the sense of
"to achieve orgasm," a pun that is treated in a playfully lighthearted way in
Rosalind's meditations on love in the fourth act of *As You Like It*, for instance, is
pushed far in the direction of a literal equivalence. It is perhaps no accident that
in *Measure for Measure* that same equivalence is writ large in the Viennese law
making fornication a capital crime. We have come a very long way, it would
seem, from the joyful anticipation of marriage and sexual intimacy in the earlier
comedies to arrive at something that anticipates far more the bloody inter-
generational conflicts of the mature tragedies, the child untimely ripped from the
womb at the expense of the mother's life (*Macbeth*, V.viii.15–16),[8] or the filial
ingratitude that is "sharper than a serpent's tooth" (*King Lear*, I.iv.288). Such
conflicts will be resolved, and even then not until they are played out and worked
through, only in the late romances, the last plays Shakespeare would write. Only
there can a father call a long lost daughter "Thou that beget'st him that did thee
beget" (*Pericles*, V.i.195).

The avoidance or denial of sexuality is a recurrent theme in *Measure for
Measure*, sounded most obviously in the fiercely repressed Angelo and the chaste
Isabella, but present as well in the Duke's denial that "the dribbling dart of love"
can pierce his "complete bosom" (I.iii.2–3). Indeed, the topography of the play is
given as a series of withdrawn enclaves—Angelo's study (ironically superseded by
his walled garden towards the middle of the play), Isabella's convent, Mariana's
"moated grange," the Duke's cherished privacy (Lucio calls him "the old

fantastical Duke of dark corners" [IV.iii.156–57]), all summed up perhaps in the prison in which much of the action takes place. Into these sequestered spaces the principal figures have retreated, apparently out of fear or disappointment or insecurity, only emerging in the face of threat or duress, and then only with a reluctance that bespeaks a kind of fragility of the self, a constructed identity that can only be precariously maintained in the rarefied atmosphere of an unthreatening solitude. It is no accident that in this play the timid Isabella, in the course of pleading with Angelo for her brother's life, speaks of man's "glassy essence" (II.ii.120) and of women as being as frail "as the glasses where they view themselves, / Which are as easy broke as they make forms" (II.iv.125–26).

Isabella's complicated and in some ways puzzling figure seems uneasily to skirt thoughts of sexuality and procreation. Mirrors ("glasses") "make forms" in reflecting images; women make forms in creating children, and it is surely significant that in Isabella's hesitant figure the idea of making forms is linked with the idea of brittle fragility. "Women? Help heaven!" she goes on to exclaim, "men their creation mar / In profiting by them" (lines 127–28). The antecedent of the possessive "their" is perhaps intentionally blurred, since we can understand Isabella to say either (or both) of two distinct but interrelated things. Men mar their own creation in taking sexual advantage of women, a sex whose representatives created them in the first place; a man's sexuality is a sin against his origin. But men mar women's creation, that is, they destroy women's being, in doing the sexual deed that will engender further life. But the protest taken in either way elides the necessary fact of sexuality in the creation of human life, the anterior sexual act on which the existence of either man or woman depends. There is in Isabella's difficult language a skittish avoidance of the topic, as there has been throughout her strangely oblique interview with Angelo, a kind of denial of the body as it is implicated in human life.

A related recoil from the flesh and its consequences is to be found in Angelo's language, even when it is at its most formal and forensic. Here, for instance, is Angelo on the bad effects of permissiveness:

> The law hath not been dead, though it hath slept.
> Those many had not dar'd to do that evil
> If the first that did th' edict infringe
> Had answer'd for his deed. Now 'tis awake,
> Takes note of what is done, and like a prophet
> Looks in a glass that shows what future evils,
> Either now, or by remissness new conceived,
> And so in progress to be hatch'd and born,
> Are now to have no successive degrees,
> But here they live, to end.
>
> (II.ii.90–99)

It is an indication of the maturity of Shakespeare's imagination in *Measure for Measure* that Angelo never quite functions as a straw man. Indeed, his arguments, including this one about deterrence, have point and weight, they suggest tenable positions, they are not to be dismissed as conscious or hypocritical dissembling. And yet the peculiar imagery of Angelo's speech here, so suggestive of procreation ("conceived," "hatch'd," "born"), can make us wonder whether what he is really taking aim at is not so much acts of fornication as their consequences, the generation that will replace him and thus seal forever the fact of his own creaturely mortality. There can be little wonder then that Angelo pursues sexual misdemeanors with such stringency, when every such act can only remind him of the process of generation, the impersonal cycle of birth and death that spells the obliteration of the individual.

Indeed, it is possible to think of Angelo's edgy defensiveness as resting on a kind of unconscious pseudo-logic involving the substitution of effect for cause and cause for effect. If we begin with the premise that we are sexual creatures because we are mortal, that is, we are given the capacity to reproduce ourselves precisely because none of us can live forever, then it is compelling (though entirely fallacious from the point of view of logic) to invert the premise and conclude that we are mortal creatures because we are sexual. From here it is not far (via another fallacy known as denying the antecedent) to the conclusion that if we are not sexual creatures we will not die. The rigorous suppression of sexuality, in oneself as well as others, comes to seem of the first importance to a man like Angelo, precisely because it becomes a means of warding off oblivion.

It must be clear that when we touch such matters we have passed far beyond the kind of delusion typical of male figures in the earlier romantic comedies. Angelo anticipates such tragic figures as Macbeth far more than he reminds us of Orlando or Orsino, because he shares with the hero of the Scottish play an intransigent unwillingness to contemplate a world that will continue without him.[9] But just as clearly, the circumscribed comic structure of *Measure for Measure* precludes the extremity of full-blown tragedy. It would be futile to insist that the play really is a tragedy in the face of the Duke's return in the fifth act and the controls he there imposes. And yet it seems equally futile to insist on any very satisfying sense of atonement or reconciliation arising out of the elaborate maneuvers of the finale. If Angelo is resigned to anything, it is to the fact of his own death, and not in the ideally philosophical sense, where consciousness of eventual mortality makes life a thing to be cherished, but in a mood very close to defeated despair, reminiscent of the condemned Claudio's remark to the Friar-Duke after his explosive interview with his sister: "I am so out of love with life that I will sue to be rid of it" (III.i.171–72). Angelo's marriage does not reconcile him to life, as his last, astonishing, words in the play indicate:

> I am sorry that such sorrow I procure,
> And so deep sticks it in my penitent heart

> That I crave death more willingly than mercy:
> 'Tis my deserving, and I do entreat it.
>   (V.i.474–77)

These may well be the words of a man who, having failed to deny death absolutely, embraces with equal fervor the opposite extreme. If he cannot live forever, he will die now, as if to retain some measure of control by willing the instant of his demise.[10]

To see Angelo from the vantage of his own mortality is at once to call in question the abstract, formal, even disinterested character of his pronouncements on law and transgression. But it is also to see the genuine pathos of his situation, where nineteenth-century critics like William Hazlitt could only protest what they understood as his cold-blooded hypocrisy. There is much in *Measure for Measure* to suggest that Angelo does not simply experience an abrupt change of heart and then go craftily to work to compass his evil will. For one thing, his steely control prior to the eruption of his passion for Isabella suggests not so much stability as the presence of chaotic forces unacknowledged by the conscious mind and kept forcefully at bay. There is a touch of desperation even early on in his first interview with Isabella:

> Be you content, fair maid,
> It is the law, not I, condemn your brother.
> Were he my kinsman, brother, or my son,
> It should be thus with him: he must die to-morrow.
>   (II.ii.79–82)

The preference for impersonal and hypothetical constructions is striking ("it is," "it should be," "he must"), here and throughout this same scene.[11] We have just heard Angelo say of Claudio, "He's sentenced; 'tis too late" (line 55), and, "Your brother is a forfeit of the law" (line 71), locutions that suggest that Angelo is at least struggling to think of himself as the mere conductor of an impersonal process, the operator of a machine that once set in motion will irrevocably pursue its destructive course.

But no code of law is really a set of instructions from which we can simply read off decisions and procedures.[12] Codified law requires interpretation—that is why in Shakespeare's time, as in ours, there were and are courts and judges. And to understand matters otherwise is badly to confuse the law with justice itself, an unacceptable conflation that runs the risk of reducing all jurisprudence to a process rather like following a recipe in a cookbook.[13] That Angelo lacks patience with the often difficult and even painful process of interpretation is amply evidenced in his delegation of the task of discovering what affront (if any) was actually offered Elbow's wife:

This will last out a night in Russia
When nights are longest there. I'll take my leave,
And leave you to the hearing of the cause,
Hoping you'll find good cause to whip them all.

(II.i.134–37)

The edginess of his impatience, and perhaps something more as well, comes out
in the rather clumsy repetitions of this exit speech ("I'll take my leave, / And leave
you"; "the hearing of the cause, / Hoping you'll find good cause"). This is clearly
a man with no sympathy for the kind of tangles typical of law applied to often
murky social situations. His preference is for the case like Claudio's, which—so
he can persuade himself at any rate—is clear-cut.

But whatever reasons we assign to Angelo's hasty retreat from the
complexities of the Elbow imbroglio, it is clear that his drive to associate himself
with impersonal principles above the sweaty disputes of ordinary men has a
defensive character and is an example of the strategy of denying by embracing
the opposite, a strategy characteristic of reaction-formation.[14] Such a man is not
merely, at least in any very simple sense, the puritan he seems to others and
perhaps himself, for he is in fact in headlong flight from the raging sensualist he
fears he may be. His view of the self is characteristically absolutist and extreme.
Either he is a rigid puritan or a creature of lust: there can be no middle ground.
And when the dam bursts, as it does in Angelo's case when he is suddenly smitten
by Isabella, his worst fears about what he takes to be his true nature seem
horribly confirmed.

In a character as complex as Angelo we may expect to find defensive
systems of extraordinary complexity as well. What we have considered so far may
be summed up as Angelo's means of retreating from his sensual nature, from the
inescapably corporeal base of his existence. If this shrinking from the body were
the whole story, *Measure for Measure* might resemble a good deal more than it
actually does the earlier romantic comedies, and Angelo might seem a ripened
version of the moonstruck Orlando in *As You Like It*, whose Petrarchism is
among other things a means of keeping his lady etherealized and at a safe
distance. But Angelo's defenses contain a distinctly active and aggressive
component as well, and this in large measure explains the tragic feel of the play
that generations of critics have responded to. In the circumstances it is difficult
to believe that singling Claudio out for execution under a statute that has gone
unenforced for so many years is either quite random or a disinterested strategy
for creating a telling example. Vienna, after all, is not exactly short of obvious
violations, with its flourishing trade in prostitution and abundant supply of
dissolute young men eager to patronize it. It is true that we hear early on in
Angelo's regency of a proclamation that "All houses in the suburbs of Vienna
must be pluck'd down" (I.ii.95–96), but the bawd who reports it seems
remarkably undisturbed by it, and there is nothing further in the play to suggest

that his cynical confidence is misplaced. No, Angelo's rigor in sentencing Claudio seems as much the enactment of a private ritual as it does the performance of a public duty. It is perhaps best understood as his displaced attack on his own sexuality, a symbolic attempt to purge his own nature of the sensuality it is irrevocably saddled with. Escalus's question to Angelo concerning Elbow, "Do you hear how he misplaces?" (II.ii.88), might be profitably put concerning Angelo as well. Such misplacement reminds us of the scapegoating that is so often a part of both comedies and tragedies. And here, as usual, it is an inevitable failure: subjecting Claudio to the ultimate penalty can only restate in uncanny fashion the equation of sex and death that Angelo is attempting to deny. In Angelo's coldly precise remark to Isabella, "It is the law, not I, condemn your brother" (II.ii.80), we are perhaps justified in hearing a very different assertion: "It is the law not—I condemn your brother."[15]

II

If we understand Angelo's attitude toward the law as a failed attempt to make of it an instrument that speaks in and through him rather than a medium in which he speaks by interpreting its language, then we have in Isabella an interestingly parallel case. Her chosen text, of course, the one in which she attempts to invest herself, is not the codified civil law but Holy Writ and its derivative, the rule of the religious order she is on the point of entering as the play begins. Concerning the figure of Isabella there has been much throwing about of critical brains, with some treating her, as Lucio does, as "a thing enskied, and sainted" (I.iv.34), others seeing in her a self-righteous religiosity and a fundamental lack of human compassion.[16] The opposing positions are typical of the kind of polarities *Measure for Measure* has inspired in its students, and it is perhaps this polarizing tendency which further explains a recurrent allegorizing strain in the criticism, a stance pressing the play in the direction of religious parable, with, for instance, the Duke "automatically comparable with Divinity," Angelo "the symbol of a false intellectualized ethic divorced from the deeper springs of human instinct," and the projected wedding of the Duke and Isabella "the marriage of understanding with purity; of tolerance with moral fervour."[17]

It is not altogether easy to see what provokes readings that seem so patently wrong. But that *Measure for Measure* has often been read as a spiritual allegory may be the effect not so much of any allegorical structure in the play itself, as of the fact that its characters ceaselessly attempt to allegorize themselves and those with whom they have to deal.[18] Angelo and Isabella in particular are both desperately embroiled in attempts to evade their own human complexity by making the self the site of an abstraction. On the brink of revealing himself to Isabella, Angelo still identifies himself as "the voice of the recorded law" (II.iv.61); and in her sudden disillusionment, doubtless out of extreme fear and confusion, Isabella can identify herself with her own chastity and weigh it against the concrete human fact of her own brother, quite as if it were a personified thing of equal or greater weight: "Then, Isabel, live chaste, and, brother, die; / More than our brother is our chastity" (II.iv.184–85). And even the Duke has a strange propensity for moralized allegory, as he delivers his famous speech on life and death, for instance, and casts life as a personified addressee:

> Reason thus with life:
> If I do lose thee, I do lose a thing
> That none but fools would keep. A breath thou art,
> Servile to all the skyey influences,
> That dost this habitation where thou keep'st
> Hourly afflict.
>   (III.i.6–11)

The futility of this allegorization is indicated in the fact that the Duke grants Life no opportunity for rejoinder (the personified abstraction remains a mere addressee, not a real interlocutor). But life, at least that irreducibly concrete bit of it that bears Claudio's name, will shortly seize the opportunity denied in the first instance and rise to an eloquent plea:

> Ay, but to die, and go we know not where;
> To lie in cold obstruction, and to rot;
> This sensible warm motion to become
> A kneaded clod; and the delighted spirit
> To bathe in fiery floods, or to reside
> In thrilling region of thick-ribbed ice.
> . . . .
> Sweet sister, let me live.
>   (III.i.117–32)

All allegory properly speaking is a reminder of the Christian idea of the Incarnation. The Divine Idea descends from above and temporarily takes up residence in the humility of the flesh, accommodates itself to human understanding, and thus becomes intelligible: "And the Word became flesh and dwelt among us" (John 1:14). The process is also reminiscent of the dramatist's problem, as he writes, then produces his play: how is he to make his words become flesh, that is, impose his disembodied script with its several parts on a troupe of actors and make them body it forth satisfactorily? But just because God, the playwright, and the allegorist share the problem of making words flesh, it does not follow that all plays and *Measure for Measure* in particular are allegorical or about the Incarnation. An allegorical play and a play that dramatizes the strategy of allegorization in its characters are separate things.

That *Measure for Measure* is an example of the latter, not of the former, has been implicit in all I have argued so far.

Indeed, allegorization in Shakespeare's characters may be understood as their attempt not to make the word flesh, but to make the flesh word, to dispose of the problems our stubbornly incarnate existence, with its vagaries of desire or gusts of anger, perhaps above all with its vulnerability to pain, is constantly posing. To ascend from the plane of fleshly turmoil to a region where all is high-minded discourse and moralizing (and moralizing, incidentally, is not quite the same thing as morality)—this begins to describe the kind of activity in which Isabella is engaged. From this ideal region she can prescribe mercy freely to those who remain below without herself having in fact to dispense it:

> Why, all the souls that were were forfeit once,
> And He that might the vantage best have took
> Found out the remedy. How would you be
> If He, which is the top of judgment, should
> But judge you as you are? O, think on that,
> And mercy then will breathe within your lips,
> Like man new made.
>
> (II.ii.73–79)

Without for a moment detracting from the undeniable beauty of these lines, we can turn Isabella's impassioned question to Angelo back on herself: how would she be, if He should but judge her as she is? And her answer is implicit later in the scene, when she offers to bribe Angelo, "Not with fond sicles of the tested gold,"

> but with true prayers,
> That shall be up at heaven, and enter there
> Ere sun-rise, prayers from preserved souls,
> From fasting maids, whose minds are dedicate
> To nothing temporal.
>
> (II.ii.151–55)

Nothing is clearer than that Isabella includes herself among those "preserved souls" and "fasting maids," the efficacy of whose prayers she apparently does not doubt. Her unworldly devaluation of material things, of "tested gold, / Or stones, whose rate are either rich or poor / As fancy values them" (lines 149–51), may be an amusing display of adolescent zeal, but it also ill conceals an overvaluation of her own purity. Mercy is evidently something only less saintly people need.

Once we become attuned to Isabella's inconsistencies, we are likely to find her lofty pronouncements somewhat less edifying and, even as her situation grows extreme, gently comic. In her second interview with Angelo, as she has begun to grasp the terms of the bargain the deputy is so haltingly proposing, she remarks with fine moral distinction, if a bit primly, "Ignomy in ransom and free pardon / Are of two houses: lawful mercy / Is nothing kin to foul redemption" (II.iv.111–13). And yet a few lines later, when the personal nature of the case Angelo has been proposing has come clear, she resorts with surprising speed to a kind of blackmail:

> I will proclaim thee, Angelo, look for't!
> Sign me a present pardon for my brother,
> Or with an outstretch'd throat I'll tell the world aloud
> What man thou art.
>
> (II.iv.151–54)

It is not entirely clear that Claudio's deliverance on such terms would constitute "ignomy in ransom" and "foul redemption," but neither would it much resemble "free pardon" or "lawful mercy." This is one of those moments in *Measure for Measure* when we encounter in its timid and ethereal heroine something hard as nails.

To remark this kind of hardness at the core is not to convict Isabella of hypocrisy, but only to realize, as in the case of Angelo, that there is more to her than she is willing to admit. Living in the body (and so far no one has devised any other way to live) brings with it for Isabella, as for the rest of us, the capacity for rage, vindictiveness, fear, desire, and pain. These are not things we are likely to escape by making the flesh a mere word. And as long as it remains a matter of mere words, Isabella is a signal failure. "I'll to my brother," she says after Angelo has delivered his cruel ultimatum and departed:

> Though he hath fall'n by prompture of the blood,
> Yet hath he in him such a mind of honor
> That had he twenty heads to tender down
> On twenty bloody blocks, he'ld yield them up,
> Before his sister should her body stoop
> To such abhorr'd pollution.
>
> (II.iv.178–83)

But Claudio does not have twenty heads, he has but one, which is even now in dire danger, and which he would understandably prefer to keep. In her bland assumption about Claudio's willingness to sacrifice his life for her virginity, Isabella can hardly be imagining the scene of her brother's impending execution, the severed head, for instance, its mouth set in a rictus of agony, the trunk spurting blood, slick, wet, and all too palpable.

Isabella's failure of imagination here at the midpoint of *Measure for Measure* reminds us of the Duke's somewhat hectic scheming in the play's latter half.[19]

For the plot he attempts to impose on the world of Vienna encounters its own difficulties in the always problematic passage from word to flesh. The magnificent Barnardine, for instance, "insensible of mortality, and desperately mortal" (IV.ii.145), not surprisingly has profound reservations about the Duke's plan to substitute his head for Claudio's; and the Provost's description of him as a "man that apprehends death no more dreadfully but as a drunken sleep" (IV.ii.142–43) throws an ironic light backward on the Duke's attempt to reconcile Claudio to his own death: "Thy best of rest is sleep, / And that thou oft provok'st, yet grossly fear'st / Thy death, which is no more" (III.i.17–19). The very necessity of substituting one head for another is brought about by the Duke's prior failure to anticipate the possibility that Angelo might renege on his bargain with Isabella and execute Claudio anyway. What finally bails the play out is not the cunning of the Duke's scheme, but an utterly fortuitous event, the death of Ragozine, an event which the Duke greets with obvious relief, if a little lamely: "O, 'tis 'an accident that heaven provides?" (IV.iii.77).

This pervasive refusal of the flesh to acquiesce in the imagination's plots and compacts may or may not reflect the playwright's puzzlement in the face of this very problematic play. Yet one thing is clear: if the attempt to make the flesh word is an evasion and the attempt to make the word flesh largely a failure, there is another sense of making the flesh word that is crucial. For language as we use it begins in the body, it is articulated by the body's means, and, as it arises from the flesh, it must first speak of the flesh. Justice and mercy are not finally abstractions, mere forms of words resulting in the homily on forgiveness Isabella reads off to Angelo in II.ii. They are not the work of the mind merely, for they involve, in a way the play makes terribly concrete, the body as well—Isabella's body, Angelo's, the Duke's. And while we must reject the attempt to make *Measure for Measure* yield up a univocal message about justice and mercy neatly reconcilable with the Gospels (or any other text), we can say that it continually returns to the idea of incarnation (but not to the Incarnation), to the word made flesh and the flesh made word, to the body not as a philosophical abstraction but in all its organic bluntness. As Claudio says in words that themselves seek to mitigate what has passed between himself and Juliet, "The stealth of our most mutual entertainment / With characters too gross is writ on Juliet" (I.ii.154–55). The mute spectacle of that particular female body, great with child and standing before us as Claudio speaks these lines, is rather more eloquent finally than any of the sermons and bookish theories offered by other characters in the play.

Perhaps what Isabella has learned by the time she kneels in the final scene to beg forgiveness of the Duke for the man she still thinks has caused her brother's death is that her own body, with all its capacity to arouse and to be aroused and to suffer pain, has been, quite literally, the price of mercy in the case of the now broken bargain with Angelo:

>   Most bounteous sir:
> Look, if it please you, on this man condemn'd
> As if my brother liv'd. I partly think
> A due sincerity governed his deeds,
> Till he did look on me. Since it is so,
> Let him not die. My brother had but justice,
> In that he did the thing for which he died;
> For Angelo,
> His act did not o'ertake his bad intent,
> And must be buried but as an intent
> That perish'd by the way. Thoughts are no subjects,
> Intents but merely thoughts.
>   (V.i.443–54)

These lines have been criticized for legalistic hairsplitting as well as personal vanity. They particularly repelled Samuel Johnson.[20] But in the context of our present argument we can admit that they show an increased awareness in Isabella, and also see that this awareness is one of a very few things the Duke's elaborate scheming actually accomplishes. What it may have accomplished for Angelo himself is impossible to say in the face of his silence at the end. And how Isabella herself may feel about the Duke's abrupt proposal of marriage we cannot know for the same reason. Whatever its small victories, *Measure for Measure* still suggests Shakespeare's fast ebbing faith in the ability of comic scheming to produce real solutions for the social malaise.

NOTES

1. Northrop Frye, *Anatomy of Criticism* (Princeton: Princeton Univ. Press, 1957), p. 163.

2. This is roughly the view of Anne Barton in her excellent introduction to the play in *The Riverside Shakespeare*, ed. G. Blakemore Evans, et al. (Boston: Houghton Mifflin, 1974), pp. 545–49. All quotations from Shakespeare's works are taken from this edition.

3. For a brilliant recent account of *Measure for Measure* richly informed by psychoanalytic lore, see Richard P. Wheeler's chapter on the play in *Shakespeare's Development and the Problem Comedies: Turn and Counter-Turn* (Berkeley: Univ. of California Press, 1981). Wheeler's argument draws largely on Freud's three essays on the psychology of love, "A Special Type of Choice of Object Made By Men" (1910), "On the Universal Tendency to Debasement in the Sphere of Love" (1912), and "The Taboo of Virginity" (1918). See *The Standard Edition of the Complete Psychological Works of Sigmund Freud*, ed. James Strachey, trans. James Strachey et al., 24 vols. (London: Hogarth Press and the Institute of Psychoanalysis, 1953–1974), 11:163–208. This edition is hereafter cited as S.E.

4. So Arthur Kirsch summarizes the shift, before going on to call in question the problematics of the problem comedies. See *Shakespeare and the Experience of Love* (Cambridge: Cambridge Univ. Press, 1981), p. 71.

5. Northrop Frye, *The Myth of Deliverance: Reflections on Shakespeare's Problem Comedies* (Toronto: Univ. of Toronto Press, 1983), p. 32.

6. On the Delphic Oracle as Lacanian voice of the Other, see the fifth chapter of Shoshana Felman's *Jacques Lacan and the Adventure of Insight: Psychoanalysis in Contemporary Culture* (Cambridge, MA: Harvard Univ. Press, 1987).

7. For a particularly cogent presentation of this view, see David Sundelson's chapter on *Measure for Measure* in *Shakespeare's Restorations of the Father* (New Brunswick: Rutgers Univ. Press, 1983).

8. On the motif of the Caesarian birth in the tragedies, in which giving the child life entails the death of the parent, see Robert N. Watson, *Shakespeare and the Hazards of Ambition* (Cambridge, MA: Harvard Univ. Press, 1984).

9. For an extended and very sensitive account of Macbeth's war on the generations, see James L. Calderwood, *If It Were Done: Macbeth and Tragic Action* (Amherst: Univ. of Massachusetts Press, 1986).

10. Terry Eagleton puts the matter succinctly: "The suicide and the martyr look alike, but are in fact opposites: the one throws away his life because he judges it worthless, the other surrenders his most valuable possession. The martyr becomes something by actively embracing nothing; the suicide simply substitutes one negativity for another. Though death finally erases all measure and distinction, you must cling provisionally to those values while you live, just as mercy ultimately undercuts the tit for tat of justice but must not be permitted to undo those mutualities completely." See Terry Eagleton, *William Shakespeare* (Oxford: Basil Blackwell, 1986), pp. 54–55.

11. For an illuminating account of rhetoric and ideology in the play, see David Aers and Gunther Kress, "The Politics of Style: Discourses of Law and Authority in *Measure for Measure*," *Style* 16, 1 (Winter 1982): 22–37.

12. This general point is made well by Terry Eagleton in his discussion of the play. See his *William Shakespeare*, pp. 48–57.

13. For evidence, however, that the formulaic approach had some sanction in contemporary legal theory, see Harold Skulsky, "Pain, Law, and Conscience in *Measure for Measure*," *JHI* 25, 2 (April–June 1964): 147–68.

14. For a brief account of reaction-formation see Freud's "Character and Anal Erotism" (1908), S.E. 9:169–75.

15. The more so because "condemn" agrees grammatically with "I," not with "the law." The punctuation of the 1623 Folio, reproduced in the Riverside text, suggests that "condemn" is certainly governed by "the law." The misagreement is doubtless the result of "attraction," so common in Shakespeare's English.

16. For a tempered example of the former view, see R.W. Chambers's chapter on *Measure for Measure* in *Man's Unconquerable Mind* (London: Jonathan Cape, 1939); for an example of the latter, Ernest Schanzer's chapter on the play in *The Problem Plays of Shakespeare* (New York: Schocken Books, 1963). The pertinent passages from both books are conveniently excerpted in *Twentieth Century Interpretations of Measure for Measure*, ed. George L. Geckle (Englewood Cliffs: Prentice-Hall, 1970), pp. 106–11.

17. The phrases in quotation marks are taken from G. Wilson Knight's essay "*Measure for Measure* and the Gospels," in *The Wheel of Fire* (1930; rpt. London: Methuen, 1967), pp. 82, 89, 95. For a truly extreme allegorized version of the play, see Roy W. Battenhouse, "*Measure for Measure* and Christian Doctrine of the Atonement," *PMLA* 61, 3 (September 1946): 1029–59.

18. A point recently touched on by Alexander Leggatt in "Substitution in *Measure for Measure*," *SQ* 39, 3 (Autumn 1988): 342–59.

19. Many have noticed that this play seems to break apart at its center. With the Duke's intervention in the explosive interview of Isabella and Claudio at III.i.351 we enter a new dramatic phase, executive rather than contemplative and plotty rather than conversational. The shift is sometimes denied by those who would smooth out the problematic knots in the play. See, for instance, Darryl J. Gless, *Measure for Measure, the Law, and the Convent* (Princeton: Princeton Univ. Press, 1979).

20. "From what extenuation of his crime can Isabel, who yet supposes her brother dead, form any plea in his favour. 'Since he was good 'till he looked on me, let him not die.' I am afraid our varlet poet intended to inculcate, that women think ill of nothing that raises the credit of their beauty, and are ready, however virtuous, to pardon any act which they think incited by their own charms." *The Yale Edition of the Works of Samuel Johnson*, 15 vols. (New Haven: Yale Univ. Press, 1958–78), vol. 7, *Johnson on Shakespeare*, ed. Arthur Sherbo, p. 213.

GRAHAM BRADSHAW

Dramatic Intentions
in Othello

OBEYING THE TIME

Although it is factitious and distracting, the theory or myth of "double time" is still respectfully trundled out in every modern scholarly edition of *Othello*, even the most recent.[22] It has been as long lived as Nahum Tate's adaptation of *King Lear*, which held the stage for a century and a half, and, like that adaptation, it deserves to be firmly laid to rest. It betrays its bad nineteenth-century provenance in three different (though related) ways. First, it expects Shakespearean poetic drama to repay an approach that (as C. P. Sanger's examination of the handling of the time scheme in *Wuthering Heights* memorably showed) is more appropriate to mid-nineteenth-century novels; this, as Jane Adamson crisply put it, leads "our attention away from Othello's obsession, towards the kind of details that might obsess an Inspector from Scotland Yard."[23] Second, it is bardolatrous, and offends against what Richard Levin has called the "undiscussed principle of Knowing When to Give Up."[24] For the theory describes and depends on what is unashamedly called a trick, a device usually seen as an occasion for bardolatrous rejoicing, except by a few scrupulous critics like Bradley and Emrys Jones. Finally, the theory cannot be separated from that nineteenth-century tendency which found its glorious apotheosis in Verdi's *Othello*. Othello is the "Noble" Moor, Desdemona is beatified, Iago is demonized—and, in the opera, even sings a satanic "Credo." There is then no need for a drastically compressed time scheme, and indeed Verdi's lovers, like

From *Misrepresentations: Shakespeare and the Materialists*. © 1993 by Cornell University.

Cinthio's in the Italian source story, have been married for some time: here Arrigo Boito, Verdi's brilliant librettist and collaborator in *Otello* and *Falstaff*, might just as well have claimed of *Otello* what he claimed of *Falstaff*—that he had returned the Shakespearean play to its native Italian source.[25] *Otello* is a work of genius, and the "double-time" scheme a product of misguided bardolatrous ingenuity; but neither makes sense of (more bluntly, the nineteenth century couldn't make sense of) the dramatic and psychological effect of Shakespeare's purposefully drastic compression of the loose, indefinite "romance" time in the Italian novella.

As Emrys Jones emphasizes in *Scenic Form in Shakespeare*,[26] it is important not to confuse "double time" with accelerated time, which is theatrically indispensable, commonplace, and usually untroubling. So, for example, nearly five hours of "stage" time and less than a minute of "real" time pass between that moment in 2.2 when we hear the Herald proclaim "full libertie of Feasting from this present houre of five," and our hearing Iago observe in 2.3 that "'tis not yet ten o'th'clock." What follows in 2.3 is more remarkable, since the first night in Cyprus passes during this scene; Jones pertinently compares this with *Richard III*, 5.3, which takes us through the night before the battle of Bosworth. So, by the time the scene ends, the triumphant Iago can tell Roderigo that

> Thou know'st we worke by Wit, and not by Witchcraft
> And Wit depends on dilatory time,

and exclaim, with self-congratulatory cheerfulness:

> Introth 'tis Morning;
> Pleasure, and Action, make the houres seeme short.
> (2.3.362–63, 368–69)

Indeed this is exuberantly and unnervingly witty: the surrogate dramatist who has produced chaos in this scene, and whose reference to "Witchcraft" gleefully recalls his earlier triumph over Brabantio, seems here to be sharing a professional joke with the real dramatist, whose own skill in managing this scene's accelerated time has helped to "make the houres seeme short."

The third act follows in similarly precipitate fashion. When Iago encounters Cassio again in 3.1 he asks, "You have not bin a-bed then?" and Cassio reminds him that "the day had broke before we parted"; Emilia then enters, telling Cassio (and us) that the "Generall and his wife are talking" of Cassio's disgrace—not were, but "are," talking of it, now. Although Emilia has heard enough of this conversation to be able to assure Cassio that Desdemona "speakes for you stoutly," while Othello "protests" that he "needs no other Suitor, but his likings" to reinstate Cassio after a prudent interval, Cassio determines to stay for "some breefe Discourse" with Desdemona "alone." The brief glimpse of Othello in 3.2 shows him already busy with the day's work: the letters for the Senate have already been written, and he sets off to inspect the "Fortification." By now the play is half over, without its being at all obvious that this is a play—the play—about "adultery" and "jealousy."

Throughout this first half of the play the only indeterminate period of time is that taken up by the voyage to Cyprus, when (it is emphasized) Othello and Desdemona are in different ships. This carefully managed compression of the Italian story's time scheme maximizes tension and the continuity between the scenes is a theatrically impressive way, but it also ensures—takes pains to ensure—that the newly married lovers have so little time together. When Othello leads Desdemona off to bed some hours after their arrival in Cyprus (and immediately after telling Cassio to report the next morning at his "earliest" convenience) he confirms that the marriage still has not been consummated:

> Come my deere Love,
> The purchase made, the fruites are to ensue,
> That profit's yet to come 'tweene me, and you.
> (2.3.10–12)

The stage direction for Iago's entrance follows these lines, leaving open the possibility that he arrives on stage just in time to hear Othello's words and perhaps register some malignantly interested response. Be that as it may, his next words show that Iago is well aware that the marriage still hasn't been consummated, and he immediately insinuates, in his busy, tirelessly malicious way, that Othello is neglecting his official duties.

> 'tis not yet ten o'th'clocke. Our Generall cast us thus earely for the love of his *Desdemona*: Who, let us not therefore blame; he hath not yet made wanton the night with her. (2.3.13–16)

Learning that the marriage still hasn't been consummated is, for the audience, a confirmation rather than a surprise—precisely because Shakespeare's handling of time has been both careful and suggestive, constantly bringing home how little time these lovers are allowed together. In the second scene they were interrupted by Iago's warning that Brabantio's posse is on its way. Then, after Desdemona's bold affirmation, in the Senate scene, that she would not be "bereft" of the "Rites," it was determined that the newlyweds would leave that night, in different ships; as Othello tells Desdemona, he has

> but an houre
> Of Love, of worldly matter, and direction
> To spend with thee. We must obey the time.
> (1.3.329–31)

And of course in 2.3 they are disturbed once again, by the riot that Iago engineers; after quelling the riot Othello goes off to dress Montano's wounds, while Desdemona goes back to bed. Indeed, the accelerated time in 2.3 makes it impossible to know how much time the lovers have together before they are disturbed; although critics assume that the marriage is consummated, it is not clear whether the consummation happens before or after the riot, or not at all.

I return to this point later, but advocates of the "double-time" theory are more concerned that Desdemona hasn't had time to sleep with Cassio. So, the "difficulty" that—as the New Arden editor puts it—threatens to make "nonsense" of the "dramatic action" is that, within the play's "short time," there is no time in which "adultery" could have occurred. Nobody doubts that (as Frank Kermode assures us in the Riverside edition) Shakespeare "is clearly aware" of this difficulty.[27] But we are to suppose that, having taken such pains to get into it, Shakespeare "resolved" it not by a real extension, or loosening, of the stage time, like that in the second half of *The Merchant of Venice*, but by what the New Arden editor, M. R. Ridley, describes as a craftily engineered "trick": "What Shakespeare is doing is to present, before our eyes, an unbroken series of events happening in 'short time', but to present them against a background, of events not presented but implied, which gives the needed impression of 'long time'" (lxx). Instead of feeling uneasy about a play that must resort to a trick "to make the whole progress of the plot credible" (lxix), the excited Ridley affirms that this "throws light on Shakespeare's astonishing skill and judgment as a practical craftsman.... He knew to a fraction of an inch how far he could go in playing a trick upon his audience, and the measure of his success is precisely the unawareness of the audience in the theatre that any trick is being played" (lxx). Dover Wilson similarly invites us to discover and marvel over "yet another piece of dramatic legerdemain, the most audacious in the whole canon, which has come to be known as Double Time."[28]

One strange feature of this argument appears in that question-begging emphasis on a needful "impression": since "short time" is also, and no less, an "impression" or dramatic illusion, it is hard to see what could prevent the one "impression" jarring against the other. Moreover, although having an "impression" of "long time" is thought to be wonderfully helpful where Desdemona's (alleged) relationship with Cassio is concerned, it wouldn't be at all helpful to any spectator who then began wondering about Desdemona's (actual) relationship with her husband. What would they be talking about? Where would Othello sleep for however many nights are in question? I hasten to add that I don't for one moment think we do ask such questions, in reading or watching Shakespeare's play. But then *Othello* is constantly making us think, whereas the presumed point of creating the "impression" of "long time" is to prevent thought.

Another general difficulty is that the "trick" can work only if we first notice, but then don't *think* about, the various alleged "instances" and "indications" of an "illusory" period of "long time."[29] Here the argument becomes alarmingly circular, and also depends on an elaborate but confidently predictive set of assumptions about what our old, dim friend—the Audience as Monolithic Entity: that fabulous beast with many bodies but a single, unimpressive mind—can be relied upon to notice or not to notice. Evidently, we *don't* reflect, when reading or watching *Othello*, that there has been no time for Desdemona to commit adultery. But then, it's assumed, we *would* notice this, or would have noticed it, were it not for all those craftily planted "indications" of an illusory period of "long time." This in turn assumes that we will notice, and be tricked by, the "indications" of "long time." Finally, this magic circle closes with the further assurance, or assumption, that we *won't* also notice and reflect on the discrepancy between the "short time" of the stage action and the illusory "impression" of "long time." Noticing this discrepancy would of course expose the very "difficulty" that the "trick" is to prevent us noticing—along with other new difficulties that, we shall see, the "trick" introduces. But later, as a kind of reward, we are also being invited to notice, and marvel at, this "legerdemain" as a supreme instance of Shakespearean art. Part of the theory's appeal is that of our feeling superior—of our being initiated into a bardolatrous inner circle that knows how the trick works and is (as Catherine Earnshaw might say, but all this is very nineteenth century) incomparably above and beyond that dumb uncomprehending block, the Audience.

Something is evidently wrong, but how much is wrong in Shakespeare's play? To take one of the "instances," it is apparent—on reflection, if not in the theater—that Lodovico's arrival in Cyprus in Act 4 is implausibly rapid, and involves the sort of discrepancy which diligent editors are quite properly expected to spot, and try to account for. As the very diligent New Arden editor observes, "the government of Venice can hardly be supposed to recall Othello till there has been time for the report of the Turkish disaster to reach them and for them to send the order for recall" (lxx). Here is a case where we might readily agree that Shakespeare has nodded. Perhaps he failed to notice the lapse; perhaps he noticed it but saw that nothing was to be done, since he could hardly postpone the play's climax for however many days would suffice to forestall such a literal-minded objection. We cannot know either way; more to the point, we have little reason to care. As long as we do regard it as an instance of nodding—of Shakespeare failing to notice what few members of his audience would notice— it is not difficult to account for as a loose end or unwanted consequence of Shakespeare's drastic compression of the Italian story's indeterminate but extended time scheme. However, it is a quite different matter to suppose that this is, as the New Arden editor tells us, a "very clear instance" of the conscious, deliberate, and wonderfully crafty way in which the Bard tricks us by including various "indications" of an illusory period of "long time." Nor could we suppose that the trick works in this "very clear instance" unless we believe what seems inherently unlikely: that the dim but sturdily reliable Audience (which, if we gave it a shape and form, might resemble Orwell's Boxer) could be counted upon to take in the "indication," though without thinking any more about it.

Let us try another, instructively different "instance." Beady-eyed sleuths have assumed that Bianca's complaint about Cassio's week-long absence (3.4.173) must refer to a period of time spent in Cyprus.

> Bianca.   'Save you (Friend *Cassio*).
> Cassio.   What make you from home?
>   How is't with you, my most faire *Bianca*?
>   Indeed (sweet Love) I was comming to your house.
> Bianca.   And I was going to your Lodging, *Cassio*.
>   What? keepe a weeke away? Seven dayes, and Nights?
>   Eight score eight houres? And Lovers absent houres
>   More tedious then the Diall, eight score times?
>   Oh weary reck'ning.
> Cassio.   Pardon me, *Bianca*:
>   I have this while with leaden thoughts beene prest,
>   But I shall in a more continuate time
>   Strike off this score of absence.
>
> (3.4.168–79)

I have quoted so much of this dreadfully undistinguished exchange because I don't want to be accused of special pleading: Cassio must live in army lodgings and Bianca clearly can't, but it's easy to see how the references to her "house" and his "Lodging" made "double-time" sleuths pounce—supposing that the week in question has passed in Cyprus, and that Cassio's fumbled excuse for his week-long absence refers back to his catastrophe on the first night in Cyprus. Nonetheless, this must be wrong. If we do take Bianca's reference to a week-long absence as another "indication" of "long time," then a moment's reflection is enough to suggest that the long time in question must be real, not "illusory," while the period of time spent in Cyprus must then be considerably longer than a week—since it is also being assumed that the liaison between Cassio and Bianca has run its whole course in Cyprus. We see the New Arden editor assuming this (without reflecting further) when he observes that, although there is "no doubt" that Iago's reference to Bianca as a "Huswife, that by selling her desires / Buyes her selfe Bread, and Cloath" (4.1.94–95) gives "Huswife" its bawdy sense, meaning that Bianca is a courtesan, "there is also little doubt that Bianca is also a housewife in the normal sense, a citizen of Cyprus, with her own house, and not a mere camp-follower" (141). Norman Sanders hedges on this point in the New Cambridge edition, saying that "there is no clear evidence in the play for or against the idea that Cassio knew Bianca before he landed in Cyprus" (189). But again a moment's reflection suggests what more is "clear," for if the relationship was going on before the journey to Cyprus, there is no need to take Bianca's reference to a week-long absence as an "indication" of "long time." Moreover, the alternative—supposing that they have been in Cyprus for more than a week—produces a quite horrendous difficulty, since the business with the handkerchief in 4.1 is so important within the main action. Nobody can suppose that 4.1 is taking place on the second day in Cyprus and more than a week after the arrival in Cyprus. Iago acquires the handkerchief in 3.3, and that scene clearly takes place on the first morning in Cyprus. In the latter part of 3.4 Cassio enters (with Iago) and gives Bianca the handkerchief he has just found in his "lodging"; in scene 4.1, she angrily returns it, having examined it and found it impossible to "take out." Time passes between and during these successive scenes, but how much time? Pressing Ridley's argument to its logical conclusion would mean having to suppose that in the handkerchief scene we have that impression of "short time" which the stage action establishes, and a cunningly contrived "impression" of an illusory period of "long time," and a logically inescapable impression of nonillusory "long time."

The "double-time" theory cannot resolve this difficulty, since the theory is what has produced it. Nor can I believe that any spectator or reader who was not already distracted by the theory, and peering excitedly round every textual corner for "evidence" to support it, could suppose that Bianca's complaint shows that a week has passed in Cyprus without also feeling some disturbance and dissatisfaction. Yet the difficulty dissolves if we forget the theory and stay with the "short time." If the meetings between Cassio and Bianca in Acts 3 and 4 take place later, on the second day in Cyprus, Bianca's complaint about a week-long absence then confirms that she was already Cassio's mistress in Venice—where he was already avoiding her, since he likes sleeping with her but has no intention of marrying her. The doting, determined Bianca has followed him to Cyprus, provoking Cassio's complacent complaint to Iago that she "haunts me in every place" (4.1.132): she is a camp-follower in this literal sense, while he, like Mann's Felix Krull, understands that since he is irresistible he should try to make some allowances.

It is not easy to believe that in inventing the Cassio–Bianca liaison Shakespeare never considered when and where it starts. If we suppose that it starts in Cyprus, this produces far more problems than the only alternative, which is to stay with the "short time." But then that also helps with two textual cruces that have led editors who are loyal to the nonsense about "double time" to pronounce Shakespeare "careless" in his handling of Cassio. They are another part of the mess the myth of "double time" has made.

We know from Othello's first speech to the Senators that he has spent the last nine months in Venice and found this first experience of civilian life enervating:

> since these Armes of mine, had seven yeares pith,
> Till now, some nine Moones wasted, they have us'd

> Their deerest action, in the Tented Field.
>
> (1.3.83–85)

We also know that during this period Cassio has been with Othello, who *prefers* him to Iago not only as his chosen lieutenant, but also as the close, trusted friend who frequently accompanied him in his secret wooing and knew of Othello's love "from first to last" (3.3–97). The obvious need for discretion in that case explains Cassio's circumspection in the play's second scene when he pretends not even to know whom Othello might have married, and asks Iago, "To who?" (1.2.53). Similarly, keeping to the "short time" yields a consistent explanation of that other much debated "crux" which is so often said to show that Shakespeare is careless or that the text needs emendation: Iago's apparently, knowing but mysterious joke about Cassio being "A Fellow almost damn'd in a faire Wife" (1.1.18) seems mysterious and is knowing because Iago already knows what we cannot yet know.[30] Cassio is "almost damn'd in a faire Wife" because, although he wants nothing more than a sexually convenient liaison with the "very faire Bianca," she is determined to marry him—and because, for Iago, to be almost married is to be almost damned.

Iago clearly knows about the Cassio–Bianca relationship and its difficulties in 4.1, when we hear him planning to make use of that knowledge:

> Now will I question *Cassio* of *Bianca*,
> A Huswife, that by selling her desires
> Buyes her selfe Bread, and Cloath. It is a Creature
> That dotes on Cassio, (as 'tis the Strumpets plague
> To be-guile many, and be be-guil'd by one)
> He, when he heares of her, cannot restraine
> From the excesse of Laughter.
>
> (4.1.93–97)

Unless we have been distracted by the "double-time" theory, it is also clear that whatever Iago knows about this liaison in 4.1, on the second day in Cyprus, must also have been known to him in the play's first scene, which takes place only hours before Iago and Cassio set off (again in different ships) for Cyprus. But the New Arden and New Cambridge editors have been distracted by the theory. Ridley explains in his long note on "A Fellow almost damn'd in a faire Wife" that this cannot allude to Cassio's liaison with Bianca, since at this "moment he has not met her" (4); similarly Barbara Everett refers to Iago's cynical joke and supposes that it cannot refer to "Cassio's future affair with the whore, Bianca" (209). And in the New Cambridge edition Norman Sanders recycles the idea that both Iago's remark and the way in which Cassio "appears to be completely ignorant of Othello's interest in Desdemona" in 1.2 are "inconsistencies" that make the character of Cassio "something of a puzzle" (189, 16).

I think this wrong but had better confront the objection that the kind of explanation I offer is embarrassingly like the argument for "double time," which hangs on an elaborate and implausible tapestry of assumptions about what an audience would or would not notice in performance. I think there is an important difference.

Certainly, no spectator watching the play for the first time could know that Cassio has reason to be discreet when he asks, "To who?". Edwin Booth's recommendation[31] that the actor playing Cassio should signal circumspection— letting on that there is something Cassio isn't letting on—is fussy and dramatically unhelpful: even if we noticed and stored the signal, we couldn't make sense of it until the revelations in 3.3, and any such signaling would threaten to make Cassio seem the kind of friend who couldn't be trusted to keep a confidence. Similarly, nobody watching the play for the first time and hearing Iago describe Cassio as "almost damn'd in a faire Wife" could know about the liaison with Bianca and its difficulties. Shakespeare is giving Iago and Cassio lines that are consistent with their characters and situation, but the first-time spectator or reader is in no position to see how.

In other words, this kind of explanation is peculiar because it addresses a peculiar kind of "problem": the problem is just as remote as its solution from theatrical experience. No spectator would see the "inconsistency" in Cassio's question or start trembling before a "crux." As for Iago's joke, since it is ambiguously phrased, a spectator might feel uncertain how to take it, or might just mistake it, supposing that Cassio must be married and, for some reason, badly matched. The play has only just begun, Cassio has only just been mentioned, and we know nothing about Bianca. We are only beginning to put things together and make sense of what is before us: in a significant sense we expect to understand, and have no reason to suspect that our information may be contradictory. In both cases the "problem" or "crux" appears only when we are studying the text closely and, as it were, reading and thinking forward and backward—or when we are reading the text in a modern scholarly edition and letting our eye be dragged down to the ballast of notes beneath the precious ribbon of Shakespearean matter. As that ribbon thins, we know that scrupulous editors have discovered a difficulty that we had better attend to, now, if we want to be sure we won't forget its existence; but unfortunately, because editors are usually more concerned with the play as text than with the text as play, they rarely point out (or notice) when a difficulty that the text throws out and that has exercised generations of editors isn't apparent in performance. The "problem" is there in the text but, like its explanation, cannot be a part of our initial dramatic experience.

This peculiar kind of problem is best considered as a question about dramatic intention. Shakespeare clearly was in a unique situation to be thinking backward and forward, and wouldn't have given Cassio his question or Iago that joke unless he thought the lines meant something when he wrote them.

Shakespeare wrote quickly, and on the whole rather well, but he could write badly, as in that slovenly verse exchange between Cassio and Bianca; he could fail to notice some problems that are there in the text and there in the play, like Lady Macbeth's giving suck or Jessica's account of conversations between Shylock and Tubal which could only have taken place after her elopement; he could be negligent about minor matters and characters, like Lodovico's implausibly rapid arrival in Cyprus. But such things aren't as surprising as it would be if, after taking pains to compress his time scheme and keep Othello and Desdemona apart, Shakespeare had carelessly given them an extra week or two in Cyprus without considering what they might do there, or talk about. As for Cassio and Bianca, Shakespeare is perfunctory about filling in the background of their relationship. Ibsen once remarked that he liked to work everything out "down to the last button" before beginning to write; Shakespeare doesn't attend to buttons so closely, but there is an important difference between not working things out and not making them clear. That an explanation is available within the play's "short time" suggests that in this case—as indeed with Iago's joke—the perfunctoriness is that of a dramatist who is writing rapidly and with a very sure sense of his characters and their situations, but hasn't paused to consider whether what is clear to him might seem less than clear to an audience. Once we comb through the text, putting together scattered references and weighing alternative possibilities, the text shows why the Cassio–Bianca relationship must have been going on during the same nine-month period as Othello's secret wooing. To say this is not to suppose that Othello's specific reference to "nine Moones" would be noticed and remembered by every attentive spectator: the theater is not a court or classroom, and we might well pay more attention to the information that this was his first experience of civilian life than to his specification of the precise period of time in question. The point is rather that we would expect, and can confirm, that Shakespeare thought carefully about what important matters need to have taken place before his play starts.

But now we can observe what is most strange about that basic assumption on which the "double-time" theory rests. It is always taken for granted that there is a "difficulty" that, as Dover Wilson proudly observes, "might well have seemed insuperable to any ordinary dramatist": "For, if Othello and Desdemona consummated their marriage during the first night in Cyprus, when could she have committed the adultery that Iago charges her with?" (Preface, New Shakespeare *Othello*, xxxii). This is true only if we are using the word "adultery" in a strict, legalistic sense, but what warrant does the play provide for supposing that Othello is concerned only with what might have happened *after* his marriage? The answer is, none.

Early in 3.3, the ever-vigilant Iago hears Desdemona protest to Othello that she should not have "so much to do" in pleading on behalf of that very friend who

came a wooing with you? and so many a time
(When I have spoke of you dispraisingly)
Hath tane your part.

(3.3.71–73)

This is news to Iago, and once he is alone with Othello he can launch his first direct assault by concentrating on that very question to which Desdemona has just provided the answer:

Iago.	Did *Michael Cassio*
	When you woo'd my Lady, know of your love?
Othello.	He did, from first to last: Why dost thou aske?
Iago.	But for a satisfaction of my Thought,
	No further harme.
Othello.	What of thy thought, *Iago*?
Iago.	I did not thinke he had bin acquainted with hir.
Othello.	O yes, and went betweene us very oft.
Iago.	Indeed?
Othello.	Indeed? I indeed. Discern'st thou aught in that?
	Is he not honest?
Iago.	Honest, my Lord?
Othello.	Honest? I, Honest.
Iago.	My Lord, for ought I know.
Othello.	What do'st thou thinke?
Iago.	Thinke, my Lord?
Othello.	Thinke, my Lord? Alas, thou ecchos't me;
	As if there were some Monster in thy thought
	Too hideous to be shewne.

(3.3.94–108)

In exploiting what Desdemona revealed, Iago must tread very carefully: if the marriage was consummated hours before, Othello is likely to know whether his wife was a virgin. Throughout this first stage of the assault, what is in question is not the absurd suggestion that Desdemona has committed adultery with Cassio since her wedding, in what would indeed be "stolen hours"; Iago's insinuation, as he feels his way forward, is that something took place *before* the wedding, something that can be expected to continue and that would explain Desdemona's passionate concern to have Cassio reinstated—and we see the "Monster" emerging in Othello's own mind as he begins to discern what is in question. Similarly, when Iago later promises Othello that he will persuade Cassio to "tell the Tale anew; / Where, how, how oft, how long ago, and when / He hath, and is againe to tope your wife" (4.1.85–86), this is not another "indication" of "long time," as editors tell us: Iago is once again conjuring up that nightmare of a promiscuous liaison which began when Cassio was the trusted friend who "very oft" went between the lovers. Part of this nightmare of betrayal is familiar; the situation in the *Sonnets* is not as irrelevant as Dover Wilson supposes.[32]

In other words there is no "difficulty" that requires a "needful impression" of "long time." Not only does the theory of "double time" not work, or work to ruinous effect; it is redundant. At this point, and with these various objections to the theory in mind, it is worth quickly running through those other alleged "indications" of "long time" which are conveniently (and confidently) set out in the New Arden introduction and notes. The first two "instances," involving references to the handkerchief, are perhaps the most troubling, but suggest negligence rather than the carefully laid foundation for the edifice of double time. The others are no more compelling than the "very clear instance" of Lodovico's premature arrival (really an instance of Shakespeare nodding) or of Cassio's week-long absence from Bianca (which makes good sense in the play's "short time," and produces nightmarish complications if taken as evidence of "long time"):

> (1) 3.3.296 [Iago's asking Emilia to steal the handkerchief's "a hundred times"]. There is no reason to suppose that Iago had not often seen it, in Othello's possession or in Desdemona's when, in her girlish way, she kisses and talks to it (3.3.295).

> (2) 3.3.313 ["so often did you bid me steale"]. Ditto; and, as Ridley himself observes, this "might have been on voyage."

> (3) 3.3.344–48 [Othello on "stolne houres of Lust" which "harm'd not me"]. Othello's speech is rapid and excited, but makes better sense in relation to the lengthy period before the marriage. His reference to "the next night" need not refer to the first night in Cyprus, unless we refuse to suppose that Othello could have kissed Desdemona before marriage.
> (4) 3.3.419 ["I lay with Cassio lately"]. That is, in Venice, where (as Iago now knows) Cassio was "very oft" alone with Desdemona; the "foregone conclusion" Othello tormentedly imagines would have preceded the marriage.

> (5) 3.4.97 ["I nev'r saw this before"]. Desdemona (who has been pursued by other suitors) is simply saying that she has never before seen any sign that Othello is prone to jealousy.

> (6) 4.1.50–51 [the "second Fit" of "Epilepsie"]. This is the first such fit; Iago is lying when he says it is the second, in order to get rid of Cassio. Any direct confrontation between Othello and Cassio could

be catastrophic, so he improvises cleverly, assuring the concerned Cassio that this has happened before and that he knows what to do.

(7) 4.1.85–86 [Iago's promise to make Cassio "tell the Tale anew"]. Iago is speaking of the whole period from the wooing to the present—and into the future.

(8) 4.1.132 ["I was the other day talking on the Sea-banke with certaine Venetians"]. The conversation took place in Venice; ironically, Ridley finds in "Sea-banke" a "suggestion of something raised above sea—level"—which might in turn have suggested Venice if Ridley were not so sure that Bianca is a Cypriot.

(9) 4.1.274 [Iago's "what I have seene and knowne"]. It is quite arbitrary to take this as an indication of "long time."

(10) 4.2.23 ["she'le kneele, and pray: I have seene her do't"]. Othello's remark makes perfectly good sense if he has only seen her kneel and pray once, on their first night in Cyprus.

(11) 4.2.1–10 [dialogue between Emilia and Othello]. This is compatible with "short time"; Emilia was with Desdemona and Cassio, at the beginning of 3.3.

(12) 5.2.213 ["a thousand times committed"]. Othello is speaking wildly, not attempting a sober calculation of what sexual feats a young hot-blooded Florentine might manage; still, the exaggeration is less grotesque if the period in question includes the months (up to nine) of the wooing.

To dismiss this horribly long-lived idea that the play depends upon a trick to make its action credible is a critical relief, but it is historically disquieting—unless we can also see why the theory has had so long a life. Here, rather than simply dismiss it as groundless, we should notice how it is grounded on that willingness to generalize about the audience as a monolithic entity which has now resurfaced in the "new" historicism and on a corresponding *interpretative* assumption about Jacobean attitudes which emerges very clearly in Dover Wilson's New Shakespeare edition: "An accusation of premarital incontinence would not have served either [Iago's] purpose or Shakespeare's, since adultery was required to make Othello a cuckold, and it is the dishonourable stigma of cuckoldry that maddens Othello once his confidence has gone and, we may add, greatly increased the excitement for a Jacobean audience" (xxxii). This of course raises fundamental questions about what Shakespeare's play is "about," but

Dover Wilson tells us: in "its simplest terms, ... the tragedy of *Othello* represents the destruction of a sublime love between two noble spirits through the intrigues of a villain devilish in his cunning and unscrupulousness" (xxx). These terms are indeed "simple," not least because they preserve the Coleridgean assumption that murdering Desdemona would have been all right, or at least compatible with being very noble, if only she had committed adultery.

"We must obey the time," Othello tells his bride: the "rites" she so eagerly awaits must wait. But here, too, critics who are obedient to the myth of "double time" get into further difficulties. As I observed earlier, there is nothing in 2.3 to tell us—and the accelerated time makes it more than ever difficult to guess— whether the marriage is consummated before the riot, or after it, or not at all. The established assumption is that it is consummated, and some readings—like Stephen Greenblatt's in his immensely influential *Renaissance Self-Fashioning*— fall apart if we think that it isn't.

Here it seems worth recording how my own experience ran counter to what critics and editors assume we "naturally" assume. Having seen the play twice as a schoolboy before I ever read it, having then read it several times before I "studied" it and consulted critics, I had always supposed that the marriage wasn't consummated. I still thought that in a 1979 article in which I referred to the murder as this marriage's "poetic consummation," giving that word "poetic" the unfairly cruel sense it has in talk of "poetic justice."[33] That was unguarded— my assuming what is by no means an inevitable reading—and I found myself prompted to a more systematic consideration in 1983, when T. G. A. Nelson and Charles Haines published an article titled "Othello's Unconsummated Marriage."[34] The authors carefully explored the question of whether the marriage is consummated, and concluded that it isn't. Since they were also arguing that Othello's behavior is the result of unbearable sexual frustration, their reading was diametrically opposed to Greenblatt's, though similarly reductive. Setting that aside, their textual arguments for thinking that the marriage is not consummated were unprecedentedly thorough, but open to three objections.

The first may well seem the most important to readers who assume that consummation takes place in 2.3. Nelson and Haines are confusing "stage" time with "real" time when they say that "Othello and Desdemona have hardly gone to bed when a brawl begins (4), and that when Othello does, "in the end, get back to bed" (after going off with the seriously injured Montano to tend his wounds), "there is, indeed, nothing left of the night" (5). Later, Desdemona's touchingly innocent assumption that the "pain" on Othello's forehead is caused by "watching" (3.3.289) confirms that Othello has spent much of the night looking after Montano, but doesn't tell us how much. In other words, Nelson and Haines don't reckon with the complications caused by accelerated time, which is not to be confused with double time. The second objection is prompted by what these critics say of the scene between the clown and the musicians at the start of Act 3.

Most critics ignore this scene; Nelson and Haines argue, picking up some suggestions of Lawrence Ross and Linda Boose,[35] that its dramatic "point" is to signal that the serenade is "ill-timed, for the event it is intended to celebrate has not yet taken place" (6). Unfortunately, the persuasive argument that the incompetently executed serenade becomes a badly timed, inadvertently mocking charivari is shackled to a far from persuasive argument about Othello's "impotence" and "temporary failure of virility" (17). The third objection, which seems to me the most important, also shows how the textual argument is weakened by the critics' interpretative assumptions. Like Leavis and Greenblatt, Nelson and Haines offer a psychologically reductive account of Othello as a "case." Because they are so sure *how* the failure to consummate the marriage matters, they aren't sufficiently concerned to specify *when* it most clearly matters, as the play unfolds, and don't see why the references to sheets are even more significant than they suppose.

The wedding sheets evidently matter very much to Desdemona in 4.2—either because she has already lost her virginity on them or because she still hasn't and still wants to. "Prythee," she carefully instructs Emilia, "Lay on my bed my wedding sheetes, remember" (4.2.105). And when Emilia returns in the next scene to assure Desdemona that she has "laid those Sheetes you bad me on the bed," she receives this unnerving reply:

All's one: good Father, how foolish are our minds?
If I do die before, prythee shrow'd me
In one of these same Sheetes.

(4.3.23–25)

And in the penultimate scene the idea of bloodied sheets is inflaming Othello's mind, as he determines, "Thy Bed, lust-stain'd, shall with Lusts blood bee spotted" (5.1.36). But is he thinking of the *wedding* sheets?

Here, if anywhere, is a "difficulty" that threatens to make "nonsense" of the "dramatic action"—or, since an interpretative choice is in question, of all those readings which depend upon the assumption that the marriage is consummated. To take the most extreme but influential case, Greenblatt's reading altogether depends upon his assumption that on the first night in Cyprus—which was "perhaps" Othello's only experience of "marital sexuality"—Othello "took" Desdemona's "virginity," "shed her blood," and then not only noticed but became violently obsessed by the condition of the wedding sheets.[36] Greenblatt doesn't notice the difficulty in this reading, because his sampling of the text is so partial, and because in offering his curious explanation of why the sheets matter so much to Othello he never explains, or asks, why they also matter so much to Desdemona. Part of the difficulty, put bluntly and indelicately, is that of understanding why, if Desdemona is no longer a virgin, she should want lust-stained sheets relaid. (Doubtless there is someone, somewhere, who believes that she wants to confront her husband with ocular proof of her chastity, so that it is a great pity when Othello decides to put out the light.) The other part of the difficulty is that of understanding what kind of mental defective could first take his wife's virginity and then, the morning after, become convinced of her continued infidelity. Here Greenblatt's reading seems to need—or, if it is not to become risible, depend upon—the "double-time" theory, a need that his "perhaps" discreetly acknowledges. Yet that theory cannot help here, since 3.3 clearly takes place the morning after the first night in Cyprus, and not even the most convinced advocates of "long time" suppose that Othello and Desdemona make love between 3.3 and the murder. In other words, if the marriage isn't consummated on that first night in Cyprus, it isn't consummated at all; here the "double-time" theory merely blurs the textual and dramatic issues.

Were it not for those dramatically prominent references to the sheets, the question whether this marriage has been consummated—whether Othello and Desdemona had slept together once, like Romeo and Juliet, or not at all—wouldn't matter in the same way. It might still occur to us to wonder how Othello could entertain the idea of Desdemona's infidelity if, as Greenblatt supposes, he so recently took her virginity and "shed her blood"; but such a worry would still be, as it were, dispersed through the latter half of the play. The references to the sheets—not to mention a strawberry-spotted handkerchief—are what make this worry immediately pressing and alarmingly definite. Another difficulty appears, as soon as we ask what on earth Shakespeare is up to. For it seems inconceivable that, in so drastically compressing the Italian novella's time scheme, making Othello and Desdemona newly married lovers, and then taking such pains to keep them physically apart, Shakespeare never considered whether this marriage was consummated. If we are to think that it is, Shakespeare should have been no less anxious than Iago that Othello shouldn't consider (and that the audience shouldn't notice Othello failing to consider) any physical evidence of Desdemona's virginity—especially in an age when it was not uncommon, after nuptials, to display the bloodied wedding sheets or a blood-spotted napkin.[37]

By now we might feel relieved that the textual evidence of whether the marriage is or is not consummated in 2.3 is so uncertain. For if we think the received idea that it is consummated throws out too many problems, we are free to prefer the alternative reading. Desdemona wants the sheets to be relaid because she is still a virgin, and still poignantly longs for "such observancie / As fits the Bridall" (3.4.147–48). When Othello determines that "Thy Bed lust-stain'd, shall with Lusts blood bee spotted" he is tormenting himself with the deluded thought of what somebody else has done: as Montaigne might say, another bed, other sheets. Virginity, like a life, can only be taken once: in Othello's diseased, self-tormenting imagination all that remains for him to do—the only way in which *he* can "shed her blood"—is bloody murder.

That tragicomic irony is horrible enough, but the final scene then gives it a still more dreadful visit. Just as Desdemona could not bring herself to say the word "whore" in 4.2, Othello tells the "chaste Starres" that he cannot "name" the "Cause," but will not—after all—"shed her blood" (5.2.2–3): "Yet Ile not shed her blood.... Yet she must dye." That tangle of yets shows that what he is talking about—what he has not changed his mind about—is not whether to kill her, but how; it also shows how this latest resolution is still insanely ensnarled with his obsessive sense of what he has never done and thinks he can never do—and what his still-virginal bride still hopes he will do, as she lies waiting for him on those relaid, unspotted wedding sheets. The murder is indeed this marriage's only consummation, and the ghastly tragicomic parody of an erotic "death."

> *Desdemona.* And yet I feare you: for you're fatall then
>   When your eyes rowle so. Why I should feare, I know not,
>   Since guiltinesse I know not: But yet I feele I feare.
> *Othello.* Thinke on thy sinnes.
> *Desdemona.*   They are Loves I beare to you.
> *Othello.* I, and for that thou dy'st.
> *Desdemona.* That death's unnaturall, that kils for loving.
>   Alas, why gnaw you so your nether-lip?
>   Some bloody passion shakes your very Frame.
>
>   (5.2.36–44)

The "Light" is finally "put out"; in that way, but only in that way, Desdemona's "Rose" is "pluck'd." I find myself wanting to ask not only Greenblatt but every critic who thinks Othello took Desdemona's virginity not long before, on this bed and these relaid sheets, how they understood Othello's wrenching words when he realizes what he has done and bends over what is now a corpse:

>   Cold, cold, my Girle?
> Even like thy Chastity.

Indeed he has never "shed her blood": that final sniffing and snuffing has indeed been his only "possession of this Heavenly sight." And that culminating tragicomic irony, perhaps the most horrible in drama, is indeed as "grim as hell."

FASHIONING *OTHELLO*

A work of art is worked, or fashioned; it isn't "out there" in the way the solar system and seas are, since it didn't precede human activity. What is absorbingly suggestive about Shakespeare's departures from Cinthio's story is that they show how he works to complicate our responses to Othello, and even Desdemona. Indeed that is the general effect and tendency of Shakespeare's dramatic perspectivism, but *Othello* is also a special case. There is no other play that so depends on rival interpretations and the destructive power of misconstructions and strong misreadings: they torment Othello in the play's second half, but they disturb the reader or spectator long before; nor does it seem implausible to suppose that they issued from or answered to some moral and imaginative disturbance in the dramatist—some compellingly creative tension between skepticism and magnanimity.

I want first to examine a series of departures from the Italian story which tend to prompt or be compatible with a magnanimous view of Othello, like that of Coleridge or Bradley; and then to examine another series of changes that tend to prompt, or be compatible with, some more unsparingly diagnostic view. The word *series* seems justified, since in each case the changes in question are intricately connected.

In the Italian story the Cassio-figure is married, while the Iago-figure is the father of a three-year-old infant. For us, it's not easy to imagine Iago as a daddy, but then Shakespeare's imagination had to work in the reverse direction, turning that daddy into his Iago while seeing why his Cassio should be a bachelor and ladies' man. In each case the critical decision about what not to do was inseparable from the creative decision about what to do instead. Doubtless, to speak of decisions is too summary as a way of representing a process of creative solicitation and divination; but the decisions that were made are our best, and usually our only, means of access to that gestatory process. I have already taken issue with the familiar charge that Shakespeare was "careless" with Cassio; it would be surprising if he hadn't thought carefully about Cassio, since he makes Cassio so much more important than his counterpart in the Italian story. In the first half of the play—up to 3.3, and using the New Cambridge edition's lineation—Cassio has 155 lines to Desdemona's 58, and is on stage for 791 lines against her 298.

Of course such tallies are a crude indication of relative importance: in 2.1, the scene at the harbor, Desdemona has 29 lines and is on stage for 123, while Cassio has 51 lines and is on stage for 163, but these ratios don't mean that she makes a weaker dramatic impression. But then Cassio is dramatically, and structurally, prominent. In this first half of the play we follow his fortunes from his new appointment to his disgrace, which prefigures Othello's devastating collapse while also providing a cautionary comparison, since Cassio is not a black outsider but a handsome young Florentine—*da noi*, or, as a Shakespearean Marlow might say, "one of us." This does not save him from Iago or the shaming, Circe-like transformation—"To be now a sensible man, by and by a Foole, and presently a Beast" (2.3.305–106). The engineering of Cassio's downfall—within minutes of our seeing him at his most attractive—tests Iago's malign skills more than manipulating Brabantio and Roderigo does, and it is also an essential preparation for the coming assault on Othello: as we watch Cassio with Desdemona at the harbor we also see Iago watching, registering the possibilities of a strong misreading, and immediately testing his "interpretation" on Roderigo in an impromptu rehearsal. Nonetheless, that most critics deal with Cassio very perfunctorily suggests a want of proportion either in the play or in critical accounts of the play. Since the distribution of interest in a Shakespearean drama is not usually so strange, this might seem one aspect of a larger problem: if Othello is to be regarded as a play about love and jealousy it would seem to follow that—as H. A. Mason argues in *Shakespeare's Tragedies of Loves*[38]—it lacks effective *données*. But this is a case where considering what Shakespeare decided not to do helps us to understand why he chose to do something else.

One result of the decision to unmarry Cassio and unfather Iago—making the one a bachelor who has no intention of marrying, and the other a married cynic who thinks that to be almost married is to be almost damned—is to emphasize the fear or distrust of domesticity that is so often heard in this play. We hear it even in Othello's references to housewives and skillets and the *wasting* effects of nine months of civilian life. It is qualified though not eliminated by an important "but," when he confides to Iago,

> But that I love the gentle *Desdemona*,
> I would not my unhoused free condition
> Put into Circumscription, and Confine,
> For the Seas worth
>   (1.2.25–28)

This play's dramatic world is a markedly military, not to say macho, world in which (to put the matter as nicely as Purcell's sailors) soldiers regularly take a boozy short leave of their nymphs on the shore, and are (as Iago knows) ready to believe that a married general's wife may be the general's general. Even in 2.3 when the soldiers are celebrating and productions sometimes bring in townswomen, girls, and camp followers (including Bianca), the stage directions do not mention women: this appears to be a male booze-up. And this male, military world has been Othello's whole world, until his nine months in Venice.

Here another effect of the Shakespearean changes is to emphasize the isolation (and consequent vulnerability) of his own very differently conceived lovers: Othello and Desdemona are the only couple in this play's dramatic world who attempt any kind of enduring love relationship. Dover Wilson's reference to "a sublime love between two noble spirits" might remind us that nobody in the play thinks about Othello and Desdemona or love and marriage in these terms. In this important respect Emilia's attitudes resemble—or are, in Kenneth Burke's sense, "consubstantial" with[39]—her husband's. To be sure, there is a crucial difference between the husband who pronounces "not I for love and dutie" and the wife who knowingly risks and loses her life, impelled by nothing other than "love and dutie." But Emilia never thinks of Desdemona as "sublime," and regrets that she "forsooke so many Noble Matches" (4.2.124)—always seeing her as a lovably innocent, inexperienced girl whose pitiful ignorance of men and marriage led her into a grotesque and disastrous union. She regards Othello with dislike, considering him a man like other men, just as her own husband regards Desdemona as a woman like other women. Cassio *does* idealize "the divine *Desdemona*" and loves his friend and general, but in ways that never impinge on what he expects from, and brings to, a sexual relationship. Even the Duke's benign comment in the Senate scene, that Othello's tale would have won his own daughter's heart, implies a worldly view of the world and young women without suggesting that he sees this union as ideal, or as "a sublime love between two noble spirits." Within this play's dramatic world it is not Iago but the lovers who are set apart, by their own idealistic and self-committed aspirations.

Such things suggest how, for Shakespeare, thinking about what to do with Cassio, Iago, or Emilia and inventing Brabantio and Bianca was part of his thinking about Othello and Desdemona and their respective places in this "world," or poetic-dramatic ensemble, of contrasted human potentialities. Unmarrying Cassio and providing him with a mistress then allows further examples of dramatic "rhyming." Othello's secret wooing takes place in the same period as Cassio's fairly public liaison, and is apparently the more questionable in Venetian terms. Like Desdemona, Bianca loves her man enough to follow him to Cyprus, and has occasion to insist that she is "no Strumpet, but of life as honest / As you that thus abuse me" (5.1.122–23). It is a fine, thought-provoking touch that Bianca's final, furious claim to respectability must be asserted against Emilia and her very different view of men and marriage, and is heard just before "It is the Cause, it is the Cause (my Soule)." Something like Bianca's outburst is what we want to hear from Desdemona; its truth is far more questionable in Bianca's case, but is also asserted with far more vigor than Desdemona can command—as is Emilia's powerful crypto-feminist denunciation of the sexual and marital double code:

> But I do thinke it is their Husbands faults
> If Wives do fall: (Say that they slacke their duties,
> And powre our Treasures into forraigne laps;
> Or else breake out in peevish jealousies,
> Throwing restraint upon us: Or say they strike us,
> Or scant our former having in despight)
> Why we have galles: and though we have some Grace,
> Yet have we some Revenge. Let Husbands know,
> Their wives have sense like them; They see, and smell,
> And have their Palats both for sweet, and sowre,
> As Husbands have. What is it that they do,
> When they change us for others? Is it Sport?
> I thinke it is: and doth Affection breed it?
> I thinke it cloth. Is't frailty that thus erres?
> It is so too? And have not we Affections?
> Desires for Sport? and Frailty, as men have?

Then let them use us well: else let them know,
The illes we do, their illes instruct us so.

(4.3.86–103)

That speech alone might have given pause to all those male champions of
the "Noble" Moor who write as though murdering Desdemona would have been
compatible with nobility if only she had committed adultery. But then Emilia's
speech, like that most famous speech of Shylock's which it recalls, is likely to
provoke a more mixed, disturbed response if we also value Desdemona's idealistic
self-commitment and don't want to see her come round, and down, to Emilia's
embittered view of the marriage hearse. Moreover, the ensemble of characters is
a means of exploring representative attitudes to sex, the other sex, and marriage,
and if we are responding to the contrasts between three *couples*, we are more
likely to see Emilia's hostility to men as the counterpart of her husband's
misogyny. In this perspective, her attitude to "Affections" and "Desires" seems as
limited as her husband's, so that the contrast between the couples is likely to
increase our sympathy for Othello and Desdemona's vulnerably isolated attempt
at a more enduring, mutually loving relationship. However, in the Shakespearean
nexus of contrasts the three couples are also presented as two male-and-female
trios, so that Desdemona, Emilia, and Bianca make up a triad of women who all
suffer from their men and from a disquietingly representative range of male
attitudes; in this perspective, we are more likely to warm to Emilia's speech as a
perceptive crypto-feminist denunciation of a double code.

This kind of dramatic structuring is light years away from Cinthio's story.
Because it requires that Cassio (the lyric tenor in operatic terms) should be
attractive but somewhat loose—decent but not rigorously principled in *unständig*,
in Wittgenstein's exacting sense—it calls for fine, not "careless," tuning. Cassio
must now be somebody whom Othello and Desdemona could like so much,
while also being the Florentine finger-kisser whose "smiles, gestures, and light
behaviours" (4.1.102) might—just—make him capable of doing what Iago says he
has done. We see the man Othello "loves" (3.1.48) in 2.3, when Cassio
innocently deflects Iago's leerily prosaic[40] nudges and worldly winks, about
Desdemona:

Iago.	She is sport for Jove.
Cassio.	She's a most exquisite Lady.
Iago.	And Ile warrant her, full of Game.
Cassio.	Indeed shes a most fresh and delicate creature.
Iago.	What an eye she has? Methinks it sounds a parley to provocation.
Cassio.	An inviting eye: and yet me thinkes right modest.
Iago.	And when she speakes, is it not an Alarum to Love?
Cassio.	She is indeed perfection.

Iago.   Well: happinesse to their Sheetes.

                                                        (2.3.17–29)

The moral comedy in that exchange is all the more welcome and enjoyable because it momentarily defeats the vulgarly reductive Iago—but only for a while; in 4.1, when Bianca rather than Desdemona is the subject of the conversation between Iago and Cassio, we see the sniggering, vain, and ruttish young buck, whom Iago can easily lead by the nose.

Emilia's speech in 3.1 provides a convenient checklist of several important departures from the Italian story, and not only where Cassio is concerned. Although it rarely figures in critical accounts of the" play—which needs some explanation-it would be difficult to exaggerate this speech's dramatic importance:

> Goodmorrow (good Lieutenant) I am sorrie
> For your displeasure: but all will sure [Q:soon] be well.
> The Generall and his wife are talking of it,
> And she speakes for you stoutly. The Moore replies,
> That he you hurt is of great Fame in Cyprus,
> And great Affinitie: and that in wholsome Wisedome
> He might not but refuse you. But he protests he loves you
> And needs no other Suitor, but his likings
> [Q: To take the safest occasion by the front]
> To bring you in againe
>
>   (3.1.41–50)

In the Italian story the Captain draws on and wounds a soldier, but the soldier is not the ex-governor of Cyprus, there is no war, and the Captain is not drunk; his offense is far less grave, so that there is more excuse for Desdemona's plea that it is minor, *un picciolo fallo*. Shakespeare's Cyprus is a garrisoned city, under martial law, and when Shakespeare's Moor asks his new lieutenant to stand in for him as commander he even gives Cassio—his closest friend, the one man he trusted in his secret wooing—a tactful warning not to "out-sport discretion." Nonetheless Cassio gets drunk and starts a riot, while the man he seriously wounds and almost kills—for trying to keep the peace—is that very ex-governor whose services to the state were commended in the Senate scene. Cassio betrays a personal as well as a professional trust, and for the first time in the play we see Othello having to fight to keep his own self-control, or "government":

>   Now by Heaven,
> My blood begins my safer Guides to rule,
> And passion (having my best judgement collied)
> Assaies to lead the way.
>
>   (2.3.204–7)

Moreover, it's important to see how Cassio yields to Iago twice: first, in committing the offense, but then—after his paroxysm of self-blame proves too painful to sustain—in allowing Iago to persuade him that he is "too severe a Moraller" and should persuade Desdemona to intervene on his behalf. That decision involves another betrayal and gives Emilia's speech a pivotal significance: if Cassio were a more intelligently loyal friend to Othello, he would abandon his (or Iago's) plan of involving Desdemona as soon as he heard Emilia's report-and the play, or the play Iago is now staging, would stop.

As it is, Othello has every reason to emphasize to Desdemona that Cassio's offense is far more serious than she appears to realize, and to explain why "in wholsome Wisdome / He might not but refuse" to reinstate him. Indeed, Emilia's report suggests that Othello was gently, and with a tact like that shown in his earlier warning to Cassio, reminding Desdemona that she is out of her depth. But here another change has momentous consequences. In Cinthio's story Desdemona's appeals really do provide the Captain with his only hope, but in Shakespeare's play the effect of Emilia's report is to make Desdemona's subsequent appeals in 3.3 redundant, and even offensive: her husband has just told her that he "loves" Cassio, has already determined to reinstate him, and "needs no other Suitor, but his likings." Although Shakespeare has made his Moor a Christian convert much concerned with his "Soule," "government," and the need for the "safer Guides to rule," this avowal reveals the Moor as a man ready to trust his own generous impulses and disregard "wholsome Wisdome" where those he "loves" are concerned. "Noble" is a word to use very cautiously in discussing the play, but Othello's decision is noble, and provides another example of finely calibrated characterization: we see both the experienced general and the man whose "free and open Nature" appeals to the impulsively generous Desdemona.

So, another effect of Emilia's speech is to suggest how, at this crucial moment, Othello is to be the victim not only of his ensign's brilliantly malignant improvisations but also of the two people he most "loves" and trusts. Not only Cassio but Desdemona herself, who has evidently not been listening to her husband—Or rather listening but not thinking. Her own report to Cassio echoes Othello's remarks about what "wholsome Wisdome" requires, but with a troubling difference:

> Do not doubt *Cassio*
> But I will have my Lord, and you againe
> As friendly as you were ...
>   ... be you well assur'd
> He shall in strangenesse stand no farther off
> Then in a politique distance.
>   (3.3.5–7, 11–13)

Instead of pondering Othello's insistence that her own role as "Suitor" is both inappropriate and redundant, Desdemona actually encourages Cassio to believe that she is the general's general and that Cassio's reinstatement really does depend on overcoming Othello's resistance with her own eager and relentless suit:

> before Æmilia here,
> I give thee warrant of thy place. Assure thee,
> If I do vow a friendship, Ile performe it
> To the last Article. My Lord shall never rest,
> Ile watch him tame, and talke him out of patience;
> His Bed shall seeme a Schoole, his Boord a Shrift;
> Ile intermingle every thing he do's
> With *Cassio's* suit. Therefore be merry, *Cassio*,
> For thy Solicitor shall rather dye,
> Then give thy cause away.
>
> (3.3.19–28)

Most astonishing, she even invites Cassio to "stay, and heare me speake." He at least knows better than that, but we soon hear her explaining to her astonished husband why he was quite mistaken about the seriousness of Cassio's offense:

> In faith hee's penitent:
> And yet his Trespasse, in our common reason
> (Save that they say the warres must make example)
> Out of her best, is not almost a fault
> T'encurre a private checke. When shall he come?
>
> (3.3.63–67)

That tripping appeal to what "they say" is all too characteristic of her behavior in the first part of this scene.

Worse, by speaking like this in front of Iago, Desdemona provides him with the two weapons he needs. Now he learns for the first time what Cassio had carefully not revealed—that Cassio accompanied Othello on his secret wooing. Secondly, Iago can see how Desdemona's behavior is so extraordinary as to *need* some explanation; *mammering* is not characteristic of Othello, but he has every reason to be astonished by this persistence, when he has already assured her that he will reinstate Cassio after a prudent interval. The first part of this scene charts his increasing astonishment and confusion, as he makes each concession:

(1) *Desdemona.*   Good Love, call him backe.
    Othello.   Not now (sweet *Desdemon*) some other time.

Desdemona.	But shall't be shortly?
Othello.	The sooner (Sweet) for you.
	(3.3.54–57)

(2) *Desdemona.*	Trust me, I could do much.
Othello.	Prythee no more: Let him come when he will:
	I will deny thee nothing.
	(3.3.74–76)

(3) *Othello.*	I will deny thee nothing.
	Whereon, I do beseech thee, grant me this,
	To leave me but a little to my selfe.
	(3.3.83–85)

(4) *Othello.*	Excellent wretch: Perdition catch my Soule
	But I do love thee: and when I love thee not,
	Chaos is come againe.
	(3.3.90–92)

Othello's bewilderment is entirely natural, and explained by the intricately connected series of changes Shakespeare has made in departing from the Italian story. What seems harder to explain is that way in which critics tend to disregard Emilia's speech and its bearing on what follows. There is, after all, something peculiar about discussing whether or not Othello is too "easily jealous" in 3.3—the issue which Coleridge saw as central, and which virtually every critic does discuss—without considering why Othello is so vulnerable to Iago's obscene way of accounting for Desdemona's passionately importunate interventions on Cassio's behalf. Is the critical elision a consequence of that nineteenth-century tendency to beatify Desdemona, instead of seeing her as a brave and generous but very green girl? In putting that question I certainly do not want to press for some moralistic (or Rymeresque) judgment of Desdemona: a severe "moraller" might insist that she behaves *badly*,[41] but I am more inclined to say that she behaves thoughtlessly and that her want of judgment is closely related to those very qualities which make her loveable. Desdemona is virtually (or virtuously) incapable of being a severe "moraller" herself, of judging those she loves—Cassio in this instance, Othello later. The worst doubt her behavior with Cassio might prompt is whether she knows herself well enough to have chosen her husband wisely. That question must be put sooner or later—if only when we are looking at her corpse and having to listen to the murderer she exonerates claiming to be what she so much more obviously is, or was: "one that loved not wisely, but too well." Charles Lamb raised that question in his characteristically mild, ironic way, but Bradley's response was quite uncharacteristically acerbic;[42] that fervently protective reaction suggests (like the resistance to Freud's almost contemporary theories of infantile sexuality) some peculiarly intense emotional investment or need.

That, at least, is one way of accounting for the otherwise puzzling critical elision of Emilia's speech—a speech that seems all the more significant because it was invented, and figures in an intricately connected series of creatively purposeful departures from the Italian story. Shakespeare's radical replotting places Othello in a situation quite unlike that of Cinthio's Moor, and the changes in question work to increase, rather than diminish, sympathy for his own Moor; they make it easier, not more difficult, to see the play as a tragedy of idealism. Significantly, the speech of Othello's that best answers to this view— "Had it pleas'd Heaven," in 4.2—is not even mentioned by Leavis or Greenblatt; yet there is nothing in it to suggest Greenblatt's deluded Christian, and the speech itself suggests what is inadequate in Leavis's view of Othello as a deluded, self-dramatizing egotist. In the preceding scene Othello was quite incapable of speaking like this, so that the verse itself measures a recovery— perhaps partial, and precarious, but remarkable after those earlier, catastrophic collapses:

> Had it pleas'd Heaven,
> To try me with Affliction, had they rain'd
> All kinds of Sores, and Shames on my bare-head:
> Steep'd me in povertie to the very lippes,
> Given to Captivitie, me, and my utmost hopes,
> I should have found in some place of my Soule
> A drop of patience. But alas, to make me
> A fixed Figure for the time of Scorne,
> To point his slow, and moving [Q: unmoving] finger at.
>
> (4.2.47–55)

True, those who take Leavis's condemnatory view of Othello's "self dramatization" can find it in this first half of the speech: the comparison with Job's afflictions, the hint of paranoia in "they," and the self-pitying reference to his exposed, enduring "bare-head," all powerfully convey Othello's sense of himself as a noble, much-tried victim. He asserts that he could still have found a "drop of patience," but the sense of himself as a "Figure" for "Scorne" to point at is harder to bear; here too is that concern with his own (shrunken) stature that might seem to support Leavis's unsparingly hostile view of Othello as a deluded egotist—were it not that Othello immediately goes on to say that he could "beare that too." These things are not what is unendurable.

Although the speech is a great swell of pain, it is also purposive and exploratory, discounting this and then that as it moves on to locate the source of the deepest, unendurable agony. Its syntax is remarkably controlled and sustained ("Had it pleas'd Heaven ... But alas ... Yet ... But there") until the idea of rejection—"To be discarded thence"— brings an annihilating sense that the basis of his moral existence has been shattered:

> Yet could I beare that too, well, very well:
> But there where I have garnerd up my heart,
> Where either I must live, or beare no life,
> The Fountaine from the which my current runnes,
> Or else dries up: to be discarded thence,
> Or keepe it as a Cesterne, for foule Toades
> To knot and gender in. Turne thy complexion there:
> Patience, thou young and Rose-lip'd Cherubin,
> I heere looke grim as hell.
>
> (4.2.56–64)

As he confronts what he cannot "beare" his mind, syntax, and sense all break down, but not, as before, into prose. His mind now floods with an image of obscene, purposeless creation and Iago-like bestiality, and *flooded* seems the right word when we notice how the imagery pursues its own dreadful inner logic: the other liquid agonies (*raining, steeping*) could all be endured (resisted by the *drop* of patience) if only his *current* still *ran* from that *fountain*, but with the idea of being "discarded" the images smash against *dries up*, and reform into the wrenchingly gross, unhinging image of "it"—"it"!—as a foul *cistern*. "Or keepe it" is the point where the thought in this hitherto remarkably controlled speech cannot keep to its trajectory: everything breaks down, so that it isn't clear whether "I" means "I" or "Ay," or what "there" is doing in relation to "heere," or whether "Patience" addresses Desdemona or a personified virtue, or where the "Cherubin" comes from. The one thing that does seem clear in these last lines is that they register a terrifying complete collapse, and are not (as the New Arden notes suggest) "a most tiresome crux, coming at a moment when any clog on apprehension is particularly vexatious."

Since this is one of the most remarkable moments poetic drama affords, its worth reflecting on what poetic drama does and doesn't do. Imagine a father discovering his dead daughter: what does he say? Quite probably nothing—he just moans or howls. Perhaps he might manage a sentence, or some broken phrases. What he certainly won't do is speak in blank verse like Lear, or sing an aria like Rigoletto. That kind of appeal to "realism"—to what in real life we would expect to see or hear—underlies Tolstoy's complaints about Shakespeare and his reductive parody of operatic conventions in *War and Peace*, when Natasha goes to the opera: people just don't speak like that or behave like that, so why prize any art in which they do? One answer—the kind of answer we might offer if we were reading *War and Peace* with *Ulysses* fresh in our minds—is that "realism" is subject to representational conventions. A representation of mental and emotional processes is never transparent, unmediated presentation; it is always something more, or less. But then how can it be, positively, more? Here it seems helpful to consider Lear's blank verse or Rigoletto's music as a species of metaphor: it doesn't merely intensify the feeling in question because poetry and music can be intense; it allows us to *see*, as well as feel, what the character is feeling. A kind of metaphorical and exploratory charting is in question, since the drama in each case is being articulated through its verse or music. We see, for example, why Othello's agony in this crucial speech is so unlike that of Leontes, so that applying the term "jealous" to both men brings out what is insentient and vague in that Gladstone-bag notion. In real life nobody subject to these feelings would speak of "garnering" and "fountains"; and Dr. Johnson objected to the mixed metaphor. Yet no transcript or video of what somebody might really say could show so much. As I suggested in *Shakespeare's Scepticism*, that "mixed" metaphor *shows* how the "idealistic Othello first endows, or invests, Desdemona with unique significance, garnering up his heart by making her his storehouse of value; and then he sees her as the fountain or source, from which his life *derives* significance and value" (4). In this sense the metaphor charts that process of disjunction through which, once someone or something has been endowed with value, the value *appears* to be inherent in the valued and detached from the valuer. There is that "tragedy of idealism."

On the other hand, those departures from the Italian story I have so far considered are, in a sense, "plotty," or situational. They make Othello more than ever vulnerable at the beginning of 3.3, but such changes don't in themselves suggest how or why he has it *in* him to become what he becomes, and do what he does do. That question isn't ever an issue for Iago, because he takes such a reductive view of Othello, and human potentialities. The question is pressing to the extent that we take, or want to take, a less reductive and Iago-like view of Othello's nature, and human nature. If, after seeing what Othello has it in him to become, we still ask, "How *could* he?" we create, in a painful way, our own problem. Iago's insouciant answer is in his last speech—"what you know, you know"—while that intricately connected series of changes I have so far been considering stops short of suggesting any more inward answer. It is all the more striking that Shakespeare makes another series of intricately connected changes that prompt, or seem to support, a more detached and even unsparingly diagnostic view of the Noble Moor: here we see how Shakespeare works, from the first, to produce what in our century has become "the Othello debate."

As has often been remarked, the first half of *Othello* owes very little to Cinthio's story in the *Hecatommithi*. Shakespeare seems more concerned to establish how and why his lovers are profoundly unlike Cinthio's. So, in the Italian story the lovers have been married long enough for Desdemona to wonder in all seriousness whether her husband's changed behavior is the result of his having grown tired of her *after using her so much*. The Italian is as blunt as that, and, in this area, so is Cinthio's Disdemona. Shakespeare's Desdemona isn't, and couldn't be; in the not very plausible reading of Nelson and Haines she should wonder whether (or simply fail to see how) her violently frustrated husband's changed behavior is the result of never having "used" her at all. But then it is important that Cinthio's Moor is physically demonstrative, assured, and direct in his expressions of passion, and in the Italian story it is the Moor who finds the prospect of a long absence unendurable, and says so: "having to leave you behind," he affirms (in Spenser's Penguin translation), "would make me intolerable to myself; for parting from you would be like parting from my very life." Shakespeare notes that speech, but then his Moor expresses no such regrets, even though he is now a bridegroom whose marriage has not yet been consummated. Instead, it is Desdemona who pleads to accompany her husband, boldly insisting—even as she acknowledges her "downright violence"—that she did love the Moor to live with him, and would not be "bereft" of "the Rites for why I love him." Why should Shakespeare make that change—in effect, a transposition—and why should he so deliberately make his lovers a newly married, idealistic couple, whose marriage is still not consummated when they arrive in Cyprus?

They are not merely newlyweds, they have eloped, and this major departure from the Italian story is the result of another, since Shakespeare decided to make so much more of the differences in age, race, culture and color. Yet another effect of—or reason for—the drastic compression of Cinthio's indeterminate "romance" time is to ensure that both the Shakespearean lovers are, unlike Cinthio's, inexperienced idealists who are idealistic in ominously different ways. They are magnificently committed to each other without knowing each other—that is, without being allowed any time in which to live together and establish, through the continuing, reciprocal intimacies of marriage (think of the Macbeths, or Brutus and Portia) any basis for that kind of domestic familiarity and trust which is wholly unlike Grand Passion and shows itself (blessedly, dangerously) in the habit of taking the other for granted.

As for the other differences between the lovers, which make it necessary for them to woo in secret and then elope, they matter so much to Brabantio that he eventually dies of a broken heart; nor would Shakespeare have included that information in a busy final act unless he wanted spectators to think about it. Here it's worth noticing, if Shakespeare's Othello had looked as magnificent as Lawrence Olivier's Caribbean Othello, or as fine as that "negro Pullman conductor" whom the New Arden editor excitedly recalls (li), any modern father with eyes to see would have been looking to his daughter. But for Brabantio (Shakespeare's invention) the differences in age, culture, color, and race had made the danger of an alliance inconceivable. His imagination reels at the very idea that his own daughter was able,

> in spight of Nature,
> Of Yeares, of Country, Credite, every thing,

To fall in Love, with what she fear'd to look on.
(1.3.96–98)

Othello's color clearly matters more in Shakespeare's play than it did in Cinthio's story; just as clearly, it is not all that matters. Brabantio's list is comprehensive, while the violence of his syntactically contorted insistence that

> For Nature, so preposterously to erre,
> (Being not deficient, blind, or lame of sense,)
> Sans witch-craft could not.
(1.3.62–64)

measures his conviction that "every thing" made this alliance unthinkable.

Here both the liberal reminders that black is beautiful and the more or less illiberal, anxious fretting about the degree of Othello's blackness can be equally distracting. Like Brabantio and like that lady from Maryland whose conviction that Othello *must* be white is preserved in the Variorum, Coleridge also thought it "monstrous" to suppose that Desdemona could love a "veritable negro." More recently Barbara Everett has argued for a tawny, "Spanish" Moor, warning that "if we visualize Othello as black, we see him as essentially standing out from the white faces around him."[43] But Othello *should* stand out; he is *the* Moor of Venice and, although our modern responses to color and miscegenation are shaped by our concerned sense that these are familiar and troubling "issues," Brabantio has seen no "thing" like Othello. Writing from a more confidently enlightened modern standpoint, Karen Newman has argued that "in *Othello*, the black Moor and the fair Desdemona are united in a marriage which all the other characters view as unthinkable" and that "for the white male characters of the play, the black man's power resides in his sexual difference from a white male norm."[44] Yet this is simply and demonstrably untrue: Cassio doesn't think like that, any more than Montano, or Lodovico. For Brabantio, and indeed Desdemona, Othello's exotic uniqueness has been part of the appeal that had hitherto made him a welcome guest. Newman discovers a "cultural aporia" involving "the play's other marginality, femininity" but aporias are a last resort, and the fear of miscegenation that Newman presents as a discovery rather works within a more inclusive, overt, and socially intelligible nexus of attitudes which make it "unthinkable" to the senator that his young daughter could be deeply attracted to this unique and impressive man as a mate.

So, although the difference in "Yeares" rarely figures in critical accounts and doesn't matter to Desdemona, it is another thing that appalls Brabantio. Iago insists that "she must change for youth" (1.3.350), and age figures in Iago's own no less comprehensive list of "all" the things "the Moor is defective in"— including "loveliness in favor, sympathy in years, manner, and beauties" (2.1.229)—while Othello anxiously weighs this difference: "I am declin'd / Into the vale of years (yet that's not much)" (3.3.265–66). As for Desdemona, although we are not told how old she is, it seems a mistake to have her played by any actress (or boy) who couldn't play Juliet: her girlishness appears in her habit of kissing and talking to the handkerchief, in her credulous, wide-eyed responses to Othello's account in 3.4 of its magical properties ("Is't possible? ... Indeed? Is't true? ... Bless us"), in her naively uncomprehending insistence that Cassio's "Trespasse" is trifling, and in all her conversations with the sexually experienced and formidable Emilia (one cannot imagine Cintio's Disdemona responding in those ways). In commenting on the harbor scene Harley Granville-Barker observed that Othello's "if it were not to die" speech "gives us the already aging, disillusioned man" while "Desdemona, in her youthfulness, is confident for happiness"; the critical resistance that observation provoked has less to do with what the text tells us than with the habit of idealizing Desdemona and having the part performed by established actresses who are no longer girls.[45] The young, virginal Desdemona is also brave and generous, like her husband, but her life stretches before her, whereas Othello characteristically— and revealingly—thinks of his as a long "pilgrimage" that has found its goal (1.3.153).

My point here is not that these changes to Cinthio's story diminish our sympathy for the lovers or Othello, but that they are what sympathy must work against. Some visual and imaginative shock is essential, both as a measure of Desdemona's youthfully idealistic high-mindedness and to produce a kind of shaming struggle in our own responses. So, any production that wants to keep faith with the problem Shakespeare is setting his audience needs to take aim at its audience. If the play were being produced in Johannesburg, or in those cities in the American South where people tooted carhorns and danced in the streets after the assassination of Martin Luther King, the "sooty bosom" would be enough; but in more hygienic zones where that isn't enough, the play's dynamics require that he should be formidably ugly, or a disturbingly old mate for this idealistic girl who sees "Othello's visage in his mind."

Let us return to that interesting "transposition"—at that moment in the Senate scene when Desdemona, who has already taken the initiative in the wooing, now both shows and acknowledges her "downright violence" by affirming that she loved the Moor to live with him, and would not be "bereft" of the amorous "rites." Before this arrestingly bold, frankly passionate speech, Shakespeare's Moor has taken for granted—and, unlike Cinthio's Moor, simply accepted—that they must be parted for some time. After directing attention to his own remarkable qualities in a suitably lofty but somewhat stilted fashion— "agnising" the natural and prompt alacrity he finds in "hardness," which wouldn't be "natural" to most men, let alone newly married husbands—he asks merely that "my wife" should have "such accommodation and besort / As levels with her breeding." It then falls to Desdemona to show her own quite different kind of natural and prompt alacrity:

> That I [Q: did] love the Moore, to live with him,
> My downe-right violence, and storme of Fortunes,
> May trumpet to the world. My heart's subdu'd
> Even to the very quality of my Lord;
> I saw *Othello's* visage in his mind,
> And to his Honours and his valiant parts,
> Did I my soule and Fortunes consecrate.
> So that (deere Lords) if I be left behind
> A Moth of Peace, and he go to the Warre,
> The Rites for why I love him, are bereft me:
> And I a heavie interim shall support
> By his deere absence. Let me go with him.
>
>   (1.3.248–59)

Othello at once supports this request, but does so by insisting in a curiously awkward, unconsciously disparaging way that *he* begs it not

> To please the pallate of my Appetite:
> Nor to comply with heat the yong affects
> In my defunct, and proper satisfaction
>   (1.3.262–64)

that is, by insisting that *he* is not subject to those youthfully intense "affects" or affections which, as we or the senators might reflect, have led the more impulsive Desdemona to the downright violence of an elopement.

"Defunct" is a shocking word here and, although it appears both in the Folio and in the 1622 Quarto, most editors habitually adopt Theobald's emendation; but the "emendation" cannot remove that more general shock which is established through another quietly purposeful departure from Cinthio's story. The youthful, passionately idealistic Disdemona declares, "I saw *Othello's* visage in his mind," while also insisting that she desires those "Rites"; but Othello's no less idealistic insistence that his wish is "to be free, and bounteous to her minde" is associated with a series of *nots* and disparaging references to the palate of appetite, sexual heat, young "affects," corrupting disports, and wanton dullness—as well as to housewives and skillets. We understand, of course, that he is drawing a contrast between maturity and youthful passion, to emphasize that he will not neglect or "scant" the Senate's "serious and great business"; yet his speech so far exceeds that brief as to suggest how he is disposed to think of those amorous "Rites"—which Desdemona desires so frankly, and with such chastely passionate eagerness—as "light wing'd Toyes / Of feather'd Cupid." (Later, when Othello is leading Desdemona off to bed in 2.3, his mercantile imagery of *purchasing* prompts in us a similar unease: she would never talk like that.) In a deeply moving way, her mind is entirely concentrated on what she feels for the unique and particular man she loves and desires: "my Lord," to whom "My heart's subdu'd." He, in a more unwelcome attempt at mature knowingness, is thinking and speaking of sex and what it is and does to other people. After Othello's long speech, the Duke, who had responded in a warmly appreciative way to the account of a wooing in which Desdemona also took the initiative, now responds with something almost like curtness: "Be it as you shall privately determine, / Either for her stay, or going."

I am trying to give an account of some qualm, some tremor of misgiving that I think Othello's speech produces in us. Since the criticism I've read doesn't suggest that many others feel this unease, it's a relief to be able to connect it to things that Shakespeare has rejected, changed, or transposed in the Italian story—while seeing how it also bears on what is to follow. Here, when the Duke goes on to say "You must hence tonight," it is Desdemona who (in the Quarto) asks in dismay, "Tonight, my lord?" and Othello who affirms, with an enthusiasm that displays the loyal soldier rather than the lover, "With all my heart." Later, when the lovers are eventually reunited at Cyprus, Othello exclaims,

> If it were now to dye,
> 'Twere now to be most happy. For I feare,
> My Soule hath her content so absolute,
> That not another comfort like to this,
> Succeedes in unknowne Fate.
> (2.1.189–93)

These lines express a feeling both rare and familiar (I imagine many or most of us have felt something like this at some time, but not often), and so touchingly, magnificently ardent that it seems almost gross to *reflect* that this marriage has still not been consummated. Yet the earlier part of this scene has emphasized Desdemona's sexuality in various ways; here, when Othello marvels at his private and "absolute" ecstasy, it is Desdemona who pulls him back to earth and her. In a more ordinarily human but undiminishing and shareable way, her reply looks forward to *their* living and loving together:

> The Heavens forbid
> But that our Loves and Comforts should encrease
> Even as our dayes do grow.
> (2.1.193–95)

As in the Senate scene, her idealistic love for her lover's "mind" is entirely consonant with her eager anticipation of the amorous "Rites"; we might even notice how her eagerness here seems less close to her husband's feeling than to the generously vicarious pleasure with which Cassio had anticipated the lovers' reunion and consummation:

> Great Jove, *Othello* guard,
> And swell his Saile with thine owne powrefull breath,
> That he may bless this Bay with his tall Ship,
> Make loves quicke pants in *Desdemonaes* Armes,
> Give renew'd fire to our extincted Spirits.
> [Q: And bring all Cypresse comfort)
>
> (2.1.77–82)

But then that frank and forward, happily human quality in Desdemona, to which fair young Cassio is so responsive, is something that Othello seems both above and below. Again the question that might, be stirring in our minds seems coarse: what is the relation between Othello's ardently soulful intensity and those earlier, disquietingly generalized references to the palate of appetite and "Disports" which will not "corrupt, and taint my businesse"? Earlier he was speaking of sex as something remote from the "Soule"; here he is overwhelmed by a love so much of the "Soule" that he has no thought of that sexual "content" which still lies ahead. There seems to be some kind of rift, or disjunction, which again has to do with the ways in which Shakespeare has made his Moor and this marriage so unlike Cinthio's.

I assume that in the first half of this play we probably don't *want* to ask this kind of question, even when we are registering some more or less inchoate sense of difference between these idealistic lovers: we resist it, rather as Cassio resists Iago's smuttier suggestions about Desdemona being "full of Game" in 2.3. But in that case what we suppress or put down earlier resurfaces later. If we had registered something momentarily disquieting or at least unwelcome in Othello's imaginative dwelling on the "pallate" of "Appetite," wouldn't our alarm at these later lines include some shock of recognition

> I had been happy, if the generall Campe,
> Pyoners and all, had tasted her sweet Body,
> So I had nothing knowne.
>
> (3.3.345–47)

That dirty Iago-like way of thinking of Desdemona as a "sweet" body to be "tasted" confirms and goes far beyond the very worst misgiving Othello's earlier reference to the palate of appetite might have prompted, while the dirtiness is all the more shocking if we remember not only that pioneers were the lowest rank of soldier but that other Shakespearean references associate them with the work of mining and countermining: Desdemona's reified body is being gang-mined as well as "tasted."[46]

Now there is an appalling sense of filth surfacing in Othello's mind. It was rising to the surface moments before, when Othello spoke of keeping "a corner in the thing I love / For others uses" (3.3.274–75); and his first reference to a

"Toad" in that speech looks forward to the later filthiness, when the "corner" becomes a *cistern* for "foule Toades / To knot and gender in" (4.2.60–61). When the play's final scene begins we again see Othello thinking of Desdemona's body as an object and gourmet dish for the palate of appetite—contemplating and appraising that "whiter skin," which is "smooth as Monumentall Alablaster," and even bending down to "smell" her defenseless body on the relaid wedding sheets. And in that same speech the Moor, whom Shakespeare had made into a Christian convert (another significant departure from Cinthio) and who is, throughout the play, much given to making references to his "Soule," addresses his soul again— but now in a monstrously deranged way, seeing the murder itself as some heavenly mission or cause to save mankind or, rather, men: "It is the Cause, it is the Cause (my Soule) ... else shee'l betray more men." Here is the dreadful culmination of that disjunction which could be glimpsed in the first acts, but which, if we thought about it then, we probably wanted to discount or dismiss as an "uncleanly Apprehension."

So far, I have directed attention to two intricately organized series of changes to the Italian story, which appear to move in different directions—on the one hand to increase, on the other to check or complicate, our sympathetic engagement with Shakespeare's Moor. Readings that insist that the Moor is "too easily jealous" make little or nothing of the first series of changes, with its radical replotting of Othello's situation; to withhold sympathy, or deny Othello's nobility, is to be drawn toward that diminished and diminishing view of human motives and relationships which Iago represents in its most virulently reductive form. But the second series of changes makes it more than ever difficult to displace the responsibility for Othello's "Monstrous Acte" onto a demonized Iago, and to sustain a view of Othello as the "Noble Moor"—not least by showing how exactly that view corresponds with Othello's view of himself in the final scene. At first Othello insists that even though "this acte shewes most horrible and grim," that is only how it "shewes," or seems: he "did proceed upon just grounds / To this extremity," since the extremity was justified by Desdemona's own "Act of shame, a thousand times committed." Then, when Emilia's revelations explode this argument, Othello's response is to try to sever the *monstrous act* from the noble *agent*, by insisting that his "Soule and Body" were "ensnar'd" by "that demy-Divell" and that he was "one that lov'd not wisely, but too well." Hearing Othello describe himself in that way—or as "an honourable Murderer, if you will," who did nothing "in hate, but all in Honour"—should make it all the more difficult for us to take that view. It is almost a relief, or compensation, to hear the disgusted Emilia reviling him as a "murd'rous Coxcombe" and insisting on Desdemona's better claim to be considered as one that loved not wisely, but too well—or, as Emilia blisteringly puts it, one "too fond of her most filthy Bargaine." Earlier, Othello's gloating, morally bestial response to the screams of the permanently crippled and, as Othello thinks and hopes, dying Cassio similarly measured the degradation of the "Noble," even as Othello used that word:

'Tis he: O brave *Iago*, honest, and just,
That hast such Noble sense of thy Friends wrong,
Thou teachest me. Minion, youre deare lyes dead,
And your unblest Fate highes: Strumpet I come.

                                             (5.1.31–34)

Nothing "in hate, but all in Honour"?

What I have called the second series of departures from the Italian story does allow a more inward view of Othello—and an answer, or range of answers, to the question of how Othello has it in him to become what he becomes, and do what he does. But the effect of these departures is to expose and chart those disturbing features in the Shakespearean Moor which have prompted various sharply diagnostic accounts of Othello as a "case": as Leavis's deluded egotist, Greenblatt's deluded Christian, Edward Snow's deranged victim of "sexual anxiety and the male order of things,"[47] and Karen Newman's "instrument of punishment" who "enacts the moral Rymer and Cinthio point, both confirming cultural prejudice by his monstrous murder of Desdemona and punishing her desire which transgresses the norms of the Elizabethan sex/race system" ("Wash the Ethiop White," 153). Although these diagnostically knowing accounts differ in their explanatory emphases—that is, in the relative importance attached to moral, psychological or historical considerations—their effect is always estranging: they are *directionally* opposed to that investment of imaginative sympathy which characterizes the accounts of Othello offered by Coleridge, Bradley, and Dover Wilson. Here Iago enters by another route, as we see if we compare Leavis's reading with Greenblatt's and notice how neither account of Othello is an account of *Othello*.[48]

A CHOICE OF DELUSIONS

Considering how Greenblatt's account of Othello resembles Leavis's is instructive if we are concerned with how the play itself—Shakespeare's play, not the simpler play Iago is staging—frames different perspectives on its main character. Although both critics take a sharply diagnostic and reductive view of Othello and represent him as being, in the limiting sense, a "case," it might seem strange to consider Greenblatt's reading as an "anti-Othello" intervention in a familiar twentieth-century debate. First, Greenblatt shows no interest in that earlier debate, and his essay is one of his more conspicuously all-American pieces: the copious references take in the work of Altman, Martz, Spivack, Snow, Kirsch, Mack, Hyman, Bersani, Fiedler, Burke, Bloom, Barber, Cavell, Stone, and Rabkin, among others, and of a few British historians and scholars like Yates, Strong, and Thomas, but there is no suggestion that British literary critics have contributed anything to twentieth-century critical thinking about *Othello*.[49] Second, although Leavis had criticized Bradley for being preoccupied with character, his own essay is more narrowly characterological than Bradley's; here the contrast of Leavis's essay with the magnificent scope and *élan* of Greenblatt's *Renaissance Self-Fashioning* might seem decisive—until we notice how its sampling of Shakespeare's play is no less partial than Leavis's, and how neither critic attempts to integrate what he sees in Othello into any account of what the play is doing. Greenblatt's essay does indeed present an "anti-Othello" reading, but in the way his account of the "Henriad" is "anti-Henry": the old-fashioned, narrowly characterological analysis is recast in gleamingly contemporary ideological terms, so that it is something of a shock to realize that the reading still centers on a diagnostic analysis of Othello's character and what this gives Iago to "play upon."

Hence the paradoxical relation between the critics' perceptions of Othello and those of Iago, who is "nothing, if not Criticall" and provides the most savagely reductive view of Othello within the play. So, for example, that "Othello music" to which Wilson Knight warily thrilled and which prompted Bradley to consider Othello as a "poet" is for Leavis related to Othello's self-regard, while for Greenblatt "Othello's rhetorical extremism" is one of the "habitual and self-limiting forms of discourse" to which Iago is so "demonically sensitive" (*Renaissance Self-Fashioning*, 235). Whether we choose to speak (like Leavis) of self-regard, or (like Greenblatt) of self-fashioning and self-limiting, or (like Martin Elliott) of "self-publication,"[50] it is clear that all these terms refer us to something in Othello which the play *makes* problematic and which has no counterpart in the Italian story. Early in the first scene we hear Iago refer, scathingly, to what Othello "evades" with "bumbast Circumstance" (or bombastic, circumlocutory padding) and "horribly stufft" epithets. Iago's view is critical and reductive: this is how an uppity Moor talks, "in loving his owne pride, and purposes." But then, to the extent that Leavis and Greenblatt see an obvious truth in Iago's diagnostic way of relating Othello's eloquence to "pride, and purposes"—to what Leavis sees as egotistical self-regard, and Greenblatt as narrative self-fashioning—they are less inclined to consider that perception as an expression of Iago's way of seeing and mode of being. Precisely because Leavis's own view of Othello resembles Iago's he can, with no sense of contradiction, demote Iago's significance within the play, and protest against a critical tradition that would salvage Othello's nobility by having him brought down by a manipulator of such satanic power. Greenblatt doesn't demote Iago, and indeed provides an exceptionally powerful, inward account of Iago's "demonic sensitivity"; but, like Leavis, he also emphasizes the extent to which Iago is a catalyst who can "play upon" and release what is already in Othello.

Obvious differences shouldn't obscure this important resemblance. Where Leavis sees Othello as a deluded egotist Greenblatt sees him as a deluded Christian convert; but both concentrate on unpacking a disabling and finally murderous delusion. Leavis's account of Othello's egotism comes perilously close to repudiating any morally and imaginatively constructive aspiration to live up to a "better self"; Greenblatt attaches more importance to Othello's Christianity than any other critic, while at the same time emptying it of any positive religious or spiritual significance. In other words, both critics assume—like Iago—that understanding Othello means seeing *through* him in a reductively diagnostic fashion. For Leavis, this is a largely moral and critical matter; in the terms of his analysis, historical considerations and cultural contexts are largely or entirely irrelevant—whereas they are crucial to Greenblatt's argument that "Christianity is the alienating yet constitutive force in Othello's identity" (245). We are to believe that the "orthodox doctrine which governs Othello's sexual attitudes" (246) is the "traditional" Christian idea that (in Calvin's reformulation) "the man who shows no modesty or comeliness in conjugal intercourse is committing adultery with his wife" (248). As a Christian convert Othello cannot protect himself from the neurotic-making, finally murderous dynamics of "orthodox" Christian teaching on sexuality, since "he cannot allow himself the moderately flexible adherence that most ordinary men have towards their formal beliefs" (245). So, the play's "symbolic center" is Othello's "tormenting identification" between "taking excessive pleasure in the marriage bed" and "adultery," and the "dark essence of Iago's whole enterprise" is to "play upon Othello's buried perception of his own sexual relations with Desdemona as adulterous" (233). This is an unexpected reading and I must say more about it, but my immediate point has to do with the way in which Greenblatt, like Leavis, diagnoses Othello as a "case."

Moreover, in developing their very different diagnoses neither critic speaks to the play by considering whether the play prompts a diagnosis in these terms, or whether there is some significant difficulty in aligning the modern critic's analytical vocabulary with that of the play: the significance of any such difficulty is usually moral and historical. But then neither Leavis nor Greenblatt is concerned to ask whether the play calls for a diagnostic account of Othello in an intelligently purposive or merely inadvertent way. Here, once again, the issue of dramatic intention enters to the degree that it is excluded. Leavis writes as though Othello were an inadequately prepared examination candidate whose failure could be contemplated with something like satisfaction: "In this testing, Othello's inner timbers begin to part at once, the stuff of which he is made begins at once to deteriorate and show itself unfit." His tone is representative, morally ugly, and rather surprising from the critic who had observed that "if we don't see ourselves in Angelo, we have taken the play very imperfectly."[51] But then Leavis never confronts the question his own analysis makes so pressing: if the main effect of *Othello* is to provoke such extraordinary animus, wouldn't the play itself be less satisfactory than he supposes? Greenblatt's reading presents an equivalent difficulty because of the way it figures in an impressively ranging and often enthralling discussion of Renaissance *mentalité*. Presenting a reductively diagnostic view of Othello is neither the essay's main aim nor an incidental effect: rather, it is a *condition* of the way *Othello* is thought to fit into that ranging argument. Yet this makes the critical difficulty: Greenblatt is providing a *cultural* context, but not a *dramatic* context, for those parts of the Shakespearean text which he discusses. Once again a play is being used to instantiate, without being allowed to test, the controlling thesis, and a thesis that is characteristically new historicist in its insistence on what *estranges* us from the Renaissance and Shakespeare: in this case seeing through Othello turns *Othello* into a period piece.

For this very reason it matters whether Shakespeare could have recognized his play in Greenblatt's conspicuously contemporary—anti-Christian and Lacanian—account of its "symbolic center." If the play can be understood in different, less estranging terms, we need to know, and so does Greenblatt. If the play itself is exploring and diagnosing the malign, neurotic-making dynamics of that "orthodox doctrine that governs Othello's sexual attitudes," it would be a revolutionary document, rather than a museum exhibit. If, on the other hand, it merely illustrates or (worse) endorses that warped, warping doctrine, then Greenblatt's diagnosis of Othello extends to the play itself—and we would then know how to unravel, or cut through, Greenblatt's elaborately poised, suavely inconclusive conclusion:

> Shakespeare approaches his culture not, like Marlowe, as rebel and blasphemer, but rather as a dutiful servant, content to improvise a part of his own within its orthodoxy. And if after centuries, that improvisation has been revealed to us as embodying an almost boundless challenge to the culture's every tenet, a devastation of every source, the author of Othello would have understood that such a revelation scarcely matters. (253)

As Geoffrey Strickland observes in *Structuralism or Criticism?*, "We cannot possibly understand what is written or said unless we understand its interest and importance for the writer or speaker; which affects inevitably its interest and importance for us. Evaluation, in this sense, and interpretation are the same."[52] That is why the student of literature is and must be a student of history, learning to see with what Michael Baxandall calls the "period eye."[53] But at this point Greenblatt's own avowedly Lacanian, psychoanalytical account of the "symbolic center" presents a peculiar difficulty: it keeps telling us that the "symbolic center" is "concealed," but not by whom, or from whom.

To take one little cluster of examples from one page of Greenblatt's essay, even when we are being told that "Othello comes close to revealing his tormenting identification of marital sexuality—limited perhaps to the night he took Desdemona's virginity—and adultery" (251), *revealing* means something so close to betraying as to imply further *concealing*. When Greenblatt goes on to observe, of Iago, who so successfully improvises "on the religious sexual doctrine in which Othello believes," that "beneath his cynical modernity and professed self-love Iago reproduces in himself the same psychic structure," the same difficulty is revealed, or betrayed, or concealed: apparently, what "assures" Iago's "access to Othello" is not in any straightforward sense apparent to Iago himself. Greenblatt then observes that the "improvisational process we have been discussing depends for its success upon the concealment of its symbolic center, but as the end approaches this center becomes increasingly visible"—not before time, since the play is nearly over, yet the interpretation still will not tell us whether what becomes increasingly visible is being *made* increasingly visible by Shakespeare or by this mode of psychoanalytical analysis, which half creates what it half perceives. (Though peculiar, this difficulty is familiar in psychoanalytical interpretations; an Iago-like cynic might associate it with the practical difficulty confronting those psychiatrists who are well paid by the healthy and wealthy to represent inner vacuity as inner life.) Disquietingly, what is said to become "increasingly visible" apparently remained invisible for nearly four centuries, and certainly wasn't visible to earlier, Christian critics like Johnson and Coleridge, writing in centuries when "orthodox" Christian doctrine didn't have to be expounded by literary critics. In all these instances the analysis equivocates by not considering whether the play is diagnosing the perverting dynamics of the "orthodox doctrine that governs Othello's sexual attitudes," or whether the play itself is "governed" by the "doctrine." This difficulty corresponds with that in Greenblatt's discussion of the "logic which governs the relation between orthodoxy and subversion" in the "Henriad," and provokes the same objection: it is the critic's own thesis—Lacanian in this case, Foucauldian in that—which actually "governs" his reading, determining when he dips into the Shakespearean text, and determining what the partial sampling of the text is to instantiate.

The most spectacular instance of the peculiar difficulty posed by this Lacanian interpretative model is also the most important for Greenblatt's thesis, since it involves that speech of Iago's which is said to show how the play's "symbolic center" if both revealed and concealed:

> *Cassio's* a proper man: Let me see now,
> To get his Place, and to plume up my will
> In double Knavery. How? How? Let's see.
> After some time, to abuse *Othello's* eares,
> That he is too familiar with his wife:
> He hath a person, and a smooth dispose
> To be suspected; fram'd to make women false.
> The Moore is of a free, and open Nature,
> That thinkes men honest, that but seeme to be so,
> And will as tenderly be lead by'th'Nose-as Asses are:
> I have't: it is engendred: Hell, and Night,
> Must bring this monstrous Birth, to the worlds light.
>
> (1.3.392–404)

Greenblatt discusses this passage twice. First, he directs attention to the "felicitous" way in which "the ambiguity of the third-person pronoun" delivers the suggestion that Othello himself is "too familiar with his wife": he adds that "though scarcely visible at this point, it is the dark essence of Iago's whole enterprise which is, as we shall see, to play upon Othello's buried perception of his own sexual relations with Desdemona as adulterous (233). Later, Greenblatt returns to this supposedly "felicitous" and more than merely "syntactic" ambiguity, to explain "how Iago manages to persuade Othello that Desdemona has committed adultery" (247). The two ways of understanding "he is too familiar with his wife" allegedly correspond with two aspects of "the centuries-old Christian doctrine": the "rigorist" condemnation of (real) adultery as "one of the most horrible of mortal sins, more detestable, in the words of the *Eruditorium penitentiale*, 'than homicide or plunder' "; and that "still darker aspect of orthodox Christian doctrine" which compares taking pleasure in "conjugal intercourse" with "adultery."

Greenblatt's exposition of this "darker" doctrine runs the course from Jerome's dictum—"An adulterer is he who is too ardent a lover of his wife"—and Augustine, to Calvin and sundry "orthodox" warnings like that in the *King's Book*, "attributed to Henry VIII," that says a man can break the Seventh Commandment and "live unchaste with his own wife, if he do unmeasurably or inordinately serve his or her fleshly appetite or lust." In other words, Greenblatt assembles an old historicist *cento* of quotations which briskly cuts through complicated historical and theological issues and is most obviously selective where it matters most—at the Renaissance end. There is no doubt that the desert fathers took up the Pauline exaltation of celibacy with an anti-sexual vengeance, or that—despite occasional dissidents, like the fifth-century Synesius of Cyrene—this dominated "orthodox" doctrine for the millennium from the fourth to the fourteenth centuries.[54] Nor can we soften the force of Jerome's enthusiastic recyclings of the stoic Xystus's leathery little maxim that "He who loves his own wife too ardently is an adulterer" (*omnis ardentior amator propriae uxoris adulter est*) by supposing that Jerome means that pleasure in marital sex should be ardent but not too ardent: in Jerome's majestic view any sexual pleasure is excessive and sinful. But this was not quite the view taken by Aquinas and Peter Lombard when they discussed Jerome's two reworkings of the maxim from Xystus, as appears in this modern theologian's explication: "The man thus denounced is not, apparently, he who entertains too warm an affection for his wife, but he whose *amor* (that is, his desire for venereal pleasure—the word here does not mean 'love,' as we understand it) is so vehement that it impels him to abandon the restraint which pays careful regard to the *bona matrimonii*, and incites him to treat her as if she were merely, like any other woman, a means of lustful gratification."[55] On this view sex is not sinful per se, even though it cannot be pursued for its own sake without sin—"a venial sin when sought within marriage, and a mortal sin when sought outside it." Greenblatt doesn't make room for Peter Lombard and Aquinas, and he quotes Calvin's warning that "the man who shows no modesty or comeliness in conjugal intercourse is committing adultery with his wife" as though Calvin thought on this matter like Jerome; yet Calvin specifically and very sternly repudiated Jerome's argument that "if it is good not to touch a woman, it is bad to touch one"—affirming that sexual intercourse is a pure institution of God and that the idea that "we are polluted by intercourse with our wives" emanates from Satan, not Paul.[56] Greenblatt quotes from the "influential" Raymond and Jacobus Ungarelli, but not from Luther, or Thomas Becon's *Book of Matrimony*, or Erasmus's colloquies on marriage—where there is a direct link, not only with the "marriage group" of Sonnets but with the witty sexual frankness of women in Shakespeare's romantic comedies.[57] After quoting Nicholas of Ausimo's warning that the conjugal act may be without sin, but only if "in the performance of this act there is no enjoyment of pleasure," Greenblatt solemnly concludes that "few *summas* and no marriage manuals take so extreme a position, but virtually all are in agreement that the active pursuit of pleasure in sexuality is damnable" (*Renaissance Self-Fashioning*, 249). But are we then to conclude that Shakespeare's audiences would have thought that Desdemona's forthright declaration in the Senate of what Greenblatt himself describes as a "frankly, though by no means exclusively sexual" passion was "damnable"? And if not, why not?

As for Iago's speech, Greenblatt's extraordinary reading is altogether severed from any dramatic context, and leaves the conscious and the unconscious to play peekaboo. Iago's speech occurs in the third scene, when the marriage has not even been consummated: far from being "too familiar with his wife" by taking "excessive pleasure" in the marriage bed, Othello hasn't taken any. Moreover, at this point in the drama, neither Iago nor the audience knows anything of Cassio's part in the secret wooing: he and we only learn in 3.3 that Cassio and Desdemona were "very oft" alone together. When Iago says "after some time" he is assuming, sensibly enough, he will have to wait before trying to convince Othello that Cassio is his wife's lover: how does one convince somebody who has just taken his wife's virginity that she is adulterous? Moreover, just as Iago cannot think that the attraction between Othello and Desdemona is anything but grossly physical and perverted, he is actually incapable of thinking that Othello is seriously committed to his Christian faith. In his soliloquy after the riot in Act 2, he sneers that Othello is so "enfetter'd" by his love for Desdemona that she could persuade him "to renownce his Baptisme, / All Seales, and Simbols of redeemed sin" (2.3.334–35). Consequently, one objection to the thesis that the "dark essence of Iago's whole enterprise" is "to play upon Othello's buried perception of his own sexual relations with Desdemona as adulterous" is that Iago doesn't and couldn't see what he is said to be doing and playing upon.

As the thesis becomes ever more ramified, we are invited to suppose that Othello unleashes upon Cassio "the fear of pollution, defilement, brutish violence that is bound up with his own experience of sexual pleasure" (250);

finally, it is "as if Othello has found in a necrophilic fantasy the secret solution to the intolerable demands of the rigorist sexual ethic, and the revelation that Cassio has not slept with Desdemona leads only to a doubling of this solution, for the adulterous sexual pleasure that Othello had projected upon his lieutenant now rebounds upon himself" (252). Yet the crucial issue, on which Greenblatt's whole reading depends, is whether the newly married Othello does tormentedly identify his own sexual pleasure with sin.

In fact, Greenblatt is surprisingly specific about what he thinks happens on that first night in Cyprus. Yet this assurance involves a very curious assumption that what (allegedly) happens onstage during the lovers' "passionate reunion" at the harbor anticipates, and explains, what will (allegedly) happen offstage during the next scene. For Greenblatt, this reunion has a "rich and disturbing pathos" that derives from the lovers' very different attitudes toward sexuality. Othello's words are said to convey both "an ecstatic acceptance of sexuality, an absolute content," and "the longing for a final release from desire"—since "for him sexuality is a menacing voyage ... one of the dangers to be passed," and a "tempest" that threatens "self-dissolution." As for Desdemona, her "response is in an entirely different key" and, although "spoken to allay Othello's fear," is far more likely to "augment it," since her own "erotic submission" threatens and "subverts her husband's carefully fashioned identity" (242–44). Yet the "ecstatic acceptance of sexuality" is Greenblatt's invention, or fantasy. When Othello speaks of that absolute content which his "Soule" already has, and which he fears can never be equaled in the future, he isn't even thinking of future sexual "content":

> If it were now to dye,
> 'Twere now to be most happy. For I feare,
> My Soule hath her content so absolute,
> That not another comfort like to this,
> Succeeds in unknowne Fate.
>
> (2.1.189–93)

It is Desdemona who then reminds Othello, in a lovingly corrective way, of the "Loves and Comforts" yet to come, which "should encrease," not diminish, his and their "content." But here Greenblatt's account of Desdemona's "erotic submissiveness" is no less curious, and disquietingly consistent with his argument that although Bianca and Emilia both have "moments of disobedience to the men who possess and abuse them," Desdemona "performs no such acts of defiance" (244). What of her "downe-right violence," her deception and defiance of her own father, her readiness to "trumpet to the world" that "I did love the Moore, to live with him," or her fatal refusal to stop pressing Cassio's case? Greenblatt's Desdemona is more tame, since he gives little or no weight to all those creatively purposeful changes through which Shakespeare made his Desdemona so unlike

Cinthio's Disdemona. Nonetheless, this part of Greenblatt's analysis is very important to his reading, since he sees Othello's speech at the harbor as a tragically accurate "premonition" of "a rent, a moving ambivalence, in his experience of the ecstatic moment itself" (243): that is, when he "took Desdemona's virginity," "shed her blood," and not only noticed but became imaginatively obsessed by the condition of their own lust-stained wedding sheets.

This explanation of what allegedly happens on the first night in Cyprus is wholly untenable if, as I argue, weighing the textual and dramatic evidence suggests that the marriage is never consummated; but I do not assume that all readers will accept my own argument about that. The objection to Greenblatt's reading is more basic, and is that when he provides local analysis and commentary he is unable to establish the basic premise—that Othello himself tormentedly identifies his own sexual pleasure with sin and "adultery." The reading is willful because it is so partial, and because it disregards whatever conflicts with the forceful thesis. As we have seen, Greenblatt's explanation of why Othello is obsessed with sheets won't explain why they also matter to Desdemona, just as Othello's speech at the harbor doesn't show any "ecstatic acceptance of sexuality" and just as the extraordinarily tenuous reading of Iago's soliloquy at the end of Act I never asks why Iago should say, "After some time." Iago is thinking about the dramatic situation, but Greenblatt isn't. The dramatic situation makes it impossible that Iago could be determining to "play upon Othello's buried perception of his own sexual relations with Desdemona as adulterous." The fact that nobody before Greenblatt ever had interpreted Iago's speech in that way suggests how the Shakespearean chapter in *Renaissance Self-Fashioning* presents yet another critical tribar. As in his "Invisible Bullets" essay, the critic keeps slithering between an ideal is (a strongly prescriptive and "original" critical account of how the play should be understood) and a material was, where what makes the reading seem "original" is also what explodes it— precisely because no earlier critic, including Christian critics like Johnson and Coleridge, had ever understood the play in this way. The result, once again, is that the reading becomes an impossible object in four-dimensional (non-historical) space.

Although I agree with Greenblatt and Snow that there are disparities between Othello's and Desdemona's attitudes toward sexuality (to put the matter narrowly), their readings also show how such disparities can be described in very different ways. In "Sexual Anxiety and the Male Order of Things," Snow himself protests against Greenblatt's "scapegoating" of Christianity, while discussing forms of sexual anxiety that are not inconceivable today; for that very reason Snow's own psychoanalytical reading wouldn't be so attractive to the new historicist: it isn't so *estranging*. The appeal of Greenblatt's argument, in new historicist terms, is that it once again posits that gulf between Them and Us: the play becomes another period piece that can then only be "understood" in alienating or estranging terms—in this case by invoking that "orthodox"

Christian "doctrine" which is said to "govern" Othello's attitude to sexuality, but really governs Greenblatt's thesis.

Some other explanation is needed for Shakespeare's decision to turn Cinthio's Moor into a Christian convert much given to making references to his "Soule." Nor should we suppose that if there is some disparity between Othello's and Desdemona's attitudes toward sexuality, it forces us to withhold sympathy from Othello and to regard him merely as a "case"; rather, I need to modify my own earlier argument that Shakespeare's departures from Cinthio's story show him moving in what appear to be opposite directions. It is indeed worth noticing how Shakespeare worked from the first, to complicate his material, and how these complications produced the twentieth-century debate about Othello in which each party to the debate disregards or plays down that "evidence" which most impresses the other. Yet the metaphor of departing in different directions is still potentially misleading, since all of Shakespeare's departures from the Italian story are directed to one end, which is to fashion—and integrate—his own work. Moreover, that work is a poetic drama, not another prose story or novella. A "novel," according to Dr. Johnson's *Dictionary*, is "a small tale, generally of love"; Cinthio's story is that, but *Othello* is not. The greatest difference between Cinthio's Moor and Shakespeare's has to do with those modes of metaphorical representation which transform the Italian story into a powerfully sustained poetic-dramatic conceit: Othello, his potentialities, and the dramatic world he inhabits are conceived and characterized in poetic-dramatic terms.

NOTES

22. See the discussions in M. R. Ridley, ed., *Othello*, New Arden ed. (London: Methuen, 1965), lxvii–lxx, and Norman Sanders, ed., *Othello*, New Cambridge ed. (Cambridge: Cambridge University Press, 1984), 14–17. These views are less skeptical than those in H. H. Furness, ed., *Othello*, New Variorum ed. (Philadelphia: Lippincott, 1886), 358–72.

23. Jane Adamson, *"Othello" as Tragedy: Some Problems of Judgment and Feeling* (Cambridge: Cambridge University Press, 1980), 7.

24. Richard Levin, "Shakespearean Defects and Shakespeareans' Defenses," in Maurice Charney, ed., *"Bad" Shakespeare: Revaluations of the Shakespeare Canon* (London: Associated University Presses; Rutherford, N.J.: Farleigh Dickenson University Press, 1988), 23–36.

25. See my epilogue, "Verdi and Boito as Translators," in James Hepokoski, *Giuseppe Verdi: Falstaff* (Cambridge: Cambridge University Press, 1983), 152–71. For a discussion of what *Otello* owes to the nineteenth-century continental understanding of Shakespeare, see Hepokoski, "Boito and F.-V. Hugo's 'Magnificent Translation': A Study in the Genesis of the *Otello* Libretto," in

Arthur Groos and Roger Parker, eds., *Reading Opera* (Princeton: Princeton University Press, 1988), 34–59.

26. See the very searching chapter "Time and Continuity" in Emrys Jones, *Scenic Form in Shakespeare* (Oxford: Clarendon Press, 1871), especially 41–43 and 54–63.

27. Frank Kermode, introduction to *Othello* in *The Riverside Shakespeare*, ed. G. Blakemore Evans et al., 2 vols. (Boston: Houghton Mifflin, 1974), 2:1199.

28. See John Dover Wilson, ed., *Othello*, New Shakespeare ed. (Cambridge: Cambridge University Press, 1957), xxxi.

29. Harley Granville-Barker, "The Ambiguity in Time: A Parenthesis," in *Prefaces to Shakespeare*, 2 vols. (London: Batsford, 1972), 2:24–30, directs attention to the unobtrusive but numerous indications of time which suggest the passage of a day from early morning to after midnight. Their unobtrusiveness is what seems telling: the point is they seem to emerge, naturally and easily, from the dramatist's own sense of when things are happening. We need not suppose that they are deliberately, consciously inserted.

About half way through 3.3—which extends through the morning just as the "dilatory time" in 2.3 extends through the night—Desdemona appears to fetch Othello to "dinner," that is, the midday meal for which the "generous Islanders / By you invited" are now arriving (280–81). Evidently, this is not just dinner but an official dinner arranged by Othello (we might recall that glimpse of his earlier activities in 3.2 and of letters he has already written), and a dinner that is then being delayed through the rest of this agonizing scene. The solidity of specification appears in those incidental details: there is a sense that as this scenario evolved fleeting matters of detail were considered. (Many great works are not like that: we may wonder but will never know how Don Alfonso persuades a regiment to help him in *Cosi fan tutte*, or why Hamlet didn't see Horatio at his father's funeral.) A few lines later, when Desdemona innocently attributes Othello's "paine upon my Forehead" to lack of sleep—"Why that's with watching, 'twill away againe"—this confirms that Othello spent hours tending Montano; we might not notice the significance of that single word "watching," but it is waiting for us if we look for it. Othello leaves with Desdemona for the dinner; within moments Iago has the handkerchief, impatiently dismisses Emilia, and is about to rush off to plant it in Cassio's lodging when Othello unexpectedly returns. By now Iago knows that time is of the essence, and he would hardly let a week pass without helping Cassio to find that handkerchief and satisfying Othello's demand for "proofes"; here "double-timers" create and then fail to notice another problem, by imagining a period of a "long time" between 3.3 and 4.1. But in 3.4 Cassio enters with the handkerchief and Iago, who has evidently lost no time; and, as Furness noticed, the idea of an appreciable lapse of time between 3.4 and 4.1 is scotched when Bianca returns that handkerchief "you gave me even now" (4.1.149–50). Again, the point is not that we would notice the significance of that "even now" but that its unemphatic casualness (which makes it easy not to notice) suggests how the dramatist is writing from a sure sense of when important matters take place.

30. Barbara Everett discusses this in Everett, *Young Hamlet: Essays on Shakespeare's Tragedies* (Oxford: Clarendon Press, 1989), 208–24, as "one of the best-known and longest-unresolved cruces in the canon," and proposes that the Folio's "damn'd" (Q: "dambd") should read *limn'd*. Sanders's long footnote in the New Cambridge *Othello* takes up most of the page, while the Furness Variorum notes cover five pages.

31. Reported in the Variorum *Othello*.

32. Wilson, in the New Shakespeare *Othello*, dismisses any idea that a suggestion of "premarital incontinence" would have served Iago's purpose, or Shakespeare's (xxxii), since he sees "cuckoldry" as the issue. But of course one might think it remarkably interesting that the *Sonnets*, *Othello*, and later *The Winter's Tale* all explore a situation in which a man believes that he has been betrayed by the male friend he most loves with the woman he most loves. In *A Lover's Complaint* the situational "rhyme" also allows a greater distancing: now the "Poet" overhears the complaint of, an innocent (not "Dark" or "blacke") maid who was seduced by a Bertram-like young man who uses sonnets as part of his seduction technique.

33. "Leavis, *Othello*, and Self-knowledge," *Dutch Quarterly Review* 9 (1979): 218–31.

34. T. R. Nelson and Charles Haines, "Othello's Unconsummated Marriage," *Essays in Criticism*, 33 (1983): 1–18.

35. See Lawrence J. Ross, "Shakespeare's 'Dull Clown' and Symbolic Music," *Shakespeare Quarterly* 17 (1966): 107–28; "The Meaning of Strawberries in Shakespeare," *Studies in the Renaissance* 7 (1960): 225–40; Linda Boose, "Othello's Handkerchief: The Recognizance and Pledge of Love," *English Literary Renaissance* 5 (1975): 360–74. Like Greenblatt, Ross and Boose consider details that might make us doubt whether the marriage ever is consummated, but without drawing that conclusion.

36. Greenblatt, *Renaissance Self-Fashioning*, 251. Although Greenblatt and Edward Snow are both concerned with Othello's "sexual anxiety," their accounts diverge sharply at this point; see note 47, below.

37. Boose is good on this; see note 35, above. François Laroque, in his absorbing discussion of Othello and the festive traditions, analyzes the charivari as one of the instances in which the play offers a "double perspective, alternately comic and tragic, derisive and pathetic"; see Laroque, *Shakespeare's Festive World: Elizabethan Seasonal Entertainment and the Popular Stage* (Cambridge: Cambridge University Press, 1991), 287–89.

38. See H.A. Mason, *Shakespeare's Tragedies of Love* (London: Chatto & Windus, 1970), especially chap. 2, on *Othello*.

39. See Kenneth Burke's discussion of the consubstantiality between Othello and Iago in Burke, *A Grammar of Motives* (New York: Prentice Hall, 1945) 413–14. This is taken up by Greenblatt and by Karen Newman. In Emilia's case, the salutary force and independence of her views of men are so engaging that there is some corrective point in noticing how they complement Iago's cynical misogyny. Burke recalls Coleridge's remark that *rivales* are "opposite banks of the same stream"; that remark is relevant here if we think there is now some danger of sentimentalizing Emilia's "crypto-feminism," remarkable though it is.

40. I discuss this passage further in the appendix.

41. S. N. Garner, "Shakespeare's Desdemona," *Shakespeare Studies* 9 (1976): 232–52. Martin Orkin (see note 43) quotes, and quite properly expects us to disapprove of, A. C. Bradley's suggestion, in *Shakespearean Tragedy* (London: Macmillan, 1960), 165, that "perhaps, if we saw Othello coal-black with the bodily eye, the aversion of our blood, an aversion which comes as near to being merely physical as anything human can, would overpower our imagination and sink us below not Shakespeare only but the audiences of the seventeenth and eighteenth centuries." This sentence concludes the first paragraph of a long, rewardingly complicated footnote. However, the offensive sentence is striking in a different way if we consider what precedes it: "I will not discuss the further question whether, granted that to Shakespeare Othello was a black, he should be represented as a black in our theatres now. I dare say not. We do not like the real Shakespeare. We like to have his language pruned and his conceptions flattened into something that suits our mouths and minds. And even if we were prepared to make an effort, still, as Lamb observes, to imagine is one thing and to see is another" (ibid.). Taking Bradley's paragraph as a whole, I would say that it recognizes, in a remarkably complicated and even courageous way, that "the real Shakespeare" may be too strong for modern sensibilities, including his own. Bradley sees how the play administers a profound shock, which challenges the audience to overcome that shock by taking something more like Desdemona's view of Othello's "visage." Bradley's assumption that this challenge will be too much for a modern audience (in 1904) seems to me less damaging to the play's dynamics than, say, Barbara Everett's attempts to reduce the shock by arguing for a merely "tawny" Moor or Karen Newman's assumption (see note 44) that we know better than to be shocked by a black Othello. Bradley sees the challenge; Everett and Newman—and Coleridge—deflect it.

42. Bradley's quarrel with Lamb takes up the second paragraph of the footnote discussed in my preceding footnote, and is again worth quoting in full: "As I have mentioned Lamb, I may observe that he differed from Coleridge as to Othello's colour, but, I am sorry to add, thought Desdemona to stand in need of excuse. 'This noble lady, with a singularity rather to be wondered at than imitated, had chosen for the object of her affections a Moor, or black.... Neither is Desdemona to be altogether condemned for unsuitableness of the person

whom she had selected for her lover' (*Tales from Shakespeare*). Others, of course, have gone much further and have treated all the calamities of the tragedy as a sort of judgment on Desdemona's rashness, wilfulness and undutifulness. There is no arguing with opinions like this; but I cannot believe that even Lamb is true to Shakespeare in implying that Desdemona is in some degree to be condemned. What is there in the play to show that Shakespeare regarded her marriage differently from Imogen's?" That last question is worth putting, but one answer—which Lamb was evidently considering, but Bradley refused to countenance—is that Imogen is alive at the end of her play, while Desdemona isn't.

43. For Coleridge, "it would be something monstrous to conceive this beautiful Venetian girl falling in love with a veritable negro. It would argue a disproportionateness, a want of balance, in Desdemona, which Shakespeare does not appear to have in the least contemplated"; T. M. Raysor, ed., *Coleridge's Shakespearean Criticism*, 2 vols. (London: Dent, 1960), 1:42. (Raysor questions the authenticity of this passage, "certainly in part and perhaps even as a whole.") It is easy to assemble such quotations, and they are angrily dissected by Martin Orkin in "Othello and the 'Plain Face' of Racism," *Shakespeare Quarterly* 38 (1987): 166–88. Barbara Everett's argument for a tawny "Spanish" Othello was originally developed in "'Spanish' Othello: The Making of Shakespeare's Moor," *Shakespeare Survey* 35 (1982), and is reprinted in Everett, *Young Hamlet*, 186–207. Apparently, when tawny Spanish Moors say "I am black" (3.3.262) we should regard that as an unhappy exaggeration: poor tawnies don't know better?

44. See Karen Newman's vigorous and challenging essay, "'And Wash the Ethiop White': Femininity and the Monstrous in *Othello*," in Jean E. Howard and Marion O'Connor, eds., *Shakespeare Reproduced: The Text in History and Ideology* (London and New York: Methuen, 1987), 143–62. Newman cites Orkin's essay but doesn't explain why she disagrees with his comment that the racist sentiment in the play is "to an important degree confined to Iago, Roderigo and Brabantio" (168).

45. Granville-Barker, *Prefaces to Shakespeare*, 2:17. The shocked Dover Wilson found this "incredible": "True, they [Othello's lines] are spoken before the wedding night, but by this placing of them Shakespeare surely meant to emphasize what Othello has said already at 1.3.26ff"; Wilson, New Shakespeare *Othello*, xxii. As usual, the word "surely" signals wishful thinking.

46. Compare "Have you quit the mines? have the pioners given o'er?" (*Henry V*, 3.2.86–87) and "Well said, old mole? canst work i'the earth so fast? A worthy pioner!" (*Hamlet*, 1.5.162–63).

47. Edward Snow, "Sexual Anxiety and the Male Order of Things in Othello," *English Literary Renaissance* 10 (1980): 384–412. For Snow, the murder "involves a repetition and undoing of the sexual experience." As this suggests, his argument overlaps with Greenblatt's at many points (each acknowledges the

other), but Snow objects to Greenblatt's emphasis on the Christian doctrine that supposedly governs Othello's sexual attitudes: "Greenblatt has an especially acute discussion ... of the theme of confession in *Othello* and its bearing on the play's insights into the malign influence of Christian doctrine on human life. But it is important not to scapegoat Christianity in turn, making it (as Greenblatt seems to do) the 'cause' of sexual disgust" (384). The reasons for the objection are not altogether clear; Snow agrees about Christianity's "malign influence" but doesn't want to see that as the main "cause" of Othello's neurosis. We might also doubt whether Greenblatt's essay ever attributes the "insights" into Christianity's "malign influence" to the play itself. If he thought that, he would presumably offer a different reading, and not suggest in his conclusion that Shakespeare is less radical than Marlowe. He might even have reflected on the dangers in taking a dramatic character together with historical characters in his discussion of Renaissance self-fashioning.

48. F.R. Leavis, "Diabolic Intellect and the Noble Hero: or, The Sentimentalist's Othello," *The Common Pursuit* (London: Chatto & Windus, 1952), 136–59; originally published in *Scrutiny* 6 (1937): 259–83.

49. This is a delicate matter. An Englishman reading the essay cannot but notice it, as an American reader would notice if an English critic's radical reading of Melville ignored twentieth-century American criticism.

50. See Martin Elliott, *Shakespeare's Invention of Othello* (London: Macmillan; New York: St. Martin's Press, 1988), which provides some remarkably detailed and perceptive "close" readings of Othello's language.

51. F.R. Leavis, "Measure for Measure," in *The Common Pursuit* (London: Chatto & Windus, 1952), 160–81.

52. Geoffrey Strickland, *Structuralism or Criticism? Thoughts on How We Read* (Cambridge: Cambridge University Press, 1981). 36.

53. See Michael Baxandall, *Painting and Experience in Fifteenth-Century Italy*, 2d ed. (Oxford: Oxford University Press, 1988), pt. 2.

54. For a magnificent study of these and related matters, see Peter Brown, *The Body and Society: Men, Women, and Sexual Renunciation in Early Christianity* (New York: Columbia University Press, 1988).

55. D.S. Bailey, *The Man–Woman Relation in Christian Thought* (London: Longmans, 1959), 137. The "Gawain-poet" was evidently unaware of the theological "state of play" when, in *Cleanness* (lines 697–708), he described God's pride in making sex so pleasurable: "Bytweene a male and his make such merthe schulde come, / Wel nygh pure Paradyse moght prove no better."

56. Ibid., 171–72; see also François Wendel, *Calvin: Origins and Development of His Religious Thought*, trans. Philip Mairet (Durham, N.C.: Labyrinth Press, 1988), 65, for the interesting memorandum where Calvin reflects, "I, whom you see so hostile to celibacy, have never taken a wife." The idea that celibacy confers

a higher spiritual state than marriage was of course repudiated by many sixteenth-century humanists. In objecting to the way in which Greenblatt's cento of quotations elides important shifts of emphasis and concern, I am not denying that unease or hostility has characterized Christian teaching on sexual pleasure. Bailey suggests that "the first express recognition in theological literature of what may be termed the relational purpose of coitus" comes in Jeremy Taylor's *Rules and Exercises of Holy Living*, when Taylor allows that one of the proper "ends" of marital intercourse is "to endear each other" (208).

57. See Craig R. Thompson, *The Colloquies of Erasmus* (Chicago: University of Chicago Press, 1965), 86–87.

WILLIAM EMPSON

Macbeth

J. Dover Wilson's arguments, in his edition of the play (1947), for an early revision by Shakespeare himself, designed to shorten it for a Court performance, seem to me valuable but untrue. Valuable, that is, because they draw attention to points you do not easily notice otherwise, and untrue because these points add to the dramatic effect when noticed: it is therefore unnecessary to suppose they are confusions due to revision.

All this is separate from the generally accepted opinion, not questioned either by Dover Wilson or myself, that the scenes and passages involving Hecate were added by Shakespeare especially to please James I. Admittedly, if that is so, it makes an unusually short play even shorter; and many critics have used that as an argument for believing in substantial cuts. I don't mean to deny the possibility, but don't feel that much can be built on it. In any case, the play gives great opportunities for trick staging with the witches (they always had a resinous white smoke, says Dover Wilson, but didn't start flying on wires till after Ariel had done it in *The Tempest*; a year or two later, on his dating, than Middleton's first vulgarisation of *Macbeth* in 1610); it was probably altered a little whenever it was done with new machinery. It doesn't seem likely that the audience would complain of being given short measure, and surely that would be the only practical objection to a short text.

However, if I may chatter about my prejudices at once, so as to help the reader's work of judging my whole position, I do feel sympathetic to a theory

From *Essays on Shakespeare*, ed. David B. Pirie. © 1986 by David B. Pirie.

which would put the first draft of the play earlier. *Macbeth* is now generally put later than *Lear*, but it seems much more satisfactory to have *Lear* at the end of the main tragic series; as a matter, that is, of the development of Shakespeare's thought and feeling, and this seems to me a stronger argument than the one from style which has also been plausibly advanced. You then have some kind of breakdown after *Lear*, rather accidentally recorded in *Timon*, and then a recovery which always remained in some important way partial, so that after this recovery he always felt somehow above his characters, even in *Antony and Cleopatra* never again really part of them. He could have fallen back on an old style, presumably, merely because it suited the case in hand; but what you are really trying to envisage is an entire development under heavy pressure. However, this kind of thing only makes me want to put *Macbeth* before *Lear* and after *Othello*; I don't see that there is a strong argument, either from style or development, to help Dover Wilson in trying to put the first draft of the play considerably earlier.

On his general thesis, that many Shakespeare plays bear marks of repeated revision, I feel less inclined to prattle about the psychology of the Bard; it is a delightful occupation, but the guesses are so liable to cancel one another out. One would think he had neither the time nor the inclination for revising, but the more you make him careless about his old work the more possible it seems that he threw away the perfect first version of *Macbeth* just to get through one Court performance quick enough. What does seem to me incredible is that the Company would allow him to do it; the decision rested with them, and it was not at all in their interest. They made their money out of the public performances, and only needed the Court for protection; at least this is commonly accepted, though perhaps one could argue that James was paying much more than Elizabeth had done (the evidence given by Harbage, for instance, seems to deal mainly with Elizabeth): but anyway the public performances were still important to them. The Globe audience was going to demand to see a play all the more after it had been honoured by performance at Court, and that audience would demand the full text—they wouldn't even know what the Court cuts had been. Dover Wilson describes many other details of procedure, but he never I think explains exactly how a full Shakespeare text so often got lost after a performance at Court; and for that matter why, if the surviving bits of *Measure for Measure* had to be dragged up to full length by a hack for the public stages after this process, the same did not have to be done for *Macbeth* too. One can hardly suppose it was left for Middleton four years later; these fighting little theatres were on a repertory basis. I presume he means they all got too drunk to carry the text home (though not their individual parts in some cases); a plausible theory, because James does seem to have gone in for tossing the drink around; but surely somebody could have been sent home with the full text, even if they had risked bringing it with them. There were plenty of servants about; one wouldn't think the actors were mingling with the throng very much anyway; surely they could manage to get drunk without losing the most important bit of property they had brought. They were rather property-minded characters. You can imagine it happening once, but there would be a good deal of fuss about not letting it happen again.

The only standard argument for putting *Macbeth* later than *Lear* seems to be the Porter's joke about equivocation, which is held to be a direct reference, beyond doubt, to the trial of the leading Jesuit Garnet from the end of March 1606 onwards (that is, none of the other arguments seem to me decisive). One cannot simply reply that the joke was added when it was topical, because it fits in with so major a cry as Macbeth saying "I now begin / To doubt the equivocation of the fiend", let alone minor phrases which merely echo the story; they cannot all have been added later, because that assumes a dramatist who didn't know what he was writing about to start with. However, I think it is dangerous in this process of dating to neglect the element of luck; in fact it seems fair to be rather superstitious about the luck of a man of genius, in such matters, because he can feel somehow what is going to become "topical". Obviously the idea that equivocation is important and harmful and above all protean did not simply become discovered at the trial of Garnet; it would be as plausible to say that the trial went off as it did because that was felt (these state trials of course were as elaborately prepared beforehand as any in recent history). The echoes of the Shakespeare play in other people's plays, usually called in evidence, come very soon after the trial—while it was topical; provokingly soon if you want to argue that Shakespeare had rushed out his masterpiece in between. Indeed the current theory, as I understand, makes him not merely write it but prepare it for a Court performance (with elaborate business presumably) between May and early August of 1606; surely that amount of pace is too hot. And on the other hand none of these echoes come early enough to support the pre-equivocation draft of 1602 posited by Dover Wilson. I think Shakespeare simply got in first with this topic, in 1605, and did not have to add anything to make it look startlingly topical in its second year. It was already about what was really happening; for that matter, I should think it just comfortably predated the actual Gunpowder Plot affair.

By the way, Dover Wilson's argument that the prattle of the child Macduff must be a later insertion intended as a reference to the Garnet trial (because he says a traitor means one who "swears and lies") does seem to me absurd. The argument is that the child uses the word in a different sense from that of Ross, who has just said it, so the effect is artificial and can't have been in the first draft; but obviously children often do do that. This seemed to need fitting in here, but I wish to avoid fussing about trivialities; probably no one would deny that there may have been cuts and insertions by Shakespeare. The very specific proposals of Dover Wilson about what was cut are what I want to examine here.

In the first place, he feels that the murder of Duncan comes too quickly, or anyway abnormally quickly; the hesitation of Macbeth is a key dramatic effect which in most plays would be given space. This is true, but the whole point about

Macbeth is that he is hurried into an ill-considered action, or that he refuses to consider it himself: "let not light see"—"the eye wink at the hand"—"which must be acted ere they may be scanned"; the play is crowded with such phrases, and its prevailing darkness is a symbol of his refusal to see the consequences of his actions. These consequences are to be long drawn out, but the choice of killing Duncan is to be shown as the effect of two or three shocks close together. Dover Wilson proposes whole scenes to be added before the murder of Duncan, and I think this would not merely be less "exciting" but off the point of the play. A. C. Bradley, to be sure, has said this already, but I don't think he recognised enough the "psychology" as the contemporary audience would see it, which was rather what we now call "existentialist". Problems about free will, which are raised particularly sharply by prophetic witches, were much in the air, and also the idea of the speed with which the self-blinded soul could be damned. One might perhaps imagine that Shakespeare cut down his first version to get the right effect, but that he really intended the effect, and wasn't merely pushed into it by a Court performance, seems hard to doubt.

Some remarks by Dover Wilson on the state of mind of Macbeth, which only bear indirectly on the question of cuts, had better be looked at next. Murderous thoughts, we are told, first come to him, not before the play nor yet on hearing the prophecy, but on hearing that he has become Thane of Cawdor so that half of the prophecy has been fulfilled. The temptation fills him with horror: "the symptoms would be meaningless" unless he were "an innocent spirit reeling under an utterly unforeseen attack". This first assault of the Tempter is viewed in moral terms, and Macbeth repels it as such, but the idea continues to "mine unseen". When Duncan appoints Malcolm his heir, though the deed seems as terrible as ever, Macbeth "has moved appreciably nearer to it". I should have thought he clearly plans to do it: the words are:

> Stars, hide your fires;
> Let not light see my black and deep desires:
> The eye wink at the hand: yet let that be
> Which the eye fears, when it is done, to see.

The chief thought here, surely, as in all these habitual metaphors of darkness, is that Macbeth wants somehow to get away from or hoodwink his consciousness and self-knowledge and do the deed without knowing it. His first meeting with his wife helps forward this process, as Dover Wilson agrees. But by the stage of the I.vii soliloquy ("if it were done ...") he has reached "a new stage of his disease"; he is thinking not morally but purely from self-interest, says Dover Wilson. Yet "the voice of the good angel can still be heard by us, though not by Macbeth, speaking through the poetry which reveals his subconscious mind". (A. C. Bradley ought to be given credit here, I think.) The proof that his objections are now only prudential is that those are the only ones he makes to his wife (but they are the only ones he *dares* make) and this is why he is won over by her plan to hide the murder—though obviously open to suspicion, it gives him "the talisman his soul craves", an *appearance* of safety (so far from that, it seems to me, what wins him over is her reckless courage). After the murder he has no morality but only bad dreams of being assassinated, which drive him on from crime to crime (but it is the suppressed feeling of guilt, surely, which emerges as neurotic fear—that is how he is "possessed", if you regard him as possessed).

All this discussion about when he is thinking "morally" seems to me to ignore the central fact that there are two moral systems in view, even though one of them is firmly called a bad system. When the witches lead off with "fair is foul and foul is fair" they are wicked; but when Macbeth says their soliciting "cannot be good, cannot be ill" he is in real doubt; and the first soliloquy of Lady Macbeth is presented as a quite laborious and earnest inversion of moral values. The Machiavellian or the Ambitious Man has his moral struggles no less than the Christian or the loyal feudalist, and what prevents Macbeth from confessing his scruples to his wife is a genuine moral shame.

> Thou wouldst be great,
> Art not without ambition, but without
> The illness should attend it; what thou wouldst highly
> That thou wouldst holily,

and so on, is not meant merely as obvious moral paradox from the author but as real moral blame from the deluded speaker; a man *should* be ambitious and *should* have the "illness" required for success in that line of effort; it is good to will highly, and slavish to will "holily". The inversion of moral values is sketched as an actual system of belief, and given strength by being tied to the supreme virtue of courage. Of course it is presented as both wicked and fallacious, but also as a thing that some people feel. (Dover Wilson indeed makes this point himself, by saying that she regards the private murder as a glorious act, just as Macbeth does killing in battle. But Macbeth is involved in this puzzle too, as is rubbed in by the irony of "nothing affeared of what thyself didst make, strange images of death".) There is a good deal of truth, in fact, in the Victorian joke that the Macbeths commit the murder as a painful duty. Indeed they never seem to regard royalty as a source of pleasure at all. Lady Macbeth regards the crown as an "ornament", a satisfaction to pride; and Macbeth says in so many words, "I have no spur / To prick the sides of my intent, but only / Vaulting ambition, which o'er-leaps itself." Unless you regard this moral paradox as already obvious, given from the start, it is natural to feel that the characters are practically unmotivated and must have been explained in early passages which are now cut.

The great question "How many children had Lady Macbeth?" had better be fitted in here. The question cannot be regarded as merely farcical, as one might say, "Who wants children anyhow?" Macbeth is far more concerned to found a royal line than to be King himself; he howls on and on against the threat that his descendants will be supplanted by Banquo's. When Lady Macbeth says she would kill her child she is felt to be ridiculous as well as devilish, because without a child the main purpose would be defeated. But the murdered or the helpless child comes echoing back into the play all through (as Cleanth Brooks pointed out); it is the one thing strong enough to defeat Macbeth and the whole philosophy he has adopted. In the story, however, we are left in doubt whether the Macbeths have any children; it would be symbolically appropriate if they hadn't, but Macbeth's talk would be absurd unless they have, as perhaps it is; and there the matter is left. It is the only crux in the play, I think, which need be regarded as a radical dramatic ambiguity.

The first of Dover Wilson's arguments for a cut scene is what he calls the "ambiguity" of Banquo. A. C. Bradley remarked that only Banquo knew what the witches had told Macbeth, and by keeping silent after the murder, though suspicious in soliloquy, he "yielded to evil". Dover Wilson says that this "shows Bradley at his weakest", because Shakespeare could not possibly have intended to show to James I the supposed founder of his line as a criminal. Besides, James believed in the Divine Right of Kings, even of usurpers once legally crowned, and would have thought Banquo's behaviour merely correct. Exactly; the King would find nothing to complain about, and other persons in the audience could look at the character in other ways—surely this second point of Dover Wilson destroys his previous argument that a scene has been cut. Besides, if James was the person to whom Banquo needed justifying, it is absurd to suppose that the scene justifying him was cut out precisely to suit performance before James.

It seems to me, in any case, that all the lords are meant to be "ambiguous", in the quite flat vague sense that we feel any of them may be playing his own game during this period of confusion, though we never get it clear. "Cruel are the times, when we are traitors, and do not know ourselves"—the point could hardly be rubbed in more firmly, with even the child Macduff prattling about whether his father is a traitor too. It is not merely a literary effect; it is what people really do feel in times of civil war, and Shakespeare had a practical and lasting fear of civil war. The witches say it is "fog" in the first scene, and fog it remains not only in Macbeth's mind but in all the nobles'; we are given two sheer scenes (II.iv and III.vi) of suspicious gossip between persons hardly worth naming, to intensify the thing merely. Ross in the first of these scenes is clearly telling lies to Old Man. Old Man tells a prodigious story about what the birds did on the night Duncan was murdered, so Ross says on that night Duncan's horses turned wild in nature and began kicking their stalls down. "Tis said they ate each other" says eager Old Man, and Ross says "They did so, to the amazement of my eyes / That looked upon it. Here comes the good Macduff." Surely even a very superstitious audience would realise that he has waited to see how much Old Man will swallow; he is "spreading alarm and despondency". But this isn't meant to reduce the magic of the play to farce; the idea is that a fog of evil really has got abroad, and as likely as not did produce prodigies; the fact that Ross is telling lies about them only makes it all worse. In short, I believe that the various muddles which have occupied the minds of critics (the kind of thing which allowed the Victorian Libby to produce a rather impressive argument that Ross was the villain all through) were deliberately planned to keep the audience guessing but fogged.

On this basis, I think, we can advance with tolerable firmness upon the baffling confusions about the previous Thane of Cawdor. At the beginning of the play messengers arrive from two battlefields; they speak obscurely, but we learn that Cawdor was assisting the King of Norway, who was at the southern battlefield. We then see Macbeth returning from the northern battlefield; he is met by Ross and Angus, who are sent to tell him he has been given the thaneship of Cawdor, and he has never heard of the treachery of Cawdor; Angus says he doesn't know whether Cawdor "was combined / With those of Norway, or did line the rebel / With hidden help and vantage"; and Ross says nothing about it, though he was the messenger from the south in the previous scene. Dover Wilson points out that the prophecy of the witches, that Macbeth will become Thane of Cawdor, "loses half its virtue." if Macbeth has just been fighting Cawdor and knows he is a traitor; but anyhow the audience must be meant to gather that he doesn't know it. "The real explanation", says Dover Wilson (thus I think giving an example of what he calls "Bradley at his weakest", the treatment of a play as a historical document) is that Cawdor had *secretly* helped both the Norwegian invader and the Scotch rebel lord; so this must have been said plainly in one of the cut lines. This rule that secrets have to be said plainly, one is tempted to observe, would lighten the work of the historian if properly carried out. But the historian has still got to worry about how Macbeth managed to fight two decisive battles, practically on the same day, in both Fife and Inverness, north and south of east Scotland and more than a hundred miles apart. The messengers came in almost simultaneously; of course he could conceivably have done it by moving as fast as the messengers—a horse relay system has to be envisaged, though we see him returning from the battle on foot. But there is nothing in the deliberately confused scene I.ii to convince a practical listener that Macbeth went to a new battlefield; so far from that, as soon as he had finished with the rebels (we are told, I.ii.30, by the messenger from the northern battlefield) he and Banquo began to fight the invaders; then Ross comes in from the southern battlefield and never mentions Macbeth, though he uses the peculiar term "Bellona's bridegroom" which practically all commentators assume to mean Macbeth in person. Duncan, to whom these things are told, expresses no interest whatever in the conduct of the campaigns but only attends to the passing phrase about the traitorship of Cawdor, adding that Macbeth shall succeed him. This need not make Duncan look weak; he is dealing with the only immediate essential point. It is only reasonable to suppose that the Norwegians, holding the sea and fully informed by the traitor, would attack at two points at once. I hope I do not appear subtle here; I am trying to follow what the first audiences would make of it. They were very much better-trained than I am on picking up the spoken word; they also thought very keenly, after succeeding in hearing words, along their own lines of military and political strategy. They would certainly notice that Duncan never examines the case of Cawdor, and is only told of Cawdor's confession by his child Malcolm, who may easily have been lied to. I do not mean that there is a story about Cawdor to be dug out of the Shakespeare text, only that the fate of the previous Thane of Cawdor (from the point of view of the first listeners) was already made a baffling and fateful thing before Macbeth began to howl out "And therefore Cawdor shall sleep no more, Macbeth shall sleep no more." In fact, everybody feels this; it is the poetry of the thing. All Macbeth's inheritance is appalling; here he inherits from a man who, in spite of a circle of contradictory gossip, remains baffling and is assumed to need no trial. The smashing irony of "There's no art / To find the mind's construction in the face ... O worthiest cousin" is transferred obviously by Duncan from Cawdor to Macbeth as soon as Macbeth enters. We do not have to worry about Cawdor; he is presumed to be in the usual fog. But his name does sound like Fate in the play, merely because Macbeth has got to be the same kind of thing all over again. Perhaps it is tedious to say something so obvious; but editors who try to tidy the play really do need to be told the obvious. So far from being a cut version of a tidy historical play now unfortunately lost, it is a rather massive effort, very consistently carried out, to convey the immense confusion in which these historical events actually occur.

Various minor arguments are often produced for believing in cuts, for example the large number of incomplete lines. It seems to me that they merely give a more dramatic and vigorous rhythm. The most extreme case of this uneasiness in the editorial ear is "Toad, that under cold stone," which practically every editor since Pope has wanted to tinker with because it "doesn't scan", whereas of course it is a wonderfully powerful sound effect. However, Dover Wilson is not particularly guilty here; and one cannot blame his ear for feeling that there is something peculiar about the beginning of the play—the whole second scene is pretty close to turgid rant. I think it was needed, however hard it may be to stomach, just to get enough pace at the beginning; the audience has to be thrown into a wild and whirling situation right away. Has to be, that is, if you are going to get to the murder of Duncan very quickly; certainly, if you are going to put in a lot of extra scenes before it, you will want a different beginning, but to argue from one to the other is only to argue in a circle. The same applies to the complaints of editors about the "abruptness" of scene iv, the way Duncan weeps for joy over the loyalty of Macbeth, dooms himself by making Malcolm his heir, and arranges an immediate death by inviting himself to Macbeth's castle, actually in three consecutive sentences. Surely it is absurd to say that this masterly piece of compression cannot have been intended, merely *because* it is so compressed. You might as well say that Wagner must have composed the first draft of his music for a single flute, because he cannot have intended to be so noisy. As to the arguments that the audience needs to be told where Macbeth's castle is before Duncan says "from hence to Inverness", so that an earlier passage must have been cut—the audience are told it in the next sentence; as soon as their interest in the subject has been aroused. As to the arguments that the appearance of a third murderer for Banquo, and Macduff's desertion of his wife and family, are puzzling and therefore must have been prepared for in earlier passages now cut-of course, they are *meant* to seem puzzling; they are part of the general atmosphere of fog and suspicion.

Dover Wilson speaks with great confidence about a passage in Malcolm's curious scene of self-accusation:

Nay, had I power, I should
Pour the sweet milk of concord into hell,

and so on. "That here we have an instance of rewriting after the completion of the original dialogue cannot, I think, be denied", he says, and the reason is that the passage is aimed at pleasing James; instead of following Holinshed and accusing himself of falsehood, he accuses himself of contentiousness, "a strange vice and expressed in strangely modern terms", says Dover Wilson (oddly), but this would please James who was a pacifist. The change was made "because Shakespeare had come to know more of his royal master's mind in the interval". This seems to me a really remarkable case of arguing in a circle. Dover Wilson himself suggests that Shakespeare went to Edinburgh in 1602 or so and wrote the first draft of the play there specifically to curry favour with a possible future King of England; if this is true, it seems quite unnecessary to suppose he had to learn a rather prominent fact about the mind of James four years later. In any case, the mind of Shakespeare himself can reasonably be considered when we wonder why he wrote something down. He thought civil war a real and horrible danger, and he was right in fearing it would come; we need not suppose he was lying to flatter the King when he says it here. And he hardly alters the Holinshed moral anecdote at all, from this point of view; he merely illustrates it. The objection to lying in kings is that by lying they make people quarrel; you don't want a child's copybook rule against lying here, you want to relate the harmfulness of lying to the appalling scene before you; and that is all he does. Surely it is absurd for Dover Wilson to call this a case where revision "cannot be denied".

However, his major thesis does not turn on these dubious minor points; it raises two important questions, and many people will feel it to give them probable and reasonable answers. He maintains that the full play of Macbeth gave a much more prolonged struggle between Macbeth and his wife, in which things that now seem baffling to a careful reader, if not to an audience, were given intelligible preparation. I do not want to treat this as absurd; in fact it seems rather wilful to argue, as I am now doing, that the first part of the play was intended to be as thin and confused as so many critics have found the existing text. On the other hand, since we cannot recover these lost scenes if there were any, it does seem at least tolerably useful to show that we can get along without them; and I think that to answer the two questions on that basis (chiefly, of course, by collecting previous opinions) improves or restores the play a good deal.

The first main argument is that Lady Macbeth, in her second soliloquy and her first two conversations with her husband, repeatedly says or appears to say that she is going to kill Duncan herself; but then without further explanation it turns out that both she and Macbeth assume Macbeth is going to do it. It does seem likely that this change of plan would at least have been mentioned. By the way, what seems to me a more immediate argument for some cut in I.vii is that she makes Macbeth change his mind so ridiculously quickly; he says with apparently settled conviction "We will proceed no further in this business", and within thirty lines he is merely asking for a good plan. The answer here, surely, is that all poetic drama uses poetry as a substitute for repetition of arguments and "sleeping on" a problem and such like; the convention feels natural because it is clearly what the stage requires—the characters talk so powerfully that the story can move forward. In real life the Macbeths would argue for half the night, but the audience is actually presented with the morning after a few minutes of action. Here you might possibly invent some arrangement about the time, but the same device is used later in the play with no break at all; the banquet at which Banquo's ghost appears leads us on to dawn in a few minutes, and this seems a natural consequence of the brief exhausted worrying of the Macbeth couple after dismissing their guests. These conventions of course have been much discussed, and they are not questioned here by Dover Wilson. I wanted to remark that we should only accept Elizabethan conventions if they are in a sense natural, that is, such as modern actors and producers can make an audience accept. It is off the point to list "the Elizabethan conventions", as some critics have done; because the Elizabethans did not formulate such things and rather imagined they were free from them. In the case of Lady Macbeth, we can say that the mere force of her two speeches is enough to prevent Macbeth from looking too ridiculous; but also that, even if it isn't, the main point of the story is that he let himself be hurried into a wrong decision.

The second main argument, from the same scene, is that she scolds him because, though unwilling to do the murder now that "time" and "place ... adhere", he had been willing to promise he would do it when he needn't act, and she finds this a typical mark of cowardice. It seems obvious to deduce that the promise was made before the battle, therefore of course before the meeting with the witches; but Dover Wilson maintains that this would spoil the whole shock of their prophecy. He therefore argues that Macbeth must have visited his wife after seeing the witches and before reporting to the King on his conduct in the battle; a scene has therefore been cut. But a definite geography can be fitted together; Macbeth has been fighting near the east coast, because the Norwegian invader could throw in fresh troops when the rebel was defeated; he walks westwards to the King's headquarters to report; and his wife is in his castle at Inverness, a day's ride to the west again. He has a positive duty to report to the King before going to her. Surely this kind of point was firm in the Elizabethan mind, however foggy everything else was made. (Even if you are determined to have him gallop between the two battlefields instead of staying at one of them, he still has an obligation to report before he goes home.) In this scene with his wife, now lost, says Dover Wilson, he must have sworn he would kill Duncan when occasion arose, and she in her turn must have insisted, probably using her now misplaced invocation to the "spirits that / tend on mortal thoughts", that she would do it herself. In our text "I.v", jammed together from bits of the lost scenes, she is still assuming she will do it herself; and the change of plan by which Macbeth does it, says Dover Wilson,

> ought by all dramatic rights to be explained to the audience. This was originally done, I suggest, by means of a further dialogue between husband and wife, preceded perhaps by a scene in which, going into the bedroom knife in hand, she cannot bring herself to do it.

So three whole scenes are to be added before we finish with Duncan. The first objection, I think, must be that this painstaking treatment would throw away the whole impression of "fog" which has been established at the start; the impression, that is, of a fatal decision made hurriedly in confusion. The play that Dover Wilson is imagining, or rather not imagining, would be like a "debate" by Racine. Also I do not see why, in the first of these lost scenes, Lady Macbeth insisted that *she* would kill Duncan, if the whole point of the scene was to make *him* swear he would do it. Also the arguments keep on being drawn from our existing text as though it were the original text, though that is what is being denied; if Lady Macbeth *didn't* say she would kill Duncan as late as our "I.v" (because her remarks to that effect have been dragged in from an earlier scene) then you can't require further scenes which presume that she *did* say it. However, this amount of confusion might be justified. What does seem clear is that the play supposed by Dover Wilson would not do what *Macbeth* does. I suspect he would have two jealous hell-hounds, each of them greedy to be first at the kill. In any case, he would not have an atmosphere of wincing and horrified determination, in which a crucial decision is scrambled through hurriedly and confusedly.

Before reaching this bold theory, Dover Wilson recalls various older suggestions about why Lady Macbeth says Macbeth had broached the enterprise before:

> (1) on psychological grounds as a bold lie or as an exaggeration, based on his letter to her, and (2) on technical grounds, as an

"episodic intensification" like the allusion to Lady Macbeth's children, or as a piece of dramatic legerdemain resorted to in order to stress at this juncture the less admirable side of Macbeth's character. The trouble with this last explanation, in some ways the most plausible of the four, is that as no spectator or reader apparently observed the point until 1865, it can hardly have been intended to stress anything.

But surely it can add to the atmosphere without the critics arguing about it first; both the actors and the audience are always doing a great deal of "interpretation" which doesn't get written down. I am anxious not to ignore these partial ways of swallowing the effect, without which it would no doubt have long been felt as obtrusively confused. Instead of that it feels like a fierce strain on your attention, intelligible somehow but intensely far from common life—new factors keep being thrown in. To that extent it should I think be called a "dramatic ambiguity"; but all the same I think the text here is meant to yield one straightforward story about what happened.

If we take "I.vii" as it stands, surely we have to believe that Macbeth *did* broach the enterprise to his wife before the battle and before meeting the witches, and before the play; what is more, we have to feel that this belated piece of news about Macbeth is credible on the spot, though it comes as a dramatic surprise. Lady Macbeth goes on to hint that he was half drunk at the time. At least, I am not sure that her metaphor in itself need carry much weight, but an actor could easily emphasise the lines so as to make it prominent:

> Was the hope drunk
> Wherein you dressed yourself? Hath it slept since
> And wakes it now, to look so green and pale ...

It is not hard to believe that she could drink with him till he talked rashly; she boasts very soon after that she drank the grooms under the table and was only made bold by it. The argument against believing in this previous conversation, according to Dover Wilson, is that the first witch scene, "depicts the terror of Macbeth's soul when the idea of murder first comes to him", and the first speech of his wife "makes it clear that so far he has refused to entertain any but honourable thoughts". As to the second point, she only makes clear that he has been deciding *against* the murder; how can she know all this, about how much he wants to do it, and fears to do it, if they have never mentioned the subject to each other? No doubt in real life she could, but surely the dramatic impression is that this kind of topic is practically the small talk of the Macbeth household. As to the first point, which I agree is stronger and must be answered by imposing a greater dramatic strain, it is a commonplace that Macbeth and Banquo react quite differently to the witches. Banquo is needed in the scene as the innocent mind, which accepts the prophecy about himself as merely a statement about the future; Macbeth, because he already has murder in view, immediately accepts his part of the prophecy as a kind of order that he must bring it about. What horrifies him so much is that the witches appear as an externalisation of his secret, guilty daydreams; partly he feels exposed, but even worse he feels that the imaginary world has become real and must now be acted upon. The reaction is immediate; the sequence is:

> 3. *Witch* All hail, Macbeth! that shalt be king hereafter.
> *Banquo* Good sir, why do you start, and seem to fear
> Things that do sound so fair?

and almost his first words alone call it "this supernatural *soliciting*"; whereas so far from tempting him to act, they have if anything told him that there is no need for action; he is sure to become King. This actually occurs to him a few lines later ("If chance will have me king, why chance may crown me, / Without my stir"), and he seems to throw the idea aside till Duncan appoints Malcolm his next heir. Then it comes back to him strongly, but he has already begun to waver away from it again by the time he meets his wife. Incidentally, the phrase "my thought, whose murder yet is but fantastical" does not sound to me as if the thought first came into his mind a few moments ago; the point is rather "in spite of hearing the witches just now, my thought is still only imaginary; the fatal decision has still not been taken". Surely none of it sounds like a man who has never thought of such a thing before. Bradley makes most of the points along this line, and I feel Dover Wilson ought to have done more to recognise them. But he might still say that they are the "weak side" of Bradley, deductions in the study which are ineffective on the stage. I do not agree, though no doubt the effect depends largely on the actor and the production. We are not meant, probably, to decide in the first witch scene that Macbeth has already discussed the murder; but we are meant to be in a position to reflect, when his wife brings out her accusation, "after all, he didn't act like a man to whom the idea was new, such as Banquo, and he has gone on wavering ever since; she is probably exaggerating, but they probably have talked about it before".

This seems to me an important point, because if accepted it would clear up a lot of muddling about the idea of Fate, which has become almost habitual in critical writing on *Macbeth*. Shakespeare I think always uses the word with a fairly clear suggestion that it stands for an excuse, and for his audience it was at best a learned classical idea, not one that they couldn't avoid taking seriously. The dramatic trick, in the structure of the first Act of *Macbeth*, is that the audience is put through what appears to be an experience of Fate but is then expected to think more sensibly. The audience is anyway expected to be frightened by the witches, and during the first meeting of Macbeth with the witches the audience might as it were be stampeded into the immediately plausible theory of Dover

Wilson, that Macbeth had an innocent mind before now but has at once been forced into a damnable intention by a supernatural power. But afterwards, listening to Lady Macbeth, and no longer frightened by the witches, they are to recover their theology; they should think "Yes, after all, a witch *couldn't* have made him do it, unless he had weakened his own will before." "Compare the case of Banquo", they could go on; and this line of thought was not difficult for them, because they had assumed Macbeth to be wicked before they came; their chief engagement in the witch scenes would be from puzzles about the limitations of the powers of devils and the free will of man. That the self-blinded soul would fall fast when pushed by witches would still be a natural expectation, fulfilled by the dramatic structure. I don't say that a modern producer could easily recover this movement of thought, but it does prevent what I have just called "a dramatic trick" from being a mere cheat.

The strongest modern attack on *Macbeth* was made by Robert Bridges, whose central charge was this:

> It would not be untrue to the facts as Shakespeare presents them to precede the drama with a scene in which Macbeth and Lady Macbeth should in Machiavellian composure deliberate together upon the murder of Duncan, but plainly such a scene would destroy the drama.

A simple distinction is needed here; to act such a scene would destroy the sequence of feelings which the audience is meant to go through, but to believe that it happened doesn't destroy the drama, in fact the audience are meant to have come round to that (apart from the "composure") by the end of the first Act. A certain amount of surprise is quite usual in plays; what Bridges seems to have felt is the old Puritanical objection to all plays, that they don't tell all the truth all the time.

Macbeth's first meeting with his wife in the play (end of I.v) requires good acting. He is gravely shaken by the thought of guilt but has still not decided to incur it. He leaves it to her to raise the topic at all. She can see just what he is feeling, and begins at once to twist him into action. She pretends that the indecision and conscience in his face are merely the outward marks of a savage determination; let him hide them, and there will be no more trouble. It is too much effort for him to start to unwind this misunderstanding; he merely says it will have to be discussed later. But meanwhile his wife, who knows he is going to say this, has cut the ground from under him by implying that *she* is going to do the murder, so he needn't worry about it again. She does not however say this in so many words, and no doubt assumes that he will not be able to leave her carrying all the burden. The words are framed with a grim and triumphant ambiguity, as is obvious at once, but one does not easily notice that the ambiguity carries this twist of personal argument as well:

He that's coming
Must be provided for; and you shall put
This night's great business into my dispatch,
Which shall to all our nights and days to come
Give solely sovereign sway and masterdom.

The whole thrill of the first phrase is that it means "I have to do my housework next; I have to get ready a grand dinner-party; don't you worry, you have only to keep your face straight" as well as "somebody has to plan how to kill the guest"; but neither idea says quite positively that she will do the killing. It is true, of course, that her soliloquy just before has prayed for cruelty enough to use a knife, which she rightly fears she may not have; but this is a matter of preparing enough determination for her share in the murder, not of saying she is determined to reject the help of her husband. The balance of the thing seems to me to be kept just right.[1]

The next great scene between them is in I.vii, after Macbeth has said "We will proceed no further in this business." She has to rally all her powers, makes a variety of accusations against him for *not* being ready to do it, and says she would have killed her baby *if* she had sworn to kill it as Macbeth has sworn to kill Duncan; she never says that *she* has sworn to kill Duncan. But there is again the obscure threat against him, very hard for him to stand up against, that perhaps if he refuses he will only be thrusting the work upon *her*. Macbeth's first words when he yields are "If *we* should fail" and from then on they both assume they will work together. Finally in II.ii, after making the chamberlains drunk and leaving the daggers beside them, she remarks that she thought of doing it herself before Macbeth came, but found she couldn't; she had already planned for him to come, and has only to ring a bell to bring him.

This seems to me a consistent story, not leaving any need for three extra scenes that would destroy the pace; hard to get across in the acting, no doubt, but that need not astonish us. The curious thing, rather typical of the combination of grasp of mind with wilfulness in Dover Wilson, is that he admits nearly all of it himself. It is agreed that Macbeth's mind has been "rendered temptable by previous dalliance of that fancy with ambitious thoughts"; it is agreed that, by offering to do the murder, his wife "leads him unconsciously forward by removing from his path the terror that immediately confronts him". Perhaps it is unnecessary to answer at such length a theory to which its propounder, very fairly, has already given the essential answers.

II

It struck me that this essay seemed rather too confident, so I turned to a work of attractive confidence and vigour by J. M. Robertson, *Literary Detection* (1931), concerned to prove that a great variety of hands mangled the play of *Macbeth*

incessantly from its first drafting by Kyd; very depressing to read, naturally. The
great days of Disintegration are over, but the subject cannot be ignored; I noticed
G. B. Harrison recently (*Shakespeare's Tragedies*, 1951) saying that the
collaborator must have written such things as

> Thoughts speculative their unsure hopes relate,
> But certain issue strokes must arbitrate.

We need not pretend it is good, but I think that Shakespeare, a peaceable man,
was usually embarrassed when he had to write something particularly soldierly;
it is rather the same even with Fortinbras. Also one cannot call the theatrical
effect bad; these laboured confusing patches somehow add to the wild foggy
background. We cannot say they are certainly not Shakespeare's because they
aren't in "his style".

The main argument for disintegration is from "tags" or repeated phrases,
and the results seem valuable in showing what a large common stock the
Elizabethans could draw upon. Robertson assumes that a "tag" could not be
repeated unless deliberately, and uses such phrases as "Shakespeare does not go
about picking from Kyd in general". I think he often echoed Kyd, but without
noticing it, and would only have been mildly interested if you had told him so.
The fact that what amounts to "Give me the daggers" is said by a woman in both
Soliman and Perseda and *Arden of Faversham* seems worth knowing as part of the
mental background of the audience (for instance, it shows they would not find
Lady Macbeth incredible); but we need not think Shakespeare would avoid
repeating it. Indeed a dramatist who worked under such a taboo would have to
become very eccentric. We might go so far as to deduce that Shakespeare did not
despise the Kyd part of his background.

Many of the objections of Robertson seem to me worth answering but in
no need of so startling an answer; for example, "the man who can see nothing
absurd in the blood-boltered Sergeant ploughing his gory way from Fife up to
Forres, ahead of the mounted nobles, is capable of any bluff" (since it is about
150 miles). But it is enough to assume there were two battles, with Macbeth and
the Sergeant at the near one; a natural presumption from the two messengers—
I don't deny that a line or two making it clearer may have got cut. The "aside" of
Macbeth at the end of "I.iv", announcing his treachery to the King in Council,
is absurd in itself and "the couplets are utterly out of place in an aside"—a good
point, but it isn't meant to be an "aside"; it is a soliloquy on the apron-stage after
the Council scene is over. "Shakespeare never brought the primary exposition of
Macbeth's growth of purpose to clearness because he was hampered by a
composite recast of an old play." But there is a positive merit in having his growth
of purpose a mystery which only gradually clears. "The juggling cauldron stuff is
extraneous to the very idea of Fate", therefore can't be Shakespeare's; "what the
play needed, for him, in that kind, was just the really thrilling sense of 'Fate and

metaphysical aid'". The devil, in short, ought to be presented as a gentleman; I think Shakespeare hadn't got all this respect for Fate, and would regard the sordidness of the witches as a traditional and proper thing to show about them.

The undue refinement in this last case is perhaps a natural result of no longer believing in the witches; I agree that they can't be seen in their original proportions by a modern audience. But I think a certain wincing away from the play causes many of Robertson's other objections, as in the sustained argument that the Porter's scene cannot be Shakespeare's. Middleton's *Blurt Master-Constable* makes the servant of a prostitute say "I am porter in Hell", so Middleton wrote it. But the familiarity of the idea was no objection to it; the audience would only see the point more readily. And the idea is not merely to provide "comic relief", which Robertson easily shows wasn't always required. The idea is that the servants regarded the victory and the visit of the King as an occasion for a gaudy night; only their masters regarded it as an occasion to enter Hell.

The repeated use of theatrical couplets at the ends of the scenes appeared particularly vulgar to Robertson, and he throws out a number of them which seem to me to sum up the thought of the play particularly vividly, such as

> The eye wink at the hand; yet let that be
> Which the eye fears, when it is done, to see.

and even "Hover through the fog and filthy air" is called a "vacuous tag-line", though it establishes from the start the theme of fog that Robertson always ignores. Even the central lines

> But cruel are the times, when we are traitors
> And do not know ourselves, when we hold rumour
> From what we fear, yet know not what we fear,
> But float upon a wild and violent sea,
> Each way, and move

are said to be certainly not Shakespeare's because they have "no sense". Here one must lose patience, I think; no one who had experienced civil war could say it had no sense. I find I take *know ourselves* to mean chiefly "ourselves know", as with a comma between the words, but "know the right name for our actions, and therefore in some degree our own natures" is also prominent; *hold rumour* could be like "hold parley with", be ready to entertain such a rumour, or simply "hold onto it" by believing it; the compactness is rather strained but surely not unlike Shakespeare. I still feel strongly what I said about *move* here in my *Ambiguity* (end of Chap. II) but the passage is still very good even if you regard it as incomplete or are determined to emend "move" to "none".

Robertson takes "Before my body / I throw my warlike shield" as admittedly intolerable, known even by its defenders to be very bad; he jeers at E.

K. Chambers for saying one could not deny it to Shakespeare merely on grounds of style, and says "Chambers does not distinguish between the sense of style and the sense of sense". This case seems worth attention, because I suspect the trouble is merely that the critics don't see the point. "I will not yield" and so on, says Macbeth,

> Though Birnam Wood *be* come to Dunsinane,
> And thou opposed, *being* of no woman born,
> Yet I will try the last; before my body
> I throw my warlike *shield*. Lay on, Macduff,
> And damned be he that first cries "hold, enough".

The argument is "*although* the protections promised by the witches have failed me, *yet* I will try the bodily protection which is all I have left"; once you notice this idea, surely, you have nothing to grumble about.

NOTE

1. As to the much discussed problem about whether Lady Macbeth "really" faints, it seems to me quite invisible; she probably wouldn't know herself. She is only keeping going by an effort of will, and she can see that this is a good time to stop the effort.

JANET ADELMAN

Nature's Piece 'gainst Fancy: Poetry and the Structure of Belief in Antony and Cleopatra

Throughout *Antony and Cleopatra*, we have seen Cleopatra indulge in visions of Antony whenever he was absent; and after his death, she creates the most monumental vision of all. Her emperor Antony is a gigantic and godlike figure, virtually a human form divine. To what extent can we share her vision, or the other hyperbolical visions of the play? The study of the traditional interpretations of myth can set her emperor in an appropriate context, but it cannot in itself verify her vision. Mythic and iconographic meaning can participate in the significance of a play only if the play first invites their participation; if the work itself does not provide a fertile seedbed, then no amount of mythic analogy will flourish. We must consequently turn back to the play itself.

SKEPTICISM AND BELIEF

You lie up to the hearing of the gods. [5.2.95]

From the first words of the play ("Nay, but"), our reactions have been at issue. We are given judgments that we must simultaneously accept and reject; we are shown the partiality of truth. But finally we are not permitted to stand aside and comment with impunity any more than Enobarbus is: we must choose either to accept or to reject the lovers' versions of themselves and of their death; and our

---

From *The Common Liar: An Essay on Antony and Cleopatra.* © 1973 by Yale University.

choice will determine the meaning of the play for us. But the choice becomes increasingly impossible to make on the evidence of our reason or our senses. How can we believe in Enobarbus's description of Cleopatra as Venus when we see the boy actor before us? The Antony whom Cleopatra describes in her dream is not the Antony whom we have seen sitting on stage in dejection after Actium or bungling his suicide. Although the lovers die asserting their postmortem reunion, all we see is the dead queen and her women, surrounded by Caesar and his soldiers. The stage action necessarily presents us with one version of the facts, the poetry with another.[1] This is the dilemma inherent in much dramatic poetry; and the more hyperbolical the poetry, the more acute the dilemma.[2] Critics are occasionally tempted to read *Antony and Cleopatra* as a very long poem; but it is essential that we be aware of it as drama at all times. For how can one stage hyperbole? Reading the play, we might imagine Antony a colossus; but what shall we do with the very human-sized Antony who has been before us for several hours? In a sonnet, for instance, an assertion contrary to fact will be true within the poem; standards must be imported from outside the work by which to find the assertions improbable. As Shakespeare points out, not every girl be-sonneted has breasts whiter than snow, despite the assertions of her sonneteer. But a play carries its own refutation within itself: even with the most advanced stage technology, the action and the human actors will undercut these assertions even as they are made. Precisely this tension is at the heart of *Antony and Cleopatra*: we can neither believe nor wholly disbelieve in the claims made by the poetry.

The poetry of the last two acts is generally acknowledged as the sleight-of-hand by which Shakespeare transforms our sympathies toward the lovers, in despite of the evidence of our reason and our senses. Although even Caesar speaks in blank verse, the language of most richness and power is in the service of the lovers: it is the language in which Enobarbus creates Cleopatra as Venus and the lovers assert the value of their love and their death. In this play, the naysayers may have reason and justice on their side; but as Plato suspected when he banished poetry from his republic, reason and justice are no match for poetry. The appeal to mere reason will not always affect fallen man; according to Renaissance theorists, it was precisely the power of poetry to *move*, occasionally against the dictates of all reason, that made it at once most dangerous and most fruitful. And modern critics are as wary of the power of poetry as their predecessors: the poetry in *Antony and Cleopatra* is almost always praised, but the praise frequently coincides with the suspicion that it has somehow taken unfair advantage of us by befuddling our clear moral judgment. It is that doubtless delightful but nonetheless dubious means by which the lovers are rescued from our condemnation at the last moment, rather as Lancelot rescues Guinevere from her trial by fire. We are pleased but suspect that strictest justice has not been done. If it is true that Shakespeare uses the poetry to dazzle our moral sense and undo the structure of criticism in the play, then we may find *Antony and Cleopatra* satisfying as a rhetorical showcase, but we cannot admire the play as a whole.[3] It is refreshing to find this charge made explicit by G. B. Shaw, who clearly enjoys expressing his contempt for a poet who finds it necessary to rescue his lovers from our moral judgment by means of a rhetorical trick.

> Shakespear's Antony and Cleopatra must needs be as intolerable to the true Puritan as it is vaguely distressing to the ordinary healthy citizen, because after giving a faithful picture of the soldier broken down by debauchery, & the typical wanton in whose arms such men perish, Shakespear finally strains all his huge command of rhetoric & stage pathos to give a theatrical sublimity to the wretched end of the business, & to persuade foolish spectators that the world was well lost by the twain. Such falsehood is not to be borne except by the real Cleopatras & Antonys (they are to be found in every public house) who would no doubt be glad enough to be transfigured by some poet as immortal lovers. Woe to the poet who stoops to such folly! ... When your Shakespears & Thackerays huddle up the matter at the end by killing somebody & covering your eyes with the undertaker's handkerchief, duly onioned with some pathetic phrase ... I have no respect for them at all: such maudlin tricks may impose on tea-house drunkards, not on me.[4]

The final poetry, detached from character and situation, does indeed give us the glorified vision of love that Shaw mistrusted, a vision not wholly consistent with the merely human Antony and Cleopatra, though Antony is far more than a debauchee and Cleopatra anything but typical, no matter how wanton. But the poetry is not a rhetorical Lancelot. Its assertions and the problems they present to our skepticism have been inherent throughout: and if the poetry strains our credulity toward the end, the strain itself is a necessary part of our experience. Are the visions asserted by the poetry mere fancies, or are they "nature's piece 'gainst fancy"? Precisely this tension between belief and disbelief has been essential from the start. When the lovers first come on stage, very much in the context of an unfriendly Roman judgment, they announce the validity of their love in a hyperbolical poetry which contrasts sharply with Philo's equally hyperbolical condemnation. Here, at the very beginning, two attitudes are set in juxtaposition by the use of two equally impossible images which appeal to two very different modes of belief. Philo uses hyperbole as *metaphor*: "his captain's heart / ... is become the bellows and the fan / To cool a gipsy's lust" (1.1.6–10). This is the deliberate exaggeration which moral indignation excites; it does not in any sense call for our literal belief. The hyperbolical metaphor is morally apt, and that is all. The Roman metaphor is carefully delineated as metaphor: it never pretends to a validity beyond the metaphoric. But what of the lovers? "Then must thou needs find out new heaven, new earth" (1.1.17); "Let Rome in Tiber melt" (1.1.33). Strictly speaking, these hyperboles are not metaphor at all.

Antony's words assert his access to a hyperbolical world where such things actually happen, a world beyond the reach of metaphor. They claim, like Cleopatra's dream, to be in the realm of nature, not of fancy. His words do not give us the protection of regarding them merely as apt metaphors: they make their claim as literal action. We may choose to disbelieve their claim; but in doing so, we are rejecting a version of reality, not the validity of a metaphor. And precisely this kind of assertion will become more insistent—and more improbable—as the play progresses.

The poetry of the final acts should not take us unawares: if at the last moment it surfaces, like the dolphin who shows his back above the element he lives in, the whole of the play and a good deal of Shakespeare's career should have prepared us for its appearance. The validity of the imaginative vision as it is asserted in the poetry is a part of Shakespeare's subject in *Antony and Cleopatra*. But the play is not therefore "about" the vision of the poet: we are presented with lovers creating the image of their love, not with poets poetizing. For the association of love with imagination or fancy is one of Shakespeare's most persistent themes. Love in Shakespeare almost always creates its own imaginative versions of reality; and it is almost always forced to test its version against the realities acknowledged by the rest of the world. Theseus in *Midsummer Night's Dream* tells us that the lover, like the lunatic and the poet, is of imagination all compact (5.1.7–8): in that play, "fancy" is generally used as synonymous with "love." We remember Juliet, valiantly making day into night in despite of the lark that sings so out of tune. Imagination is essential to love; but if it is totally unmoored to reality, it becomes love's greatest threat. Othello's love will turn to hate as Iago poisons his imagination. Spenser circumscribes his book of chaste love (*The Faerie Queene*, book 3) with just this kind of warning about the uses and misuses of imagination in love. Britomart falls in love with Artegall when she sees him in Merlin's magic mirror; she immediately assumes that the vision has no basis in reality and that she is doomed to "feed on shadowes" (*FQ* 3.2.44). But her vision is directed by Merlin's art: her Artegall exists, though she does not recognize him when she first meets him in the real world. The vision here is no shadow but an idealized version of reality; and in time Britomart will recognize the real Artegall whose ideal form she has seen. Her love depends initially on the idealizing vision, but it passes the test of reality. But at the end of book 3, we see the consequences of an abandonment to self-willed imagination. Amoret is subject to Busirane's tormented perversion of love: and the masque of Cupid which holds her captive is led by Fancy (*FQ* 3.12.7).

Love is an act of imagination, but it cannot be an act of *mere* imagination. In the plays that deal with lovers, Shakespeare continually emphasizes the need to circumscribe the tyranny of imagination in love. The arbitrary loves of *Midsummer Night's Dream* must be subjected to the chaos of unbridled fancy (stage-managed by Puck) before they can be sorted out. At the end of *As You*

Like It, Orlando proclaims that he can live no longer by thinking (5.2.55). But in the Forest of Arden, thinking makes it so: Orlando's imagined Rosalind can reveal herself as the real Rosalind because her game has permitted her to test the realities of love. The matter is more complex in *Twelfth Night*, where mere imagination prevails in the self-willed loves of Olivia and Orsino. Here the emblem for the dangerous prevalence of the imagination in love is Malvolio, reading the supposed letter from Olivia and finding himself in every word. Malvolio here is exactly like any lover, searching reality for clues to confirm his own delusions; that the letter is constructed precisely so that he will find such confirmation simply emphasizes the process. Given all this imagination run rampant, it is no wonder that Viola insists on testing her imagination, even to the point of stubbornness "Prove true, imagination, O, prove true" (*Twelfth Night* 3.4.409), she says, and then quizzes Sebastian extensively about his parentage and his early history before she will allow herself to believe that he is her brother.

If the theme of imagination in love is a concern in these plays, it is an obsession in *Troilus and Cressida*, where the consequences of mere imagination are delineated with chilling accuracy. Before Troilus meets with Cressida, "expectation" whirls him round; "th' imaginary relish is so sweet" (3.2.19–20) that it enchants his sense. But even Troilus knows that the imaginary relish will exceed the act; and his description of the physiology of sex is true of all enterprise in this world of frustration

> This is the monstruosity in love, lady, that the will is infinite and the
> execution confin'd, that the desire is boundless and the act a slave to
> limit. [*Troilus and Cressida* 3.2.87–90]

Troilus watching Cressida give herself to Diomed will learn exactly how much desire or imaginary relish is bound by the limits of reality. He has throughout the play assumed that thinking makes it so: during the council scene he asks, "What is aught, but as 'tis valu'd?" (2.2.52). At the end, he will learn the hard facts of value, the facts implicit in Hector's answer to his question

> But value dwells not in particular will;
> It holds his estimate and dignity
> As well wherein 'tis precious of itself
> As in the prizer.
>
> [*Troilus and Cressida* 2.2.53–56]

Troilus and Cressida is Shakespeare's most horrifying vision of untested imagination in love. In that sense, it is a necessary counterpoise both to the earlier comedies and to *Antony and Cleopatra*. For *Antony and Cleopatra* is *Troilus and Cressida* revisited: if *Troilus and Cressida* portrays desire as a slave to limit,

Antony and Cleopatra asserts the power of desire to transcend limits; if Troilus's subjection to mere imagination nearly destroys him, Cleopatra's imagination of her Antony virtually redeems them both. Later, in the romances, the desires of the lovers will usually become their realities: the art itself is nature, and imagination purely redemptive. *Troilus* and the romances are in this sense at opposite ends of the scale: in *Troilus and Cressida*, our credulity is at the mercy of our skepticism, as Troilus himself will discover; in the romances, our skepticism is banished by an act of total poetic faith. But *Antony and Cleopatra* is poised in a paradoxical middle region in which skepticism and credulity must be balanced. In this sense, the perspectives of both *Troilus and Cressida* and the romances are included within *Antony and Cleopatra*; and it is precisely because of this inclusiveness that imagination can emerge triumphant.

The process of testing the imagination is essential to the assertion of its validity: for only through an exacting balance of skepticism and assent can it prove true. And more than any other play, *Antony and Cleopatra* insists on both our skepticism and our assent. For it is simultaneously the most tough-minded and the most triumphant of the tragedies, and it is necessarily both at once. Throughout, Shakespeare disarms criticism by allowing the skeptics their full say: the whole play is in effect a test of the lovers' visions of themselves. Cleopatra herself. presents the most grotesquely skeptical view of her own play:

> ... The quick comedians
> Extemporally will stage us, and present
> Our Alexandrian revels: Antony
> Shall be brought drunken forth, and I shall see
> Some squeaking Cleopatra boy my greatness
> I' the posture of a whore.
>
>   [5.2.215–20]

Once she has spoken, this Roman version of her greatness becomes untenable; we know that Shakespeare's *Antony and Cleopatra* is not an item in Caesar's triumph. It is only in the context of "Nay, but" that we can answer "yes": if the imaginative affirmations were not so persistently questioned, they could not emerge triumphant. The extreme of skepticism itself argues for affirmation: and here the affirmations are no less extreme than the skepticism. Throughout the play, we are not permitted to see Cleopatra merely as a fallen woman: we are asked to see her in the posture of a whore. And when the time has come for affirmation, we are asked to believe not in the probable but in the palpably impossible: not that the lovers are worthy though misguided, but that they are semidivine creatures whose love has somehow managed to escape the bonds of time and space, and even of death. Whore or goddess, strumpet's fool or colossus: the play allows us no midpoint. After all the doubt which has been central to our experience, we are asked to participate in a secular act of faith. This is the final contrariety that the play demands of us: that the extreme of skepticism itself must be balanced by an extreme of assent.

If we come to believe in the assertions of the poetry, it is, I think, precisely because they are so unbelievable. One of the tricks of the human imagination is that an appeal to the rationally possible is not always the most effective means of insuring belief: occasionally an appeal to the impossible, an appeal to doubt, works wonders. *Antony and Cleopatra* embodies in its structure the paradox of faith: the exercise of faith is necessary only when our reason dictates doubt; we believe only in the things that we know are not true. The central strategy of *Antony and Cleopatra* depends upon this process: we achieve faith by deliberately invoking doubt. And in fact this process dictates not only the broad structure of the play but also its poetic texture. The imaginative vision of the play is based firmly on the two rhetorical figures that are themselves dependent on this strategy: paradox and hyperbole.[5]

The incidence of paradox and hyperbole in *Antony and Cleopatra* is not merely an accident or Shakespeare's sleight-of-hand: these figures inform the shape and the substance of the play. For they posit in their very structure the tension between imaginative assertion and literal fact that is part of the state of love. Even Bacon is willing to concede that love is appropriately expressed in hyperbole, precisely because its assertions are palpably untrue.

> It is a strange thing to note the excess of this passion, and how it braves the nature and value of things, by this: that the speaking in a perpetual hyperbole is comely in nothing but love. Neither is it merely in the phrase; for whereas it hath been well said that the arch-flatterer, with whom all the petty flatterers have intelligence, is a man's self; certainly the lover is more. For there was never proud man thought so absurdly well of himself as the lover doth of the person loved.[6]

As Bacon points out, love infects the thought as well as the language of lovers with hyperbole. Biron and the other lovers fall hopelessly into paradox as they fall in love in *Love's Labour's Lost*; even Hamlet is subject to paradox and hyperbole in love, as his poem to Ophelia demonstrates. Only the contradictions of paradox are capable of expressing the contradictions of love: for paradox is a stylistic *discordia concors*, a knot intrinsicate like love itself. In his discussion of the Neoplatonic doctrine of Blind Love, Wind says,

> In reducing the confusions of the senses to reason, the intellect clarifies but it also contracts: for it clarifies by setting limits; and to transcend these limits we require a new and more lasting confusion,

which is supplied by the blindness of love. Intellect excludes
contradictions; love embraces them.[7]

In embracing contradictions, love transcends the limits of the intellect and of
reality as the intellect normally perceives it: and no figure more vehemently
asserts this transcendence than hyperbole, Puttenham's overreacher. Shakespeare
expresses his sense that love transcends the limits of reason and fact in the
overreaching paradoxes of "The Phoenix and the Turtle" here the lovers can
transcend number ("Two distincts, division none," line 27), space ("Distance, and
no space was seen / 'Twixt this turtle and his queen," lines 30–31), and identity
("Property was thus appalled, / That the self was not the same," lines 37–38).
Reason itself is confounded by these paradoxes and cries: "Love hath Reason,
Reason none, / If what parts can so remain" (lines 47–48).

Antony and Cleopatra is the exploration of this if: it is the working out of
these paradoxes in human terms, with all their human contradictions. The
paradoxes so easily stated in "The Phoenix and the Turtle" are the hard-won
conclusions of the lovers: that one must lose oneself to gain oneself; that the only
life is in death, the only union in separation. To regard either paradox or
hyperbole as merely rhetorical ornament is to overlook their enormous potency
in the play: in a very literal way, they shape not only the language but also the
presentation of character, the structure, and the themes. And if the tension
between skepticism and belief is resolved for a moment at the end, it is resolved
only insofar as we for a moment accept paradox and hyperbole as literally true,
despite their logical impossibilities. These are large claims; in order to
substantiate them, I shall have to discuss the figures and some related concepts at
length.

The structure of Antony and Cleopatra is the structure of paradox and
hyperbole themselves: according to Renaissance figurists, both gain our credence
by appealing to our doubt.

> Paradoxon, is a forme of speech by which the Orator affirmeth some
> thing to be true, by saying he would not have beleeved it, or that it
> is so straunge, so great, or so wonderfull, that it may appeare to be
> incredible.[8]

Thus Henry Peacham defines paradox.[9] The figure paradoxon, or as Puttenham
calls it, "the wondrer,"[10] affirms faith by appealing to doubt.[11] Paradox was for
the Renaissance a figure pliable to any use: if John Donne as a young man could
use it as an occasion for the display of witty and cynical extravagance, he could
also use it in his sermons to express the central tenets of Christianity. A
seventeenth-century theologian cast these tenets into the form of paradox
precisely because they impose such a strain on our logical categories and
nonetheless are not to be questioned—that is to say, because they demand the

operation of our faith, not our reason.[12] All paradox demands an act of faith; but hyperbole is that species of paradox which poses the crisis in its most acute form.[13] Hyperbole must, by, definition, assert that which is literally untrue. George Puttenham in *The Arte of English Poesie* discusses hyperbole along with other figures which work by altering the meaning of words or phrases:

> As figures be the instruments of ornament in every language, so be they also in a sorte abuses or rather trespasses in speech, because they passe the ordinary limits of common utterance, and be occupied of purpose to deceive the eare and also the minde, drawing it from plainnesse and simplicitie to a certaine doublenesse, whereby our talke is the more guilefull & abusing, for what els is your *Metaphor* but an inversion of sense by transport; your *allegorie* by a duplicitie of meaning or dissimulation under covert and darke intendments: one while speaking obscurely and in riddle called *Aenigma*: another while by common proverbe or Adage called *Paremia*: then by merry skoffe called *Ironia*: ... then by incredible comparison giving credit, as by your *Hyperbole*.[14]

"By incredible comparison giving credit": this is the paradox of hyperbole. And if all these figures are in some sense deceivers, then the worst in this kind are the hyperboles. Puttenham later says,

> Ye have yet two or three other figures that smatch a spice of the same *false semblant* but in another sort and maner of phrase, whereof one is when we speake in the superlative and beyond the limites of credit, that is by the figure which the Greeks called *Hiperbole*, the Latines *Dementiens* or the lying figure. I for his immoderate excesse cal him the over reacher right with his originall or [lowd lyar] & me thinks not amisse: now when I speake that which neither I my selfe thinke to be true, nor would have any other body beleeve, it must needs be a great dissimulation, because I mean nothing lesse than that I speake.[15]

Precisely this great dissimulation gives credit, as Puttenham has told us earlier; and although the speaker does not believe himself and expects no one else to believe him, he means no less than what he says. This very illogical state of affairs reduces Puttenham to a similar illogic; but with this illogic he suggests the central force of hyperbole and its fascination for poets at the end of the sixteenth century. If we are to take it seriously, hyperbole must elicit some sort of belief or assent: that is to say that it demands of us the simultaneous perception of its literal falsehood and its imaginative relevance. It presents the spectacle of man making his own imaginative universe in despite of all reality, in despite of all human limitation: the struggle of Tamburlaine, or Richard II, or the lover in Donne's love poetry.

But can we take paradox and hyperbole seriously? If the two figures challenge our reason by their very structure, the play takes up that challenge: for paradox and hyperbole are to some extent embodied in the lovers; and the degree to which we can believe in these figures will determine our response to the play. Cleopatra herself seems to embrace contradictions; she is usually described in terms which confound all our logical categories. One need only look at Shakespeare's additions to Plutarch's description of Cleopatra at Cydnus for confirmation: by the use of paradox, Shakespeare transforms Plutarch's beautiful but entirely probable description into something rich and strange.[16] The wind from the fans of her Cupids "did seem / To glow the delicate cheeks which they did cool" (2.2.203–4). Her barge burns on the water. She animates nature with love for her: the waters follow her barge, "As amorous of their strokes" (2.2.197), as Antony will follow her at Actium. "She did make defect perfection, / And, breathless, power breathe forth" (2.2.231–32). She embodies all the paradoxes of sexual appetite, which grows the more by reaping: she "makes hungry, / Where most she satisfies" (2.2.237–38). Like the woman in the sonnets, she is black with Phoebus's amorous pinches (1.5.28) and yet the day of the world (4.8.13): black and wholly fair.[17] She is wrinkled deep in time (1.5.29), and yet age cannot wither her. And if Cleopatra is paradoxical in her nature, Antony is hyperbolical in all that he does: in his rage, his valor, his love, and his folly.[18] From Philo's description of him as Mars to Cleopatra's description of him as her colossus, he is seen in hyperbolic terms; and his own passionate use of hyperbole confirms its association with him.

The paradoxes surrounding Cleopatra are in a sense verified early in the play by Enobarbus's portrait of her at Cydnus. Enobarbus's speech is placed between Antony's resolution to marry Octavia and his decision to leave her; placed here, it serves to tell us why Antony will return to Cleopatra. In this sense, it functions as a substitute for a soliloquy in which Antony could announce his intentions to us. But a soliloquy would tell us about Cleopatra only as Antony perceives her this description comes from Enobarbus, the most consistently skeptical voice in the play. That Enobarbus is the spokesman for Cleopatra's paradoxes establishes the portrait of her as one of the facts of the play.[19] We are presented with her paradoxical nature as a fait accompli, as one of the premises from which the action of the play springs. In this sense, paradox itself is embodied in the person of Cleopatra, and we are forced to acknowledge its presence on stage.[20] Her nature is fixed from that moment: and although she changes constantly, paradox can accommodate all the change; it is, after all, central to the paradox that everything becomes her and that she becomes everything. Cleopatra's definition by paradox comes early in the play and remains relatively static; Antony's definition by hyperbole is a continuing process, a continuing attempt to redefine him. And our education is at stake in his definition: for we are continually reeducated in the possibilities of hyperbole and in the kind of belief we can accord it. If Antony's hyperboles are verified, it is only at the end of the play, after a continual process of testing. The entire play leads us to Cleopatra's hyperbolical portrait of him; but it leads us there by subjecting hyperbole to skepticism as well as to assent.

Like the play itself, Antony's hyperboles can be verified only by surviving the test of the comic structure. Hyperbole can indicate either the similarity or the discrepancy between assertion and reality; or it can indicate both together. Whether the effect of the hyperbole is comic or tragic depends largely on the extent to which we are permitted to believe in the untruth it asserts.[21] In purely comic hyperbole, the effect lies precisely in the discrepancy between the fact and the assertion. The hyperbolical claims about Antony are frequently subject to just such mockery. For Ventidius, who has just won a battle by his own harsh labor, Antony's name is "that magical word of war" (3.1.31). Agrippa and Enobarbus mock Lepidus's sycophantic love for his two masters by citing his hyperbolical praise of them

> *Eno.* Caesar? Why he's the Jupiter of men.
> *Agr.* What's Antony? The god of Jupiter.
> *Eno.* Spake you of Caesar? How, the nonpareil?
> *Agr.* O Antony, O thou Arabian bird!
>
> [3.2.9–12]

But not all the hyperboles in the play are comic: and as hyperbole becomes imaginatively relevant, it begins to invoke our belief, in despite of all reason. For *Antony and Cleopatra* is virtually an experiment in establishing the imaginative relevance of hyperbole and consequently the kind of belief we can accord it: and our final sense of Antony depends on this process.

Throughout the play, we are given a medley of hyperboles ranging from the purely comic to the purely tragic. Antony, as one of the three triumvirs, is "the triple pillar of the world," according to Philo (1.1.12); and even Antony seems to imagine that when he takes his support from the world, a significant portion of it will collapse ("Let Rome in Tiber melt, and the wide arch / Of the rang'd empire fall!" 1.1.33–34). Cleopatra later imagines Antony bearing up the heavens rather than the earth: her Antony is "the demi-Atlas of this earth" (1.5.23).[22] But these very hyperboles are mocked when the drunken Lepidus is carried offstage:

> *Eno.* There's a strong fellow, Menas.
> *Men.* Why?
> *Eno.* 'A bears the third part of the world, man; see'st not?
> *Men.* The third part, then, is drunk.
>
> [2.7.88–91]

When Octavius hears of Antony's death, he comments, "The breaking of so great a thing should make / A greater crack" (5.1.14–15). In his words, the concept of universal order crumbles; but so does our hyperbolical vision of Antony upholding earth and heaven. At his death, there is no crack. But the effect of this sequence of hyperboles is balanced by another sequence. When the serving men on Pompey's barge compare the drunken Lepidus to a star, the poetical clothing is clearly too large for him, and the effect is comic:

> To be called into a huge sphere, and not to be seen to move in't, are
> the holes where eyes should be, which pitifully disaster the cheeks.
> [2.7.14–16]

The servant's shift from the cosmic and outsized to the human and minute in mid-metaphor is wholly appropriate: for poor Lepidus is in a sense a mere mortal caught in a world filled with hyperbolical figures. But when we find Antony dressed in the same poetical clothing, he wears it with grace. Lepidus compares his faults to the spots of heaven (1.4.12–13); and the comparison is not ludicrous. By the time the second guardsman responds to Antony's suicide by reiterating the hyperbolical association ("The star is fall'n" 4.14.106), we are, I think, quite prepared to believe him. And he in turn prepares us for Cleopatra's assertion that the crown of the earth doth melt and the soldier's pole is fallen.

If the hyperboles that describe Antony are subject to a continual process of testing, so are the hyperboles that Antony himself uses. In his education in the hyperbolical, Antony appeals to his ancestor Hercules as teacher:

> The shirt of Nessus is upon me, teach me,
> Alcides, thou mine ancestor, thy rage.
> Let me lodge Lichas on the horns o' the moon,
> And with those hands that grasp'd the heaviest club,
> Subdue my worthiest self.
>
> [4.12.43–47]

But Antony does not even manage to subdue his worthiest self. What is possible for the god inevitably remains impossible for the mortal—impossible and consequently slightly foolish. Cleopatra suggests by her mockery at the beginning of the play that this emulation is folly in a mere mortal: she notes to Charmian "how this Herculean Roman does become / The carriage of his chafe" (1.3.84–85). In imitating his ancestor's gigantic rage in act 1, Antony is merely playacting and is as foolish as Pistol or any other Herculean stage braggart whose language is clearly too big for his worth—he is a slightly larger version of Moth.[23] The frequent reference to Herod, the conventional stage blusterer, would remind the audience of the dangers inherent in the use of hyperbole: it was the language of tyrants.²⁴ For much of the play, Antony's hyperbolical passion is subject to this kind of comic testing. The long scene in which Antony rages in Hercules' vein and Enobarbus consistently undercuts him (act 3, scene 13) is fundamentally comic in structure; as I have noted elsewhere, it follows the classical pattern of *miles gloriosus* and servant. His rage here does not fully engage our sympathy; when he says, "O that I were / Upon the hill of Basan, to outroar / The horned herd, for I have savage cause" (3.13.126–28), we are disinclined to believe in the extent of his grievances or in his hyperbolical expression of an action appropriate to them. The hyperbole here dissuades us from belief and becomes mere rant. But the situation is more complex after the Egyptian fleet has joined with Caesar's. Antony in calling on his ancestor for instruction seems to recognize that his own hyperbolical language is not altogether equal to the occasion. His language here is proportionate to the cause of his rage: it is not merely rant, and it is surely no longer comic. Moreover, Cleopatra immediately verifies the heroic extent of his rage: "O, he's more mad / Than Telamon for his shield, the boar of Thessaly / Was never so emboss'd" (4.13.1–3). Though we still cannot believe in Antony's hyperbolical actions as literal, at least we believe in his rage. The hyperbole becomes an appropriate expression for the gigantic rage and, in that sense, imaginatively relevant. And after Antony hears of Cleopatra's death, he echoes her reference to Ajax in an image which sounds hyperbolical but is in fact absolutely literal: "The seven-fold shield of Ajax cannot keep / The battery from my heart" (4.14.38–39).

If Cleopatra is the first to mock Antony's hyperboles, she is also the final advocate of their truth. Cleopatra asserts to Dolabella that her dream of Antony belongs to the realm of nature, not of fancy: "to imagine / An Antony were nature's piece, 'gainst fancy, / Condemning shadows quite" (5.2.98–100). But this assertion comes only after five acts of continual testing. Even while Antony is dying, Cleopatra can acknowledge the folly of hyperbole. As she struggles to lift him into her monument, she says,

> ... Had I great Juno's power,
> The strong-wing'd Mercury should fetch thee up,
> And set thee by Jove's side. Yet come a little,
> Wishers were ever fools.
>
> [4.15.34–37]

Yet side by side with this quiet resignation to the literal is her hyperbolical appeal to the sun ("Burn the great sphere thou mov'st in" 4.15.10): precisely the crack the absence of which Caesar notes. "Wishers were ever fools": "O, see, my women: / The crown o' the earth doth melt" (4.15.62–63). If we are finally able to believe Cleopatra's hyperbolical portrait of her Antony, it is only because she herself tells us that wishers are fools.

POETIC PROCESS AS POETIC THEME

... this dotage of our general's
O'er flows the measure. [1.1.1–2]

The descriptive hyperboles that surround Antony and Cleopatra are essential to our understanding of them: for the lovers and the world they inhabit are themselves hyperbolical. *Antony and Cleopatra* is preeminently about immoderate excess: excess which the Roman world successfully measures and subdues. But Puttenham chides hyperbole itself for its immoderate excess; like the Nile, hyperbole continually overflows the measure. And if hyperbole is the rhetorical figure appropriate to excess, it is also the remembrance of time past, when the hyperbolical was still available to man: as *Hamlet* gives us the Denmark of Hamlet's father or *Richard II* the England of John of Gaunt, so *Antony and Cleopatra* gives us a glimpse of a past when men were greater than they are now, when in fact excess was the rule. At the same time, the play suggests that the lovers' escape from the world is a literal achievement of the hyperbolical and the paradoxical: that the contradictions of these figures are embodied in the lovers as they die. In this sense, the two rhetorical figures shape the themes as well as the structure and the poetic texture of the play: poetic process becomes poetic theme.

When Pompey encounters Octavius and Antony, he gives them a lesson in recent Roman history:

> ... What was't
> That mov'd pale Cassius to conspire? And what
> Made the all-honour'd, honest Roman, Brutus,
> With the arm'd rest, courtiers of beauteous freedom,
> To drench the Capitol, but that they would
> Have one man but a man?
>
> [2.6.14–19]

To have one man but a man: according to Pompey, the effort of the revolution was in effect to abolish the hyperbolical from Rome. If that was indeed their goal, the Romans seem to have learned the lessons of history well: the first words of the play introduce us to the Roman scale of measurement, on which man is but a man. Antony's dotage overflows the measure: his heart "reneges all temper" (1.1.8). Implicit in the word "measure" are two significantly related concepts: *moderation* and *measurement*. Here moderation, temperance, are the measuring rods for man: it is literally by his temperance that a man must be measured. Antony plays on these two concepts when he tells Octavia, "I have not kept my square, but that to come / Shall all be done by the rule" (2.3.6–7): in the Roman world, the rule is that by which one is measured. The same cluster of concepts is implicit in Cleopatra's description of the "mechanic slaves / With greasy aprons, rules, and hammers" (5.2.208–9), whose presence she so dreads in the Roman triumph: they will attempt to measure her by their rules and will presumably proclaim her whore. In fact, this play on concepts was traditionally associated with the virtue of temperance, the "temper" which Antony's heart reneges: the Palmer, that repository of common knowledge, makes precisely this association early in book 2 of *The Faerie Queene*. Guyon has just announced that man is inevitably doomed by either pleasure or pain, but the Palmer reassures him: "'But Temperaunce,' (said he), 'with golden squire / Betwixt them both can measure out a meane'" (*FQ* 2.1.38).[25] And before long we are on our way to the house of the Golden Mean herself.

To have one man but a man: the association between temperance and the merely human was implicit in the Renaissance understanding of the virtue itself. Temperance is the virtue of the unaided human reason: it dictates man's behavior, not toward God or toward his fellowman, but toward his own body. It is the virtue most often associated by the Renaissance with the period before the birth of Christ and the literal entrance of Godhead into the world of men. Thus for Spenser, it is the second virtue necessary for the fashioning of a moral gentleman, the classical complement to the Christian virtue of holiness. If Redcrosse attempts to know the New Jerusalem at the House of Holiness, then Guyon discovers his own body, his Shamefastness, and his ancestry at the House of Temperance. The dictate *know thyself* is at the moral center of classical civilization; and temperance is that virtue by which self-knowledge is most readily achieved.[26] Hence the prime danger throughout book 2 of *The Faerie Queene* is the loss of self: Furor causes poor Guyon to overthrow himself (*FQ* 2.4.8).

Guyon goes on his way to self-knowledge and self-control guided by the reasonable advice of the Palmer; he leaves the only spectacular battle in the book to Prince Arthur, a figure associated with supernatural powers of grace. For temperance is in fact somewhat equivocal as a virtue: Spenser implies that it is the best unaided man can do but not all in all sufficient. Octavius is the exemplar of measure in *Antony and Cleopatra*: and his virtue is scarcely heartwarming. His victory promises a civil peace for the world

> The time of universal peace is near:
> Prove this a prosperous day, the three-nook'd world
> Shall bear the olive freely.
>
> [4.6.5–7]

Peace is of course highly desirable, but we see how freely Caesar's peace will be borne in his treatment of Lepidus and the kings who have revolted from Antony and in his plans for Cleopatra. Octavius's comparative sobriety on Pompey's galley suggests both the negative and the positive aspects of the virtue. There is no question that his measured behavior is more suitable for a world leader than Antony's excess: but at the same time, there is something niggardly in his refusal to be a child of the time, to give himself to the situation. Temperance will keep man under control, but it does not allow room for love or grace. Both love and grace must necessarily overflow: they are inimical to measure. There is no love in book 2 of *The Faerie Queene*: and the only grace comes while Temperance is conspicuously absent by virtue of being asleep. Proculeius asks Cleopatra not to abuse his "master's bounty, by / The undoing of yourself" (5.2.43–44); but we have already seen a fine instance of Octavius's bounty. It is while Proculeius is proclaiming Caesar "so full of grace, that it flows over / On all that need" (5.2.24–25), that Gallus and the soldiers trap Cleopatra; obviously Octavius overflows only in expediency. The man of measure is necessarily miserly in his relations with other people; he will commit no excesses, but neither will he give himself. And if he never loses himself, it is at least partly, we suspect, because he has no self to lose. We are never permitted to see Octavius in a private context. We see him always in the light of an insistent publicity; moreover, he seems to determine his own emotions by public and political effect. His love for his sister does not prevent his pawning her for political gain. His grief at Antony's death seems designed to emphasize his own greatness: he mourns for Antony as "the arm of mine own body" (5.1.45). And his tears for his great competitor are too public to be entirely convincing; they are easily interrupted as soon as business intervenes (5.1.48–50).

If Octavius is the exemplar of measure, Antony is the exemplar of that loss of self which intemperance necessitates. His attempt to live by the rule must fail; his dotage will overflow the measure. From the Roman perspective, Antony illustrates precisely the results of sexual intemperance: when feminine passion dominates masculine reason, effeminacy and loss of manhood are necessarily the results. Antony's act of overflow is specifically sexual: and he pays the consequences. Early in the play, Philo finds the symptoms of this loss of self:

> ... sometimes, when he is not Antony,
> He comes too short of that great property
> Which still should go with Antony.
>
> [1.1.57–59]

When Antony is under the influence of his Egyptian fetters, Enobarbus cannot tell him from his queen (1.2.76); like Cleopatra's description of the exchange of clothing, Enobarbus's error suggests the diminution of Antony's masculine identity. Octavius enters the play condemning Antony's intemperance and his consequent loss of manhood (1.4.1–7). And immediately after Antony's flight at Actium, Scarus says,

> I never saw an action of such shame;
> Experience, manhood, honour, ne'er before

Did violate so itself.

[3.10.22–24]

But we learn the value of measure less from Antony's Roman critics than from his own perception of his loss: throughout, he sees his own folly and intemperance with a Roman clarity of moral vision. He knows from the start that he is losing himself: "These strong Egyptian fetters I must break, / Or lose myself in dotage" (1.2.113–14). And after Actium, when he has quite literally lost himself, he perceives his loss more clearly than anyone else. He bids his followers fly to Caesar because his own flight has instructed them in desertion: "I have fled myself, and have instructed cowards / To run, and show their shoulders" (3.1.17–8). As he overflows the measure, he feels himself becoming "indistinct / As water is in water" (4.14.10–11).

Antony loses himself and feels his boundaries dissolving; and without boundaries, he can contain nothing. As Antony's worldly fortunes worsen, there is an implied contrast between his emptiness and Octavius's fullness: Antony overflows his measure and becomes empty, while Octavius is filled with fortune's gifts. At Antony's death, he is wholly empty: his body is merely "the case of that huge spirit" (4.15.89). And Octavius has become "full-fortun'd Caesar" (1.15.24), "the fullest man" (3.13.87). Enobarbus makes the contrast explicit when he comments on Antony's folly in expecting Octavius to accept his challenge to single combat:

> ... that he should dream,
> Knowing all measures, the full Caesar will
> Answer his emptiness.

[3.13.34–36]

But it is part of Antony's folly that he no longer knows all measures; for measure is the necessary virtue in the realm of fortune, the realm of business which Octavius manages so well and Antony so poorly. As Antony overflows his measure and loses himself to Cleopatra, he becomes a strumpet's fool; as Octavius maintains his measure and is filled with fortune's gifts, he becomes fortune's knave. The choice is not attractive: and Rome allows us no other alternatives.

At his most Roman, Antony will accuse Cleopatra of intemperance: "I am sure, / Though you can guess what temperance should be, / You know not what it is" (3.13.120–22). Despite his tone of disappointed surprise, we can no more imagine a temperate Cleopatra than a Nile which behaves like the Tiber or the Thames. For Egypt is itself hyperbolical: everything there overflows the measure, and excess is the normal state of affairs. However abhorrent to Roman notions of agriculture, the survival of Egypt is dependent on the mingled fertility of the overflowing Nile, breeding both crops and serpents. In Rome, overflow is a human vice; in Egypt, it is a natural necessity. Overflow here is neither moral nor immoral; it breeds good and evil indifferently. The sense of an enormous and mingled fertility is everywhere in the play. Antony swears "By the fire / That quickens Nilus' slime" (1.3.68-69); Lepidus tells us that "Your serpent of Egypt is bred now of your mud by the operation of your sun: so is your crocodile" (2.7.26–27). Cleopatra imagines the water flies on Nile breeding a corrupt vitality in her dead body: "on Nilus' mud / Lay me stark-nak'd, and let the water-flies / Blow me into abhorring" (5.2.58–60). But this corruption of the overflowing Nile is essential to its fertility; without serpents, there would be no crops.

Antony, like the Nile, overflows the measure: and that overflow which is purely loss from the perspective of Rome is partly gain in Egypt. The mingled abundance of the Nile serves as an analogy for the mingled abundance of Antony himself, excessive in all he does. The opening lines of the play associate Antony's overflowing with the fecundity of the overflowing Nile; the association is emphasized a few moments later when Charmian mocks the chastity presaged in Iras's oily palm by comparing it to the famine presaged by "o'erflowing Nilus" (1.2.47). Like the Nile itself, Antony will breed serpents. His idleness breeds multiple dangers in the political sphere: he himself tells us that "we bring forth weeds, / When our quick minds lie still" (1.2.106–7) and that "ten thousand harms, more than the ills I know, / My idleness doth hatch" (1.2.126–27). In his absence from the political sphere, "Much is breeding, / Which like the courser's hair, hath yet but life, / And not a serpent's poison" (1.2.190–92). But not all his children are serpents. His dotage overflows the measure, but so do his courage, his generosity, and his love. For Octavius, any unnecessary expenditure of time or supplies is waste: he tells us that Antony "wastes / the lamps of night in revel" (1.4.5); he himself will agree to feast his victorious soldiers (feast in moderation) because "we have store to do't, / And they have earn'd the waste" (4.1.15–16). But in Antony's world there is an apparently endless abundance of food, drink, and gold and an endless abundance of time to enjoy them in: "There's not a minute of our lives should stretch / Without some pleasure now" (1.1.46–47). Octavius will not be bountiful even to those who have deserted Antony for him: Alexas is hanged; Canidius and the rest have "no honourable trust" (4.6.18). But Antony's bounty overflows even toward those who are disloyal to him. After Enobarbus has deserted, one of Octavius's soldiers tells him that "Antony / Hath after thee sent all thy treasure, with / His bounty. overplus" (4.6.20–22). Antony "continues still a Jove" in generosity (4.6.29); to Enobarbus, he is a "mine of bounty" (4.6.32).

Antony's Jove-like generosity is a central element in Cleopatra's hyperbolical vision of him:

> ... For his bounty,
> There was no winter in't: an autumn 'twas

That grew the more by reaping.

[5.2.86–88]

To grow by reaping: like the Nile itself, Antony's excess breeds life out of death. In this world the only life comes from loss and death: the autumnal vitality of the lovers, which grows the more by reaping. And if Antony overflows the Roman scale, on which man is but a man, he will find a new scale in Egypt. For Egypt is itself hyperbolical; here, the only adequate scale is one which will measure the overflow. As Antony is telling Lepidus about the mysteries of Egypt on Pompey's galley, he gives us just such a scale:

> Thus do they, sir: they take the flow o' the Nile
> By certain scales i' the pyramid; they know,
> By the height, the lowness, or the mean, if dearth
> Or foison follow. The higher Nilus swells,
> The more it promises.

[2.7.17–21]

On this scale, fecundity and corruption are seen as necessarily part of the same process. The pyramid, the tomb of Egypt, becomes the measure of fertility; death quite literally becomes the measure of life.[27] The overflowing Nile and the scale that measures it can stand as the defining image for the tragic experience to which Rome is immune; for the Nile itself, like Antony, grows the more by reaping. And it is only this scale that is adequate to Antony's autumnal bounty. In this fluid world, only the capacity for loss and death can measure the life of man; only by the scales of the pyramid can we measure Antony's fatal and triumphant excess.

In Rome, it is an easy matter to measure a man; and in Rome, Antony loses himself and becomes empty. But in Egypt, loss is the only way to gain. For Antony's enormous bounty is entirely dependent upon his generosity of self, finally upon his loss of himself. He will give himself wholly and without that regard for consequences that reason dictates. He will give himself away. And if Rome (and Antony himself in his Roman mood) will see that loss of self as the result of effeminate intemperance, it can also be seen as evidence of a final and overwhelming generosity. Love demands precisely that loss of self which temperance abhors: if Guyon as patron of temperance must learn always to be master of himself, then Redcrosse as patron of holiness must learn to lose himself. In this knot intrinsicate of life, both kinds of loss are necessarily bound up together. Antony's overflowing excess is as equivocal as the Nile's: it too will breed serpents as well as crops. But the man of measure—the man who never overflows—will not breed at all. One takes one's choice: either a world of lavish overflow and the attendant risk of serpents; or a world of measure and the attendant risk of sterility. Once again there is no middle ground: the only way to fertility is through dissolution.

Both Cleopatra and Octavius are in a sense absolutes, untainted with their opposites. Both are free from the moral contradictions that so plague Antony, who will continue to think like a Roman even after he has chosen to act like an Egyptian. But in this world of violent extremes, the only safety is in the purity which both Octavius and Cleopatra possess; to be mixed in composition is disastrous. Enobarbus, like Antony, is mixed. He chooses to obey his reasonable sense of expediency, to behave like a man of measure. But once he has left Antony, his own spiritual niggardliness is mocked by Antony's overwhelming generosity; and the contrast kills him:

> ... O, Antony,
> Thou mine of bounty, how wouldst thou have paid
> My better service, when my turpitude
> Thou dost so crown with gold! This blows my heart.
>   [4.6.31–34][28]

Enobarbus is a figure of moderation who attempts to live in a world of excess: generous enough to be loyal to Antony against the dictates of his reason but not generous enough to be loyal to the end. He is in this sense the pivotal figure in the play. His death not only deprives us of our most skeptical spokesman; it also teaches us precisely the cost of skepticism. For Enobarbus is unable to commit himself to either measure or overflow. He attempts to maintain an equilibrium between the two worlds; and for his attempt, he suffers the fate of Antony in little and in reverse. He chooses to obey the Roman dictates of his reason and then sees the pettiness of his choice with an overflowing generosity of spirit. And if he is foolish to stay with Antony (3.13.42–43), he is equally foolish to leave him. For those who are mixed in composition, there can be no resolution.

Cleopatra's Egypt is associated with overflow and Octavius's Rome with measure: but Octavius's is not the only Rome we see. Although Octavius is the spokesman for measure, he is by no means the spokesman for the idea of Rome itself: our sense of ancient Roman virtue comes not from Octavius but from the descriptions of Antony as he used to be. And in these descriptions, Rome itself is hyperbolical: Antony's excess is associated not only with Egypt and Cleopatra but also with his own past glory as a Roman soldier. Even as a Roman, Antony is consistently opposed to Roman measure: the heroic virtue which Philo, Pompey, and Octavius extol is quite as inconsistent with measure as the love which they deplore.[29] Bursting the buckles of one's breast and drinking the stale of horses are hardly the marks of a temperate man. Philo's portrait of his warrior is as excessive as Cleopatra's of her lover: hyperbole is the mode used to describe him in either arena. The Roman valor associated with Antony's past and the Egypt of overflow are both equally excessive and equally inimical to the measured Rome of the present. For Octavius's moderate world necessarily excludes heroic virtue:

just as it allows no room for the overflowing of human emotion, so it allows no room for the outsized individual who may in some respects be more than man. Prince Arthur, not Guyon, is the warrior hero in Spenser's book of Temperance: temperance is itself inimical to heroism. Antony accepts Octavius's challenge to fight at sea against great odds merely because the challenge must be accepted; Octavius mocks Antony's challenge to hand-to-hand combat. Why should he fight with Antony, He has a marvelously efficient army to do his fighting for him. Heroism, like love, is sacrificed to expediency: measure is the virtue of the efficiently run bureaucracy. *Antony and Cleopatra* is usually seen as some sort of debate between Egypt and Rome; but if this is the debate, then the debaters are grossly unbalanced. In fact, the opposition is never between the Rome of honor and heroic virtue and the Egypt of the senses: Octavius firmly rejects heroic virtue, and Roman honor has dwindled to Pompey's scrupulous desire for clean hands, for murder by proxy.

The Roman virtues of valor and heroism in the play are distinctly in the past tense: we must look to Antony's own past and to the fathers of our modern Romans. And however much Shakespeare may have challenged the grandeur of Julius Caesar in *Julius Caesar*, he is "great Caesar" or "broad-fronted Caesar" in this play, an almost mythic figure who towers over the generation of his heir. The play similarly insists on the elder Pompey's greatness. These were the great exemplars of Roman virtue; and they seem to belong to a time when one man was more than a man. Compared to this near-mythic generation, the sons have dwindled in stature. Octavius and Pompey are Cleopatra's harshest critics; but their fathers were her lovers. Shakespeare makes the point abundantly clear:

> ... Broad-fronted Caesar,
> When thou wast here above the ground, I was
> A morsel for a monarch: and great Pompey
> Would stand and make his eyes grow in my brow,
> There would he anchor his aspect, and die
> With looking on his life.

[1.5.29–34]

Almost every allusion to these great Romans links them with Cleopatra. Antony in a Roman mood will remind Cleopatra that he found her

> ... as a morsel, cold upon
> Dead Caesar's trencher: nay, you were a fragment
> Of Gnaeus Pompey's.

[3.13.116–18]

Cleopatra asks Charmian to recall her love for Caesar (1.4); Pompey has heard that Apollodorus carried a certain queen to Caesar in a mattress (2.6.67–70).

Agrippa knows "She made great Caesar lay his sword to bed; / He plough'd her, and she cropp'd" (2.2.227–28); Octavius will later refer to this crop as "Caesarion, whom they call my father's son" (3.6.6). Cleopatra tells Thidias, "Your Caesar's father oft, / When he hath mus'd of taking kingdoms in, / Bestow'd his lips on that unworthy place, / As it rain'd kisses" (3.13.82–85). The play insistently reminds us that the fathers of Cleopatra's harshest critics were her lovers. This insistence is particularly striking because Shakespeare has rearranged historical fact to make his point: Octavius was actually Julius Caesar's nephew, his son only by adoption; and it was our Pompey's older brother (not particularly "great") rather than his father, Pompey the Great, who loved Cleopatra. The historical facts are plain in Plutarch; Shakespeare has done an admirable job of obscuring them.[30] We associate Roman virtue with these great men of the preceding generation: but they were not so prim as their sons. They were able to incorporate Egypt and its immoderate excesses into themselves. For them, Rome and Egypt were not irreconcilable; they were able quite literally to embrace Cleopatra. For the fathers, the mighty excesses of heroic virtue and passion can be conjoined; but the sons are so shrunk in grandeur that they can never embrace Egypt. They must ward it off as a curse. The younger Caesar is apparently immune to Cleopatra's charms. He may dally with her for political purposes, but we know that his very dallying is passionless. But in the past, when men were more than men, the greatest Romans themselves overflowed the measure.

Insofar as the greatest exemplars of Roman virtue were also in some sense Egyptians, our critical vision of the play as a balanced debate between Rome and Egypt is seriously befuddled. Side by side with this debate is another of more permanent consequence: that between the past and the present, the heroic excess of the fathers and the moderation of the sons. And standing behind the near-mythic figures of the past is a figure even more remote and more heroic: the gigantic figure of Hercules himself. Hercules is presented here as a god rather than as a human hero: placed firmly in a mythic past, inaccessible to mere mortals.[31] The role of Hercules as moral analogue in the play has often been noted; but it seems to me much less significant than his role as poetic analogue. Eugene Waith suggests the complex of ideas associating Hercules with heroic virtue, the virtue of excess, magnanimity, and all that which overflows ordinary human limits:[32] the labors and loves of Hercules were equally excessive. After Seneca, his gigantic rage and madness became stage properties as commonplace as his gigantic heroism, and inevitably bound up with it. Indeed, *Antony and Cleopatra* consistently emphasizes the hyperbolical proportions of his rage rather than the moral significance of his acts. For Hercules is the type of gigantic excess, a figure whose native region is the impossible and whose native speech is hyperbole;[33] he is a hyperbolical braggart who always makes good his claims.[34] He functions in the play neither as Roman nor Egyptian but rather as a distant and godlike figure of achieved excess: a figure who overflows every human scale.

For Antony's hyperboles are Hercules' literal actions: he presumably could lodge Lichas on the horns of the moon in fact, while Antony can lodge him there only in rhetoric. At the allusive center of the play, then, is the shadowy figure of one for whom hyperbole is not in fact hyperbole but rather literal truth.

Antony and Hercules are relatives with the same taste for the excessive, no matter how diminished Antony is in power. Both Antony's folly and his grandeur have their literary roots in Hercules: *miles gloriosus* and hero are two sides of the same coin; and Antony inherits both literary traditions from his great ancestor. The allusions to Hercules serve partly to remind us of the discrepancy between Hercules' actions and Antony's pretensions, of the degree to which Antony has dwindled from the heroic stature of his great ancestor.[35] Yet Hercules does not serve merely as a contrast to Antony. Here again Shakespeare disarms skepticism by including its perspective within the play. If the presence of Hercules emphasizes the folly of Antony's ventures into the realm of hyperbole, it also emphasizes their grandeur. Hercules becomes in effect a model for hyperbole which we can take perfectly literally: he shows us the way toward belief in the impossible. And although Antony is not Hercules, at the end of the play the hyperbolical realm has become his as well as his ancestor's. Even as Hercules withdraws from Antony, he in effect asserts their likeness: we need only try to imagine his withdrawing from Octavius to demonstrate the point.

We become fully aware of the god only as he is departing from his descendant, withdrawing in effect from the present world entirely. The withdrawal of the god is a scene of enormous imaginative potency, perhaps because it is so wholly irrelevant to the plot. If Hercules had withdrawn before Actium, then we could find in him a cause or at least a portent of Antony's desertion of himself at Actium. But he withdraws after Actium. The departure may signal Antony's loss of heroic virtue, since he has refused to fight; in this sense, Hercules seems to participate in the Roman judgment about Antony. But if Antony has managed to shame himself in the presence of the god, he manages to redeem himself in the god's absence: Hercules' withdrawal is followed immediately by the victorious land battle. But even as the god withdraws from the world, the possibility for significant heroic action goes with him. Antony momentarily recaptures his heroic valor, but to no avail. We are no longer in a world where individual heroism matters. Despite Cleopatra's pride in the valor of her man of men, she knows how little valor ultimately counts for in this world

> ... that he and Caesar might
> Determine this great war in single fight!
> Then Antony—; but now—Well, on.

[4.4.36–38]

This is no world for single combat. Antony has promised Cleopatra that he will be "treble-sinew'd, hearted, breath'd" (3.13.178), and he keeps his hyperbolical promise, but it no longer matters. The loss at Actium has put us squarely in the realm of present-day Rome, where a man is but a man, the realm most antithetical to Hercules. Hence the withdrawal of Hercules gives us the sense of heroic virtue, of excess and magnanimity itself, withdrawing from the earth, leaving in preparation for the triumph of measure. Our own sense of loss and betrayal here is extraordinarily complex: though the scene signals Antony's self-betrayal and his loss of grandeur, it simultaneously functions to suggest the consequences of the Roman victory. The gods will depart. And at the same time, the scene anticipates our sense of desolation when Antony himself withdraws from the earth.

No matter how diminished Antony was in grandeur, he was nonetheless the only grandeur we had: at his death, there *is* nothing left remarkable beneath the visiting moon. For Antony's place is midway between the generation of the fathers and the generation of the sons: his own Roman glory is past, but it is the only Roman glory of which there is any hint in the play. He comes to maturity after the assassination and is in that sense after the fall from the heroic and the hyperbolical, when one man is but a man; but he is associated with the generation of the fathers by his heroism and his love for Cleopatra. The old balance of Rome and Egypt is no longer possible for him; but neither is the modern Roman's total rejection of Egypt. Antony is caught between the generations he lives with the values of the old in the world of the new. In this sense he is a throwback to the time when men were more than men, an uncomfortably outsized figure, a grand remnant of the past living on into a dwindled present.

Even in his age, Antony is associated with the giants of the past. Antony's age and Octavius's youth are continually emphasized: Octavius is the "scarce-bearded Caesar" (1.1.21) and "the young man" (3.11.62); "the rose/ Of youth" (3.13.20–21) is upon him. Antony advises Cleopatra: "To the boy Caesar send this grizzled head" (3.13.17). Caesar in turn complains that Antony "calls me boy" (4.1.1); he calls Antony "the old ruffian" (4.1.4). And if Antony is significantly older than Octavius, Cleopatra has the aura of an age which outdistances them both: compared to her, Octavius and his family are parvenus. Charmian stresses the antiquity of Cleopatra's race during the last moments of the play: she is "a princess / Descended of so many royal kings" (5.2.325–26). She is associated with the antiquity of Egypt itself and of its serpents: she is the serpent of old Nile. And although "age cannot wither her" (2.2.235), she is "wrinkled deep in time" (1.3.29). She and Antony are the only characters in the play with fully imagined pasts: throughout the play, we see the past history of her conquests in a warfare very different from Antony's but no less heroic in its excess. Both Antony and Cleopatra are sharply distinguished from the youth and business of Octavius's present Rome: if Antony's age associates him with a past of grandeur and excess, then Cleopatra's age associates her with an antiquity outside the range of time altogether, certainly outside the range of Caesar's time.

The contest between Antony and Octavius is a contest of generations, though hardly the contest we would expect between lovers and society. Throughout, there is an insistent emphasis on Antony's dotage; the folly of love is explicitly associated with the folly of old age (3.11.13–15). In this emphasis on the age of the lovers, Shakespeare inverts the common pattern of romantic comedy or tragedy, the pattern which informs most of his middle comedies, *Romeo and Juliet*, and the late romances. This is essentially the pattern of new comedy: the struggle is between the young lovers and the older and overly rigid generation of the parents or the political authorities. The young, whether they succeed or fail, provide some sort of regeneration for the old society.[36] By subverting the rigid values of the older generation, they assure that life will go on. But here the older generation commits itself to love, while the younger generation presents the obstacles of society, custom, and business. The young world does not regenerate the old; youth here harries age to death.

Antony and Cleopatra suggests the extent to which we have dwindled from the time of giants. We descend from Hercules to Julius Caesar and Pompey the Great to Antony to Octavius and Pompey—from the heroic to the merely bureaucratic. Octavius's youth and Antony's age, the Roman glory of Antony's past, the sins of the fathers, the figure of Antony's gigantic ancestor Hercules: all serve to delineate this descent into the present, where man is but a man. Only Antony is somehow still more than a man; when he dies, the last remnant of the heroic past dies with him, and we are left in the absolutely flat world of the young Octavius. The victory of the "universal landlord" is final; we are "under his shroud" (3.13.71) indeed, with no hope of regeneration. The implicit reversal of the Menandrian pattern makes our loss more poignant: the old lovers have been destroyed and the new world is desolate without them; there will be no second chance. The guardsmen's apocalyptic commentary on Antony's suicide is wholly fitting: the old time is at its period. In this new world,

> ... young boys and girls
> Are level now with men: the odds is gone,
> And there is nothing left remarkable
> Beneath the visiting moon.

> [4.15.65–68]

The young boys have won: the hyperbolical, with all its foolish excess, has successfully been exorcised.

If at the start of the play Antony overflows the measure, by its end he has become the measure: at his death, the odds is gone. But even at the first entrance of the lovers, Antony renounces the concept of ordinary measure as irrelevant to their love

Cleo. If it be love indeed, tell me how much.
Ant. There's beggary in the love that can be reckon'd.
Cleo. I'll set a bourn how far to be belov'd.
Ant. Then must thou needs find out new heaven, new earth.

[1.1.14–17]

If Cleopatra demands measurement, limits larger than those of the Roman Empire must be found. In the attempt to find out new heaven, new earth, Antony must abandon the limits of Rome: "Let Rome in Tiber melt." And as Antony destroys the Roman Empire in a phrase, he destroys Philo's Roman measure. For an objective measurement of space, he substitutes a subjective measurement of emotion: "Here is my space" (1.1.34). On this scale, one tear may be worth the world:

Fall not a tear, I say, one of them rates
All that is won and lost: give me a kiss,
Even this repays me.

[3.11.69–71]

It is no wonder that Antony's attempt to keep his square in his marriage with Octavia is doomed: for he has renounced Roman measure in favor of a new scale. In the scene on Pompey's galley, he gives us the scales of the pyramid, which assume overflow as the norm and measure life only through death. A few moments later, he mocks the entire concept of measurement: the crocodile that he describes to Lepidus is "shap'd, sir, like itself, and it is as broad as it hath breadth: it is just so high as it is" (2.7.41–42). On Antony's Egyptian scale, everything is its own measure: man, like the crocodile, is as broad as he hath breadth and as high as he is. Cleopatra's hyperbolical vision of her emperor Antony is on this scale measured: for Antony himself is the odds, the means of measurement.

The lovers are not the only ones who must renounce the concept of ordinary measurement: if we are to participate in the play, we must also renounce it. Cleopatra's outrageously excessive portrait of her Antony is only part of the excess to which the play subjects us: we are asked to accept a play with too many short scenes and too many minor characters, with passions generally in excess of their objects and characters who claim to be larger than life: a play which gives us the whole world and then demands that we exchange it for a kiss. We cannot measure this play by any ordinary scale: it violates every principle of classical decorum and establishes a new decorum of its own. Shakespeare seems deliberately to challenge our sense of what is artistically measured, or fitting, throughout the play; and ultimately we must take it on its own terms, like the crocodile. Even within the play, Shakespeare insists that we notice his new decorum, a decorum tolerant of excess. Early in the play, Iras prays to Isis to "keep decorum" (1.2.71) by cuckolding Alexas; later, Cleopatra will define her own thoroughly unclassical decorum:

> ... our size of sorrow,
> Proportion'd to our cause, must be as great
> As that which makes it.

[4.15.4–6][37]

Cleopatra asserts her Egyptian decorum to Proculeius:

> ... If your master
> Would have a queen his beggar, you must tell him,
> That majesty, to keep decorum, must
> No less beg than a kingdom.

[5.2.15–18]

And even the Roman Dolabella will respect Cleopatra's decorum: "Your loss is as yourself, great; and you bear it / As answering to the weight" (5.2.101–2). At the end of the play, Charmian insists on the correctness of Cleopatra's decorum of excess when the first guardsman discovers Cleopatra dead and asks, "Is this well done?" Charmian replies, "It is well done, and fitting for a princess / Descended of so many royal kings" (5.2.325–26). Egyptian decorum is hyperbolical: it overflows the Roman concept of decorum itself. And in the course of the play, we must learn to accept it as our own: in its very form, the play insists that we acknowledge the limitations of measurement.

The process of measurement is at issue in *Antony and Cleopatra* ultimately because identity itself is at issue. In the Roman world, the object retains its visible shape and is measurable; but in Egypt, the very measures dissolve. We are introduced to a world of continual metamorphosis, in which everything seems to become everything else. Nothing maintains its shape for long enough to be measured: the size and shape shifts that occur even in mid-metaphor and so baffle our critical senses are the manifestation of a world in which no scale is adequate. And if we can assent to Cleopatra's outrageously unmeasured vision of Antony, it is partly because we have become thoroughly inured to the shifting scales and shifting identities that constitute the play. Philo's first words present a world in which nothing is to scale: the triple pillar of the world is become a strumpet's fool; Antony's heart has become a bellows and a fan. These shifts in shape and size are everywhere in the play. According to Lepidus, Antony's flaws are the spots of heaven (1.4.12). Lepidus is simultaneously eyes and stars, or rather the empty eye socket which pitifully disasters the cheeks (2.7.14–16). Enobarbus will not call Cleopatra's "winds and waters sighs and tears: they are greater storms and tempests than almanacs can report" (1.2.146–48). All these instances of shape shifting may be seen as at least partly ironic and hence explicable; but what of the inexplicably grotesque metaphoric transformations characteristic of the most serious moments in the play? Antony bids his servants farewell and tells them,

> I wish I could be made so many men, And all of you clapp'd up together in An Antony; that I might do you service, So good as you have done.
>
> [4.2.16–19]

The servants understandably reply, "The gods forbid!" The metaphor in which Cleopatra protests her fidelity to Antony is similarly grotesque

> From my cold heart let heaven engender hail,
> And poison it in the source, and the first stone
> Drop in my neck: as it determines, so
> Dissolve my life; the next Caesarion smite
> Till by degrees the memory of my womb,
> Together with my brave Egyptians all,
> By the discandying of this pelleted storm,
> Lie graveless, till the flies and gnats of Nile
> Have buried them for prey!
>
> [3.13.159–67]

Antony thus greets Cleopatra after his victorious land battle

> ... O thou day o' the world,
> Chain mine arm'd neck; leap thou, attire and all,
> Through proof of harness to my heart, and there
> Ride on the pants triumphing!
>
> [4.8.13–16]

Antony sees that his fleet has joined with Caesar's and laments.

> ... The hearts
> That spaniel'd me at heels, to whom I gave
> Their wishes, do discandy, melt their sweets
> On blossoming Caesar: and this pine is bark'd,
> That overtopp'd them all.
>
> [4.12.20–24]

By what scale can such a world adequately be measured? Antony's initial act of overflow seems to have doomed us to a world in which all measures dissolve and discandy. It is in this world of fluid size and dissolving measurements that the lovers make their hyperbolical claims. It is a simple matter to determine the measure of man in Rome, but what is the measure of man here? Puttenham accuses hyperbole of immoderate excess: but how do we measure excess when the very measuring rods dissolve?

This shape shifting is characteristic of a world in which nothing stays to scale because everything overflows its own boundaries. It is to this dangerous and vital world that Antony commits himself. And here he will both lose himself and find himself: only here can we find a scale adequate to him. In this world, everything is in process; nothing can hold its visible shape. Antony "is not more manlike / Than Cleopatra; nor the queen of Ptolemy / More womanly than he" (1.4.5–6): the normal boundaries of sexuality begin to fuse into their own *discordia concors*. We know that Cleopatra makes defect perfection: our logical categories themselves begin to lose their boundaries. Everything here is in process: flaws become virtues, as stars become eyes which pitifully disaster the face. According to Egyptian decorum, everything is becoming: "everything becomes" Cleopatra (1.1.49); even "vilest things / Become themselves in her" (2.2.238–39). If everything becomes Cleopatra, she also becomes everything: she becomes sad and merry for Antony, as she becomes Venus at Cydnus or fire and air at her death; for process—infinite variety—is her decorum. Cleopatra herself plays on the double meaning of "becoming" when she tells Antony, "My becomings kill me, when they do not / Eye well to you" (1.3.96–97): both the things that are becoming to her and the things she becomes must eye well to him. When she reacts to Antony's rage by playing dead, her becomings kill him–and ultimately her as well. And if her becomings kill her in Antony's displeasure, they revive her as she performs her final act for his pleasure. Antony has his becomings as well as Cleopatra: the violence of either sadness or mirth becomes him (1.5.60); and Octavius tells Thidias to "observe how Antony becomes his flaw" (3.12.34). For Octavius, Antony becomes merely his flaw; for Cleopatra, he becomes a colossus. Identity in *Antony and Cleopatra* is not merely a question of Antony's Romanness or of his manhood by its merging and blending of all things, the play questions the very concept of identity. And if there is an answer, it is not in the realm of being at all but in the realm of becoming: identity is defined not by static measurement but by flux. As Antony loses his soldiership, his authority, and even his visible shape, he is nonetheless Antony. Both lovers become each other and themselves: and, in their infinite variety, they virtually become all the world besides. Other figures in the play retain their visible shape: they are precisely what they are. Octavius never loses himself: but neither does he become anything. But our lovers lose their boundaries and absorb everything into themselves.

It is no wonder that this world of fluid size and shape in which nothing stays to scale is reflected throughout the play in the water imagery: this watery world must overflow the measure. The Nile itself is, of course, the central image of overflow; but water is associated throughout with all that does not hold its bounds. Virtually all the uncertain motion in the play is associated with water. Pompey, who depends upon the fickle favor of the people, is strong at sea; his supporters flock to the ports. The favor of the people,

> Like to a vagabond flag upon the stream,
> Goes to, and back, lackeying the varying tide,
> To rot itself with motion.
>
> [1.4.45–47]

Octavia's varying love for her two world leaders is

> ... the swan's down feather,
> That stands upon the swell at the full of tide,
> And neither way inclines.
>
> [3.2.48–50]

Lepidus nearly sinks upon the "quick-sands" of drunkenness (2.7.59); Pompey's galley, upon which treason is plotted only to be resisted and friendships are formed only to be broken, is at sea. Bacchus, the god of drunkenness, is naturally the presiding deity on this drunken boat: the whole scene is emblematic of the giddy and uncertain motion of this world. After Actium, Antony himself becomes an unstable boat: Enobarbus decides, "Sir, sir, thou art so leaky / That we must leave thee to thy sinking" (3.13.63–64). All the varying and unreliable emotions of the play are characterized by weeping, tears that are wet. Even the shore of the world is "varying" (4.15.11): water itself is formlessness and motion.

It is in this metaphoric context that Antony's decision to fight by sea at Actium must be considered. This decision is the turning point in the play: until that time, Antony's military defeat is by no means certain; after that decision, not even the victorious land battle can restore Antony's losses. For it is at this moment that Antony emblematically gives himself up to the world of motion and of overflow. Enobarbus warns him of the consequences of his choice to fight by sea:

> ... you therein throw away
> The absolute soldiership you have by land,
>
> .   .   .   .
>
> ... quite forgo
> The way which promises assurance, and
> Give up yourself merely to chance and hazard,
> From firm security.
>
> [3.7.41–48]

Enobarbus associates the sea with chance and hazard: it suggests fortune itself, that realm in which Caesar is necessarily supreme.[38] The soldier also advises

Antony not to trust "rotten planks" (3.7.62). Their unsteady motion may be appropriate for Egyptians but not for Romans; the soldier associates land with Roman firmness:

> ... Let the Egyptians
> And the *Phoenicians* go a-ducking: we
> Have us'd to conquer standing on the earth,
> And fighting foot to foot.
>
> [3.7.63–66]

But Antony rejects the Roman firmness; and at this moment, the fluid metaphors of the play become a reality. Antony chooses to immerse in the destructive element: it is inherent in the element itself that Cleopatra will flee and that he will follow her. After he has rejected the firmness of land and given himself to the world of chance, he senses that the land itself rejects him: "The land bids me tread no more upon't" (3.11.1). On land, during the next battle, he will retain his soldiership; but once again on sea, his fleet will mysteriously disperse and join with Caesar's.

It is only after Antony has decided to fight at sea that he becomes entirely part of a world melting, dissolving, discandying, overflowing. He has indeed lost himself: but nothing in this world can hold its visible form. Rome melts into Tiber (1.1.33) and Egypt into Nile (2.5.78), at least in the wishes of the lovers; even "the crown o' the earth doth melt" (4.15.63). Enobarbus asks the moon to "disponge" the poisonous damp of night upon him (4.9.13). Cleopatra's poisoned hail discandies (3.12.165) as the hearts of Antony's followers will discandy (4.12.22). Here nothing stands firm; the boundaries cannot hold. Antony feels the dissolution of himself; like Lear, he tells us, "Authority melts from me" (3.13.90). Identity becomes as uncertain as the dislimning clouds.

> *Ant.* That which is now a horse, even with a thought
>   The rack dislimns, and makes it indistinct
>   As water is in water.
> *Eros.*   It does, my lord.
> *Ant.* My good knave Eros, now thy captain is
>   Even such a body: here I am Antony,
>   Yet cannot hold this visible shape, my knave.
>
> [4.14.9–14]

Even the word "dislimns" suggests the process of liquefaction: the painter limns his visible shapes, but the paint turns to liquid and the shapes vanish. There can be no measure in this world of dissolution; all forms blur and merge, and the scale itself is lost.

In this watery world, Antony loses himself and becomes empty: that the shifts of size and shape throughout the play are insistently associated with water emphasizes the sexual basis of Antony's dissolution. Water in all its ambiguity is the emblem of the world of generation: if melting and dissolving are associated with lust and its consequences, overflowing is associated with all fecundity.[39] The sea is the birthplace of the great generative principle: and if the water leads us to Actium and Antony's desertion of himself, it also leads us to Cydnus, where Cleopatra reigns as Venus, surrounded by Nereids and mermaids (2.2.206–9). For water is, in a sense, Cleopatra's terrain: and if Cleopatra is a whore, she is also a generative goddess. The emotional and imagistic nexus of the play lies in the sexual process itself, where one must lose oneself in order to form a new union. The Roman horror of that loss and the ecstatic union which the lovers feel as they die are two elements in the same process: for the dissolution of personal boundaries is both our greatest fear and our highest desire. One must become as indistinct as water is in water to enter this world of enormous loss and enormous fecundity: only here, where all measures dissolve, can the frail case of nature be cracked and the hyperbolical be achieved.

If the hyperbolical is exorcised from the world, the world itself proves too small to contain these lovers. Like the phoenix and the turtle, they are "fled / In a mutual flame from hence" ("The Phoenix and the Turtle," lines 23–24). They may lose the world, but the world is infinitely impoverished by their loss. Ultimately the loss is ours, not theirs: at the same time that we are left in the flat world of the present, the lovers gain access to a region in which man is more than man. For Antony and Cleopatra overflow the measure itself: they burst through their own boundaries and become everything.

The limitations of nature itself will not suffice for these two. Early in the play, Cleopatra complains that "the sides of nature / Will not sustain it" (1.3.16–17); although she is at the time merely indulging in a feminine fainting fit, her words suggest the force of spirit bursting through natural form, violently exceeding its own measure. When she hears the news of Antony's marriage, Charmian tells her, "Keep yourself within yourself" (2.5.75); but how can the woman whom everything becomes keep herself within herself? Philo has told us at the very start that Antony's captain's heart "in the scuffles of great fights hath burst/ The buckles on his breast" (1.1.6–7); later in the play, his lover's heart will also strain to burst its limits. Antony echoes Cleopatra's words when Mardian reports her dead:

> ... O, cleave, my sides!
> Heart, once be stronger than thy continent,
> Crack thy frail case!
>
> [4.14.39–41]

But Antony's heart does not crack its case; though for Enobarbus, "thought will do't" (4.6.36), Antony needs a more mechanical means of death. After his death, Antony's body is merely the "case of that huge spirit" (4.15.89). For the sides of nature cannot sustain such spirits: in death, Antony breaks through the measurements of his body and is freed into Cleopatra's hyperbolical realm.

> His face was as the heavens, and therein stuck
> A sun and moon, which kept their course, and lighted
> The little O, the earth....
> His legs bestrid the ocean, his rear'd arm
> Crested the world.
>
> [5.2.79–83]

In death, Antony achieves the hyperbolical in Cleopatra's vision; as she dies, Cleopatra herself asserts that she is exempt from the natural limitation of death. She is again for Cydnus to meet Mark Antony: and she returns to no literal Cydnus but to the Cydnus of Enobarbus's description, where the limitations of nature itself were defied. And if there is beggary in the love that can be reckoned, there is beggary in ordinary language when it attempts to describe her there. Only unmeasured language is adequate to her; decorum itself demands its use. Enobarbus tells Agrippa, "For her own person, / It beggar'd all description" (2.2.197–98). He valiantly tries to describe Cleopatra despite his own pronouncement and moves immediately into convoluted hyperbole:

> ... she did lie
> In her pavilion—cloth of gold, of tissue—
> O'er-picturing that Venus where we see
> The fancy outwork nature.
>
> [2.2.198–20]

Obviously overcome by his task, he passes to the description of the pretty dimpled boys surrounding her. "O'er-picturing," "outwork": the description itself must overflow the measure and outwork nature. Cleopatra can confer hyperbolical eternity on Antony because she herself has throughout been virtually exempt from natural limitation: according to Enobarbus, she nearly confounds nature itself. He describes Antony sitting in the empty marketplace,

> Whistling to the air; which, but for vacancy,
> Had gone to gaze on Cleopatra too,
> And made a gap in nature.
>
> [2.2.216–18]

And if Cleopatra cannot quite make a gap in nature, she can make a gap in time and achieve eternity.

In their deaths, the lovers escape from time itself. At Antony's suicide, the first guard asserts that "time is at his period" (4.14.107); and as Cleopatra dies, she fulfills her "immortal longings" (5.2.280) in the bite of the worm, "for his biting is immortal" (5.2.245–46). Their escape from the world is an escape from time: for time is preeminently the realm of Caesar.[40] Roman time is a measurable and inescapable quantity, the medium of action and business.[41] This is the time which Octavius will "possess" (2.7.100) and which will allow him to move to Toryne with such incredible speed, the time which Antony himself evokes when he tells Cleopatra that he must return to Rome:

> The strong necessity of time commands
> Our services awhile; but my full heart
> Remains in use with you.
>
> [1.3.42–44]

The strong necessity of time may command Antony's Roman services; but Cleopatra will offer him escape from the necessity of time itself. Opposed to the Roman time of measure, of which Octavius is both master and knave, is the hyperbolical time of which Cleopatra is mistress: time which contracts or expands at will. Antony tells Cleopatra early in the play, "There's not a minute of our lives should stretch / Without some pleasure now" (1.1.46–47). If time can be stretched, it can also be contracted. Cleopatra asks for mandragora to "sleep out this great gap of time / My Antony is away" (1.5.5–6). For Antony, time itself becomes grotesquely unproportioned when he hears of Cleopatra's death: it stretches beyond all measure, so that "now / All length is torture" (4.14.45–46). Only a few moments (about twenty lines) after Mardian's report, Antony speaks as though her death were in the infinitely remote past

> Since Cleopatra died,
> I have liv'd in such dishonour that the gods
> Detest my baseness.
>
> [4.14.55–57]

Cleopatra and her Egypt are both immersed in time and exempt from time: she is "wrinkled deep in time" (1.5.29), but "age cannot wither her" (2.2.235). In Egypt, time itself overflows the measure and moves toward eternity: as Antony determines to obey the strong necessity of time, Cleopatra reminds him that "Eternity was in our lips, and eyes" (1.3.35).

Time is the medium of drama as well as of history, but Shakespeare's manipulation of dramatic time insures that we, as well as Antony, will participate in Cleopatra's eternity. Throughout the first two acts, the bustle of the Roman scenes has been sharply contrasted with the languor of the Egyptian scenes, in which little happens: the dramatic effect is to suggest the slowness of time in Egypt. And in dramatic terms, Cleopatra manages to create a quite literal gap in time. In act 2, scene 5, Cleopatra receives the news of Antony's marriage and harries the messenger until he leaves her presence. At the end of the scene, she decides to extort more information from the poor man and sends Alexas to find him:

> Go to the fellow, good Alexas, bid him
> Report the feature of Octavia; her years,
> Her inclination, let him not leave out
> The colour of her hair: bring me word quickly.
>
> [2.5.111–14]

"Bring me word quickly": we can assume that the queen was accustomed to being obeyed. But four very crowded Roman scenes intervene before the messenger returns and Cleopatra is given the information she wants: four scenes that take us to the farthest corners of the empire and obviously occupy a great deal of Roman time. All the major Roman figures of the play are introduced while Cleopatra waits for the messenger: Pompey, Caesar, and Antony meet and are accorded; the world leaders participate in the drunken feast on Pompey's galley; Ventidius triumphs over the Parthians and discreetly decides to pursue them no further; Octavia and Antony part from Caesar. Then at last we return to Egypt and find that nothing there has changed. Cleopatra's first words make it clear that no time whatever has elapsed:

> *Cleo.*   Where is the fellow?
> *Alex.*   Half afeard to come.
> *Cleo.*   Go to, go to. Come hither, sir.
>
> [3.3.1–2]

Time has rushed on in Rome; it has virtually stood still in Egypt.

The only Roman eternity is achieved through due process of time: Caesar asks Proculeius to guard Cleopatra from suicide, "For her life in Rome / Would be eternal in our triumph" (5.1.65–66), the eternity of history. But Cleopatra exists in a gap of time: and her eternity is achieved not by measure but by overflow. For it is an eternity that can be achieved only through immersion in time and in the world of generation. Octavius possesses the time and remains its knave; Antony is the child of time and escapes it. Despite Caesar, death, not history, is the way to eternity.

Although Cleopatra is mutability itself, only she can offer release from mutability and the realm of fortune. Octavius, who possesses time, is fortune's darling: Antony says,

... The very dice obey him,
And in our sports my better cunning faints
Under his chance.

[2.3.33–35]

The games of chance at which Caesar, fortune's knave, always beats Antony are analogous to that much larger game of fortune which Caesar will win. But Cleopatra, in her sport, wins release from fortune itself. Throughout, she is associated with sport and game: Antony asks, "What sport tonight?" (1.1.47); Cleopatra reminisces about her fishing matches with Antony. Antony assumes that her disloyalty is all part of her game: she beguiles him at the game of fast and loose (4.12.28); she has "pack'd cards with Caesar" (4.14.19). But Cleopatra's final sport will demonstrate her loyalty to Antony. For deep in the texture of the play, there is a gaiety transfiguring all that dread, so that, in the last moments, even death is play. As Cleopatra lifts Antony into her monument, she says, "Here's sport indeed!" (4.15.32). And in the end, as she dies, Cleopatra's sport takes on the self-consciousness of art itself: "Show me, my women, like a queen" (5.2.226). Cleopatra promises Charmian release from her service: "And when thou hast done this chare, I'll give thee leave / To play till doomsday" (5.2.230–31). But even for Charmian, the only play is death: "Your crown's awry, / I'll mend it, and then play" (5.2.317–18). Cleopatra in her death becomes marble-constant, like a work of art: and in her constancy, she escapes from the flux of fortune and nature.

... it is great
To do that thing that ends all other deeds,
Which shackles accidents, and bolts up change;
Which sleeps, and never palates more the dung,
The beggar's nurse, and Caesar's.

[5.2.4–8]

Cleopatra will sleep out the great gap of time her Antony's away; and by that sleep she will rejoin him in the hyperbolical realm to which they had no access while alive: "O such another sleep, that I might see / But such another man!" (5.2.77–78). And the paradoxical impossibility that could never be wholly true in the realm of flux becomes true here:

Our separation so abides and flies,
That thou, residing here, goes yet with me;
And I, hence fleeting, here remain with thee.

[1.3.102–4]

Throughout this play, we are in the presence of the most Christian of paradoxes: that man must lose himself in order to gain himself. This paradox informs the shipwrecks in the romances; and it informs our sense of what is won and lost here. Here, as in the romances, life itself can grow the more only by reaping. Antony must lose his visible shape to become infinite; the only measure of overflow is on the scales of the pyramid. Only by giving himself wholly to nature can he out-measure it; only by giving himself wholly to flux and dissolution can he attain release from flux in death and in Cleopatra's vision. For death and life meet at once in Cleopatra: and one is not possible without the other.

> ... great Pompey
> Would stand and make his eyes grow in my brow,
> There would he anchor his aspect, and die
> With looking on his life.
>
> [1.5.31–34]

And at Antony's literal death, the paradox is repeated

> ... Die when thou hast liv'd,
> Quicken with kissing: had my lips that power,
> Thus would I wear them out.
>
> [4.15.38–40]

As Antony must lose his visible shape to become infinite, so the lovers must die to find their life.

Throughout the play, transcendence of any kind is achieved only by immersion in the realm of nature, with all its limitations. As the lovers die, they are united sexually in a vast act of overflow: so that death is simultaneously their means of escaping from the mutability of nature and their means of participating in it. In its emphasis on changes of size and shape and on all that overflows the measure, the play poses the mysteries of the sexual process: Antony grows the more by reaping. Enobarbus makes the paradox explicit in his description of Cleopatra:

> ... other women cloy
> The appetites they feed, but she makes hungry,
> Where most she satisfies.
>
> [2.2.236–38]

The sense of spirit violently bursting through the case of nature is appropriate to the double nature of man as spirit incarnate, literally embodied; and it is also appropriate to human sexuality on the most literal and physiological level. The ultimate paradox of the play is that even its transcendence is part of the natural world of flux: measure and overflow, flux and stasis, time and eternity, life and death, are all inseparable, a knot intrinsicate.

The Structure of Assent

Pass the size of dreaming [5.2.97]

When Cleopatra somewhat coyly asks poor Dolabella whether or not there could be such a man as the Antony she dreamed of, Dolabella denies the possibility of her dream. Her answer is immediate: "You lie up to the hearing of the gods" (5.2.95). The entire play has led us to the point where we, as well as Cleopatra, can find Dolabella's denial of the dream at least as suspect as the dream itself. In what sense do we come to believe in the lovers' assertions, and how are we led to this belief?[42]

One of the paths of assent open to us is that which would see the lovers' paradoxical and hyperbolical assertions as accurate metaphors for psychological facts, as descriptions of the world as it appears to the lovers. Antony says, "Fall not a tear, I say, one of them rates/ All that is won and lost" (3.11.69–70). If one of Cleopatra's tears is worth the world to Antony, then one tear *is* worth the world—insofar as we agree to see the world from his perspective. What we think of the bargain is, for the moment, irrelevant. In these matters there need be no "objective correlative": if Hamlet's situation drives him to despair, then it is for him a desperate situation. But does "His legs bestrid the ocean" mean only, "As far as Cleopatra was concerned, Antony's legs bestrid the ocean"? Do we accept the lovers' assertions only as evaluative truths, only as we would perforce accept the truth of the statement, "It looks red to me" (even though the object looks very blue to us)?[43] Is Cleopatra's dream only one more judgment in the long series of partial and erroneous judgments in the play? I think not. To believe in these assertions only as psychological metaphors is Philo's Roman way and does not seem adequate to our experience. "Cleopatra dies at one with Antony in her love for him" simply does not do justice to our sense of affirmation when she says, "Husband, I come"; we cannot translate the impossible statement of fact into any possible statement of emotion without losing its force. As Cleopatra's dream of Antony is in the realm of nature, not of fancy, so these assertions leave the realm of fancy and begin to claim our belief as fact.

To the extent that we are engaged with the protagonist, his judgment will be our judgment; and to that extent it will be dramatic fact. Throughout most of *Antony and Cleopatra*, we are not permitted to become wholly engaged with the protagonists. In fact, most of the structural devices of the play prevent our engagement (see chapter 1). But toward the end of the play the dramatic technique changes radically. We tend more often to accept the lovers' evaluation of themselves, to take them at their word, because we are more often permitted to identify ourselves with them. The entire structure of framing commentary and of shifts of scene had forced us to remain relatively detached from them; after act 4, scene 12, it tends to disappear. No one intervenes between us and the lovers;

there are no radical and disjunctive shifts in perspective. The final scene of the play is almost twice as long as the next longest scene (364 lines as opposed to 201 in act 3, scene 13): and it is Cleopatra's scene virtually from beginning to end. For once, she is allowed to undercut Caesar by her commentary: "He words me, girls, he words me" (5.2.190). The Clown interrupts Cleopatra, but she turns his presence to her own account: his banter serves as an impetus to her immortal longings. Though he qualifies the solemnity of her death, he does not provide the radical shift in perspective that we have come to expect in this play. We can here take her as seriously as she takes herself, participate with her in the tragic perspective. The critical structure drops away from Antony in act 4, scene 14, in much the same manner. And as we are permitted to become involved with the lovers, their evaluations tend to take on the status of emotional fact even in despite of the literal fact.

If the dramatic structure now permits us to become engaged with the lovers, it also works to give us the feeling of assent in spite of all logic. For most of the play, we have been subjected to the wear and tear of numerous short scenes, to the restless shifts of perspective. Now, as the lovers leave the world of business, we are permitted to rest.[44] The scenes become longer and more leisurely; the entire pace of the play slows. In some ways, the rhythm of the play suggests the rhythm of the sexual act itself, especially in the quiescent melting of its end. And as the lovers come together, even the quality of the language changes. The word "come," used so frequently by the lovers as they prepare to die, suggests that death is a reunion, not a separation—a suggestion not at all mitigated by the secondary sexual meaning of the word.[45] But the sound of the word may be as significant as its meaning. We move from the complexity, rapidity, and lightness of "Our separation so abides and flies, / That thou, residing here, goes yet with me; / And I, hence fleeting, here remain with thee" (1.3.102–4) to the simple slowness of "I come, my queen" (4.14.50). The restless tension in the language seems to be replaced by a new ease. If we participate in the lovers' sense of release from life, it is at least partly because we are ourselves released from the strain which action and language had imposed on us earlier.

At the same time, we are released from the doubts and scruples which have hedged us in throughout the play. Ultimately our sense of assent probably comes from the fact that the psychological roots of the play are our psychological roots too. Insofar as *Antony and Cleopatra* concerns overflow, the dissolution of boundaries, bisexuality, and the association of both death and sexual love with loss of self and ecstatic union, it touches many of us where we live.[46] One of the most difficult problems in love of any kind is to strike a balance between the desire to give oneself wholly to another and the desire to keep oneself wholly intact: We have had both sides of this conflict exacerbated in us as we watch the play: and most of the time, the spokesmen for the terrors of dissolution and loss of self have had the upper hand. Antony's fear that he is losing his visible shape may come dangerously close to home: for it is to some extent the fear of everyone in love. When this fear at last becomes desire, when mere loss of self is transformed into "I come, my queen," we are bound to feel the release as well as Antony. As the lovers die asserting that death is union, they temporarily resolve the tension for us; and in that sense, their resolution is bound to be ours.

This sense of resolution prepares us, I think, for the leap of faith necessary at the end of the play; and if we are given the feeling of assent, the play supports our feeling with a logic of its own. Antony's assertion that he and Cleopatra will meet in Elysium has sometimes been regarded as evidence of his delusion-unto-death; but if it is a delusion, it must in some sense be our delusion too. The play has throughout insisted on the possibility of the impossible: Caesar is in fact at Toryne, however impossible; the Clown echoes the particular impossibility of a death which is not final in his tale of the immortal woman who reports how she died of the biting of the worm. Throughout, we have been told that death may be sleep. At Enobarbus's death, the Roman guardsmen assume that he is asleep; even when he does not awaken, they think that "he may recover yet" (4.9.33). Even the crocodile "transmigrates" instead of dying. Cleopatra faints when Antony dies, and Iras assumes that "she's dead too" (4.15.69). Her recovery gives us a precedent and a dramatic image for immortality.

Antony's impossibility is in some sense confirmed by Cleopatra's independent expression of the same impossibility: "I am again for Cydnus, / To meet Mark Antony" (5.2.227–28). These may be shared delusions, but they nonetheless create in us the sense that the lovers have grown together in death. The lovers are apart or acting at cross-purposes during most of the play: despite the verbal assertions of love and union, the sense we get is of their disunity. But after Antony dies, the feeling of union is gradually created, not only through Cleopatra's resolve to join him in death (as everyone has noted, she is not entirely resolute) but also through the dramatic structure. She begins to echo his phrases as though the lovers were in fact becoming one. But the lovers are not the only ones who assert their impossible reunion. Toward the end of the play, the possibility of the impossible is repeatedly confirmed by a striking technique: the assertions are reiterated by the most unexpected allies. In the end, the lovers do not need to rely on each other for support in their assertions: for their hyperbolical assertions are echoed by characters not ordinarily prone to the hyperbolical vision. Cleopatra finds in Antony's death the signs of the great Apocalypse: "darkling stand the varying shore o' the world"; "The soldier's pole is fall'n." But even the guardsmen greet Antony's suicide as an apocalyptic event:

> *Sec. Guard.*   The star is fall'n.
> *First Guard.* And time is at his period.
>
> [4.14.106–7]

Both independently see Antony as a fallen star; we need not depend on the testimony of his mistress alone. Their reaction authenticates her hyperbolical vision. The lovers' assertions that death is a sleep in which they will be reunited are authenticated by the same means. Antony senses in Cleopatra's death the coming of night: "Unarm, Eros, the long day's task is done, /And we must sleep" (4.14.35–36). While she lived, she was "thou day o' the world" (4.8.13); at her death, only darkness is left. Iras urges her mistress to sleep in strikingly similar language: "Finish, good lady, the bright day is done, / And we are for the dark" (5.2.192–93). For Cleopatra, the asp is the baby "that sucks the nurse asleep" (5.2.309). Antony's sleep will permit him to meet Cleopatra where souls do couch on flowers; Cleopatra calls for "such another sleep" (5.2.77) to repossess her dream of Antony. At the last moment in the play, even Octavius hints that perhaps death is a sleep which will permit them to be reunited: "she looks like sleep, / As she would catch another Antony / In her strong toil of grace" (5.2.344–46). The repeated assertion from unexpected perspectives forces us to consider that, despite all probability, the impossible may be true.

After Actium, Thidias bestows some excellent Roman advice on Cleopatra:

Wisdom and fortune combating together,
If that the former dare but what it can,
No chance may shake it.

[3.13.79–81]

Roman wisdom consists in confining oneself to the possible; but Egyptian wisdom always dares more than what it can. Antony may be a strumpet's fool (1.1.13), but Octavius is after all only fortune's knave (5.2.3). Cleopatra tells us as she lifts Antony into the monument that wishers were ever fools. Perhaps so: but there are many kinds of folly.[47] Enobarbus in his Roman wisdom knows that "The loyalty well held to fools does make / Our faith mere folly" (3.13.42–43); yet his refusal to abide by his folly finally kills him. For despite the judgment of our reason, man is most noble when he is most foolish when Enobarbus has obeyed his reason, he feels himself "alone the villain of the earth" (4.6.30). Antony in his foolish passion kills himself at the news of Cleopatra's death; but his folly insures his nobility. Wishers and fools may see more deeply than men of reason: the Soothsayer who sees a little into nature's infinite book of secrecy (1.2.9) is a fool.

Char.	... prithee, how many boys and wenches must I have?
Sooth.	If every of your wishes had a womb,
	And fertile every wish, a million.
Char.	Out, fool! I forgive thee for a witch.

[1.2.35–39]

Cleopatra, like the Soothsayer, is both witch and wisher: and not all her wishes are fertile. But in the end, her folly is the folly of vision; and the whole play moves us toward the acknowledgment of its truth.

Throughout, the play has insisted on the unreliability of all report and the uncertainty of truth itself (see chapter 1, pp. 24–39). Is Mardian's false report false after all? It becomes true after the fact when Cleopatra does kill herself for Antony. And what of the Clown's witness for the immortal worm, "a very honest woman, but something given to lie, as a woman should not do, but in the way of honesty" (5.2.251–53)? Not all judgments are equally verifiable: Cleopatra's dream of Antony is not susceptible to proof in the way that Pompey's prediction of his whereabouts is. The play teaches us that there are different modes of belief for different kinds of statement. It forces us to acknowledge a fundamental paradox of the human imagination: that occasionally truth can be told only in lies.[48] Cleopatra's dream is her lie in the way of honesty; it is the central paradox of the play that we must both deny it and find it true. Like the other assertions of the impossible, it remains in the unverifiable domain of the true lie. And however impervious to logic this domain is, it occasionally comes closer to our experience than the tidy categories of logic can. There are lies and dreams that are more true than truth itself; the hyperbolical version of their story which the lovers present at the end of the play is one of these lies. The poetry in which the lovers create their version of the story may be only true lies; but the paradoxical true lie may be the only sort of truth available to us in this world.

Cleopatra's lips do not have the power to quicken with kissing. Only in *The Winter's Tale* do lips have that power: it is Leontes' kiss that reawakens Hermione. In *Antony and Cleopatra* we must take the impossible on faith; in the romances, these very impossibilities will become actual on stage. The poetic assertions of *Antony and Cleopatra* become the literal facts of the romances. We *see* Cleopatra's gap of time and the eternity which it confers in *The Winter's Tale*. Antony asserts his own version of pastoral rebirth when he says, "Where souls do couch on flowers, we'll hand in hand" (4.14.51); this rebirth will become literal in act 4 of *The Winter's Tale*. In the romances the world itself embodies the impossible. There is no longer a discrepancy between fact and poetic vision: the two have become one. As *Antony and Cleopatra* moves toward the attainment of the impossible, it leaves the realm of tragedy and moves toward romance.[49] The tension between fact and assertion is always essential in *Antony and Cleopatra*, as it is not in the romances; but nonetheless, the poetic credibility of the romances can serve as an analogue for the process of our assent at the end of *Antony and Cleopatra*.

In the major tragedies, the poetry does not contradict the action. Macbeth's poetry perfectly reflects his moral state; it never asserts anything which we do not find verified by the action. When Othello says,

It is the cause, it is the cause, my soul,
Let me not name it to you, you chaste stars:
. . . .
... she must die, else she'll betray more men.

> [*Othello* 5.2.1–6]

the language makes claims which are inconsistent with the action; but just this inconsistency is the reflection of Othello's delusion. We do not for a moment believe the assertions of the poetry. We know that he is committing murder: his tragedy is that he has been duped into regarding this murder as a sacrificial act. The poetry here illuminates his delusion and makes no claim to the status of fact; but in *Antony and Cleopatra*, when the poetry and action are inconsistent, poetry begins to make this claim. In both *Othello* and *Antony and Cleopatra*, the concept of the afterlife is significant at the end of the play; but the quality of belief accorded each is strikingly disparate. Othello pictures a reunion of lovers rather different from Antony's:

... when we shall meet at count,
This look of thine will hurl my soul from heaven,
And fiends will snatch at it.

> [*Othello* 5.2.274–76]

Othello is set in a context which is thoroughly Christian: his prevision here is perfectly literal; the reaction of the audience would probably depend on their belief that it was essentially accurate. This is no mere poetic assertion of the impossible; it does not strain our credulity in any way. Indeed, it is a statement about the highest reality which is terrifying precisely in its literalness. But in *Antony and Cleopatra*, there is no context which demands that we believe in the literal possibility of the afterlife; there is no evidence that either the Egyptians or the Romans in the play take the belief seriously. The entire effect of the lovers' assertions depends upon the fact that we cannot take their belief literally. These assertions are contrary to any literal fact; and yet we do not see them merely as expressions of delusion.

In *Antony and Cleopatra*, when the poetry conflicts with the literal situation, it nonetheless can make some claim to our belief. Cleopatra's dream has a certain validity, although it is a dream; in the romances, the dream is usually revealed as the reality. For the metaphors of the earlier plays become the literal actions of the romances. Lear says to Kent in the storm,

... where the greater malady is fix'd
The lesser is scarce felt. Thou'ldst shun a bear;
But if thy flight lay toward the roaring sea,
Thou'ldst meet the bear i' th' mouth.

> [*King Lear* 3.4.8–11]

Lear expresses the most extreme situation imaginable here by the metaphor; but in *The Winter's Tale*, precisely this metaphor will become the literal action. Antigonus will be caught between the bear and the raging sea and will face the bear in the mouth. In *Hamlet*, we are told about the flights of angels that will sing the prince to his rest; in *The Tempest*, we see Ariel singing Ferdinand to his rest. Pericles hears the music of the spheres and sleeps: in his dream, Diana appears and reveals the real pattern behind his apparently random wanderings. His dream is not a poetic assertion or a metaphor but a vision which is literally true: for Diana herself appears on stage before us. We are given momentary access to a truth usually concealed; the miraculous takes place before our eyes. The impossible is no longer a matter of poetic assertion: it actually takes place on stage. When Hermione steps down from her pedestal in *The Winter's Tale*, the impossible has been achieved. In these plays, the symbolic pattern asserted in the poetry takes precedence over any considerations of realism: each play dares far more than what it can. No one would think of questioning Hermione about her perverse sadomasochistic desire to torment Leontes by remaining hidden until Perdita is found or about her living arrangements during that period; nor in fact do we take the rationalization that she has remained hidden very seriously. We know that she has come back to life. We do not, that is to say, seek to explain the impossible away. Instead, we gladly accept the impossibility for the sake of the symbolic pattern: she must remain hidden until her daughter has grown up and returned; only thus can the validity of the natural process of regeneration be asserted.

In both romance and tragedy, then, the poetry and the action are in accord: in tragedy, the poetry is usually at the service of the action; in romance, the action is usually at the service of the poetry. *Antony and Cleopatra* stands between the two: poetry and action conflict; and each makes its own assertions and has its own validity. We do not literally believe in such poetic assertions as the postmortem reunion, and we certainly do not see them achieved on stage; but at moments the symbolic pattern of reunion begins to take precedence over any literal-minded questions about how precisely the lovers plan to be together. At these moments, the modes of tragedy and romance are competing; and we must be willing to acknowledge the claims of both. At the end of *Antony and Cleopatra*, death bolts up change for Cleopatra, and she becomes almost statuelike in her attainment of stasis: "I am marble-constant: now the fleeting moon / No planet is of mine" (5.2.239–40). Octavia is subject to Cleopatra's scorn for being more "a statue, than a breather" (3.3.21) in life; but Cleopatra will attain her eternity by becoming statuesque in death. This transformation is emblematic of the power accorded art in this play: the poetic assertion itself will confer a kind of eternity. In *The Winter's Tale*, art or poetic assertion becomes a literal fact of nature: the statue moves from her pedestal and comes to life. And in *Antony and Cleopatra* the art does not remain lifeless: the poetic assertion moves into the realm of nature. Cleopatra overpictures the mere picture of Venus; her Antony is natures piece 'gainst fancy. The art here is not pure nature, as it is in *The Winter's Tale*: it is after all the *imagination* of an Antony which is nature's piece. The assertion remains poised in the middle region, where we can neither believe it nor disbelieve it: and finally this balance is essential to the whole.

NOTES

1. Harry Levin's discussion in *The Overreacher* (Cambridge, 1952) first made me aware of the problem of staged hyperbole, though his view of it is very different from mine. He says, "The stage becomes a vehicle for hyperbole, not merely by accrediting the incredible or supporting rhetoric with a platform and sounding board, but by taking metaphors literally and acting concepts out. Operating visually as well as vocally, it converts symbols into properties; triumph must ride across in a chariot, hell must flare up in fireworks; students, no longer satisfied to read about Helen of Troy, must behold her in her habit as she lived. Whereas poetry is said to transport us to an imaginative level, poetic drama transports that level to us: hyperbolically speaking, it brings the mountains to Mohammed" (p. 24). But we can never see Helen; any actual face is a poor substitute for the face that launched a thousand ships. In fact, the literal action will always to some extent contradict the assertions of the poetry: it will be up to the individual playwright to emphasize these contradictions or to ignore them, as he chooses.

2. This concern with the problem of staged hyperbole may have been suggested to Shakespeare by Marlowe's *Dido, Queen of Carthage*; Marlowe insists upon the discrepancy between literal action and verbal assertion throughout *Dido*. For a fuller discussion of staged hyperbole in *Dido*, see appendix B.

3. In fact, many of the critics who praise the poetry extravagantly seem by implication to condemn the play as a whole, as though it were necessary for us to adjudicate between the claims of the Poetry and those of the Play. G. B. Harrison, for instance, says, "*Antony and Cleopatra* is gorgeous, with the loveliest word-music, but it never reaches down to the depths of emotion" ("*Antony and Cleopatra*," *Shakespeare's Tragedies* [London, 1951], p. 226). A. C. Bradley ("Shakespeare's *Antony and Cleopatra*," *Oxford Lectures on Poetry* [London, 1909]) suggests that in praising the play, we are praising "the artist and his activity, while in the case of the four famous tragedies it is the product of this activity, the thing presented, that first engrosses us" (p. 282). In fact, very few people attempt to reconcile the final claims of the poetry with the play as a whole. Those who wish for certainty inevitably wish that Shakespeare had condemned the lovers a little more, or exalted them a little more; and according to their preference, they either minimize or emphasize the poetry. In either case, the poetry becomes in effect detachable from the play. Thus Bethell, Griffiths, and Knight rely too exclusively on the poetry; Danby, Rosen, et al. are too eager to ignore it

altogether. Proser suggests that the lovers create their own poetic universe which can compete with the everyday universe, but he does not show how this poetic universe is related to the rest of the play. Though his discussion is suggestive, he still seems to regard the poetry as finally detachable. Traversi is almost alone among major critics in insisting that the "lyrical" and "realistic" visions of the play are part of the same organic whole: "It is the play's achievement to leave room for *both* estimates of the personal tragedy, the realistic as well as the lyrical; and if each has to be continually balanced against its opposite, so that the total impression can never, even at the last, depend upon one to the exclusion of the other, full understanding of what is intended rests upon an appreciation of the poetic quality so marvelously, richly present throughout the play. The gap between what is clearly, from one point of view, a sordid infatuation, and the triumphant feeling which undoubtedly, though never exclusively, prevails in the final scenes is bridged by a wonderful modification of connected imagery. Rottenness becomes the ground for fertility, opulence becomes royalty, infatuation turns into transcendent passion, all by means of an *organic* process which ignores none of its own earlier stages, which, while never denying the validity of the realistic estimates of the situation which accompany it to the last, integrates these in the more ample unity of its creative purpose" (*An Approach to Shakespeare* [Garden City, 1969], 2: 224–25). In his view, the lyricism grows from the realism as all the vitality in the play grows from its corruption. The central metaphor for this process is Nilus's' slime, quickened by the fire of the sun (p. 230). Though the terms of our arguments are very different, Traversi's demonstration that the poetry is not detachable from the play and his emphasis on the corrupt vitality of the Nile are similar to my own; see especially pp. 127 ff., below.

4. Bernard Shaw, *Three Plays for Puritans* (London, 1930), pp. xxx–xxxi.

5. Both figures have been recognized as essential to the poetic texture of the play; sec, for example, Benjamin T. Spencer, "*Antony and Cleopatra* and the Paradoxical Metaphor," *Shakespeare Quarterly* 9 (1958): 373–78; and Madeleine Doran, "'High Events as These': The Language of Hyperbole in *Antony and Cleopatra*," *Queen's Quarterly* 72 (1965): 25–51. Spencer notes most of the paradoxes in the play and finds paradox "the matrix from which much of the characterization and the action sprang" (p. 376). He finds it characteristic of a discourse "obliged to take account of the contradictions and unpredictability and irrationality of human affection and passion" (p. 373). His suggestion that at the end "the paradoxical hints at the transcendental" (p. 375) is tantalizing; unfortunately he does not tell us how, nor does he discuss the tension between belief and disbelief which is, I think, essential to paradox in the play. Doran's essay is particularly useful insofar as it discusses hyperbole as part of the Elizabethan tendency toward "the ideal, the excellent, the distinguished, the quintessential" in all areas (p. 28).

6. "On Love," *The Works of Francis Bacon*, ed. James Spedding, Robert Leslie Ellis, and Douglas Denon Heath (London, 1859), 6: 397–98.

7. Edgar Wind, *Pagan Mysteries in the Renaissance* (New York, 1968), pp. 55–56.

8. Henry Peacham, *The Garden of Eloquence* (1593), ed. William G. Crane (Gainesville, Fla., 1954), p. 112.

9. It is suggestive that Peacham's only example of the figure is Paul's words to King Agrippa, a skeptic about the miracles of Christianity: "'Why should it be thought a thing incredible unto you: that God should raise againe the dead. I also thought in my selfe that I ought to do many contrary things against the name of Jesus of *Nazareth*....' Here Paul sheweth, that not long before he was of the same opinion that his adversaries and the judge were now of, and was in the like maner an open enemy to the professor of that name" (pp. 112–13).

10. George Puttenham, *The Arte of English Poesie*, ed. Gladys Doidge Willcock and Alice Walker (Cambridge, 1936), p. 226.

11. Peacham, Puttenham, and the other English figurists seem to regard paradox as a strictly verbal phenomenon, in which the doubt is expressed explicitly in so many words. Thus Day's example of paradox is, "Could it possibly bee thought that learning and place of good education might ever have produced such monstrous effects?" (Angel Day, *The English Secretary* [1599], ed. Robert O. Evans [Gainesville, Fla., 1967], pt. 2, p. 90). James Blair Leishman (*Themes and Variations in Shakespeare's Sonnets* [London, 1963]) eloquently warns against the danger of putting the cart before the horse in this matter: the use of "hyperbole" as "a rhetorical or literary-critical term represents an attempt by rhetoricians and 'grammarians' to describe something which had struck them in the practice of great poets, not an attempt by great poets to realise something which had first been suggested as a possibility by rhetoricians and grammarians. This may perhaps seem too obvious to require insistence, but I think it is not so at a time when so many scholars, especially in America, seem to have persuaded themselves, not only that we can learn something really valuable from a study of medieval or semi-medieval textbooks on rhetoric which great Renaissance poets may or may not have read at school, but also that it was from such textbooks that great poets learnt to use rhetorical devices which, long before any textbooks existed, had been used by Homer and Aeschylus and Pindar" (p. 152). The rhetoricians may suggest traditional attitudes toward a figure, but they can never suggest the function a figure actually serves in an author as complex as Shakespeare.

12. The "Christian Paradoxes," originally printed under Bacon's name, are almost certainly not by him. According to the editors of the collected *Works*, "It is the work of an orthodox Churchman of the early part of the 17th century, who fully and unreservedly accepting on the authority of revelation the entire scheme of Christian theology, and believing that the province of faith is altogether

distinct from that of reason, found a pleasure in bringing his spiritual loyalty into stronger relief by confronting and numbering up the intellectual paradoxes which it involved" (*Works*, 7: 290). Paradox in the Renaissance has recently received much attention. See, for instance, A. E. Malloch, "The Technique and Function of the Renaissance Paradox," *Studies in Philology* 53 (1956): 191–203. Malloch gives the philosophical background in Aquinas and More and emphasizes the importance of the readers response to the illogic of the paradox. His conclusion is suggestive for *Antony and Cleopatra*: "Logic operates upon concepts, which are by definition abstracts from the world of existent things. Paradox controls and makes intelligible this multiple world much as two negative units in algebra, when multiplied, bring forth a positive answer" (p. 203). Rosalie Colie defines the traditional *topoi* of paradox in *Paradoxia Epidemica: The Renaissance Tradition of Paradox* (Princeton, 1966). Her discussion is illuminating for *Antony and Cleopatra*, particularly in her emphasis on the self-reflexive quality of paradox (p. 7); on its involvement in dialectic (paradox exploits "the fact of relative, or competing, value systems" [p. 10]); and on the necessity for belief in the impossible expressed through paradox (p. 23).

13. The figurists generally give paradox and hyperbole approximately equal billing as figures; but nonetheless hyperbole is defined in a way which permits us to see it as a species of paradox in the broadest sense. In fact, the terms of the figurists constitute a quicksand quite as dangerous as the one in which Lepidus almost sinks. One of the few flaws in Sister Miriam Joseph's useful study (*Shakespeare's Use of the Arts of Language* (New York, 1947]) is that she makes the rhetoricians appear far more consistent than they actually are. According to Sister Miriam Joseph, it is very probable that Shakespeare knew Puttenham (p. 44); and there is some evidence to suggest his knowledge of Peacham (pp. 113–14). For most of the figurists, *paradoxon* does not imply logical contradiction, though this implication is present in Donne's use of the word. The term *oxymoron* had not yet come into use. The closest approximation to it was *sinaciosis* or *synaeceosis*, defined by Peacham as "a figure which teacheth to conjoine diverse things or contraries, and to repugne common opinion with reason, thus: The covetous & the prodigall are both alike in fault, for neither of them knoweth to use their wealth aright, for they both abuse it, and both get shame by it" (p. 170). Puttenham defines it as "the *Crossecouple*, because it takes me two contrary words, and tieth them as it were in a paire of couples, and so makes them agree like good fellowes" (p. 206). He uses the same example as Peacham. (Day also uses the same example, incidentally, on p. 95: apparently synaeceosis was scarce.) Despite the apparent similarity to paradox in function, these figurists did not connect the two in any way. But I suspect that they would have considered Shakespeare's additions to Plutarch's description of Cleopatra synaeceosis rather than paradox. In general, these figurists tended to divide the figures into three categories: *tropes*, in which the signification of a word or sentence was changed, such as metaphor or allegory (Puttenham calls these

"sensable figures"); *grammatical schemes* such as zeugma, in which the order or spelling of words was changed without affecting the signification (Puttenham calls these "auricular figures"); and *rhetorical schemes*, in which both the arrangement of words and the signification is changed (Puttenham calls these "sententious figures"). Unfortunately, hyperbole is by this system a trope and paradox is a rhetorical scheme, and never the twain shall meet, despite their similarity of function. In any event, since hyperbole can be used to create precisely the effect prescribed for paradox, I have chosen perhaps arbitrarily to consider hyperbole as a species of paradox. Colie also concludes that paradox is "primarily a figure of thought, in which the various suitable figures of speech are inextricably impacted" (p. 22).

14. Puttenham, p. 154.

15. Puttenham, pp. 191–92.

16. Our sense of Cleopatra as a creature who embodies paradox within herself comes largely from Enobarbus's speech; Shakespeare's addition of paradox to Plutarch's description is the more striking because he otherwise follows Plutarch's wording so exactly. The barge in Plutarch has a gold poop and purple sails, but it does not burn on the water. The winds are not lovesick with the sails. Plutarch's oars are silver and move in time to flutes; the water does not follow, amorous of their strokes. Plutarch's Cleopatra does not beggar description. She is "apparelled and attired like the goddesse Venus, commonly drawen in picture" and surrounded by boys, "apparelled as painters doe set forth god Cupide," who are fanning her; but Plutarch's Cleopatra does not overpicture Venus, the picture of Venus does not outwork nature, and the winds fanned by the Cupids do not glow the cheeks which they did cool. The inhabitants of Plutarch's city run to gaze at Cleopatra; but his air seems untempted to follow suit and make a gap in nature.

17. Theseus tells us that it is part of love's madness to see "Helen's beauty in a brow of Egypt" (*Midsummer Night's Dream* 5.2.11). For an extended discussion of Cleopatra's blackness, see appendix C.

18. In one sense, of course, this distinction is specious: Antony's hyperboles are paradoxical and Cleopatra's paradoxes hyperbolical. The two figures of thought are thoroughly intertwined in the play. Nonetheless, as purely verbal phenomena, the paradoxes tend to be associated with Cleopatra and the hyperboles with Antony.

19. To rectify this obvious implausibility, Dryden transferred the speech to Antony; by the same process, he transferred the mystery out of the speech. There have been other, equally ingenious, solutions to the problems which Enobarbus's speech creates. In Michael Langham's Stratford, Ont., production of the play (1967), Enobarbus assumed the guise of a city sharpy gulling Roman rednecks, thus obliterating the audience's dangerous tendency to believe the speech.

20. Mack says of Enobarbus's description of Cleopatra at Cydnus, "This is

clearly not a portrait of a mere intriguing woman, but a kind of absolute oxymoron" (introduction to the Pelican *Antony and Cleopatra* (Baltimore, 1960], p. 19).

21. Puttenham cautions against the abuse of this figure on just these grounds: "this maner of speech is used, when either we would greatly advaunce or greatly abase the reputation of any thing or person, and must be used very discreetly, or els it will seeme odious, for although a prayse or other report may be allowed bey?d credit, it may not be beyd all measure" (p. 192). He tells the story of a speaker who compared the task of reciting the virtues of Henry VIII to numbering the stars of the sky and consequently made of himself "a grosse flattering foole": and though he does not say so, by his own law the speaker probably did nothing to enhance Henry's reputation. The effect of the hyperbole was comic, independent of the speakers, intentions, because the discrepancy between fact and assertion was too great. Puttenham then suggests his own "more moderate lye" as a substitute for this gross flattery (p. 192).

22. It is not clear whether Cleopatra imagines Antony upholding the heavens (as the Atlas myth would suggest) or the earth: "of the earth" may imply either that this Atlas belongs to the earth or that he upholds the earth instead of the heavens. The second alternative would be more consistent with the imagery of the play, especially with the collapse of the wide arch of the rang'd empire; but perhaps we should not expect consistency from Cleopatra. According to the myth, Hercules once relieved Atlas of his task; since Caesar, and Antony now share the task between them, Antony is only a demi-Atlas, by implication only half as strong as his great ancestor.

23. The hyperbolical braggart is in fact associated with Antony in *Henry V*: Fluellen tells us that he thinks Pistol "is as valiant a man as Mark Antony" *Henry V* (3.6.13–15).

24. For a discussion of the stage representations of Herod, see Douglas Cole, *Suffering and Evil in the Plays of Christopher Marlowe* (Princeton, 1962), pp. 11–22. Geoffrey Bullough accounts for the references to Herod by suggesting that Shakespeare probably knew the tradition that Cleopatra had attempted to seduce Herod and failed (*Narrative and Dramatic Sources of Shakespeare* (London, 1964], 5: 219). We probably need not refer to any tradition to explain his presence: it is part of the spaciousness of *Antony and Cleopatra* that the grand tyrant himself is in effect one of the superfluous kings who have served as Antony's messengers. When Charmian imagines herself mother of a son to whom Herod will do homage, her fantasy is a comic version of the other grandiose ambitions in the play. But at the same time, her mock ambition makes us strangely conscious of Herod's real power as a tyrant in the Christian context. Stephen Booth has pointed out to me that this curious half allusion to Christ produces a good deal of gratuitous hyperbolical energy at this moment in the play.

25. According to A. D. S. Fowler ("Emblems of Temperance in *The Faerie*

Queene, Book II," *Review of English Studies*, n.s. 11 (1960): 143), the golden set square was a common emblem for temperance; as the "norm of temperance" it occurs in Achille Bocchi's *Symbolicarum quaestionum libri quinque* (Bologna, 1574) as emblem 144.

26. I am indebted here (as everywhere in my discussion of Spenser) to John C. Pope.

27. Shakespeare's use of this scale is the more striking since, as far as I know, it is his own invention. Everyone agrees that the overflow of the Nile determines the size of the crop, but the use of the pyramids as a scale is not mentioned by Conti, Cartari, Spenser, Whitney, or any of the other mythographers, emblem writers, Egyptologists, or poets with whom I am familiar. According to Pliny, the overflow is measured by "certaine pits" (*The Historie of the World, Commonly called, the Naturall Historie of C. Plinius Secundus*, vol. 5, sec. 9, trans. Philemon Holland [London, 1601], p. 98). According to Plutarch, the crocodile lays her eggs at the point to which the Nile will reach ("Of Isis and Osiris," *The Morals*, trans. Philemon Holland [London, 1603], p. 1316); this measurement of overflow is repeated in the emblemists. Leo Africanus tells us that "the Egyptians according to the increase of Nilus doe foresee the plentie or dearth of the yeere following" (*The History and Description of Africa* [London, 1896], 3: 860), Leo's wording in this 1600 translation by Pory is similar to Shakespeare's "they know / ... if dearth / Or foison follow." Later in Leo's account, he describes "the isle of measure, in which isle (according to the inundation of Nilus) they haue a kinde of deuise inuented by the ancient Egyptians, whereby they most certainely foresee the plentie or scarcitie of the yeere following.... Vpon another side of the Island standeth an house alone by it selfe, in the midst whereof there is a fouresquare cestern or chanell of eighteene cubits deepe, whereinto the water of Nilus is conueied by a certaine sluce vnder the ground. And in the midst of the cestern there is erected a certaine piller, which is marked and diuided into so many cubits as the cesterne it selfe containeth in depth" (p. 879). Leo then recounts the consequences of the various degrees of overflow and the festivities which attend a propitious measurement. Malone first suggested this passage in Leo Africanus as a source for Shakespeare's scale; his suggestion has been accepted by several scholars. If this passage is indeed a source, Shakespeare has deliberately substituted his own pyramid for Leo's pillar. In his discussion of Shakespeare's use of Leo, Eldred Jones (*Othello's Countrymen: The African in English Renaissance Drama* [London, 1965]) notes another important divergence between Shakespeare's scale and Leo's: "the higher Nilus swells / The more it promises," but only up to a point; according to Leo, an excessive overflow will also cause scarcity (Jones, p. 24). Jones suggests that Shakespeare omits this detail "probably in order to demonstrate Antony's inebriation" (p. 24); but Shakespeare's omission is not simply an indication of Antony's befuddled state. It is a commonplace that too much overflow is as disastrous as too little: see Pliny, p. 98; *Mandeville's Travels*, ed. M. C. Seymour (Oxford, 1967), p. 31; George

Abbot, *A briefe description of the whole worlde* (London, 1599), Ciiij recto. The natural history of the Nile as presented in this commonplace is a celebration of temperance: only the mean is fertile. But temperance is totally foreign to Shakespeare's Nile. Shakespeare may have suppressed the implicit warning about the disastrous effects of excessive overflow because it was untrue to the scheme of his play, where the only fertility comes through excess.

28. In Plutarch, Enobarbus dies of ague, compounded, no doubt, by grief (*Life of Marcus Antonius* in *Shakespeare's Plutarch*, ed. T. J. B. Spencer [Baltimore, 1964], p. 253).

29. Roman heroic virtue is also hyperbolical in *Coriolanus*, where the hero makes a habit of murdering impossibilities. And he, like Antony, is without peer in his excess: "he is himself alone, / To answer all the city" (*Coriolanus* 1.4.51–52).

30. Waino S. Nyland, in "Pompey as the Mythical Lover of Cleopatra," *Modern Language Notes* 64 (1949): 515–16, explicates Shakespeare's confusion of the two Pompeys but attributes it to "the hurried sweep of his imagination" (p. 516). Otherwise, Shakespeare's rearrangement seems to have gone unnoticed.

31. He is not always portrayed as godlike. In *Midsummer Night's Dream*, he is Hippolyta's hunting companion (4.1.115). It is part of the multiple time scheme of that play that Bottom thinks of him as the legendary hero (1.2.30) and Hippolyta thinks of him as her contemporary.

32. *The Herculean Hero in Marlowe, Chapman, Shakespeare, and Dryden* (New York, 1962), especially pp. 37–49.

33. Waith suggests that the greatness of the Herculean hero "is a marvel which only the suggestiveness of poetic image can convey" (p. 37). Hyperbole seems, then, to be the necessary mode of representation. Waith later notes the extravagant language associated with Hercules and the frequent Elizabethan parodies of it (p. 208). See, for instance, Bottom's concept of "Ercles' vein":

> The raging rocks
> And shivering shocks
> Shall break the locks
>   Of prison gates;
> And Phibbus' car
> Shall shine from far,
> And make and mar
>   The foolish Fates.

> [*Midsummer Night's Dream* 1.2.32–39]

34. In Thomas Heywood's *The Silver Age*, for instance, the pattern of hyperbolical boast and instantaneous achievement is so mechanical that it becomes comic. When Ceres asks Hercules to rescue Proserpine, Hercules promises to

> ... vndertake what neither *Jupiter*,
>   *Neptune*, nor all the Gods dare make their taske:

> The Stygian. *Pluto* shall restore the moone,
> Or feele the masse of this my ponderous club.

[p. 145]

He tells Cerberus,

> At euery stroke that lights vpon thy skull,
> Il'e make thee thinke the weight of all the world
> And the earths huge masse shall crowne thee
>
> . . . .
> Il'e make thee ease my club.
>
> . . . .
> Hels bowels I must pierce, and rouze blacke *Dis*,
> Breake (with my fists) these Adamantine gates.

[p. 158]

After each boast, the stage direction calls for the action to be done (*Dramatic Works of Thomas Heywood* [New York, 1964], vol. 3).

35. Here my emphasis is slightly different from Waith's. He tends to see the figure of Hercules as an analogy for Antony and the other Herculean heroes; I think that the presence of Hercules in this play operates simultaneously to suggest both the analogy and the discrepancy between Hercules and Antony.

36. This comic pattern is explicated in Northrop Frye, "The Argument of Comedy," *English Institute Essays* (New York, 1948, 1949), pp. 58–73.

37. The suggestion that extreme sorrow may demand its own decorum is made, surprisingly, by that most decorous of authors, Marc Garnier. His chorus of Egyptians says,

> Our plaints no limits stay,
> No more than doo our woes;
> Both infinitely straie
> And neither measure knowes.
> *In measure let them plaine*:
> *Who measur'd griefes sustain*.

[*Antonie*, lines 331–86]

38. The association of the sea with fortune was traditional; Daniel speaks of the "overwhelming seas of fortune" (*Cleopatra*, line 140).

39. The association of water both with lust and with fertility was commonplace. Spenser's characters seem always to be melting in lust. Redcrosse during his dalliance with Duessa is "pourd out in loosnesse on the grassy grownd" (*FQ* 1.7.7); Cymochles, the lustful knight of book 2, is of course associated with water. But the sea itself was the birthplace of Venus; Spenser says,

> So fertile be the clouds in generation,
> So huge their numbers, and so numberlesse their nation.
> Therefore the antique wisards well invented,

That Venus of the fomy sea was bred.

FQ 4.12.1–2]

40. The association of temperance with time was common: a clock was part of Temperance's standard iconological equipment in some traditions. See Rosemond Tuve, *Allegorical Imagery: Some Medieval Books and Their Posterity* (Princeton, 1966), p. 74.

41. Roman time is the medium of the histories, time as Henry IV sees it and Hal learns to see it, time which cannot be wasted and determines the success or failure of our actions. Lepidus promises Caesar "to front this present time" (1.4.79); later, he will remind the other triumvirs that "time calls upon's" (2.2.158). Caesar lays the blame for his sister's sorrow conveniently at the feet of time itself: "Be you not troubled with the time, which drives / O'er your content these strong necessities" (3.6.82–83). Antony particularly infuriates Octavius by his disregard for time:

> ... to confound such time,
> That drums him from *his* sport, and speaks as loud
> As his own state, and ours.

[1.4.28–30]

42. If we accept the distinction between the emotive and symbolic functions of language proposed by C. K. Ogden and I. A. Richards in *The Meaning of Meaning* (New York, Harvest Books, n.d.) and elaborated in later books, then the poetic assertions of the play can be seen as purely emotive; we are thus relieved of the responsibility for taking them seriously as statement or according them any degree of belief at all. "So far as words are used emotively no question as to their truth in the strict sense can directly arise. Indirectly, no doubt, truth in this strict sense is often involved. Very much poetry consists of statements, symbolic arrangements capable of truth or falsity, which are used not for the sake of their truth or falsity but for the sake of the attitudes which their acceptance will evoke. For this purpose it fortunately happens, or rather it is part of the poet's business to make it happen, that the truth or falsity matters not at all to the acceptance" (Ogden and Richards, p. 150). For Ogden and Richards, any use of language which makes assertions not scientifically verifiable must be considered emotive: "The best test of whether our use of words is essentially symbolic or emotive is the question—'Is this true or false in the ordinary strict scientific sense?' If this question is relevant then the use is symbolic, if it is clearly irrelevant then we have an emotive utterance" (p. 150). There is of course no denying that Shakespeare creates in us an emotion of belief quite out of proportion to any scientifically verifiable belief in the lovers' assertions as fact. But insofar as *Antony and Cleopatra* continually questions the validity of its assertions (by the technique of staged hyperbole, for instance, or by Dolabella's denial of Cleopatra's dream), it seems unwise to deny that their truth value is to some extent at issue. For this reason, the ending of *Antony and Cleopatra* poses a critical test for any theory

which separates the emotive from the symbolic (or cognitive) function of language: our emotions here will depend very largely on the degree to which we are willing to believe in the truth value of the poetic assertions. When Danby speaks of the lovers' "autotoxic exaltations" (*Poets on Fortune's Hill* (London, 1952), p. 145) before they die, his emotion (contempt) is clearly based on his estimate of the cognitive value of their words (they are deluded); when Knight rhapsodizes about the lovers, he is clearly willing to assume that what they say is true. Sense and emotion are thoroughly interdependent; the emotive function should not be used to rescue the symbolic function from itself. The poetic assertions are to some extent statements, and belief in them is very much at issue. William Empson suggests the complexity of our belief in *Antony and Cleopatra* in the course of dissenting from Richards's view of emotive language: "Cleopatra says repeatedly that she expects some kind of happiness after her death ...; we seem meant to feel that her belief is pathetically untrue but has something profound about it. The atheist and the Christian presumably disbelieve her about equally, because the Christian consigns her to a very hot part of Hell. But on the other hand the pantheistic belief that we are somehow absorbed into Nature seems to have remained so natural to us that people of all opinions can follow the last act of the play without feeling positively that her assertions are wrong" (*The Structure of Complex Words* (London, 1952), pp. 8–9). As Empson suggests, we both believe and disbelieve in the lovers' assertions; and our emotions depend on our balance of belief and disbelief. A theory which suggests that the poetic language is purely emotive seems to me inadequate to our experience of the play: the poetic language makes its claim as cognitive statement; and our emotion will depend partly on our judgment of the truth of the statement.

43. A.P. Riemer thinks so. "Wilson Knight's fulsome statements about this section of the play are accurate, but only in so far as they describe Cleopatra's own emotions and attitudes; the play does not share these feelings and ideas.... While it is not possible for us to share her emotions, our observations of her experiencing them produces a curious excitement and exhilaration" (*A Reading of Shakespeare's "Antony and Cleopatra"* [Sydney, 1968], p. 100). But the play does not present her passion at the end merely as a curiosity of character for us to observe. We must, I think, share her, emotions at least momentarily, even while we are aware of all that qualifies them.

44. Stephen Booth has suggested to me that this effect of rest is partly dependent on the monument as *place*: "Consider the monument; it's the first assertive place in the play; we are at it and things come to and go from it. Crudely put: I think we get intellectually comfortable in the monument; we are *with* Cleopatra in the *cum* sense. Geography has been important, also terrain, but this is the first locale to which we and the characters are not in fluid relationship. Compare the bedroom in *Othello*, Gertrude's closet in *Hamlet*, the Volsci camp in *Coriolanus*, Philippi in *Julius Caesar*, and—curiously—Macduff's castle in

Macbeth." This perception seems to me very useful for all the tragedies.

45. The number of times that the lovers use the word within the space of a few lines is astonishing. See 4.14.50–101; 4.15.29–90; 5.2.47; 5.2.286–322.

46. The desire to merge and the desire to remain intact are probably psychic components of any personality to some extent; when they become obsessive, they are characteristic of what Philip Slater calls the "oral-narcissistic dilemma" (*The Glory of Hera* [Boston, 1968], p. 88). Many of the concerns of *Antony and Cleopatra* are characteristic of this dilemma: so many, in fact, that Slater's book is suggestive for *Antony and Cleopatra* at every turn. I have already made use of his work on serpents as emblems of boundary ambiguity; see chap. 2, nn. 29 and 31. Boundary dissolution and bisexuality are Slater's main concerns; see especially his pp. 84–118. Slater's work provides particular insight into the metaphoric structure linking death and love: for the oral personality, both represent an engulfment of self which is terrifying and ecstatic. Antony's fear that he is dissolving and his decision, to die are part of the same process. According to Slater, "it is only form and structure which are individual, matter and energy being common to all.... One way of viewing the 'death instinct' of Freud is as a withdrawal of cathexis from this particular structure, and abandonment of the boundaries which hold it apart from other forms. This also involves a release from the responsibility and burden of maintaining intact and fostering the development of this particular organization" (pp. 90–91). The sexual act may sere the same function: "The ego dissolves, inundated with impulse, and this may be experienced as a kind of death—as complete submersion in unconsciousness.... At the oral level, ecstasy is feared as a bursting or disintegrating of the boundaries of the self" (p. 101). Slater notes that in the sexual encounters of simpler species, the two individuals actually do fuse; he then comments, "In multicellular organisms this fusion is delegated to a single cell, but human fantasy often recreates the more primitive process in the context and language of love" (p. 101). Since the bulk of this book was written before I had read Slater s work, I was particularly struck by the similarity of concern. I do not mean to suggest that Shakespeare (or Antony) is necessarily suffering from an oral-narcissistic dilemma, but rather that the play deals with fears and desires to which we are all prone but which are exaggerated—and therefore clarified—in the particular neurosis which is Slater's subject.

47. When Charmian advises Cleopatra to cross Antony in nothing, she teaches like a fool (1.3.10); though age gives Cleopatra freedom from childishness, it cannot give her freedom from folly (1.3.57). Antony leaves her, deaf to her "unpitied folly" (1.3.98).

48. This is the paradox with which Sidney had wrestled in *An Apologie for Poetrie*; he resolved it by asserting that the fictions of poetry have access to Ideas and hence to a higher truth than history can deliver. Shakespeare apparently was absorbed by this problem sometime around 1595: *Richard II, Romeo and Juliet,*

and many of the sonnets set up tensions between verbal assertion and fact; all ask whether or not wishers are fools. His resolution was dramatic rather than philosophical: Juliet asserting against the evidence of lark and envious streaks of dawn that it is still night or Richard asserting in the face of Bolingbroke's troops that stones shall prove armed soldiers are both in a sense fools; but when the forces of ordinary reality win out, the world in which we are left is bleak indeed. Bolingbroke will pay the consequences of his lack of imagination through the rest of his life. Concern with this problem then seems to diminish for about ten years; it returns with increased urgency and complexity in *Macbeth*, *Antony and Cleopatra*, and the romances.

   49. Many critics have felt a tendency toward romance at the end of this play. Bradley finds the degree of reconciliation uncharacteristic of tragedy; Donald A. Stauffer asserts that in the end the play "is less a tragedy than a victorious vision.... In the sense that its protagonists finally create their own glowing worlds, the play is not the next-to-last of the tragedies, but the first and greatest of the dramatic romances. The tragic notion of acceptance and abnegation is given expression. But in contrast, the idea that imagination and resolution may reshape or transcend life is whispered, and man is seen as the creator of his fate" (*Shakespeare's World of Images* [New York, 1949], p. 247). Charney also notes that in the primacy given to poetry, *Antony and Cleopatra* moves toward romance: "Rather than being resolved, the conflict between Egypt and Rome ceases to exist, and the hard 'visible shapes' of Rome are dissolved into an ecstatic, poetic reality. In this sense *Antony and Cleopatra* looks ahead to the mood of Shakespeare's last plays" (*Shakespeare's Roman Plays* [Cambridge, 1961], p. 141). Schanzer distinguishes between formal, affective, and experiential elements in tragedy and suggests that, seen affectively, *Antony and Cleopatra* may be close to *The Winter's Tale* but, seen formally or experientially, it is a tragedy. The degree to which we find the similarity to romance depends largely on the degree to which we believe in the reunion which the lovers assert as they die: and there is little critical agreement here. Danby most vigorously opposes any form of belief in their reunion: he speaks of "the Egypt-beyond-the-grave of Antony and Cleopatra in their autotoxic exaltations before they kill themselves" (p. 145). Ribner also finds their belief mere delusion (*Patterns in Shakespearean Tragedy* [New York, 1960], p. 181). On the other hand, Pogson finds it literal as the mystical union of Man and Soul. Goddard seems to believe in the "transcendental reunion of the lovers" (*The Meaning of Shakespeare* [Chicago, 1951], p. 592) and notes that the motif is the same as in *Othello*. Stauffer and Knight believe wholly in the reunion, though it is difficult to decide with what degree of literalness. But none of these critics relates this belief to the play as a whole and to the process of belief. The play does not move magically toward romance at the end: the perspective of romance is implicit throughout. And there is an essential distinction between the poetic assertion at the end of *Antony and Cleopatra* and that of the romances.

STEPHEN ORGEL

The Poetics of Incomprehensibility:
The Winter's Tale

Stage procedures and their importance, as embedded in the texts that
remain to us, have yet to be looked at outside of the rubric of the
assumptions about method that we have inherited from the
Enlightenment.

—Marion Trousdale[1]

I want to begin with two notoriously obscure passages in *The Winter's Tale*—by
no means the most obscure, at least for modern readers. Both are from
Hermione's trial scene. The first has Hermione, in the course of her objections
to the proceedings, say to Leontes,

> I appeale
> To your owne Confcience (Sir) before *Polixenes*
> Came to your Court, how I was in your grace,
> How merited to be fo: Since he came,
> With what encounter fo vncurrant, I
> Haue ftrayn'd t' appeale thus;[2]

For the past hundred years or so, the last two lines have been taken to mean
"with what behavior so unacceptable I have transgressed that I should appear
thus [i.e., on trial]." This interpretation represents the consensus of three mid-

From *Shakespeare Quarterly* 42, no. 4 (1991): 431-37. © 1991 by the Folger Shakespeare Library.

Victorian editors, Halliwell, Staunton, and White, and it has become, for us, simply the meaning of the passage. But to gloss the passage in this way is, at the very least, to conceal more than a century of debate and bafflement. The lines were, in fact, considered incomprehensible by most eighteenth-century editors, including Johnson, who wrote of them

> These lines I do not understand; with the licence of all editors, what
> I cannot understand I suppose unintelligible, and therefore propose
> that they may be altered....

Johnson's testimony in this matter is especially *à propos* given his characteristic genius for finding a plain prose sense in the most elaborately conceited Shakespearean verse. In default of an interpretation, he produced a felicitous, if unconvincingly rationalized, emendation: "With what encounter so uncurrent *have I /* Been stain'd to appear thus?"[3] Even this, though it certainly makes a kind of sense, depends on its emendation to render the crucially ambiguous words encounter and uncurrent comprehensible. A detailed consideration of the history of similar attempts at elucidation would show no more than do the relevant *OED* entries for encounter, uncurrent, and strain: namely, that the modern interpretation represents an essentially arbitrary selection of meanings from a list of diverse and often contradictory possibilities and does not so much resolve the linguistic problem as enable us to ignore it.

Consider another example. Hermione, later in the same scene, recalling her recent childbirth confinement, objects that she has been

>   hurried
> Here, to this place, i'th open ayre, before
> I haue got ftrength of limit.[4]

In this case the Victorian editors were as divided as their predecessors. Theobald thought "strength of limit" must mean "strength enough for coming abroad, going never so little a way." Heath, in 1765, found a rather garrulous sense in the passage: "before I have recovered that degree of strength which women to my circumstances usually acquire by a longer confinement to their chamber." Halliwell produced a different and more economical paraphrase, "that is, before even I have regained a limited degree of strength," and explained that "strength of limit" is limited strength. White, in 1858, endorsed a version of Heath's interpretation of a century earlier: "before I have regained strength by limit, restraint, confinement after childbirth." Furness, reviewing the controversy in 1898, rendered a characteristically judicious opinion: "If it could be proved that 'limit' had a special meaning, corresponding to what is now called, with a special meaning, confinement, the interpretations referring to childbirth would be unquestionable, but, without this proof, I think Halliwell's paraphrase the best."

Johnson, the greatest of explicators, had once again confessed himself baffled and once again took refuge in an emendation: "I know not well how 'strength of limit' can mean strength *to pass the limits* of the child-bed chamber; which yet it must mean in this place, unless we read in a more easy phrase, 'strength of *limb*.'" It is only in the present century that a consensus has been reached. Dover Wilson and Quiller-Couch, in the Cambridge New Shakespeare *Winter's Tale*, followed by virtually all subsequent editors, returned to Heath's explanation of 1765, glossing the crucial words, "the strength which returns to a woman when she has rested the prescribed period after childbirth."[5] Their confident note gives no hint of two centuries of uncertainty, debate, and disagreement.

But convenient as the modern interpretation is, the *OED* in fact offers little support for it. The entry for *limit* cites only two examples of the word meaning a prescribed time, Hermione's passage and one from *Measure for Measure*, "between which time of the contract and limit of the solemnity." It is not, however, clear to me that this is in fact the same usage: "limit" here means not a period of time but a *terminus ad quem*, the date fixed for Mariana's marriage to Angelo. Pafford adds a more persuasive example from *Richard III*, "the limit of your life is out."[6] This example, however, is much less elliptical than Hermione's, and the expression in relation to childbed is otherwise unparalleled. By 1664 the phrase in *The Winter's Tale* was already being emended; in F3, F4, Rowe, Pope, and Hammer, Hermione's "limit" became "limbs." And though the emendation was not generally accepted after this time, the interpretive problem remained, and, as we have seen, Johnson found the emendation attractive enough to return to it.

I have focused on these two cases because they are relatively simple ones; though the particular expressions are obscure, Hermione's general drift is clear enough for us to see what we have to get her words to mean. What is concealed in the process of interpretation—to which Johnson's methods constitute a striking exception—is the effort of will, or even willfulness, involved. This method of elucidation assumes that behind the obscurity and confusion of the text is a clear meaning, and that the obscurity, moreover, is not part of the meaning.

2

But what are the implications for drama of a text that works in this way? Hermione's speeches are, as I have said, simple cases, discrete moments that at least appear to leave the larger sense of the passage intact. Leontes' invective in Act 1 gives us no such confidence:

>   Can thy Dam, may't be
> Affection? thy Intention ſtabs the Center.
> Thou do'ſt make poſſible things not ſo held,

Communicat'ft with Dreames (how can this be?)
With what's vnreall: thou coactiue art,
And fellow'ft nothing. Then 'tis very credent,
Thou may'ft co-ioyne with fomething, and thou do'ft,
(And that beyond Commiffion) and I find it[7]

Find *what?* From Rowe onward, the passage has defied any consensus. Indeed, it is one of the rare places where Rowe, normally the most tolerant of editors, felt moved to radical revision: "Can thy dam? may't be— / Imagination! thou dost stab to th'center." This can hardly be called emendation. And though no subsequent editor was persuaded, most editions since Rowe's time have adopted his equally radical repointing, whereby "may't be—" stands alone, and "Affection," no longer a predicate nominative in the simple question "may't be Affection?", is now the vocative subject of a new sentence, "Affection, thy intention stabs the center!"

My purpose is not to propose a new reading or to announce the matter solved (though I cannot help remarking that I find some of the problems greatly simplified if we reject the ubiquitous and quite unnecessary repunctuation). What interests me is how little attention the editorial tradition has paid to the fact of a drama that speaks in this way—few commentators get beyond Pafford's observation that "the speech is meant to be incoherent";[8] i.e., Leontes is crazy, and his language is an index to his character. The problem with this is not merely that it commits the play to the imitative fallacy but that this sort of linguistic opacity is not at all limited to Leontes. Hermione, Camillo, Antigonus, and Polixenes all exhibit it on occasion as well. It is a feature of the play.

3

What does it mean that a drama speaks incomprehensibly? Even if we were persuaded that we had successfully elucidated all the play's obscurities, no actor can speak meaning rather than words, and no audience, least of all Shakespeare's in 1611, comes supplied with the necessary glosses. Of course, we assume that we are, by elucidating, recovering meaning, not imposing it; but is this assumption really defensible? How do we know that the obscurity of the text was not in fact precisely what it expressed to the Renaissance audience? Is meaning, in any case, a transhistorical phenomenon? To take only a famous and obvious example, the history of interpretations of *ut pictura poesis* would suggest that it is not. The phrase for us is quite unambiguous: Horace says simply that poems, like paintings, have various ways of pleasing, some by detail, some by their broad sweep. Nothing in the Horatian context appears to us to admit of the standard Renaissance interpretation, that poetry should be pictorial. Our interpretation is plain common sense; the Renaissance version is strained and illogical, wrenching the phrase from its context, "contaminated," as we would say, by Simonides' equally famous dictum that poetry is a speaking picture, with which it was usually equated.

Clearly, however, there is nothing common about common sense; it is as culturally specific as anything else in our intellectual lives. Renaissance strategies of interpretation call into question our axiomatic assumption that a plain prose paraphrase is the bottom line in unlocking the mysteries of an occluded text. If we look at what gets elucidated in the marginal glosses and footnotes of Renaissance editions, the idea that we are *recovering* meaning by looking up hard words and sorting out syntax becomes very difficult to maintain. E. K.'s glosses to *The Shepheardes Calender*, for example, deal with sources and analogues, but they seem designed primarily as a legitimating strategy for what is being presented as a radically new kind of text.[9] E. K. very occasionally undertakes to explain a hard word, which is invariably conceived to be hard only because it is archaic. Syntactical and conceptual matters are not dealt with at all. The reason may, of course, be that to the sixteenth-century reader they were perfectly clear (whatever "clear" meant to such a reader); but it may also be that in some different and much larger way they were not felt to be problematic—that their complexities and obscurities were, for the commentator, an essential part of the meaning and not to be removed by elucidation. In this respect the claims of Spenser for his "dark conceit," of Chapman and Jonson for the virtues of the mysterious in poetry, may be less uncharacteristic of the age than our construction of literary history has assumed.[10] The glosses of the great sixteenth-century humanist editions of the classics exhibit a similar pattern: historical, ethical, and philosophical commentaries, crossreferences, analogues, and sources fill the margins. Confusions or solecisms are dealt with only as part of the editorial process, by emendation, usually silent—these matters certainly bear on interpretation, but they are considered prior to elucidation. Obscurity, or perhaps obscurantism, had by 1607 begun to be an issue primarily in legal texts, as the publication of John Cowell's *The interpreter: or booke containing the signification of ... such words and terms as are mentioned in the lawe writers or statutes* testifies.[11] It also testifies to the dangers of elucidation: the book was suppressed by royal proclamation because of its absolutist interpretation of such terms as "prerogative" and "subsidy"[12]—an interpretation that the king certainly would not have found unsympathetic, but that was, precisely for that reason, better left a mystery.

4

But in the largest sense, all this is profoundly irrelevant, an answer to the question of how a Jacobean commentator would have glossed a Shakespeare text. The idea is not inconceivable—Jonson, after all, annotated a number of his plays and masques—but this was part of a systematic reconceiving of the theatrical as textual, the transformation of scripts into books, and, moreover, into classics.

Jonson's Folio of 1616, with its novel (and, to a number of his contemporaries, ludicrous) claim that plays were "works," provided the essential model not only for the Shakespeare Folio but for the subsequent editorial treatment of the Shakespeare canon. In this form the play becomes a transaction between the author and the reader, enabled and mediated by the editor.

What this version of the play omits is precisely what Jonson wanted to omit: actors and audiences. The actor playing Polixenes, when we first see him in *The Winter's Tale*, is required to tell Leontes,

> I am queftion'd by my feares, of what may chance,
> Or breed vpon our abfence, that may blow
> No fneaping Winds at home, to make vs fay.
> This is put forth too truly:[13]

Warburton declared this "nonsense," but doubtless a sense can be got out of it. Shakespeare had *something* in mind, and editors since the late eighteenth century have invariably assumed that this something must have been a paraphrasable meaning, which it is their task to recover. The problematic part of the passage, "that may blow / No sneaping Winds," etc., is generally glossed more or less as follows: "so that no destructive events may arise at home to persuade me that my fears were only too well founded." Some editors take "that" to imply a wish rather than a contingency, and gloss the line "*oh* that no biting winds," etc. The passage has, over the centuries, suffered much inconclusive elucidation. Polixenes obviously wants to go home, but his reasons are elliptical and obscure, and his metaphor changes in mid-sentence. The kingdom is conceived as a garden; with the gardener absent, the plants have no protection against the "sneaping winds," whatever these may be. Attempts to make "This is put forth too truly" part of the same metaphor have resulted in outright revision and paraphrases that wander very far from the text: Hanmer changed "truly" to "early," understanding "put forth" to imply the unseasonable appearance of buds. Some editors have adopted this, but it makes the relevance of the metaphor even more obscure. Quiller-Couch and Dover Wilson, who thought Hanmer's emendation was "probably ... right," saw the sneaping winds as Polixenes' response to some conspiracy he fears is breeding at home, and which, were he on the spot, could be nipped in the bud.[14] Pafford wants Polixenes' fears to be tormenting him precisely "in order that no biting winds may indeed blast affairs at home...."[15] And so forth.

Such interpretations strike me as excessively arbitrary, though of course there is no way of determining whether they are right or wrong; and if it is really the sensibility of Shakespeare we are concerned with, it is difficult to see what alternative there might be to addressing linguistic problems in this fashion: the playwright must, as I say, have meant something. But in a larger sense, we are not, or at least not only, concerned with Shakespeare's mind. Plays may start as private musings; but they end as scripts performed by actors for spectators, and their success depends on what they convey to those spectators. What did an audience hearing the speech in 1611 think it meant?

What does an audience think it means now? We need to remember that the Renaissance tolerated, and indeed courted, a much higher degree of ambiguity and opacity than we do; we tend to forget that the age often found in incomprehensibility a positive virtue. The discontinuity between image and text in Renaissance iconographic structures has in recent years become a commonplace; symbolic imagery was *not* a universal language—on the contrary, it was radically indeterminate and always depended on explanation to establish its meaning. When the explanation was not provided—as was often the case—the spectators remained unenlightened. But this was not a problem: "no doubt," as Ben Jonson put it, "their grounded judgments did gaze, said it was fine, and were satisfied."[16] This particular observation described the response of uneducated spectators, but even writing for an intellectual elite, Jonson strove for what he called "more removed mysteries,"[17] and his printed texts included explanatory commentaries designed, as he put it, finally, months or years after the event, "to make the spectators understanders."[18] The satisfaction in such cases derived precisely from the presence of the mystery, which assured the audience at abstruse spectacles, whether groundlings or scholars, that they participated in a world of higher meaning. We are familiar with such strategies in court masques, but they are also not alien to popular drama. *Pericles*, which Jonson attacked for pandering to popular taste, includes a procession of knights bearing symbolic shields and mottos that require elucidation to be understood but which are not elucidated.

As editors, we all subscribe, however uncomfortably, to some version of Burckhardt's Renaissance, an integrated culture that still spoke a universal language. For theater historians this view of the period was, or at least should have been, seriously compromised when Aby Warburg analyzed two of the learned spectators' accounts of the famous Medici *intermezzi* of 1589, probably the best documented of the great Renaissance festivals, and observed that the meaning of the performance, and indeed the very identity of the symbolic figures, was opaque to even the most erudite members of the audience.[19] Since Warburg's essay was published in 1895, it is time Renaissance studies began to take it into account: it bears on our general sense of the nature of Renaissance public discourse as a whole. The spectator of *The Winter's Tale* in 1611, we implicitly assume, would have understood it all. What we are recovering, we tell ourselves, is only what every Renaissance audience already knew. I want to argue on the contrary that Shakespeare's audience was more like the audience constructed by Warburg than like the audience constructed by Burckhardt; that what Polixenes' speech conveyed to the Renaissance audience was pretty much what it conveys to us: vagueness and confusion. It is clear that the king of Bohemia is insisting he must go home; if anything is clear about his reasons it is that they are utterly unclear, despite the attempts of almost three centuries of commentary to clarify them. How we interpret this obscurity—as a function of Polixenes' character, or of the Sicilian court, of the language of kings, of the complexities of public discourse, of the nature of stage plays themselves in the Renaissance—is the real textual question, and it remains an open one. The Shakespearean text, characteristically, gives us no guidance on the matter. We do it wrong when we deny that it is problematic and has always been so, and reduce it to our own brand of common sense.

NOTES

In addition to the friends and colleagues mentioned in the notes, I am indebted for references and valuable suggestions to A. R. Braunmuller, Randall S. Nakayama, David Riggs, and Marion Trousdale. This paper was delivered at the annual meeting of the Shakespeare Association of America, March 1991, in Vancouver, Canada.

1. "A Second Look at Critical Bibliography and the Acting of Plays," *Shakespeare Quarterly*, 41 (1990), 87–96, esp. p. 95.

2. p. 286, First Folio, Folger copy 38. This and other reproductions of Folio passages have been photographed from copies 38 and 39 of Shakespeare's First Folio (London: Isaac Jaggard, 1623), courtesy of the Folger Shakespeare Library. In the Charlton Hinman facsimile of the First Folio (New York: W. W. Norton, 1968), this speech occurs at through-line number 1219–24; in the Arden Shakespeare *The Winter's Tale*, ed. J.H.P. Pafford (London: Methuen, 1963), at 3.2.45–50.

3. Quotations from eighteenth- and nineteenth-century editors can be found collected in the *Variorum Shakespeare: The Winter's Tale*, ed. H. H. Furness (Philadelphia, Pa.: J. B. Lippincott Co., 1898).

4. p. 287, First Folio, copy 38; TLN 1283–85 in Hinman; 3.2.104–6 in Pafford's Arden edition.

5. The Cambridge New Shakespeare *The Winter's Tale*, ed. Arthur Quiller-Couch and John Dover Wilson (Cambridge: At the Univ. Press, 1931), p. 153.

6. p. 60.

7. p. 278, First Folio, copy 38; TLN 213–20 in Hinman; 1.2.137–44 in Pafford's Arden edition.

8. p. 166.

9. Edmund Spenser, *The Shepheardes Calender* (London: H. Singleton, 1579).

10. See, for example, Spenser's *Letter to Ralegh*, Chapman's preface ("To the Understander") to *Achilles' Shield*, Jonson's preface to *Hymenaei*.

11. Cambridge: J. Legate, 1607. The major exception is in biblical commentary, where the glosses bear heavily on interpretive questions deriving from issues raised by the process of translation; the marginalia to the Geneva Bible are a striking instance. Barbara Bono has suggested to me that these constitute a Protestant strategy to counteract Catholic interpretive modes, characteristically symbolic and allegorical. I am also indebted to a member of the audience at the SAA meeting who cited a large number of practical texts—handbooks, guides, and the like—that have elucidative glosses. These would naturally depend on clarity for their usefulness; it is to the point that imaginative works are not glossed in this way.

12. See the note on the entry for STC 5900.

13. p. 277, First Folio, copy 39; TLN 62–65 in Hinman; 1.2.11–14 in Pafford's Arden edition.

14. p. 131.

15. p. 6.

16. *Part of the Kings entertainment, in passing to his Coronation* in *Ben Jonson*, ed. C. H. Herford and Percy and Evelyn Simpson, 11 vols. (Oxford: Clarendon Press, 1938–52), Vol. 7, p. 91, ll. 266–67.

17. *Hymenaei*, ll. 16–17.

18. *Love's Triumph Through Callipolis*, l. 1.

19. "I Costumi Teatrali per gli Intermezzi del 1589," *Atti dell'Accademia del Reale Istituto Musicale di Firenze: Commemorazione della Riforma Melodrammatica* (Florence, 1895), pp. 125–26. For a recent study with a similar point, see A. R. Braunmuller, "'To the Globe I rowed': John Holles Sees *A Game At Chess*," *English Literary Renaissance*, 20 (1990), 940–56.

A.D. NUTTALL

Two Concepts of Allegory
in The Tempest

One of the reasons why *The Tempest* is hard to classify lies in its parentage. It has two sets of sources, first a body of romantic, fairy-tale literature and second a collection of travellers' reports. If its mother was a mermaid, its father was a sailor. It must be acknowledged that on the fairy side there is no story which we can point to as a direct influence on Shakespeare, but Iakob Ayrer's *Die Schöne Sidea* (published posthumously in his Opus *Theatricum*) and the story of Dardano and Nicephorus in the fourth chapter of Antonio de Eslava's *Noches de Invierno*[1] show, besides a strong similarity of plot, an occasional correspondence of detail, as in the episode of the log-carrying. The late date at which Ayrer's play was published makes it very unlikely that it was Shakespeare's source, but there is just enough similarity between the two plays to let us postulate a common origin. Some close analogues have been found in the *scenari* for Italian *commedia dell'arte*[2] but Kermode observes[3] that all extant *scenari* postdate Shakespeare's play. Other analogues are Diego Ortunez de Calahorra's *Espejo de Príncipes y Caballeros*, and *Fiamella*, a pastoral comedy by Bartolomeo Rossi. Here, at all events, are hints of a story available to Shakespeare, and very amenable to the Romantic style of composition he had learned in company with Beaumont and Fletcher.[4]

On the other side of the family correspondences are more striking, and we can speak of direct influences. There is no doubt that the Bermuda pamphlets describing the wreck of the *Sea-Adventure* on her way to Virginia were known to

From *Two Concepts of Allegory*. © 1967 by A.D. Nuttall.

Shakespeare. Sylvester Jourdain's *Discovery of the Barmudas* (1610), the Council of Virginia's *True Declaration of the State of the Colonie in Virginia, with a confutation of such scandalous reports as have tended to the disgrace of so worthy an enterprise* (1610), and William Strachey's *True Reportory of the Wrack*, first published in *Purchas his Pilgrimes*, 1625, but accessible to Shakespeare from 1610, have all left traces in *The Tempest*.

The peculiar wedding of the marvellous and the circumstantial which we find in *The Tempest* may thus be attributed, in some measure, to the stuff of which it is made. But, nevertheless, we must be careful not to make too much of the contrast between the documentary naval reports and the fabulous tales of princes and sorcerers. *Purchas his Pilgrimes*, though not so extravagant and romantic as it appeared to the author of *The Ancient Mariner* centuries later, was nevertheless not entirely innocent of the marvellous. Geography itself was still soaked with imaginative significance, for the Royal Society had not yet done its judicious work of scientific desiccation. Spatial conceptions of Paradise, unacknowledged allegories, and 'tall stories' were all a normal part of the literature of travel. In the sixth century the monk Cosmas had, as Raleigh noted, laid down the object of many a later quest.

> If Paradise were really on the surface of the world, is there not a man among those who are so keen to learn and search out everything, that would not let himself be deterred from reaching it? When we see that there are men who will not be deterred from penetrating to the ends of the earth in search of silk, and all for the sake of filthy lucre, how can we believe that they would be deterred from going to get a sight of Paradise?[5]

Columbus (quite seriously) took the mouths of the Orinoco for the threshold of Paradise, and in 1512 the Governor of Puerto Rico landed in Florida while sailing in search of a miraculous Fountain of Youth. It is hard to know whether to call George Chapman's *De Guina Carmen Epicum* (1596) a Utopian or a Paradisal account of that place. It is well known that Spenser places his fairyland at once in England and in the human heart. But there is another place, the prologue of the second book of the *Faerie Queene*, where he suggests, more than half seriously, that explorers may at any time *discover* Fairyland in some other part of the Globe.

The interesting thing is that none of these three suggestions is felt to be incompatible with the other two, just as no conflict was recognized between Paradise as a lost primal state of felicity and Paradise as a place somewhere out in the unknown Atlantic seas. Marlowe seems to see no important distinction between geographical exploration and philosophical inquiry-at least, he speaks of them in one breath in *Doctor Faustus*:

Shall I make spirits fetch me what I please,
Resolve me of all ambiguities,
Performe what desperate enterprise I will?
Ile have them flye to *India* for gold,
Ransacke the Ocean for orient pearle,
And search all corners of the newfound world
For pleasant fruites and princely delicates:
Ile have then reade mee straunge philosophie,
An tell the secrets of all forraine kings ...

(ll. 107–15, my italics in ll. 112–14)

All the same, the distinction between frank fancy and documentary report remains, and if fabulous elements appear in naval records they merely gain a more startling appearance of factual truth thereby. And there is no doubt that *The Tempest* owes much of its power to an air of circumstantial actuality. Nothing could be more different than *The Tempest* from the Gothic ghost stories of the earlier Shakespeare, all graveyards and darkness. The spectres of the Enchanted Isle move in the daylight, and are for that reason twice as frightening. The Jacobeans were after all much more ready to credit the *actual* existence of the supernatural than are we. There are no sorcerers of repute in England now, but an historical Prospero can easily be found—Dr. John Dee[6] for example. Lytton Strachey's astonishing statement to turn from Theseus and Titania and Bottom to the Enchanted Island, is to step out of a country lane into a conservatory[7] is almost the flat opposite of the truth.

Yet there is no doubt that *The Tempest* is a queer play. The strangeness of the island, the sounds in the air, the unnatural languor that intermittently envelops the characters, have the sinister quality of Phaedria's Isle in the *Faerie Queene*. Though the strange events of the play are in large measure accounted for by the arts of Prospero, certain things remain odd to the end. Playgoers are fairly well accustomed to that sane and purposive magic which saves a drowning man or refreshes him with sleep, but the music in the air, the voice crying in the wave, the 'strange, hollow and confused noise' which accompanies the vanishing of the reapers and nymphs at the end of the masque, the somnolence of Miranda—these gratuitous paranorma are more disturbing. Ariel mocking the drunkards by playing the song back to them on the tabor and pipe does not really worry us; we have seen similar things before in *A Midsummer Night's Dream*. But these causeless and capricious portents propel the sensibility into an unfamiliar region, and abandon it to uneasy speculation.

At the same time, the miracles and prodigies of the Enchanted Isle are related in a curiously intimate way to our experience. The hearing of strange sounds which are never properly identified, the swift recourse to useless weapons in the moments between sleep and waking—these things are especially alarming because especially near the bone. We have all lain in a twilight of inarticulate apprehension through the moments of waking. We have all known times in our everyday lives when our inattentive faculties have been surprised by confused noises, or the sound as of a name being called. E.R. Dodds in *The Greeks and The Irrational*[8] observes that dreams are a fertile source of inference to another world in primitive thought. In Shakespeare's hands, these half-glimpsed sights, half-heard sounds, this ἀπορία felt by men surprised by the nameless, become once more a means of alerting apprehensive speculation. And in the unpredictable island of *The Tempest*, we are denied that prosaic awakening which vividly refutes the night. It seems as if the poet is bent on drawing from us a different sort of credence from that ordinarily given to plays—perhaps a more primitive sort. At III.iii.83 the Shapes (we are given no clearer stage-direction) carry out the banquet 'with mops and mows', and we never learn what they are or what their dance is about. At V.i.231 we are told how the sleeping sailors awoke to hear strange and horrific sounds and we are never told what made them. Yet to call these things loose ends would be foolish criticism. They are there to heat our imaginations. One feels that one can hardly call the metaphysically speculative reaction inappropriate.

Shakespeare has another instrument for piercing to the more primitive levels of our consciousness in the unpleasing shape of Caliban. Caliban, though horribly unchildlike, belongs to a world most of us have known as children. He lives in an intellectual half-light of bites, pinches, nettle-stings, terrors, cupboard-love, glimpses of extraordinary and inexplicable beauty. These things play a negligible part in the society of adults, but most of us remember a society in which they were intensely familiar. It was Caliban who, like a child, 'cried to dream again', was taught how to talk, and shown the Man in the Moon. The character of Caliban shows us objects which are too close to be seen in the ordinary way of things. His world is near-sighted, tactile, downward-looking, lacking in distant prospects.

But, despite the probing imagery of Caliban, the island itself seems very remote. We are given the feeling of immense distances, enforced by many images: 'Now would I give a thousand furlongs of sea for an acre of barren ground; long heath, brown furze, anything', 'Canst thou remember A time before we came unto this cell? ... 'Tis far off; and rather like a dream than an assurance', 'What seest thou else In the dark backward and abysm of time?' 'She that dwells Ten leagues beyond man's life; she that from Naples Can have no note, unless the sun were post—The man i' th' moon's too slow—till new-born chins Be rough and razorable: she that from whom We all were sea-swallowed ...', 'A space whose every cubit Seems to cry out ...' 'In this most desolate isle', together with the use of far-away place-names like Arabia, Tunis and Angier.

The combination of a feeling of remoteness with an equally strong feeling of nearness, of intimacy, is an ambiguity characteristic of dreams, and of things half perceived in the instant of awaking. There are several wakings from sleep in the play, all drawn with an emphasis on the equivocal character of perception in such circumstances—Gonzalo and others in II.i., the sailors in V.i., and Caliban's

> ... and sometime voices,
> That, if I then had wak'd after long sleep,
> Will make me sleep again ...   III. ii. 144–6

Miranda compares her dim memory image of the ladies who attended her in her infancy to a dream (I. ii. 45). To these we may add the wonderful description in the minutest terms of an image glimmering upon the sight—'The fringed curtains of thine eye advance' (I. ii. 405). There is another reference to eyelids at IV. i. 177.

The nature poetry of the play (much of it Caliban's) is extremely interesting. It, too, is full of minute observations and gigantic distances, with a strange salt-sweetness hardly to be found elsewhere. We may skim the play, creaming off images which illustrate its special flavour—'the ooze of the salt deep ... the veins of the earth when it is baked with frost', 'unwholesome fen ... berries ... brine-pits', 'yellow sands ... the wild waves whist', 'sea-water ... fresh brook mussels, withered roots and husks, wherein the acorn cradles', 'bogs, fens, flats', 'a rock by the sea-side', 'show thee a jay's nest and instruct thee how To snare the nimble marmoset; I'll bring thee To clust'ring filberts, and sometimes I'll get thee Young scamels from the rock', 'Where crabs grow ... pignuts', 'the quick freshes'—and the nature hymn at IV. i. 60 ff., bristling with grain and grasses, wet with rain and dew. It is strange that this great nature poem is not better loved. It may be that the focus is too clear for our post-romantic eyes. Perhaps most of us would prefer 'showery April' to Shakespeare's more intimate, tactile 'spongy April'. This truthful clarity in the natural imagery, like the circumstantial elements in the plot, helps to draw from us that special credence, at once lively and in a state of suspense, which is proper to the play. When the picture blurs we look for the emergence of bright, if unfamiliar, realities, not Gothic spectres. While the smoky ghosts of the old Histories seemed to repel our gaze, the supernatural in *The Tempest* seems to invite our minute attention or even to arise from it.

Once charmed into such an expectant frame of mind, we are quick to speculate, to postulate new 'planes of being' and vague spiritual hierarchies. The play begins with a desperate storm and shipwreck, and then the scene shifts abruptly to Prospero's cell. The crackling oaths of the rough-lunged castaways give place to the tranquil discourse of two angelic beings who might have stepped out of Blake's illustration to his *Songs of Innocence*. No sound of tempest now, the father and daughter talk together in an elaborately beautiful language, the sense variously drawn out from one line to another, which is very difficult to describe. They talk as no human beings ever talked and yet seem all the closer to our humanity for it. The difference between the diction of the castaways and that of

Prospero and Miranda, like the different systems of perspective which Michelangelo gives to his *Ignudi* and his Biblical personages in the Sistine Chapel, prompt us to assign to them different 'orders of being'.

But we are also informed that Prospero is an Italian, an old acquaintance of the castaways, sometime Duke of Milan. His discontents and ambitions are extremely worldly. He is to be given no dramatic walk-over as a type of Spiritual Virtue. Again we wish to use the prefix 'half-', as often in discussing this play, and say that Prospero and Miranda are half-dipped in another world. This recurrent sense of ambiguity and suspension is extremely potent dramatically.

In the first scene of Act II we have an excellent specimen of this dramatic avoidance of the univocal. In it the 'honest old Counsellor' Gonzalo is baited by the wicked plotters. The dialogue in which this is carried out is not to be understood or enjoyed by a lazy mind. Let us not deceive ourselves, Antonio and Sebastian are truly witty; Gonzalo really does talk like an old fool. But Antonio and Sebastian are themselves both foolish and wicked, while Gonzalo is not really a fool at all. Had Shakespeare made Gonzalo's discourse less ponderous and the witticisms of the rest feebler, instead of allowing merit to prevail by its own sinews, the scene would have had one-tenth of its present power. As it stands, it is taut as a bowstring. As the scene proceeds the laughter of the plotters, and our own laughter also, grows harsher in our ears. Between interruptions, Gonzalo makes several pertinent observations: that they are better off than they had reason to expect, that though the island seems to be uninhabited the necessities of life are all to hand. He also remarks the disturbing state of their garments, dry and unstained by the sea. The others laugh on, and their laughter seems an echo of another laughter, in a Flemish tavern, where other similarly jovial fellows gaily proposed to slay Death-the *riotoures* of Chaucer's *Pardoner's Tale*.

In turning to this scene, we passed over the meeting of Ferdinand and Miranda, which is oddly colourless and at the same time entirely glorious. Prospero, a little less than omniscient, directs the course of the encounter. Miranda glimmers upon Ferdinand's sight like something divine (as he says). The haunting image of Adam's dream ('he awoke and found it Truth') seems strangely relevant. Samuel Pepys (who seems to have seen *The Tempest* at least six times) called it 'the most innocent play that ever I saw'.[9] This is perhaps the first meagre hint of the imagery of Eden which was to gather round the play in the writings of Coleridge, Lamb, Meredith and others.[10] Miranda speaks the forthright language of the late-Shakespearean heroine, without coquetry or irony, yet full of humanity. Ferdinand is, I feel, the lesser creature of the two. He has the air of youthful nobility which allows Miranda to take him for a spirit, yet at the same time he has something in common with other young pup heroes (to whom Shakespeare is strangely indulgent) such as Posthumus, or even Claudio. He is a flawed object, uncertainly idealistic, and lacks the sweet earthbound candour of his lady.

As the play unfolds the character of Caliban is introduced, and, a little later, the comedians, Trinculo and Stephano. The marvellous animal poetry of Caliban contrasts strangely with the myopic inebriation of Stephano and the folly of the fool. We feel a slight shiver when Caliban deifies the drunken butler. Long ago Schlegel and Hazlitt[11] pointed out the vulgarity of the comedians and the utter absence of it in Caliban, who is without convention. One is reminded of E. M. Forster's distinction[12] between coarseness and vulgarity, the first revealing something and the second concealing something. Caliban belongs to one order, the comedians to another, Prospero to another and Miranda perhaps to yet another. The play begins to shimmer and the allegorist critic is 'amazed with matter'.

The beginning of Act III is in symmetrical contrast with the beginning of the previous scene. There we had the brutish Caliban bearing wood for his master. Here we have Ferdinand bearing wood for his lady. Ferdinand, like Caliban, is given a soliloquy. But this is no animal poetry. We hear nothing now of stings or hedgehogs. Instead we have a rounded little philosophical discourse, and breathe the upper air of the polite Renascence intellect. Yet he is not entirely satisfactory. We feel that where the play requires him to be luminous he is merely grey. It seems hard that Caliban should so engross the nature poetry of the play, for if a little were given to Ferdinand (as it is given to Florizel in *The Winter's Tale*) he might gain in radiance.

The crazy plot of Caliban and the comedians against Prospero is carried forward with great dramatic dexterity. We are never allowed to abandon ourselves to unreserved laughter, largely because of the character of Caliban. On the one hand his sheer nastiness (notice that he merits the conceptually primitive charge of 'nastiness' rather than the fully-fledged moral opprobrium of 'wickedness') as in his plans for Prospero—

> I'll yield him thee asleep,
> Where thou may'st knock a nail into his head.
>
> III. ii. 65–66

> Batter his skull, or paunch him with a stake,
> Or cut his wezand with thy knife.
>
> III. ii. 95–96

—and, on the other hand, his glimpses of inexplicable beauty leave the scene with an uneasy status. Caliban's description of his heart-tearing visions creates a perfect suspension in time, to which the illogical tense-sequence may be allowed to contribute.[13]

> Be not afeard: the isle is full of noises,
> Sounds and sweet airs, that give delight, and hurt not.

504

Sometimes a thousand twangling instruments
Will hum about mine ears; and sometime voices,
That, if I then had wak'd after long sleep,
Will make me sleep again: and then, in dreaming,
The clouds methought would open and show riches
Ready to drop upon me; that, when I wak'd
I cried to dream again.

III. ii. 141–9

The effect is increased a few lines later when Stephano suddenly sees all that they have been doing and plotting for the immediate future in the light of a tale told to him long ago—

That shall be by and by: I remember the story.

III. ii. 153

The bewilderment grows in the next scene, where Alonso, Sebastian and the rest find that they are lost. Gonzalo describes the island as a maze (III. iii. 2–3), an image which is to recur at V. i. 242. As they talk, the sound of music comes to their ears. As before, when each saw the island with different eyes, so now their perceptions diverge in the presence of the supernatural. Gonzalo is at first content with the mere beauty of it—'marvellous sweet music!' (III. iii. 19). Sebastian and Antonio are flippant. Prospero watches, invisible, and approves Gonzalo. He mocks them with the banquet, snatched from them by Harpies. Ariel appears and denounces the villains. They draw, only to be mocked by Ariel, who all but says to them, in the best Oxford manner, 'You have made a category mistake.' Again the feeling of ἀπορία, of utter helplessness is conveyed to us. There is nothing remote from our experience in this, despite the elaborate apparatus of sorcery and fairies with which it is presented. There must be few people who have never awoken from a nightmare still grappling with an insubstantial enemy—attempting to bring physical slings and arrows to subdue a 'mental phenomenon'. Less closely connected but not irrelevant is the *feeling* which accompanies the making of a category mistake, or an attempt to yoke incomparables; as P. G. Wodehouse would say, the mind boggles. The villains boggle.

Ariel vanishes in thunder, the 'Shapes' carry out the table, and Alonso tells how he heard the name 'Prosper' in the withdrawing roar of the waves, and then in the wind and thunder. Again, the empirical character is strong. Experience will supply many such false configurations which have left us momentarily in doubt whether to form a natural or a supernatural interpretation. The play, with its life-size magician and veritable bombardment of miracles, determines us in favour of the supernatural. Sebastian and Antonio, still bemused by their own folly, cry out in hysterical defiance of the spirits that they will 'fight their legions o'er' (III. iii. 103).

Act IV opens with the sweet and orderly betrothal of Ferdinand and Miranda. Prospero, a heavyish father, enjoins the observance of the sacrament of marriage. Ariel is dispatched to invite the rabble to the ceremony, the crown of the play, where all are to be joined. It is the turning point of the plot, where δέσις gives place to λύσις—though with this particular story it is tempting to reverse Aristotle's metaphor, and refer to the end as the Sluts or binding up of the play. The betrothal is attended by a masque, and therefore, we may suppose, by elaborate music and décor. Juno and Ceres come, heralded by the rainbow messenger Iris—represented by players, it is true, but then the players are spirits—and the play seems to move into yet another dimension.[14] The transformation is almost worth calling a change of medium, and is comparable in its effect to the introduction of human voices in the last movement of Beethoven's Ninth Symphony. Goddesses, nymphs and sunburned reapers (in addition to the other characters) all come to the betrothal. The blessings of plenty are called down upon the future bride and bridegroom.

But the masque ends abruptly in a chaos of discords—'a strange, hollow and confused noise'. Prospero at once attributes this to the conspiracy against his life. We find ourselves being propelled into the mental entertainment of a cosmic harmony, in which an impulse of ill will entails a physical dislocation elsewhere in the system. It is uncertain whether the disturbance we are watching is deemed to have taken place in objective reality or in Prospero's mind alone, of which the masquers are mere figments. Really, at this stage of the game, it seems to matter very little. Prospero sorrowfully meditates that we, too, shall pass like spirits. Here occurs the finest sleep image of a play filled with sleepers,

> We are such stuff
> As dreams are made on, and our little life
> Is rounded with a sleep.
>
> IV. i. 15 6–8

The ground is cut from under our feet and we are left with the intuition of a regress of fictions. The note has already been heard faintly in the play–at II. i. 253–4, where Antonio speaks as though he and his companions were characters in a play, but this has little effect on us. It has too much Fancy and not enough Imagination about it. Stephano's relegation of his own recent actions to a story heard long before (III. ii. 153) touches us more nearly. The idea is, of course, a Shakespearean commonplace, frequently appearing at poetic high-points, anthology pieces, ranging from Jaques's 'All the world's a stage'[15] through Lear's 'When we are born, we cry that we are come To this great stage of fools',[16] to Macbeth's 'tale Told by an idiot, full of sound and fury, signifying nothing'.[17] The history of this metaphysical idea and its derivation from Plato have been briefly discussed in an earlier chapter.[18] It is perhaps worth adding that something very like this idea can be found in the Greek poets who lived before

Plato; for example, Pindar, *Pythian*, VIII. 137 sq.; Aeschylus, *Prometheus Vinctus*, 547–50; Sophocles, *Ajax*, 125–6.[19] I hope it will not be thought perverse if I describe this poetry as metaphysical. Certainly Shakespeare is not affirming that we last for ever, but rather the exact reverse. Yet the nature of the denial is metaphysical in its assumption of pathos. It only makes sense in the context of immortal longings. The man who has never felt, however faintly, the tug of everlastingness will find little to admire in these lines—a pleasing description of cloudy towers, perhaps, but nothing more; the observation that things decay shrinks into triviality; what else should they do? Such a man will have no need, in the face of such thoughts, to take a turn or two 'to still [his] beating mind'.

The fundamentally metaphysical status of Prospero's lines emerges very clearly if we compare them with the epilogue to *A Midsummer Night's Dream*, spoken by Puck. Indeed, the comparison will be found to have a certain property of reverberation, for each passage is in a way typical of the play in which it appears. It is necessary to give the two speeches in full:

> If we shadows have offended,
> Think but this, and all is mended,
> That you have but slumber'd here
> While these visions did appear.
> And this weak and idle theme,
> No more yielding but a dream,
> Gentles, do not reprehend:
> If you pardon, we will mend.
> And, as I'm an honest Puck,
> If we have unearned luck
> Now to 'scape the serpent's tongue,
> We will make amends ere long;
> Else the Puck a liar call:
> So, good night unto you all.
> Give me your hands, if we be friends,
> And Robin shall restore amends.
>   *A Midsummer Night's Dream*, V. ii. 54–69

And now Prospero:

> Our revels now are ended. These our actors,
> As I foretold you, were all spirits and
> Are melted into air, into thin air
> And, like the baseless fabric of this vision,
> The cloud-capp'd towers, the gorgeous palaces,
> The solemn temples, the great globe itself,
> Yea, all which it inherit, shall dissolve

And, like this insubstantial pageant faded,
Leave not a rack behind. We are such stuff
As dreams are made on, and our little life
Is rounded with a sleep.—Sir, I am vex'd:
Bear with my weakness; my old brain is troubled.
Be not disturb'd with my infirmity.
If you be pleas'd, retire into my cell
And there repose: a turn or two I'll walk,
To still my beating mind.

                The Tempest, IV. i. 148–63

Puck's speech is ingenious, delightful and undisturbing. If anything, it is reassuring. Common sense is not unseated by this play with reality and unreality, for the simple reason that the normal scope of the terms has suffered no metaphysical revision. It is the players who are 'shadows', the play which is 'a dream'. The audience is allowed to be utterly real. The speech is designed to end with applause. Plainly, after such a preparation, the sudden clapping from hundreds of hands will sound very human and solid. The epilogue carefully leads the audience back to a consciousness of its own ordinary humanity, before sending it home in happy complacency The ending is wholly appropriate to the play. *A Midsummer Night's Dream* is, no doubt, a miracle of expressionist grace and ingenuity, a gossamer construction of fictions within fictions, dreams within a dream. But when we compare it with *The Tempest* it seems virtually innocent of any metaphysical impact. In it Shakespeare is almost as far removed from Plato as is Pirandello. I say 'almost' because I have no doubt that any Elizabethan regress of fictions will have *some* smell of Plato about it. But *A Midsummer Night's Dream* is singularly down to earth in its conceptual structure. There is one place only where the play seems likely, for a moment, to take on another dimension-a brief exchange between Demetrius and Hermia:

DEMETRIUS. These things seem small and undistinguishable,
    Like far-off mountains turned into clouds.
HERMIA. Methinks I see these things with parted eye,
    When everything seems double.

                IV. i. 189–92

Curiously, these are, of all the lines in the play, the most reminiscent of *The Tempest*. They begin to 'get at' the intimate experience[20] of the audience in a way which is untypical of the play as a whole. But the idea is not developed.

Now turn to Prospero's lines. Where Puck's speech was comfortable, Prospero's is uncomfortable. Where *A Midsummer Night's Dream*, at the last, assured us of our reality, *The Tempest* deprives us of that assurance. Observe how the thing is done: Prospero begins with what appears to be a consoling speech, addressed to Ferdinand, explaining the disruption of the masque. But the audience knows from the start that it is an odd sort of consolation, delivered not from a mood of easy benevolence, but from anger. Before he actually speaks, Ferdinand and Miranda watch him in consternation

> FERDINAND. This is strange: your father's in some passion
>   That works him strongly.
> MIRANDA. Never till this day
>   Saw I him touch'd with anger so distemper'd.
>
> IV. i. 143–5

It is something of a surprise to find Prospero addressing Ferdinand at all. The opening of the speech is probably best played abruptly. Further, as the speech unfolds we find that the comfort offered at the beginning is in no way realized. At the end Prospero turns his back on Ferdinand and Miranda, in order, as he says, to settle his disturbed thoughts. It is worth while reminding ourselves of the occasion of the speech as a whole. We suspect that the conspiracy of Caliban and the rest is the cause of the break-up of the masque, but this is rather suspicion than knowledge. Certainly we are quite unable to explain *how* the behaviour of the conspirators has led to this result. The whole episode is extremely odd, and the oddity is never cleared up. It belongs with all those other examples of the imperfectly explained supernatural which were discussed at the beginning of this chapter. In *A Midsummer Night's Dream* we may be cheated for a moment by the intricacy of the plot, but we know what form an explanation would take—for example 'You see, he has just used the love-philtre', or something of that sort. But in *The Tempest* we are led into a wilderness where we have lost even the proper form of explanation. Hence, even before Prospero begins his 'explanation in which nothing is explained', we are, so to speak, disorientated. As we have seen, Prospero's speech does nothing to cure this.

In Puck's speech it was quite easy to see what was supposed to be real, and what unreal; easy, because the unreal things were things which in any case everyone knows to be unreal—a simulated Duke of Athens, a personated Queen of the Amazons, the King and Queen of the Fairies—while the real things were, simply, ourselves. But in Prospero's speech the area of unreality has ceased to be constant and familiar. In a way it has got out of control. He begins by talking about the actor-spirits (themselves a regress of fictions). So far there is nothing absolutely unprecedented. Puck himself was capable of stepping outside the play in order to discuss it. But the circle of darkness, of unreality, continues to widen, passing over the audience itself, beyond the walls of the theatre, to engulf palace and church, and, at last, the whole world. From making the stage shimmer before our eyes Prospero passes on to cast the same spell of doubt on the earth itself. Words alone retain a vivid life, cutting deep at our inmost memories and perceptions.[21]

Act V opens with the entry of Prospero, attired, as the Folio stage-direction tells us, *in his Magicke robes*. Ariel reports that the King and his followers are thoroughly distracted. Prospero announces that he will break his charms, so that all 'shall be themselves' once more. We have a sensation as of passing from the inner world to the outer. In a great speech the spirits are dispelled and we feel ourselves falling back into Italy, into things civil and political (though, in a way, the play is all about politics). The sleeping sailors are awakened by Ariel. Assorted ἀναγνωρίσεις follow. In the interview between Alonso and Prospero we feel the link with the other late plays, with their theme of children lost in tempest and found to the playing of sweet music. We remember Perdita and Marina.

> ALONSO. When did you lose your daughter?
> PROSPERO. In this last tempest.
>
> V. i. 152–3

As the play closes the theme of reconciliation and restoration grows stronger still, until at last all set sail for home with the 'calm seas' and 'auspicious gales' that Ariel gives them for his last service.

This play is obviously not an explicit allegory in which both the figure and its significance are clearly expressed in the text, in the manner of the *Psychomachia* of Prudentius. This can be shortly proved by pointing to the names of the personages in either work. The names Prospero, Miranda, Ariel might be held to be faint hints towards allegorical significance, but they are faint indeed compared with the strident labels which Prudentius has pasted on the brows of all his characters—*Patientia, Ira, Sodomita Libido*, and so on. *The Winter's Tale* might be thought more explicit, since scholarship has shown that *Hermione* was in the seventeenth century identified with *Harmonia*. Yet both were the names of a person, associated with the Theban Cycle long before Shakespeare appeared. So even here we hardly have a clear case of an abstraction personified.

But if *The Tempest* is not explicit, formal allegory, cannot it be *allegorised?* Of course, it can; but anything can. No one has yet written a story which is utterly proof against the efforts of a determined allegorical exegete. If a character exemplifies any quality (and all characters do) he may be said to figure that quality. This is the mere licence of ordinary linguistic usage; the 'semantic areas' of 'exemplify' and 'figure' overlap.

It remains to ask whether *The Tempest* can be *shown* to be allegorical; whether the basic logical structure which is explicit in the *Psychomachia* can be shown to be implicit—that is less obviously present but present all the same—in *The Tempest*. The various attempts to do this, have been, almost without exception, metaphysical in character. In my second chapter I argued at some length against the crude opposition of allegory and transcendentalism, and suggested that allegory was, in fact, a very frequent medium for the expression of transcendentalist metaphysics. But this habit of viewing the whole world as an allegory, and then expressing the fact allegorically, can lead, as one might expect, to some tricky situations. Where allegory becomes, as it were, the natural habit of the mind, it is often difficult for the more literal-minded person to satisfy himself as to what exactly is being asserted at all. A good example of the *anima naturaliter allegorica* in modern times is Professor J.R. Tolkien. He says (describing the dragon in *Beowulf*)

> There are in the poem some vivid touches of the right kind—as *pa se wyrm onwoc, wroht wæs geniwad; stonc oefter stane*[22] ... in which this dragon is real worm, with a bestial life and thought of his own, but the conception, none the less, approaches *draconitas* rather than *draco*: a personification of malice, greed, destruction (the evil side of heroic life) and of the undiscriminating cruelty of fortune that distinguishes not good or bad (the evil aspect of all life).[23]

It is clear that Tolkien is telling us something about the structure of the universe, as well as about the Beowulfian dragon. The Old Worm, merely by becoming indeterminate, is transformed into *draconitas*. The metaphysical opinion that malice is something active, operating in the world like an interpenetrating spirit, and that 'dragonishness' is a sort of huge, diffused, dragon, infused like a gas through the universe, denied idiosyncratic shape and thoughts but still having the authentic dragon stench about him—this metaphysical opinion is not so much the concomitant of Professor Tolkien's observations as the very condition of them. And now we may ask the question. Does Professor Tolkien suggest that *Beowulf* is an allegory? It is almost impossible to answer. If we say yes, we must allow that, for such a sensibility, all undifferentiated, morally simple characters will be allegorical, since they will resemble more closely (while never expressing literally) the great archetypal Exemplars which properly enjoy the name of universals. Otherwise we may say 'No, clearly he doesn't mistake it for a Prudentian formal allegory; it's just his manner of speaking.' But this will blind us to the fact that Tolkien's poem is different in kind from the literal-minded man's poem.

To bring the argument back within, the pale of Shakespearian criticism, we may take a passage from the critical writings of Professor Nevill Coghill:

> If I use the word 'allegory' in connection with Shakespeare I do not mean that the characters are abstractions representing this or that vice or virtue (as they do in some allegories, say the *Roman de la Rose* or *The Castle of Perseverance* itself). I mean that they contain and adumbrate certain principles, not in a crude or neat form, but mixed with other human qualities; but that these principles, taken as operating in human life, do in fact give shape and direction to the course, and therefore to the meaning of the play.[24]

How, then, is this special sort of allegory, in which principles are contained and adumbrated, to be distinguished from any other play, from which principles can be extracted? Apparently, in virtue of the activity of those principles. They *operate* 'in human life', and 'give shape and direction to the course ... of the play'. I do not understand how a 'principle' is to do this unless it is turned into a spirit, that is, into an active, influential individual. I think we can conclude that Professor Coghill is not so much suggesting that Shakespeare's comedies are allegorical as proposing a metaphysical view of virtues and vices as active (a view authorized by much Christian religious language) and suggesting that this view was shared by Shakespeare and expressed in his plays. And indeed, he may be right.

For the nineteenth-century critics of our first chapter, proving *The Tempest* an allegory and proving it metaphysical were very nearly the same thing. It might be objected that if only we would revive the much-despised opposition between allegory and metaphysics we might be lifted out of this confusing state of affairs; either a poem is allegorical—that is, a fictitious reification of qualities, etc.—or else it is metaphysical, in which case the reification, since it is ontologically asserted, must be taken as literal; hence a poem must be described as either metaphysical or allegorical, certainly not both. Unfortunately, this lucid distinction proves to be of little use when applied to actual specimens of metaphysical/allegorical poetry, since, when the metaphysician wishes to make an ontological assertion, he is seldom *able* to make it literally at all. It is evident that almost all those who have wished to call *The Tempest* allegorical have done so on the ground that it represents metaphysical truths about the world allegorically.

That Shakespeare's poetry betrays a tendency towards metaphysics is, I think, impossible to deny. The suggestion that his metaphysical imagery may be solely intensive in function we have already considered and rejected.[25]

Allegoristic criticism was almost normal in the nineteenth century. In the twentieth, though still vigorous,[26] it has come to be considered eccentric. But one good result of the general retreat from enthusiastic allegorizing is that when a critic does brave disapproval, and allegorize, we can be tolerably sure that he is describing the play, and not just indulging in verbal high flights of his own.

The twentieth-century arguments for describing *The Tempest* as a metaphysical allegory may be classified under two heads; first those drawn from a comparison of the story-patterns of the late Romances with one other and with the plots and imagery of the earlier Tragedies; second, arguments drawn from the internal character of *The Tempest* itself, its characterization, treatment of morality, use of the supernatural. The first class may be represented by G. Wilson Knight and E. M. W. Tillyard and the second by Derek Traversi and Patrick Cruttwell.

The former critics point out that the late Romances, *Pericles*, *Cymbeline*, *The Winter's Tale* and *The Tempest*, are all concerned with restoration and reconciliation of persons thought to be dead. The recurring feature of the storm is associated with their loss, and music with their reconciliation. This pattern may be compared with another pattern, discernible in the tragedies, in which the breakdown and death of a man is externally reflected in violent storm, and a hint of reconciliation beyond the grave is held out in the metaphors used by the heroes in their 'moments of fifth act transcendental speculation'.[27] It is thus argued that the Romances in their veritable reconciliation after tempests represent an acting out of those metaphors. It is therefore suggested that they are symbolic of a theological afterlife in which all manner of things shall be well. The necessity of supposing that Shakespeare intends a life beyond the grave may well be questioned, particularly since the most explicit metaphysics in *The Tempest* is to be found in the speech in which Prospero stresses the transitoriness of this life which is rounded with a sleep (IV. i. 146–63). So long as eternal happiness is conceived in terms of extended duration, it will be difficult to find unequivocal Shakespearian support for it.

But the relation of the story-pattern of the Romances to that of the Tragedies could be accounted for with a more modest set of presumptions. For example, one might suggest that Shakespeare thought what a wonderful wish-fulfilment type of play could be written if one gave these tragic heroes their whole desire, in this world; if, after all, the beloved person were shown never to have died at all. The dramatic use of the delightfulness of reconciliation after all hope has been lost does not necessarily imply a theological belief in resurrection. If *The Tempest* is really to be taken as an account of survival after death, since it certainly is not literal it must undoubtedly be allegorical. However, I should be much happier with the alternative suggestion, hazier and perhaps unpalatable to Christian sensibilities, that the 'story' of life after death and the story of *The Tempest* both stand as myths of some mysterious state of affairs, closely connected with moral questions, which may elude literal description together.

This approach is extremely unmanageable and vague, and perhaps it is for that very reason that it admits more readily an alliance with the second approach, the approach by way of the nature of characterization and treatment of ethics in the last plays. There are indeed certain features in the Romances which are easily connected with the separation and 'eternizing' of love-value which we found in the Sonnets and elsewhere.[28] D. A. Traversi says, of Florizel's comparison[29] of Perdita to a wave of the sea in *The Winter's Tale* (IV. iii. 140 ff.)

> This image, like the speech of which it forms a part, is, of course, much more than a beautiful piece of decorative poetry. It is rather the particular expression of a vital theme of the play ... the relation between the values of human life which postulate timelessness, and the impersonal, 'devouring' action of time which wears these values ceaselessly away. The wave image conveys perfectly the necessary relation between the mutability of life and the infinite value of

human experience which it conditions, but which is finally incommensurate with it.[30]

Traversi is quick, too, to point out the association in *The Tempest* of supernatural imagery with intuitions of value.[31] Yet the task is less easily performed for *The Tempest* than it is for *The Winter's Tale*. What we may call the Affirmation of Paradise has in *The Tempest* a far less confident tone. Miranda's first perception of the 'noble vessel' has a visionary quality, yet it is belied, as Traversi acknowledges, by the presence of the plotters in the ship. In *The Tempest* alone of the Romances the divine masque is broken up in confusion. The whole play, as compared with *The Winter's Tale*, is strangely perverse, like a piece of flawed glass. Bonamy Dobrée, in a brilliant essay,[32] pointed out the unique flavour of *The Tempest*, more shimmering, less full-bloodedly confident in its paradisal intuitions that its immediate predecessors; the wooing of Ferdinand, though piercingly ideal, is less warm than the wooing of Florizel; the forgiveness of Prospero has a touch of the priggish Senecan.

It is as if a second wave of scepticism has passed over the poet. It is quite different from the coprologous indignation of *Troilus and Cressida*. He no longer, for the sake of one transgression, denies the authenticity of love itself. But a reservation as to the truth-value of the assertions love provokes seems to have reappeared. Time, the old grey destroyer of the Sonnets, was not, after all, put down by love. After the enthusiastic reaffirmation of the later Sonnets and the first three Romances, a sadder and more complex reaction has set in, slightly ironical perhaps, but not at all cynical. The world has not been wholly redeemed by love; look at it. The subjective vision of the lover may transcend objective facts, but it does not obliterate them. The lover has one level, the hater another; perhaps there are a thousand more such levels, each as unreal as the rest.

Thus the quasi-mystical ethical intuitions are undermined by a doubt about reality, about the comparative status of different kinds of perception. My summary of the play in the first half of this chapter was, of course, selective. It may be as well to proclaim here the principle of selection involved. I was concerned to show Shakespeare's preoccupation, throughout the play, with the more nearly subliminal aspects of perception. It is as if Shakespeare himself became concerned, as I was in the third and fourth chapters of this book, to retreat into the preconceptual area of the mind. The chapters and the play have, in a sense, very similar subject-matter. Certainly, *The Tempest* is not related to that psychological theorizing in just the same way as the poetic specimens I cited were related to it. Those poems *exemplified* the indeterminate, configurative imagination. *The Tempest* is, for much of its length, *about* people configurating, imagining without actualizing, and so on. Patrick Cruttwell argues[33] that Shakespeare in his last plays began to take seriously the allegorical transcendental images of his youthful poetry. In *The Winter's Tale*, indeed, it may be that an ontological force is given to such imagery. But in *The Tempest* the prominence given to the ambiguous lower reaches of our conceptual and perceptual apparatus infects all ontological dogmatism with uncertainty. Shakespeare repeatedly restricts his characters to the primitive stages of perception in their apprehension of the island and its denizens. In this way he builds up a sense of a shimmering multiplicity of levels, which, together with the gratuitous operations of the supernatural, produce in the audience a state of primitive apprehension similar to that in which the characters find themselves. We are given the impression that the island may, after all, belong wholly to the unassertive world of dreams and ambiguous perceptions. Such material is naturally baffling to the critic who wishes to sort out symbol and statement. The allegorical exegete feels he has been cheated of his proper prey.

But we have also to reckon with the intuitions of value which are expressed in the meeting of Ferdinand and Miranda, and also (possibly) in the masque. That value is in these passages supernaturally conceived according to the logic treated in the earlier chapters of this book, I have little doubt. But it is somewhat puzzling to encounter these intuitions in a context so instinct with the atmosphere of ambiguous imagery. The proper relation of these ethical intuitions to the more elusive intuition that the island is only a dream or figment of the configurative imagination is difficult to determine. Certainly there is no sign of any attempt on Shakespeare's part to postulate a *genetic* relationship, to suggest that primitive configurations are the psychological parents of intuitions of value. After all, the two elements are presented in a totally different manner, the first involving the use of metaphor, the second dramatically. The imaginary status of the island is hinted by the behaviour of the characters, sometimes baffled, sometimes inconsistent. The value-intuitions are explicitly stated, by certain characters in theological imagery, and also (possibly) in the terms of a mythological spectacle. Yet it is easy to feel that some part of the vague scepticism created by the recurrence of half-subliminal perceptions has attached itself to the lovers and the persons of the masque. The differing visions which the castaways have of the island[34] may be held to throw a pale cast of doubt on the vision of Ferdinand when he falls in love with Miranda. We must allow that Shakespeare's motive in associating perceptual ambiguity with supernatural encounters is quite different from the motives behind chapter III of this book. He is not concerned to provide an instantial correlative for universals. But in our inquiry into perceptual imagery we discovered the peculiar indulgence of that area of the mind to the combining of things incompatible and the admission of things impossible. It is surely this character which it is Shakespeare's object to exploit. That property of the imagination which makes possible the instantial 'universal' is the same property as that which gives *The Tempest* its peculiar atmosphere of ontological suspension. This Shakespeare effects by giving the imaginative 'limbo of possibles' a dramatic impulse in the direction of reality, that is, by backing up the glimpses enjoyed by his characters with just enough magical apparatus to determine us in favour of a supernatural explanation without losing our sense of the 'internal' flavour of the experience. The truth is that these ambiguities have at least two functions. If they make the reports of the characters dubious, they make the playwright convincing. We cannot trust characters who contradict one another and continually stumble in their encounters with the supernatural. But we must trust the playwright who shows us both their insights and their stumblings.

Shakespeare has, in a perfectly legitimate manner, contrived to have his cake and eat it. He gives us the heart-tearing intuitions of heavenly value, but in a radically empirical and undogmatic way which disarms the cynical critic. He seems to say, 'I have seen this, and this, and this. You receive it as I found it. The interpretation I leave to you.' Certainly, the challenge has been accepted!

Is *The Tempest* allegorical? If I have done my work properly, the question should have shrunk in importance. The principal object of this book has been to show that allegorical poetry is more curiously and intimately related to life than was allowed by the petrifying formula of C. S. Lewis. One result of this is that the question 'Is this work allegorical?' ceases to have the clear significance it would have for a man to whom allegory, as the most ostentatiously fictitious of all literary forms, is directly opposed to a serious preoccupation with the real universe. Nevertheless, I am willing to give a few arbitrary rulings. The simplified characters of the play are not *ipso facto* allegorical, but it is no great sin to take them as types. The sense that beauty and goodness and harmony are ontologically prior to their subjects does not become full-bloodedly allegorical until the masque, where the spirits, nymphs, etc., may without straining be taken as a mythological acting out of the mystery of the betrothal. It is hardly worth while to call the island itself allegorical ('the mind of man' and so on). Certainly it shimmers between subjectivity and objectivity, presents itself differently to different eyes, yet it will not keep still long enough for one to affix an allegorical label. For the island, as for most of the elements of the play, I should prefer to coin a rather ugly term—'pre-allegorical'. Ariel and Caliban of all the characters in the play come nearest to being allegories of the psychic processes, but it would certainly be a mistake not to realize that they are very much more besides. If the suggestion of the unique authority of love and value were only a little more explicit, we might allow the word 'allegorical' for the play as a whole, and consider the restoration of the supposedly dead as a myth of this ethic, but, as things are, we cannot.

The minutely perceptive scepticism of *The Tempest* defeats the stony allegorist and the rigid cynic equally. The mystery is never allowed to harden into an ontological dogma to be reduced to symbols or rejected with contempt. Instead we have an extraordinarily delicate and dramatic play, which, until the Last Day makes all things clear, will never be anything but immensely suggestive.

One important claim can be made. The suggestiveness of *The Tempest* is metaphysical in tendency, and the indeterminate *concepts* adumbrated do have the logical oddity which we have followed through from the first chapter. Love *is* conceived as a supernatural force, and any number of protestations of metaphor and apologetic inverted commas cannot do away with the fact that a sort of deification, and therefore *a fortiori* reification has taken place. Whether these concepts should be allowed to be meaningful, or whether they should be permitted only a 'merely aesthetic' force (and that presumably spurious) I do not know. The unassertive candour of Shakespeare's imagination has left the question open. But the nineteenth-century allegorists were at any rate concerning themselves with the right (i.e. the peculiar) sort of concept. Their heresy is less than that of the hard-headed, poetry-has-nothing-to-do-with-ideas school. Their claims to have found *the* exclusive allegorical interpretation may be left to their foolish internecine strife, but their noses told them truly that the smell of metaphysics was in the air. If we look upon their effusions less as appraisals of the play than as reactions to it, they will be more acceptable. We may think of them as we think of the women who miscarried on seeing the Eumenides of Aeschylus: as critics they may have been injudicious, but as an audience they were magnificent—though perhaps a little too lively.

NOTES

1. A collection of Spanish romances published in 1609 or 1610.

2. The notion appears to have originated in F. Neri's *Scenari delle Maschere in Arcadia*, 1913. See also Hardin Craig, *An Interpretation of Shakespeare*, New York 1948, p. 345, and H.D. Gray, *Studies in Philology*, XVIII (192.1), p. 129.

3. In his Arden Edition of *The Tempest*, 6th ed., 1958, p. lxvii.

4. See A.H. Thorndike, *The Influence of Beaumont and Fletcher on Shakespeare*, Cambridge, Mass. 1901.

5. Quoted in W. Raleigh, *The English Voyages*, London 1928, p. 16.

6. See Bonamy Dobrée, 'The Tempest', *E & S*, NS V (1952), p. 18.

7. 'Shakespeare's Final Period', in *Books and Characters*, p. 62.

8. London, 1951. See especially pp. 102–34.

9. *The Diary of Samuel Pepys, M.A., F.R.S.*, ed. H.B. Wheatley, London 186, entry for 7 November 1667.

10. See *Coleridge's Shakespearean Criticism*, ed. T.M. Raysor, London 1930, vol. I, p. 133; Charles Lamb, *On the Tragedies of Shakespeare, considered with reference to their fitness for Stage Representation*, first published in *The Reflector*, 1811, printed in *The Complete Works of Charles Lamb*, ed. R.H. Shepherd, London 1892, p. 264; George Meredith, *The Ordeal of Richard Feverel*, first published 1859, in the Standard Edition, London 1914, p. 120. See also above, pp. 3ff.

11. See above.

12. In *The Longest Journey* (first published 1907), The World's Classics Edition, London 1960, p. 241.

13. As Robert Graves suggests in *The White Goddess*, emended and enlarged edition, London 1948, p. 425.

14. The true complexity of this is well caught by E.M.W. Tillyard, *Shakespeare's Last Plays*, London 1938, p. 80: 'On the actual stage the Masque is executed by players pretending to be spirits, pretending to be real actors, pretending to be supposed goddesses and rustics.'

15. *As You Like It*, II.vii.139.

16. *King Lear*, IV.vi.183–4.

17. *Macbeth*, V.v.26–8.

18. See above.

19. All three references are to the Oxford Texts of these authors, the editions of C.M. Bowra (1947), Gilbert Murray (1955) and A. C. Pearson (1931), respectively.

20. It seems that Shakespeare's interest in the minutiae of perception was present from the first. It supplies the most brilliant image of *Venus and Adonis*:

Upon his hurt she looks so steadfastly,
That her sight dazzling makes the wound seem three;
And then she reprehends her mangling eye,
That makes more gashes where no breach should be ...
(ll. 1063–6)

But it is only in *The Tempest* that the idea of the whole work adequately reflects this piercing imaginative insight.

21. I reached my conclusions about this speech before I read Anne Righter's *Shakespeare and the Idea of the Play*. I was delighted to find my analysis confirmed by hers.

22. Taking *stonc* to mean 'moved rapidly', 'slid', translate: 'Then the worm arose, the struggle was begun; it slid over the stone.' But *stonc* could, just possibly, mean 'stank' or 'sniffed'.

23. 'Beowulf, the Monsters and the Critics', *PBA*, XXII (1936), pp. 258–9.

24. ' The Basis of Shakespearian Comedy', *E & S*, NS III (1950), p. 21.

25. See above.

26. The most elaborate of all Tempest allegorizings was published in 1921— Colin Still's *Shakespeare's Mystery Play, a study of 'The Tempest'*.

27. G.W. Knight, *The Crown of Life*, London 1948, p. 208.

28. See above.

29. Quoted above.

30. *Shakespeare: the Last Phase*, London 1954, pp. 151–2.

31. *ibid.*, e.g. pp. 202, 207.

32. 'The Tempest', *E & S*, NS V (1952), pp. 13–25.

33. *The Shakespearean Moment*, London 1954. pp. 73–106.

34. II. i. 46–55.

Chronology

1564	William Shakespeare is born at Stratford-on-Avon to John Shakespeare, a butcher, and Mary Arden. He is baptized on April 26.
1582	Marries Anne Hathaway in November.
1583	Daughter Susanna is born, and is baptized on May 26.
1585	Twins Hamnet and Judith are born, and are baptized on February 2.
1587–90	Sometime during these years, Shakespeare goes to London, without his family; first plays are performed in London.
1589–91	Three parts of *Henry VI*.
1592–93	*Richard III, Two Gentlemen of Verona, The Comedy of Errors*.
1593–94	Publication of *Venus and Adonis* and *The Rape of Lucrece*, two narrative poems dedicated to Earl of Southampton; Shakespeare joins the Lord Chamberlain's Men, adding to its repertoire *The Taming of the Shrew, Titus Andronicus*, and perhaps the first version of *Hamlet*.
1595–96	*King John, Love's Labor's Lost, Richard II, Romeo and Juliet, A Midsummer Night's Dream*.
1596	Son Hamnet dies; grant of arms to Shakespeare's father.
1597	*The Merchant of Venice, Henry IV, Part 1, The Merry Wives of Windsor*; Purchases New Place in Stratford.
1598–99	*Henry IV, Part 2, Much Ado About Nothing, Henry V, Julius Caesar, As You Like It*; Lord Chamberlain's Men moves to new Globe Theatre.

1601	*Hamlet*, The poem *The Phoenix and the Turtle*; Shakespeare's father dies and is buried on September 8.
1601–02	*Twelfth Night, Troilus and Cressida*.
1603	*All's Well That Ends Well*; death of Queen Elizabeth; James VI of Scotland becomes James I of England; Shakespeare's company becomes the King's Men.
1604	*Measure for Measure, Othello*.
1605–06	*King Lear, Macbeth, Antony and Cleopatra*.
1607–08	*Coriolanus, Timon of Athens, Pericles*.
1609	*Cymbeline*; publication of *Sonnets*.
1610–11	*The Winter's Tale, The Tempest*; Shakespeare retires to Stratford.
1612–13	*Henry VIII, The Noble Kinsmen* (with John Fletcher).
1616	Shakespeare dies at Stratford on April 23.
1623	Publication of the first Folio of Shakespeare's plays.

Contributors

HAROLD BLOOM is Sterling Professor of the Humanities at Yale University and Henry W. and Albert A. Berg Professor of English at the New York University Graduate School. He is the author of over 20 books, including *Shelley's Mythmaking* (1959), *The Visionary Company* (1961), *Blake's Apocalypse* (1963), *Yeats* (1970), *A Map of Misreading* (1975), *Kabbalah and Criticism* (1975), *Agon: Toward a Theory of Revisionism* (1982), *The American Religion* (1992), *The Western Canon* (1994), and *Omens of Millennium: The Gnosis of Angels, Dreams, and Resurrection* (1996). *The Anxiety of Influence* (1973) sets forth Professor Bloom's provocative theory of the literary relationships between the great writers and their predecessors. His most recent books include *Shakespeare: The Invention of the Human* (1998), a 1998 National Book Award finalist, *How to Read and Why* (2000), *Genius: A Mosaic of One Hundred Exemplary Creative Minds* (2002), and *Hamlet: Poem Unlimited* (2003). In 1999, Professor Bloom received the prestigious American Academy of Arts and Letters Gold Medal for Criticism, and in 2002 he received the Catalonia International Prize.

FRANK O'CONNOR was born in Ireland, and made his name as a fiction writer, dramatist, and literary critic. He is perhaps best remembered for his short stories, and his books include *Guests of the Nation, Bones of Contention, Irish Miles* and *Mirror in the Roadway*.

E. PEARLMAN is Professor of English at the University of Colorado, Denver. He has written a book on Shakespeare's history plays and an article about "*Macbeth* on film."

ERICH SEGAL has taught at Harvard, Yale, and Princeton, and is currently a

Fellow at Wolfson College, Oxford University. He has written on Caesar Augustus, Roman comedy, Greek tragedy, and is also the author of nine novels.

THOMAS M. GREENE was Professor Emeritus of comparative literature and English at Yale University. His books include *The Light in Troy: Imitation and Discovery in Renaissance Poetry*, the essay collection *The Vulnerable Text*, and *Calling from Diffusion: Hermeneutics of the Promenade*. A posthumous collection of essays, *Poetry, Signs, and Magic*, is forthcoming.

HAROLD C. GODDARD was a well known educator and literary critic during the first half of the twentieth century. He also wrote on Chaucer, Blake, and the New England Transcendentalists.

G.K. CHESTERTON, poet, novelist, and essayist, was best known as a reviewer for *The Bookman* and as the author of the 'Father Brown' stories.

NORTHROP FRYE, preeminent among Canadian literary critics, was Professor of English at University of Toronto (Victoria College) and later the chancellor at Victoria University. Of his many books, some of the best known are *Fearful Symmetry: A Study of William Blake*, *Anatomy of Criticism*, *The Well-Tempered Critic*, *T.S. Eliot*, *Fables of Identity*, and *The Great Code*.

A.C. BRADLEY served as Oxford Professor of Poetry and is best remembered for *Shakespearean Tragedy*, a character-centered study that has been reprinted more than a dozen times.

JOSEPH WESTLUND is the author of *Shakespeare's Reparative Comedies: A Psychoanalytic View of the Middle Plays*, and more recently he has written on *All's Well that Ends Well*. He has taught at Northeastern University.

BARBARA EVERETT, a lecturer at Oxford University (Somerville College), has also taught at Cambridge University and the University of Hull. Her recent books include *Poets in Their Time: Essays on English Poetry from Donne to Larkin* and *Young Hamlet: Essays on Shakespeare's Tragedies*.

WILLIAM HAZLITT was the foremost English literary critic during the early nineteenth century, and he remains one of the great prose stylists in the language. A popular lecturer, reviewer, and biographer, his books include *Characaters of Shakespeare's Plays*, *Criticisms and Dramatic Essays of the English Stage*, *Lectures on the English Comic Writers*, *Liber amoris*, and *Spirit of the Age*, a collection of contemporary biographical portraits.

DAVID QUINT is the George M. Bodman Professor of English and

Comparative Literature at Yale University. His books include *Origin and Originality in Renaissance Literature* and *Epic and Empire*. He has also published a study of Montaigne and translations of Poliziano's *Stanze* and Ariosto's *Cinque Canti*. A book on Don Quixote is forthcoming.

LAWRENCE DANSON is an English Professor at Princeton University. His publications include *Tragic Alphabet: Shakespeare's Drama of Language*, as well as studies of *The Merchant of Venice* and *King Lear*. He has also written on Max Beerbohm and Oscar Wilde.

JAMES P. BEDNARZ is Professor of English at the C.W. Post campus of Long Island University. He is the author of *Shakespeare and the Poets' War*, and his articles have appeared in journals such as *ELH*, *Shakespeare Studies*, *Renaissance Drama*, and *The Huntington Library Quarterly*.

JOHN HOLLANDER, Sterling Professor Emeritus of English at Yale University, is the author and editor of many books. The latest of his nineteen volumes of poetry is *Picture Window*, and his critical works include *Vision and Resonance: Two Senses of Poetic Form*, *Melodious Guile: Fictive Pattern in Poetic Language*, and more recently, *The Poetry of Everyday Life* and *The Work of Poetry*.

RICHARD A. LANHAM is a Professor of English at UCLA. Besides *The Motives of Eloquence*, he has also published studies of *Tristram Shandy* and Philip Sidney's *Arcadia* and the reference book *A Handlist of Rhetorical Terms*. Other works include *Literacy and the Survival of Humanism* and *Electronic Word: democracy, technology, and the arts*.

PATRICIA PARKER is the Margery Bailey Professor in English and Dramatic Literature at Stanford University. In addition to *Shakespeare From the Margins*, she has written *Literary Fat Ladies: rhetoric, gender, property* and *Inescapable Romance*. She has also co-edited five collections of essays.

RONALD R. MACDONALD was Professor of English at Smith College. His publications include *The Burial Places of Memory: Epic Underworlds in Vergil, Dante, and Milton*, and a study of Shakespeare's comedies.

GRAHAM BRADSHAW is the author of *Misrepresentations: Shakespeare and the Materialists* and an earlier study, *Shakespeare's Skepticism*.

SIR WILLIAM EMPSON was a highly original voice among modern poet-critics. He taught for many years in China and later at Sheffield University. His principal writings include his *Collected Poems*, *Seven Types of Ambiguity*, *Some Versions of Pastoral*, and *The Structure of Complex Words*.

JANET ADELMAN, Professor of English at the University of California, Berkeley, has published many articles on Shakespeare, as well as *The Common Liar* (her book-length study of *Antony and Cleopatra*) and *Suffocating Mothers: Fantasies of Maternal Origin in Shakespeare, from* Hamlet *to* The Tempest. She is currently working on a study of conversion, race, and identity in *The Merchant of Venice*.

STEPHEN ORGEL is the Jackson Eli Reynolds Professor of Humanities at Stanford University. His books include *The Jonsonian Masque*, *The Illusion of Power*, and most recently, *Authentic Shakespeare*. He has also edited Ben Jonson's masques, the poems of Christopher Marlowe, and Shakespeare's *The Tempest*.

A.D. NUTTALL has written several books on a wide range of literary and philosophical topics, from tragedy and mimesis to stoicism and gnosticism. His work on Shakespeare includes book-length studies of *Timon of Athens*, *The Winter's Tale*, and *The Tempest*.

Bibliography

Adelman, Janet. *The Common Liar: An Essay on* Antony and Cleopatra. New Haven: Yale University Press, 1973.

Barber, C.L. *Shakespeare's Festive Comedy*. Princeton: Princeton University Press, 1959.

Barkan, Leonard. "The Theatrical Consistency of *Richard II*." *Shakespeare Quarterly* 29 (1978): 5–19.

Barton, Anne. *The Names of Comedy*. Toronto: University of Toronto Press, 1990.

Bate, Jonathan. *The Genius of Shakespeare*. Oxford: Oxford University Press, 1998.

Bednarz, James P. *Shakespeare and the Poets' War*. New York: Columbia University Press, 2001.

Belsey, Catherine. "Disrupting sexual difference: meaning and gender in the comedies." *Alternative Shakespeares*. Ed. John Drakakis. New York: Methuen & Co., 1985.

Berryman, John. *Berryman's Shakespeare*. Ed. John Haffenden. New York: Farrar, Straus & Giroux, 1999.

Bevington, David, ed. *Henry the Fourth Parts I and II: Critical Essays*. New York: Garland, 1986.

Bloom, Harold. *Hamlet: Poem Unlimited*. New York: Riverhead Books, 2003.

———. *Shakespeare: The Invention of the Human*. New York: Riverhead Books, 1998.

Booth, Stephen. *King Lear, Macbeth, Indefinition and Tragedy*. New Haven: Yale University Press, 1983.

Bradley, A.C. *Oxford Lectures on Poetry*. New York: Macmillan & Co., 1909.

———. *Shakespearean Tragedy*. 1904. 3rd ed. New York: St. Martin's Press, 1992.

Bradshaw, Graham. *Misrepresentations: Shakespeare and the Materialists*. Ithaca: Cornell University Press, 1993.

Brockbank, Philip, Russell Jackson, and Robert Smallwood, eds. *Players of Shakespeare*, vols. 1–3. Cambridge: Cambridge University Press, 1985, 1988, 1993.

Burnett, Mark Thornton. "Giving and Receiving: *Love's Labour's Lost* and the Politics of Exchange." *English Literary Renaissance* 23 (1993): 287–313.

Calderwood, James L. *"A Midsummer Night's Dream*: Anamorphism and Theseus' Dream." *Shakespeare Quarterly* 42 (1991): 409–30.

Chesterton, G.K. *Chesterton on Shakespeare*. Ed. Dorothy Collins. n.p.: Dufour, 1971.

Clarke, Kate. "Reading *As You Like It*." *Shakespeare, Aphra Behn, and the Canon*. Eds. W.R. Owens and Lizbeth Goodman. London: Routledge, 1996.

Cole, Rosalie. *Shakespeare's Living Art*. Princeton: Princeton University Press, 1974.

Danson, Lawrence. *Tragic Alphabet: Shakespeare's Drama of Language*. New Haven: Yale University Press, 1974.

Di Biase, Carmine. "Ovid, Pettie, and the Mythic Foundation of *Cymbeline*." *Cahiers Elisabethans* 46 (October 1994): 59–70.

Empson, William. *Essays on Shakespeare*. Ed. David B. Pirie. Cambridge: Cambridge University Press, 1986.

Erickson, Peter B. *Patriarchal Structures in Shakespeare's Drama*. Berkeley: University of California Press, 1985.

Everett, Barbara. *"Much Ado About Nothing*: the unsociable comedy." In *English Comedy*. Eds. Michael Cordner, Peter Holland, and John Kerrigan. Cambridge: Cambridge University Press, 1994.

Foakes, R.A. *Shakespeare, the Dark Comedies to the Last Plays: From Satire to Celebration*. Charlottesville: University Press of Virginia, 1971.

Frye, Northrop. *A Natural Perspective: The Development of Shakespearean Comedy and Romance*. New York: Columbia University Press, 1955.

———. *Northrop Frye on Shakespeare*. Ed. Robert Sandler. New Haven: Yale University Press, 1986.

Garber, Majorie. "The Education of Orlando." *Comedy from Shakespeare to Sheridan*. Eds. A.R. Braunmuller and J.C. Bulman. Newark: University of Delaware Press, 1986.

Gay, Penny. *As She Likes It: Shakespeare's Unruly Women*. London: Routledge, 1994.

Girard, René. *A Theater of Envy: William Shakespeare*. Oxford: Oxford University Press, 1991.

Goddard, Harold C. *The Meaning of Shakespeare*. Chicago: The University of Chicago Press, 1951.

Greenblatt, Stephen. *Hamlet in Purgatory*. Princeton: Princeton University Press, 2001.

————. *Shakespearean Negotiations: The Circulation of Social Energy in Renaissance England.* Berkeley: University of California Press, 1988.

Greene, Thomas M. *The Vulnerable Text: Essays on Renaissance Literature.* New York: Columbia University Press, 1986.

Gross, John, ed. *After Shakespeare.* Oxford: Oxford University Press, 2002.

Gross, Kenneth. *Shakespeare's Noise.* Chicago: The University of Chicago Press, 2001.

Harner, James. *The World Shakespeare Bibliography on CD-ROM: 1900–Present.*

Hawkes, Terence. *Shakespeare in the Present.* London: Routledge, 2002.

Hazlitt, William. *Characters of Shakespeare's Plays.* Oxford: Oxford University Press, 1916.

Hillman, Richard. "'The Tempest' as Romance and Anti-Romance." *University of Toronto Quarterly* 55 (Winter 1985–86): 141–60.

Hinman, Charlton. *The Norton Facsimile: The First Folio of Shakespeare.* New York: W.W. Norton, 1968.

Hollander, John. "*Twelfth Night* and the Morality of Indulgence." *The Sewanee Review* 68 (1959): 220–38.

Honan, Park. *Shakespeare: A Life.* Oxford: Oxford University Press, 1998.

Howard, Jean E. *The Stage and Social Struggle in Early Modern England.* London: Routledge, 1994.

Hughes, Ted. *Shakespeare and the Goddess of Complete Being.* New York: Farrar, Straus & Giroux, 1992.

Kermode, Frank. *William Shakespeare: The Final Plays.* London: Longmans, Green, 1963.

Kinney, Arthur F. "Shakespeare's *Comedy of Errors* and the Nature of Kinds." *Studies in Philology* 85 (1988): 29–52.

Knapp, Jeffrey. *Shakespeare's Tribe: Church, Nation, and Theater in Renaissance England.* Chicago: The University of Chicago Press, 2002.

Knight, G. Wilson. *The Wheel of Fire.* 1930. 4th ed. London: Methuen, 1978.

Knights, L.C. "Integration in 'The Winter's Tale.'" *Sewanee Review* 84 (Fall 1976): 595–613.

Kott, Jan. *Shakespeare Our Contemporary.* London: Methuen & Co., 1965.

Lanham, Richard A. *The Motives of Eloquence: Literary Rhetoric in the Renaissance.* New Haven: Yale University Press, 1976.

Macdonald, Ronald R. "Measure for Measure: The Flesh Made Word." *Studies in English Literature 1500–1900* 30 (1990): 265–82.

Marcus, Leah S. *Puzzling Shakespeare: Local Reading and Its Discontents.* Berkeley: University of California Press, 1988.

McFarland, Thomas. *Shakespeare's Pastoral Comedy.* Chapel Hill: University of North Carolina Press, 1972.

Miles, Gary. "How Roman Are Shakespeare's 'Romans'?" *Shakespeare Quarterly* 40 (1989): 257–83.

Muir, Kenneth. *Shakespeare as Collaborator*. London: Methuen, 1960.

Nevo, Ruth. *Comic Transformations in Shakespeare*. New York and London: Methuen, 1980.

———. *Shakespeare's Other Language*. London: Methuen, 1987.

———. *Tragic Form in Shakespeare*. Princeton: Princeton University Press, 1972.

Nuttall, A.D. *Shakespeare: The Winter's Tale*. London: Edward Arnold, 1966.

———. *Two Concepts of Allegory*. London: Routledge & Kegan Paul, 1967.

O'Connor, Frank. *Shakespeare's Progress*. Cleveland: World Publishing Co., 1960.

Orgel, Stephen. *Authentic Shakespeare*. New York: Routledge, 2002.

———. *Impersonations*. Cambridge: Cambridge University Press, 1996.

———. "The Poetics of Incomprehensibility." *Shakespeare Quarterly* 42, no. 4 (1991): 43–37.

Parker, Patricia. *Shakespeare from the Margins: Language, Culture, Context*. Chicago: The University of Chicago Press, 1996.

———, and Geoffrey Hartman, eds. *Shakespeare & the Question of Theory*. London: Methuen, 1985.

Pearlman, E. "The Invention of Richard of Gloucester." *Shakespeare Quarterly* 43, no. 4 (1992): 420–29.

Quint, David. "'Alexander the Pig': Shakespeare on History and Poetry." *Boundary 2*, no. 10 (1982): 49–67.

Schmidt, Alexander. *Shakespeare Lexicon and Quotation Dictionary*. 1874. 2 vols. New York: Dover, 1971.

Schwartz, Murray M. and Kahn, Coppelia, eds. *Representing Shakespeare*. Baltimore: The Johns Hopkins University Press, 1980.

Segal, Erich. *The Death of Comedy*. Cambridge, MA: Harvard University Press, 2001.

Shapiro, James. *Shakespeare and the Jews*. Chicago: The University of Chicago Press, 1996.

Shirley, Frances, ed. King John *and* Henry VIII: *Critical Essays*. New York: Garland, 1988.

Shuger, Debora Kuller. *Political Theologies in Shakespeare's England*. Houndmills, Basingstoke: Palgrave, 2001.

Smith, Bruce R. "The Passionate Shepherd." *Homosexual Desire in Shakespeare's England: A Cultural Poetics*. Chicago: The University of Chicago Press, 1991.

Snyder, Susan, ed. Othello: *Critical Essays*. New York: Garland, 1988.

Steiner, George. "Shakespeare—Four Hundreth." *Language & Silence*. New York: Atheneum, 1972.

Taylor, Michael. "The Pastoral Reckoning in *Cymbeline*" *Shakespeare Survey: An Annual Survey of Shakespearean Study and Production* 36 (1983): 97–106.

Traub, Valerie. "The Homoerotics of Shakespearean Comedy." *Desire and Anxiety: Circulations of Sexuality in Shakespearean Drama*. London: Routledge, 1992.

Uphaus, Robert W. *Beyond Tragedy: Structure and Experience in Shakespeare's Romances.* Lexington, KY: The University Press of Kentucky, 1981.

Westlund, Joseph. *Shakespeare's Reparative Comedies: A Psychoanalytical View of the Middle Plays.* Chicago: The University of Chicago Press, 1984.

Wills, Garry. *Witches & Jesuits: Shakespeare's* Macbeth. Oxford: Oxford University Press, 1995.

Yates, Francis A. *Shakespeare's Last Plays: A New Approach.* London: Routledge & Kegan Paul, 1975.

Young, David. *The Heart's Forest: A Study of Shakespeare's Pastoral Plays.* New Haven: Yale University Press, 1972.

Acknowledgments

"Foregrounding" by Harold Bloom. From *Shakespeare: The Invention of the Human*. © 1998 by the author. Used by permission of Riverhead Books, an imprint of Penguin Group (USA) Inc.

"Masterpieces" by Frank O'Connor. From *Shakespeare's Progress*. © 1960 by the author. Reprinted by permission.

"The Invention of Richard of Gloucester in *3 Henry VI* and *Richard III*" by E. Pearlman. From *Shakespeare Quarterly* 43, no. 4 (1992): 410–29. © 1992 by the Folger Shakespeare Library. Reprinted with permission of the Johns Hopkins University Press.

"Shakespeare: Errors and *Erōs*" by Erich Segal. From *The Death of Comedy*. © 2001 by the President and Fellows of Harvard College. Reprinted by permission.

"Romantic Comedy and Farce: *The Taming of the Shrew*" by Harold Bloom. From *Shakespeare: The Invention of the Human*. © 1998 by the author. Used by permission of Riverhead Books, an imprint of Penguin Group (USA) Inc.

"*Love's Labour's Lost*: The Grace of Society" by Thomas M. Greene. From *The Vulnerable Text: Essays on Renaissance Literature*. © 1986 by Columbia University. Reprinted by permission.

"The Meaning of Shakespeare: *Romeo and Juliet*" by Harold C. Goddard. From *The Meaning of Shakespeare*. © 1951 by the University of Chicago. Reprinted by permission.

531

"*A Midsummer Night's Dream*" by G.K. Chesteron. From *Chesterton on Shakespeare*, ed. Dorothy Collins. © 1971 by Dorothy E. Collins. Reprinted by permission.

"*Richard II*" by Northrop Frye. From *Northrop Frye on Shakespeare*, ed. Robert Sandler. © 1986 by the author. Reprinted by permission.

"The Rejection of Falstaff" by A.C. Bradley. From *Oxford Lectures on Poetry*. © 1909 by Macmillan and Co. Reprinted by permission.

"*The Merchant of Venice*: Merging with a Perfect World" by Joseph Westlund. From *Shakespeare's Reparative Comedies: A Psychoanalytic View of the Middle Plays*. © 1984 by the University of Chicago. Reprinted by permission.

"*Much Ado About Nothing*: the unsociable comedy" by Barbara Everett. From *English Comedy*, eds. Michael Cordner, Peter Holland, and John Kerrigan. © 1994 by Cambridge University Press. Reprinted by permission.

"Shakespeare's Characters: Henry V and Coriolanus" by William Hazlitt. From *Characters of Shakespeare's Plays*. © 1916 by Oxford University Press. Reprinted by permission.

"'Alexander the Pig': Shakespeare on History and Poetry" by David Quint. From *Boundary 2* 10 (1982): 49–67. © 1982, *Boundary* 2– SUNY Binghampton. All rights reserved. Used by permission of the publisher.

"*Julius Caesar*" by Lawrence Danson. From *Tragic Alphabet: Shakespeare's Drama of Language*. © 1974 by Yale University. Reprinted by permission.

"*As You Like It* and the Containment of Comical Satire" by James P. Bednarz. From *Shakespeare and the Poets' War*. © 2001 by Columbia University Press. Reprinted by permission.

"*Twelfth Night* and the Morality of Indulgence" by John Hollander. From *The Sewanee Review* 67.2 (Spring 1959): 220–38. © 1959 by the University of the South. Reprinted with permission of the editor and the author.

"Superposed Plays: *Hamlet*" by Richard A. Lanham. From *The Motives of Eloquence: Literary Rhetoric in the Renaissance*. © 1976 by Yale University. Reprinted by permission.

"Dilation and Inflation: Shakespearean Increase in *All's Well That Ends Well* and

Troilus and Cressida" by Patricia Parker. From *Shakespeare From the Margins: Language, Culture, Context*. © 1996 by the University of Chicago. Reprinted by permission.

"*Measure for Measure*: The Flesh Made Word" by Ronald R. Macdonald. From *Studies in English Literature 1500–1900* 30, 2 (1990): 265–82. © 1990 by William Marsh Rice University. Reprinted by permission.

"Dramatic Intentions in *Othello*" by Graham Bradshaw. From *Misrepresentations: Shakespeare and the Materialists*. © 1993 by Cornell University. Used by permission of the publisher, Cornell University Press.

"*Macbeth*" by William Empson. From *Essays on Shakespeare*, ed. David B. Piric. © 1986 by the author. Reprinted by permission.

"Nature's Piece 'gainst Fancy: Poetry and the Structure of Belief in *Antony and Cleopatra*" by Janet Adelman. From *The Common Liar: An Essay on* Antony and Cleopatra. © 1973 by Yale University. Reprinted by permission.

"The Poetics of Incomphrensibility: *The Winter's Tale*" by Stephen Orgel. From *Shakespeare Quarterly* 12.4 (1991): 431–37. © 1991 by the Folger Shakespeare Library. Reprinted by permission.

"Two Concepts of Allegory in *The Tempest*" by A.D. Nuttall. From *Two Concepts of Allegory*. © 1967 by the author. Reprinted by permission.

Index